Americans and Their Homes

Demographics of Homeownership

Americans and Their Homes

Demographics of Homeownership

BY THE EDITORS OF NEW STRATEGIST PUBLICATIONS

New Strategist Publications, Inc.
Ithaca, New York

New Strategist Publications, Inc.
P.O. Box 242, Ithaca, New York 14851
800/848-0842; 607/273-0913
www.newstrategist.com

ISBN 978-1-935775-29-4 (hardcover)
ISBN 978-1-935775-30-0 (paper)

Table of Contents

List of Tables

Chapter 5. Renters by Region

Introduction

The real estate market is in turmoil thanks to the housing bubble, the collapse in housing prices, the plunging mobility rate of homeowners, and the paralysis in home sales. This all-new third edition of *Americans and Their Homes* shows you where the nation stands in the aftermath of the Great Recession. *Americans and Their Homes* is a reference tool that provides you with the latest demographic data, profiling the nation's homeowners and renters. Compiling and comparing statistics from the 2009 American Housing Survey and the 2010 Housing Vacancy Survey, and detailing trends between the peak of the housing market and today, *Americans and Their Homes* reveals where we are and where the housing market might be headed.

Some of it is good news. Despite the turmoil, homeowners and homeownership remain remarkably stable in the United States. The homeownership rate has not declined as much as some feared. Most homeowners still have plenty of equity in their home. But a growing number are underwater. *Americans and Their Homes* shows you these trends.

New to this edition of *Americans and Their Homes* are chapters examining the demographics of renters and the characteristics of their houses and apartments. As it becomes more difficult to buy and sell houses, renting has become a viable alternative for millions of Americans—especially young adults. Developers are taking note and building more rental housing. *Americans and Their Homes* shows you who rents and what they rent.

American dream or nightmare?

Homeownership has long been one of the key elements of the American dream. A majority of American households achieved that dream during the 1940s, when the federal government made mortgage terms less stringent and more accessible to the average family. Homeownership in the United States climbed upwards from there, reaching a record high of 65.6 percent in 1980. Then it hit a 16-year slump. It was not until 1997 that the homeownership rate finally surpassed the high of 1980.

Behind the 16-year slump was the baby-boom generation in the young-adult life stage. In 1980, boomers spanned the ages of 16 to 34. As they inflated the number of young adults in the population, they depressed the homeownership rate, since most young adults do not own homes. The slump ended as boomers hit middle age, buying homes and boosting the homeownership rate. As if this was not enough to spur the housing market, financial regulators lowered interest rates and relaxed mortgage rules, creating a housing bubble. Housing prices began to soar as millions of Americans attempted to buy homes before prices escalated even more. Many tried to profit from the home buying frenzy. The homeownership rate peaked in 2004 at 69.0 percent then began to fall along with housing prices. Today, 66.9 percent of households own their home. The presence of the large baby-boom generation at the peak ages of homeownership explains why the rate has changed relatively little despite record numbers of foreclosures. The large baby-boom generation, most of them homeowners, is stabilizing the housing market.

For most Americans, housing is their greatest expense. For most businesses, homeowners are their primary customers. Understanding the characteristics of homeowners and the homes in which they live is the key to understanding American attitudes and lifestyles. This has never been truer than it is today. With homeowners under extreme stress—many underwater, others unable to sell their home and move—it has never been more important to understand the complex relationship between Americans and their homes. As the number of renters grows by the millions—some renting by choice, others because of hardship—it also has never been more important to understand who rents, why they rent, and what they rent. With the publication of the third edition of *Americans and Their Homes: The Demographics of Homeownership*, you hold those facts in your hand.

Americans and Their Homes examines in detail the demographics of homeowners and renters and the characteristics of their housing. By cutting through the statistical clutter with clear tables extracted and produced by New Strategist's editors and with explanatory text accompanying each table, *Americans and Their Homes* reveals the story behind the tattered American Dream.

How to use this book

Americans and Their Homes: The Demographics of Homeownership is designed to be easy to use. Its 10 chapters look at homeowners and renters from a variety of perspectives.

Chapter 1, Trends in Homeownership, shows changes in the number and percentage of Americans who own or rent their home by a variety of demographic characteristics such as age, income, race and Hispanic origin, household type, and education. It also examines trends in housing quality, including changes in the number of bedrooms, bathrooms, and square footage of housing units.

Chapter 2, Homeowners and Their Homes, compares the characteristics of the nation's homeowners with those of the average household to reveal the unique qualities of owners.

Chapter 3, Renters and Their Homes, compares the characteristics of the nation's renters with those of the average household to reveal the unique qualities of the growing rental market.

Chapter 4, Homeowners by Region, reveals the important ways in which homeowners and their homes differ by region. Those differences are often striking, creating distinct markets.

Chapter 5, Renters by Region, reveals the important ways in which renters differ by region. Understanding those differences is vital for policymakers, real estate developers, and landlords large and small.

Chapter 6, Owners of New Homes, examines a once vibrant segment of the housing market that is now under stress. A large percentage of these homeowners are underwater and trapped in homes they are unable to sell.

Chapter 7, Renters of New Homes, presents the characteristics of perhaps the hottest segment of the housing market. Renters of new homes are more affluent than the average renter, and more choosey. Many could buy, but are opting to rent. This chapter tells you who they are and what they rent.

Chapter 8, Owners of Mobile Homes, examines the large segment of homeowners who live in this type of affordable housing. Mobile homes are prevalent throughout the United States, but especially in the South. Mobile homes make homeownership affordable for many young adults and minorities.

Chapter 9, Renters of Mobile Homes, examines perhaps the most downscale segment of the rental market. Because a growing share of Americans are renting rather than buying, and because so many households are struggling to make ends meet, mobile home renters may become an even bigger portion of the nation's rental market.

Chapter 10, Spending of Owners and Renters, looks at what homeowners and renters spend on all products and services, from mortgage interest to fast food. This chapter shows you where the money goes. Based on unpublished data from the Consumer Expenditure Survey, the chapter also compares the spending of homeowners with mortgages to the spending of homeowners without mortgages. There are striking differences.

Within each chapter, easy-to-read tables tell the housing story by presenting both numbers and percent distributions. A caption accompanies each table, explaining the most important points. *Americans and Their Homes* contains a comprehensive table list at the front of the book to help readers locate the information they need. For an even more detailed search, use the index in the back of the book. Also in the back of the book is the glossary, which defines many of the terms commonly used in the tables and text.

Sources of data

In creating *Americans and Their Homes*, the editors of New Strategist Publications extracted data from spreadsheets on government web sites, constructed tables, analyzed numbers, and described trends. The Census Bureau's American Housing Survey is one of the primary databases used to create *Americans and Their Homes*. The American Housing Survey is the best source of up-to-date, reliable information on the characteristics of the nation's housing, homeowners, and renters. The Census Bureau conducts the housing survey every two years, using a national sample of 60,000 housing units. The first such survey, called the Annual Housing Survey, was taken in 1973 and repeated every year through 1981. Beginning in 1981, the survey became biennial and was renamed the American Housing Survey. It is now taken only in odd-numbered years, and the most recent data available are for 2009. For more about the American Housing Survey, go to http://www.census.gov/hhes/www/housing/ahs/ahs.html.

New Strategist's editors extracted the information on homeownership rates, which appear in Chapter 1, from the Census Bureau's Housing Vacancy Survey. This survey is taken each quarter to collect information on rental and homeowner vacancy rates, which are part of the index of leading economic indicators. About 60,000 housing units are included in the sample, providing homeownership rates for the nation, regions, states, and metropolitan areas by age of householder and other demographic characteristics. For more about the Housing Vacancy Survey, go to http://www.census.gov/hhes/www/housing/hvs.html.

The spending data in Chapter 10, which are not available online, were obtained by special request from the Bureau of Labor Statistics Consumer Expenditure Survey. New Strategist's editors created the spending tables to compare and contrast what homeowners and renters do with their money. For more about the Consumer Expenditure Survey, go to http://www.bls.gov/cex/home.htm.

Although most of the statistics presented in *Americans and Their Homes* are available online, they are buried in giant spreadsheets of numbers without context or analysis. In *Americans and Their Homes*, New Strategist's editors have extracted the data, created hundreds of tables that give context to the housing market, and analyzed the trends. With *Americans and Their Homes* in hand, you no longer need to wade through countless spreadsheets to locate the number you need. You do not need a calculator or personal assistant to determine percent distributions, indexes, and percent changes. *Americans and Their Homes* has done the work for you, saving you from the chore of downloading spreadsheets and performing time-consuming calculations to determine the trends.

Americans and Their Homes tells the story. Thumbing through its pages, you can gain more insight into the housing market than you could by surfing the Internet all afternoon. You can get instant answers to your questions by having it on your computer desktop (with each table linked to its Excel version) or on your bookshelf for thumbing through. New Strategist's unique analysis unlocks the numbers and brings the all-important housing market to life.

CHAPTER

1

Trends in Homeownership

The homeownership rate peaked in 2004, and then fell as the bubble in housing prices inflated and burst.

As of 2010, only 66.9 percent of American households owned their home, well below the peak homeownership rate of 69.0 percent reached in 2004. The bubble in the housing market first inflated prices, spurring millions to jump on the homeownership bandwagon to cash in on the rise. Then housing prices began to fall, an important cause of the Great Recession. Many people lost their home through foreclosure, and young adults have become much more hesitant to buy. Consequently, the homeownership rate fell by 2.1 percentage points since its peak. The rate is likely to trend downward for several more years.

■ Homeownership rates fell in all but the oldest age group between 2004 and 2010, with the biggest decline occurring among 30-to-34-year-olds.

■ The number of renters grew by 12 percent between 2004 and 2010, to 37 million, as homeownership rates fell.

■ The collapse of the housing market has hit the construction industry particularly hard. The number of new single-family homes sold fell sharply in every region, with the West seeing a 76 percent decline between 2005 (the peak year in that region) and 2009.

The homeownership rate was lower in 2010 than in 2000

(percent of households that own their home, 2000 to 2010)

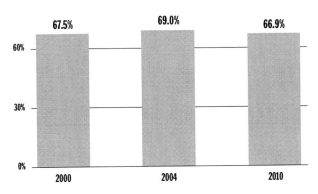

Table 1.1 Housing Inventory and Homeownership, 2000 to 2010

The homeownership rate peaked in 2004 at 69.0 percent. The number
of homeowners peaked in 2006 at 75.6 million. In 2010, the homeownership
rate was 2.1 percentage points below the 2004 peak, and the
number of homeowners was 805,000 below the 2006 peak.

(total number of housing units, number of occupied units, number of owner-occupied housing units, and owner-occupied units as a percent of total occupied units, selected years 2000 to 2010; numbers in thousands)

	total housing units	occupied housing units	owner-occupied housing units	
			number	percent of occupied units
2010	130,599	111,860	74,791	66.9%
2009	129,944	111,159	74,892	67.4
2008	129,211	110,637	75,043	67.8
2007	128,017	110,351	75,192	68.1
2006	126,383	109,896	75,596	68.8
2005	124,600	108,814	74,962	68.9
2004	122,766	107,089	73,929	69.0
2003	121,023	105,722	72,170	68.3
2002	119,396	105,053	71,342	67.9
2001	117,831	103,804	70,434	67.9
2000	116,236	102,560	69,206	67.5

	percent change			percentage point change
2004 to 2010	6.4%	4.5%	1.2%	−2.1
2000 to 2010	12.4	9.1	8.1	−0.6

Source: Bureau of the Census, Housing Vacancies and Homeownership surveys, Internet site http://www.census.gov/hhes/www/housing/hvs/hvs.html; calculations by New Strategist

Table 1.2 Homeownership Rate by Age, 2000 to 2010

Householders aged 30 to 34 experienced the biggest decline in homeownership since the rate peaked in 2004, a 5.8 percentage point decline.

(percent of householders who own their home by age of householder, selected years 2000 to 2010; percentage point change in rate, 2000–10 and 2004–10)

	2010	2004	2000	percentage point change	
				2000–10	2004–10
Total households	**66.9%**	**69.0%**	**67.5%**	**–0.6**	**–2.1**
Under age 35	39.1	43.1	40.7	–1.7	–4.0
Aged 35 to 44	65.0	69.2	68.0	–2.9	–4.2
Aged 45 to 54	73.5	77.2	76.7	–3.2	–3.7
Aged 55 to 64	79.0	81.7	80.2	–1.2	–2.7
Aged 65 or older	80.5	81.1	80.5	0.1	–0.5
Under age 25	22.9	25.2	21.8	1.1	–2.3
Aged 25 to 29	36.8	40.2	37.8	–1.0	–3.4
Aged 30 to 34	51.6	57.4	54.5	–2.9	–5.8
Aged 35 to 39	61.9	66.2	65.2	–3.3	–4.2
Aged 40 to 44	67.9	71.9	70.6	–2.7	–4.1
Aged 45 to 49	72.0	76.3	75.0	–3.0	–4.3
Aged 50 to 54	75.0	78.3	78.7	–3.7	–3.2
Aged 55 to 59	77.7	81.2	79.8	–2.1	–3.5
Aged 60 to 64	80.4	82.4	80.6	–0.2	–2.0
Aged 65 to 69	81.6	83.2	83.4	–1.8	–1.6
Aged 70 to 74	82.4	83.4	81.6	0.9	–1.0
Aged 75 or older	78.9	78.8	78.2	0.7	0.1

Source: Bureau of the Census, Housing Vacancies and Homeownership surveys, Internet site http://www.census.gov/hhes/www/housing/hvs/hvs.html; calculations by New Strategist

Table 1.3 Homeownership Rate by Race and Hispanic Origin, 2000 to 2010

Homeownership rates fell in every racial and ethnic group between 2004 (when the overall homeownership rate peaked) and 2010. Despite the decline, Asians, Hispanics, and non-Hispanic whites had a higher homeownership rate in 2010 than in 2000.

(percent of householders who own their home by race and Hispanic origin of householder, selected years 2000 to 2010; percentage point change in rate, 2000–10 and 2004–10)

	2010	2004	2000	percentage point change 2000–10	percentage point change 2004–10
Total households	**66.9%**	**69.0%**	**67.5%**	**–0.6**	**–2.1**
American Indian	52.3	55.6	56.2	–3.9	–3.3
Asian	58.9	59.8	52.8	6.1	–0.9
Black	45.4	49.1	47.2	–1.8	–3.7
Hispanic	47.5	48.1	46.3	1.2	–0.6
White, non-Hispanic	74.4	76.0	73.8	0.6	–1.6

Source: Bureau of the Census, Housing Vacancies and Homeownership surveys, Internet site http://www.census.gov/hhes/www/housing/hvs/hvs.html; calculations by New Strategist

Table 1.4 Homeownership Rate by Household Type, 2000 to 2010

All but one household type saw their homeownership rate decline between 2004 (when the overall homeownership rate peaked) and 2010. The homeownership rate of men who live alone increased during those years.

(percent of householders who own their home by household type, selected years 2000 to 2010; percentage point change in rate, 2000–10 and 2004–10)

	2010	2004	2000	percentage point change 2000–10	percentage point change 2004–10
Total households	**66.9%**	**69.0%**	**67.5%**	**–0.6**	**–2.1**
Married couples	82.1	84.0	82.4	–0.3	–1.9
Female-headed families	48.6	50.9	48.9	–0.3	–2.3
Male-headed families	56.9	59.6	58.6	–1.7	–2.7
Women living alone	58.6	59.9	57.9	0.7	–1.3
Men living alone	51.3	50.5	47.8	3.5	0.8
Two-or-more-person nonfamily households	41.9	42.4	39.1	2.8	–0.5

Source: Bureau of the Census, Housing Vacancies and Homeownership surveys, Internet site http://www.census.gov/hhes/www/housing/hvs/hvs.html; calculations by New Strategist

Table 1.5 Homeownership Rate of Married Couples by Age, 2000 to 2010

Married couples in every age group saw their homeownership rate decline between 2004 (the year when overall homeownership peaked) and 2010. The biggest decline was among couples aged 30 to 34, down 6.4 percentage points.

(percent of married-couple householders who own their home by age of householder, selected years 2000 to 2010; percentage point change in rate, 2000–10 and 2004–10)

				percentage point change	
	2010	2004	2000	2000–10	2004–10
Total married couples	**82.1%**	**84.0%**	**82.4%**	**–0.3**	**–1.9**
Under age 35	58.3	63.1	61.0	–2.7	–4.8
Aged 35 to 44	79.0	83.0	81.8	–2.8	–4.0
Aged 45 to 54	87.0	89.6	88.6	–1.6	–2.6
Aged 55 to 64	90.7	92.0	90.5	0.2	–1.3
Aged 65 or older	91.8	92.7	92.2	–0.4	–0.9
Under age 25	33.8	37.7	35.1	–1.3	–3.9
Aged 25 to 29	54.4	58.4	55.9	–1.5	–4.0
Aged 30 to 34	66.1	72.5	71.3	–5.2	–6.4
Aged 35 to 39	75.9	80.6	79.3	–3.4	–4.7
Aged 40 to 44	81.9	85.1	84.3	–2.4	–3.2
Aged 45 to 49	85.8	89.0	87.4	–1.6	–3.2
Aged 50 to 54	88.2	90.3	89.9	–1.7	–2.1
Aged 55 to 59	90.0	91.4	90.8	–0.8	–1.4
Aged 60 to 64	91.3	92.7	90.1	1.2	–1.4
Aged 65 to 69	92.3	93.1	93.3	–1.0	–0.8
Aged 70 to 74	93.3	93.9	92.6	0.7	–0.6
Aged 75 or older	90.3	91.5	90.8	–0.5	–1.2

Source: Bureau of the Census, Housing Vacancies and Homeownership surveys, Internet site http://www.census.gov/hhes/www/ housing/hvs/hvs.html; calculations by New Strategist

Table 1.6 Homeownership Rate of Female-Headed Families by Age, 2000 to 2010

Female-headed families saw their homeownership rate decline in all but one age group between 2004 (the year when the overall homeownership rate peaked) and 2010. Householders aged 75 or older were the only ones to make homeownership gains during those years.

(percent of female-headed family householders who own their home by age of householder, selected years 2000 to 2010; percentage point change in rate, 2000–10 and 2004–10)

	2010	2004	2000	percentage point change 2000–10	2004–10
Total female-headed families	**48.6%**	**50.9%**	**49.1%**	**–0.5**	**–2.3**
Under age 35	25.8	27.7	25.2	0.6	–1.9
Aged 35 to 44	42.3	48.7	47.2	–4.9	–6.4
Aged 45 to 54	58.6	63.3	59.7	–1.1	–4.7
Aged 55 to 64	67.1	70.2	69.8	–2.7	–3.1
Aged 65 or older	80.5	81.8	81.4	–0.9	–1.3
Under age 25	24.4	25.7	20.7	3.7	–1.3
Aged 25 to 29	22.2	22.3	22.4	–0.2	–0.1
Aged 30 to 34	30.6	34.5	31.5	–0.9	–3.9
Aged 35 to 39	37.8	42.8	43.3	–5.5	–5.0
Aged 40 to 44	46.9	54.1	50.8	–3.9	–7.2
Aged 45 to 49	56.7	62.6	57.7	–1.0	–5.9
Aged 50 to 54	61.1	64.4	62.5	–1.4	–3.3
Aged 55 to 59	65.7	69.5	67.3	–1.6	–3.8
Aged 60 to 64	69.0	71.2	73.1	–4.1	–2.2
Aged 65 to 69	72.6	76.0	76.6	–4.0	–3.4
Aged 70 to 74	78.6	82.4	79.4	–0.8	–3.8
Aged 75 or older	85.7	84.2	85.2	0.5	1.5

Source: Bureau of the Census, Housing Vacancies and Homeownership surveys, Internet site http://www.census.gov/hhes/www/housing/hvs/hvs.html; calculations by New Strategist

Table 1.7 Homeownership Rate of Male-Headed Families by Age, 2000 to 2010

Male-headed families saw their homeownership rate decline in
all but two age groups between 2004 (the year when the overall
homeownership rate peaked) and 2010. Householders aged 75 or older
saw a 2 percentage point increase in homeownership during those years,
and householders aged 65 to 69 made a small 0.3 percentage point gain.

*(percent of male-headed family householders who own their home by age of householder, selected years 2000 to
2010; percentage point change in rate, 2000–10 and 2004–10)*

				percentage point change	
	2010	2004	2000	2000–10	2004–10
Total male-headed families	**56.9%**	**59.6%**	**57.5%**	**–0.6**	**–2.7**
Under age 35	41.0	44.9	39.9	1.1	–3.9
Aged 35 to 44	56.5	59.6	60.0	–3.5	–3.1
Aged 45 to 54	67.3	70.8	68.2	–0.9	–3.5
Aged 55 to 64	75.0	78.0	72.1	2.9	–3.0
Aged 65 or older	82.0	81.9	82.8	–0.8	0.1
Under age 25	39.2	44.5	38.0	1.2	–5.3
Aged 25 to 29	38.7	39.5	34.5	4.2	–0.8
Aged 30 to 34	46.6	52.0	47.6	–1.0	–5.4
Aged 35 to 39	51.3	55.7	56.2	–4.9	–4.4
Aged 40 to 44	61.8	62.9	63.6	–1.8	–1.1
Aged 45 to 49	65.5	71.0	68.6	–3.1	–5.5
Aged 50 to 54	69.4	70.5	67.6	1.8	–1.1
Aged 55 to 59	74.2	75.0	73.8	0.4	–0.8
Aged 60 to 64	76.3	82.3	70.1	6.2	–6.0
Aged 65 to 69	75.5	75.2	77.2	–1.7	0.3
Aged 70 to 74	79.4	81.9	83.0	–3.6	–2.5
Aged 75 or older	87.2	85.2	85.9	1.3	2.0

*Source: Bureau of the Census, Housing Vacancies and Homeownership surveys, Internet site http://www.census.gov/hhes/www/
housing/hvs/hvs.html; calculations by New Strategist*

Table 1.8 Homeownership Rate of Women Living Alone by Age, 2000 to 2010

The homeownership rate of women who live alone fell between 2004
(when the overall homeownership rate peaked) and 2010. Only the
oldest women, aged 75 or older, saw any gains during those years.

(percent of women living alone who own their home by age of householder, selected years 2000 to 2010; percentage point change in rate, 2000–10 and 2004–10)

	2010	2004	2000	percentage point change 2000–10	2004–10
Total women living alone	**58.6%**	**59.9%**	**58.1%**	**0.5**	**–1.3**
Under age 35	22.3	24.3	19.8	2.5	–2.0
Aged 35 to 44	45.9	49.1	44.5	1.4	–3.2
Aged 45 to 54	53.9	58.4	58.9	–5.0	–4.5
Aged 55 to 64	64.2	67.6	65.5	–1.3	–3.4
Aged 65 or older	70.4	70.6	69.7	0.7	–0.2
Under age 25	11.6	13.0	9.8	1.8	–1.4
Aged 25 to 29	20.8	23.9	18.3	2.5	–3.1
Aged 30 to 34	35.2	37.3	30.1	5.1	–2.1
Aged 35 to 39	45.4	46.8	41.6	3.8	–1.4
Aged 40 to 44	46.3	51.0	47.1	–0.8	–4.7
Aged 45 to 49	50.3	54.5	54.5	–4.2	–4.2
Aged 50 to 54	56.6	61.6	62.5	–5.9	–5.0
Aged 55 to 59	60.4	66.2	64.9	–4.5	–5.8
Aged 60 to 64	67.7	69.1	66.1	1.6	–1.4
Aged 65 to 69	70.3	71.3	70.6	–0.3	–1.0
Aged 70 to 74	71.7	72.3	73.5	–1.8	–0.6
Aged 75 or older	70.1	69.9	68.1	2.0	0.2

Source: Bureau of the Census, Housing Vacancies and Homeownership surveys, Internet site http://www.census.gov/hhes/www/housing/hvs/hvs.html; calculations by New Strategist

Table 1.9 Homeownership Rate of Men Living Alone by Age, 2000 to 2010

Men who live alone experienced a small increase in homeownership between 2004 (when the overall homeownership rate peaked) and 2010. Those aged 60 to 64 saw the biggest gain, an increase of 1.2 percentage points during those years.

(percent of men living alone who own their home by age of householder, selected years 2000 to 2010; percentage point change in rate, 2000–10 and 2004–10)

	2010	2004	2000	percentage point change 2000–10	2004–10
Total men living alone	**51.3%**	**50.5%**	**47.4%**	**3.9**	**0.8**
Under age 35	28.7	29.1	26.0	2.7	–0.4
Aged 35 to 44	46.0	48.0	44.8	1.2	–2.0
Aged 45 to 54	52.2	53.1	50.9	1.3	–0.9
Aged 55 to 64	60.7	59.7	57.1	3.6	1.0
Aged 65 or older	68.3	69.4	68.0	0.3	–1.1
Under age 25	16.1	16.9	12.9	3.2	–0.8
Aged 25 to 29	29.0	29.4	26.0	3.0	–0.4
Aged 30 to 34	37.4	37.5	33.6	3.8	–0.1
Aged 35 to 39	45.7	45.5	41.2	4.5	0.2
Aged 40 to 44	46.3	50.2	48.0	–1.7	–3.9
Aged 45 to 49	49.9	51.6	48.7	1.2	–1.7
Aged 50 to 54	54.4	54.7	53.6	0.8	–0.3
Aged 55 to 59	59.0	58.5	57.3	1.7	0.5
Aged 60 to 64	62.5	61.3	56.7	5.8	1.2
Aged 65 to 69	63.3	66.3	60.9	2.4	–3.0
Aged 70 to 74	65.3	65.7	67.4	–2.1	–0.4
Aged 75 or older	72.6	72.3	71.4	1.2	0.3

Source: Bureau of the Census, Housing Vacancies and Homeownership surveys, Internet site http://www.census.gov/hhes/www/housing/hvs/hvs.html; calculations by New Strategist

Table 1.10 Homeownership Rate for Nonfamily Households with Two or More Persons by Age, 2000 to 2010

Homeownership rates fell for two-or-more-person nonfamily households between 2004 (when the overall homeownership rate peaked) and 2010. Householders aged 65 or older saw their homeownership rate rise during those years, however.

(percent of nonfamily householders with two or more persons who own their home by age of householder, selected years 2000 to 2010; percentage point change in rate, 2000–10 and 2004–10)

| | 2010 | 2004 | 2000 | percentage point change | |
				2000–10	2004–10
TWO-OR-MORE-PERSON NONFAMILY HOUSEHOLDS					
Female householders	**41.9%**	**43.5%**	**40.6%**	**1.3**	**–1.6**
Under age 35	21.8	22.4	19.1	2.7	–0.6
Aged 35 to 44	46.8	54.6	53.5	–6.7	–7.8
Aged 45 to 54	63.4	63.2	68.5	–5.1	0.2
Aged 55 to 64	71.5	77.8	72.2	–0.7	–6.3
Aged 65 or older	80.3	75.1	72.3	8.0	5.2
Male householders	**40.7**	**41.7**	**38.0**	**2.7**	**–1.0**
Under age 35	25.2	25.5	23.5	1.7	–0.3
Aged 35 to 44	45.3	52.0	46.8	–1.5	–6.7
Aged 45 to 54	59.5	62.0	58.1	1.4	–2.5
Aged 55 to 64	65.2	74.5	69.3	–4.1	–9.3
Aged 65 or older	73.3	73.1	71.1	2.2	0.2

Source: Bureau of the Census, Housing Vacancies and Homeownership surveys, Internet site http://www.census.gov/hhes/www/ housing/hvs/hvs.html; calculations by New Strategist

Table 1.11 Homeownership Rate by Age, 2000 to 2010: Northeast

The homeownership rate in the Northeast fell slightly between 2004 (the year when the overall homeownership rate peaked) and 2010. Despite the decline, the 2010 homeownership rate in the Northeast was still above the rate in 2000, especially among the youngest and oldest householders.

(percent of householders in the Northeast who own their home by age, selected years 2000 to 2010; percentage point change in rate, 2000–10 and 2004–10)

	2010	2004	2000	percentage point change	
				2000–10	2004–10
Total Northeast households	**64.1%**	**65.0%**	**63.4%**	**0.7**	**–0.9**
Under age 35	36.9	39.9	37.7	–0.8	–3.0
Aged 35 to 44	62.6	65.5	63.6	–1.0	–2.9
Aged 45 to 54	70.6	72.3	72.2	–1.6	–1.7
Aged 55 to 64	74.9	76.2	74.6	0.3	–1.3
Aged 65 or older	73.4	72.4	71.6	1.8	1.0
Under age 25	21.1	24.7	17.8	3.3	–3.6
Aged 25 to 29	32.6	34.6	33.0	–0.4	–2.0
Aged 30 to 34	49.7	51.9	49.6	0.1	–2.2
Aged 35 to 39	59.2	61.9	60.5	–1.3	–2.7
Aged 40 to 44	65.5	68.5	66.6	–1.1	–3.0
Aged 45 to 49	69.6	71.9	71.2	–1.6	–2.3
Aged 50 to 54	71.6	72.6	73.3	–1.7	–1.0
Aged 55 to 59	73.2	77.0	75.0	–1.8	–3.8
Aged 60 to 64	76.7	75.2	74.2	2.5	1.5
Aged 65 to 69	75.6	74.5	75.0	0.6	1.1
Aged 70 to 74	74.3	75.4	74.3	0.0	–1.1
Aged 75 or older	71.8	70.1	68.5	3.3	1.7

Source: Bureau of the Census, Housing Vacancies and Homeownership surveys, Internet site http://www.census.gov/hhes/www/ housing/hvs/hvs.html; calculations by New Strategist

Table 1.12 Homeownership Rate by Age, 2000 to 2010: Midwest

Every age group in the Midwest saw its homeownership rate decline between 2004 (the year when the overall homeownership rate peaked) and 2010. Most age groups were less likely to be homeowners in 2010 than in 2000. The decline was greatest among householders aged 30 to 34.

(percent of householders in the Midwest who own their home by age, selected years 2000 to 2010; percentage point change in rate, 2000–10 and 2004–10)

| | 2010 | 2004 | 2000 | percentage point change | |
				2000–10	2004–10
Total Midwestern households	**70.8%**	**73.8%**	**72.5%**	**−1.7**	**−3.0**
Under age 35	43.5	49.1	47.7	−4.2	−5.6
Aged 35 to 44	71.5	76.5	74.8	−3.3	−5.0
Aged 45 to 54	78.3	82.5	81.8	−3.5	−4.2
Aged 55 to 64	82.1	84.8	83.4	−1.3	−2.7
Aged 65 or older	81.2	82.5	82.3	−1.1	−1.3
Under age 25	23.0	27.8	24.8	−1.8	−4.8
Aged 25 to 29	42.8	47.9	45.7	−2.9	−5.1
Aged 30 to 34	58.2	65.0	64.3	−6.1	−6.8
Aged 35 to 39	67.9	74.2	72.6	−4.7	−6.3
Aged 40 to 44	74.8	78.5	76.9	−2.1	−3.7
Aged 45 to 49	77.6	81.4	80.4	−2.8	−3.8
Aged 50 to 54	79.0	83.8	83.4	−4.4	−4.8
Aged 55 to 59	80.5	84.7	83.6	−3.1	−4.2
Aged 60 to 64	83.9	84.8	83.2	0.7	−0.9
Aged 65 to 69	83.4	86.6	86.6	−3.2	−3.2
Aged 70 to 74	84.9	86.0	84.6	0.3	−1.1
Aged 75 or older	78.2	79.1	78.9	−0.7	−0.9

Source: Bureau of the Census, Housing Vacancies and Homeownership surveys, Internet site http://www.census.gov/hhes/www/housing/hvs/hvs.html; calculations by New Strategist

Table 1.13 Homeownership Rate by Age, 2000 to 2010: South

The homeownership rate in the South fell by 1.9 percentage points
between 2004 (the year when the overall homeownership rate peaked)
and 2010. Every age group lost ground during those years.
The biggest losers were householders aged 30 to 34.

(percent of householders in the South who own their home by age, selected years 2000 to 2010; percentage point change in rate, 2000–10 and 2004–10)

	2010	2004	2000	percentage point change 2000–10	2004–10
Total Southern households	69.0%	70.9%	69.6%	–0.6	–1.9
Under age 35	40.5	43.7	42.4	–1.9	–3.2
Aged 35 to 44	67.0	70.7	69.7	–2.7	–3.7
Aged 45 to 54	74.8	79.2	78.0	–3.2	–4.4
Aged 55 to 64	81.6	83.8	83.1	–1.5	–2.2
Aged 65 or older	84.9	86.3	84.9	0.0	–1.4
Under age 25	24.7	26.2	23.7	1.0	–1.5
Aged 25 to 29	38.2	40.8	40.1	–1.9	–2.6
Aged 30 to 34	53.1	58.8	56.6	–3.5	–5.7
Aged 35 to 39	65.1	67.9	66.9	–1.8	–2.8
Aged 40 to 44	68.7	73.2	72.4	–3.7	–4.5
Aged 45 to 49	73.3	78.3	75.7	–2.4	–5.0
Aged 50 to 54	76.3	80.2	80.7	–4.4	–3.9
Aged 55 to 59	80.3	83.2	82.8	–2.5	–2.9
Aged 60 to 64	83.1	84.6	83.4	–0.3	–1.5
Aged 65 to 69	84.8	87.7	85.8	–1.0	–2.9
Aged 70 to 74	87.0	87.7	86.4	0.6	–0.7
Aged 75 or older	83.9	84.8	83.5	0.4	–0.9

Source: Bureau of the Census, Housing Vacancies and Homeownership surveys, Internet site http://www.census.gov/hhes/www/housing/hvs/hvs.html; calculations by New Strategist

Table 1.14 Homeownership Rate by Age, 2000 to 2010: West

The homeownership rate in the West fell by a steep 2.8 percentage points between 2004 (the year when the overall homeownership rate peaked) and 2010. All but one age group lost ground during those years. Householders aged 75 or older were the only ones to make gains.

(percent of householders in the West who own their home by age, selected years 2000 to 2010; percentage point change in rate, 2000–10 and 2004–10)

| | | | | percentage point change | |
	2010	2004	2000	2000–10	2004–10
Total Western households	61.4%	64.2%	61.7%	–0.3	–2.8
Under age 35	33.9	38.3	33.6	0.3	–4.4
Aged 35 to 44	57.3	62.6	61.4	–4.1	–5.3
Aged 45 to 54	68.6	72.7	72.1	–3.5	–4.1
Aged 55 to 64	74.8	79.8	77.7	–2.9	–5.0
Aged 65 or older	78.8	79.0	78.7	0.1	–0.2
Under age 25	20.8	21.0	17.4	3.4	–0.2
Aged 25 to 29	31.2	35.4	30.7	0.5	–4.2
Aged 30 to 34	44.6	52.1	46.1	–1.5	–7.5
Aged 35 to 39	53.1	58.8	57.8	–4.7	–5.7
Aged 40 to 44	61.5	66.1	64.8	–3.3	–4.6
Aged 45 to 49	65.8	71.5	70.1	–4.3	–5.7
Aged 50 to 54	71.4	74.0	74.4	–3.0	–2.6
Aged 55 to 59	74.4	78.0	77.7	–3.3	–3.6
Aged 60 to 64	75.3	82.2	77.7	–2.4	–6.9
Aged 65 to 69	79.2	80.2	81.6	–2.4	–1.0
Aged 70 to 74	78.9	80.5	80.0	–1.1	–1.6
Aged 75 or older	78.5	77.6	76.4	2.1	0.9

Source: Bureau of the Census, Housing Vacancies and Homeownership surveys, Internet site http://www.census.gov/hhes/www/housing/hvs/hvs.html; calculations by New Strategist

Table 1.15 Homeownership Rate of Married Couples by Age, 2000 to 2010: Northeast

The homeownership rate of married couples in the Northeast fell slightly between 2004 (the year when the overall homeownership rate peaked) and 2010. Despite the decline, married couples in the Northeast were still more likely to own a home in 2010 than in 2000, especially the youngest.

(percent of married-couple householders in the Northeast who own their home by age, selected years 2000 to 2010; percentage point change in rate, 2000–10 and 2004–10)

				percentage point change	
	2010	2004	2000	2000–10	2004–10
Northeastern married couples	**82.0%**	**82.5%**	**80.6%**	**1.4**	**–0.5**
Under age 35	60.2	61.8	59.4	0.8	–1.6
Aged 35 to 44	78.7	81.9	80.2	–1.5	–3.2
Aged 45 to 54	87.4	86.9	87.0	0.4	0.5
Aged 55 to 64	88.8	89.2	88.0	0.8	–0.4
Aged 65 or older	87.1	88.0	86.0	1.1	–0.9
Under age 25	32.1	34.4	26.0	6.1	–2.3
Aged 25 to 29	53.2	55.3	51.8	1.4	–2.1
Aged 30 to 34	68.2	69.3	67.6	0.6	–1.1
Aged 35 to 39	75.5	78.8	78.2	–2.7	–3.3
Aged 40 to 44	81.4	84.5	82.0	–0.6	–3.1
Aged 45 to 49	86.8	87.2	86.1	0.7	–0.4
Aged 50 to 54	87.9	86.6	88.0	–0.1	1.3
Aged 55 to 59	88.6	89.3	89.2	–0.6	–0.7
Aged 60 to 64	89.2	88.9	86.5	2.7	0.3
Aged 65 to 69	89.7	88.6	88.0	1.7	1.1
Aged 70 to 74	89.4	89.8	86.7	2.7	–0.4
Aged 75 or older	83.3	86.3	83.7	–0.4	–3.0

Source: Bureau of the Census, Housing Vacancies and Homeownership surveys, Internet site http://www.census.gov/hhes/www/ housing/hvs/hvs.html; calculations by New Strategist

Table 1.16 Homeownership Rate of Married Couples by Age, 2000 to 2010: Midwest

Midwestern married couples in most age groups saw their homeownership rate decline between 2004 (the year when the overall homeownership rate peaked) and 2010. The decline was greatest among householders aged 30 to 34, an 8.6 percentage point decline.

(percent of married-couple householders in the Midwest who own their home by age, selected years 2000 to 2010; percentage point change in rate, 2000–10 and 2004–10)

	2010	2004	2000	percentage point change 2000–10	2004–10
Midwestern married couples	**87.2%**	**89.3%**	**87.7%**	**–0.5**	**–2.1**
Under age 35	66.3	73.3	71.3	–5.0	–7.0
Aged 35 to 44	86.2	89.1	88.4	–2.2	–2.9
Aged 45 to 54	91.4	93.6	92.1	–0.7	–2.2
Aged 55 to 64	94.0	94.8	92.9	1.1	–0.8
Aged 65 or older	93.5	95.2	94.1	–0.6	–1.7
Under age 25	41.2	47.9	43.1	–1.9	–6.7
Aged 25 to 29	64.1	69.0	66.1	–2.0	–4.9
Aged 30 to 34	73.2	81.8	81.7	–8.5	–8.6
Aged 35 to 39	83.6	88.4	86.5	–2.9	–4.8
Aged 40 to 44	88.5	89.7	90.1	–1.6	–1.2
Aged 45 to 49	91.0	93.0	90.9	0.1	–2.0
Aged 50 to 54	91.8	94.2	93.5	–1.7	–2.4
Aged 55 to 59	93.1	94.8	92.8	0.3	–1.7
Aged 60 to 64	95.2	94.9	93.1	2.1	0.3
Aged 65 to 69	93.9	96.5	95.5	–1.6	–2.6
Aged 70 to 74	94.7	94.8	94.6	0.1	–0.1
Aged 75 or older	92.3	94.3	92.5	–0.2	–2.0

Source: Bureau of the Census, Housing Vacancies and Homeownership surveys, Internet site http://www.census.gov/hhes/www/housing/hvs/hvs.html; calculations by New Strategist

Table 1.17 Homeownership Rate of Married Couples by Age, 2000 to 2010: South

The homeownership rate of married couples in the South fell by 1.9 percentage points between 2004 (the year when the overall homeownership rate peaked) and 2010. Every age group lost ground during those years. The biggest losers were couples aged 30 to 34.

(percent of married-couple householders in the South who own their home by age, selected years 2000 to 2010; percentage point change in rate, 2000–10 and 2004–10)

				percentage point change	
	2010	2004	2000	2000–10	2004–10
Southern married couples	**83.1%**	**85.0%**	**83.8%**	**−0.7**	**−1.9**
Under age 35	59.5	63.5	62.7	−3.2	−4.0
Aged 35 to 44	80.8	84.0	82.8	−2.0	−3.2
Aged 45 to 54	87.1	91.0	89.9	−2.8	−3.9
Aged 55 to 64	91.6	93.0	92.3	−0.7	−1.4
Aged 65 or older	94.2	95.2	95.0	−0.8	−1.0
Under age 25	36.5	39.1	39.1	−2.6	−2.6
Aged 25 to 29	55.4	59.1	59.4	−4.0	−3.7
Aged 30 to 34	67.7	73.7	72.7	−5.0	−6.0
Aged 35 to 39	78.7	81.7	80.0	−1.3	−3.0
Aged 40 to 44	82.9	86.2	85.4	−2.5	−3.3
Aged 45 to 49	85.5	90.4	88.7	−3.2	−4.9
Aged 50 to 54	88.8	91.7	91.3	−2.5	−2.9
Aged 55 to 59	91.0	92.7	92.6	−1.6	−1.7
Aged 60 to 64	92.2	93.5	91.9	0.3	−1.3
Aged 65 to 69	94.3	95.4	95.7	−1.4	−1.1
Aged 70 to 74	95.9	96.2	95.0	0.9	−0.3
Aged 75 or older	92.8	94.1	94.3	−1.5	−1.3

Source: Bureau of the Census, Housing Vacancies and Homeownership surveys, Internet site http://www.census.gov/hhes/www/housing/hvs/hvs.html; calculations by New Strategist

Table 1.18 **Homeownership Rate of Married Couples by Age, 2000 to 2010: West**

The homeownership rate of married couples in the West fell by 2.8 percentage points between 2004 (the year when the overall homeownership rate peaked) and 2010. All but one age group lost ground during those years. Married couples with a householder aged 75 or older were the only ones to make gains.

(percent of married-couple householders in the West who own their home by age, selected years 2000 to 2010; percentage point change in rate, 2000–10 and 2004–10)

	2010	2004	2000	percentage point change	
				2000–10	2004–10
Western married couples	**75.1%**	**77.9%**	**75.6%**	**–0.5**	**–2.8**
Under age 35	47.8	54.0	49.2	–1.4	–6.2
Aged 35 to 44	69.5	75.8	74.8	–5.3	–6.3
Aged 45 to 54	81.6	85.3	84.1	–2.5	–3.7
Aged 55 to 64	86.9	89.6	87.0	–0.1	–2.7
Aged 65 or older	89.8	89.8	90.5	–0.7	0.0
Under age 25	24.0	28.7	24.9	–0.9	–4.7
Aged 25 to 29	44.0	49.1	43.0	1.0	–5.1
Aged 30 to 34	55.7	64.0	61.3	–5.6	–8.3
Aged 35 to 39	64.9	72.6	71.4	–6.5	–7.7
Aged 40 to 44	74.1	78.8	78.1	–4.0	–4.7
Aged 45 to 49	79.5	84.1	82.8	–3.3	–4.6
Aged 50 to 54	83.6	86.8	85.5	–1.9	–3.2
Aged 55 to 59	86.3	87.8	87.0	–0.7	–1.5
Aged 60 to 64	87.5	92.1	86.9	0.6	–4.6
Aged 65 to 69	88.8	89.3	90.6	–1.8	–0.5
Aged 70 to 74	90.4	92.2	91.6	–1.2	–1.8
Aged 75 or older	90.2	88.5	89.7	0.5	1.7

Source: Bureau of the Census, Housing Vacancies and Homeownership surveys, Internet site http://www.census.gov/hhes/www/housing/hvs/hvs.html; calculations by New Strategist

Table 1.19 Homeownership Rate by State, 2000 to 2010

Homeownership rates fell in most states between 2004 (when the overall homeownership rate peaked) and 2010. The biggest decline was in Nevada, where the homeownership rate fell 6 percentage points during those years.

(percent of householders who own their home by state, selected years 2000 to 2010; percentage point change in rate, 2000–10 and 2004–10)

				percentage point change	
	2010	2004	2000	2000–10	2004–10
Total households	**66.9%**	**69.0%**	**67.4%**	**−0.5**	**−2.1**
Alabama	73.2	78.0	73.2	0.0	−4.8
Alaska	65.7	67.2	66.4	−0.7	−1.5
Arizona	66.6	68.7	68.0	−1.4	−2.1
Arkansas	67.9	69.1	68.9	−1.0	−1.2
California	56.1	59.7	57.1	−1.0	−3.6
Colorado	68.5	71.1	68.3	0.2	−2.6
Connecticut	70.8	71.7	70.0	0.8	−0.9
Delaware	74.7	77.3	72.0	2.7	−2.6
District of Columbia	45.6	45.6	41.9	3.7	0.0
Florida	69.3	72.2	68.4	0.9	−2.9
Georgia	67.1	70.9	69.8	−2.7	−3.8
Hawaii	56.1	60.6	55.2	0.9	−4.5
Idaho	72.4	73.7	70.5	1.9	−1.3
Illinois	68.8	72.7	67.9	0.9	−3.9
Indiana	71.2	75.8	74.9	−3.7	−4.6
Iowa	71.1	73.2	75.2	−4.1	−2.1
Kansas	67.4	69.9	69.3	−1.9	−2.5
Kentucky	70.3	73.3	73.4	−3.1	−3.0
Louisiana	70.4	70.6	68.1	2.3	−0.2
Maine	73.8	74.7	76.5	−2.7	−0.9
Maryland	68.9	72.1	69.9	−1.0	−3.2
Massachusetts	65.3	63.8	59.9	5.4	1.5
Michigan	74.5	77.1	77.2	−2.7	−2.6
Minnesota	72.6	76.4	76.1	−3.5	−3.8
Mississippi	74.8	74.0	75.2	−0.4	0.8
Missouri	71.2	72.4	74.2	−3.0	−1.2
Montana	68.1	72.4	70.2	−2.1	−4.3
Nebraska	70.4	71.2	70.2	0.2	−0.8
Nevada	59.7	65.7	64.0	−4.3	−6.0
New Hampshire	74.9	73.3	69.2	5.7	1.6
New Jersey	66.5	68.8	66.2	0.3	−2.3
New Mexico	68.6	71.5	73.7	−5.1	−2.9
New York	54.5	54.8	53.4	1.1	−0.3
North Carolina	69.5	69.8	71.1	−1.6	−0.3
North Dakota	67.1	70.0	70.7	−3.6	−2.9

| | 2010 | 2004 | 2000 | percentage point change | |
				2000–10	2004–10
Ohio	69.7%	73.1%	71.3%	−1.6	−3.4
Oklahoma	69.2	71.1	72.7	−3.5	−1.9
Oregon	66.3	69.0	65.3	1.0	−2.7
Pennsylvania	72.2	74.9	74.7	−2.5	−2.7
Rhode Island	62.8	61.5	61.5	1.3	1.3
South Carolina	74.8	76.2	76.5	−1.7 ·	−1.4
South Dakota	70.6	68.5	71.2	−0.6	2.1
Tennessee	71.0	71.6	70.9	0.1	−0.6
Texas	65.3	65.5	63.8	1.5	−0.2
Utah	72.5	74.9	72.7	−0.2	−2.4
Vermont	73.6	72.0	68.7	4.9	1.6
Virginia	68.7	73.4	73.9	−5.2	−4.7
Washington	64.4	66.0	63.6	0.8	−1.6
West Virginia	79.0	80.3	75.9	3.1	−1.3
Wisconsin	71.0	73.3	71.8	−0.8	−2.3
Wyoming	73.4	72.8	71.0	2.4	0.6

Source: Bureau of the Census, Housing Vacancy Surveys, Internet site http://www.census.gov/hhes/www/housing/hvs/hvs.html; calculations by New Strategist

Table 1.20 Homeownership Rate by Metropolitan Area, 2005 and 2010

Homeownership rates fell in most of the 75 largest metropolitan areas
between 2005 (the earliest year for which data are available) and 2010.
The biggest decline was in Toledo, Ohio, an 8.5 percentage point drop.
The biggest gain was in Albany, New York, a 6.5 percentage point increase.

(percent of householders who own their home in the 75 largest metropolitan areas, 2005 and 2010; percentage point change, 2005–10)

	2010	2005	percentage point change 2005–10
Total inside metropolitan areas	**65.4%**	**67.4%**	**–2.0**
Akron, OH	76.9	78.1	–1.2
Albany–Schenectady–Troy, NY	72.8	66.3	6.5
Alburquerque, NM	65.5	69.2	–3.7
Allentown–Bethlehem–Easton, PA–NJ	71.5	73.5	–2.0
Atlanta–Sandy Springs–Marietta, GA	67.2	66.4	0.8
Austin–Round Rock, TX	65.8	63.9	1.9
Bakersfield, CA	61.7	60.5	1.2
Baltimore–Towson, MD	65.7	70.6	–4.9
Baton Rouge, LA	70.3	71.0	–0.7
Birmingham–Hoover, AL	76.2	75.1	1.1
Boston–Cambridge–Quincy, MA–NH	66.0	63.0	3.0
Bridgeport–Stamford–Norwalk, CT	71.3	68.2	3.1
Buffalo–Cheektowaga–Tonawanda, NY	64.5	66.3	–1.8
Charlotte–Gastonia–Concord, NC–SC	66.1	65.8	0.3
Chicago–Naperville–Joliet, IL	68.2	70.0	–1.8
Cincinnati–Middletown, OH–KY–IN	62.8	68.4	–5.6
Cleveland–Elyria–Mentor, OH	70.7	74.4	–3.7
Columbia, SC	74.1	76.3	–2.2
Columbus, OH	62.2	68.9	–6.7
Dallas–Ft Worth–Arlington, TX	63.8	62.3	1.5
Dayton, OH	67.4	66.1	1.3
Denver–Aurora, CO	65.7	70.7	–5.0
Detroit–Warren–Livonia, MI\13	73.6	75.1	–1.5
El Paso, TX	70.1	72.6	–2.5
Fresno, CA	49.3	51.8	–2.5
Grand Rapids–Wyoming, MI	76.4	72.6	3.8
Greensboro–High Point, NC	68.8	66.3	2.5
Hartford–West Hartford–East Hartford, CT	71.3	72.2	–0.9
Honolulu, HI	54.9	58.0	–3.1
Houston–Baytown–Sugar Land, TX	61.4	61.7	0.3
Indianapolis, IN	68.8	77.1	–8.3
Jacksonville, FL	70.0	67.9	2.1
Kansas City, MO–KS	68.8	71.3	–2.5
Las Vegas–Paradise, NV	55.7	61.4	–5.7
Los Angeles–Long Beach–Santa Ana, CA	49.7	54.6	–4.9

	2010	2005	percentage point change 2005–10
Louisville, KY–IN	63.4%	62.9%	0.5
Memphis, TN–AR–MS	61.9	64.8	–2.9
Miami–Fort Lauderdale–Miami Beach, FL	63.8	69.2	–5.4
Milwaukee–Waukesha–West Allis, WI	62.4	65.7	–3.3
Minneapolis–St. Paul–Bloomington, MN–WI	71.2	74.9	–3.7
Nashville–Davidson–Murfreesboro, TN	70.4	73.0	–2.6
New Haven–Milford, CT	65.6	66.9	–1.3
New Orleans–Metairie–Kenner, LA	66.9	71.2	–4.3
New York–Northern New Jersey–Long Island, NY	51.6	54.6	–3.0
Oklahoma City, OK	70.0	72.9	–2.9
Omaha–Council Bluffs, NE–IA	73.2	69.7	3.5
Orlando, FL	70.8	70.5	0.3
Oxnard–Thousand Oaks–Ventura, CA	67.1	73.4	–6.3
Philadelphia–Camden–Wilmington, PA	70.7	73.5	–2.8
Phoenix–Mesa–Scottsdale, AZ	66.5	71.2	–4.7
Pittsburgh, PA	70.4	73.1	–2.7
Portland–Vancouver–Beaverton, OR–WA	63.7	68.3	–4.6
Poughkeepsie–Newburgh–Middletown, NJ	70.8	74.2	–3.4
Providence–New Bedford–Fall River RI–MA	61.0	63.1	–2.1
Raleigh–Cary, NC	65.9	71.4	–5.5
Richmond, VA	68.1	69.7	–1.6
Riverside–San Bernardino–Ontario, CA	63.9	68.5	–4.6
Rochester, NY	71.4	74.9	–3.5
Sacramento–Arden-Arcade–Roseville, CA	61.1	64.1	–3.0
St. Louis, MO–IL	72.2	74.4	–2.2
Salt Lake City, UT	65.5	68.8	–3.3
San Antonio, TX	70.1	66.0	4.1
San Diego–Carlsbad–San Marcos	54.4	60.5	–6.1
San Francisco–Oakland–Fremont, CA	58.0	57.8	0.2
San Jose–Sunnyvale–Santa Clara, CA	58.9	59.2	–0.3
Seattle–Bellevue–Everett, WA	60.9	64.5	–3.6
Springfield, MA	67.1	64.5	2.6
Syracuse, NY	61.1	59.8	1.3
Tampa–St. Petersburg–Clearwater, FL	68.3	71.7	–3.4
Toledo, OH	63.9	72.4	–8.5
Tucson, AZ	64.3	66.1	–1.8
Tulsa, OK	64.2	71.7	–7.5
Virginia Beach–Norfolk–Newport News, VA	61.4	68.0	–6.6
Washington–Arlington–Alexandria, DC–VA–MD–WV	67.3	68.4	–1.1
Worcester, MA	64.1	65.3	–1.2

Note: 2004 was the peak year for homeownership nationwide, but 2005 is the earliest year for which comparable metropolitan area data are available.

Source: Bureau of the Census, Housing Vacancy Survey, Internet site http://www.census.gov/hhes/www/housing/hvs/hvs.html; calculations by New Strategist

Table 1.21 Number of Homeowners by Age, 2000 to 2010

The number of homeowners rose 8 percent between 2000
and 2010. The biggest increase was in the number of
homeowners aged 60 to 64, a figure that rose 55 percent.

*(number and percent distribution of householders who own their home, by age of householder, selected years 2000
to 2010; percent change in number, 2000–10 and 2004–10; numbers in thousands)*

	2010		2004		2000		percent change in number	
	number	percent	number	percent	number	percent	2000–10	2004–10
Total homeowners	**74,791**	**100.0%**	**73,929**	**100.0%**	**69,206**	**100.0%**	**8.1%**	**1.2%**
Under age 35	9,601	12.8	10,779	14.6	9,813	14.2	–2.2	–10.9
Aged 35 to 44	13,209	17.7	15,444	20.9	16,028	23.2	–17.6	–14.5
Aged 45 to 54	17,212	23.0	16,986	23.0	15,541	22.5	10.8	1.3
Aged 55 to 64	15,625	20.9	13,172	17.8	10,798	15.6	44.7	18.6
Aged 65 or older	19,144	25.6	17,548	23.7	17,027	24.6	12.4	9.1
Under age 25	1,385	1.9	1,655	2.2	1,299	1.9	6.6	–16.3
Aged 25 to 29	3,327	4.4	3,431	4.6	3,097	4.5	7.4	–3.0
Aged 30 to 34	4,890	6.5	5,694	7.7	5,416	7.8	–9.7	–14.1
Aged 35 to 39	6,065	8.1	6,938	9.4	7,545	10.9	–19.6	–12.6
Aged 40 to 44	7,144	9.6	8,506	11.5	8,483	12.3	–15.8	–16.0
Aged 45 to 49	8,418	11.3	8,875	12.0	8,130	11.7	3.5	–5.1
Aged 50 to 54	8,793	11.8	8,111	11.0	7,411	10.7	18.6	8.4
Aged 55 to 59	8,112	10.8	7,283	9.9	5,951	8.6	36.3	11.4
Aged 60 to 64	7,513	10.0	5,889	8.0	4,847	7.0	55.0	27.6
Aged 65 to 69	5,744	7.7	4,731	6.4	4,735	6.8	21.3	21.4
Aged 70 to 74	4,492	6.0	4,245	5.7	4,421	6.4	1.6	5.8
Aged 75 or older	8,908	11.9	8,572	11.6	7,870	11.4	13.2	3.9

*Source: Bureau of the Census, Housing Vacancy Survey, Internet site http://www.census.gov/hhes/www/housing/hvs/hvs.html;
calculations by New Strategist*

Table 1.22 Number of Renters by Age, 2000 to 2010

The number of renters increased 11 percent between 2000 and 2010, the entire increase occurring since 2004. The biggest gain was in the 55-to-64 age group as it filled with boomers.

(number and percent distribution of householders who rent their home, by age of householder, selected years 2000 to 2010; percent change in number, 2000–10 and 2004–10; numbers in thousands)

	2010		2004		2000		percent change in number	
	number	percent	number	percent	number	percent	2000–10	2004–10
Total renters	**37,069**	**100.0%**	**33,160**	**100.0%**	**33,354**	**100.0%**	**11.1%**	**11.8%**
Under age 35	14,977	40.4	14,236	42.9	14,287	42.8	4.8	5.2
Aged 35 to 44	7,110	19.2	6,865	20.7	7,558	22.7	−5.9	3.6
Aged 45 to 54	6,199	16.7	5,016	15.1	4,708	14.1	31.7	23.6
Aged 55 to 64	4,156	11.2	2,943	8.9	2,669	8.0	55.7	41.2
Aged 65 or older	4,628	12.5	4,100	12.4	4,131	12.4	12.0	12.9
Under age 25	4,675	12.6	4,916	14.8	4,665	14.0	0.2	−4.9
Aged 25 to 29	5,714	15.4	5,101	15.4	5,100	15.3	12.0	12.0
Aged 30 to 34	4,587	12.4	4,218	12.7	4,523	13.6	1.4	8.7
Aged 35 to 39	3,729	10.1	3,548	10.7	4,028	12.1	−7.4	5.1
Aged 40 to 44	3,381	9.1	3,317	10.0	3,530	10.6	−4.2	1.9
Aged 45 to 49	3,272	8.8	2,762	8.3	2,705	8.1	21.0	18.5
Aged 50 to 54	2,928	7.9	2,253	6.8	2,003	6.0	46.2	30.0
Aged 55 to 59	2,325	6.3	1,686	5.1	1,504	4.5	54.6	37.9
Aged 60 to 64	1,832	4.9	1,256	3.8	1,164	3.5	57.4	45.9
Aged 65 to 69	1,294	3.5	952	2.9	944	2.8	37.1	35.9
Aged 70 to 74	957	2.6	844	2.5	999	3.0	−4.2	13.4
Aged 75 or older	2,377	6.4	2,305	7.0	2,189	6.6	8.6	3.1

Source: Bureau of the Census, Housing Vacancy Survey, Internet site http://www.census.gov/hhes/www/housing/hvs/hvs.html; calculations by New Strategist

Table 1.23 Number of Homeowners by Household Type, 2000 to 2010

Married couples account for 60 percent of homeowners. The number of married couple homeowners fell 2 percent between 2004 and 2010.

(number and percent distribution of householders who own their home, by household type, selected years 2000 to 2010; percent change in number, 2000–10 and 2004–10; numbers in thousands)

	2010		2004		2000		percent change in number	
	number	percent	number	percent	number	percent	2000–10	2004–10
Total households	**74,791**	**100.0%**	**73,929**	**100.0%**	**69,206**	**100.0%**	**8.1%**	**1.2%**
Married couples	45,068	60.3	45,972	62.2	44,255	63.9	1.8	–2.0
Female-headed families	6,846	9.2	6,568	8.9	6,100	8.8	12.2	4.2
Male-headed families	3,138	4.2	2,871	3.9	2,385	3.4	31.6	9.3
Women living alone	9,842	13.2	9,716	13.1	8,818	12.7	11.6	1.3
Men living alone	7,002	9.4	6,205	8.4	5,347	7.7	31.0	12.8
Two-or-more-person nonfamily households	2,895	3.9	2,598	3.5	2,302	3.3	25.8	11.4

Source: Bureau of the Census, Housing Vacancies and Homeownership surveys, Internet site http://www.census.gov/hhes/www/housing/hvs/hvs.html; calculations by New Strategist

Table 1.24 Number of Renters by Household Type, 2000 to 2010

The number of renters increased 12 percent between 2004 and 2010. The biggest percent increase was among male-headed families.

(number and percent distribution of householders who rent their home, by household type, selected years 2000 to 2010; percent change in number, 2000–10 and 2004–10; numbers in thousands)

	2010		2004		2000		percent change in number	
	number	percent	number	percent	number	percent	2000–10	2004–10
Total households	**37,069**	**100.0%**	**33,160**	**100.0%**	**33,354**	**100.0%**	**11.1%**	**11.8%**
Married couples	9,830	26.5	8,767	26.4	9,439	28.3	4.1	12.1
Female-headed families	7,236	19.5	6,326	19.1	6,377	19.1	13.5	14.4
Male-headed families	2,375	6.4	1,946	5.9	1,683	5.0	41.1	22.0
Women living alone	6,959	18.8	6,515	19.6	6,408	19.2	8.6	6.8
Men living alone	6,650	17.9	6,078	18.3	5,846	17.5	13.8	9.4
Two-or-more-person nonfamily households	4,020	10.8	3,527	10.6	3,601	10.8	11.6	14.0

Source: Bureau of the Census, Housing Vacancies and Homeownership surveys, Internet site http://www.census.gov/hhes/www/housing/hvs/hvs.html; calculations by New Strategist

Table 1.25 Number of Married-Couple Homeowners by Age, 2000 to 2010

The number of married-couple homeowners fell 2 percent between 2004 (when the overall homeownership rate peaked) and 2010. The declines occurred among married couples under age 50.

(number and percent distribution of married couples who own their home, by age of householder, selected years 2000 to 2010; percent change in number, 2000–10 and 2004–10; numbers in thousands)

	2010		2004		2000		percent change in number	
	number	percent	number	percent	number	percent	2000–10	2004–10
Total married-couple homeowners	**45,068**	**100.0%**	**45,972**	**100.0%**	**44,255**	**100.0%**	**1.8%**	**−2.0%**
Under age 35	5,373	11.9	6,539	14.2	6,301	14.2	−14.7	−17.8
Aged 35 to 44	9,250	20.5	10,714	23.3	11,401	25.8	−18.9	−13.7
Aged 45 to 54	11,230	24.9	11,428	24.9	10,780	24.4	4.2	−1.7
Aged 55 to 64	9,835	21.8	8,673	18.9	7,327	16.6	34.2	13.4
Aged 65 or older	9,379	20.8	8,618	18.7	8,445	19.1	11.1	8.8
Under age 25	358	0.8	508	1.1	485	1.1	−26.2	−29.5
Aged 25 to 29	1,771	3.9	2,082	4.5	1,984	4.5	−10.7	−14.9
Aged 30 to 34	3,244	7.2	3,949	8.6	3,832	8.7	−15.3	−17.9
Aged 35 to 39	4,272	9.5	4,884	10.6	5,492	12.4	−22.2	−12.5
Aged 40 to 44	4,978	11.0	5,830	12.7	5,910	13.4	−15.8	−14.6
Aged 45 to 49	5,584	12.4	5,982	13.0	5,691	12.9	−1.9	−6.7
Aged 50 to 54	5,647	12.5	5,447	11.8	5,090	11.5	10.9	3.7
Aged 55 to 59	5,163	11.5	4,865	10.6	4,092	9.2	26.2	6.1
Aged 60 to 64	4,673	10.4	3,808	8.3	3,235	7.3	44.5	22.7
Aged 65 to 69	3,472	7.7	2,921	6.4	2,981	6.7	16.5	18.9
Aged 70 to 74	2,478	5.5	2,411	5.2	2,405	5.4	3.0	2.8
Aged 75 or older	3,428	7.6	3,286	7.1	3,060	6.9	12.0	4.3

Source: Bureau of the Census, Housing Vacancy Survey, Internet site http://www.census.gov/hhes/www/housing/hvs/hvs.html; calculations by New Strategist

Table 1.26 Number of Married-Couple Renters by Age, 2000 to 2010

The number of married couples who rent their home
increased 12 percent between 2004 and 2010. By age,
the only loss was among married renters under age 25.

(number and percent distribution of married couples who rent their home, by age of householder, selected years 2000 to 2010; percent change in number, 2000–10 and 2004–10; numbers in thousands)

	2010		2004		2000		percent change in number	
	number	percent	number	percent	number	percent	2000–10	2004–10
Total married-couple renters	**9,830**	**100.0%**	**8,767**	**100.0%**	**9,439**	**100.0%**	**4.1%**	**12.1%**
Under age 35	3,849	39.2	3,816	43.5	4,075	43.2	–5.5	0.9
Aged 35 to 44	2,452	24.9	2,193	25.0	2,503	26.5	–2.0	11.8
Aged 45 to 54	1,678	17.1	1,326	15.1	1,362	14.4	23.2	26.5
Aged 55 to 64	1,015	10.3	754	8.6	784	8.3	29.5	34.6
Aged 65 or older	836	8.5	678	7.7	716	7.6	16.8	23.3
Under age 25	700	7.1	840	9.6	939	9.9	–25.5	–16.7
Aged 25 to 29	1,483	15.1	1,483	16.9	1,591	16.9	–6.8	0.0
Aged 30 to 34	1,666	16.9	1,494	17.0	1,545	16.4	7.8	11.5
Aged 35 to 39	1,355	13.8	1,173	13.4	1,397	14.8	–3.0	15.5
Aged 40 to 44	1,097	11.2	1,021	11.6	1,104	11.7	–0.6	7.4
Aged 45 to 49	924	9.4	740	8.4	796	8.4	16.1	24.9
Aged 50 to 54	753	7.7	585	6.7	565	6.0	33.3	28.7
Aged 55 to 59	571	5.8	454	5.2	432	4.6	32.2	25.8
Aged 60 to 64	442	4.5	299	3.4	352	3.7	25.6	47.8
Aged 65 to 69	290	3.0	215	2.5	198	2.1	46.5	34.9
Aged 70 to 74	178	1.8	157	1.8	198	2.1	–10.1	13.4
Aged 75 or older	369	3.8	305	3.5	319	3.4	15.7	21.0

Source: Bureau of the Census, Housing Vacancy Survey, Internet site http://www.census.gov/hhes/www/housing/hvs/hvs.html; calculations by New Strategist

Table 1.27 Number of Female-Headed Family Homeowners by Age, 2000 to 2010

The number of female-headed families that own their
home grew by 12 percent between 2000 and 2010.

(number and percent distribution of female-headed families who own their home, by age of householder, selected years 2000 to 2010; percent change in number, 2000–10 and 2004–10; numbers in thousands)

	2010		2004		2000		percent change in number	
	number	percent	number	percent	number	percent	2000–10	2004–10
Total female-head-of-family homeowners	**6,846**	**100.0%**	**6,568**	**100.0%**	**6,100**	**100.0%**	**12.2%**	**4.2%**
Under age 35	1,129	16.5	1,152	17.5	992	16.3	13.8	–2.0
Aged 35 to 44	1,362	19.9	1,650	25.1	1,635	26.8	–16.7	–17.5
Aged 45 to 54	1,721	25.1	1,595	24.3	1,392	22.8	23.6	7.9
Aged 55 to 64	1,078	15.7	859	13.1	729	12.0	47.9	25.5
Aged 65 or older	1,556	22.7	1,311	20.0	1,352	22.2	15.1	18.7
Under age 25	327	4.8	347	5.3	263	4.3	24.3	–5.8
Aged 25 to 29	340	5.0	299	4.6	280	4.6	21.4	13.7
Aged 30 to 34	462	6.7	506	7.7	449	7.4	2.9	–8.7
Aged 35 to 39	617	9.0	694	10.6	697	11.4	–11.5	–11.1
Aged 40 to 44	745	10.9	956	14.6	938	15.4	–20.6	–22.1
Aged 45 to 49	920	13.4	939	14.3	773	12.7	19.0	–2.0
Aged 50 to 54	800	11.7	656	10.0	619	10.1	29.2	22.0
Aged 55 to 59	623	9.1	497	7.6	395	6.5	57.7	25.4
Aged 60 to 64	456	6.7	362	5.5	334	5.5	36.5	26.0
Aged 65 to 69	370	5.4	296	4.5	343	5.6	7.9	25.0
Aged 70 to 74	369	5.4	310	4.7	332	5.4	11.1	19.0
Aged 75 or older	817	11.9	706	10.7	676	11.1	20.9	15.7

Source: Bureau of the Census, Housing Vacancy Survey, Internet site http://www.census.gov/hhes/www/housing/hvs/hvs.html; calculations by New Strategist

Table 1.28 Number of Female-Headed Family Renters by Age, 2000 to 2010

The number of female-headed families that rent their
home grew by 13 percent between 2000 and 2010.

(number and percent distribution of female-headed families who rent their home, by age of householder, selected years 2000 to 2010; percent change in number, 2000–10 and 2004–10; numbers in thousands)

	2010		2004		2000		percent change in number	
	number	percent	number	percent	number	percent	2000–10	2004–10
Total female-head-of-family renters	**7,236**	**100.0%**	**6,326**	**100.0%**	**6,377**	**100.0%**	**13.5%**	**14.4%**
Under age 35	3,256	45.0	3,006	47.5	2,962	46.4	9.9	8.3
Aged 35 to 44	1,860	25.7	1,739	27.5	1,831	28.7	1.6	7.0
Aged 45 to 54	1,213	16.8	922	14.6	907	14.2	33.7	31.6
Aged 55 to 64	530	7.3	365	5.8	332	5.2	59.6	45.2
Aged 65 or older	376	5.2	294	4.6	346	5.4	8.7	27.9
Under age 25	1,013	14.0	1,002	15.8	1,003	15.7	1.0	1.1
Aged 25 to 29	1,193	16.5	1,044	16.5	976	15.3	22.2	14.3
Aged 30 to 34	1,050	14.5	960	15.2	982	15.4	6.9	9.4
Aged 35 to 39	1,017	14.1	929	14.7	925	14.5	9.9	9.5
Aged 40 to 44	843	11.7	811	12.8	906	14.2	–7.0	3.9
Aged 45 to 49	705	9.7	560	8.9	565	8.9	24.8	25.9
Aged 50 to 54	510	7.0	362	5.7	342	5.4	49.1	40.9
Aged 55 to 59	325	4.5	218	3.4	212	3.3	53.3	49.1
Aged 60 to 64	204	2.8	148	2.3	120	1.9	70.0	37.8
Aged 65 to 69	140	1.9	94	1.5	124	1.9	12.9	48.9
Aged 70 to 74	100	1.4	66	1.0	99	1.6	1.0	51.5
Aged 75 or older	135	1.9	133	2.1	123	1.9	9.8	1.5

Source: Bureau of the Census, Housing Vacancy Survey, Internet site http://www.census.gov/hhes/www/housing/hvs/hvs.html; calculations by New Strategist

Table 1.29 Number of Male-Headed Family Homeowners by Age, 2000 to 2010

The number of male-headed families that own their home
grew by an enormous 32 percent between 2000 and 2010.

(number and percent distribution of male-headed families who own their home, by age of householder, selected years 2000 to 2010; percent change in number, 2000–10 and 2004–10; numbers in thousands)

	2010		2004		2000		percent change in number	
	number	percent	number	percent	number	percent	2000–10	2004–10
Total male head-of-family homeowners	**3,138**	**100.0%**	**2,871**	**100.0%**	**2,385**	**100.0%**	**31.6%**	**9.3%**
Under age 35	887	28.3	849	29.6	592	24.8	49.8	4.5
Aged 35 to 44	632	20.1	660	23.0	678	28.4	−6.8	−4.2
Aged 45 to 54	765	24.4	698	24.3	510	21.4	50.0	9.6
Aged 55 to 64	481	15.3	317	11.0	260	10.9	85.0	51.7
Aged 65 or older	373	11.9	347	12.1	345	14.5	8.1	7.5
Under age 25	350	11.2	377	13.1	238	10.0	47.1	−7.2
Aged 25 to 29	268	8.5	221	7.7	135	5.7	98.5	21.3
Aged 30 to 34	270	8.6	251	8.7	219	9.2	23.3	7.6
Aged 35 to 39	285	9.1	280	9.8	302	12.7	−5.6	1.8
Aged 40 to 44	347	11.1	379	13.2	376	15.8	−7.7	−8.4
Aged 45 to 49	401	12.8	409	14.2	288	12.1	39.2	−2.0
Aged 50 to 54	364	11.6	290	10.1	222	9.3	64.0	25.5
Aged 55 to 59	291	9.3	181	6.3	151	6.3	92.7	60.8
Aged 60 to 64	191	6.1	135	4.7	109	4.6	75.2	41.5
Aged 65 to 69	101	3.2	82	2.9	87	3.6	16.1	23.2
Aged 70 to 74	79	2.5	68	2.4	102	4.3	−22.5	16.2
Aged 75 or older	192	6.1	196	6.8	156	6.5	23.1	−2.0

Source: Bureau of the Census, Housing Vacancy Survey, Internet site http://www.census.gov/hhes/www/housing/hvs/hvs.html; calculations by New Strategist

Table 1.30 Number of Male-Headed Family Renters by Age, 2000 to 2010

The number of male-headed families that rent their home
grew by a substantial 41 percent between 2000 and 2010.

(number and percent distribution of male-headed families who rent their home, by age of householder, selected years 2000 to 2010; percent change in number, 2000–10 and 2004–10; numbers in thousands)

	2010		2004		2000		percent change in number	
	number	percent	number	percent	number	percent	2000–10	2004–10
Total male head-of-family renters	**2,375**	**100.0%**	**1,946**	**100.0%**	**1,683**	**100.0%**	**41.1%**	**22.0%**
Under age 35	1,275	53.7	1,044	53.6	879	52.2	45.1	22.1
Aged 35 to 44	485	20.4	448	23.0	401	23.8	20.9	8.3
Aged 45 to 54	372	15.7	289	14.9	243	14.4	53.1	28.7
Aged 55 to 64	161	6.8	89	4.6	90	5.3	78.9	80.9
Aged 65 or older	81	3.4	77	4.0	71	4.2	14.1	5.2
Under age 25	542	22.8	472	24.3	367	21.8	47.7	14.8
Aged 25 to 29	424	17.9	339	17.4	276	16.4	53.6	25.1
Aged 30 to 34	309	13.0	232	11.9	236	14.0	30.9	33.2
Aged 35 to 39	271	11.4	224	11.5	218	13.0	24.3	21.0
Aged 40 to 44	214	9.0	225	11.6	182	10.8	17.6	–4.9
Aged 45 to 49	211	8.9	166	8.5	139	8.3	51.8	27.1
Aged 50 to 54	161	6.8	122	6.3	103	6.1	56.3	32.0
Aged 55 to 59	101	4.3	60	3.1	52	3.1	94.2	68.3
Aged 60 to 64	59	2.5	30	1.5	38	2.3	55.3	96.7
Aged 65 to 69	33	1.4	28	1.4	24	1.4	37.5	17.9
Aged 70 to 74	21	0.9	16	0.8	17	1.0	23.5	31.3
Aged 75 or older	29	1.2	35	1.8	29	1.7	0.0	–17.1

Source: Bureau of the Census, Housing Vacancy Survey, Internet site http://www.census.gov/hhes/www/housing/hvs/hvs.html; calculations by New Strategist

Table 1.31 Number of Women Living Alone Who Are Homeowners by Age, 2000 to 2010

The number of women homeowners who live alone fell in many age groups between 2004 (when the overall homeownership rate peaked) and 2010.

(number and percent distribution of women living alone who own their home, by age of householder, selected years 2000 to 2010; percent change in number, 2000–10 and 2004–10; numbers in thousands)

	2010		2004		2000		percent change in number	
	number	percent	number	percent	number	percent	2000–10	2004–10
Total women who live alone who are homeowners	**9,842**	**100.0%**	**9,716**	**100.0%**	**8,818**	**100.0%**	**11.6%**	**1.3%**
Under age 35	506	5.1	555	5.7	428	4.9	18.2	−8.8
Aged 35 to 44	561	5.7	731	7.5	654	7.4	−14.2	−23.3
Aged 45 to 54	1,294	13.1	1,383	14.2	1,262	14.3	2.5	−6.4
Aged 55 to 64	2,090	21.2	1,827	18.8	1,453	16.5	43.8	14.4
Aged 65 or older	5,390	54.8	5,219	53.7	5,021	56.9	7.3	3.3
Under age 25	77	0.8	103	1.1	65	0.7	18.5	−25.2
Aged 25 to 29	194	2.0	185	1.9	138	1.6	40.6	4.9
Aged 30 to 34	235	2.4	267	2.7	225	2.6	4.4	−12.0
Aged 35 to 39	252	2.6	309	3.2	284	3.2	−11.3	−18.4
Aged 40 to 44	309	3.1	422	4.3	370	4.2	−16.5	−26.8
Aged 45 to 49	511	5.2	582	6.0	538	6.1	−5.0	−12.2
Aged 50 to 54	783	8.0	802	8.3	723	8.2	8.3	−2.4
Aged 55 to 59	930	9.4	888	9.1	734	8.3	26.7	4.7
Aged 60 to 64	1,160	11.8	939	9.7	719	8.2	61.3	23.5
Aged 65 to 69	1,088	11.1	909	9.4	921	10.4	18.1	19.7
Aged 70 to 74	1,037	10.5	1,031	10.6	1,119	12.7	−7.3	0.6
Aged 75 or older	3,266	33.2	3,279	33.7	2,981	33.8	9.6	−0.4

Source: Bureau of the Census, Housing Vacancy Survey, Internet site http://www.census.gov/hhes/www/housing/hvs/hvs.html; calculations by New Strategist

Table 1.32 Number of Women Living Alone Who Are Renters by Age, 2000 to 2010

The number of women renters who live alone fell 7 percent between 2004 (when the overall homeownership rate peaked) and 2010.

(number and percent distribution of women living alone who rent their home, by age of householder, selected years 2000 to 2010; percent change in number, 2000–10 and 2004–10; numbers in thousands)

	2010		2004		2000		percent change in number	
	number	percent	number	percent	number	percent	2000–10	2004–10
Total women who live alone who are renters	**6,959**	**100.0%**	**6,515**	**100.0%**	**6,408**	**100.0%**	**8.6%**	**6.8%**
Under age 35	1,763	25.3	1,728	26.5	1,685	26.3	4.6	2.0
Aged 35 to 44	662	9.5	756	11.6	841	13.1	−21.3	−12.4
Aged 45 to 54	1,107	15.9	985	15.1	897	14.0	23.4	12.4
Aged 55 to 64	1,165	16.7	874	13.4	782	12.2	49.0	33.3
Aged 65 or older	2,263	32.5	2,172	33.3	2,202	34.4	2.8	4.2
Under age 25	592	8.5	687	10.5	552	8.6	7.2	−13.8
Aged 25 to 29	738	10.6	592	9.1	615	9.6	20.0	24.7
Aged 30 to 34	433	6.2	450	6.9	519	8.1	−16.6	−3.8
Aged 35 to 39	303	4.4	350	5.4	431	6.7	−29.7	−13.4
Aged 40 to 44	359	5.2	406	6.2	410	6.4	−12.4	−11.6
Aged 45 to 49	506	7.3	485	7.4	442	6.9	14.5	4.3
Aged 50 to 54	602	8.7	500	7.7	456	7.1	32.0	20.4
Aged 55 to 59	611	8.8	453	7.0	415	6.5	47.2	34.9
Aged 60 to 64	554	8.0	421	6.5	367	5.7	51.0	31.6
Aged 65 to 69	459	6.6	367	5.6	378	5.9	21.4	25.1
Aged 70 to 74	409	5.9	395	6.1	466	7.3	−12.2	3.5
Aged 75 or older	1,394	20.0	1,411	21.7	1,357	21.2	2.7	−1.2

Source: Bureau of the Census, Housing Vacancy Survey, Internet site http://www.census.gov/hhes/www/housing/hvs/hvs.html; calculations by New Strategist

Table 1.33 Number of Men Living Alone Who Are Homeowners by Age, 2000 to 2010

The number of male homeowners who live alone increased
substantially between 2000 and 2010, rising by 31 percent.

*(number and percent distribution of men living alone who own their home, by age of householder, selected years
2000 to 2010; percent change in number, 2000–10 and 2004–10; numbers in thousands)*

	2010		2004		2000		percent change in number	
	number	percent	number	percent	number	percent	2000–10	2004–10
Total men who live alone who are homeowners	**7,002**	**100.0%**	**6,205**	**100.0%**	**5,347**	**100.0%**	**31.0%**	**12.8%**
Under age 35	857	12.2	888	14.3	767	14.3	11.7	−3.5
Aged 35 to 44	968	13.8	1,158	18.7	1,114	20.8	−13.1	−16.4
Aged 45 to 54	1,540	22.0	1,298	20.9	1,116	20.9	38.0	18.6
Aged 55 to 64	1,592	22.7	1,084	17.5	742	13.9	114.6	46.9
Aged 65 or older	2,044	29.2	1,776	28.6	1,607	30.1	27.2	15.1
Under age 25	115	1.6	134	2.2	95	1.8	21.1	−14.2
Aged 25 to 29	363	5.2	337	5.4	284	5.3	27.8	7.7
Aged 30 to 34	379	5.4	418	6.7	388	7.3	−2.3	−9.3
Aged 35 to 39	434	6.2	513	8.3	482	9.0	−10.0	−15.4
Aged 40 to 44	534	7.6	645	10.4	632	11.8	−15.5	−17.2
Aged 45 to 49	705	10.1	655	10.6	591	11.1	19.3	7.6
Aged 50 to 54	836	11.9	644	10.4	524	9.8	59.5	29.8
Aged 55 to 59	810	11.6	600	9.7	412	7.7	96.6	35.0
Aged 60 to 64	782	11.2	485	7.8	330	6.2	137.0	61.2
Aged 65 to 69	552	7.9	425	6.8	312	5.8	76.9	29.9
Aged 70 to 74	417	6.0	357	5.8	404	7.6	3.2	16.8
Aged 75 or older	1,075	15.4	994	16.0	891	16.7	20.7	8.1

*Source: Bureau of the Census, Housing Vacancy Survey, Internet site http://www.census.gov/hhes/www/housing/hvs/hvs.html;
calculations by New Strategist*

Table 1.34 Number of Men Living Alone Who Are Renters by Age, 2000 to 2010

The number of male renters who live alone increased 14 percent between 2000 and 2010. The number of those aged 30 to 44 declined, however.

(number and percent distribution of men living alone who rent their home, by age of householder, selected years 2000 to 2010; percent change in number, 2000–10 and 2004–10; numbers in thousands)

	2010		2004		2000		percent change in number	
	number	percent	number	percent	number	percent	2000–10	2004–10
Total men who live alone who are renters	**6,650**	**100.0%**	**6,078**	**100.0%**	**5,846**	**100.0%**	**13.8%**	**9.4%**
Under age 35	2,128	32.0	2,163	35.6	2,175	37.2	–2.2	–1.6
Aged 35 to 44	1,133	17.0	1,255	20.6	1,382	23.6	–18.0	–9.7
Aged 45 to 54	1,409	21.2	1,148	18.9	1,018	17.4	38.4	22.7
Aged 55 to 64	1,032	15.5	731	12.0	565	9.7	82.7	41.2
Aged 65 or older	949	14.3	782	12.9	707	12.1	34.2	21.4
Under age 25	601	9.0	659	10.8	586	10.0	2.6	–8.8
Aged 25 to 29	890	13.4	807	13.3	806	13.8	10.4	10.3
Aged 30 to 34	636	9.6	697	11.5	783	13.4	–18.8	–8.8
Aged 35 to 39	515	7.7	614	10.1	699	12.0	–26.3	–16.1
Aged 40 to 44	619	9.3	641	10.5	683	11.7	–9.4	–3.4
Aged 45 to 49	708	10.6	615	10.1	605	10.3	17.0	15.1
Aged 50 to 54	700	10.5	532	8.8	414	7.1	69.1	31.6
Aged 55 to 59	562	8.5	426	7.0	317	5.4	77.3	31.9
Aged 60 to 64	470	7.1	305	5.0	248	4.2	89.5	54.1
Aged 65 to 69	321	4.8	216	3.6	194	3.3	65.5	48.6
Aged 70 to 74	222	3.3	186	3.1	193	3.3	15.0	19.4
Aged 75 or older	406	6.1	380	6.3	321	5.5	26.5	6.8

Source: Bureau of the Census, Housing Vacancy Survey, Internet site http://www.census.gov/hhes/www/housing/hvs/hvs.html; calculations by New Strategist

Table 1.35 Number of Nonfamily Households with Two or More Persons Who Are Homeowners by Age, 2000 to 2010

The number of two-or-more-person nonfamily households that own their home increased by 26 percent between 2000 and 2010. Owners aged 30 to 44 were the only ones whose numbers shrank.

(number and percent distribution of nonfamily households with two or more persons who own their home, by age of householder, selected years 2000 to 2010; percent change in number, 2000–10 and 2004–10; numbers in thousands)

	2010		2004		2000		percent change in number	
	number	percent	number	percent	number	percent	2000–10	2004–10
Total nonfamily households with two or more persons, homeowners	**2,895**	**100.0%**	**2,598**	**100.0%**	**2,302**	**100.0%**	**25.8%**	**11.4%**
Under age 35	848	29.3	795	30.6	733	31.8	15.7	6.7
Aged 35 to 44	437	15.1	532	20.5	546	23.7	−20.0	−17.9
Aged 45 to 54	661	22.8	582	22.4	481	20.9	37.4	13.6
Aged 55 to 64	548	18.9	412	15.9	287	12.5	90.9	33.0
Aged 65 or older	402	13.9	277	10.7	257	11.2	56.4	45.1
Under age 25	157	5.4	186	7.2	154	6.7	1.9	−15.6
Aged 25 to 29	391	13.5	306	11.8	275	11.9	42.2	27.8
Aged 30 to 34	300	10.4	302	11.6	302	13.1	−0.7	−0.7
Aged 35 to 39	205	7.1	258	9.9	289	12.6	−29.1	−20.5
Aged 40 to 44	231	8.0	273	10.5	257	11.2	−10.1	−15.4
Aged 45 to 49	298	10.3	309	11.9	249	10.8	19.7	−3.6
Aged 50 to 54	363	12.5	272	10.5	233	10.1	55.8	33.5
Aged 55 to 59	297	10.3	252	9.7	166	7.2	78.9	17.9
Aged 60 to 64	251	8.7	159	6.1	120	5.2	109.2	57.9
Aged 65 to 69	161	5.6	97	3.7	90	3.9	78.9	66.0
Aged 70 to 74	112	3.9	69	2.7	60	2.6	86.7	62.3
Aged 75 or older	130	4.5	111	4.3	106	4.6	22.6	17.1

Source: Bureau of the Census, Housing Vacancy Survey, Internet site http://www.census.gov/hhes/www/housing/hvs/hvs.html; calculations by New Strategist

Table 1.36 Number of Nonfamily Households with Two or More Persons Who Are Renters by Age, 2000 to 2010

The number of two-or-more-person nonfamily households that rent their home increased by 12 percent between 2000 and 2010. Renters aged 35 to 39 were the only ones whose numbers shrank.

(number and percent distribution of nonfamily households with two or more persons who rent their home, by age of householder, selected years 2000 to 2010; percent change in number, 2000–10 and 2004–10; numbers in thousands)

	2010		2004		2000		percent change in number	
	number	percent	number	percent	number	percent	2000–10	2004–10
Total nonfamily households with two or more persons, renters	4,020	100.0%	3,527	100.0%	3,601	100.0%	11.6%	14.0%
Under age 35	2,707	67.3	2,480	70.3	2,510	69.7	7.8	9.2
Aged 35 to 44	516	12.8	473	13.4	601	16.7	−14.1	9.1
Aged 45 to 54	419	10.4	347	9.8	282	7.8	48.6	20.7
Aged 55 to 64	255	6.3	130	3.7	116	3.2	119.8	96.2
Aged 65 or older	123	3.1	96	2.7	90	2.5	36.7	28.1
Under age 25	1,228	30.5	1,257	35.6	1,216	33.8	1.0	−2.3
Aged 25 to 29	985	24.5	838	23.8	838	23.3	17.5	17.5
Aged 30 to 34	494	12.3	387	11.0	458	12.7	7.9	27.6
Aged 35 to 39	268	6.7	259	7.3	356	9.9	−24.7	3.5
Aged 40 to 44	249	6.2	215	6.1	245	6.8	1.6	15.8
Aged 45 to 49	218	5.4	196	5.6	157	4.4	38.9	11.2
Aged 50 to 54	202	5.0	153	4.3	122	3.4	65.6	32.0
Aged 55 to 59	153	3.8	75	2.1	78	2.2	96.2	104.0
Aged 60 to 64	102	2.5	55	1.6	39	1.1	161.5	85.5
Aged 65 to 69	51	1.3	33	0.9	27	0.7	88.9	54.5
Aged 70 to 74	27	0.7	23	0.7	25	0.7	8.0	17.4
Aged 75 or older	43	1.1	41	1.2	39	1.1	10.3	4.9

Source: Bureau of the Census, Housing Vacancy Survey, Internet site http://www.census.gov/hhes/www/housing/hvs/hvs.html; calculations by New Strategist

Table 1.37 Number of Homeowners by Region, 2000 to 2010

The number of homeowners in the Midwest fell between 2004 (the year when the homeownership rate peaked) and 2010. Despite the decline, the number of homeowners increased in every region between 2000 and 2010.

(number and percent distribution of households that own their home, by age of householder, selected years 2000 to 2010; percent change in number, 2000–10 and 2004–10; numbers in thousands)

	2010		2004		2000		percent change in number	
	number	percent	number	percent	number	percent	2000–10	2004–10
Total homeowners	**74,791**	**100.0%**	**73,929**	**100.0%**	**69,206**	**100.0%**	**8.1%**	**1.2%**
Northeast	13,102	17.5	13,030	17.6	12,548	18.1	4.4	0.6
Midwest	18,107	24.2	18,373	24.9	17,552	25.4	3.2	–1.4
South	28,611	38.3	27,549	37.3	25,460	36.8	12.4	3.9
West	14,971	20.0	14,978	20.3	13,646	19.7	9.7	0.0

Source: Bureau of the Census, Housing Vacancy Survey, Internet site http://www.census.gov/hhes/www/housing/hvs/hvs.html; calculations by New Strategist

Table 1.38 Number of Renters by Region, 2000 to 2010

The number of renters increased in every region between 2000 and 2010. The biggest gain occurred in the South.

(number and percent distribution of households that rent their home, by age of householder, selected years 2000 to 2010; percent change in number, 2000–10 and 2004–10; numbers in thousands)

	2010		2004		2000		percent change in number	
	number	percent	number	percent	number	percent	2000–10	2004–10
Total renters	**37,069**	**100.0%**	**33,160**	**100.0%**	**33,354**	**100.0%**	**11.1%**	**11.8%**
Northeast	7,329	19.8	7,005	21.1	7,170	21.5	2.2	4.6
Midwest	7,458	20.1	6,517	19.7	6,644	19.9	12.3	14.4
South	12,866	34.7	11,285	34.0	11,196	33.6	14.9	14.0
West	9,416	25.4	8,355	25.2	8,343	25.0	12.9	12.7

Source: Bureau of the Census, Housing Vacancy Survey, Internet site http://www.census.gov/hhes/www/housing/hvs/hvs.html; calculations by New Strategist

Table 1.39 Number of New Single-Family Homes Sold by Region, 2000 to 2009

The number of new single-family houses sold peaked
in 2005 and has fallen to a record low since then.

(number and percent distribution of new single-family houses sold by region, 2000 to 2009; numbers in thousands)

	total new houses	Northeast	Midwest	South	West
2009	375	31	54	202	87
2008	485	35	70	266	114
2007	776	65	118	411	181
2006	1,051	63	161	559	267
2005	1,283	81	205	638	358
2004	1,203	83	210	562	348
2003	1,086	79	189	511	307
2002	973	65	185	450	273
2001	908	66	164	439	239
2000	877	71	155	406	244
Percent distribution by region					
2009	100.0%	8.3%	14.4%	53.9%	23.2%
2008	100.0	7.2	14.4	54.8	23.5
2007	100.0	8.4	15.2	53.0	23.3
2006	100.0	6.0	15.3	53.2	25.4
2005	100.0	6.3	16.0	49.7	27.9
2004	100.0	6.9	17.5	46.7	28.9
2003	100.0	7.3	17.4	47.1	28.3
2002	100.0	6.7	19.0	46.2	28.1
2001	100.0	7.3	18.1	48.3	26.3
2000	100.0	8.1	17.7	46.3	27.8

Source: Bureau of the Census, Survey of Construction, Internet site http://www.census.gov/const/www/charindex.html#sold

Table 1.40 Median Sales Price of New Single-Family Houses Sold by Region, 2000 to 2009

The median sales price of new single-family homes peaked in 2007 and has fallen over the past few years. Despite the decline, home prices are still well above the 2000 level.

(median sales price of new single-family houses sold by region, 2000 to 2009, percent change in price for selected years, and index of regional to national sales price)

	total new houses	Northeast	Midwest	South	West
2009	$216,700	$302,500	$189,200	$194,800	$263,700
2008	232,100	343,600	198,900	203,700	294,800
2007	247,900	320,200	208,600	217,700	330,900
2006	246,500	346,000	213,500	208,200	337,700
2005	240,900	343,800	216,900	197,300	332,600
2004	221,000	315,800	205,000	181,100	283,100
2003	195,000	264,500	184,300	168,100	260,900
2002	187,600	264,300	178,000	163,400	238,500
2001	175,200	246,400	172,600	155,400	213,600
2000	169,000	227,400	169,700	148,000	196,400

Percent change

	total new houses	Northeast	Midwest	South	West
2006 to 2009	−10.0%	−12.0%	−12.8%	−1.3%	−20.7%
2000 to 2009	28.2	33.0	11.5	31.6	34.3

Index of regional to national sales price

	total new houses	Northeast	Midwest	South	West
2009	100	140	87	90	122
2008	100	148	86	88	127
2007	100	129	84	88	133
2006	100	140	87	84	137
2005	100	143	90	82	138
2004	100	143	93	82	128
2003	100	136	95	86	134
2002	100	141	95	87	127
2001	100	141	99	89	122
2000	100	135	100	88	116

Source: Bureau of the Census, Survey of Construction, Internet site http://www.census.gov/const/www/charindex.html#sold; calculations by New Strategist

Table 1.41 Median Square Footage in New Single-Family Homes Sold by Region, 2000 to 2009

New single-family homes sold in 2009 were slightly smaller
than those sold a few years earlier. New homes sold in the
Northeast and Midwest in 2009 were smaller than those sold in 2000.

(median square feet of floor area in new single-family houses sold by region, 2000 to 2009; percent change, 2000–09)

	total new houses	Northeast	Midwest	South	West
2009	2,202	2,287	1,933	2,284	2,121
2008	2,234	2,438	1,999	2,267	2,209
2007	2,235	2,278	2,001	2,300	2,220
2006	2,237	2,412	2,019	2,281	2,249
2005	2,235	2,365	2,049	2,255	2,261
2004	2,169	2,406	2,003	2,222	2,126
2003	2,125	2,276	1,916	2,146	2,168
2002	2,134	2,323	1,946	2,158	2,166
2001	2,099	2,301	1,936	2,137	2,062
2000	2,077	2,323	1,982	2,092	2,042
Percent change					
2000 to 2009	6.0%	−1.5%	−2.5%	9.2%	3.9%

Source: Bureau of the Census, Survey of Construction, Internet site http://www.census.gov/const/www/charindex.html#sold; calculations by New Strategist

Table 1.42 Bedrooms in New Single-Family Homes Sold, 2000 to 2009

The majority of new single-family homes sold have three bedrooms.
The proportion with four or more bedrooms fell to 38 percent in 2009.

(total number of new single-family houses sold, and percent distribution by number of bedrooms, 2000 to 2009; numbers in thousands)

	total new houses		number of bedrooms		
	number	percent	two or fewer	three	four or more
2009	375	100%	9%	53%	38%
2008	485	100	9	50	41
2007	776	100	10	50	40
2006	1,051	100	10	48	42
2005	1,283	100	10	48	42
2004	1,203	100	10	49	42
2003	1,086	100	10	49	41
2002	973	100	10	49	41
2001	908	100	9	51	40
2000	877	100	9	52	40

Source: Bureau of the Census, Survey of Construction, Internet site http://www.census.gov/const/www/charindex.html#sold

Table 1.43 Bathrooms in New Single-Family Homes Sold, 2000 to 2009

The share of new single-family homes sold in 2009 with three or more
bathrooms fell to 24 percent, down from 27 percent in 2007 and 2008.

(total number of new single-family houses sold, and percent distribution by number of bathrooms, 2000 to 2009; numbers in thousands)

	total new houses		number of bathrooms			
	number	percent	1.5 or fewer	2	2.5	3 or more
2009	375	100%	3%	37%	36%	24%
2008	485	100	2	36	35	27
2007	776	100	2	35	35	27
2006	1,051	100	3	35	36	26
2005	1,283	100	3	36	36	25
2004	1,203	100	3	38	35	24
2003	1,086	100	3	38	36	22
2002	973	100	4	38	37	21
2001	908	100	4	39	37	19
2000	877	100	4	39	37	20

Source: Bureau of the Census, Survey of Construction, Internet site http://www.census.gov/const/www/charindex.html#sold

Table 1.44 Air Conditioning in New Single-Family Homes Sold, 2000 to 2009

Fully 93 percent of new single-family homes sold in 2009
were air conditioned, up from 87 percent in 2000.

(total number of new single-family houses sold, and percent distribution by presence of air conditioning, 2000 to 2009; numbers in thousands)

	total new houses		with air conditioning	without air conditioning
	number	percent		
2009	375	100%	93%	7%
2008	485	100	93	7
2007	776	100	93	7
2006	1,051	100	93	7
2005	1,283	100	92	8
2004	1,203	100	92	8
2003	1,086	100	91	9
2002	973	100	89	11
2001	908	100	89	11
2000	877	100	87	13

Source: Bureau of the Census, Survey of Construction, Internet site http://www.census.gov/const/www/charindex.html#sold

2

Homeowners and Their Homes

The majority of homeowners have plenty of equity left in their home, although less than they once had.

Most Americans still think owning a home is a safe investment, although homeowners are more likely to feel that way (72 percent) than renters (54 percent). Among the nation's 76 million homeowners, 32 percent own their home free and clear. Among the two-thirds of homeowners with a mortgage, only 12 percent were underwater in 2009—owing more than their home was worth. Despite setbacks in the housing market, homeowners still dominate the nation's economy. Not only do they outnumber renters, but they are also older, more affluent, and better educated.

■ Median home value fell 11 percent between 2007 and 2009, from $191,471 to $170,000. Five states saw double-digit declines in median home value during those years: Arizona, California, Florida, Michigan, and Nevada.

■ Most homeowners with mortgages have considerable equity in their home despite declining home values. In 2009, homeowners with mortgages owed a median of 63 percent of the value of their home, up from 54 percent in 2007.

■ Owned homes have a median of 1,800 square feet, most have three or more bedrooms and two or more bathrooms. Seventy-seven percent of homeowners rate their home an 8 or higher on a scale of 1 (worst) to 10 (best).

Twelve percent of homeowners are underwater

(percent distribution of homeowners with mortgages by current total loan as a percent of home value, 2009)

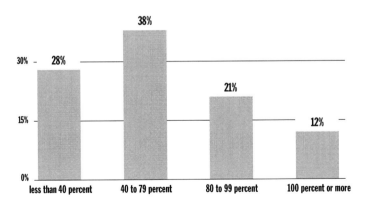

Table 2.1 Attitudes toward Homeownership, 2010

Most Americans still think buying a home is a safe investment, but
the percentage who feel that way fell slightly during 2010. In 2003 (not shown),
the figure was 83 percent—16 percentage points higher than today.

(percent agreeing with statement, by homeownership status, 2010)

PERCENT AGREEING WITH STATEMENT	June–July 2010	January 2010
Homeownership is important to the economy	**82%**	**80%**
Among owners only	84	80
Among renters only	72	77
Buying a home is a safe investment	**67**	**70**
Among owners only	72	73
Among renters only	54	61
It is a good time to buy a house	**70**	**64**
Among owners only	68	62
Among renters only	59	58
It is a bad time to sell a house	**83**	**82**
Home prices will rise over the next year	**31**	–
Among owners only	29	–
Among renters only	35	–
Home prices will decline over the next year	**18**	–
Among owners only	18	–
Among renters only	19	–
Rents will rise over the next year	**39**	–
Among owners only	38	–
Among renters only	46	–
Owning a home makes more sense than renting	**84**	**85**
Among owners only	91	89
Among renters only	69	75
If moving, would be more likely to rent next home	**33**	**30**
Among owners only	21	18
Among renters only	60	54
It would be difficult for you to get home loan today	**54**	**60**
Among owners only	44	46
Among renters only	73	78
It will be harder for the next generation to buy a home than it is today	**71**	**68**
Among owners only	72	69
Among renters only	70	65

	June–July 2010	January 2010
Know someone in your area or neighborhood who has defaulted on their mortgage	**39%**	**39%**
Among owners only	38	34
Among renters only	38	36
Know someone who has defaulted on their mortgage though they could afford to pay	**19**	–
Among owners only	18	–
Among renters only	18	–
Owner likely to sell house in the next three years	**15**	–
Likely to buy a house in the next three years	**24**	–
Among owners only	16	–
Among renters only	38	–
Plans to purchase a home have changed in past year		
Yes, later than planned	12	13
Yes, sooner than planned	6	8
Nothing has changed	37	43
Never did and still don't plan to purchase (another) home	43	34
Percent with debt, by type		
First home mortgage	29	27
Credit card debt that you do not pay off each month	27	28
Car loans	26	25
School loans	15	16
Second mortgage or home equity line of credit	8	10
Other loans/debt	6	5
Back taxes	4	4
No debt	30	29

Note: "–" means data are not available.
Source: Fannie Mae National Housing Survey, June-July, 2010, Internet site http://www.fanniemae.com/about/housing-survey-091610.html

Table 2.2 Homeowners by Age, 2009

Half the nation's homeowners are aged 52 or older. This is well
above the median age of 48 for all householders because
homeownership peaks in the older age groups.

(number and percent distribution of total householders and homeowners, by age of householder, 2009; numbers in thousands)

	total		homeowners		
	number	percent distribution	number	percent distribution	percent of total
Total households	**111,806**	**100.0%**	**76,428**	**100.0%**	**68.4%**
Under age 25	6,083	5.4	1,284	1.7	21.1
Aged 25 to 29	8,614	7.7	3,541	4.6	41.1
Aged 30 to 34	10,093	9.0	5,532	7.2	54.8
Aged 35 to 44	21,908	19.6	14,932	19.5	68.2
Aged 45 to 54	23,505	21.0	17,743	23.2	75.5
Aged 55 to 64	18,509	16.6	14,924	19.5	80.6
Aged 65 to 74	11,938	10.7	9,818	12.8	82.2
Aged 75 or older	11,157	10.0	8,653	11.3	77.6
Median age	48	–	52	–	–

Note: "–" means not applicable.
Source: Bureau of the Census, American Housing Survey for the United States: 2009, Internet site http://www.census.gov/hhes/ www/housing/ahs/ahs09/ahs09.html; calculations by New Strategist

Table 2.3 Homeowners by Household Type and Age of Householder, 2009

Married couples account for only half of the nation's householders,
but for more than 60 percent of the nation's homeowners.

(number and percent distribution of total households and homeowners, by type of household and age of household, 2009; numbers in thousands)

	total		homeowners		
	number	percent distribution	number	percent distribution	percent of total
Total households	**111,806**	**100.0%**	**76,428**	**100.0%**	**68.4%**
MARRIED-COUPLE HOUSEHOLDS	**55,817**	**49.9**	**47,008**	**61.5**	**84.2**
Under age 25	1,203	1.1	495	0.6	41.2
Aged 25 to 29	3,320	3.0	2,007	2.6	60.4
Aged 30 to 34	5,143	4.6	3,646	4.8	70.9
Aged 35 to 44	12,504	11.2	10,336	13.5	82.7
Aged 45 to 64	23,681	21.2	21,352	27.9	90.2
Aged 65 or older	9,967	8.9	9,174	12.0	92.0
TWO-OR-MORE-PERSON HOUSEHOLDS					
Female householders, no spouse present	**16,496**	**14.8**	**7,931**	**10.4**	**48.1**
Under age 45	9,066	8.1	2,948	3.9	32.5
Aged 45 to 64	5,426	4.9	3,397	4.4	62.6
Aged 65 or older	2,004	1.8	1,587	2.1	79.2
Male householders, no spouse present	**9,385**	**8.4**	**4,712**	**6.2**	**50.2**
Under age 45	5,800	5.2	2,170	2.8	37.4
Aged 45 to 64	2,773	2.5	1,878	2.5	67.7
Aged 65 or older	813	0.7	663	0.9	81.6
SINGLE-PERSON HOUSEHOLDS	**30,108**	**26.9**	**16,777**	**22.0**	**55.7**
Female householders	**16,750**	**15.0**	**10,007**	**13.1**	**59.7**
Under age 45	3,980	3.6	1,547	2.0	38.9
Aged 45 to 64	5,212	4.7	3,231	4.2	62.0
Aged 65 or older	7,558	6.8	5,230	6.8	69.2
Male householders	**13,357**	**11.9**	**6,770**	**8.9**	**50.7**
Under age 45	5,682	5.1	2,142	2.8	37.7
Aged 45 to 64	4,922	4.4	2,810	3.7	57.1
Aged 65 or older	2,754	2.5	1,818	2.4	66.0

Source: Bureau of the Census, American Housing Survey for the United States: 2009, Internet site http://www.census.gov/hhes/ www/housing/ahs/ahs09/ahs09.html; calculations by New Strategist

Table 2.4 Homeowners by Race and Hispanic Origin, 2009

Blacks and Hispanics are less likely than non-Hispanic whites
to own a home. In 2009, only 47 percent of black and
51 percent of Hispanic householders were homeowners.

(number and percent distribution of total households and homeowners, by race and Hispanic origin of householder, 2009; numbers in thousands)

	total		homeowners		
	number	percent distribution	number	percent distribution	percent of total
Total households	**111,806**	**100.0%**	**76,428**	**100.0%**	**68.4%**
American Indian	968	0.9	503	0.7	51.9
Asian	4,003	3.6	2,516	3.3	62.9
Black	13,993	12.5	6,547	8.6	46.8
Hispanic	12,739	11.4	6,439	8.4	50.5
White, non-Hispanic	79,333	71.0	59,905	78.4	75.5

Note: American Indians, Asians, blacks, and whites are those who identify themselves as being of the race alone. Numbers do not add to total because not all races are shown and Hispanics may be of any race.
Source: Bureau of the Census, American Housing Survey for the United States: 2009, Internet site http://www.census.gov/hhes/ www/housing/ahs/ahs09/ahs09.html; calculations by New Strategist

Table 2.5 Homeowners by Age, Race, and Hispanic Origin, 2009

Most black householders aged 45 or older and Hispanic householders aged 35 or older are homeowners.

(number and percent distribution of total households and homeowners, by race, Hispanic origin, and age of householder, 2009; numbers in thousands)

	total		homeowners		
	number	percent distribution	number	percent distribution	percent of total
Black households	**13,993**	**100.0%**	**6,547**	**100.0%**	**46.8%**
Under age 25	949	6.8	74	1.1	7.8
Aged 25 to 29	1,245	8.9	240	3.7	19.3
Aged 30 to 34	1,287	9.2	352	5.4	27.4
Aged 35 to 44	3,005	21.5	1,399	21.4	46.6
Aged 45 to 54	3,049	21.8	1,669	25.5	54.8
Aged 55 to 64	2,214	15.8	1,352	20.7	61.1
Aged 65 to 74	1,374	9.8	887	13.5	64.5
Aged 75 or older	872	6.2	573	8.8	65.8
Hispanic households	**12,739**	**100.0**	**6,439**	**100.0**	**50.5**
Under age 25	955	7.5	136	2.1	14.2
Aged 25 to 29	1,418	11.1	426	6.6	30.0
Aged 30 to 34	1,712	13.4	668	10.4	39.0
Aged 35 to 44	3,128	24.6	1,682	26.1	53.8
Aged 45 to 54	2,441	19.2	1,487	23.1	60.9
Aged 55 to 64	1,604	12.6	1,046	16.2	65.2
Aged 65 to 74	877	6.9	606	9.4	69.1
Aged 75 or older	604	4.7	389	6.0	64.3

Note: Blacks are those who identify themselves as being of the race alone. Hispanics may be of any race.
Source: Bureau of the Census, American Housing Survey for the United States: 2009, Internet site http://www.census.gov/hhes/ www/housing/ahs/ahs09/ahs09.html; calculations by New Strategist

Table 2.6 Homeowners by Household Income, 2009

The nation's homeowners have higher incomes than the average householder because they are older, with many in their peak earning years.

(number and percent distribution of total householders and homeowners by household income, 2009; numbers in thousands)

	total		homeowners		
	number	percent distribution	number	percent distribution	percent of total
Total households	**111,806**	**100.0%**	**76,428**	**100.0%**	**68.4%**
Under $10,000	10,532	9.4	4,423	5.8	42.0
$10,000 to $19,999	12,025	10.8	5,911	7.7	49.2
$20,000 to $29,999	13,598	12.2	7,617	10.0	56.0
$30,000 to $39,999	11,559	10.3	7,082	9.3	61.3
$40,000 to $49,999	10,290	9.2	6,852	9.0	66.6
$50,000 to $59,999	8,654	7.7	6,328	8.3	73.1
$60,000 to $79,999	13,780	12.3	10,535	13.8	76.5
$80,000 to $99,999	10,073	9.0	8,409	11.0	83.5
$100,000 to $119,999	6,840	6.1	6,007	7.9	87.8
$120,000 or more	14,456	12.9	13,264	17.4	91.8
Median income	$47,000	–	$60,000	–	–

Note: "–" means not applicable.
Source: Bureau of the Census, American Housing Survey for the United States: 2009, Internet site http://www.census.gov/hhes/www/housing/ahs/ahs09/ahs09.html; calculations by New Strategist

Table 2.7 Homeowners by Educational Attainment, 2009

Thirty-four percent of homeowners have at least a bachelor's degree compared with 30 percent of all householders.

(number and percent distribution of total households and homeowners, by educational attainment of householder, 2009; numbers in thousands)

	total		homeowners		
	number	percent distribution	number	percent distribution	percent of total
Total households	**111,806**	**100.0%**	**76,428**	**100.0%**	**68.4%**
Not a high school graduate	15,229	13.6	8,542	11.2	56.1
High school graduate only	34,389	30.8	22,665	29.7	65.9
Some college, no degree	19,583	17.5	12,659	16.6	64.6
Associate's degree	9,244	8.3	6,722	8.8	72.7
Bachelor's degree	21,077	18.9	15,894	20.8	75.4
Graduate or professional degree	12,285	11.0	9,947	13.0	81.0
High school graduate or higher	96,577	86.4	67,886	88.8	70.3
Some college or higher	62,188	55.6	45,221	59.2	72.7
Bachelor's degree or higher	33,361	29.8	25,840	33.8	77.5

Source: Bureau of the Census, American Housing Survey for the United States: 2009, Internet site http://www.census.gov/hhes/www/housing/ahs/ahs09/ahs09.html; calculations by New Strategist

Table 2.8 Homeowners by Household Size, 2009

Homeowners are less likely to live alone than the average householder. Twenty-two percent of homeowners live alone versus 27 percent of all householders.

(number and percent distribution of total households and homeowners, by number of persons in home, 2009; numbers in thousands)

	total		homeowners		
	number	percent distribution	number	percent distribution	percent of total
Total households	**111,806**	**100.0%**	**76,428**	**100.0%**	**68.4%**
One person	30,108	26.9	16,777	22.0	55.7
Two persons	37,086	33.2	27,633	36.2	74.5
Three persons	17,568	15.7	12,223	16.0	69.6
Four persons	15,807	14.1	11,791	15.4	74.6
Five persons	7,117	6.4	5,207	6.8	73.2
Six persons	2,577	2.3	1,797	2.4	69.7
Seven or more persons	1,543	1.4	1,000	1.3	64.8

Source: Bureau of the Census, American Housing Survey for the United States: 2009, Internet site http://www.census.gov/hhes/www/housing/ahs/ahs09/ahs09.html; calculations by New Strategist

Table 2.9 Homeowners by Type of Structure, 2009

Homeowners are more likely than the average householder to live in a single-family detached home. They are also more likely to live in mobile homes.

(number and percent distribution of total households and homeowners, by number of units in structure, 2009; numbers in thousands)

	total		homeowners		
	number	percent distribution	number	percent distribution	percent of total
Total households	**111,806**	**100.0%**	**76,428**	**100.0%**	**68.4%**
One, detached	73,079	65.4	63,324	82.9	86.7
One, attached	5,973	5.3	3,952	5.2	66.2
Multiunit buildings	25,915	23.2	3,734	4.9	14.4
Two to four	8,350	7.5	1,353	1.8	16.2
Five to nine	5,269	4.7	632	0.8	12.0
10 to 19	4,661	4.2	483	0.6	10.4
20 to 49	3,630	3.2	499	0.7	13.7
50 or more	4,004	3.6	768	1.0	19.2
Mobile home	6,839	6.1	5,418	7.1	79.2

Source: Bureau of the Census, American Housing Survey for the United States: 2009, Internet site http://www.census.gov/hhes/www/housing/ahs/ahs09/ahs09.html; calculations by New Strategist

Table 2.10 Homeowners by Year Structure Built, 2009

Homeowners live in slightly newer homes than the average householder.
Fourteen percent live in homes built since 2000.

(number and percent distribution of total households and homeowners, by year structure was built, 2009; numbers in thousands)

	total		homeowners		
	number	percent distribution	number	percent distribution	percent of total
Total households	**111,806**	**100.0%**	**76,428**	**100.0%**	**68.4%**
2005 to 2009	5,884	5.3	4,601	6.0	78.2
2000 to 2004	8,102	7.2	6,371	8.3	78.6
1995 to 1999	7,825	7.0	6,221	8.1	79.5
1990 to 1994	5,995	5.4	4,715	6.2	78.6
1985 to 1989	7,648	6.8	5,159	6.8	67.5
1980 to 1984	6,380	5.7	4,201	5.5	65.8
1975 to 1979	11,835	10.6	7,471	9.8	63.1
1970 to 1974	9,413	8.4	5,696	7.5	60.5
1960 to 1969	13,326	11.9	8,917	11.7	66.9
1950 to 1959	11,771	10.5	8,528	11.2	72.4
1940 to 1949	6,745	6.0	4,423	5.8	65.6
1930 to 1939	4,828	4.3	2,904	3.8	60.1
1920 to 1929	4,331	3.9	2,520	3.3	58.2
1919 or earlier	7,724	6.9	4,703	6.2	60.9
Median year	1974	–	1975	–	–

Note: "–" means not applicable.
Source: Bureau of the Census, American Housing Survey for the United States: 2009, Internet site http://www.census.gov/hhes/ www/housing/ahs/ahs09/ahs09.html; calculations by New Strategist

Table 2.11 Homeowners by Year Moved into Home, 2009

Homeowners are less likely—and less able—to move than the average house-holder. Consequently, they have lived in their current home longer.

(number and percent distribution of total households and homeowners, by year householder moved into unit, 2009; numbers in thousands)

	total		homeowners		
	number	percent distribution	number	percent distribution	percent of total
Total households	**111,806**	**100.0%**	**76,428**	**100.0%**	**68.4%**
2005 to 2009	46,108	41.2	20,126	26.3	43.6
2000 to 2004	22,490	20.1	17,520	22.9	77.9
1995 to 1999	13,131	11.7	11,217	14.7	85.4
1990 to 1994	8,763	7.8	7,706	10.1	87.9
1985 to 1989	5,844	5.2	5,362	7.0	91.8
1980 to 1984	3,436	3.1	3,124	4.1	90.9
1975 to 1979	3,978	3.6	3,734	4.9	93.9
1970 to 1974	2,698	2.4	2,548	3.3	94.4
1960 to 1969	3,300	3.0	3,142	4.1	95.2
1950 to 1959	1,592	1.4	1,522	2.0	95.6
1940 to 1949	357	0.3	334	0.4	93.5
1939 or earlier	110	0.1	93	0.1	84.5
Median year moved into home	2003	–	1999	–	–

Note: "–" means not applicable.
Source: Bureau of the Census, American Housing Survey for the United States: 2009, Internet site http://www.census.gov/hhes/www/housing/ahs/ahs09/ahs09.html; calculations by New Strategist

Table 2.12 Homeowners by Square Footage of Unit and Lot Size, 2009

Half of homeowners live in homes less than 1,800 square feet
in size, and half live in larger homes.

(number and percent distribution of total households and homeowners, by size of unit and lot, 2009; numbers in thousands)

	total		homeowners		
	number	percent distribution	number	percent distribution	percent of total
Square footage of home, total*	**79,918**	**100.0%**	**68,742**	**100.0%**	**86.0%**
Less than 500 square feet	603	0.8	383	0.6	63.5
500 to 749 square feet	1,771	2.2	1,085	1.6	61.3
750 to 999 square feet	5,014	6.3	3,519	5.1	70.2
1,000 to 1,499 square feet	18,419	23.0	14,978	21.8	81.3
1,500 to 1,999 square feet	18,519	23.2	16,284	23.7	87.9
2,000 to 2,499 square feet	13,190	16.5	12,057	17.5	91.4
2,500 to 2,999 square feet	7,050	8.8	6,622	9.6	93.9
3,000 to 3,999 square feet	6,692	8.4	6,391	9.3	95.5
4,000 or more square feet	4,030	5.0	3,787	5.5	94.0
Not reported	4,630	5.8	3,638	5.3	78.6
Median square footage	1,800	–	1,800	–	–
Lot size, total**	**83,466**	**100.0**	**70,643**	**100.0**	**84.6**
Less than one-eighth acre	11,824	14.2	9,107	12.9	77.0
One-eighth up to one-quarter acre	21,793	26.1	17,771	25.2	81.5
One-quarter up to one-half acre	15,921	19.1	13,837	19.6	86.9
One-half up to one acre	10,036	12.0	8,874	12.6	88.4
One to five acres	17,014	20.4	14,895	21.1	87.5
Five to 10 acres	2,750	3.3	2,545	3.6	92.5
10 or more acres	4,127	4.9	3,614	5.1	87.6
Median lot size (acres)	0.27	–	0.32	–	–

* *Single-family detached and mobile homes only.*
** *Homes in two-or-more-unit buildings are excluded.*
Note: "–" means not applicable.
Source: Bureau of the Census, American Housing Survey for the United States: 2009, Internet site http://www.census.gov/hhes/ www/housing/ahs/ahs09/ahs09.html; calculations by New Strategist

Table 2.13 Homeowners by Number of Rooms in Home, 2009

Most homeowners have three or more bedrooms and two or more bathrooms. More than one-third have a room used for business.

(number and percent distribution of total households and homeowners, by number and type of rooms in home, 2009; numbers in thousands)

	total		homeowners		
	number	percent distribution	number	percent distribution	percent of total
Total households	**111,806**	**100.0%**	**76,428**	**100.0%**	**68.4%**
Number of rooms					
One room	352	0.3	26	0.0	7.3
Two rooms	946	0.8	68	0.1	7.2
Three rooms	8,711	7.8	1,036	1.4	11.9
Four rooms	17,828	15.9	6,475	8.5	36.3
Five rooms	25,444	22.8	17,232	22.5	67.7
Six rooms	24,596	22.0	20,364	26.6	82.8
Seven rooms	16,489	14.7	14,754	19.3	89.5
Eight rooms	10,033	9.0	9,410	12.3	93.8
Nine rooms	4,344	3.9	4,130	5.4	95.1
10 or more rooms	3,063	2.7	2,933	3.8	95.7
Number of bedrooms					
None	789	0.7	45	0.1	5.7
One bedroom	11,434	10.2	1,714	2.2	15.0
Two bedrooms	27,671	24.7	13,471	17.6	48.7
Three bedrooms	48,082	43.0	39,723	52.0	82.6
Four or more bedrooms	23,830	21.3	21,475	28.1	90.1
Number of bathrooms					
None	403	0.4	175	0.2	43.3
One bathroom	38,662	34.6	15,767	20.6	40.8
One-and-one-half bathrooms	15,656	14.0	12,081	15.8	77.2
Two or more bathrooms	57,085	51.1	48,405	63.3	84.8
With room used for business	**34,148**	**30.5**	**26,108**	**34.2**	**76.5**
Business only	15,236	13.6	11,479	15.0	75.3
Business and other use	18,912	16.9	14,629	19.1	77.4

Source: Bureau of the Census, American Housing Survey for the United States: 2009, Internet site http://www.census.gov/hhes/ www/housing/ahs/ahs09/ahs09.html; calculations by New Strategist

Table 2.14 Homeowners by Presence of Kitchen, Laundry, and Safety Equipment, 2009

Homeowners are more likely than the average householder to have
a washer and dryer. Seventy-five percent of homeowners have
a dishwasher compared with 66 percent of all householders.

(number and percent of total households and homeowners, by presence of kitchen, laundry, and safety equipment, 2009; numbers in thousands)

	total		homeowners		
	number	percent distribution	number	percent distribution	percent of total
Total households	**111,806**	**100.0%**	**76,428**	**100.0%**	**68.4%**
With complete kitchen equipment	110,054	98.4	76,050	99.5	69.1
Dishwasher	73,584	65.8	57,191	74.8	77.7
Washing machine	93,372	83.5	73,826	96.6	79.1
Clothes dryer	90,905	81.3	72,562	94.9	79.8
Disposal in kitchen sink	56,531	50.6	40,597	53.1	71.8
Trash compactor	3,896	3.5	3,166	4.1	81.3
Working smoke detector	104,362	93.3	71,797	93.9	68.8
Fire extinguisher	49,902	44.6	37,922	49.6	76.0
Sprinkler system inside home	5,167	4.6	2,086	2.7	40.4
Carbon monoxide detector	40,698	36.4	31,691	41.5	77.9

Note: Complete kitchen equipment includes a sink, refrigerator, and oven or burners.
Source: Bureau of the Census, American Housing Survey for the United States: 2009, Internet site http://www.census.gov/hhes/ www/housing/ahs/ahs09/ahs09.html; calculations by New Strategist

Table 2.15 Homeowners by Type of Heating Equipment, 2009

More than two-thirds of homeowners use a warm-air
furnace as their main heating equipment.

(number and percent distribution of total households and homeowners, by presence and type of heating equipment, 2009; numbers in thousands)

	total		homeowners		
	number	percent distribution	number	percent distribution	percent of total
Total households	111,806	100.0%	76,428	100.0%	68.4%
Main heating equipment					
Warm-air furnace	71,141	63.6	51,691	67.6	72.7
Steam or hot water system	12,506	11.2	7,494	9.8	59.9
Electric heat pump	13,264	11.9	9,764	12.8	73.6
Built-in electric units	4,761	4.3	2,120	2.8	44.5
Floor, wall, or other built-in hot air units without ducts	4,802	4.3	2,043	2.7	42.5
Room heaters with flue	950	0.8	580	0.8	61.0
Room heaters without flue	1,109	1.0	694	0.9	62.6
Portable electric heaters	1,167	1.0	535	0.7	45.8
Stoves	1,035	0.9	845	1.1	81.6
Fireplaces with inserts	172	0.2	155	0.2	89.7
Fireplaces without inserts	43	0.0	35	0.0	82.5
Other	386	0.3	232	0.3	60.1
Cooking stove	84	0.1	34	0.0	41.2
None	386	0.3	206	0.3	53.4
Households with additional heating equipment					
Warm-air furnace	251	0.2	225	0.3	89.7
Steam or hot water system	56	0.1	51	0.1	91.9
Electric heat pump	97	0.1	91	0.1	94.1
Built-in electric units	1,882	1.7	1,428	1.9	75.9
Floor, wall, or other built-in hot air units without ducts	75	0.1	63	0.1	83.6
Room heaters with flue	822	0.7	716	0.9	87.1
Room heaters without flue	1,471	1.3	1,207	1.6	82.0
Portable electric heaters	13,719	12.3	9,886	12.9	72.1
Stoves	4,165	3.7	3,740	4.9	89.8
Fireplaces with inserts	5,205	4.7	4,742	6.2	91.1
Fireplaces without inserts	5,765	5.2	4,869	6.4	84.5
Other	790	0.7	707	0.9	89.5
Cooking stove	66	0.1	50	0.1	74.8
None	80,034	71.6	51,171	67.0	63.9

Source: Bureau of the Census, American Housing Survey for the United States: 2009, Internet site http://www.census.gov/hhes/www/housing/ahs/ahs09/ahs09.html; calculations by New Strategist

Table 2.16 Homeowners with Air Conditioning, 2009

Seventy-two percent of homeowners have central air conditioning.

(number and percent distribution of total households and homeowners, by presence of air conditioning equipment, 2009; numbers in thousands)

	total		homeowners		
	number	percent distribution	number	percent distribution	percent of total
TOTAL HOUSEHOLDS	**111,806**	**100.0%**	**76,428**	**100.0%**	**68.4%**
Households with air conditioning	**97,390**	**87.1**	**68,355**	**89.4**	**70.2**
Central	72,808	65.1	54,647	71.5	75.1
Additional central	5,629	5.0	4,709	6.2	83.7
One room unit	11,532	10.3	5,303	6.9	46.0
Two room units	8,132	7.3	4,800	6.3	59.0
Three or more room units	4,918	4.4	3,604	4.7	73.3

Source: Bureau of the Census, American Housing Survey for the United States: 2009, Internet site http://www.census.gov/hhes/www/housing/ahs/ahs09/ahs09.html; calculations by New Strategist

Table 2.17 Homeowners by Primary Source of Water and Sewage Disposal System, 2009

More than one in four homeowners is not connected to a public sewer.

(number and percent distribution of total households and homeowners, by primary source of water and type of sewage disposal system, 2009; numbers in thousands)

	total		homeowners		
	number	percent distribution	number	percent distribution	percent of total
Total households	**111,806**	**100.0%**	**76,428**	**100.0%**	**68.4%**
Source of water					
Public system or private company	98,027	87.7	64,372	84.2	65.7
Well	13,430	12.0	11,769	15.4	87.6
Safety of primary source of water					
Safe to drink	102,247	91.5	71,152	93.1	69.6
Not safe to drink	8,412	7.5	4,530	5.9	53.9
Sewage disposal system					
Public sewer	89,467	80.0	56,736	74.2	63.4
Septic tank, cesspool, chemical toilet	22,307	20.0	19,667	25.7	88.2

Note: Numbers may not sum to total because "other" and "not reported" are not shown.
Source: Bureau of the Census, American Housing Survey for the United States: 2009, Internet site http://www.census.gov/hhes/www/housing/ahs/ahs09/ahs09.html; calculations by New Strategist

Table 2.18 Homeowners by Fuels Used, 2009

Homeowners are slightly less likely than the average householder to have an all-electric home.

(number and percent distribution of total households and homeowners, by type of fuels used, 2009; numbers in thousands)

	total		homeowners		
	number	percent distribution	number	percent distribution	percent of total
Total households	**111,806**	**100.0%**	**76,428**	**100.0%**	**68.4%**
Electricity	111,746	99.9	76,378	99.9	68.3
All-electric homes	30,166	27.0	17,951	23.5	59.5
Piped gas	67,886	60.7	46,700	61.1	68.8
Bottled gas	9,816	8.8	8,391	11.0	85.5
Fuel oil	9,208	8.2	6,409	8.4	69.6
Kerosene or other liquid fuel	616	0.6	451	0.6	73.3
Coal or coke	104	0.1	97	0.1	93.2
Wood	1,787	1.6	1,510	2.0	84.5
Solar energy	147	0.1	130	0.2	88.4
Other	405	0.4	254	0.3	62.8

Note: Numbers do not add to total because many households use more than one fuel.
Source: Bureau of the Census, American Housing Survey for the United States: 2009, Internet site http://www.census.gov/hhes/ www/housing/ahs/ahs09/ahs09.html; calculations by New Strategist

Table 2.19 Homeowners by Primary Heating Fuel Used, 2009

Most homeowners use piped gas as their main heating fuel.

(number and percent distribution of total households and homeowners, by primary heating fuel used, 2009; numbers in thousands)

	total		homeowners		
	number	percent distribution	number	percent distribution	percent of total
Primary heating fuel	**111,806**	**100.0%**	**76,428**	**100.0%**	**68.4%**
Households using heating fuel	111,420	100.0	76,222	100.0	68.4
Electricity	37,851	34.0	22,219	29.2	58.7
Piped gas	56,806	51.0	41,233	54.1	72.6
Bottled gas	5,817	5.2	4,889	6.4	84.0
Fuel oil	8,214	7.4	5,693	7.5	69.3
Kerosene or other liquid fuel	599	0.5	444	0.6	74.2
Coal or coke	98	0.1	91	0.1	92.8
Wood	1,780	1.6	1,503	2.0	84.4
Solar energy	11	0.0	8	0.0	73.7
Other	243	0.2	142	0.2	58.4

Source: Bureau of the Census, American Housing Survey for the United States: 2009, Internet site http://www.census.gov/hhes/ www/housing/ahs/ahs09/ahs09.html; calculations by New Strategist

Table 2.20 Homeowners by Cooking, Water Heating, and Clothes Dryer Fuels Used, 2009

There are few differences between homeowners and the average householder in the types of fuels used for cooking, water heating, or clothes drying.

(number and percent distribution of total households and homeowners, by cooking, water heating, and clothes dryer fuels used, 2009; numbers in thousands)

	total		homeowners		
	number	percent distribution	number	percent distribution	percent of total
COOKING FUEL					
Households using cooking fuel	**111,623**	**100.0%**	**76,388**	**100.0%**	**68.4%**
Electricity	67,078	60.1	45,512	59.6	67.8
Piped gas	39,476	35.4	26,553	34.8	67.3
Bottled gas	5,001	4.5	4,274	5.6	85.5
Kerosene or other liquid fuel	14	0.0	7	0.0	48.4
Wood	29	0.0	17	0.0	58.2
Other	23	0.0	25	0.0	100.0
WATER HEATING FUEL					
Households with hot piped water	**111,691**	**100.0**	**76,371**	**100.0**	**68.4**
Electricity	45,435	40.7	29,341	38.4	64.6
Piped gas	57,145	51.2	40,280	52.7	70.5
Bottled gas	4,057	3.6	3,365	4.4	83.0
Fuel oil	4,692	4.2	3,087	4.0	65.8
Kerosene or other liquid fuel	21	0.0	18	0.0	87.3
Coal or coke	23	0.0	23	0.0	100.0
Wood	104	0.1	96	0.1	91.8
Solar energy	135	0.1	121	0.2	89.6
Other	78	0.1	40	0.1	50.5
CLOTHES DRYER FUEL					
Households with clothes dryers	**90,905**	**100.0**	**72,562**	**100.0**	**79.8**
Electricity	70,497	77.5	55,059	75.9	78.1
Piped gas	19,111	21.0	16,326	22.5	85.4
Other	1,298	1.4	1,178	1.6	90.7

Source: Bureau of the Census, American Housing Survey for the United States: 2009, Internet site http://www.census.gov/hhes/www/housing/ahs/ahs09/ahs09.html; calculations by New Strategist

Table 2.21 Homeowners by Amenities of Home, 2009

Eighty percent of homeowners have a garage or carport,
versus 66 percent of all householders.

(number and percent distribution of total households and homeowners, by selected amenities of home, 2009; numbers in thousands)

	total		homeowners		
	number	percent distribution	number	percent distribution	percent of total
Total households	**111,806**	**100.0%**	**76,428**	**100.0%**	**68.4%**
Porch, deck, balcony, or patio	95,406	85.3	70,421	92.1	73.8
Telephone available	109,325	97.8	75,129	98.3	68.7
Usable fireplace	38,998	34.9	34,458	45.1	88.4
Separate dining room	53,676	48.0	43,717	57.2	81.4
With two or more living or recreation rooms	33,912	30.3	30,978	40.5	91.3
Garage or carport					
Yes	74,236	66.4	60,979	79.8	82.1
No, but off-street parking included	30,963	27.7	13,287	17.4	42.9
No cars, trucks, or vans	8,738	7.8	2,069	2.7	23.7

Source: Bureau of the Census, American Housing Survey for the United States: 2009, Internet site http://www.census.gov/hhes/ www/housing/ahs/ahs09/ahs09.html; calculations by New Strategist

Table 2.22 Homeowners by Deficiencies of Home, 2009

More than 5 percent of homeowners have seen
signs of mice in the past three months.

(number and percent distribution of total households and homeowners, by selected deficiencies of housing unit, 2009; numbers in thousands)

	total		homeowners		
	number	percent distribution	number	percent distribution	percent of total
Total households	**111,806**	**100.0%**	**76,428**	**100.0%**	**68.4%**
Signs of rats in last three months	613	0.5	354	0.5	57.9
Signs of mice in last three months	6,122	5.5	3,984	5.2	65.1
Signs of rodents, not sure which kind, in last three months	353	0.3	164	0.2	46.5
Holes in floor	1,141	1.0	581	0.8	50.9
Open cracks or holes (interior)	5,517	4.9	3,101	4.1	56.2
Broken plaster, peeling paint (interior)	2,378	2.1	1,246	1.6	52.4
No electrical wiring	84	0.1	57	0.1	68.4
Exposed wiring	355	0.3	221	0.3	62.2
Rooms without electric outlets	1,274	1.1	650	0.8	51.0

Source: Bureau of the Census, American Housing Survey for the United States: 2009, Internet site http://www.census.gov/hhes/ www/housing/ahs/ahs09/ahs09.html; calculations by New Strategist

Table 2.23 Homeowners by Housing Equipment Failures, 2009

Eight percent of homeowners were uncomfortably cold for 24 or more hours last winter. The most common cause was a utility interruption.

(number and percent distribution of total households and homeowners, by type of equipment failure, 2009; numbers in thousands)

	total		homeowners		
	number	percent distribution	number	percent distribution	percent of total
WATER SUPPLY STOPPAGE					
Households with piped water	**111,691**	**100.0%**	**76,371**	**100.0%**	**68.4%**
No stoppage in last three months	106,864	95.7	73,494	96.2	68.8
With stoppage in last three months	3,632	3.3	2,031	2.7	55.9
Not reported	1,194	1.1	846	1.1	70.8
FLUSH TOILET BREAKDOWNS					
Households with flush toilets	**111,704**	**100.0**	**76,391**	**100.0**	**68.4**
With at least one working toilet at all times, last three months	108,440	97.1	74,674	97.8	68.9
With no working toilet at least once in last three months	2,094	1.9	884	1.2	42.2
Not reported	1,170	1.0	833	1.1	71.2
WATER LEAKAGE DURING LAST 12 MONTHS					
Total households	**111,806**	**100.0**	**76,428**	**100.0**	**68.4**
No leakage from within structure	101,540	90.8	70,356	92.1	69.3
With leakage from within structure*	9,007	8.1	5,170	6.8	57.4
Fixtures backed up or overflowed	2,141	1.9	1,188	1.6	55.5
Pipes leaked	3,809	3.4	2,145	2.8	56.3
Broken water heater	1,041	0.9	714	0.9	68.6
Other or unknown	2,351	2.1	1,263	1.7	53.7
Leakage not reported	1,260	1.1	902	1.2	71.6
No leakage from outside structure	99,592	89.1	67,686	88.6	68.0
With leakage from outside structure*	10,963	9.8	7,842	10.3	71.5
Roof	5,747	5.1	4,168	5.5	72.5
Basement	2,847	2.5	2,309	3.0	81.1
Walls, windows, or doors	1,960	1.8	1,165	1.5	59.5
Other or not reported	1,101	1.0	691	0.9	62.8
Leakage not reported	1,250	1.1	900	1.2	72.0

	total		homeowners		
	number	percent distribution	number	percent distribution	percent of total
HEATING PROBLEMS					
Households with heating equipment and occupying home last winter	**106,459**	**100.0%**	**75,215**	**100.0%**	**70.7%**
Not uncomfortably cold for 24 or more hours last winter	94,725	89.0	67,769	90.1	71.5
Uncomfortably cold for 24 or more hours last winter*	9,677	9.1	6,055	8.1	62.6
Equipment breakdown	2,738	2.6	1,594	2.1	58.2
Utility interruption	2,635	2.5	2,139	2.8	81.2
Inadequate heating capacity	1,025	1.0	350	0.5	34.1
Inadequate insulation	917	0.9	394	0.5	42.9
Cost of heating	1,200	1.1	778	1.0	64.9
Other	1,699	1.6	1,022	1.4	60.1
Not reported	2,057	1.9	1,391	1.8	67.6
ELECTRICAL PROBLEMS					
Households with electrical wiring	**111,722**	**100.0**	**76,371**	**100.0**	**68.4**
No fuses or breakers blown in last three months	100,576	90.0	68,697	90.0	68.3
With fuses or breakers blown in last three months	9,767	8.7	6,685	8.8	68.4
Not reported	1,380	1.2	989	1.3	71.7

* Figures may not add to total because more than one problem may have occurred.
Source: Bureau of the Census, American Housing Survey for the United States: 2009, Internet site http://www.census.gov/hhes/www/housing/ahs/ahs09/ahs09.html; calculations by New Strategist

Table 2.24 Homeowners by Purchase Price of Home, 2009

Half of homeowners paid more than $107,500 for their home
and half paid less. Only 11 percent paid $300,000 or more.

(number and percent distribution of homeowners by purchase price of home, 2009; numbers in thousands)

	number	percent distribution
TOTAL HOMEOWNERS	**76,428**	**100.0%**
Home purchased or built	**71,877**	**94.0**
Under $10,000	2,799	3.7
$10,000 to $19,999	4,229	5.5
$20,000 to $29,999	3,648	4.8
$30,000 to $39,999	3,489	4.6
$40,000 to $49,999	3,002	3.9
$50,000 to $59,999	3,076	4.0
$60,000 to $69,999	3,126	4.1
$70,000 to $79,999	2,968	3.9
$80,000 to $99,999	5,662	7.4
$100,000 to $119,999	4,288	5.6
$120,000 to $149,999	6,691	8.8
$150,000 to $199,999	8,055	10.5
$200,000 to $249,999	5,029	6.6
$250,000 to $299,999	3,024	4.0
$300,000 or more	8,594	11.2
Not reported	4,196	5.5
Median purchase price	$107,500	–
Received as inheritance or gift	**3,388**	**4.4**
Not reported	**1,163**	**1.5**

Note: "–" means not applicable.
Source: Bureau of the Census, American Housing Survey for the United States: 2009, Internet site http://www.census.gov/hhes/www/housing/ahs/ahs09/ahs09.html; calculations by New Strategist

Table 2.25 Homeowners by Value of Home, 2007 and 2009

Median home value fell 11 percent between 2007 and 2009.

(number of homeowners by current self-reported value of home, 2007 and 2009, percent change in number of homeowners by value, 2007–09; numbers in thousands)

	2009	2007	percent change
Total homeowners	**76,428**	**75,647**	**1.0%**
Under $10,000	1,696	1,988	−14.7
$10,000 to $19,999	1,311	1,175	11.6
$20,000 to $29,999	1,073	1,088	−1.4
$30,000 to $39,999	1,187	1,196	−0.7
$40,000 to $59,999	3,155	3,111	1.4
$60,000 to $79,999	5,261	4,722	11.4
$80,000 to $99,999	6,002	5,499	9.1
$100,000 to $119,999	4,980	4,313	15.5
$120,000 to $149,999	7,629	6,735	13.3
$150,000 to $199,999	11,141	9,643	15.5
$200,000 to $299,999	13,494	13,132	2.8
$300,000 to $399,999	7,924	8,060	−1.7
$400,000 to $499,999	4,200	4,740	−11.4
$500,000 to $749,999	4,577	6,234	−26.6
$750,000 or more	2,798	4,013	−30.3
Median home value	$170,000	$191,471	−11.2

Source: Bureau of the Census, American Housing Survey for the United States: 2009, Internet site http://www.census.gov/hhes/ www/housing/ahs/ahs09/ahs09.html; calculations by New Strategist

Table 2.26 Distribution of Homeowners by Value of Home, 2007 and 2009

The number of homeowners who think their home is worth $300,000
or more fell from 23 million to 19 million between 2007 and 2009.

(number and percent distribution of homeowners by current self-reported value of home, 2007 and 2009; numbers in thousands)

	2009		2007	
	number	percent distributon	number	percent distributon
Total homeowners	**76,428**	**100.0%**	**75,647**	**100.0%**
Under $100,000	19,685	25.8	18,779	24.8
Under $10,000	1,696	2.2	1,988	2.6
$10,000 to $19,999	1,311	1.7	1,175	1.6
$20,000 to $29,999	1,073	1.4	1,088	1.4
$30,000 to $39,999	1,187	1.6	1,196	1.6
$40,000 to $59,999	3,155	4.1	3,111	4.1
$60,000 to $79,999	5,261	6.9	4,722	6.2
$80,000 to $99,999	6,002	7.9	5,499	7.3
$100,000 to $199,999	23,750	31.1	20,691	27.4
$100,000 to $119,999	4,980	6.5	4,313	5.7
$120,000 to $149,999	7,629	10.0	6,735	8.9
$150,000 to $199,999	11,141	14.6	9,643	12.7
$200,000 to $299,999	13,494	17.7	13,132	17.4
$300,000 or more	19,499	25.5	23,047	30.5
$300,000 to $399,999	7,924	10.4	8,060	10.7
$400,000 to $499,999	4,200	5.5	4,740	6.3
$500,000 to $749,999	4,577	6.0	6,234	8.2
$750,000 or more	2,798	3.7	4,013	5.3
Median home value	$170,000	–	$191,471	–

Note: "–" means not applicable.
Source: Bureau of the Census, American Housing Survey for the United States: 2009, Internet site http://www.census.gov/hhes/ www/housing/ahs/ahs09/ahs09.html; calculations by New Strategist

Table 2.27 Homeowners by Major Source of Down Payment, 2009

The largest share of homeowners used savings as their major source of down payment. Twelve percent did not make a down payment.

(number and percent distribution of homeowners by major source of down payment, 2009; numbers in thousands)

	number	percent distribution
Total homes purchased or built	**71,877**	**100.0%**
Sale of previous home	21,946	30.5
Savings or cash on hand	31,437	43.7
Sale of other investment	750	1.0
Borrowing, other than mortgage on this property	2,409	3.4
Inheritance or gift	1,358	1.9
Land where building built used for financing	639	0.9
Other	3,125	4.3
No down payment	8,346	11.6
Not reported	1,867	2.6

Source: Bureau of the Census, American Housing Survey for the United States: 2009, Internet site http://www.census.gov/hhes/www/housing/ahs/ahs09/ahs09.html; calculations by New Strategist

Table 2.28 Homeowners by First Home and Mortgage Status, 2009

Forty-one percent of homeowners live in the first home they
have ever owned. Most homeowners have a mortgage.
Only 32 percent own their home free and clear.

(number and percent distribution of homeowners by first-home and mortgage status, 2009; numbers in thousands)

	number	percent distribution
FIRST-HOME STATUS		
Total homeowners	**76,428**	**100.0%**
First home ever owned	31,676	41.4
Not first home	43,233	56.6
Not reported	1,519	2.0
MORTGAGE STATUS		
Total homeowners	**76,428**	**100.0**
None, owned free and clear	24,206	31.7
Reverse mortgage	252	0.3
With regular and/or home-equity mortgage	50,300	65.8
Regular mortgage	46,703	61.1
Home-equity lump-sum mortgage	4,022	5.3
Home-equity line of credit	9,184	12.0
Not reported	1,670	2.2

Source: Bureau of the Census, American Housing Survey for the United States: 2009, Internet site http://www.census.gov/hhes/ www/housing/ahs/ahs09/ahs09.html; calculations by New Strategist

Table 2.29 Year of Origination for Primary Mortgage, 2009

Half of the nation's homeowners with mortgages obtained
their primary mortgage in 2004 or later.

(number and percent distribution of homeowners with mortgages by year primary mortgage originated, 2009; numbers in thousands)

	number	percent distribution
Total homeowners with mortgages	**47,945**	**100.0%**
2005 to 2009	21,064	43.9
2000 to 2004	14,175	29.6
1995 to 1999	6,152	12.8
1990 to 1994	2,953	6.2
1985 to 1989	1,808	3.8
1980 to 1984	767	1.6
1975 to 1979	564	1.2
1970 to 1974	434	0.9
1969 or earlier	28	0.1
Median year of origination	2004	–

Note "–" means not applicable.
Source: Bureau of the Census, American Housing Survey for the United States: 2009, Internet site http://www.census.gov/hhes/ www/housing/ahs/ahs09/ahs09.html; calculations by New Strategist

Table 2.30 Homeowners by Mortgage Characteristics, 2007 and 2009

As home values have declined, mortgage loans as a percentage
of home value have increased from 54 to 63 percent.

*(number and percent distribution of homeowners with mortgages by mortgage characteristics, 2007 and 2009;
numbers in thousands)*

	2009		2007	
	number	percent	number	percent
TOTAL HOMEOWNERS	76,428	100.0%	75,647	100.0%
Homeowners with mortgages	47,945	62.7	46,461	61.4
REMAINING YEARS MORTGAGED				
Homeowners with mortgages	47,945	100.0	46,461	100.0
Less than eight years	6,160	12.8	5,981	12.9
Eight to 12 years	5,188	10.8	5,549	11.9
13 to 17 years	5,077	10.6	4,602	9.9
18 to 22 years	6,568	13.7	4,879	10.5
23 to 27 years	14,948	31.2	12,263	26.4
28 to 32 years	9,569	20.0	12,791	27.5
33 years or more	164	0.3	241	0.5
Variable	271	0.6	156	0.3
Median years remaining	23	–	24	–
TOTAL OUTSTANDING PRINCIPAL				
Homeowners with mortgages	47,945	100.0	46,461	100.0
Under $10,000	2,797	5.8	3,122	6.7
$10,000 to $19,999	1,972	4.1	2,011	4.3
$20,000 to $29,999	1,877	3.9	2,038	4.4
$30,000 to $39,999	1,978	4.1	2,188	4.7
$40,000 to $49,999	2,338	4.9	2,220	4.8
$50,000 to $59,999	2,328	4.9	2,246	4.8
$60,000 to $69,999	2,504	5.2	2,373	5.1
$70,000 to $79,999	2,484	5.2	2,414	5.2
$80,000 to $99,999	4,420	9.2	4,447	9.6
$100,000 to $119,999	3,751	7.8	3,790	8.2
$120,000 to $149,999	5,029	10.5	4,751	10.2
$150,000 to $199,999	5,926	12.4	5,511	11.9
$200,000 to $249,999	3,575	7.5	3,081	6.6
$250,000 to $299,999	2,267	4.7	2,008	4.3
$300,000 or more	4,700	9.8	4,261	9.2
Median outstanding principal	$106,909	–	$100,904	–

	2009		2007	
	number	percent	number	percent
CURRENT TOTAL LOAN AS PERCENT OF VALUE				
Homeowners with mortgages	**47,945**	**100.0%**	**46,461**	**100.0%**
Less than 20 percent	6,174	12.9	7,204	15.5
20 to 39 percent	7,478	15.6	9,102	19.6
40 to 59 percent	8,524	17.8	9,626	20.7
60 to 79 percent	9,924	20.7	10,365	22.3
80 to 89 percent	5,128	10.7	4,489	9.7
90 to 99 percent	4,928	10.3	3,220	6.9
100 percent or more	5,789	12.1	2,456	5.3
Median percent of value	63.0%	–	54.4%	–

Note: "–" means not applicable.
Source: Bureau of the Census, American Housing Survey for the United States: 2007 and 2009, Internet site http://www.census .gov/hhes/www/housing/ahs/nationaldata.html; calculations by New Strategist

Table 2.31 Refinancing of Primary Mortgage, 2009

Twenty-five percent of homeowners have refinanced their primary mortgage, the majority doing so to lower their interest rate.

(number and percent distribution of homeowners with mortgages by refinancing of primary mortgage status, reason for refinancing, and cash received, 2009; numbers in thousands)

	number	percent distribution
HOMEOWNERS WITH MORTGAGES	**47,945**	**100.0%**
Homeowners with a refinanced primary mortgage	**12,220**	**25.5**
REASON FOR REFINANCING OF PRIMARY MORTGAGE		
Homeowners with a refinanced primary mortgage	**12,220**	**100.0**
To get lower interest rate	9,228	75.5
To reduce the monthly payment	1,552	12.7
To increase payment period	180	1.5
To reduce payment period	573	4.7
To renew or extend a loan that has fallen due	123	1.0
To receive cash	1,587	13.0
Other reasons	1,655	13.5
CASH RECEIVED IN PRIMARY MORTGAGE REFINANCING		
Homeowners receiving cash in mortgage refinancing	**1,587**	**100.0**
Under $10,000	125	7.9
$10,000 to $19,999	231	14.5
$20,000 to $29,999	226	14.3
$30,000 to $39,999	157	9.9
$40,000 to $49,999	93	5.9
$50,000 to $59,999	99	6.3
$60,000 to $69,999	46	2.9
$70,000 to $79,999	25	1.6
$80,000 to $99,999	93	5.9
$100,000 to $119,999	90	5.7
$120,000 to $149,999	30	1.9
$150,000 or more	95	6.0
Not reported	276	17.4
Median amount of cash received	$30,000	–
Percent of cash used for home improvement, repairs	15.0%	–

Note: "–" means not applicable.
Source: Bureau of the Census, American Housing Survey for the United States: 2009, Internet site http://www.census.gov/hhes/ www/housing/ahs/ahs09/ahs09.html; calculations by New Strategist

Table 2.32 Homeowners by Home Equity Line of Credit Status, 2009

Only 19 percent of homeowners have a home equity line of credit, and an even smaller 11 percent have an outstanding balance on their loan.

(number and percent distribution of homeowners by home equity line of credit status, outstanding loan amount, and monthly payment, 2009; numbers in thousands)

	number	percent distribution
HOMEOWNERS WITH MORTGAGES	**47,945**	**100.0%**
Homeowners with home equity line-of-credit	**9,184**	**19.2**
Homeowners with home equity loan outstanding	**5,306**	**11.1**
LINE-OF-CREDIT LOANS OUTSTANDING		
Homeowners with outstanding line-of-credit loans	**5,306**	**100.0**
Under $10,000	837	15.8
$10,000 to $19,999	982	18.5
$20,000 to $29,999	748	14.1
$30,000 to $39,999	460	8.7
$40,000 to $49,999	354	6.7
$50,000 to $59,999	227	4.3
$60,000 to $69,999	237	4.5
$70,000 to $79,999	151	2.9
$80,000 to $99,999	264	5.0
$100,000 to $119,999	159	3.0
$120,000 to $149,999	111	2.1
$150,000 or more	245	4.6
Not reported	523	9.9
Median outstanding line-of-credit loan	$26,000	–
LINE-OF-CREDIT MONTHLY PAYMENT		
Homeowners with outstanding line-of-credit loans	**5,306**	**100.0**
Less than $100	532	10.0
$100 to $199	1,010	19.0
$200 to $299	965	18.2
$300 to $399	594	11.2
$400 to $499	349	6.6
$500 to $599	414	7.8
$600 to $699	183	3.5
$700 to $799	109	2.1
$800 to $999	146	2.8
$1,000 or more	457	8.6
Not reported	546	10.3
Median monthly payment	$260	–

Note: "–" means not applicable.
Source: Bureau of the Census, American Housing Survey for the United States: 2009, Internet site http://www.census.gov/hhes/www/housing/ahs/ahs09/ahs09.html; calculations by New Strategist

Table 2.33 Homeowners by Monthly Principal and Interest Payments, 2009

Homeowners with mortgages pay a median of $878 a month in principal and interest. Twelve percent pay more than $2,000 per month.

(number and percent distribution of homeowners with mortgages by monthly payment for principal and interest, 2009; numbers in thousands)

	number	percent distribution
Homeowners with mortgages	**47,945**	**100.0%**
Less than $100	1,327	2.8
$100 to $199	1,072	2.2
$200 to $299	1,757	3.7
$300 to $399	2,873	6.0
$400 to $499	3,338	7.0
$500 to $599	3,816	8.0
$600 to $699	3,859	8.0
$700 to $799	3,443	7.2
$800 to $999	6,162	12.9
$1,000 to $1,249	5,879	12.3
$1,250 to $1,499	4,059	8.5
$1,500 to $1,999	4,786	10.0
$2,000 or more	5,574	11.6
Median monthly payment	$878	–

Note: "–" means not applicable.
Source: Bureau of the Census, American Housing Survey for the United States: 2009, Internet site http://www.census.gov/hhes/ www/housing/ahs/ahs09/ahs09.html; calculations by New Strategist

Table 2.34 Homeowners by Monthly Housing Costs, 2009

Monthly housing costs for homeowners are only slightly above average,
a median of $1,000 per month versus $909 for all householders.

(number and percent distribution of total households and homeowners, by monthly housing costs, 2009; numbers in thousands)

	total		homeowners		
	number	percent distribution	number	percent distribution	percent of total
Total households	**111,806**	**100.0%**	**76,428**	**100.0%**	**68.4%**
Less than $100	723	0.6	475	0.6	65.7
$100 to $199	2,889	2.6	2,161	2.8	74.8
$200 to $299	6,732	6.0	5,351	7.0	79.5
$300 to $399	7,381	6.6	6,022	7.9	81.6
$400 to $499	7,402	6.6	5,308	6.9	71.7
$500 to $599	7,392	6.6	4,407	5.8	59.6
$600 to $699	7,542	6.7	3,735	4.9	49.5
$700 to $799	7,306	6.5	3,597	4.7	49.2
$800 to $999	13,200	11.8	7,139	9.3	54.1
$1,000 to $1,249	12,933	11.6	8,156	10.7	63.1
$1,250 to $1,499	9,459	8.5	6,828	8.9	72.2
$1,500 or $1,999	11,692	10.5	9,445	12.4	80.8
$2,000 to $2,499	6,140	5.5	5,422	7.1	88.3
$2,500 or more	8,980	8.0	8,383	11.0	93.4
No cash rent	2,037	1.8	–	–	
Median monthly cost	$909	–	$1,000	–	–

Note: Housing costs include utilities, mortgages, real estate taxes, property insurance, and regime fees. "–" means not applicable.
Source: Bureau of the Census, American Housing Survey for the United States: 2009, Internet site http://www.census.gov/hhes/www/housing/ahs/ahs09/ahs09.html; calculations by New Strategist

Table 2.35 Homeowners by Monthly Utility and Property Insurance Costs, 2009

Homeowners pay more per month for electricity and
piped gas than the average householder.

(number and percent distribution of total households and homeowners, by average monthly costs for utilities and property insurance, 2009; numbers in thousands)

	total		homeowners		
	number	percent distribution	number	percent distribution	percent of total
MONTHLY COST OF ELECTRICITY					
Households using electricity	**111,746**	**100.0%**	**76,378**	**100.0%**	**68.3%**
Less than $25	1,701	1.5	442	0.6	26.0
$25 to $49	9,851	8.8	4,425	5.8	44.9
$50 to $74	17,551	15.7	11,016	14.4	62.8
$75 to $99	18,444	16.5	12,975	17.0	70.3
$100 to $149	27,826	24.9	21,237	27.8	76.3
$150 to $199	14,959	13.4	12,164	15.9	81.3
$200 or more	14,451	12.9	12,110	15.9	83.8
Included in rent, other fee, or obtained free	6,964	6.2	2,010	2.6	28.9
Median monthly cost	$107	–	$117	–	–
MONTHLY COST OF PIPED GAS					
Households using piped gas	**67,886**	**100.0**	**46,700**	**100.0**	**68.8**
Less than $25	3,856	5.7	1,410	3.0	36.6
$25 to $49	12,402	18.3	7,933	17.0	64.0
$50 to $74	14,777	21.8	11,196	24.0	75.8
$75 to $99	10,648	15.7	8,595	18.4	80.7
$100 to $149	11,578	17.1	9,694	20.8	83.7
$150 to $199	4,341	6.4	3,698	7.9	85.2
$200 or more	3,200	4.7	2,682	5.7	83.8
Included in rent, other fee, or obtained free	7,082	10.4	1,494	3.2	21.1
Median monthly cost	$73	–	$80	–	–
MONTHLY COST OF FUEL OIL					
Households using fuel oil	**9,208**	**100.0**	**6,409**	**100.0**	**69.6**
Less than $25	228	2.5	176	2.8	77.2
$25 to $49	395	4.3	325	5.1	82.3
$50 to $74	581	6.3	490	7.6	84.3
$75 to $99	825	9.0	725	11.3	87.9
$100 to $149	1,566	17.0	1,403	21.9	89.6
$150 to $199	1,161	12.6	1,052	16.4	90.7
$200 or more	1,848	20.1	1,701	26.5	92.1
Included in rent, other fee, or obtained free	2,604	28.3	536	8.4	20.6
Median monthly cost	$133	–	$133	–	–

	total		homeowners		
	number	percent distribution	number	percent distribution	percent of total
Water paid separately	62,789	–	53,552	–	85.3%
Median monthly cost	$35	–	$38	–	–
Trash paid separately	52,525	–	44,974	–	85.6
Median monthly cost	$21	–	$21	–	–
Property insurance paid separately	81,711	–	72,313	–	88.5
Median monthly cost	$50	–	$55	–	–

Note: "–" means not applicable.
Source: Bureau of the Census, American Housing Survey for the United States: 2009, Internet site http://www.census.gov/hhes/ www/housing/ahs/ahs09/ahs09.html; calculations by New Strategist

Table 2.36 Homeowners by Real Estate Taxes, 2009

Homeowners pay a median of $150 per month for real estate taxes.

(number and percent distribution of homeowners by monthly costs for real estate taxes and taxes per $1,000 assessed value, 2003; numbers in thousands)

	number	percent distribution
Total homeowners	**76,428**	**100.0%**
Monthly cost of real estate taxes		
Less than $25	7,751	10.1
$25 to $49	6,017	7.9
$50 to $74	6,565	8.6
$75 to $99	5,883	7.7
$100 to $124	6,494	8.5
$125 to $149	4,880	6.4
$150 to $199	9,140	12.0
$200 to $299	11,727	15.3
$300 to $399	6,171	8.1
$400 to $499	3,655	4.8
$500 to $599	2,884	3.8
$600 or more	5,260	6.9
Median monthly cost	$150	–
Annual taxes paid per $1,000 value		
Less than $5	12,710	16.6
$5 to $9	21,383	28.0
$10 to $14	17,473	22.9
$15 to $19	9,992	13.1
$20 to $24	6,058	7.9
$25 or more	8,812	11.5
Median amount per $1,000 assessed	$10	–

Note: "–" means not applicable.
Source: Bureau of the Census, American Housing Survey for the United States: 2009, Internet site http://www.census.gov/hhes/ www/housing/ahs/ahs09/ahs09.html; calculations by New Strategist

Table 2.37 Homeowners by Opinion of Home, 2009

Homeowners have a higher opinion of their home than the average householder, 31 percent giving their home the highest rating.

(number and percent distribution of total households and homeowners, by opinion of home, 2009; numbers in thousands)

	total		homeowners		
	number	percent distribution	number	percent distribution	percent of total
Total households	**111,806**	**100.0%**	**76,428**	**100.0%**	**68.4%**
1 (worst)	530	0.5	203	0.3	38.4
2	331	0.3	122	0.2	37.0
3	611	0.5	175	0.2	28.6
4	1,153	1.0	444	0.6	38.6
5	5,275	4.7	2,365	3.1	44.8
6	5,208	4.7	2,655	3.5	51.0
7	15,045	13.5	8,899	11.6	59.1
8	30,667	27.4	21,042	27.5	68.6
9	17,844	16.0	13,627	17.8	76.4
10 (best)	30,909	27.6	23,967	31.4	77.5
Not reported	4,233	3.8	2,926	3.8	69.1

Note: "–" means not applicable.
Source: Bureau of the Census, American Housing Survey for the United States: 2009, Internet site http://www.census.gov/hhes/ www/housing/ahs/ahs09/ahs09.html; calculations by New Strategist

Table 2.38 Homeowners by Opinion of Neighborhood, 2009

Homeowners have a slightly higher opinion of their neighborhood
than the average householder does, 27 percent giving
their neighborhood the highest rating.

(number and percent distribution of total households and homeowners, by opinion of neighborhood, 2009; numbers in thousands)

	total		homeowners		
	number	percent distribution	number	percent distribution	percent of total
Total households	**111,806**	**100.0%**	**76,428**	**100.0%**	**68.4%**
1 (worst)	837	0.7	338	0.4	40.4
2	637	0.6	289	0.4	45.4
3	1,002	0.9	459	0.6	45.8
4	1,633	1.5	766	1.0	46.9
5	6,332	5.7	3,356	4.4	53.0
6	5,919	5.3	3,454	4.5	58.3
7	14,767	13.2	9,603	12.6	65.0
8	29,794	26.6	20,808	27.2	69.8
9	18,017	16.1	13,454	17.6	74.7
10 (best)	28,465	25.5	20,891	27.3	73.4
No neighborhood	60	0.1	31	0.0	51.0
Not reported	4,341	3.9	2,979	3.9	68.6

Source: Bureau of the Census, American Housing Survey for the United States: 2009, Internet site http://www.census.gov/hhes/ www/housing/ahs/ahs09/ahs09.html; calculations by New Strategist

Table 2.39 Homeowners by Neighborhood Problems, 2009

Fifteen percent of homeowners say there has been serious crime
in their neighborhood in the past 12 months.

(number and percent distribution of total households and homeowners with neighborhood problems, 2009; numbers in thousands)

	total		homeowners		
	number	percent distribution	number	percent distribution	percent of total
Total households	**111,806**	**100.0%**	**76,428**	**100.0%**	**68.4%**
Bothersome street noise or heavy traffic	25,381	22.7	15,223	19.9	60.0
Serious crime in neighborhood in past 12 months	19,299	17.3	11,649	15.2	60.4
Bothersome odor problem	5,434	4.9	3,278	4.3	60.3
Noise problem	2,950	2.6	1,733	2.3	58.7
Litter or housing deterioration	1,691	1.5	1,101	1.4	65.1
With poor city or county services	694	0.6	440	0.6	63.4
Undesirable commercial, institutional, industrial properties	415	0.4	247	0.3	59.5
People problem	4,521	4.0	2,706	3.5	59.9
Other problems	9,539	8.5	6,748	8.8	70.7

Source: Bureau of the Census, American Housing Survey for the United States: 2009, Internet site http://www.census.gov/hhes/ www/housing/ahs/ahs09/ahs09.html; calculations by New Strategist

Table 2.40 Homeowners by Community Characteristics, 2009

Only 7 percent of homeowners live in a gated community. Forty-three percent live near open space, park, woods, farm, or ranchland.

(number and percent distribution of total households and homeowners, by community characteristics, 2009; numbers in thousands)

	total		homeowners		
	number	percent distribution	number	percent distribution	percent of total
Total households	**111,806**	**100.0%**	**76,428**	**100.0%**	**68.4%**
SECURED COMMUNITIES					
Total households	**111,806**	**100.0**	**76,428**	**100.0**	**68.4**
Community access secured with walls or fences	10,759	9.6	5,337	7.0	49.6
Special entry system present	6,091	5.4	2,682	3.5	44.0
Special entry system not present	4,653	4.2	2,648	3.5	56.9
Community access not secured	100,124	89.6	70,410	92.1	70.3
SENIOR CITIZEN COMMUNITIES					
Households with persons 55 or older	**45,684**	**100.0**	**36,591**	**100.0**	**80.1**
Community age restricted	3,080	6.7	1,457	4.0	47.3
No age restriction	42,603	93.3	35,134	96.0	82.5
Community age specific	10,302	22.6	8,867	24.2	86.1
Community not age specific	29,683	65.0	24,100	65.9	81.2
COMMUNITY AMENITIES					
Total households	**111,806**	**100.0**	**76,428**	**100.0**	**68.4**
Community center or clubhouse	24,410	21.8	14,707	19.2	60.2
Golf in community	16,709	14.9	12,762	16.7	76.4
Trails in community	21,609	19.3	15,300	20.0	70.8
Shuttle bus available	9,933	8.9	5,718	7.5	57.6
Daycare center	15,883	14.2	10,633	13.9	66.9
Private or restricted beach, park, or shoreline	21,432	19.2	15,124	19.8	70.6
DESCRIPTION OF AREA WITHIN 300 FEET OF HOME					
Total households	**111,806**	**100.0**	**76,428**	**100.0**	**68.4**
Single-family detached homes	95,916	85.8	68,909	90.2	71.8
Single-family attached homes	21,832	19.5	10,973	14.4	50.3
Multiunit residential buildings	33,635	30.1	11,514	15.1	34.2
One-to-three-story multiunit tallest	25,143	22.5	9,014	11.8	35.8
Four-to-six-story multiunit tallest	4,937	4.4	1,464	1.9	29.7
Seven-or-more-story multiunit tallest	3,172	2.8	929	1.2	29.3
Manufactured/mobile homes	13,388	12.0	10,276	13.4	76.8
Commercial or institutional	35,649	31.9	16,992	22.2	47.7
Industrial or factories	5,376	4.8	2,520	3.3	46.9
Open space, park, woods, farm, ranch	45,816	41.0	33,110	43.3	72.3
Four-or-more-lane highway, railroad, or airport	19,612	17.5	10,380	13.6	52.9

	total		homeowners		
	number	percent distribution	number	percent distribution	percent of total
BODIES OF WATER WITHIN 300 FEET OF HOME					
Total households	**111,806**	**100.0%**	**76,428**	**100.0%**	**68.4%**
Water in area	18,656	16.7	13,824	18.1	74.1
With waterfront property	3,331	3.0	2,653	3.5	79.6
With flood plain	2,622	2.3	1,929	2.5	73.6
No water in area	92,474	82.7	62,083	81.2	67.1

Note: Numbers may not add to total because "not reported" is not shown.
Source: Bureau of the Census, American Housing Survey for the United States: 2009, Internet site http://www.census.gov/hhes/ www/housing/ahs/ahs09/ahs09.html; calculations by New Strategist

Table 2.41 Homeowners by Public Services Available, 2009

Most homeowners do not have public transportation in their neighborhood.

(number and percent distribution of total households and homeowners, by public services available in neighborhood, 2009; numbers in thousands)

	total		homeowners		
	number	percent distribution	number	percent distribution	percent of total
Total households	**111,806**	**100.0%**	**76,428**	**100.0%**	**68.4%**
LOCAL ELEMENTARY SCHOOL					
Households with children under age 14	**30,976**	**100.0**	**20,490**	**100.0**	**66.1**
Satisfactory public elementary school	25,297	81.7	16,966	82.8	67.1
Unsatisfactory public elementary school	2,146	6.9	1,422	6.9	66.3
Unsatisfactory public elementary school	**2,146**	**100.0**	**1,422**	**100.0**	**66.3**
Better than other area elementary schools	216	10.1	154	10.8	71.0
Same as other area elementary schools	714	33.3	490	34.4	68.6
Worse than other area elementary schools	1,082	50.4	696	49.0	64.3
Households with children under age 14	**30,976**	**100.0**	**20,490**	**100.0**	**66.1**
Public elementary school less than one mile	18,667	60.3	11,571	56.5	62.0
Public elementary school more than one mile	10,526	34.0	7,785	38.0	74.0
PUBLIC TRANSPORTATION IN AREA					
Total households	**111,806**	**100.0**	**76,428**	**100.0**	**68.4**
With public transportation	60,257	53.9	35,616	46.6	59.1
No public transportation	48,532	43.4	38,848	50.8	80.0
With public transportation, travel time to nearest stop	**60,257**	**100.0**	**35,616**	**100.0**	**59.1**
Less than 5 minutes	21,258	35.3	10,929	30.7	51.4
5 to 9 minutes	21,699	36.0	12,830	36.0	59.1
10 to 14 minutes	8,606	14.3	5,853	16.4	68.0
15 to 29 minutes	4,224	7.0	3,125	8.8	74.0
30 minutes or longer	618	1.0	449	1.3	72.7
With public transportation	**60,257**	**100.0**	**35,616**	**100.0**	**59.1**
Household uses it regularly for commute to school or work	10,212	16.9	3,817	10.7	37.4
Household does not use it regularly for commute to school or work	49,681	82.4	31,606	88.7	63.6
SHOPPING IN AREA					
Total households	**111,806**	**100.0**	**76,428**	**100.0**	**68.4**
Grocery stores or drugstores within 15 minutes of home	106,737	95.5	72,548	94.9	68.0
Satisfactory	103,482	92.6	70,400	92.1	68.0
Unsatisfactory	2,769	2.5	1,805	2.4	65.2
No grocery stores or drugstores within 15 minutes of home	3,596	3.2	2,819	3.7	78.4

	total		homeowners		
	number	percent distribution	number	percent distribution	percent of total
POLICE PROTECTION					
Total households	**111,806**	**100.0%**	**76,428**	**100.0%**	**68.4%**
Satisfactory police protection	101,373	90.7	69,633	91.1	68.7
Unsatisfactory police protection	7,356	6.6	4,800	6.3	65.3

Note: Numbers may not add to total because "not reported" is not shown.
Source: Bureau of the Census, American Housing Survey for the United States: 2009, Internet site http://www.census.gov/hhes/
www/housing/ahs/ahs09/ahs09.html; calculations by New Strategist

Table 2.42 Changes in Housing and Costs for Owners Who Moved, 2009

Homeowners who recently moved are much more likely than the average mover to have experienced an increase in housing costs—61 versus 48 percent.

(number and percent distribution of total householders and homeowners who moved in the past year, by structure type of previous residence, ownership of previous residence, and change in housing costs, 2009; numbers in thousands)

	total		homeowners		
	number	percent distribution	number	percent distribution	percent of total
STRUCTURE TYPE OF PREVIOUS RESIDENCE					
Householders who moved within United States	**16,763**	**100.0%**	**4,341**	**100.0%**	**25.9%**
House	8,531	50.9	2,595	59.8	30.4
Apartment	6,437	38.4	1,208	27.8	18.8
Mobile home	783	4.7	238	5.5	30.3
Other	499	3.0	119	2.7	23.8
Not reported	513	3.1	182	4.2	35.4
OWNERSHIP OF PREVIOUS RESIDENCE					
Householders who moved from house, apartment, or mobile home within United States	**15,751**	**100.0**	**4,041**	**100.0**	**25.7**
Owner-occupied	5,023	31.9	2,032	50.3	40.5
Renter-occupied	10,728	68.1	2,009	49.7	18.7
CHANGE IN HOUSING COSTS					
Householders who moved from house, apartment, or mobile home within United States	**15,751**	**100.0**	**4,041**	**100.0**	**25.7**
Increased with move	7,590	48.2	2,455	60.8	32.3
Decreased	4,520	28.7	801	19.8	17.7
Stayed about the same	3,107	19.7	663	16.4	21.3
Don't know	310	2.0	60	1.5	19.2
Not reported	223	1.4	62	1.5	27.8

Source: Bureau of the Census, American Housing Survey for the United States: 2009, Internet site http://www.census.gov/hhes/ www/housing/ahs/ahs09/ahs09.html; calculations by New Strategist

Table 2.43 Reasons for Choosing Home among Owners Who Moved, 2009

Homeowners who recently moved are less likely than the average mover to have chosen their home for financial reasons.

(number and percent distribution of total respondents and homeowner respondents who moved in the past year, by reasons for choosing home, 2009; numbers in thousands)

	total		homeowners		
	number	percent distribution	number	percent distribution	percent of total
Total respondents who moved	**17,463**	**100.0%**	**4,623**	**100.0%**	**26.5%**
Main reason for choice of present home					
All reported reasons equal	2,256	12.9	808	17.5	35.8
Financial reasons	4,854	27.8	1,008	21.8	20.8
Room layout/design	2,540	14.5	797	17.2	31.4
Kitchen	98	0.6	33	0.7	33.7
Size	1,775	10.2	377	8.2	21.3
Exterior appearance	475	2.7	125	2.7	26.3
Yard/trees/view	699	4.0	287	6.2	41.1
Quality of construction	417	2.4	186	4.0	44.6
Only one available	684	3.9	76	1.6	11.1
Other	2,834	16.2	636	13.7	22.4
Not reported	830	4.8	290	6.3	35.0
Present home compared with previous home					
Better	9,209	52.7	3,017	65.3	32.8
Worse	3,102	17.8	426	9.2	13.7
About the same	4,418	25.3	920	19.9	20.8
Not reported	734	4.2	261	5.6	35.5
Home search					
Now in house	8,129	100.0	3,929	100.0	48.3
Did not look at apartments	6,318	77.7	3,430	87.3	54.3
Looked at apartments too	1,467	18.0	305	7.8	20.8
Now in manufactured/mobile home	960	100.0	410	100.0	42.7
Did not look at apartments	663	69.1	304	74.1	45.8
Looked at apartments too	250	26.0	69	16.9	27.7
Now in apartment	8,374	100.0	285	100.0	3.4
Did not look at houses	5,907	70.5	181	63.6	3.1
Looked at houses too	2,148	25.6	92	32.2	4.3

Note: Total number of movers does not equal total movers in other tables because this table shows survey respondents who moved, not necessarily householders. Numbers may not add to total because "not reported" may not be shown.
Source: Bureau of the Census, American Housing Survey for the United States: 2009, Internet site http://www.census.gov/hhes/www/housing/ahs/ahs09/ahs09.html; calculations by New Strategist

Table 2.44 Reasons for Choosing Neighborhood among Owners Who Moved, 2009

Most homeowners who recently moved looked at more than one neighborhood before moving, with the particular house the single most important factor in their neighborhood choice.

(number and percent distribution of total respondents and homeowning respondents who moved in the past year, by reasons for choosing neighborhood, 2009; numbers in thousands)

	total		homeowners		
	number	percent distribution	number	percent distribution	percent of total
Total respondents who moved	**17,463**	**100.0%**	**4,623**	**100.0%**	**26.5%**
Neighborhood search					
Looked at just this neighborhood	7,490	42.9	1,590	34.4	21.2
Looked at other neighborhoods	9,335	53.5	2,802	60.6	30.0
Not reported	638	3.7	231	5.0	36.2
Main reason for choice of present neighborhood					
All reported reasons equal	1,905	10.9	551	11.9	28.9
Convenient to job	3,535	20.2	611	13.2	17.3
Convenient to friends or relatives	2,485	14.2	570	12.3	22.9
Convenient to leisure activities	331	1.9	87	1.9	26.4
Convenient to public transportation	266	1.5	29	0.6	11.0
Good schools	1,087	6.2	289	6.3	26.6
Other public services	221	1.3	36	0.8	16.4
Looks/design of neighborhood	1,798	10.3	635	13.7	35.3
House most important consideration	1,765	10.1	801	17.3	45.4
Other	3,313	19.0	750	16.2	22.6
Not reported	757	4.3	264	5.7	34.8
Present neighborhood compared with previous neighborhood					
Better	7,206	41.3	2,253	48.7	31.3
Worse	2,303	13.2	347	7.5	15.1
About the same	6,471	37.1	1,555	33.6	24.0
Same neighborhood	699	4.0	179	3.9	25.6
Not reported	786	4.5	290	6.3	36.9

Note: Total number of movers does not equal total movers in other tables because this table shows survey respondents who moved, not necessarily householders.
Source: Bureau of the Census, American Housing Survey for the United States: 2009, Internet site http://www.census.gov/hhes/ www/housing/ahs/ahs09/ahs09.html; calculations by New Strategist

Table 2.45 Main Reason for Moving among Owners Who Moved, 2009

Only 8 percent of homeowners who recently moved did so because of a new job or job transfer. A larger share moved for housing-related reasons.

(number and percent distribution of total respondents and homeowning respondents who moved in the past year, by main reason for move, 2009; numbers in thousands)

	total		homeowners		
	number	percent distribution	number	percent distribution	percent of total
Total respondents who moved	**17,463**	**100.0%**	**4,623**	**100.0%**	**26.5%**
All reported reasons equal	653	3.7	203	4.4	31.1
Private displacement	123	0.7	5	0.1	4.4
Government displacement	53	0.3	8	0.2	14.5
Disaster loss (fire, flood, etc.)	149	0.9	24	0.5	15.8
New job or job transfer	1,590	9.1	370	8.0	23.3
To be closer to work/school/other	1,634	9.4	217	4.7	13.3
Other financial, employment related	646	3.7	119	2.6	18.4
To establish own household	1,876	10.7	594	12.8	31.6
Needed larger house or apartment	1,534	8.8	431	9.3	28.1
Married, widowed, divorced, or separated	912	5.2	284	6.1	31.1
Other family or personal reasons	1,372	7.9	368	8.0	26.8
Wanted better home	1,186	6.8	305	6.6	25.7
Change from owner to renter or renter to owner	804	4.6	685	14.8	85.1
Wanted lower rent or maintenance	927	5.3	60	1.3	6.4
Other housing-related reasons	782	4.5	168	3.6	21.5
Evicted from residence	126	0.7	14	0.3	11.0
Other	2,032	11.6	484	10.5	23.8
Not reported	1,065	6.1	286	6.2	26.8

Note: Total number of movers does not equal total movers in other tables because this table shows survey respondents who moved, not necessarily householders.
Source: Bureau of the Census, American Housing Survey for the United States: 2009, Internet site http://www.census.gov/hhes/www/housing/ahs/ahs09/ahs09.html; calculations by New Strategist

Table 2.46 Median Home Values by State, 2009

Median home values were highest in Hawaii, according to the 2009 American Community Survey.

(median self-reported value of owner-occupied homes by state and index of home value to national median, 2009)

	median value	index		median value	index
United States	**$185,200**	**100**	Missouri	$139,700	75
Alabama	119,600	65	Montana	176,300	95
Alaska	232,900	126	Nebraska	123,300	67
Arizona	187,700	101	Nevada	207,600	112
Arkansas	102,900	56	New Hampshire	249,700	135
California	384,200	207	New Jersey	348,300	188
Colorado	237,800	128	New Mexico	160,900	87
Connecticut	291,200	157	New York	306,000	165
Delaware	249,400	135	North Carolina	155,500	84
District of Columbia	443,700	240	North Dakota	116,800	63
Florida	182,400	98	Ohio	134,600	73
Georgia	162,800	88	Oklahoma	107,700	58
Hawaii	517,600	279	Oregon	257,400	139
Idaho	171,700	93	Pennsylvania	164,700	89
Illinois	202,200	109	Rhode Island	267,100	144
Indiana	123,100	66	South Carolina	137,500	74
Iowa	122,000	66	South Dakota	126,200	68
Kansas	125,500	68	Tennessee	137,300	74
Kentucky	117,800	64	Texas	125,800	68
Louisiana	135,400	73	Utah	224,700	121
Maine	177,500	96	Vermont	216,300	117
Maryland	318,600	172	Virginia	252,600	136
Massachusetts	338,500	183	Washington	287,200	155
Michigan	132,200	71	West Virginia	94,500	51
Minnesota	200,400	108	Wisconsin	170,800	92
Mississippi	98,000	53	Wyoming	184,000	99

Source: Bureau of the Census, 2009 American Community Survey, Internet site http://factfinder.census.gov/home/saff/main .html?_lang=en&_ts=; calculations by New Strategist

Table 2.47 Median Home Values by State, 2007 and 2009

Home values have fallen the most in Nevada, California, Arizona, and Florida.

(median self-reported value of owner-occupied homes by state, 2007 and 2009; percent change in value, 2007–09)

	2009	2007	percent change
United States	**$185,200**	**$194,300**	**–4.7%**
Alabama	119,600	115,600	3.5
Alaska	232,900	231,300	0.7
Arizona	187,700	237,700	–21.0
Arkansas	102,900	101,000	1.9
California	384,200	532,300	–27.8
Colorado	237,800	233,900	1.7
Connecticut	291,200	309,200	–5.8
Delaware	249,400	239,700	4.0
District of Columbia	443,700	450,900	–1.6
Florida	182,400	230,400	–20.8
Georgia	162,800	164,500	–1.0
Hawaii	517,600	555,400	–6.8
Idaho	171,700	178,100	–3.6
Illinois	202,200	208,800	–3.2
Indiana	123,100	122,900	0.2
Iowa	122,000	117,900	3.5
Kansas	125,500	121,200	3.5
Kentucky	117,800	114,300	3.1
Louisiana	135,400	126,800	6.8
Maine	177,500	176,000	0.9
Maryland	318,600	347,000	–8.2
Massachusetts	338,500	366,400	–7.6
Michigan	132,200	153,100	–13.7
Minnesota	200,400	213,600	–6.2
Mississippi	98,000	96,000	2.1
Missouri	139,700	138,600	0.8
Montana	176,300	170,000	3.7
Nebraska	123,300	122,200	0.9
Nevada	207,600	311,300	–33.3
New Hampshire	249,700	261,800	–4.6
New Jersey	348,300	372,300	–6.4
New Mexico	160,900	155,400	3.5
New York	306,000	311,000	–1.6
North Carolina	155,500	145,700	6.7
North Dakota	116,800	106,800	9.4
Ohio	134,600	137,800	–2.3
Oklahoma	107,700	103,000	4.6
Oregon	257,400	257,300	0.0

	2009	2007	percent change
Pennsylvania	164,700	155,000	6.3%
Rhode Island	267,100	292,800	−8.8
South Carolina	137,500	133,900	2.7
South Dakota	126,200	118,700	6.3
Tennessee	137,300	130,800	5.0
Texas	125,800	120,900	4.1
Utah	224,700	218,700	2.7
Vermont	216,300	205,400	5.3
Virginia	252,600	262,100	−3.6
Washington	287,200	300,800	−4.5
West Virginia	94,500	96,000	−1.6
Wisconsin	170,800	168,800	1.2
Wyoming	184,000	172,300	6.8

Source: Bureau of the Census, 2007 and 2009 American Community Survey, Internet site http://factfinder.census.gov/home/saff/ main.html?_lang=en&_ts=; calculations by New Strategist

3

Renters and Their Homes

Renters are growing in number as young adults postpone buying a home.

The number of households that rent rather than own their home grew 12 percent between 2004 (the year the homeownership rate peaked) and 2009. The biggest percentage point increase in rentership rates occurred among younger adults as many postponed buying a home because of more stringent mortgage requirements and the fear of being stuck with a depreciating asset. Sixty-three percent of renters live in multiunit buildings, 28 percent are in single-family homes, 6 percent dwell in duplexes, and 4 percent inhabit mobile homes.

■ Renters have a median age of 39, well below the median age of 48 for all householders. In part because they are younger, the median household income of renters is also well below average—just $28,400 in 2009.

■ Renters live in homes with a median size of 1,300 square feet. Most have only one or two bedrooms and one bathroom. Only 46 percent of renters have a dishwasher, and 55 percent have a washing machine.

■ Most renters are happy with their home. The 59 percent majority rate their home an 8 or higher on a scale from 1 (worst) to 10 (best).

Most renters live in multi-unit buildings

(percent distribution of renters by number of units in structure, 2009)

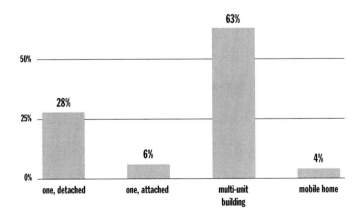

Table 3.1 Renters by Age, 2009

Half the nation's renters are aged 39 or younger. This is well below
the median age of 48 for all householders because renting is
most likely in the youngest age groups.

*(number and percent distribution of total householders and renters, by age of householder, 2009; numbers in
thousands)*

	total		renters		
	number	percent distribution	number	percent distribution	percent of total
Total households	**111,806**	**100.0%**	**35,378**	**100.0%**	**31.6%**
Under age 25	6,083	5.4	4,799	13.6	78.9
Aged 25 to 29	8,614	7.7	5,072	14.3	58.9
Aged 30 to 34	10,093	9.0	4,561	12.9	45.2
Aged 35 to 44	21,908	19.6	6,976	19.7	31.8
Aged 45 to 54	23,505	21.0	5,762	16.3	24.5
Aged 55 to 64	18,509	16.6	3,585	10.1	19.4
Aged 65 to 74	11,938	10.7	2,120	6.0	17.8
Aged 75 or older	11,157	10.0	2,503	7.1	22.4
Median age	48	–	39	–	–

Note: "–" means not applicable.
Source: Bureau of the Census, American Housing Survey for the United States: 2009, Internet site http://www.census.gov/hhes/
www/housing/ahs/ahs09/ahs09.html; calculations by New Strategist

Table 3.2 Renters by Household Type and Age of Householder, 2009

People who live alone account for more than one-third of the nation's renters.

(number and percent distribution of total households and renters, by type of household and age of householder, 2009; numbers in thousands)

	total		renters		
	number	percent distribution	number	percent distribution	percent of total
Total households	**111,806**	**100.0%**	**35,378**	**100.0%**	**31.6%**
MARRIED-COUPLE HOUSEHOLDS	**55,817**	**49.9**	**8,808**	**24.9**	**15.8**
Under age 25	1,203	1.1	707	2.0	58.8
Aged 25 to 29	3,320	3.0	1,313	3.7	39.6
Aged 30 to 34	5,143	4.6	1,497	4.2	29.1
Aged 35 to 44	12,504	11.2	2,168	6.1	17.3
Aged 45 to 64	23,681	21.2	2,329	6.6	9.8
Aged 65 or older	9,967	8.9	793	2.2	8.0
TWO-OR-MORE-PERSON HOUSEHOLDS					
Female householders, no spouse present	**16,496**	**14.8**	**8,565**	**24.2**	**51.9**
Under age 45	9,066	8.1	6,119	17.3	67.5
Aged 45 to 64	5,426	4.9	2,030	5.7	37.4
Aged 65 or older	2,004	1.8	417	1.2	20.8
Male householders, no spouse present	**9,385**	**8.4**	**4,673**	**13.2**	**49.8**
Under age 45	5,800	5.2	3,629	10.3	62.6
Aged 45 to 64	2,773	2.5	895	2.5	32.3
Aged 65 or older	813	0.7	150	0.4	18.4
SINGLE-PERSON HOUSEHOLDS	**30,108**	**26.9**	**13,331**	**37.7**	**44.3**
Female householders	**16,750**	**15.0**	**6,743**	**19.1**	**40.3**
Under age 45	3,980	3.6	2,434	6.9	61.1
Aged 45 to 64	5,212	4.7	1,981	5.6	38.0
Aged 65 or older	7,558	6.8	2,328	6.6	30.8
Male householders	**13,357**	**11.9**	**6,588**	**18.6**	**49.3**
Under age 45	5,682	5.1	3,540	10.0	62.3
Aged 45 to 64	4,922	4.4	2,112	6.0	42.9
Aged 65 or older	2,754	2.5	936	2.6	34.0

Source: Bureau of the Census, American Housing Survey for the United States: 2009, Internet site http://www.census.gov/hhes/www/housing/ahs/ahs09/ahs09.html; calculations by New Strategist

Table 3.3 Renters by Race and Hispanic Origin, 2009

Blacks and Hispanics together account for
more than one-third of the nation's renters.

(number and percent distribution of total households and renters, by race and Hispanic origin of householder, 2009; numbers in thousands)

	total		renters		
	number	percent distribution	number	percent distribution	percent of total
Total households	**111,806**	**100.0%**	**35,378**	**100.0%**	**31.6%**
American Indian	968	0.9	466	1.3	48.1
Asian	4,003	3.6	1,487	4.2	37.1
Black	13,993	12.5	7,446	21.0	53.2
Hispanic	12,739	11.4	6,300	17.8	49.5
White, non-Hispanic	79,333	71.0	19,427	54.9	24.5

Note: American Indians, Asians, blacks, and whites are those who identify themselves as being of the race alone. Numbers do not add to total because not all races are shown and Hispanics may be of any race.
Source: Bureau of the Census, American Housing Survey for the United States: 2009, Internet site http://www.census.gov/hhes/www/housing/ahs/ahs09/ahs09.html; calculations by New Strategist

Table 3.4 Renters by Age, Race, and Hispanic Origin, 2009

Renters account for most Hispanic householders under age 35
and black householders under age 45.

(number and percent distribution of total households and renters, by race, Hispanic origin, and age of householder, 2009; numbers in thousands)

	total		renters		
	number	percent distribution	number	percent distribution	percent of total
Black households	**13,993**	**100.0%**	**7,446**	**100.0%**	**53.2%**
Under age 25	949	6.8	874	11.7	92.2
Aged 25 to 29	1,245	8.9	1,005	13.5	80.7
Aged 30 to 34	1,287	9.2	934	12.5	72.6
Aged 35 to 44	3,005	21.5	1,606	21.6	53.4
Aged 45 to 54	3,049	21.8	1,379	18.5	45.2
Aged 55 to 64	2,214	15.8	861	11.6	38.9
Aged 65 to 74	1,374	9.8	487	6.5	35.5
Aged 75 or older	872	6.2	298	4.0	34.2
Hispanic households	**12,739**	**100.0**	**6,300**	**100.0**	**49.5**
Under age 25	955	7.5	819	13.0	85.8
Aged 25 to 29	1,418	11.1	993	15.8	70.0
Aged 30 to 34	1,712	13.4	1,044	16.6	61.0
Aged 35 to 44	3,128	24.6	1,446	23.0	46.2
Aged 45 to 54	2,441	19.2	954	15.1	39.1
Aged 55 to 64	1,604	12.6	558	8.9	34.8
Aged 65 to 74	877	6.9	271	4.3	30.9
Aged 75 or older	604	4.7	216	3.4	35.7

Note: Blacks are those who identify themselves as being of the race alone. Hispanics may be of any race.
Source: Bureau of the Census, American Housing Survey for the United States: 2009, Internet site http://www.census.gov/hhes/ www/housing/ahs/ahs09/ahs09.html; calculations by New Strategist

Table 3.5 Renters by Household Income, 2009

The nation's renters have much lower incomes than the
average household because they are younger.

(number and percent distribution of total householders and renters by household income, 2009; numbers in thousands)

	total		renters		
	number	percent distribution	number	percent distribution	percent of total
Total households	**111,806**	**100.0%**	**35,378**	**100.0%**	**31.6%**
Under $10,000	10,532	9.4	6,109	17.3	58.0
$10,000 to $19,999	12,025	10.8	6,115	17.3	50.8
$20,000 to $29,999	13,598	12.2	5,981	16.9	44.0
$30,000 to $39,999	11,559	10.3	4,477	12.7	38.7
$40,000 to $49,999	10,290	9.2	3,438	9.7	33.4
$50,000 to $59,999	8,654	7.7	2,326	6.6	26.9
$60,000 to $79,999	13,780	12.3	3,244	9.2	23.5
$80,000 to $99,999	10,073	9.0	1,663	4.7	16.5
$100,000 to $119,999	6,840	6.1	833	2.4	12.2
$120,000 or more	14,456	12.9	1,192	3.4	8.2
Median income	$47,000	–	$28,400	–	–

Note: "–" means not applicable.
Source: Bureau of the Census, American Housing Survey for the United States: 2009, Internet site http://www.census.gov/hhes/ www/housing/ahs/ahs09/ahs09.html; calculations by New Strategist

Table 3.6 Renters by Educational Attainment, 2009

Renters are less educated than the average householder,
in part because many are still in school.

(number and percent distribution of total households and renters, by educational attainment of householder, 2009; numbers in thousands)

	total		renters		
	number	percent distribution	number	percent distribution	percent of total
Total households	**111,806**	**100.0%**	**35,378**	**100.0%**	**31.6%**
Not a high school graduate	15,229	13.6	6,687	18.9	43.9
High school graduate only	34,389	30.8	11,724	33.1	34.1
Some college, no degree	19,583	17.5	6,924	19.6	35.4
Associate's degree	9,244	8.3	2,522	7.1	27.3
Bachelor's degree	21,077	18.9	5,183	14.7	24.6
Graduate or professional degree	12,285	11.0	2,338	6.6	19.0
High school graduate or higher	96,577	86.4	28,691	81.1	29.7
Some college or higher	62,188	55.6	16,967	48.0	27.3
Bachelor's degree or higher	33,361	29.8	7,521	21.3	22.5

Source: Bureau of the Census, American Housing Survey for the United States: 2009, Internet site http://www.census.gov/hhes/ www/housing/ahs/ahs09/ahs09.html; calculations by New Strategist

Table 3.7 Renters by Household Size, 2009

Renters are more likely to live alone than the average householder. Thirty-eight percent of renters live by themselves versus 27 percent of all householders.

(number and percent distribution of total households and renters, by number of persons in home, 2009; numbers in thousands)

	total		renters		
	number	percent distribution	number	percent distribution	percent of total
Total households	**111,806**	**100.0%**	**35,378**	**100.0%**	**31.6%**
1 person	30,108	26.9	13,331	37.7	44.3
2 persons	37,086	33.2	9,453	26.7	25.5
3 persons	17,568	15.7	5,345	15.1	30.4
4 persons	15,807	14.1	4,016	11.4	25.4
5 persons	7,117	6.4	1,910	5.4	26.8
6 persons	2,577	2.3	780	2.2	30.3
7 or more persons	1,543	1.4	543	1.5	35.2

Note: "–" means not applicable.
Source: Bureau of the Census, American Housing Survey for the United States: 2009, Internet site http://www.census.gov/hhes/ www/housing/ahs/ahs09/ahs09.html; calculations by New Strategist

Table 3.8 Renters by Type of Structure, 2009

Renters account for more than 80 percent of householders
in structures with two or more housing units.

(number and percent distribution of total households and renters, by number of units in structure, 2009; numbers in thousands)

	total		renters		
	number	percent distribution	number	percent distribution	percent of total
Total households	**111,806**	**100.0%**	**35,378**	**100.0%**	**31.6%**
One, detached	73,079	65.4	9,755	27.6	13.3
One, attached	5,973	5.3	2,021	5.7	33.8
Multiunit buildings	25,915	23.2	22,181	62.7	85.6
Two to four	8,350	7.5	6,998	19.8	83.8
Five to nine	5,269	4.7	4,637	13.1	88.0
10 to 19	4,661	4.2	4,178	11.8	89.6
20 to 49	3,630	3.2	3,131	8.9	86.3
50 or more	4,004	3.6	3,237	9.1	80.8
Mobile home	6,839	6.1	1,421	4.0	20.8

Source: Bureau of the Census, American Housing Survey for the United States: 2009, Internet site http://www.census.gov/hhes/ www/housing/ahs/ahs09/ahs09.html; calculations by New Strategist

Table 3.9 Renters by Year Structure Built, 2009

Renters live in slightly older homes than the average householder.
Only 17 percent live in homes built since 1990.

(number and percent distribution of total households and renters, by year structure was built, 2009; numbers in thousands)

	total		renters		
	number	percent distribution	number	percent distribution	percent of total
Total households	**111,806**	**100.0%**	**35,378**	**100.0%**	**31.6%**
2005 to 2009	5,884	5.3	1,283	3.6	21.8
2000 to 2004	8,102	7.2	1,731	4.9	21.4
1995 to 1999	7,825	7.0	1,603	4.5	20.5
1990 to 1994	5,995	5.4	1,280	3.6	21.4
1985 to 1989	7,648	6.8	2,489	7.0	32.5
1980 to 1984	6,380	5.7	2,179	6.2	34.2
1975 to 1979	11,835	10.6	4,364	12.3	36.9
1970 to 1974	9,413	8.4	3,718	10.5	39.5
1960 to 1969	13,326	11.9	4,409	12.5	33.1
1950 to 1959	11,771	10.5	3,243	9.2	27.6
1940 to 1949	6,745	6.0	2,322	6.6	34.4
1930 to 1939	4,828	4.3	1,924	5.4	39.9
1920 to 1929	4,331	3.9	1,811	5.1	41.8
1919 or earlier	7,724	6.9	3,021	8.5	39.1
Median year	1974	–	1971	–	–

Note: "–" means not applicable.
Source: Bureau of the Census, American Housing Survey for the United States: 2009, Internet site http://www.census.gov/hhes/www/housing/ahs/ahs09/ahs09.html; calculations by New Strategist

Table 3.10 Renters by Year Moved into Home, 2009

Because renters are relatively young, half have lived in
their current housing unit only since 2007.

*(number and percent distribution of total households and renters, by year householder moved into unit, 2009;
numbers in thousands)*

	total		renters		
	number	percent distribution	number	percent distribution	percent of total
Total households	**111,806**	**100.0%**	**35,378**	**100.0%**	**31.6%**
2005 to 2009	46,108	41.2	25,982	73.4	56.4
2000 to 2004	22,490	20.1	4,970	14.0	22.1
1995 to 1999	13,131	11.7	1,914	5.4	14.6
1990 to 1994	8,763	7.8	1,057	3.0	12.1
1985 to 1989	5,844	5.2	482	1.4	8.2
1980 to 1984	3,436	3.1	312	0.9	9.1
1975 to 1979	3,978	3.6	244	0.7	6.1
1970 to 1974	2,698	2.4	151	0.4	5.6
1960 to 1969	3,300	3.0	158	0.4	4.8
1950 to 1959	1,592	1.4	70	0.2	4.4
1940 to 1949	357	0.3	23	0.1	6.5
1939 or earlier	110	0.1	17	0.0	15.5
Median year moved into home	2003	–	2007	–	–

Note: "–" means not applicable.
*Source: Bureau of the Census, American Housing Survey for the United States: 2009, Internet site http://www.census.gov/hhes/
www/housing/ahs/ahs09/ahs09.html; calculations by New Strategist*

Table 3.11 Renters by Square Footage of Unit and Lot Size, 2009

Renters who live in a single-family detached or mobile home have a median of 1,300 square feet of living space, considerably less than the average householder.

(number and percent distribution of total households and renters, by square footage of unit and lot size, 2009; numbers in thousands)

	total		renters		
	number	percent distribution	number	percent distribution	percent of total
Square footage of home, total*	**79,918**	**100.0%**	**11,176**	**100.0%**	**14.0%**
Less than 500 square feet	603	0.8	220	2.0	36.5
500 to 749 square feet	1,771	2.2	686	6.1	38.7
750 to 999 square feet	5,014	6.3	1,495	13.4	29.8
1,000 to 1,499 square feet	18,419	23.0	3,441	30.8	18.7
1,500 to 1,999 square feet	18,519	23.2	2,235	20.0	12.1
2,000 to 2,499 square feet	13,190	16.5	1,134	10.1	8.6
2,500 to 2,999 square feet	7,050	8.8	429	3.8	6.1
3,000 to 3,999 square feet	6,692	8.4	301	2.7	4.5
4,000 or more square feet	4,030	5.0	243	2.2	6.0
Not reported	4,630	5.8	992	8.9	21.4
Median square footage	1,800	–	1,300	–	–
Lot size, total**	**83,466**	**100.0**	**12,823**	**100.0**	**15.4**
Less than one-eighth acre	11,824	14.2	2,717	21.2	23.0
One-eighth up to one-quarter acre	21,793	26.1	4,022	31.4	18.5
One-quarter up to one-half acre	15,921	19.1	2,084	16.3	13.1
One-half up to one acre	10,036	12.0	1,162	9.1	11.6
One to five acres	17,014	20.4	2,120	16.5	12.5
Five to 10 acres	2,750	3.3	205	1.6	7.5
10 or more acres	4,127	4.9	513	4.0	12.4
Median lot size (acres)	0.27	–	0.22	–	–

* Single-family detached and mobile homes only.
** Homes in two-or-more-unit buildings are excluded.
Note: "–" means not applicable.
Source: Bureau of the Census, American Housing Survey for the United States: 2009, Internet site http://www.census.gov/hhes/www/housing/ahs/ahs09/ahs09.html; calculations by New Strategist

Table 3.12 Renters by Number of Rooms in Home, 2009

Most renters have two or fewer bedrooms and only one bathroom.
Twenty-three percent have a room used for business.

(number and percent distribution of total households and renters, by number and type of rooms in home, 2009; numbers in thousands)

	total		renters		
	number	percent distribution	number	percent distribution	percent of total
Total households	**111,806**	**100.0%**	**35,378**	**100.0%**	**31.6%**
Number of rooms					
One room	352	0.3	326	0.9	92.7
Two rooms	946	0.8	879	2.5	92.8
Three rooms	8,711	7.8	7,675	21.7	88.1
Four rooms	17,828	15.9	11,354	32.1	63.7
Five rooms	25,444	22.8	8,212	23.2	32.3
Six rooms	24,596	22.0	4,232	12.0	17.2
Seven rooms	16,489	14.7	1,735	4.9	10.5
Eight rooms	10,033	9.0	622	1.8	6.2
Nine rooms	4,344	3.9	214	0.6	4.9
10 or more rooms	3,063	2.7	130	0.4	4.3
Number of bedrooms					
None	789	0.7	744	2.1	94.3
One bedroom	11,434	10.2	9,720	27.5	85.0
Two bedrooms	27,671	24.7	14,200	40.1	51.3
Three bedrooms	48,082	43.0	8,359	23.6	17.4
Four or more bedrooms	23,830	21.3	2,354	6.7	9.9
Number of bathrooms					
None	403	0.4	229	0.6	56.7
One bathroom	38,662	34.6	22,894	64.7	59.2
One-and-one-half bathrooms	15,656	14.0	3,575	10.1	22.8
Two or more bathrooms	57,085	51.1	8,680	24.5	15.2
With room used for business	**34,148**	**30.5**	**8,040**	**22.7**	**23.5**
Business only	15,236	13.6	3,757	10.6	24.7
Business and other use	18,912	16.9	4,283	12.1	22.6

Source: Bureau of the Census, American Housing Survey for the United States: 2009, Internet site http://www.census.gov/hhes/ www/housing/ahs/ahs09/ahs09.html; calculations by New Strategist

Table 3.13 Renters by Presence of Kitchen, Laundry, and Safety Equipment, 2009

Just over half of renters have a washer and dryer.
Only 46 percent have a dishwasher.

(number and percent of total households and renters, by presence of kitchen, laundry, and safety equipment, 2009; numbers in thousands)

	total		renters		
	number	percent distribution	number	percent distribution	percent of total
Total households	**111,806**	**100.0%**	**35,378**	**100.0%**	**31.6%**
With complete kitchen equipment	110,054	98.4	34,004	96.1	30.9
Dishwasher	73,584	65.8	16,393	46.3	22.3
Washing machine	93,372	83.5	19,545	55.2	20.9
Clothes dryer	90,905	81.3	18,343	51.8	20.2
Disposal in kitchen sink	56,531	50.6	15,933	45.0	28.2
Trash compactor	3,896	3.5	730	2.1	18.7
Working smoke detector	104,362	93.3	32,565	92.0	31.2
Fire extinguisher	49,902	44.6	11,980	33.9	24.0
Sprinkler system inside home	5,167	4.6	3,081	8.7	59.6
Carbon monoxide detector	40,698	36.4	9,007	25.5	22.1

Note: Complete kitchen equipment includes a sink, refrigerator, and oven or burners.
Source: Bureau of the Census, American Housing Survey for the United States: 2009, Internet site http://www.census.gov/hhes/ www/housing/ahs/ahs09/ahs09.html; calculations by New Strategist

Table 3.14 Renters by Type of Heating Equipment, 2009

Most renters use a warm-air furnace as their main heating equipment.
More than one in ten also use portable heaters.

(number and percent distribution of total households and renters, by presence and type of heating equipment, 2009; numbers in thousands)

	total		renters		
	number	percent distribution	number	percent distribution	percent of total
Total households	**111,806**	**100.0%**	**35,378**	**100.0%**	**31.6%**
Main heating equipment					
Warm-air furnace	71,141	63.6	19,450	55.0	27.3
Steam or hot water system	12,506	11.2	5,012	14.2	40.1
Electric heat pump	13,264	11.9	3,500	9.9	26.4
Built-in electric units	4,761	4.3	2,641	7.5	55.5
Floor, wall, or other built-in hot air units without ducts	4,802	4.3	2,760	7.8	57.5
Room heaters with flue	950	0.8	370	1.0	39.0
Room heaters without flue	1,109	1.0	414	1.2	37.4
Portable electric heaters	1,167	1.0	632	1.8	54.2
Stoves	1,035	0.9	190	0.5	18.4
Fireplaces with inserts	172	0.2	18	0.0	10.3
Fireplaces without inserts	43	0.0	7	0.0	17.5
Other	386	0.3	154	0.4	39.9
Cooking stove	84	0.1	49	0.1	58.8
None	386	0.3	180	0.5	46.6
Households with additional heating equipment					
Warm-air furnace	251	0.2	26	0.1	10.3
Steam or hot water system	56	0.1	5	0.0	8.1
Electric heat pump	97	0.1	6	0.0	5.9
Built-in electric units	1,882	1.7	454	1.3	24.1
Floor, wall, or other built-in hot air units without ducts	75	0.1	12	0.0	16.4
Room heaters with flue	822	0.7	106	0.3	12.9
Room heaters without flue	1,471	1.3	264	0.7	18.0
Portable electric heaters	13,719	12.3	3,832	10.8	27.9
Stoves	4,165	3.7	425	1.2	10.2
Fireplaces with inserts	5,205	4.7	464	1.3	8.9
Fireplaces without inserts	5,765	5.2	896	2.5	15.5
Other	790	0.7	83	0.2	10.5
Cooking stove	66	0.1	17	0.0	25.2
None	80,034	71.6	28,863	81.6	36.1

Source: Bureau of the Census, American Housing Survey for the United States: 2009, Internet site http://www.census.gov/hhes/www/housing/ahs/ahs09/ahs09.html; calculations by New Strategist

Table 3.15 Renters with Air Conditioning, 2009

Most renters have central air conditioning.
Thirty-one percent have room air conditioners.

(number and percent distribution of total households and renters, by presence of air conditioning equipment, 2009; numbers in thousands)

	total		renters		
	number	percent distribution	number	percent distribution	percent of total
TOTAL HOUSEHOLDS	**111,806**	**100.0%**	**35,378**	**100.0%**	**31.6%**
Households with air conditioning	**97,390**	**87.1**	**29,035**	**82.1**	**29.8**
Central	72,808	65.1	18,161	51.3	24.9
Additional central	5,629	5.0	920	2.6	16.3
One room unit	11,532	10.3	6,229	17.6	54.0
Two room units	8,132	7.3	3,332	9.4	41.0
Three or more room units	4,918	4.4	1,314	3.7	26.7

Source: Bureau of the Census, American Housing Survey for the United States: 2009, Internet site http://www.census.gov/hhes/www/housing/ahs/ahs09/ahs09.html; calculations by New Strategist

Table 3.16 Renters by Primary Source of Water and Sewage Disposal System, 2009

Eleven percent of renters say their primary source of water is not safe to drink.

(number and percent distribution of total households and renters, by primary source of water and type of sewage disposal system, 2009; numbers in thousands)

	total		renters		
	number	percent distribution	number	percent distribution	percent of total
Total households	**111,806**	**100.0%**	**35,378**	**100.0%**	**31.6%**
Source of water					
Public system or private company	98,027	87.7	33,655	95.1	34.3
Well	13,430	12.0	1,660	4.7	12.4
Safety of primary source of water					
Safe to drink	102,247	91.5	31,095	87.9	30.4
Not safe to drink	8,412	7.5	3,882	11.0	46.1
Sewage disposal system					
Public sewer	89,467	80.0	32,732	92.5	36.6
Septic tank, cesspool, chemical toilet	22,307	20.0	2,640	7.5	11.8

Note: Numbers may not sum to total because "other" and "not reported" are not shown.
Source: Bureau of the Census, American Housing Survey for the United States: 2009, Internet site http://www.census.gov/hhes/www/housing/ahs/ahs09/ahs09.html; calculations by New Strategist

Table 3.17 Renters by Fuels Used, 2009

More than one-third of renters have all-electric homes.

(number and percent distribution of total households and renters, by type of fuels used, 2009; numbers in thousands)

	total		renters		
	number	percent distribution	number	percent distribution	percent of total
Total households	**111,806**	**100.0%**	**35,378**	**100.0%**	**31.6%**
Electricity	111,746	99.9	35,368	100.0	31.7
All-electric homes	30,166	27.0	12,215	34.5	40.5
Piped gas	67,886	60.7	21,186	59.9	31.2
Bottled gas	9,816	8.8	1,425	4.0	14.5
Fuel oil	9,208	8.2	2,800	7.9	30.4
Kerosene or other liquid fuel	616	0.6	164	0.5	26.7
Coal or coke	104	0.1	7	0.0	6.8
Wood	1,787	1.6	278	0.8	15.5
Solar energy	147	0.1	17	0.0	11.6
Other	405	0.4	151	0.4	37.2

Note: Numbers do not add to total because many households use more than one fuel.
Source: Bureau of the Census, American Housing Survey for the United States: 2009, Internet site http://www.census.gov/hhes/www/housing/ahs/ahs09/ahs09.html; calculations by New Strategist

Table 3.18 Renters by Primary Heating Fuel Used, 2009

Electricity and piped gas are equally popular as the main heating fuel of renters.

(number and percent distribution of total households and renters, by primary heating fuel used, 2009; numbers in thousands)

	total		renters		
	number	percent distribution	number	percent distribution	percent of total
Primary heating fuel	**111,806**	**100.0%**	**35,378**	**100.0%**	**31.6%**
Households using heating fuel	111,420	100.0	35,198	100.0	31.6
Electricity	37,851	34.0	15,632	44.4	41.3
Piped gas	56,806	51.0	15,573	44.2	27.4
Bottled gas	5,817	5.2	929	2.6	16.0
Fuel oil	8,214	7.4	2,521	7.2	30.7
Kerosene or other liquid fuel	599	0.5	154	0.4	25.8
Coal or coke	98	0.1	7	0.0	7.2
Wood	1,780	1.6	277	0.8	15.6
Solar energy	11	0.0	3	0.0	26.3
Other	243	0.2	101	0.3	41.6

Source: Bureau of the Census, American Housing Survey for the United States: 2009, Internet site http://www.census.gov/hhes/www/housing/ahs/ahs09/ahs09.html; calculations by New Strategist

Table 3.19 Renters by Cooking, Water Heating, and Clothes Dryer Fuels Used, 2009

There are few differences between renters and the average householder in the types of fuels used for cooking, water heating, or clothes drying.

(number and percent distribution of total households and renters, by cooking, water heating, and clothes dryer fuels used, 2009; numbers in thousands)

	total		renters		
	number	percent distribution	number	percent distribution	percent of total
COOKING FUEL					
Households using cooking fuel	**111,623**	**100.0%**	**35,235**	**100.0%**	**31.6%**
Electricity	67,078	60.1	21,567	61.2	32.2
Piped gas	39,476	35.4	12,923	36.7	32.7
Bottled gas	5,001	4.5	726	2.1	14.5
Kerosene or other liquid fuel	14	0.0	7	0.0	51.6
Wood	29	0.0	12	0.0	41.8
Other	25	0.0	0	0.0	-
WATER HEATING FUEL					
Households with hot piped water	**111,691**	**100.0**	**35,319**	**100.0**	**31.6**
Electricity	45,435	40.7	16,095	45.6	35.4
Piped gas	57,145	51.2	16,865	47.7	29.5
Bottled gas	4,057	3.6	692	2.0	17.0
Fuel oil	4,692	4.2	1,604	4.5	34.2
Kerosene or other liquid fuel	21	0.0	3	0.0	12.7
Coal or coke	23	0.0	0	0.0	-
Wood	104	0.1	9	0.0	8.2
Solar energy	135	0.1	14	0.0	10.4
Other	78	0.1	39	0.1	49.5
CLOTHES DRYER FUEL					
Households with clothes dryers	**90,905**	**100.0**	**18,343**	**100.0**	**20.2**
Electricity	70,497	77.5	15,438	84.2	21.9
Piped gas	19,111	21.0	2,785	15.2	14.6
Other	1,298	1.4	120	0.7	9.3

Source: Bureau of the Census, American Housing Survey for the United States: 2009, Internet site http://www.census.gov/hhes/www/housing/ahs/ahs09/ahs09.html; calculations by New Strategist

Table 3.20 Renters by Amenities of Home, 2009

Seventy-one percent of renters have a porch, deck, balcony, or patio. Thirty-seven percent have a garage or carport, and another 50 percent have off-street parking.

(number and percent distribution of total households and renters, by selected amenities of home, 2009; numbers in thousands)

	total		renters		
	number	percent distribution	number	percent distribution	percent of total
Total households	**111,806**	**100.0%**	**35,378**	**100.0%**	**31.6%**
Porch, deck, balcony, or patio	95,406	85.3	24,984	70.6	26.2
Telephone available	109,325	97.8	34,196	96.7	31.3
Usable fireplace	38,998	34.9	4,540	12.8	11.6
Separate dining room	53,676	48.0	9,959	28.2	18.6
With two or more living or recreation rooms	33,912	30.3	2,934	8.3	8.7
Garage or carport					
Yes	74,236	66.4	13,258	37.5	17.9
No, but off-street parking included	30,963	27.7	17,676	50.0	57.1
No cars, trucks, or vans	8,738	7.8	6,669	18.9	76.3

Source: Bureau of the Census, American Housing Survey for the United States: 2009, Internet site http://www.census.gov/hhes/ www/housing/ahs/ahs09/ahs09.html; calculations by New Strategist

Table 3.21 Renters by Deficiencies of Home, 2009

Renters are about as likely as the average householder to
have deficiencies in their home. Six percent of renters
have seen signs of mice in the past three months.

*(number and percent distribution of total households and renters, by selected deficiencies of housing unit, 2009;
numbers in thousands)*

	total		renters		
	number	percent distribution	number	percent distribution	percent of total
Total households	**111,806**	**100.0%**	**35,378**	**100.0%**	**31.6%**
Signs of rats in last three months	613	0.5	258	0.7	42.1
Signs of mice in last three months	6,122	5.5	2,138	6.0	34.9
Signs of rodents, not sure which kind, in last three months	353	0.3	189	0.5	53.5
Holes in floor	1,141	1.0	560	1.6	49.1
Open cracks or holes (interior)	5,517	4.9	2,416	6.8	43.8
Broken plaster, peeling paint (interior)	2,378	2.1	1,132	3.2	47.6
No electrical wiring	84	0.1	26	0.1	31.6
Exposed wiring	355	0.3	134	0.4	37.8
Rooms without electric outlets	1,274	1.1	624	1.8	49.0

*Source: Bureau of the Census, American Housing Survey for the United States: 2009, Internet site http://www.census.gov/hhes/
www/housing/ahs/ahs09/ahs09.html; calculations by New Strategist*

Table 3.22 Renters by Housing Equipment Failures, 2009

Twelve percent of renters were uncomfortably cold for 24 or more hours last winter. The most common cause was an equipment breakdown.

(number and percent distribution of total households and renters, by type of equipment failure, 2009; numbers in thousands)

	total		renters		
	number	percent distribution	number	percent distribution	percent of total
WATER SUPPLY STOPPAGE					
Households with piped water	**111,691**	**100.0%**	**35,319**	**100.0%**	**31.6%**
No stoppage in last three months	106,864	95.7	33,370	94.5	31.2
With stoppage in last three months	3,632	3.3	1,601	4.5	44.1
Not reported	1,194	1.1	348	1.0	29.2
FLUSH TOILET BREAKDOWNS					
Households with flush toilets	**111,704**	**100.0**	**35,313**	**100.0**	**31.6**
With at least one working toilet at all times, last three months	108,440	97.1	33,766	95.6	31.1
With no working toilet at least once in last three months	2,094	1.9	1,210	3.4	57.8
Not reported	1,170	1.0	337	1.0	28.8
WATER LEAKAGE DURING LAST 12 MONTHS					
Total households	**111,806**	**100.0**	**35,378**	**100.0**	**31.6**
No leakage from within structure	101,540	90.8	31,184	88.1	30.7
With leakage from within structure*	9,007	8.1	3,836	10.8	42.6
Fixtures backed up or overflowed	2,141	1.9	952	2.7	44.5
Pipes leaked	3,809	3.4	1,664	4.7	43.7
Broken water heater	1,041	0.9	327	0.9	31.4
Other or unknown	2,351	2.1	1,088	3.1	46.3
Leakage not reported	1,260	1.1	357	1.0	28.4
No leakage from outside structure	99,592	89.1	31,906	90.2	32.0
With leakage from outside structure*	10,963	9.8	3,121	8.8	28.5
Roof	5,747	5.1	1,579	4.5	27.5
Basement	2,847	2.5	538	1.5	18.9
Walls, windows, or doors	1,960	1.8	795	2.2	40.5
Other or not reported	1,101	1.0	410	1.2	37.2
Leakage not reported	1,250	1.1	350	1.0	28.0

	total		renters		
	number	percent distribution	number	percent distribution	percent of total
HEATING PROBLEMS					
Households with heating equipment and occupying home last winter	**106,459**	**100.0%**	**31,244**	**100.0%**	**29.3%**
Not uncomfortably cold for 24 or more hours last winter	94,725	89.0	26,957	86.3	28.5
Uncomfortably cold for 24 or more hours last winter*	9,677	9.1	3,622	11.6	37.4
Equipment breakdown	2,738	2.6	1,144	3.7	41.8
Utility interruption	2,635	2.5	496	1.6	18.8
Inadequate heating capacity	1,025	1.0	675	2.2	65.9
Inadequate insulation	917	0.9	523	1.7	57.1
Cost of heating	1,200	1.1	421	1.3	35.1
Other	1,699	1.6	677	2.2	39.9
Not reported	2,057	1.9	666	2.1	32.4
ELECTRICAL PROBLEMS					
Households with electrical wiring	**111,722**	**100.0**	**35,351**	**100.0**	**31.6**
No fuses or breakers blown in last three months	100,576	90.0	31,879	90.2	31.7
With fuses or breakers blown in last three months	9,767	8.7	3,082	8.7	31.6
Not reported	1,380	1.2	391	1.1	28.3

Figures may not add to total because more than one problem may have occurred.
Source: Bureau of the Census, American Housing Survey for the United States: 2009, Internet site http://www.census.gov/hhes/ www/housing/ahs/ahs09/ahs09.html; calculations by New Strategist

Table 3.23 Renters by Monthly Housing Costs, 2009

Monthly housing costs for renters are below average, a median
of $808 per month versus $909 for all householders.

(number and percent distribution of total households and renters, by monthly housing costs, 2009; numbers in thousands)

	total		renters		
	number	percent distribution	number	percent distribution	percent of total
Total households	**111,806**	**100.0%**	**35,378**	**100.0%**	**31.6%**
Less than $100	723	0.6	248	0.7	34.3
$100 to $199	2,889	2.6	728	2.1	25.2
$200 to $299	6,732	6.0	1,381	3.9	20.5
$300 to $399	7,381	6.6	1,359	3.8	18.4
$400 to $499	7,402	6.6	2,094	5.9	28.3
$500 to $599	7,392	6.6	2,985	8.4	40.4
$600 to $699	7,542	6.7	3,808	10.8	50.5
$700 to $799	7,306	6.5	3,709	10.5	50.8
$800 to $999	13,200	11.8	6,060	17.1	45.9
$1,000 to $1,249	12,933	11.6	4,777	13.5	36.9
$1,250 to $1,499	9,459	8.5	2,631	7.4	27.8
$1,500 or $1,999	11,692	10.5	2,247	6.4	19.2
$2,000 to $2,499	6,140	5.5	718	2.0	11.7
$2,500 or more	8,980	8.0	596	1.7	6.6
No cash rent	2,037	1.8	2,037	5.8	100.0
Median monthly cost	$909	–	$808	–	–

Note: Housing costs include utilities, mortgages, real estate taxes, property insurance, and regime fees. "–" means not applicable.
Source: Bureau of the Census, American Housing Survey for the United States: 2009, Internet site http://www.census.gov/hhes/www/housing/ahs/ahs09/ahs09.html; calculations by New Strategist

Table 3.24 Renters by Monthly Utility and Property Insurance Costs, 2009

Renters pay less per month for electricity than the average household does, in part because their homes are smaller.

(number and percent distribution of total households and renters, by average monthly costs for utilities and property insurance, 2009; numbers in thousands)

	total		renters		
	number	percent distribution	number	percent distribution	percent of total
MONTHLY COST OF ELECTRICITY					
Households using electricity	**111,746**	**100.0%**	**35,368**	**100.0%**	**31.7%**
Less than $25	1,701	1.5	1,259	3.6	74.0
$25 to $49	9,851	8.8	5,426	15.3	55.1
$50 to $74	17,551	15.7	6,535	18.5	37.2
$75 to $99	18,444	16.5	5,469	15.5	29.7
$100 to $149	27,826	24.9	6,589	18.6	23.7
$150 to $199	14,959	13.4	2,795	7.9	18.7
$200 or more	14,451	12.9	2,341	6.6	16.2
Included in rent, other fee or obtained free	6,964	6.2	4,954	14.0	71.1
Median monthly cost	$107	–	$84	–	–
MONTHLY COST OF PIPED GAS					
Households using piped gas	**67,886**	**100.0**	**21,186**	**100.0**	**31.2**
Less than $25	3,856	5.7	2,447	11.5	63.4
$25 to $49	12,402	18.3	4,469	21.1	36.0
$50 to $74	14,777	21.8	3,581	16.9	24.2
$75 to $99	10,648	15.7	2,054	9.7	19.3
$100 to $149	11,578	17.1	1,884	8.9	16.3
$150 to $199	4,341	6.4	643	3.0	14.8
$200 or more	3,200	4.7	518	2.4	16.2
Included in rent, other fee or obtained free	7,082	10.4	5,588	26.4	78.9
Median monthly cost	$73	–	$55	–	–
MONTHLY COST OF FUEL OIL					
Households using fuel oil	**9,208**	**100.0**	**2,800**	**100.0**	**30.4**
Less than $25	228	2.5	52	1.9	22.8
$25 to $49	395	4.3	70	2.5	17.7
$50 to $74	581	6.3	91	3.3	15.7
$75 to $99	825	9.0	100	3.6	12.1
$100 to $149	1,566	17.0	163	5.8	10.4
$150 to $199	1,161	12.6	108	3.9	9.3
$200 or more	1,848	20.1	146	5.2	7.9
Included in rent, other fee or obtained free	2,604	28.3	2,068	73.9	79.4
Median monthly cost	$133	–	$100	–	–

	total		renters		
	number	percent distribution	number	percent distribution	percent of total
Water paid separately	62,789	–	9,237	–	14.7%
Median monthly cost	$35	–	$29	–	–
Trash paid separately	52,525	–	7,551	–	14.4
Median monthly cost	$21	–	$20	–	–
Property insurance paid separately	81,711	–	9,397	–	11.5
Median monthly cost	$50	–	$16	–	–

Note: "–" means not applicable.
Source: Bureau of the Census, American Housing Survey for the United States: 2009, Internet site http://www.census.gov/hhes/ www/housing/ahs/ahs09/ahs09.html; calculations by New Strategist

Table 3.25 Renters by Opinion of Home, 2009

Renters have a lower opinion of their home than the average householder. Still, most give their home a rating of 8 or higher.

(number and percent distribution of total households and renters, by opinion of home, 2009; numbers in thousands)

	total		renters		
	number	percent distribution	number	percent distribution	percent of total
Total households	**111,806**	**100.0%**	**35,378**	**100.0%**	**31.6%**
1 (worst)	530	0.5	327	0.9	61.6
2	331	0.3	209	0.6	63.0
3	611	0.5	436	1.2	71.4
4	1,153	1.0	708	2.0	61.4
5	5,275	4.7	2,910	8.2	55.2
6	5,208	4.7	2,553	7.2	49.0
7	15,045	13.5	6,146	17.4	40.9
8	30,667	27.4	9,625	27.2	31.4
9	17,844	16.0	4,217	11.9	23.6
10 (best)	30,909	27.6	6,941	19.6	22.5
Not reported	4,233	3.8	1,306	3.7	30.9

Source: Bureau of the Census, American Housing Survey for the United States: 2009, Internet site http://www.census.gov/hhes/www/housing/ahs/ahs09/ahs09.html; calculations by New Strategist

Table 3.26 Renters by Opinion of Neighborhood, 2009

Sixty percent of renters give their neighborhood a rating of 8 or higher.

(number and percent distribution of total households and renters, by opinion of neighborhood, 2009; numbers in thousands)

	total		renters		
	number	percent distribution	number	percent distribution	percent of total
OPINION OF NEIGHBORHOOD					
Total households	**111,806**	**100.0%**	**35,378**	**100.0%**	**31.6%**
1 (worst)	837	0.7	499	1.4	59.6
2	637	0.6	348	1.0	54.6
3	1,002	0.9	543	1.5	54.2
4	1,633	1.5	867	2.5	53.1
5	6,332	5.7	2,976	8.4	47.0
6	5,919	5.3	2,465	7.0	41.7
7	14,767	13.2	5,164	14.6	35.0
8	29,794	26.6	8,986	25.4	30.2
9	18,017	16.1	4,563	12.9	25.3
10 (best)	28,465	25.5	7,575	21.4	26.6
No neighborhood	60	0.1	29	0.1	49.0
Not reported	4,341	3.9	1,362	3.8	31.4

Source: Bureau of the Census, American Housing Survey for the United States: 2009, Internet site http://www.census.gov/hhes/ www/housing/ahs/ahs09/ahs09.html; calculations by New Strategist

Table 3.27 Renters by Neighborhood Problems, 2009

Twenty-two percent of renters say there has been serious crime
in their neighborhood in the past 12 months.

(number and percent distribution of total households and renters with neighborhood problems, 2009; numbers in thousands)

	total		renters		
	number	percent distribution	number	percent distribution	percent of total
Total households	**111,806**	**100.0%**	**35,378**	**100.0%**	**31.6%**
Bothersome street noise or heavy traffic	25,381	22.7	10,158	28.7	40.0
Serious crime in neighborhood in past 12 months	19,299	17.3	7,650	21.6	39.6
Bothersome odor problem	5,434	4.9	2,156	6.1	39.7
Noise problem	2,950	2.6	1,217	3.4	41.3
Litter or housing deterioration	1,691	1.5	590	1.7	34.9
Poor city or county services	694	0.6	254	0.7	36.6
Undesirable commercial, institutional, industrial properties	415	0.4	168	0.5	40.5
People problem	4,521	4.0	1,815	5.1	40.1
Other problems	9,539	8.5	2,791	7.9	29.3

Source: Bureau of the Census, American Housing Survey for the United States: 2009, Internet site http://www.census.gov/hhes/ www/housing/ahs/ahs09/ahs09.html; calculations by New Strategist

Table 3.28 Renters by Community Characteristics, 2009

Fifteen percent of renters live in a gated community. Thirty-six percent
live near open space, park, woods, farm, or ranchland.

(number and percent distribution of total households and renters, by community characteristics, 2009; numbers in thousands)

	total		renters		
	number	percent distribution	number	percent distribution	percent of total
Total households	**111,806**	**100.0%**	**35,378**	**100.0%**	**31.6%**
SECURED COMMUNITIES					
Total households	**111,806**	**100.0**	**35,378**	**100.0**	**31.6**
Community access secured with walls or fences	10,759	9.6	5,422	15.3	50.4
Special entry system present	6,091	5.4	3,410	9.6	56.0
Special entry system not present	4,653	4.2	2,005	5.7	43.1
Community access not secured	100,124	89.6	29,714	84.0	29.7
SENIOR CITIZEN COMMUNITIES					
Households with persons 55 or older	**45,684**	**100.0**	**9,093**	**100.0**	**19.9**
Community age restricted	3,080	6.7	1,624	17.9	52.7
No age restriction	42,603	93.3	7,469	82.1	17.5
Community age specific	10,302	22.6	1,435	15.8	13.9
Community not age specific	29,683	65.0	5,583	61.4	18.8
COMMUNITY AMENITIES					
Total households	**111,806**	**100.0**	**35,378**	**100.0**	**31.6**
Community center or clubhouse	24,410	21.8	9,703	27.4	39.8
Golf in community	16,709	14.9	3,947	11.2	23.6
Trails in community	21,609	19.3	6,309	17.8	29.2
Shuttle bus available	9,933	8.9	4,215	11.9	42.4
Daycare center	15,883	14.2	5,249	14.8	33.1
Private or restricted beach, park, or shoreline	21,432	19.2	6,308	17.8	29.4
DESCRIPTION OF AREA WITHIN 300 FEET OF HOME					
Total households	**111,806**	**100.0**	**35,378**	**100.0**	**31.6**
Single-family detached homes	95,916	85.8	27,007	76.3	28.2
Single-family attached homes	21,832	19.5	10,860	30.7	49.7
Multiunit residential buildings	33,635	30.1	22,121	62.5	65.8
One-to-three-story multiunit tallest	25,143	22.5	16,130	45.6	64.2
Four-to-six-story multiunit tallest	4,937	4.4	3,473	9.8	70.3
Seven-or-more-story multiunit tallest	3,172	2.8	2,243	6.3	70.7
Manufactured/mobile homes	13,388	12.0	3,112	8.8	23.2
Commercial or institutional	35,649	31.9	18,657	52.7	52.3
Industrial or factories	5,376	4.8	2,856	8.1	53.1
Open space, park, woods, farm, ranch	45,816	41.0	12,706	35.9	27.7
Four-or-more-lane highway, railroad, or airport	19,612	17.5	9,232	26.1	47.1

	total		renters		
	number	percent distribution	number	percent distribution	percent of total
BODIES OF WATER WITHIN 300 FEET OF HOME					
Total households	**111,806**	**100.0%**	**35,378**	**100.0%**	**31.6%**
Water in area	18,656	16.7	4,832	13.7	25.9
With waterfront property	3,331	3.0	678	1.9	20.4
With flood plain	2,622	2.3	692	2.0	26.4
No water in area	92,474	82.7	30,390	85.9	32.9

Note: Numbers may not add to total because "not reported" is not shown.
Source: Bureau of the Census, American Housing Survey for the United States: 2009, Internet site http://www.census.gov/hhes/ www/housing/ahs/ahs09/ahs09.html; calculations by New Strategist

Table 3.29 Renters by Public Services Available, 2009

Seventy percent of renters have public transportation in their neighborhood.
Among those who do, only 26 percent use it regularly.

(number and percent distribution of total households and renters, by public services available in neighborhood, 2009; numbers in thousands)

	total		renters		
	number	percent distribution	number	percent distribution	percent of total
Total households	**111,806**	**100.0%**	**35,378**	**100.0%**	**31.6%**
LOCAL ELEMENTARY SCHOOL					
Households with children under age 14	**30,976**	**100.0**	**10,486**	**100.0**	**33.9**
Satisfactory public elementary school	25,297	81.7	8,331	79.5	32.9
Unsatisfactory public elementary school	2,146	6.9	724	6.9	33.7
Unsatisfactory public elementary school	**2,146**	**100.0**	**724**	**100.0**	**33.7**
Better than other area elementary schools	216	10.1	63	8.7	29.0
Same as other area elementary schools	714	33.3	224	31.0	31.4
Worse than other area elementary schools	1,082	50.4	386	53.3	35.7
Households with children under age 14	**30,976**	**100.0**	**10,486**	**100.0**	**33.9**
Public elementary school less than one mile	18,667	60.3	7,096	67.7	38.0
Public elementary school more than one mile	10,526	34.0	2,741	26.1	26.0
PUBLIC TRANSPORTATION IN AREA					
Total households	**111,806**	**100.0**	**35,378**	**100.0**	**31.6**
With public transportation	60,257	53.9	24,641	69.6	40.9
No public transportation	48,532	43.4	9,684	27.4	20.0
With public transportation, travel time					
to nearest stop	**60,257**	**100.0**	**24,641**	**100.0**	**40.9**
Less than 5 minutes	21,258	35.3	10,328	41.9	48.6
5 to 9 minutes	21,699	36.0	8,869	36.0	40.9
10 to 14 minutes	8,606	14.3	2,753	11.2	32.0
15 to 29 minutes	4,224	7.0	1,099	4.5	26.0
30 minutes or longer	618	1.0	169	0.7	27.3
With public transportation	**60,257**	**100.0**	**24,641**	**100.0**	**40.9**
Household uses it regularly for commute to school or work	10,212	16.9	6,395	26.0	62.6
Household does not use it regularly for commute to school or work	49,681	82.4	18,075	73.4	36.4
SHOPPING IN AREA					
Total households	**111,806**	**100.0**	**35,378**	**100.0**	**31.6**
Grocery stores or drugstores within 15 minutes of home	106,737	95.5	34,189	96.6	32.0
Satisfactory	103,482	92.6	33,082	93.5	32.0
Unsatisfactory	2,769	2.5	964	2.7	34.8
No grocery stores or drugstores within 15 minutes of home	3,596	3.2	777	2.2	21.6

	total		renters		
	number	percent distribution	number	percent distribution	percent of total
POLICE PROTECTION					
Total households	**111,806**	**100.0%**	**35,378**	**100.0%**	**31.6%**
Satisfactory police protection	101,373	90.7	31,740	89.7	31.3
Unsatisfactory police protection	7,356	6.6	2,556	7.2	34.7

Note: Numbers may not add to total because "not reported" is not shown.
Source: Bureau of the Census, American Housing Survey for the United States: 2009, Internet site http://www.census.gov/hhes/ www/housing/ahs/ahs09/ahs09.html; calculations by New Strategist

Table 3.30 Changes in Housing and Costs for Renters Who Moved, 2009

Twenty-six percent of renters who moved in the past 12 months had previously lived in an owner-occupied home.

(number and percent distribution of total householders and renters who moved in the past year, by structure type of previous residence, ownership of previous residence, and change in housing costs, 2009; numbers in thousands)

	total		renters		
	number	percent distribution	number	percent distribution	percent of total
STRUCTURE TYPE OF PREVIOUS RESIDENCE					
Householders who moved within United States	**16,763**	**100.0%**	**12,422**	**100.0%**	**74.1%**
House	8,531	50.9	5,936	47.8	69.6
Apartment	6,437	38.4	5,228	42.1	81.2
Mobile home	783	4.7	545	4.4	69.7
Other	499	3.0	380	3.1	76.2
Not reported	513	3.1	331	2.7	64.6
OWNERSHIP OF PREVIOUS RESIDENCE					
Householders who moved from house, apartment, or mobile home within United States	**15,751**	**100.0**	**11,710**	**100.0**	**74.3**
Owner-occupied	5,023	31.9	2,991	25.5	59.5
Renter-occupied	10,728	68.1	8,719	74.5	81.3
CHANGE IN HOUSING COSTS					
Householders who moved from house, apartment, or mobile home within United States	**15,751**	**100.0**	**11,710**	**100.0**	**74.3**
Increased with move	7,590	48.2	5,135	43.8	67.7
Decreased	4,520	28.7	3,719	31.8	82.3
Stayed about the same	3,107	19.7	2,444	20.9	78.7
Don't know	310	2.0	250	2.1	80.8
Not reported	223	1.4	161	1.4	72.2

Source: Bureau of the Census, American Housing Survey for the United States: 2009, Internet site http://www.census.gov/hhes/ www/housing/ahs/ahs09/ahs09.html; calculations by New Strategist

Table 3.31 Reasons for Choosing Home among Renters Who Moved, 2009

Thirty percent of renters who recently moved say they
chose their current home for financial reasons.

(number and percent distribution of total respondents and renter respondents who moved in the past year, by reasons for choosing home, 2009; numbers in thousands)

	total		renters		
	number	percent distribution	number	percent distribution	percent of total
Total respondents who moved	**17,463**	**100.0%**	**12,840**	**100.0%**	**73.5%**
Main reason for choice of present home					
All reported reasons equal	2,256	12.9	1,448	11.3	64.2
Financial reasons	4,854	27.8	3,846	30.0	79.2
Room layout/design	2,540	14.5	1,743	13.6	68.6
Kitchen	98	0.6	65	0.5	66.3
Size	1,775	10.2	1,398	10.9	78.7
Exterior appearance	475	2.7	350	2.7	73.7
Yard/trees/view	699	4.0	412	3.2	58.9
Quality of construction	417	2.4	231	1.8	55.4
Only one available	684	3.9	608	4.7	88.9
Other	2,834	16.2	2,198	17.1	77.6
Not reported	830	4.8	540	4.2	65.0
Present home compared with previous home					
Better	9,209	52.7	6,192	48.2	67.2
Worse	3,102	17.8	2,676	20.8	86.3
About the same	4,418	25.3	3,498	27.2	79.2
Not reported	734	4.2	474	3.7	64.5
Home search					
Now in house	8,129	100.0	4,200	100.0	51.7
Did not look at apartments	6,318	77.7	2,888	68.8	45.7
Looked at apartments too	1,467	18.0	1,162	27.7	79.2
Now in manufactured/mobile home	960	100.0	551	100.0	57.3
Did not look at apartments	663	69.1	360	65.3	54.2
Looked at apartments too	250	26.0	181	32.8	72.3
Now in apartment	8,374	100.0	8,090	100.0	96.6
Did not look at houses	5,907	70.5	5,726	70.8	96.9
Looked at houses too	2,148	25.6	2,056	25.4	95.7

Note: Total number of movers does not equal total movers in other tables because this table shows survey respondents who moved, not necessarily householders. Numbers may not add to total because "not reported" may not be shown.
Source: Bureau of the Census, American Housing Survey for the United States: 2009, Internet site http://www.census.gov/hhes/ www/housing/ahs/ahs09/ahs09.html; calculations by New Strategist

Table 3.32 Reasons for Choosing Neighborhood among Renters Who Moved, 2009

Most renters who recently moved looked at more than one neighborhood before moving, with the convenience to friends or relatives one of the most important factors in their neighborhood choice.

(number and percent distribution of total respondents and renting respondents who moved in the past year, by reasons for choosing neighborhood, 2009; numbers in thousands)

	total		renters		
	number	percent distribution	number	percent distribution	percent of total
Total respondents who moved	**17,463**	**100.0%**	**12,840**	**100.0%**	**73.5%**
Neighborhood search					
Looked at just this neighborhood	7,490	42.9	5,900	46.0	78.8
Looked at other neighborhoods	9,335	53.5	6,533	50.9	70.0
Not reported	638	3.7	407	3.2	63.8
Main reason for choice of present neighborhood					
All reported reasons equal	1,905	10.9	1,354	10.5	71.1
Convenient to job	3,535	20.2	2,924	22.8	82.7
Convenient to friends or relatives	2,485	14.2	1,915	14.9	77.1
Convenient to leisure activities	331	1.9	244	1.9	73.6
Convenient to public transportation	266	1.5	237	1.8	89.0
Good schools	1,087	6.2	798	6.2	73.4
Other public services	221	1.3	185	1.4	83.6
Looks/design of neighborhood	1,798	10.3	1,163	9.1	64.7
House most important consideration	1,765	10.1	964	7.5	54.6
Other	3,313	19.0	2,563	20.0	77.4
Not reported	757	4.3	493	3.8	65.2
Present neighborhood compared with previous neighborhood					
Better	7,206	41.3	4,953	38.6	68.7
Worse	2,303	13.2	1,955	15.2	84.9
About the same	6,471	37.1	4,916	38.3	76.0
Same neighborhood	699	4.0	520	4.1	74.4
Not reported	786	4.5	496	3.9	63.1

Note: Total number of movers does not equal total movers in other tables because this table shows survey respondents who moved, not necessarily householders.
Source: Bureau of the Census, American Housing Survey for the United States: 2009, Internet site http://www.census.gov/hhes/ www/housing/ahs/ahs09/ahs09.html; calculations by New Strategist

Table 3.33 Main Reason for Moving among Renters Who Moved, 2009

Ten percent of renters who recently moved did so
to establish their own household.

(number and percent distribution of total respondents and renting respondents who moved in the past year, by main reason for move, 2009; numbers in thousands)

	total		renters		
	number	percent distribution	number	percent distribution	percent of total
Total respondents who moved	**17,463**	**100.0%**	**12,840**	**100.0%**	**73.5%**
All reported reasons equal	653	3.7	450	3.5	68.9
Private displacement	123	0.7	118	0.9	95.6
Government displacement	53	0.3	45	0.4	85.5
Disaster loss (fire, flood, etc.)	149	0.9	126	1.0	84.2
New job or job transfer	1,590	9.1	1,220	9.5	76.7
To be closer to work/school/other	1,634	9.4	1,416	11.0	86.7
Other financial, employment related	646	3.7	527	4.1	81.6
To establish own household	1,876	10.7	1,282	10.0	68.4
Needed larger house or apartment	1,534	8.8	1,103	8.6	71.9
Married, widowed, divorced, or separated	912	5.2	628	4.9	68.9
Other family or personal reasons	1,372	7.9	1,004	7.8	73.2
Wanted better home	1,186	6.8	881	6.9	74.3
Change from owner to renter or renter to owner	804	4.6	120	0.9	14.9
Wanted lower rent or maintenance	927	5.3	867	6.8	93.6
Other housing-related reasons	782	4.5	614	4.8	78.5
Evicted from residence	126	0.7	112	0.9	89.0
Other	2,032	11.6	1,548	12.1	76.2
Not reported	1,065	6.1	779	6.1	73.2

Note: Total number of movers does not equal total movers in other tables because this table shows survey respondents who moved, not necessarily householders.
Source: Bureau of the Census, American Housing Survey for the United States: 2009, Internet site http://www.census.gov/hhes/ www/housing/ahs/ahs09/ahs09.html; calculations by New Strategist

4

Homeowners by Region

The collapse of the housing market affected some regions more than others.

Median housing values fell the most in the West between 2007 and 2009, down 24 percent to $270,000. Home values fell the least in the Midwest during those years, but median housing value there is lower than in the other regions—just $134,000 in 2009. Homeowners in the South are much more likely to live in mobile homes (11 percent) than homeowners in the other regions. The largest homes are found in the Northeast (2,000 square feet on average). Homeowners in the Midwest are most likely to heat with piped gas (73 percent). Homeowners in the West are most likely to say their water is not safe to drink (8 percent).

■ Homeowners in the West are most likely to be underwater on their mortgage. Seventeen percent of those with mortgages in 2009 owed more than their home was worth. In the Northeast, a much smaller 8 percent were underwater, and in the Midwest and South the figure was 12 percent.

■ In every region, the majority of owned homes have air conditioning. The figure ranges from a low of 71 percent in the West to a high of 98 percent in the South.

■ The 51 percent majority of homeowners in the Northeast are living in the first home they have ever owned. In the West, only 38 percent of homeowners are in their first home.

Median home value fell in every region between 2007 and 2009

(percent change in home value 2007–09, by region)

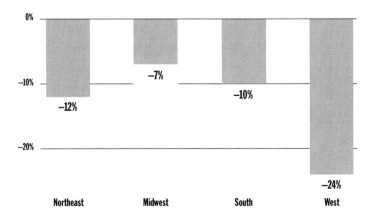

Table 4.1 Homeowners by Age and Region, 2009

The age distribution of homeowners varies little by region. The median age of homeowners is 51 in the Midwest and West and 52 in the Northeast and South.

(number and percent distribution of total homeowners and homeowners by region, by age of householder; 2009; numbers in thousands)

	total	Northeast	Midwest	South	West
Total homeowners	**76,428**	**13,378**	**18,249**	**29,193**	**15,607**
Under age 25	1,284	180	347	516	241
Aged 25 to 29	3,541	466	986	1,384	705
Aged 30 to 34	5,532	782	1,365	2,159	1,227
Aged 35 to 44	14,932	2,709	3,597	5,551	3,075
Aged 45 to 54	17,743	3,224	4,248	6,563	3,708
Aged 55 to 64	14,924	2,650	3,430	5,781	3,063
Aged 65 to 74	9,818	1,733	2,294	3,932	1,860
Aged 75 or older	8,653	1,636	1,983	3,307	1,728
Median age (years)	52	52	51	52	51
PERCENT DISTRIBUTION BY AGE					
Total homeowners	**100.0%**	**100.0%**	**100.0%**	**100.0%**	**100.0%**
Under age 25	1.7	1.3	1.9	1.8	1.5
Aged 25 to 29	4.6	3.5	5.4	4.7	4.5
Aged 30 to 34	7.2	5.8	7.5	7.4	7.9
Aged 35 to 44	19.5	20.2	19.7	19.0	19.7
Aged 45 to 54	23.2	24.1	23.3	22.5	23.8
Aged 55 to 64	19.5	19.8	18.8	19.8	19.6
Aged 65 to 74	12.8	13.0	12.6	13.5	11.9
Aged 75 or older	11.3	12.2	10.9	11.3	11.1
PERCENT DISTRIBUTION BY REGION					
Total homeowners	**100.0%**	**17.5%**	**23.9%**	**38.2%**	**20.4%**
Under age 25	100.0	14.0	27.0	40.2	18.8
Aged 25 to 29	100.0	13.2	27.8	39.1	19.9
Aged 30 to 34	100.0	14.1	24.7	39.0	22.2
Aged 35 to 44	100.0	18.1	24.1	37.2	20.6
Aged 45 to 54	100.0	18.2	23.9	37.0	20.9
Aged 55 to 64	100.0	17.8	23.0	38.7	20.5
Aged 65 to 74	100.0	17.6	23.4	40.0	18.9
Aged 75 or older	100.0	18.9	22.9	38.2	20.0

Source: Bureau of the Census, American Housing Survey for the United States: 2009, Internet site http://www.census.gov/hhes/www/housing/ahs/ahs09/ahs09.html; calculations by New Strategist

Table 4.2 Homeowners by Household Type and Age of Householder, 2009: Northeast

Sixty-one percent of homeowning households in the Northeast are headed by married couples. Twenty-two percent are headed by people who live alone.

(number and percent distribution of total homeowners and homeowners in the Northeast, and Northeastern homeowners as a percent of total, by type of household and age of householder, 2009; numbers in thousands)

	total		Northeast		
	number	percent distribution	number	percent distribution	percent of total
Total homeowners	**76,428**	**100.0%**	**13,378**	**100.0%**	**17.5%**
MARRIED-COUPLE HOUSEHOLDS	**47,008**	**61.5**	**8,207**	**61.3**	**17.5**
Under age 25	495	0.6	77	0.6	15.6
Aged 25 to 29	2,007	2.6	243	1.8	12.1
Aged 30 to 34	3,646	4.8	516	3.9	14.2
Aged 35 to 44	10,336	13.5	1,930	14.4	18.7
Aged 45 to 64	21,352	27.9	3,883	29.0	18.2
Aged 65 or older	9,174	12.0	1,559	11.7	17.0
TWO-OR-MORE-PERSON HOUSEHOLDS					
Female householder, no spouse present	**7,931**	**10.4**	**1,415**	**10.6**	**17.8**
Under age 45	2,948	3.9	484	3.6	16.4
Aged 45 to 64	3,397	4.4	657	4.9	19.4
Aged 65 or older	1,587	2.1	274	2.0	17.3
Male householder, no spouse present	**4,712**	**6.2**	**811**	**6.1**	**17.2**
Under age 45	2,170	2.8	314	2.3	14.5
Aged 45 to 64	1,878	2.5	384	2.9	20.4
Aged 65 or older	663	0.9	113	0.8	17.1
SINGLE-PERSON HOUSEHOLDS	**16,777**	**22.0**	**2,944**	**22.0**	**17.6**
Female householder	**10,007**	**13.1**	**1,805**	**13.5**	**18.0**
Under age 45	1,547	2.0	247	1.8	15.9
Aged 45 to 64	3,231	4.2	514	3.8	15.9
Aged 65 or older	5,230	6.8	1,044	7.8	20.0
Male householder	**6,770**	**8.9**	**1,140**	**8.5**	**16.8**
Under age 45	2,142	2.8	326	2.4	15.2
Aged 45 to 64	2,810	3.7	436	3.3	15.5
Aged 65 or older	1,818	2.4	378	2.8	20.8

Source: Bureau of the Census, American Housing Survey for the United States: 2009, Internet site http://www.census.gov/hhes/ www/housing/ahs/ahs09/ahs09.html; calculations by New Strategist

Table 4.3 Homeowners by Household Type and Age of Householder, 2009: Midwest

Nearly one-fourth of the nation's homeowners live in the Midwest,
a proportion that varies little by age or household type.

(number and percent distribution of total homeowners and homeowners in the Midwest, and Midwestern homeowners as a percent of total, by type of household and age of householder, 2009; numbers in thousands)

	total		Midwest		
	number	percent distribution	number	percent distribution	percent of total
Total homeowners	**76,428**	**100.0%**	**18,249**	**100.0%**	**23.9%**
MARRIED-COUPLE HOUSEHOLDS	**47,008**	**61.5**	**11,418**	**62.6**	**24.3**
Under age 25	495	0.6	127	0.7	25.7
Aged 25 to 29	2,007	2.6	564	3.1	28.1
Aged 30 to 34	3,646	4.8	930	5.1	25.5
Aged 35 to 44	10,336	13.5	2,482	13.6	24.0
Aged 45 to 64	21,352	27.9	5,133	28.1	24.0
Aged 65 or older	9,174	12.0	2,184	12.0	23.8
TWO-OR-MORE-PERSON HOUSEHOLDS					
Female householder, no spouse present	**7,931**	**10.4**	**1,721**	**9.4**	**21.7**
Under age 45	2,948	3.9	705	3.9	23.9
Aged 45 to 64	3,397	4.4	710	3.9	20.9
Aged 65 or older	1,587	2.1	306	1.7	19.3
Male householder, no spouse present	**4,712**	**6.2**	**1,124**	**6.2**	**23.9**
Under age 45	2,170	2.8	568	3.1	26.2
Aged 45 to 64	1,878	2.5	419	2.3	22.3
Aged 65 or older	663	0.9	136	0.7	20.5
SINGLE-PERSON HOUSEHOLDS	**16,777**	**22.0**	**3,986**	**21.8**	**23.8**
Female householder	**10,007**	**13.1**	**2,349**	**12.9**	**23.5**
Under age 45	1,547	2.0	343	1.9	22.2
Aged 45 to 64	3,231	4.2	744	4.1	23.0
Aged 65 or older	5,230	6.8	1,262	6.9	24.1
Male householder	**6,770**	**8.9**	**1,637**	**9.0**	**24.2**
Under age 45	2,142	2.8	576	3.2	26.9
Aged 45 to 64	2,810	3.7	673	3.7	23.9
Aged 65 or older	1,818	2.4	389	2.1	21.4

Source: Bureau of the Census, American Housing Survey for the United States: 2009, Internet site http://www.census.gov/hhes/www/housing/ahs/ahs09/ahs09.html; calculations by New Strategist

Table 4.4 Homeowners by Household Type and Age of Householder, 2009: South

Thirty-eight percent of the nation's homeowners live in the South. Among homeowners in the South, the 61 percent majority are married couples.

(number and percent distribution of total homeowners and homeowners in the South, and Southern homeowners as a percent of total, by type of household and age of householder, 2009; numbers in thousands)

	total		South		
	number	percent distribution	number	percent distribution	percent of total
Total homeowners	**76,428**	**100.0%**	**29,193**	**100.0%**	**38.2%**
MARRIED-COUPLE HOUSEHOLDS	**47,008**	**61.5**	**17,724**	**60.7**	**37.7**
Under age 25	495	0.6	219	0.7	44.1
Aged 25 to 29	2,007	2.6	795	2.7	39.6
Aged 30 to 34	3,646	4.8	1,396	4.8	38.3
Aged 35 to 44	10,336	13.5	3,793	13.0	36.7
Aged 45 to 64	21,352	27.9	7,904	27.1	37.0
Aged 65 or older	9,174	12.0	3,617	12.4	39.4
TWO-OR-MORE-PERSON HOUSEHOLDS					
Female householder, no spouse present	**7,931**	**10.4**	**3,128**	**10.7**	**39.4**
Under age 45	2,948	3.9	1,148	3.9	39.0
Aged 45 to 64	3,397	4.4	1,323	4.5	39.0
Aged 65 or older	1,587	2.1	656	2.2	41.4
Male householder, no spouse present	**4,712**	**6.2**	**1,722**	**5.9**	**36.5**
Under age 45	2,170	2.8	790	2.7	36.4
Aged 45 to 64	1,878	2.5	676	2.3	36.0
Aged 65 or older	663	0.9	256	0.9	38.6
SINGLE-PERSON HOUSEHOLDS	**16,777**	**22.0**	**6,619**	**22.7**	**39.5**
Female householder	10,007	13.1	4,037	13.8	40.3
Under age 45	1,547	2.0	691	2.4	44.7
Aged 45 to 64	3,231	4.2	1,339	4.6	41.5
Aged 65 or older	5,230	6.8	2,006	6.9	38.4
Male householder	**6,770**	**8.9**	**2,582**	**8.8**	**38.1**
Under age 45	2,142	2.8	778	2.7	36.3
Aged 45 to 64	2,810	3.7	1,100	3.8	39.2
Aged 65 or older	1,818	2.4	704	2.4	38.7

Source: Bureau of the Census, American Housing Survey for the United States: 2009, Internet site http://www.census.gov/hhes/ www/housing/ahs/ahs09/ahs09.html; calculations by New Strategist

Table 4.5 Homeowners by Household Type and Age of Householder, 2009: West

Sixty-two percent of homeowning households in the West are headed by married couples. Twenty-one percent are people who live alone.

(number and percent distribution of total homeowners and homeowners in the West, and Western homeowners as a percent of total, by type of household and age of householder, 2009; numbers in thousands)

	total		West		
	number	percent distribution	number	percent distribution	percent of total
Total homeowners	**76,428**	**100.0%**	**15,607**	**100.0%**	**20.4%**
MARRIED-COUPLE HOUSEHOLDS	**47,008**	**61.5**	**9,658**	**61.9**	**20.5**
Under age 25	495	0.6	73	0.5	14.7
Aged 25 to 29	2,007	2.6	405	2.6	20.2
Aged 30 to 34	3,646	4.8	804	5.1	22.0
Aged 35 to 44	10,336	13.5	2,131	13.7	20.6
Aged 45 to 64	21,352	27.9	4,432	28.4	20.8
Aged 65 or older	9,174	12.0	1,814	11.6	19.8
TWO-OR-MORE-PERSON HOUSEHOLDS					
Female householder, no spouse present	**7,931**	**10.4**	**1,667**	**10.7**	**21.0**
Under age 45	2,948	3.9	611	3.9	20.7
Aged 45 to 64	3,397	4.4	706	4.5	20.8
Aged 65 or older	1,587	2.1	351	2.2	22.1
Male householder, no spouse present	**4,712**	**6.2**	**1,054**	**6.8**	**22.4**
Under age 45	2,170	2.8	498	3.2	22.9
Aged 45 to 64	1,878	2.5	399	2.6	21.2
Aged 65 or older	663	0.9	158	1.0	23.8
SINGLE-PERSON HOUSEHOLDS	**16,777**	**22.0**	**3,227**	**20.7**	**19.2**
Female householder	**10,007**	**13.1**	**1,817**	**11.6**	**18.2**
Under age 45	1,547	2.0	266	1.7	17.2
Aged 45 to 64	3,231	4.2	633	4.1	19.6
Aged 65 or older	5,230	6.8	918	5.9	17.6
Male householder	**6,770**	**8.9**	**1,410**	**9.0**	**20.8**
Under age 45	2,142	2.8	462	3.0	21.5
Aged 45 to 64	2,810	3.7	601	3.9	21.4
Aged 65 or older	1,818	2.4	347	2.2	19.1

Source: Bureau of the Census, American Housing Survey for the United States: 2009, Internet site http://www.census.gov/hhes/ www/housing/ahs/ahs09/ahs09.html; calculations by New Strategist

Table 4.6 Homeowners by Race, Hispanic Origin, and Region, 2009

Non-Hispanic whites account for 70 percent of homeowners
in the West and 88 percent of homeowners in the Midwest.

(number and percent distribution of total homeowners and homeowners by region, by race and Hispanic origin of householder, 2009; numbers in thousands)

	total	Northeast	Midwest	South	West
Total homeowners	**76,428**	**13,378**	**18,249**	**29,193**	**15,607**
American Indian	503	32	82	138	250
Asian	2,516	444	309	558	1,206
Black	6,547	903	1,120	4,014	510
Hispanic	6,439	522	589	2,788	2,540
White, non-Hispanic	59,905	11,450	16,062	21,481	10,912

PERCENT DISTRIBUTION BY RACE AND HISPANIC ORIGIN

	total	Northeast	Midwest	South	West
Total homeowners	**100.0%**	**100.0%**	**100.0%**	**100.0%**	**100.0%**
American Indian	0.7	0.2	0.4	0.5	1.6
Asian	3.3	3.3	1.7	1.9	7.7
Black	8.6	6.8	6.1	13.7	3.3
Hispanic	8.4	3.9	3.2	9.6	16.3
White, non-Hispanic	78.4	85.6	88.0	73.6	69.9

PERCENT DISTRIBUTION BY REGION

	total	Northeast	Midwest	South	West
Total homeowners	**100.0%**	**17.5%**	**23.9%**	**38.2%**	**20.4%**
American Indian	100.0	6.4	16.3	27.6	49.7
Asian	100.0	17.6	12.3	22.2	47.9
Black	100.0	13.8	17.1	61.3	7.8
Hispanic	100.0	8.1	9.1	43.3	39.4
White, non-Hispanic	100.0	19.1	26.8	35.9	18.2

Note: American Indians, Asians, blacks, and whites are those who identify themselves as being of the race alone. Numbers do not add to total because not all races are shown and Hispanics may be of any race.
Source: Bureau of the Census, American Housing Survey for the United States: 2009, Internet site http://www.census.gov/hhes/ www/housing/ahs/ahs09/ahs09.html; calculations by New Strategist

Table 4.7 Homeowners by Household Income and Region, 2009

Homeowners in the South have the lowest incomes, a median of $52,000 in 2009.
Homeowners in the West have the highest incomes, a median of $70,000.

(number and percent distribution of total homeowners and homeowners by region, by household income, 2009; numbers in thousands)

	total	Northeast	Midwest	South	West
Total homeowners	**76,428**	**13,378**	**18,249**	**29,193**	**15,607**
Under $10,000	4,423	654	893	2,052	823
$10,000 to $19,999	5,911	906	1,357	2,730	918
$20,000 to $29,999	7,617	1,284	1,900	3,204	1,229
$30,000 to $39,999	7,082	978	1,825	3,061	1,219
$40,000 to $49,999	6,852	1,035	1,791	2,783	1,243
$50,000 to $59,999	6,328	1,026	1,665	2,453	1,184
$60,000 to $79,999	10,535	1,758	2,764	3,775	2,239
$80,000 to $99,999	8,409	1,485	2,163	2,902	1,859
$100,000 to $119,999	6,007	1,290	1,323	1,973	1,421
$120,000 or more	13,264	2,962	2,570	4,260	3,472
Median income	$60,000	$68,000	$57,000	$52,000	$70,000

PERCENT DISTRIBUTION BY HOUSEHOLD INCOME

	total	Northeast	Midwest	South	West
Total homeowners	**100.0%**	**100.0%**	**100.0%**	**100.0%**	**100.0%**
Under $10,000	5.8	4.9	4.9	7.0	5.3
$10,000 to $19,999	7.7	6.8	7.4	9.4	5.9
$20,000 to $29,999	10.0	9.6	10.4	11.0	7.9
$30,000 to $39,999	9.3	7.3	10.0	10.5	7.8
$40,000 to $49,999	9.0	7.7	9.8	9.5	8.0
$50,000 to $59,999	8.3	7.7	9.1	8.4	7.6
$60,000 to $79,999	13.8	13.1	15.1	12.9	14.3
$80,000 to $99,999	11.0	11.1	11.9	9.9	11.9
$100,000 to $119,999	7.9	9.6	7.2	6.8	9.1
$120,000 or more	17.4	22.1	14.1	14.6	22.2

PERCENT DISTRIBUTION BY REGION

	total	Northeast	Midwest	South	West
Total homeowners	**100.0%**	**17.5%**	**23.9%**	**38.2%**	**20.4%**
Under $10,000	100.0	14.8	20.2	46.4	18.6
$10,000 to $19,999	100.0	15.3	23.0	46.2	15.5
$20,000 to $29,999	100.0	16.9	24.9	42.1	16.1
$30,000 to $39,999	100.0	13.8	25.8	43.2	17.2
$40,000 to $49,999	100.0	15.1	26.1	40.6	18.1
$50,000 to $59,999	100.0	16.2	26.3	38.8	18.7
$60,000 to $79,999	100.0	16.7	26.2	35.8	21.3
$80,000 to $99,999	100.0	17.7	25.7	34.5	22.1
$100,000 to $119,999	100.0	21.5	22.0	32.8	23.7
$120,000 or more	100.0	22.3	19.4	32.1	26.2

Source: Bureau of the Census, American Housing Survey for the United States: 2009, Internet site http://www.census.gov/hhes/ www/housing/ahs/ahs09/ahs09.html; calculations by New Strategist

Table 4.8 Homeowners by Educational Attainment and Region, 2009

Homeowners in the Northeast and West have the highest level of education. Thirty-eight percent are college graduates. In the Midwest and South, a smaller 31 percent of homeowners are college graduates.

(number and percent distribution of total homeowners and homeowners by region, by educational attainment of householder, 2009; numbers in thousands)

	total	Northeast	Midwest	South	West
Total homeowners	**76,428**	**13,378**	**18,249**	**29,193**	**15,607**
Not a high school graduate	8,542	1,060	1,689	4,336	1,457
High school graduate only	22,665	4,290	6,244	8,501	3,630
Some college, no degree	12,659	1,727	3,000	4,802	3,129
Associate's degree	6,722	1,246	1,638	2,393	1,444
Bachelor's degree	15,894	2,862	3,605	5,806	3,620
Graduate or professional degree	9,947	2,192	2,073	3,354	2,327
High school graduate or higher	67,886	12,318	16,560	24,858	14,150
Some college or higher	45,221	8,028	10,317	16,356	10,520
Bachelor's degree or higher	25,840	5,054	5,678	9,161	5,947

PERCENT DISTRIBUTION BY EDUCATIONAL ATTAINMENT

	total	Northeast	Midwest	South	West
Total homeowners	**100.0%**	**100.0%**	**100.0%**	**100.0%**	**100.0%**
Not a high school graduate	11.2	7.9	9.3	14.9	9.3
High school graduate only	29.7	32.1	34.2	29.1	23.3
Some college, no degree	16.6	12.9	16.4	16.4	20.0
Associate's degree	8.8	9.3	9.0	8.2	9.3
Bachelor's degree	20.8	21.4	19.8	19.9	23.2
Graduate or professional degree	13.0	16.4	11.4	11.5	14.9
High school graduate or higher	88.8	92.1	90.7	85.1	90.7
Some college or higher	59.2	60.0	56.5	56.0	67.4
Bachelor's degree or higher	33.8	37.8	31.1	31.4	38.1

PERCENT DISTRIBUTION BY REGION

	total	Northeast	Midwest	South	West
Total homeowners	**100.0%**	**17.5%**	**23.9%**	**38.2%**	**20.4%**
Not a high school graduate	100.0	12.4	19.8	50.8	17.1
High school graduate only	100.0	18.9	27.5	37.5	16.0
Some college, no degree	100.0	13.6	23.7	37.9	24.7
Associate's degree	100.0	18.5	24.4	35.6	21.5
Bachelor's degree	100.0	18.0	22.7	36.5	22.8
Graduate or professional degree	100.0	22.0	20.8	33.7	23.4
High school graduate or higher	100.0	18.1	24.4	36.6	20.8
Some college or higher	100.0	17.8	22.8	36.2	23.3
Bachelor's degree or higher	100.0	19.6	22.0	35.5	23.0

Source: Bureau of the Census, American Housing Survey for the United States: 2009, Internet site http://www.census.gov/hhes/ www/housing/ahs/ahs09/ahs09.html; calculations by New Strategist

Table 4.9 Homeowners by Household Size and Region, 2009

Although only 20 percent of the nation's homeowners live in the West, the region is home to 30 percent of homeowners with the largest households—those that include six or more people.

(number and percent distribution of total homeowners and homeowners by region, by number of persons living in home, 2009; numbers in thousands)

	total	Northeast	Midwest	South	West
Total homeowners	**76,428**	**13,378**	**18,249**	**29,193**	**15,607**
One person	16,777	2,944	3,986	6,619	3,227
Two persons	27,633	4,615	6,785	10,717	5,516
Three persons	12,223	2,233	2,657	4,871	2,461
Four persons	11,791	2,206	2,937	4,300	2,348
Five persons	5,207	943	1,283	1,760	1,222
Six persons	1,797	281	392	587	537
Sevent or more persons	1,000	156	209	339	296

PERCENT DISTRIBUTION BY HOUSEHOLD SIZE

	total	Northeast	Midwest	South	West
Total homeowners	**100.0%**	**100.0%**	**100.0%**	**100.0%**	**100.0%**
One person	22.0	22.0	21.8	22.7	20.7
Two persons	36.2	34.5	37.2	36.7	35.3
Three persons	16.0	16.7	14.6	16.7	15.8
Four persons	15.4	16.5	16.1	14.7	15.0
Five persons	6.8	7.0	7.0	6.0	7.8
Six persons	2.4	2.1	2.1	2.0	3.4
Seven or more persons	1.3	1.2	1.1	1.2	1.9

PERCENT DISTRIBUTION BY REGION

	total	Northeast	Midwest	South	West
Total homeowners	**100.0%**	**17.5%**	**23.9%**	**38.2%**	**20.4%**
One person	100.0	17.6	23.8	39.5	19.2
Two persons	100.0	16.7	24.6	38.8	20.0
Three persons	100.0	18.3	21.7	39.9	20.1
Four persons	100.0	18.7	24.9	36.5	19.9
Five persons	100.0	18.1	24.6	33.8	23.5
Six persons	100.0	15.7	21.8	32.7	29.9
Seven or more persons	100.0	15.6	20.9	33.9	29.6

Source: Bureau of the Census, American Housing Survey for the United States: 2009, Internet site http://www.census.gov/hhes/www/housing/ahs/ahs09/ahs09.html; calculations by New Strategist

Table 4.10 Homeowners by Type of Structure and Region, 2009

The Northeast is home to a disproportionate share of homeowners
who live in apartment buildings. More than half the owners
of manufactured/mobile homes live in the South.

(number and percent distribution of total homeowners and homeowners by region, by type of structure, 2009; numbers in thousands)

	total	Northeast	Midwest	South	West
Total homeowners	**76,428**	**13,378**	**18,249**	**29,193**	**15,607**
One, detached	63,324	10,439	15,964	23,924	12,998
One, attached	3,952	1,294	682	1,265	711
Multi-unit buildings	3,734	1,210	661	932	932
Two to four	1,353	607	251	221	274
Five to nine	632	114	102	186	230
10 to 19	483	75	102	166	140
20 to 49	499	133	64	177	124
50 or more	768	281	142	181	164
Manufactured or mobile home	5,418	436	943	3,072	966

PERCENT DISTRIBUTION BY UNITS IN STRUCTURE

	total	Northeast	Midwest	South	West
Total homeowners	**100.0%**	**100.0%**	**100.0%**	**100.0%**	**100.0%**
One, detached	82.9	78.0	87.5	82.0	83.3
One, attached	5.2	9.7	3.7	4.3	4.6
Multi-unit buildings	4.9	9.0	3.6	3.2	6.0
Two to four	1.8	4.5	1.4	0.8	1.8
Five to nine	0.8	0.9	0.6	0.6	1.5
10 to 19	0.6	0.6	0.6	0.6	0.9
20 to 49	0.7	1.0	0.4	0.6	0.8
50 or more	1.0	2.1	0.8	0.6	1.0
Manufactured or mobile home	7.1	3.3	5.2	10.5	6.2

PERCENT DISTRIBUTION BY REGION

	total	Northeast	Midwest	South	West
Total homeowners	**100.0%**	**17.5%**	**23.9%**	**38.2%**	**20.4%**
One, detached	100.0	16.5	25.2	37.8	20.5
One, attached	100.0	32.7	17.2	32.0	18.0
Multi-unit buildings	100.0	32.4	17.7	25.0	25.0
Two to four	100.0	44.9	18.5	16.4	20.2
Five to nine	100.0	18.0	16.2	29.5	36.4
10 to 19	100.0	15.5	21.1	34.4	29.0
20 to 49	100.0	26.6	12.8	35.6	25.0
50 or more	100.0	36.6	18.5	23.5	21.3
Manufactured or mobile home	100.0	8.1	17.4	56.7	17.8

Source: Bureau of the Census, American Housing Survey for the United States: 2009, Internet site http://www.census.gov/hhes/ www/housing/ahs/ahs09/ahs09.html; calculations by New Strategist

Table 4.11 Homeowners by Year Structure Built and Region, 2009

Homeowners in the Northeast own the oldest homes, with half built before 1960. Homeowners in the South own the newest homes, with half built since 1980.

(number and percent distribution of total homeowners and homeowners by region, by year structure was built, 2009; numbers in thousands)

	total	Northeast	Midwest	South	West
Total homeowners	**76,428**	**13,378**	**18,249**	**29,193**	**15,607**
2005 to 2009	4,601	387	797	2,342	1,075
2000 to 2004	6,371	555	1,348	3,021	1,447
1995 to 1999	6,221	607	1,269	3,022	1,324
1990 to 1994	4,715	494	1,066	2,017	1,137
1985 to 1989	5,159	884	970	2,202	1,102
1980 to 1984	4,201	448	727	2,067	960
1975 to 1979	7,471	906	1,708	3,135	1,722
1970 to 1974	5,696	791	1,260	2,439	1,205
1960 to 1969	8,917	1,664	2,132	3,277	1,844
1950 to 1959	8,528	1,969	2,306	2,559	1,693
1940 to 1949	4,423	1,063	1,123	1,370	867
1930 to 1939	2,904	787	860	733	524
1920 to 1929	2,520	854	909	414	342
1919 or earlier	4,703	1,970	1,774	593	366
Median year	1975	1960	1970	1980	1978

PERCENT DISTRIBUTION BY YEAR BUILT

Total homeowners	**100.0%**	**100.0%**	**100.0%**	**100.0%**	**100.0%**
2005 to 2009	6.0	2.9	4.4	8.0	6.9
2000 to 2004	8.3	4.1	7.4	10.3	9.3
1995 to 1999	8.1	4.5	7.0	10.4	8.5
1990 to 1994	6.2	3.7	5.8	6.9	7.3
1985 to 1989	6.8	6.6	5.3	7.5	7.1
1980 to 1984	5.5	3.3	4.0	7.1	6.2
1975 to 1979	9.8	6.8	9.4	10.7	11.0
1970 to 1974	7.5	5.9	6.9	8.4	7.7
1960 to 1969	11.7	12.4	11.7	11.2	11.8
1950 to 1959	11.2	14.7	12.6	8.8	10.9
1940 to 1949	5.8	7.9	6.2	4.7	5.6
1930 to 1939	3.8	5.9	4.7	2.5	3.4
1920 to 1929	3.3	6.4	5.0	1.4	2.2
1919 or earlier	6.2	14.7	9.7	2.0	2.3

	total	Northeast	Midwest	South	West
PERCENT DISTRIBUTION BY REGION					
Total homeowners	**100.0%**	**17.5%**	**23.9%**	**38.2%**	**20.4%**
2005 to 2009	100.0	8.4	17.3	50.9	23.4
2000 to 2004	100.0	8.7	21.2	47.4	22.7
1995 to 1999	100.0	9.8	20.4	48.6	21.3
1990 to 1994	100.0	10.5	22.6	42.8	24.1
1985 to 1989	100.0	17.1	18.8	42.7	21.4
1980 to 1984	100.0	10.7	17.3	49.2	22.8
1975 to 1979	100.0	12.1	22.9	42.0	23.1
1970 to 1974	100.0	13.9	22.1	42.8	21.2
1960 to 1969	100.0	18.7	23.9	36.8	20.7
1950 to 1959	100.0	23.1	27.0	30.0	19.9
1940 to 1949	100.0	24.0	25.4	31.0	19.6
1930 to 1939	100.0	27.1	29.6	25.2	18.0
1920 to 1929	100.0	33.9	36.1	16.4	13.6
1919 or earlier	100.0	41.9	37.7	12.6	7.8

Source: Bureau of the Census, American Housing Survey for the United States: 2009, Internet site http://www.census.gov/hhes/ www/housing/ahs/ahs09/ahs09.html; calculations by New Strategist

Table 4.12 Homeowners by Year Moved into Home and Region, 2009

There is little variation by region in the median year homeowners moved into their home, ranging from 1997 in the Northeast to 2001 in the West.

(number and percent distribution of total homeowners and homeowners by region, by year householder moved into unit, 2009; numbers in thousands)

	total	Northeast	Midwest	South	West
Total homeowners	**76,428**	**13,378**	**18,249**	**29,193**	**15,607**
2005 to 2009	20,126	2,898	4,558	8,170	4,500
2000 to 2004	17,520	2,697	4,120	6,760	3,944
1995 to 1999	11,217	1,965	2,660	4,282	2,310
1990 to 1994	7,706	1,353	1,914	2,946	1,494
1985 to 1989	5,362	1,042	1,345	1,926	1,048
1980 to 1984	3,124	763	737	1,121	503
1975 to 1979	3,734	766	1,009	1,330	629
1970 to 1974	2,548	550	622	1,000	376
1960 to 1969	3,142	802	805	1,063	472
1950 to 1959	1,522	408	380	454	280
1940 to 1949	334	110	78	109	37
1939 or earlier	93	24	22	32	15
Median year moved into home	1999	1997	1999	2000	2001
PERCENT DISTRIBUTION BY YEAR					
Total homeowners	**100.0%**	**100.0%**	**100.0%**	**100.0%**	**100.0%**
2005 to 2009	26.3	21.7	25.0	28.0	28.8
2000 to 2004	22.9	20.2	22.6	23.2	25.3
1995 to 1999	14.7	14.7	14.6	14.7	14.8
1990 to 1994	10.1	10.1	10.5	10.1	9.6
1985 to 1989	7.0	7.8	7.4	6.6	6.7
1980 to 1984	4.1	5.7	4.0	3.8	3.2
1975 to 1979	4.9	5.7	5.5	4.6	4.0
1970 to 1974	3.3	4.1	3.4	3.4	2.4
1960 to 1969	4.1	6.0	4.4	3.6	3.0
1950 to 1959	2.0	3.0	2.1	1.6	1.8
1940 to 1949	0.4	0.8	0.4	0.4	0.2
1939 or earlier	0.1	0.2	0.1	0.1	0.1

	total	Northeast	Midwest	South	West
PERCENT DISTRIBUTION BY REGION					
Total homeowners	**100.0%**	**17.5%**	**23.9%**	**38.2%**	**20.4%**
2005 to 2009	100.0	14.4	22.6	40.6	22.4
2000 to 2004	100.0	15.4	23.5	38.6	22.5
1995 to 1999	100.0	17.5	23.7	38.2	20.6
1990 to 1994	100.0	17.6	24.8	38.2	19.4
1985 to 1989	100.0	19.4	25.1	35.9	19.5
1980 to 1984	100.0	24.4	23.6	35.9	16.1
1975 to 1979	100.0	20.5	27.0	35.6	16.8
1970 to 1974	100.0	21.6	24.4	39.2	14.8
1960 to 1969	100.0	25.5	25.6	33.8	15.0
1950 to 1959	100.0	26.8	25.0	29.9	18.4
1940 to 1949	100.0	32.9	23.4	32.7	11.0
1939 or earlier	100.0	26.0	23.2	34.6	16.2

Source: Bureau of the Census, American Housing Survey for the United States: 2009, Internet site http://www.census.gov/hhes/ www/housing/ahs/ahs09/ahs09.html; calculations by New Strategist

Table 4.13 Homeowners by Square Footage of Unit and Lot Size, 2009: Northeast

Homeowners in the Northeast have larger-than-average homes, with a median of 2,000 square feet. Lot size is also larger than average in the Northeast.

(number and percent distribution of total homeowners and homeowners in the Northeast, and Northeastern home-owners as a percent of total, by square footage of unit and lot size, 2009; numbers in thousands)

	total		Northeast		
	number	percent distribution	number	percent distribution	percent of total
Square footage of home, total*	**68,742**	**100.0%**	**10,875**	**100.0%**	**15.8%**
Less than 500 sq. ft.	383	0.6	58	0.5	15.1
500 to 749 sq. ft.	1,085	1.6	182	1.7	16.7
750 to 999 sq. ft.	3,519	5.1	493	4.5	14.0
1,000 to 1,499 sq. ft.	14,978	21.8	1,828	16.8	12.2
1,500 to 1,999 sq. ft.	16,284	23.7	2,248	20.7	13.8
2,000 to 2,499 sq. ft.	12,057	17.5	1,896	17.4	15.7
2,500 to 2,999 sq. ft.	6,622	9.6	1,162	10.7	17.5
3,000 to 3,999 sq. ft.	6,391	9.3	1,069	9.8	16.7
4,000 or more sq. ft.	3,787	5.5	751	6.9	19.8
Not reported	3,638	5.3	1,189	10.9	32.7
Median square footage	1,800	–	2,000	–	–
Lot size, total**	**70,643**	**100.0**	**11,742**	**100.0**	**16.6**
Less than one-eighth acre	9,107	12.9	1,710	14.6	18.8
One-eighth up to one-quarter acre	17,771	25.2	2,305	19.6	13.0
One-quarter up to one-half acre	13,837	19.6	2,176	18.5	15.7
One-half up to one acre	8,874	12.6	1,803	15.4	20.3
One to five acres	14,895	21.1	2,771	23.6	18.6
Five to 10 acres	2,545	3.6	424	3.6	16.7
10 or more acres	3,614	5.1	551	4.7	15.3
Median lot size (acres)	0.32	–	0.39	–	–

* Single-family detached and mobile homes only.
** Homes in two-or-more-unit buildings are excluded.
Note: "–" means not applicable.
Source: Bureau of the Census, American Housing Survey for the United States: 2009, Internet site http://www.census.gov/hhes/www/housing/ahs/ahs09/ahs09.html; calculations by New Strategist

Table 4.14 Homeowners by Square Footage of Unit and Lot Size, 2009: Midwest

Owned homes in the Midwest are average in size, with 1,800 square feet.
Lot size is also average, at about one-third of an acre.

(number and percent distribution of total homeowners and homeowners in the Midwest, and Midwestern homeowners as a percent of total, by square footage of unit and lot size, 2009; numbers in thousands)

	total		Midwest		
	number	percent distribution	number	percent distribution	percent of total
Square footage of home, total*	**68,742**	**100.0%**	**16,907**	**100.0%**	**24.6%**
Less than 500 sq. ft.	383	0.6	86	0.5	22.5
500 to 749 sq. ft.	1,085	1.6	264	1.6	24.4
750 to 999 sq. ft.	3,519	5.1	986	5.8	28.0
1,000 to 1,499 sq. ft.	14,978	21.8	3,684	21.8	24.6
1,500 to 1,999 sq. ft.	16,284	23.7	3,672	21.7	22.6
2,000 to 2,499 sq. ft.	12,057	17.5	3,054	18.1	25.3
2,500 to 2,999 sq. ft.	6,622	9.6	1,529	9.0	23.1
3,000 to 3,999 sq. ft.	6,391	9.3	1,617	9.6	25.3
4,000 or more sq. ft.	3,787	5.5	951	5.6	25.1
Not reported	3,638	5.3	1,063	6.3	29.2
Median square footage	1,800	–	1,800	–	–
Lot size, total**	**70,643**	**100.0**	**17,073**	**100.0**	**24.2**
Less than one-eighth acre	9,107	12.9	2,075	12.2	22.8
One-eighth up to one-quarter acre	17,771	25.2	4,371	25.6	24.6
One-quarter up to one-half acre	13,837	19.6	3,655	21.4	26.4
One-half up to one acre	8,874	12.6	1,818	10.7	20.5
One to five acres	14,895	21.1	3,281	19.2	22.0
Five to 10 acres	2,545	3.6	693	4.1	27.2
10 or more acres	3,614	5.1	1,181	6.9	32.7
Median lot size (acres)	0.32	–	0.32	–	–

* Single-family detached and mobile homes only.
** Homes in two-or-more-unit buildings are excluded.
Note: "–" means not applicable.
Source: Bureau of the Census, American Housing Survey for the United States: 2009, Internet site http://www.census.gov/hhes/www/housing/ahs/ahs09/ahs09.html; calculations by New Strategist

Table 4.15 Homeowners by Square Footage of Unit and Lot Size, 2009: South

Owned homes in the South are average in size, with 1,800 square feet.
Lot size is above average, with a median of one-half acre.

(number and percent distribution of total homeowners and homeowners in the South, and Southern homeowners as a percent of total, by square footage of unit and lot size, 2009; numbers in thousands)

	total		South		
	number	percent distribution	number	percent distribution	percent of total
Square footage of home, total*	**68,742**	**100.0%**	**26,996**	**100.0%**	**39.3%**
Less than 500 sq. ft.	383	0.6	146	0.5	38.2
500 to 749 sq. ft.	1,085	1.6	493	1.8	45.4
750 to 999 sq. ft.	3,519	5.1	1,391	5.2	39.5
1,000 to 1,499 sq. ft.	14,978	21.8	6,193	22.9	41.3
1,500 to 1,999 sq. ft.	16,284	23.7	6,585	24.4	40.4
2,000 to 2,499 sq. ft.	12,057	17.5	4,677	17.3	38.8
2,500 to 2,999 sq. ft.	6,622	9.6	2,623	9.7	39.6
3,000 to 3,999 sq. ft.	6,391	9.3	2,400	8.9	37.6
4,000 or more sq. ft.	3,787	5.5	1,442	5.3	38.1
Not reported	3,638	5.3	1,047	3.9	28.8
Median square footage	1,800	–	1,800	–	–
Lot size, total**	**70,643**	**100.0**	**27,712**	**100.0**	**39.2**
Less than one-eighth acre	9,107	12.9	2,581	9.3	28.3
One-eighth up to one-quarter acre	17,771	25.2	5,693	20.5	32.0
One-quarter up to one-half acre	13,837	19.6	5,493	19.8	39.7
One-half up to one acre	8,874	12.6	4,262	15.4	48.0
One to five acres	14,895	21.1	7,204	26.0	48.4
Five to 10 acres	2,545	3.6	1,012	3.7	39.8
10 or more acres	3,614	5.1	1,466	5.3	40.6
Median lot size (acres)	0.32	–	0.50	–	–

* Single-family detached and mobile homes only.
** Homes in two-or-more-unit buildings are excluded.
Note: "–" means not applicable.
Source: Bureau of the Census, American Housing Survey for the United States: 2009, Internet site http://www.census.gov/hhes/ www/housing/ahs/ahs09/ahs09.html; calculations by New Strategist

Table 4.16 Homeowners by Square Footage of Unit and Lot Size, 2009: West

Owned homes in the West are average in size, with a median of 1,800 square feet.
Lot size is well below average, with a median of just .19 acres.

(number and percent distribution of total homeowners and homeowners in the West, and Western homeowners as a percent of total, by square footage of unit and lot size, 2009; numbers in thousands)

	total		West		
	number	percent distribution	number	percent distribution	percent of total
Square footage of home, total*	**68,742**	**100.0%**	**13,964**	**100.0%**	**20.3%**
Less than 500 sq. ft.	383	0.6	93	0.7	24.2
500 to 749 sq. ft.	1,085	1.6	146	1.0	13.5
750 to 999 sq. ft.	3,519	5.1	650	4.7	18.5
1,000 to 1,499 sq. ft.	14,978	21.8	3,273	23.4	21.8
1,500 to 1,999 sq. ft.	16,284	23.7	3,778	27.1	23.2
2,000 to 2,499 sq. ft.	12,057	17.5	2,429	17.4	20.1
2,500 to 2,999 sq. ft.	6,622	9.6	1,308	9.4	19.8
3,000 to 3,999 sq. ft.	6,391	9.3	1,304	9.3	20.4
4,000 or more sq. ft.	3,787	5.5	644	4.6	17.0
Not reported	3,638	5.3	339	2.4	9.3
Median square footage	1,800	–	1,800	–	–
Lot size, total**	**70,643**	**100.0**	**14,116**	**100.0**	**20.0**
Less than one-eighth acre	9,107	12.9	2,742	19.4	30.1
One-eighth up to one-quarter acre	17,771	25.2	5,401	38.3	30.4
One-quarter up to one-half acre	13,837	19.6	2,513	17.8	18.2
One-half up to one acre	8,874	12.6	991	7.0	11.2
One to five acres	14,895	21.1	1,638	11.6	11.0
Five to 10 acres	2,545	3.6	416	2.9	16.3
10 or more acres	3,614	5.1	416	2.9	11.5
Median lot size (acres)	0.32	–	0.19	–	–

* Single-family detached and mobile homes only.
** Homes in two-or-more-unit buildings are excluded.
Note: "–" means not applicable.
Source: Bureau of the Census, American Housing Survey for the United States: 2009, Internet site http://www.census.gov/hhes/ www/housing/ahs/ahs09/ahs09.html; calculations by New Strategist

Table 4.17 Homeowners by Number of Rooms in Home, 2009: Northeast

Homeowners in the Northeast have fewer bathrooms than the average homeowner, in part because their homes are older. Only 47 percent of owned homes in the Northeast have two or more bathrooms versus 63 percent of all owned homes.

(number and percent distribution of total homeowners and homeowners in the Northeast, and Northeastern home-owners as a percent of total, by number and type of rooms in home, 2009; numbers in thousands)

	total		Northeast		
	number	percent distribution	number	percent distribution	percent of total
Total homeowners	**76,428**	**100.0%**	**13,378**	**100.0%**	**17.5%**
Number of rooms					
1 room	26	0.0	5	0.0	18.4
2 rooms	68	0.1	21	0.2	30.6
3 rooms	1,036	1.4	303	2.3	29.2
4 rooms	6,475	8.5	1,147	8.6	17.7
5 rooms	17,232	22.5	2,431	18.2	14.1
6 rooms	20,364	26.6	3,645	27.2	17.9
7 rooms	14,754	19.3	2,815	21.0	19.1
8 rooms	9,410	12.3	1,789	13.4	19.0
9 rooms	4,130	5.4	714	5.3	17.3
10 or more rooms	2,933	3.8	509	3.8	17.3
Number of bedrooms					
None	45	0.1	16	0.1	35.9
1 bedroom	1,714	2.2	526	3.9	30.7
2 bedrooms	13,471	17.6	2,595	19.4	19.3
3 bedrooms	39,723	52.0	6,457	48.3	16.3
4 or more bedrooms	21,475	28.1	3,785	28.3	17.6
Number of bathrooms					
None	175	0.2	25	0.2	14.3
1 bathroom	15,767	20.6	3,705	27.7	23.5
1–1/2 bathrooms	12,081	15.8	3,411	25.5	28.2
2 or more bathrooms	48,405	63.3	6,237	46.6	12.9
With room used for business	**26,108**	**34.2**	**3,893**	**29.1**	**14.9**
Business only	11,479	15.0	1,745	13.0	15.2
Business and other use	14,629	19.1	2,148	16.1	14.7

Source: Bureau of the Census, American Housing Survey for the United States: 2009, Internet site http://www.census.gov/hhes/ www/housing/ahs/ahs09/ahs09.html; calculations by New Strategist

Table 4.18 Homeowners by Number of Rooms in Home, 2009: Midwest

Homeowners in the Midwest have an average number of bedrooms.
But they have fewer than average bathrooms, only
53 percent of Midwestern homes having two or more.

(number and percent distribution of total homeowners and homeowners in the Midwest, and Midwestern home-owners as a percent of total, by number and type of rooms in home, 2009; numbers in thousands)

	total		Midwest		
	number	percent distribution	number	percent distribution	percent of total
Total homeowners	**76,428**	**100.0%**	**18,249**	**100.0%**	**23.9%**
Number of rooms					
1 room	26	0.0	7	0.0	27.4
2 rooms	68	0.1	3	0.0	4.0
3 rooms	1,036	1.4	220	1.2	21.2
4 rooms	6,475	8.5	1,576	8.6	24.3
5 rooms	17,232	22.5	4,151	22.7	24.1
6 rooms	20,364	26.6	4,582	25.1	22.5
7 rooms	14,754	19.3	3,552	19.5	24.1
8 rooms	9,410	12.3	2,344	12.8	24.9
9 rooms	4,130	5.4	1,086	6.0	26.3
10 or more rooms	2,933	3.8	728	4.0	24.8
Number of bedrooms					
None	45	0.1	10	0.1	21.9
1 bedroom	1,714	2.2	366	2.0	21.3
2 bedrooms	13,471	17.6	3,444	18.9	25.6
3 bedrooms	39,723	52.0	9,413	51.6	23.7
4 or more bedrooms	21,475	28.1	5,017	27.5	23.4
Number of bathrooms					
None	175	0.2	51	0.3	29.1
1 bathroom	15,767	20.6	4,668	25.6	29.6
1–1/2 bathrooms	12,081	15.8	3,875	21.2	32.1
2 or more bathrooms	48,405	63.3	9,656	52.9	19.9
With room used for business	**26,108**	**34.2**	**6,020**	**33.0**	**23.1**
Business only	11,479	15.0	2,527	13.8	22.0
Business and other use	14,629	19.1	3,493	19.1	23.9

Source: Bureau of the Census, American Housing Survey for the United States: 2009, Internet site http://www.census.gov/hhes/ www/housing/ahs/ahs09/ahs09.html; calculations by New Strategist

Table 4.19 Homeowners by Number of Rooms in Home, 2009: South

Homeowners in the South are much more likely than the average homeowner to have two or more bathrooms—73 versus 63 percent.

(number and percent distribution of total homeowners and homeowners in the South, and Southern homeowners as a percent of total, by number and type of rooms, 2009; numbers in thousands)

	total		South		
	number	percent distribution	number	percent distribution	percent of total
Total homeowners	**76,428**	**100.0%**	**29,193**	**100.0%**	**38.2%**
Number of rooms					
1 room	26	0.0	3	0.0	9.8
2 rooms	68	0.1	24	0.1	35.0
3 rooms	1,036	1.4	230	0.8	22.2
4 rooms	6,475	8.5	2,379	8.1	36.7
5 rooms	17,232	22.5	7,052	24.2	40.9
6 rooms	20,364	26.6	8,234	28.2	40.4
7 rooms	14,754	19.3	5,498	18.8	37.3
8 rooms	9,410	12.3	3,304	11.3	35.1
9 rooms	4,130	5.4	1,404	4.8	34.0
10 or more rooms	2,933	3.8	1,067	3.7	36.4
Number of bedrooms					
None	45	0.1	5	0.0	11.3
1 bedroom	1,714	2.2	409	1.4	23.9
2 bedrooms	13,471	17.6	4,487	15.4	33.3
3 bedrooms	39,723	52.0	16,501	56.5	41.5
4 or more bedrooms	21,475	28.1	7,791	26.7	36.3
Number of bathrooms					
None	175	0.2	72	0.2	41.0
1 bathroom	15,767	20.6	4,955	17.0	31.4
1–1/2 bathrooms	12,081	15.8	2,957	10.1	24.5
2 or more bathrooms	48,405	63.3	21,211	72.7	43.8
With room used for business	**26,108**	**34.2**	**9,918**	**34.0**	**38.0**
Business only	11,479	15.0	4,587	15.7	40.0
Business and other use	14,629	19.1	5,331	18.3	36.4

Source: Bureau of the Census, American Housing Survey for the United States: 2009, Internet site http://www.census.gov/hhes/ www/housing/ahs/ahs09/ahs09.html; calculations by New Strategist

Table 4.20 Homeowners by Number of Rooms in Home, 2009: West

Homeowners in the West are more likely than the average homeowner to have two or more bathrooms. Forty percent of homeowners in the West have a room used for business.

(number and percent distribution of total homeowners and homeowners in the West, and Western homeowners as a percent of total, by number and type of rooms, 2009; numbers in thousands)

	total		West		
	number	percent distribution	number	percent distribution	percent of total
Total homeowners	**76,428**	**100.0%**	**15,607**	**100.0%**	**20.4%**
Number of rooms					
1 room	26	0.0	11	0.1	44.4
2 rooms	68	0.1	21	0.1	30.5
3 rooms	1,036	1.4	283	1.8	27.3
4 rooms	6,475	8.5	1,372	8.8	21.2
5 rooms	17,232	22.5	3,598	23.1	20.9
6 rooms	20,364	26.6	3,903	25.0	19.2
7 rooms	14,754	19.3	2,890	18.5	19.6
8 rooms	9,410	12.3	1,973	12.6	21.0
9 rooms	4,130	5.4	926	5.9	22.4
10 or more rooms	2,933	3.8	629	4.0	21.5
Number of bedrooms					
None	45	0.1	14	0.1	30.9
1 bedroom	1,714	2.2	413	2.6	24.1
2 bedrooms	13,471	17.6	2,945	18.9	21.9
3 bedrooms	39,723	52.0	7,353	47.1	18.5
4 or more bedrooms	21,475	28.1	4,883	31.3	22.7
Number of bathrooms					
None	175	0.2	27	0.2	15.6
1 bathroom	15,767	20.6	2,440	15.6	15.5
1–1/2 bathrooms	12,081	15.8	1,838	11.8	15.2
2 or more bathrooms	48,405	63.3	11,302	72.4	23.3
With room used for business	**26,108**	**34.2**	**6,277**	**40.2**	**24.0**
Business only	11,479	15.0	2,620	16.8	22.8
Business and other use	14,629	19.1	3,657	23.4	25.0

Source: Bureau of the Census, American Housing Survey for the United States: 2009, Internet site http://www.census.gov/hhes/www/housing/ahs/ahs09/ahs09.html; calculations by New Strategist

Table 4.21 Homeowners by Presence of Kitchen, Laundry, and Safety Equipment, 2009: Northeast

Homeowners in the Northeast are much more likely than the average homeowner to have a carbon monoxide detector in their home.

(number and percent distribution of total homeowners and homeowners in the Northeast, and Northeastern home- owners as a percent of total, by presence of kitchen, laundry, and safety equipment, 2009; numbers in thousands)

	total		Northeast		
	number	percent distribution	number	percent distribution	percent of total
Total homeowners	**76,428**	**100.0%**	**13,378**	**100.0%**	**17.5%**
With complete kitchen equipment	76,050	99.5	13,272	99.2	17.5
Dishwasher	57,191	74.8	9,885	73.9	17.3
Washing machine	73,826	96.6	12,576	94.0	17.0
Clothes dryer	72,562	94.9	12,221	91.4	16.8
Disposal in kitchen sink	40,597	53.1	4,110	30.7	10.1
Trash compactor	3,166	4.1	375	2.8	11.8
Working smoke detector	71,797	93.9	12,821	95.8	17.9
Fire extinguisher	37,922	49.6	7,146	53.4	18.8
Sprinkler system inside home	2,086	2.7	295	2.2	14.2
Carbon monoxide detector	31,691	41.5	8,757	65.5	27.6

Note: Complete kitchen equipment includes a sink, refrigerator, and oven or burners.
Source: Bureau of the Census, American Housing Survey for the United States: 2009, Internet site http://www.census.gov/hhes/ www/housing/ahs/ahs09/ahs09.html; calculations by New Strategist

Table 4.22 Homeowners by Presence of Kitchen, Laundry, and Safety Equipment, 2009: Midwest

Homeowners in the Midwest are more likely than the average homeowner to have a carbon monoxide detector in their home.

(number and percent distribution of total homeowners and homeowners in the Midwest, and Midwestern homeowners as a percent of total, by presence of kitchen, laundry, and safety equipment, 2009; numbers in thousands)

	total		Midwest		
	number	percent distribution	number	percent distribution	percent of total
Total homeowners	**76,428**	**100.0%**	**18,249**	**100.0%**	**23.9%**
With complete kitchen equipment	76,050	99.5	18,167	99.6	23.9
Dishwasher	57,191	74.8	12,704	69.6	22.2
Washing machine	73,826	96.6	17,763	97.3	24.1
Clothes dryer	72,562	94.9	17,620	96.6	24.3
Disposal in kitchen sink	40,597	53.1	9,911	54.3	24.4
Trash compactor	3,166	4.1	500	2.7	15.8
Working smoke detector	71,797	93.9	17,411	95.4	24.2
Fire extinguisher	37,922	49.6	8,860	48.5	23.4
Sprinkler system inside home	2,086	2.7	308	1.7	14.7
Carbon monoxide detector	31,691	41.5	10,421	57.1	32.9

Note: Complete kitchen equipment includes a sink, refrigerator, and oven or burners.
Source: Bureau of the Census, American Housing Survey for the United States: 2009, Internet site http://www.census.gov/hhes/ www/housing/ahs/ahs09/ahs09.html; calculations by New Strategist

Table 4.23 Homeowners by Presence of Kitchen, Laundry, and Safety Equipment, 2009: South

Homeowners in the South are less likely than the average
homeowner to have a carbon monoxide detector in their home.

*(number and percent distribution of total homeowners and homeowners in the South, and Southern homeowners
as a percent of total, by presence of kitchen, laundry, and safety equipment, 2009; numbers in thousands)*

	total		South		
	number	percent distribution	number	percent distribution	percent of total
Total homeowners	**76,428**	**100.0%**	**29,193**	**100.0%**	**38.2%**
With complete kitchen equipment	76,050	99.5	29,074	99.6	38.2
Dishwasher	57,191	74.8	21,879	74.9	38.3
Washing machine	73,826	96.6	28,400	97.3	38.5
Clothes dryer	72,562	94.9	27,858	95.4	38.4
Disposal in kitchen sink	40,597	53.1	14,506	49.7	35.7
Trash compactor	3,166	4.1	1,265	4.3	39.9
Working smoke detector	71,797	93.9	26,833	91.9	37.4
Fire extinguisher	37,922	49.6	14,434	49.4	38.1
Sprinkler system inside home	2,086	2.7	766	2.6	36.7
Carbon monoxide detector	31,691	41.5	8,130	27.8	25.7

Note: Complete kitchen equipment includes a sink, refrigerator, and oven or burners.
*Source: Bureau of the Census, American Housing Survey for the United States: 2009, Internet site http://www.census.gov/hhes/
www/housing/ahs/ahs09/ahs09.html; calculations by New Strategist*

Table 4.24 Homeowners by Presence of Kitchen, Laundry, and Safety Equipment, 2009: West

Homeowners in the West are much more likely than the average homeowner to have a disposal in their kitchen sink.

(number and percent distribution of total homeowners and homeowners in the West, and Western homeowners as a percent of total, by presence of kitchen, laundry, and safety equipment, 2009; numbers in thousands)

	total		West		
	number	percent distribution	number	percent distribution	percent of total
Total homeowners	**76,428**	**100.0%**	**15,607**	**100.0%**	**20.4%**
With complete kitchen equipment	76,050	99.5	15,538	99.6	20.4
Dishwasher	57,191	74.8	12,723	81.5	22.2
Washing machine	73,826	96.6	15,088	96.7	20.4
Clothes dryer	72,562	94.9	14,864	95.2	20.5
Disposal in kitchen sink	40,597	53.1	12,071	77.3	29.7
Trash compactor	3,166	4.1	1,026	6.6	32.4
Working smoke detector	71,797	93.9	14,733	94.4	20.5
Fire extinguisher	37,922	49.6	7,481	47.9	19.7
Sprinkler system inside home	2,086	2.7	717	4.6	34.4
Carbon monoxide detector	31,691	41.5	4,383	28.1	13.8

Note: Complete kitchen equipment includes a sink, refrigerator, and oven or burners.
Source: Bureau of the Census, American Housing Survey for the United States: 2009, Internet site http://www.census.gov/hhes/ www/housing/ahs/ahs09/ahs09.html; calculations by New Strategist

Table 4.25 Homeowners by Type of Heating Equipment, 2009: Northeast

Homeowners in the Northeast account for the 74 percent majority of all homeowners whose main heating system is steam or hot water.

(number and percent distribution of total homeowners and homeowners in the Northeast, and Northeastern homeowners as a percent of total, by presence and type of heating equipment, 2009; numbers in thousands)

| | total | | Northeast | | |
	number	percent distribution	number	percent distribution	percent of total
Total homeowners	**76,428**	**100.0%**	**13,378**	**100.0%**	**17.5%**
Main heating equipment					
Warm-air furnace	51,691	67.6	6,459	48.3	12.5
Steam or hot water system	7,494	9.8	5,541	41.4	73.9
Electric heat pump	9,764	12.8	260	1.9	2.7
Built-in electric units	2,120	2.8	545	4.1	25.7
Floor, wall, other built-in hot air units without ducts	2,043	2.7	200	1.5	9.8
Room heaters with flue	580	0.8	71	0.5	12.2
Room heaters without flue	694	0.9	13	0.1	1.9
Portable electric heaters	535	0.7	8	0.1	1.4
Stoves	845	1.1	213	1.6	25.2
Fireplaces with inserts	155	0.2	21	0.2	13.8
Fireplaces without inserts	35	0.0	3	0.0	8.2
Other	232	0.3	41	0.3	17.7
Cooking stove	34	0.0	0	0.0	0.0
None	206	0.3	3	0.0	1.7
Homeowners with additional heating equipment					
Warm-air furnace	225	0.3	47	0.4	20.9
Steam or hot water system	51	0.1	27	0.2	51.7
Electric heat pump	91	0.1	9	0.1	9.5
Built-in electric units	1,428	1.9	256	1.9	17.9
Floor, wall, other built-in hot air units without ducts	63	0.1	9	0.1	14.0
Room heaters with flue	716	0.9	186	1.4	25.9
Room heaters without flue	1,207	1.6	184	1.4	15.2
Portable electric heaters	9,886	12.9	1,533	11.5	15.5
Stoves	3,740	4.9	1,142	8.5	30.5
Fireplaces with inserts	4,742	6.2	660	4.9	13.9
Fireplaces without inserts	4,869	6.4	499	3.7	10.2
Other	707	0.9	177	0.1	25.0
Cooking stove	50	0.1	7	1.3	14.1
None	51,171	67.0	9,041	67.6	17.7

Source: Bureau of the Census, American Housing Survey for the United States: 2009, Internet site http://www.census.gov/hhes/ www/housing/ahs/ahs09/ahs09.html; calculations by New Strategist

Table 4.26 Homeowners by Type of Heating Equipment, 2009: Midwest

Nearly 86 percent of homeowners in the Midwest have
a warm-air furnace as their main heating equipment.

(number and percent distribution of total homeowners and homeowners in the Midwest, and Midwestern homeowners as a percent of total, by presence and type of heating equipment, 2009; numbers in thousands)

	total		Midwest		
	number	percent distribution	number	percent distribution	percent of total
Total homeowners	**76,428**	**100.0%**	**18,249**	**100.0%**	**23.9%**
Main heating equipment					
Warm-air furnace	51,691	67.6	15,653	85.8	30.3
Steam or hot water system	7,494	9.8	1,072	5.9	14.3
Electric heat pump	9,764	12.8	547	3.0	5.6
Built-in electric units	2,120	2.8	460	2.5	21.7
Floor, wall, other built-in hot air units without ducts	2,043	2.7	177	1.0	8.7
Room heaters with flue	580	0.8	69	0.4	11.9
Room heaters without flue	694	0.9	29	0.2	4.2
Portable electric heaters	535	0.7	43	0.2	8.1
Stoves	845	1.1	132	0.7	15.6
Fireplaces with inserts	155	0.2	34	0.2	21.8
Fireplaces without inserts	35	0.0	6	0.0	16.9
Other	232	0.3	28	0.2	11.8
Cooking stove	34	0.0	0	0.0	0.0
None	206	0.3	0	0.0	0.0
Homeowners with additional heating equipment					
Warm-air furnace	225	0.3	55	0.3	24.4
Steam or hot water system	51	0.1	18	0.1	34.6
Electric heat pump	91	0.1	31	0.2	34.3
Built-in electric units	1,428	1.9	331	1.8	23.2
Floor, wall, other built-in hot air units without ducts	63	0.1	13	0.1	20.7
Room heaters with flue	716	0.9	122	0.7	17.0
Room heaters without flue	1,207	1.6	315	1.7	26.1
Portable electric heaters	9,886	12.9	3,130	17.2	31.7
Stoves	3,740	4.9	806	4.4	21.6
Fireplaces with inserts	4,742	6.2	1,035	5.7	21.8
Fireplaces without inserts	4,869	6.4	803	4.4	16.5
Other	707	0.9	170	0.9	24.0
Cooking stove	50	0.1	9	0.1	19.0
None	51,171	67.0	11,972	65.6	23.4

Source: Bureau of the Census, American Housing Survey for the United States: 2009, Internet site http://www.census.gov/hhes/ www/housing/ahs/ahs09/ahs09.html; calculations by New Strategist

Table 4.27 Homeowners by Type of Heating Equipment, 2009: South

Twenty-seven percent of homeowners in the South use an electric heat pump as their main heating equipment, accounting for 82 percent of the nation's homeowners who use heat pumps.

(number and percent distribution of total homeowners and homeowners in the South, and Southern homeowners as a percent of total, by presence and type of heating equipment, 2009; numbers in thousands)

	total		South		
	number	percent distribution	number	percent distribution	percent of total
Total homeowners	**76,428**	**100.0%**	**29,193**	**100.0%**	**38.2%**
Main heating equipment					
Warm-air furnace	51,691	67.6	17,862	61.2	34.6
Steam or hot water system	7,494	9.8	388	1.3	5.2
Electric heat pump	9,764	12.8	7,995	27.4	81.9
Built-in electric units	2,120	2.8	502	1.7	23.7
Floor, wall, other built-in hot air units without ducts	2,043	2.7	678	2.3	33.2
Room heaters with flue	580	0.8	303	1.0	52.2
Room heaters without flue	694	0.9	633	2.2	91.2
Portable electric heaters	535	0.7	364	1.2	68.0
Stoves	845	1.1	266	0.9	31.4
Fireplaces with inserts	155	0.2	32	0.1	20.5
Fireplaces without inserts	35	0.0	16	0.1	44.8
Other	232	0.3	106	0.4	45.8
Cooking stove	34	0.0	29	0.1	85.2
None	206	0.3	19	0.1	9.3
Homeowners with additional heating equipment					
Warm-air furnace	225	0.3	53	0.2	23.7
Steam or hot water system	51	0.1	4	0.0	8.2
Electric heat pump	91	0.1	31	0.1	33.7
Built-in electric units	1,428	1.9	492	1.7	34.5
Floor, wall, other built-in hot air units without ducts	63	0.1	28	0.1	45.3
Room heaters with flue	716	0.9	273	0.9	38.1
Room heaters without flue	1,207	1.6	611	2.1	50.6
Portable electric heaters	9,886	12.9	3,240	11.1	32.8
Stoves	3,740	4.9	890	3.1	23.8
Fireplaces with inserts	4,742	6.2	1,751	6.0	36.9
Fireplaces without inserts	4,869	6.4	2,213	7.6	45.4
Other	707	0.9	205	0.7	29.0
Cooking stove	50	0.1	26	0.1	51.8
None	51,171	67.0	20,356	69.7	39.8

Source: Bureau of the Census, American Housing Survey for the United States: 2009, Internet site http://www.census.gov/hhes/ www/housing/ahs/ahs09/ahs09.html; calculations by New Strategist

Table 4.28 Homeowners by Type of Heating Equipment, 2009: West

The West accounts for 89 percent of the nation's homeowners
with no heating equipment, many of them living in Hawaii.

(number and percent distribution of total homeowners and homeowners in the West, and Western homeowners as a percent of total, by presence and type of heating equipment, 2009; numbers in thousands)

	total		West		
	number	percent distribution	number	percent distribution	percent of total
Total homeowners	**76,428**	**100.0%**	**15,607**	**100.0%**	**20.4%**
Main heating equipment					
Warm-air furnace	51,691	67.6	11,717	75.1	22.7
Steam or hot water system	7,494	9.8	494	3.2	6.6
Electric heat pump	9,764	12.8	962	6.2	9.9
Built-in electric units	2,120	2.8	612	3.9	28.9
Floor, wall, other built-in hot air units without ducts	2,043	2.7	987	6.3	48.3
Room heaters with flue	580	0.8	138	0.9	23.8
Room heaters without flue	694	0.9	19	0.1	2.7
Portable electric heaters	535	0.7	120	0.8	22.4
Stoves	845	1.1	234	1.5	27.7
Fireplaces with inserts	155	0.2	68	0.4	43.9
Fireplaces without inserts	35	0.0	11	0.1	30.1
Other	232	0.3	57	0.4	24.7
Cooking stove	34	0.0	5	0.0	14.8
None	206	0.3	183	1.2	89.1
Homeowners with additional heating equipment					
Warm-air furnace	225	0.3	70	0.4	31.1
Steam or hot water system	51	0.1	3	0.0	5.4
Electric heat pump	91	0.1	20	0.1	22.5
Built-in electric units	1,428	1.9	348	2.2	24.4
Floor, wall, other built-in hot air units without ducts	63	0.1	13	0.1	20.0
Room heaters with flue	716	0.9	136	0.9	19.0
Room heaters without flue	1,207	1.6	98	0.6	8.1
Portable electric heaters	9,886	12.9	1,983	12.7	20.1
Stoves	3,740	4.9	901	5.8	24.1
Fireplaces with inserts	4,742	6.2	1,297	8.3	27.3
Fireplaces without inserts	4,869	6.4	1,354	8.7	27.8
Other	707	0.9	155	1.0	21.9
Cooking stove	50	0.1	7	0.0	15.0
None	51,171	67.0	9,802	62.8	19.2

Source: Bureau of the Census, American Housing Survey for the United States: 2009, Internet site http://www.census.gov/hhes/ www/housing/ahs/ahs09/ahs09.html; calculations by New Strategist

Table 4.29 Homeowners with Air Conditioning, 2009: Northeast

Only 40 percent of homeowners in the Northeast have central air conditioning, but a larger 46 percent use room air conditioning units.

(number and percent distribution of total homeowners and homeowners in the Northeast, and Northeastern homeowners as a percent of total, by presence of air conditioning equipment, 2009; numbers in thousands)

| | total | | Northeast | | |
	number	percent distribution	number	percent distribution	percent of total
Total homeowners	**76,428**	**100.0%**	**13,378**	**100.0%**	**17.5%**
Households with air conditioning	68,355	89.4	11,550	86.3	16.9
Central	54,647	71.5	5,371	40.2	9.8
Additional central	4,709	6.2	298	2.2	6.3
One room unit	5,303	6.9	1,820	13.6	34.3
Two room units	4,800	6.3	2,250	16.8	46.9
Three or more room units	3,604	4.7	2,109	15.8	58.5

Source: Bureau of the Census, American Housing Survey for the United States: 2009, Internet site http://www.census.gov/hhes/ www/housing/ahs/ahs09/ahs09.html; calculations by New Strategist

Table 4.30 Homeowners with Air Conditioning, 2009: Midwest

Seventy-eight percent of homeowners in the Midwest have central air conditioning.

(number and percent distribution of total homeowners and homeowners in the Midwest, and Midwestern homeowners as a percent of total, by presence of air conditioning equipment, 2009; numbers in thousands)

| | total | | Midwest | | |
	number	percent distribution	number	percent distribution	percent of total
Total homeowners	**76,428**	**100.0%**	**18,249**	**100.0%**	**23.9%**
Households with air conditioning	68,355	89.4	16,981	93.1	24.8
Central	54,647	71.5	14,165	77.6	25.9
Additional central	4,709	6.2	572	3.1	12.1
One room unit	5,303	6.9	1,324	7.3	25.0
Two room units	4,800	6.3	1,071	5.9	22.3
Three or more room units	3,604	4.7	422	2.3	11.7

Source: Bureau of the Census, American Housing Survey for the United States: 2009, Internet site http://www.census.gov/hhes/ www/housing/ahs/ahs09/ahs09.html; calculations by New Strategist

Table 4.31 Homeowners with Air Conditioning, 2009: South

Eighty-nine percent of homeowners in the South have central
air conditioning. They account for 47 percent of all homeowners
with central air conditioning in the United States.

(number and percent distribution of total homeowners and homeowners in the South, and Southern homeowners as a percent of total, by presence of air conditioning equipment, 2009; numbers in thousands)

	total		South		
	number	percent distribution	number	percent distribution	percent of total
Total homeowners	**76,428**	**100.0%**	**29,193**	**100.0%**	**38.2%**
Households with air conditioning	68,355	89.4	28,745	98.5	42.1
Central	54,647	71.5	25,902	88.7	47.4
Additional central	4,709	6.2	3,018	10.3	64.1
One room unit	5,303	6.9	819	2.8	15.4
Two room units	4,800	6.3	1,121	3.8	23.4
Three or more room units	3,604	4.7	902	3.1	25.0

Source: Bureau of the Census, American Housing Survey for the United States: 2009, Internet site http://www.census.gov/hhes/www/housing/ahs/ahs09/ahs09.html; calculations by New Strategist

Table 4.32 Homeowners with Air Conditioning, 2009: West

Only 59 percent of homeowners in the West have central
air conditioning, well below the national average.

(number and percent distribution of total homeowners and homeowners in the West, and Western homeowners as a percent of total, by presence of air conditioning equipment, 2009; numbers in thousands)

	total		West		
	number	percent distribution	number	percent distribution	percent of total
Total homeowners	**76,428**	**100.0%**	**15,607**	**100.0%**	**20.4%**
Households with air conditioning	68,355	89.4	11,078	71.0	16.2
Central	54,647	71.5	9,209	59.0	16.9
Additional central	4,709	6.2	821	5.3	17.4
One room unit	5,303	6.9	1,340	8.6	25.3
Two room units	4,800	6.3	358	2.3	7.5
Three or more room units	3,604	4.7	171	1.1	4.7

Source: Bureau of the Census, American Housing Survey for the United States: 2009, Internet site http://www.census.gov/hhes/www/housing/ahs/ahs09/ahs09.html; calculations by New Strategist

Table 4.33 Homeowners by Primary Source of Water and Sewage Disposal System, 2009: Northeast

In the Northeast, homeowners are more likely than average
to depend on wells for drinking water.

(number and percent distribution of total homeowners and homeowners in the Northeast, and Northeastern homeowners as a percent of total, by primary source of water and type of sewage disposal system, 2009; numbers in thousands)

	total		Northeast		
	number	percent distribution	number	percent distribution	percent of total
Total homeowners	**76,428**	**100.0%**	**13,378**	**100.0%**	**17.5%**
Source of water					
Public system or private company	64,372	84.2	10,416	77.9	16.2
Well	11,769	15.4	2,904	21.7	24.7
Safety of primary source of water					
Safe to drink	71,152	93.1	12,571	94.0	17.7
Not safe to drink	4,530	5.9	661	4.9	14.6
Sewage disposal system					
Public sewer	56,736	74.2	9,662	72.2	17.0
Septic tank, cesspool, chemical toilet	19,667	25.7	3,716	27.8	18.9

Note: Numbers do not sum to total because "other" and "not reported" are not shown.
Source: Bureau of the Census, American Housing Survey for the United States: 2009, Internet site http://www.census.gov/hhes/ www/housing/ahs/ahs09/ahs09.html; calculations by New Strategist

Table 4.34 Homeowners by Primary Source of Water and Sewage Disposal System, 2009: Midwest

In the Midwest, homeowners are slightly more likely
than average to depend on wells for drinking water.

(number and percent distribution of total homeowners and homeowners in the Midwest, and Midwestern home-owners as a percent of total, by primary source of water and type of sewage disposal system, 2009; numbers in thousands)

	total		Midwest		
	number	percent distribution	number	percent distribution	percent of total
Total homeowners	**76,428**	**100.0%**	**18,249**	**100.0%**	**23.9%**
Source of water					
Public system or private company	64,372	84.2	14,720	80.7	22.9
Well	11,769	15.4	3,479	19.1	29.6
Safety of primary source of water					
Safe to drink	71,152	93.1	17,368	95.2	24.4
Not safe to drink	4,530	5.9	773	4.2	17.1
Sewage disposal system					
Public sewer	56,736	74.2	13,797	75.6	24.3
Septic tank, cesspool, chemical toilet	19,667	25.7	4,447	24.4	22.6

Note: Numbers do not sum to total because "other" and "not reported" are not shown.
Source: Bureau of the Census, American Housing Survey for the United States: 2009, Internet site http://www.census.gov/hhes/www/housing/ahs/ahs09/ahs09.html; calculations by New Strategist

Table 4.35 Homeowners by Primary Source of Water and Sewage Disposal System, 2009: South

In the South, homeowners are more likely than average to
depend on septic tanks or cesspools for sewage disposal.

(number and percent distribution of total homeowners and homeowners in the South, and Southern homeowners as a percent of total, by primary source of water and type of sewage disposal system, 2009; numbers in thousands)

	total		South		
	number	percent distribution	number	percent distribution	percent of total
Total homeowners	**76,428**	**100.0%**	**29,193**	**100.0%**	**38.2%**
Source of water					
Public system or private company	64,372	84.2	24,892	85.3	38.7
Well	11,769	15.4	4,164	14.3	35.4
Safety of primary source of water					
Safe to drink	71,152	93.1	27,081	92.8	38.1
Not safe to drink	4,530	5.9	1,798	6.2	39.7
Sewage disposal system					
Public sewer	56,736	74.2	20,173	69.1	35.6
Septic tank, cesspool, chemical toilet	19,667	25.7	9,004	30.8	45.8

Note: Numbers do not sum to total because "other" and "not reported" are not shown.
Source: Bureau of the Census, American Housing Survey for the United States: 2009, Internet site http://www.census.gov/hhes/ www/housing/ahs/ahs09/ahs09.html; calculations by New Strategist

Table 4.36 Homeowners by Primary Source of Water and Sewage Disposal System, 2009: West

In the West, homeowners are more likely than average
to have unsafe drinking water.

(number and percent distribution of total homeowners and homeowners in the West, and Western homeowners as a percent of total, by primary source of water and type of sewage disposal system, 2009; numbers in thousands)

	total		West		
	number	percent distribution	number	percent distribution	percent of total
Total homeowners	**76,428**	**100.0%**	**15,607**	**100.0%**	**20.4%**
Source of water					
Public system or private company	64,372	84.2	14,345	91.9	22.3
Well	11,769	15.4	1,222	7.8	10.4
Safety of primary source of water					
Safe to drink	71,152	93.1	14,132	90.5	19.9
Not safe to drink	4,530	5.9	1,299	8.3	28.7
Sewage disposal system					
Public sewer	56,736	74.2	13,103	84.0	23.1
Septic tank, cesspool, chemical toilet	19,667	25.7	2,500	16.0	12.7

Note: Numbers do not sum to total because "other" and "not reported" are not shown.
Source: Bureau of the Census, American Housing Survey for the United States: 2009, Internet site http://www.census.gov/hhes/ www/housing/ahs/ahs09/ahs09.html; calculations by New Strategist

Table 4.37 Homeowners by Fuels Used by Region, 2009

Forty-five percent of homeowners in the South have all-electric homes compared with only 14 percent of homeowners in the West, 9 percent in the Midwest, and 6 percent in the Northeast.

(number and percent distribution of total homeowners and homeowners by region, by types of fuels used, 2009; numbers in thousands)

	total	Northeast	Midwest	South	West
Total homeowners	**76,428**	**13,378**	**18,249**	**29,193**	**15,607**
Electricity	76,378	13,364	18,223	29,183	15,607
All-electric homes	17,951	840	1,611	13,268	2,232
Piped gas	46,700	7,819	13,959	12,638	12,284
Bottled gas	8,391	1,724	2,370	3,332	966
Fuel oil	6,409	4,846	550	845	167
Kerosene or other liquid fuel	451	203	12	218	18
Coal or coke	97	78	8	6	6
Wood	1,510	375	385	412	338
Solar energy	130	17	8	21	84
Other	254	49	83	63	59

PERCENT DISTRIBUTION BY FUELS USED

	total	Northeast	Midwest	South	West
Total homeowners	**100.0%**	**100.0%**	**100.0%**	**100.0%**	**100.0%**
Electricity	99.9	99.9	99.9	100.0	100.0
All-electric homes	23.5	6.3	8.8	45.4	14.3
Piped gas	61.1	58.4	76.5	43.3	78.7
Bottled gas	11.0	12.9	13.0	11.4	6.2
Fuel oil	8.4	36.2	3.0	2.9	1.1
Kerosene or other liquid fuel	0.6	1.5	0.1	0.7	0.1
Coal or coke	0.1	0.6	0.0	0.0	0.0
Wood	2.0	2.8	2.1	1.4	2.2
Solar energy	0.2	0.1	0.0	0.1	0.5
Other	0.3	0.4	0.5	0.2	0.4

PERCENT DISTRIBUTION BY REGION

	total	Northeast	Midwest	South	West
Total homeowners	**100.0%**	**17.5%**	**23.9%**	**38.2%**	**20.4%**
Electricity	100.0	17.5	23.9	38.2	20.4
All-electric homes	100.0	4.7	9.0	73.9	12.4
Piped gas	100.0	16.7	29.9	27.1	26.3
Bottled gas	100.0	20.5	28.2	39.7	11.5
Fuel oil	100.0	75.6	8.6	13.2	2.6
Kerosene or other liquid fuel	100.0	44.9	2.7	48.4	4.0
Coal or coke	100.0	79.9	8.5	5.8	5.8
Wood	100.0	24.8	25.5	27.3	22.4
Solar energy	100.0	13.2	5.9	16.1	64.8
Other	100.0	19.5	32.6	24.8	23.1

Note: Numbers do not add to total because many households use more than one fuel.
Source: Bureau of the Census, American Housing Survey for the United States: 2009, Internet site http://www.census.gov/hhes/ www/housing/ahs/ahs09/ahs09.html; calculations by New Strategist

Table 4.38 Homeowners by Primary Heating Fuel Used, 2009: Northeast

Thirty-three percent of homeowners in the Northeast use fuel oil as their primary heating fuel, accounting for 78 percent of all homeowners who do.

(number and percent distribution of total homeowners and homeowners in the Northeast, and Northeastern homeowners as a percent of total, by primary heating fuel used, 2009; numbers in thousands)

	total		Northeast		
	number	percent distribution	number	percent distribution	percent of total
Total homeowners	**76,428**	**100.0%**	**13,378**	**100.0%**	**17.5 %**
Homeowners using heating fuel	76,222	100.0	13,375	100.0	17.5
Electricity	22,219	29.2	1,140	8.5	5.1
Piped gas	41,233	54.1	6,596	49.3	16.0
Bottled gas	4,889	6.4	554	4.1	11.3
Fuel oil	5,693	7.5	4,416	33.0	77.6
Kerosene or other liquid fuel	444	0.6	200	1.5	45.0
Coal or coke	91	0.1	75	0.6	81.9
Wood	1,503	2.0	375	2.8	24.9
Solar energy	8	0.0	3	0.0	36.0
Other	142	0.2	16	0.1	11.1

Source: Bureau of the Census, American Housing Survey for the United States: 2009, Internet site http://www.census.gov/hhes/ www/housing/ahs/ahs09/ahs09.html; calculations by New Strategist

Table 4.39 Homeowners by Primary Heating Fuel Used, 2009: Midwest

Seventy-three percent of homeowners in the Midwest
use piped gas as their primary heating fuel.

(number and percent distribution of total homeowners and homeowners in the Midwest, and Midwestern homeowners as a percent of total, by primary heating fuel used, 2009; numbers in thousands)

	total		Midwest		
	number	percent distribution	number	percent distribution	percent of total
Total homeowners	**76,428**	**100.0%**	**18,249**	**100.0%**	**23.9%**
Homeowners using heating fuel	76,222	100.0	18,249	100.0	23.9
Electricity	22,219	29.2	2,112	11.6	9.5
Piped gas	41,233	54.1	13,353	73.2	32.4
Bottled gas	4,889	6.4	1,881	10.3	38.5
Fuel oil	5,693	7.5	438	2.4	7.7
Kerosene or other liquid fuel	444	0.6	8	0.0	1.9
Coal or coke	91	0.1	8	0.0	9.1
Wood	1,503	2.0	385	2.1	25.6
Solar energy	8	0.0	2	0.0	29.8
Other	142	0.2	62	0.3	43.7

Source: Bureau of the Census, American Housing Survey for the United States: 2009, Internet site http://www.census.gov/hhes/www/housing/ahs/ahs09/ahs09.html; calculations by New Strategist

Table 4.40 Homeowners by Primary Heating Fuel Used, 2009: South

Fifty-four percent of homeowners in the South use electricity as their primary
heating fuel, accounting for 70 percent of all homeowners who do.

*(number and percent distribution of total homeowners and homeowners in the South, and Southern homeowners
as a percent of total, by primary heating fuel used, 2009; numbers in thousands)*

	total		South		
	number	percent distribution	number	percent distribution	percent of total
Total homeowners	**76,428**	**100.0%**	**29,193**	**100.0%**	**38.2%**
Homeowners using heating fuel	76,222	100.0	29,174	99.9	38.3
Electricity	22,219	29.2	15,644	53.6	70.4
Piped gas	41,233	54.1	10,386	35.6	25.2
Bottled gas	4,889	6.4	1,788	6.1	36.6
Fuel oil	5,693	7.5	696	2.4	12.2
Kerosene or other liquid fuel	444	0.6	218	0.7	49.1
Coal or coke	91	0.1	3	0.0	2.8
Wood	1,503	2.0	406	1.4	27.0
Solar energy	8	0.0	0	0.0	0.0
Other	142	0.2	33	0.1	23.6

*Source: Bureau of the Census, American Housing Survey for the United States: 2009, Internet site http://www.census.gov/hhes/
www/housing/ahs/ahs09/ahs09.html; calculations by New Strategist*

Table 4.41 Homeowners by Primary Heating Fuel Used, 2009: West

Seventy percent of homeowners in the West use piped gas as
their primary heating fuel, and 21 percent use electricity.

(number and percent distribution of total homeowners and homeowners in the West, and Western homeowners as a percent of total, by primary heating fuel used, 2009; numbers in thousands)

	total		West		
	number	percent distribution	number	percent distribution	percent of total
Total homeowners	**76,428**	**100.0%**	**15,607**	**100.0%**	**20.4%**
Homeowners using heating fuel	76,222	100.0	15,424	98.8	20.2
Electricity	22,219	29.2	3,323	21.3	15.0
Piped gas	41,233	54.1	10,897	69.8	26.4
Bottled gas	4,889	6.4	665	4.3	13.6
Fuel oil	5,693	7.5	143	0.9	2.5
Kerosene or other liquid fuel	444	0.6	18	0.1	4.0
Coal or coke	91	0.1	6	0.0	6.2
Wood	1,503	2.0	338	2.2	22.5
Solar energy	8	0.0	3	0.0	34.2
Other	142	0.2	31	0.2	21.5

Source: Bureau of the Census, American Housing Survey for the United States: 2009, Internet site http://www.census.gov/hhes/ www/housing/ahs/ahs09/ahs09.html; calculations by New Strategist

Table 4.42 Homeowners by Cooking, Water Heating, and Clothes Dryer Fuels Used, 2009: Northeast

Northeastern homeowners are more likely than the average homeowner
to use piped gas as their cooking fuel—44 versus 35 percent.

(number and percent distribution of total homeowners and homeowners in the Northeast, and Northeastern homeowners as a percent of total, by cooking, water heating, and clothes dryer fuels used, 2009; numbers in thousands)

	total		Northeast		
	number	percent distribution	number	percent distribution	percent of total
COOKING FUEL					
Households using cooking fuel	**76,388**	**100.0%**	**13,374**	**100.0%**	**17.5%**
Electricity	45,512	59.6	6,291	47.0	13.8
Piped gas	26,553	34.8	5,853	43.8	22.0
Bottled gas	4,274	5.6	1,220	9.1	28.6
Kerosene or other liquid fuel	7	0.0	3	0.0	41.0
Wood	17	0.0	1	0.0	5.9
Other	25	0.0	6	0.0	23.7
WATER HEATING FUEL					
Households with hot piped water	**76,371**	**100.0**	**13,371**	**100.0**	**17.5**
Electricity	29,341	38.4	3,000	22.4	10.2
Piped gas	40,280	52.7	6,744	50.4	16.7
Bottled gas	3,365	4.4	577	4.3	17.2
Fuel oil	3,087	4.0	2,956	22.1	95.8
Kerosene or other liquid fuel	18	0.0	11	0.1	59.4
Coal or coke	23	0.0	17	0.1	74.9
Wood	96	0.1	38	0.3	39.5
Solar energy	121	0.2	14	0.1	11.7
Other	40	0.1	13	0.1	33.9
CLOTHES DRYER FUEL					
Households with clothes dryers	**72,562**	**100.0**	**12,221**	**100.0**	**16.8**
Electricity	55,059	75.9	8,179	66.9	14.9
Piped gas	16,326	22.5	3,635	29.7	22.3
Other	1,178	1.6	407	3.3	34.6

Source: Bureau of the Census, American Housing Survey for the United States: 2009, Internet site http://www.census.gov/hhes/ www/housing/ahs/ahs09/ahs09.html; calculations by New Strategist

Table 4.43 Homeowners by Cooking, Water Heating, and Clothes Dryer Fuels Used, 2009: Midwest

Midwestern homeowners are more likely than the average homeowner to use piped gas as their water heating fuel—67 versus 53 percent.

(number and percent distribution of total homeowners and homeowners in the Midwest, and Midwestern homeowners as a percent of total, by cooking, water heating, and clothes dryer fuels used, 2009; numbers in thousands)

	total		Midwest		
	number	percent distribution	number	percent distribution	percent of total
COOKING FUEL					
Households using cooking fuel	**76,388**	**100.0%**	**18,234**	**100.0%**	**23.9%**
Electricity	45,512	59.6	10,351	56.8	22.7
Piped gas	26,553	34.8	6,810	37.3	25.6
Bottled gas	4,274	5.6	1,056	5.8	24.7
Kerosene or other liquid fuel	7	0.0	4	0.0	59.0
Wood	17	0.0	2	0.0	11.8
Other	25	0.0	11	0.1	43.5
WATER HEATING FUEL					
Households with hot piped water	**76,371**	**100.0**	**18,235**	**100.0**	**23.9**
Electricity	29,341	38.4	4,772	26.2	16.3
Piped gas	40,280	52.7	12,240	67.1	30.4
Bottled gas	3,365	4.4	1,140	6.3	33.9
Fuel oil	3,087	4.0	27	0.1	0.9
Kerosene or other liquid fuel	18	0.0	0	0.0	0.0
Coal or coke	23	0.0	3	0.0	11.9
Wood	96	0.1	43	0.2	44.4
Solar energy	121	0.2	5	0.0	4.3
Other	40	0.1	6	0.0	15.1
CLOTHES DRYER FUEL					
Households with clothes dryers	**72,562**	**100.0**	**17,620**	**100.0**	**24.3**
Electricity	55,059	75.9	11,887	67.5	21.6
Piped gas	16,326	22.5	5,370	30.5	32.9
Other	1,178	1.6	362	2.1	30.8

Source: Bureau of the Census, American Housing Survey for the United States: 2009, Internet site http://www.census.gov/hhes/www/housing/ahs/ahs09/ahs09.html; calculations by New Strategist

Table 4.44 Homeowners by Cooking, Water Heating, and Clothes Dryer Fuels Used, 2009: South

Southern homeowners are more likely than the average homeowner to use electricity as their cooking, water heating, and clothes dryer fuel.

(number and percent distribution of total homeowners and homeowners in the South, and Southern homeowners as a percent of total, by cooking, water heating, and clothes dryer fuels used, 2009; numbers in thousands)

	total		South		
	number	percent distribution	number	percent distribution	percent of total
COOKING FUEL					
Households using cooking fuel	**76,388**	**100.0%**	**29,179**	**100.0%**	**38.2%**
Electricity	45,512	59.6	21,255	72.8	46.7
Piped gas	26,553	34.8	6,427	22.0	24.2
Bottled gas	4,274	5.6	1,482	5.1	34.7
Kerosene or other liquid fuel	7	0.0	0	0.0	0.0
Wood	17	0.0	12	0.0	70.7
Other	25	0.0	3	0.0	10.8
WATER HEATING FUEL					
Households with hot piped water	**76,371**	**100.0**	**29,164**	**100.0**	**38.2**
Electricity	29,341	38.4	18,029	61.8	61.4
Piped gas	40,280	52.7	9,975	34.2	24.8
Bottled gas	3,365	4.4	1,006	3.4	29.9
Fuel oil	3,087	4.0	104	0.4	3.4
Kerosene or other liquid fuel	18	0.0	5	0.0	27.7
Coal or coke	23	0.0	3	0.0	13.2
Wood	96	0.1	10	0.0	10.2
Solar energy	121	0.2	21	0.1	17.1
Other	40	0.1	11	0.0	28.3
CLOTHES DRYER FUEL					
Households with clothes dryers	**72,562**	**100.0**	**27,858**	**100.0**	**38.4**
Electricity	55,059	75.9	25,526	91.6	46.4
Piped gas	16,326	22.5	2,108	7.6	12.9
Other	1,178	1.6	224	0.8	19.0

Source: Bureau of the Census, American Housing Survey for the United States: 2009, Internet site http://www.census.gov/hhes/ www/housing/ahs/ahs09/ahs09.html; calculations by New Strategist

Table 4.45 **Homeowners by Cooking, Water Heating, and Clothes Dryer Fuels Used, 2009: West**

Western homeowners are more likely than the average homeowner
to use piped gas as their cooking fuel—48 versus 35 percent.

*(number and percent distribution of total homeowners and homeowners in the West, and Western homeowners as
a percent of total, by cooking, water heating, and clothes dryer fuels used, 2009; numbers in thousands)*

	total		West		
	number	percent distribution	number	percent distribution	percent of total
COOKING FUEL					
Households using cooking fuel	**76,388**	**100.0%**	**15,601**	**100.0%**	**20.4%**
Electricity	45,512	59.6	7,614	48.8	16.7
Piped gas	26,553	34.8	7,463	47.8	28.1
Bottled gas	4,274	5.6	516	3.3	12.1
Kerosene or other liquid fuel	7	0.0	0	0.0	0.0
Wood	17	0.0	2	0.0	10.3
Other	25	0.0	6	0.0	23.2
WATER HEATING FUEL					
Households with hot piped water	**76,371**	**100.0**	**15,601**	**100.0**	**20.4**
Electricity	29,341	38.4	3,539	22.7	12.1
Piped gas	40,280	52.7	11,322	72.6	28.1
Bottled gas	3,365	4.4	642	4.1	19.1
Fuel oil	3,087	4.0	0	0.0	0.0
Kerosene or other liquid fuel	18	0.0	2	0.0	12.9
Coal or coke	23	0.0	0	0.0	0.0
Wood	96	0.1	6	0.0	5.9
Solar energy	121	0.2	81	0.5	66.9
Other	40	0.1	9	0.1	22.7
CLOTHES DRYER FUEL					
Households with clothes dryers	**72,562**	**100.0**	**14,864**	**100.0**	**20.5**
Electricity	55,059	75.9	9,467	63.7	17.2
Piped gas	16,326	22.5	5,212	35.1	31.9
Other	1,178	1.6	184	1.2	15.6

*Source: Bureau of the Census, American Housing Survey for the United States: 2009, Internet site http://www.census.gov/hhes/
www/housing/ahs/ahs09/ahs09.html; calculations by New Strategist*

Table 4.46 Homeowners by Amenities of Home and Region, 2009

The 58 percent majority of owned homes in the West include a usable fireplace, much higher than the percentage in any other region.

(number and percent distribution of total homeowners and homeowners by region, by selected amenities of home, 2009; numbers in thousands)

	total	Northeast	Midwest	South	West
Total homeowners	**76,428**	**13,378**	**18,249**	**29,193**	**15,607**
Porch, deck, balcony, or patio	70,421	11,742	16,799	27,257	14,623
Telephone available	75,129	13,054	17,904	28,752	15,419
Usable fireplace	34,458	5,096	7,578	12,728	9,056
Separate dining room	43,717	8,906	9,812	16,781	8,219
With two or more living or recreation rooms	30,978	5,462	8,088	10,863	6,565
Garage or carport					
Yes	60,979	9,346	15,978	21,441	14,214
No, but off-street parking is included	13,287	3,083	1,907	7,089	1,209
No cars, trucks, or vans	2,069	701	391	716	261
PERCENT DISTRIBUTION BY AMENITY					
Total homeowners	**100.0%**	**100.0%**	**100.0%**	**100.0%**	**100.0%**
Porch, deck, balcony, or patio	92.1	87.8	92.1	93.4	93.7
Telephone available	98.3	97.6	98.1	98.5	98.8
Usable fireplace	45.1	38.1	41.5	43.6	58.0
Separate dining room	57.2	66.6	53.8	57.5	52.7
With two or more living or recreation rooms	40.5	40.8	44.3	37.2	42.1
Garage or carport					
Yes	79.8	69.9	87.6	73.4	91.1
No, but off-street parking is included	17.4	23.0	10.5	24.3	7.7
No cars, trucks, or vans	2.7	5.2	2.1	2.5	1.7
PERCENT DISTRIBUTION BY REGION					
Total homeowners	**100.0%**	**17.5%**	**23.9%**	**38.2%**	**20.4%**
Porch, deck, balcony, or patio	100.0	16.7	23.9	38.7	20.8
Telephone available	100.0	17.4	23.8	38.3	20.5
Usable fireplace	100.0	14.8	22.0	36.9	26.3
Separate dining room	100.0	20.4	22.4	38.4	18.8
With two or more living or recreation rooms	100.0	17.6	26.1	35.1	21.2
Garage or carport					
Yes	100.0	15.3	26.2	35.2	23.3
No, but off-street parking is included	100.0	23.2	14.4	53.3	9.1
No cars, trucks, or vans	100.0	33.9	18.9	34.6	12.6

Source: Bureau of the Census, American Housing Survey for the United States: 2009, Internet site http://www.census.gov/hhes/ www/housing/ahs/ahs09/ahs09.html; calculations by New Strategist

Table 4.47 Homeowners by Deficiencies of Home and Region, 2009

Few homeowners report deficiencies in their home, regardless of region. The most common deficiency is signs of mice, reported by 7 percent of homeowners in the Northeast in the past three months.

(number and percent distribution of total homeowners and homeowners by region, by selected deficiencies of home, 2009; numbers in thousands)

	total	Northeast	Midwest	South	West
Total homeowners	**76,428**	**13,378**	**18,249**	**29,193**	**15,607**
Signs of rats in last three months	354	29	29	182	114
Signs of mice in last three months	3,984	1,002	1,050	1,443	489
Signs of rodents, not sure which kind, in last three months	164	27	29	79	30
Holes in floor	581	96	129	234	122
Open cracks or holes (interior)	3,101	536	814	1,188	562
Broken plaster or peeling paint (interior)	1,246	263	373	444	166
No electrical wiring	57	15	21	18	3
Exposed wiring	221	24	61	112	24
Rooms without electric outlets	650	116	227	228	78
PERCENT DISTRIBUTION BY DEFICIENCY					
Total homeowners	**100.0%**	**100.0%**	**100.0%**	**100.0%**	**100.0%**
Signs of rats in last three months	0.5	0.2	0.2	0.6	0.7
Signs of mice in last three months	5.2	7.5	5.8	4.9	3.1
Signs of rodents, not sure which kind, in last three months	0.2	0.2	0.2	0.3	0.2
Holes in floor	0.8	0.7	0.7	0.8	0.8
Open cracks or holes (interior)	4.1	4.0	4.5	4.1	3.6
Broken plaster or peeling paint (interior)	1.6	2.0	2.0	1.5	1.1
No electrical wiring	0.1	0.1	0.1	0.1	0.0
Exposed wiring	0.3	0.2	0.3	0.4	0.2
Rooms without electric outlets	0.8	0.9	1.2	0.8	0.5
PERCENT DISTRIBUTION BY REGION					
Total homeowners	**100.0%**	**17.5%**	**23.9%**	**38.2%**	**20.4%**
Signs of rats in last three months	100.0	8.3	8.3	51.2	32.2
Signs of mice in last three months	100.0	25.2	26.3	36.2	12.3
Signs of rodents, not sure which kind, in last three months	100.0	16.3	17.7	48.0	18.0
Holes in floor	100.0	16.6	22.1	40.3	21.0
Open cracks or holes (interior)	100.0	17.3	26.3	38.3	18.1
Broken plaster or peeling paint (interior)	100.0	21.1	29.9	35.7	13.3
No electrical wiring	100.0	26.3	36.1	31.6	6.0
Exposed wiring	100.0	10.7	27.8	50.7	10.8
Rooms without electric outlets	100.0	17.8	35.0	35.2	12.0

Source: Bureau of the Census, American Housing Survey for the United States: 2009, Internet site http://www.census.gov/hhes/www/housing/ahs/ahs09/ahs09.html; calculations by New Strategist

Table 4.48 Homeowners by Housing Equipment Failures, 2009: Northeast

Homeowners in the Northeast are more likely than average to have problems with outside water leakage. Twelve percent report water leaking into their home from outside the structure during the past year.

(number and percent distribution of total homeowners and homeowners in the Northeast, and Northeastern homeowners as a percent of total, by type of equipment failure, 2009; numbers in thousands)

	total		Northeast		
	number	percent distribution	number	percent distribution	percent of total
WATER SUPPLY STOPPAGE					
Homeowners with piped water	**76,371**	**100.0%**	**13,371**	**100.0%**	**17.5%**
No stoppage in last three months	73,494	96.2	12,888	96.4	17.5
With stoppage in last three months	2,031	2.7	337	2.5	16.6
Not reported	846	1.1	147	1.1	17.4
FLUSH TOILET BREAKDOWNS					
Homeowners with flush toilets	**76,391**	**100.0**	**13,376**	**100.0**	**17.5**
With at least one working toilet at all times, last three months	74,674	97.8	13,092	97.9	17.5
With no working toilet at least once in last three months	884	1.2	138	1.0	15.6
Not reported	833	1.1	146	1.1	17.5
WATER LEAKAGE DURING LAST 12 MONTHS					
Total homeowners	**76,428**	**100.0**	**13,378**	**100.0**	**17.5**
No leakage from within structure	70,356	92.1	12,345	92.3	17.5
With leakage from within structure*	5,170	6.8	893	6.7	17.3
Fixtures backed up or overflowed	1,188	1.6	168	1.3	14.2
Pipes leaked	2,145	2.8	443	3.3	20.7
Broken water heater	714	0.9	94	0.7	13.1
Other or unknown	1,263	1.7	212	1.6	16.7
Leakage not reported	902	1.2	141	1.1	15.6
No leakage from outside structure	67,686	88.6	11,578	86.5	17.1
With leakage from outside structure*	7,842	10.3	1,660	12.4	21.2
Roof	4,168	5.5	841	6.3	20.2
Basement	2,309	3.0	655	4.9	28.3
Walls, windows, or doors	1,165	1.5	189	1.4	16.3
Other or not reported	691	0.9	119	0.9	17.3
Leakage not reported	900	1.2	140	1.0	15.6

	total		Northeast		
	number	percent distribution	number	percent distribution	percent of total
HEATING PROBLEMS					
Homeowners with heating equipment and occupying home last winter	**75,215**	**100.0%**	**13,220**	**100.0%**	**17.6%**
Not uncomfortably cold for 24 or more hours last winter	67,769	90.1	11,565	87.5	17.1
Uncomfortably cold for 24 or more hours last winter*	6,055	8.1	1,364	10.3	22.5
Equipment breakdown	1,594	2.1	363	2.7	22.8
Utility interruption	2,139	2.8	495	3.7	23.2
Inadequate heating capacity	350	0.5	62	0.5	17.8
Inadequate insulation	394	0.5	88	0.7	22.4
Cost of heating	778	1.0	173	1.3	22.3
Other	1,022	1.4	235	1.8	23.0
Not reported	1,391	1.8	291	2.2	20.9
ELECTRICAL PROBLEMS					
Homeowners with electrical wiring	**76,371**	**100.0**	**13,363**	**100.0**	**17.5**
No fuses or breakers blown in last three months	68,697	90.0	12,059	90.2	17.6
With fuses or breakers blown in last three months	6,685	8.8	1,158	8.7	17.3
Not reported	989	1.3	146	1.1	14.8

* Figures do not add to total because more than one problem may have occurred.
Source: Bureau of the Census, American Housing Survey for the United States: 2009, Internet site http://www.census.gov/hhes/www/housing/ahs/ahs09/ahs09.html; calculations by New Strategist

Table 4.49 Homeowners by Housing Equipment Failures, 2009: Midwest

Homeowners in the Midwest are more likely than average to have problems with outside water leakage. Fifteen percent report water leaking into their home from outside the structure during the past year.

(number and percent distribution of total homeowners and homeowners in the Midwest, and Midwestern homeowners as a percent of total, by type of equipment failure, 2009; numbers in thousands)

	total		Midwest		
	number	percent distribution	number	percent distribution	percent of total
WATER SUPPLY STOPPAGE					
Homeowners with piped water	**76,371**	**100.0%**	**18,235**	**100.0%**	**23.9%**
No stoppage in last three months	73,494	96.2	17,566	96.3	23.9
With stoppage in last three months	2,031	2.7	519	2.8	25.6
Not reported	846	1.1	150	0.8	17.7
FLUSH TOILET BREAKDOWNS					
Homeowners with flush toilets	**76,391**	**100.0**	**18,236**	**100.0**	**23.9**
With at least one working toilet at all times, last three months	74,674	97.8	17,901	98.2	24.0
With no working toilet at least once in last three months	884	1.2	192	1.1	21.7
Not reported	833	1.1	143	0.8	17.2
WATER LEAKAGE DURING LAST 12 MONTHS					
Total homeowners	**76,428**	**100.0**	**18,249**	**100.0**	**23.9**
No leakage from within structure	70,356	92.1	16,695	91.5	23.7
With leakage from within structure*	5,170	6.8	1,406	7.7	27.2
Fixtures backed up or overflowed	1,188	1.6	349	1.9	29.3
Pipes leaked	2,145	2.8	526	2.9	24.5
Broken water heater	714	0.9	169	0.9	23.7
Other or unknown	1,263	1.7	401	2.2	31.8
Leakage not reported	902	1.2	149	0.8	16.5
No leakage from outside structure	67,686	88.6	15,346	84.1	22.7
With leakage from outside structure*	7,842	10.3	2,750	15.1	35.1
Roof	4,168	5.5	1,040	5.7	25.0
Basement	2,309	3.0	1,329	7.3	57.6
Walls, windows, or doors	1,165	1.5	385	2.1	33.0
Other or not reported	691	0.9	219	1.2	31.7
Leakage not reported	900	1.2	153	0.8	17.0

	total		Midwest		
	number	percent distribution	number	percent distribution	percent of total
HEATING PROBLEMS					
Homeowners with heating equipment and occupying home last winter	**75,215**	**100.0%**	**18,033**	**100.0%**	**24.0%**
Not uncomfortably cold for 24 or more hours last winter	67,769	90.1	16,140	89.5	23.8
Uncomfortably cold for 24 or more hours last winter*	6,055	8.1	1,649	9.1	27.2
Equipment breakdown	1,594	2.1	494	2.7	31.0
Utility interruption	2,139	2.8	579	3.2	27.1
Inadequate heating capacity	350	0.5	93	0.5	26.5
Inadequate insulation	394	0.5	94	0.5	24.0
Cost of heating	778	1.0	202	1.1	25.9
Other	1,022	1.4	258	1.4	25.3
Not reported	1,391	1.8	244	1.4	17.5
ELECTRICAL PROBLEMS					
Homeowners with electrical wiring	**76,371**	**100.0**	**18,229**	**100.0**	**23.9**
No fuses or breakers blown in last three months	68,697	90.0	16,144	88.6	23.5
With fuses or breakers blown in last three months	6,685	8.8	1,922	10.5	28.7
Not reported	989	1.3	163	0.9	16.5

* Figures do not add to total because more than one problem may have occurred.
Source: Bureau of the Census, American Housing Survey for the United States: 2009, Internet site http://www.census.gov/hhes/www/housing/ahs/ahs09/ahs09.html; calculations by New Strategist

Table 4.50 Homeowners by Housing Equipment Failures, 2009: South

Homeowners in the South are slightly less likely than the average homeowner to have been uncomfortably cold for 24 or more hours last winter.

(number and percent distribution of total homeowners and homeowners in the South, and Southern homeowners as a percent of total, by type of equipment failure, 2009; numbers in thousands)

	total		South		
	number	percent distribution	number	percent distribution	percent of total
WATER SUPPLY STOPPAGE					
Homeowners with piped water	**76,371**	**100.0%**	**29,164**	**100.0%**	**38.2%**
No stoppage in last three months	73,494	96.2	28,034	96.1	38.1
With stoppage in last three months	2,031	2.7	713	2.4	35.1
Not reported	846	1.1	417	1.4	49.3
FLUSH TOILET BREAKDOWNS					
Homeowners with flush toilets	**76,391**	**100.0**	**29,175**	**100.0**	**38.2**
With at least one working toilet at all times, last three months	74,674	97.8	28,412	97.4	38.0
With no working toilet at least once in last three months	884	1.2	351	1.2	39.7
Not reported	833	1.1	412	1.4	49.5
WATER LEAKAGE DURING LAST 12 MONTHS					
Total homeowners	**76,428**	**100.0**	**29,193**	**100.0**	**38.2**
No leakage from within structure	70,356	92.1	26,922	92.2	38.3
With leakage from within structure*	5,170	6.8	1,825	6.3	35.3
Fixtures backed up or overflowed	1,188	1.6	369	1.3	31.1
Pipes leaked	2,145	2.8	797	2.7	37.2
Broken water heater	714	0.9	283	1.0	39.6
Other or unknown	1,263	1.7	418	1.4	33.1
Leakage not reported	902	1.2	446	1.5	49.5
No leakage from outside structure	67,686	88.6	26,381	90.4	39.0
With leakage from outside structure*	7,842	10.3	2,365	8.1	30.2
Roof	4,168	5.5	1,683	5.8	40.4
Basement	2,309	3.0	190	0.7	8.2
Walls, windows, or doors	1,165	1.5	367	1.3	31.5
Other or not reported	691	0.9	230	0.8	33.3
Leakage not reported	900	1.2	447	1.5	49.7

	total		South		
	number	percent distribution	number	percent distribution	percent of total
HEATING PROBLEMS					
Homeowners with heating equipment and occupying home last winter	**75,215**	**100.0%**	**28,839**	**100.0%**	**38.3%**
Not uncomfortably cold for 24 or more hours last winter	67,769	90.1	26,272	91.1	38.8
Uncomfortably cold for 24 or more hours last winter*	6,055	8.1	1,945	6.7	32.1
Equipment breakdown	1,594	2.1	460	1.6	28.9
Utility interruption	2,139	2.8	793	2.7	37.1
Inadequate heating capacity	350	0.5	106	0.4	30.2
Inadequate insulation	394	0.5	106	0.4	27.0
Cost of heating	778	1.0	203	0.7	26.1
Other	1,022	1.4	313	1.1	30.6
Not reported	1,391	1.8	621	2.2	44.6
ELECTRICAL PROBLEMS					
Homeowners with electrical wiring	76,371	100.0	29,175	100.0	38.2
No fuses or breakers blown in last three months	68,697	90.0	26,408	90.5	38.4
With fuses or breakers blown in last three months	6,685	8.8	2,254	7.7	33.7
Not reported	989	1.3	512	1.8	51.8

Figures do not add to total because more than one problem may have occurred.
Source: Bureau of the Census, American Housing Survey for the United States: 2009, Internet site http://www.census.gov/hhes/ www/housing/ahs/ahs09/ahs09.html; calculations by New Strategist

Table 4.51 Homeowners by Housing Equipment Failures, 2009: West

Homeowners in the West are less likely than average to have problems with outside water leakage. Only 7 percent report water leaking into their home from outside the structure during the past year.

(number and percent distribution of total homeowners and homeowners in the West, and Western homeowners as a percent of total, by type of equipment failure, 2009; numbers in thousands)

	total		West		
	number	percent distribution	number	percent distribution	percent of total
WATER SUPPLY STOPPAGE					
Homeowners with piped water	**76,371**	**100.0%**	**15,601**	**100.0%**	**20.4 %**
No stoppage in last three months	73,494	96.2	15,007	96.2	20.4
With stoppage in last three months	2,031	2.7	461	3.0	22.7
Not reported	846	1.1	133	0.9	15.7
FLUSH TOILET BREAKDOWNS					
Homeowners with flush toilets	**76,391**	**100.0**	**15,604**	**100.0**	**20.4**
With at least one working toilet at all times, last three months	74,674	97.8	15,269	97.9	20.4
With no working toilet at least once in last three months	884	1.2	203	1.3	23.0
Not reported	833	1.1	132	0.8	15.9
WATER LEAKAGE DURING LAST 12 MONTHS					
Total homeowners	**76,428**	**100.0**	**15,607**	**100.0**	**20.4**
No leakage from within structure	70,356	92.1	14,394	92.2	20.5
With leakage from within structure*	5,170	6.8	1,047	6.7	20.2
Fixtures backed up or overflowed	1,188	1.6	302	1.9	25.4
Pipes leaked	2,145	2.8	379	2.4	17.7
Broken water heater	714	0.9	169	1.1	23.6
Other or unknown	1,263	1.7	232	1.5	18.4
Leakage not reported	902	1.2	167	1.1	18.5
No leakage from outside structure	67,686	88.6	14,381	92.1	21.2
With leakage from outside structure*	7,842	10.3	1,067	6.8	13.6
Roof	4,168	5.5	603	3.9	14.5
Basement	2,309	3.0	135	0.9	5.8
Walls, windows, or doors	1,165	1.5	225	1.4	19.3
Other or not reported	691	0.9	123	0.8	17.7
Leakage not reported	900	1.2	159	1.0	17.7

	total		West		
	number	percent distribution	number	percent distribution	percent of total
HEATING PROBLEMS					
Homeowners with heating equipment and occupying home last winter	**75,215**	**100.0%**	**15,123**	**100.0%**	**20.1%**
Not uncomfortably cold for 24 or more hours last winter	67,769	90.1	13,791	91.2	20.3
Uncomfortably cold for 24 or more hours last winter*	6,055	8.1	1,098	7.3	18.1
Equipment breakdown	1,594	2.1	277	1.8	17.4
Utility interruption	2,139	2.8	272	1.8	12.7
Inadequate heating capacity	350	0.5	89	0.6	25.5
Inadequate insulation	394	0.5	105	0.7	26.6
Cost of heating	778	1.0	200	1.3	25.7
Other	1,022	1.4	215	1.4	21.1
Not reported	1,391	1.8	234	1.5	16.8
ELECTRICAL PROBLEMS					
Homeowners with electrical wiring	**76,371**	**100.0**	**15,604**	**100.0**	**20.4**
No fuses or breakers blown in last three months	68,697	90.0	14,085	90.3	20.5
With fuses or breakers blown in last three months	6,685	8.8	1,351	8.7	20.2
Not reported	989	1.3	168	1.1	17.0

*Figures do not add to total because more than one problem may have occurred.
Source: Bureau of the Census, American Housing Survey for the United States: 2009, Internet site http://www.census.gov/hhes/www/housing/ahs/ahs09/ahs09.html; calculations by New Strategist

Table 4.52 Homeowners by Purchase Price of Home, 2009: Northeast

The median purchase price of owned homes in the Northeast was
slightly greater than the national median—$115,000 versus $107,500.

(number and percent distribution of total homeowners and homeowners in the Northeast, by purchase price, 2009; numbers in thousands)

	total		Northeast		
	number	percent distribution	number	percent distribution	percent of total
TOTAL HOMEOWNERS	**76,428**	**100.0%**	**13,378**	**100.0%**	**17.5%**
Home purchased or built	**71,877**	**94.0**	**12,346**	**92.3**	**17.2**
Under $10,000	2,799	3.7	460	3.4	16.4
$10,000 to $19,999	4,229	5.5	747	5.6	17.7
$20,000 to $29,999	3,648	4.8	683	5.1	18.7
$30,000 to $39,999	3,489	4.6	682	5.1	19.5
$40,000 to $49,999	3,002	3.9	511	3.8	17.0
$50,000 to $59,999	3,076	4.0	459	3.4	14.9
$60,000 to $69,999	3,126	4.1	450	3.4	14.4
$70,000 to $79,999	2,968	3.9	412	3.1	13.9
$80,000 to $99,999	5,662	7.4	780	5.8	13.8
$100,000 to $119,999	4,288	5.6	643	4.8	15.0
$120,000 to $149,999	6,691	8.8	962	7.2	14.4
$150,000 to $199,999	8,055	10.5	1,408	10.5	17.5
$200,000 to $249,999	5,029	6.6	886	6.6	17.6
$250,000 to $299,999	3,024	4.0	553	4.1	18.3
$300,000 or more	8,594	11.2	1,766	13.2	20.5
Not reported	4,196	5.5	944	7.1	22.5
Median purchase price	$107,500	–	$115,000	–	–
Received as inheritance or gift	**3,388**	**4.4**	**729**	**5.5**	**21.5**
Not reported	**1,163**	**1.5**	**303**	**2.3**	**26.0**

Note: "–" means not applicable.
Source: Bureau of the Census, American Housing Survey for the United States: 2009, Internet site http://www.census.gov/hhes/www/housing/ahs/ahs09/ahs09.html; calculations by New Strategist

Table 4.53 Homeowners by Purchase Price of Home, 2009: Midwest

The median purchase price of owned homes in the Midwest was
well below the national median—$89,900 versus $107,500.

*(number and percent distribution of total homeowners and homeowners in the Midwest, by purchase price, 2009;
numbers in thousands)*

	total		Midwest		
	number	percent distribution	number	percent distribution	percent of total
TOTAL HOMEOWNERS	**76,428**	**100.0%**	**18,249**	**100.0%**	**23.9%**
Home purchased or built	**71,877**	**94.0**	**17,380**	**95.2**	**24.2**
Under $10,000	2,799	3.7	694	3.8	24.8
$10,000 to $19,999	4,229	5.5	1,174	6.4	27.7
$20,000 to $29,999	3,648	4.8	979	5.4	26.8
$30,000 to $39,999	3,489	4.6	958	5.2	27.4
$40,000 to $49,999	3,002	3.9	850	4.7	28.3
$50,000 to $59,999	3,076	4.0	945	5.2	30.7
$60,000 to $69,999	3,126	4.1	921	5.0	29.5
$70,000 to $79,999	2,968	3.9	805	4.4	27.1
$80,000 to $99,999	5,662	7.4	1,569	8.6	27.7
$100,000 to $119,999	4,288	5.6	1,210	6.6	28.2
$120,000 to $149,999	6,691	8.8	1,806	9.9	27.0
$150,000 to $199,999	8,055	10.5	1,939	10.6	24.1
$200,000 to $249,999	5,029	6.6	1,006	5.5	20.0
$250,000 to $299,999	3,024	4.0	565	3.1	18.7
$300,000 or more	8,594	11.2	1,032	5.7	12.0
Not reported	4,196	5.5	928	5.1	22.1
Median purchase price	$107,500	–	$89,900	–	–
Received as inheritance or gift	**3,388**	**4.4**	**683**	**3.7**	**20.2**
Not reported	**1,163**	**1.5**	**186**	**1.0**	**16.0**

Note: "–" means not applicable.
Source: Bureau of the Census, American Housing Survey for the United States: 2009, Internet site http://www.census.gov/hhes/www/housing/ahs/ahs09/ahs09.html; calculations by New Strategist

Table 4.54 Homeowners by Purchase Price of Home, 2009: South

The median purchase price of owned homes in the South was
well below the national median—$91,500 versus $107,500.

(number and percent distribution of total homeowners and homeowners in the South, by purchase price, 2009; numbers in thousands)

	total		South		
	number	percent distribution	number	percent distribution	percent of total
TOTAL HOMEOWNERS	**76,428**	**100.0%**	**29,193**	**100.0%**	**38.2%**
Home purchased or built	**71,877**	**94.0**	**27,307**	**93.5**	**38.0**
Under $10,000	2,799	3.7	1,265	4.3	45.2
$10,000 to $19,999	4,229	5.5	1,684	5.8	39.8
$20,000 to $29,999	3,648	4.8	1,515	5.2	41.5
$30,000 to $39,999	3,489	4.6	1,429	4.9	41.0
$40,000 to $49,999	3,002	3.9	1,239	4.2	41.3
$50,000 to $59,999	3,076	4.0	1,335	4.6	43.4
$60,000 to $69,999	3,126	4.1	1,343	4.6	43.0
$70,000 to $79,999	2,968	3.9	1,333	4.6	44.9
$80,000 to $99,999	5,662	7.4	2,426	8.3	42.9
$100,000 to $119,999	4,288	5.6	1,685	5.8	39.3
$120,000 to $149,999	6,691	8.8	2,647	9.1	39.6
$150,000 to $199,999	8,055	10.5	2,755	9.4	34.2
$200,000 to $249,999	5,029	6.6	1,680	5.8	33.4
$250,000 to $299,999	3,024	4.0	1,004	3.4	33.2
$300,000 or more	8,594	11.2	2,238	7.7	26.0
Not reported	4,196	5.5	1,729	5.9	41.2
Median purchase price	$107,500	–	$91,500	–	–
Received as inheritance or gift	**3,388**	**4.4**	**1,411**	**4.8**	**41.7**
Not reported	**1,163**	**1.5**	**475**	**1.6**	**40.8**

Note: "–" means not applicable.
Source: Bureau of the Census, American Housing Survey for the United States: 2009, Internet site http://www.census.gov/hhes/ www/housing/ahs/ahs09/ahs09.html; calculations by New Strategist

Table 4.55 Homeowners by Purchase Price of Home, 2009: West

The median purchase price of owned homes in the West was much
greater than the national median—$165,000 versus $107,500.

(number and percent distribution of total homeowners and homeowners in the West, by purchase price, 2009;
numbers in thousands)

	total		West		
	number	percent distribution	number	percent distribution	percent of total
TOTAL HOMEOWNERS	**76,428**	**100.0%**	**15,607**	**100.0%**	**20.4%**
Home purchased or built	**71,877**	**94.0**	**14,843**	**95.1**	**20.7**
Under $10,000	2,799	3.7	381	2.4	13.6
$10,000 to $19,999	4,229	5.5	625	4.0	14.8
$20,000 to $29,999	3,648	4.8	472	3.0	12.9
$30,000 to $39,999	3,489	4.6	421	2.7	12.1
$40,000 to $49,999	3,002	3.9	403	2.6	13.4
$50,000 to $59,999	3,076	4.0	337	2.2	10.9
$60,000 to $69,999	3,126	4.1	411	2.6	13.2
$70,000 to $79,999	2,968	3.9	418	2.7	14.1
$80,000 to $99,999	5,662	7.4	887	5.7	15.7
$100,000 to $119,999	4,288	5.6	751	4.8	17.5
$120,000 to $149,999	6,691	8.8	1,275	8.2	19.1
$150,000 to $199,999	8,055	10.5	1,953	12.5	24.2
$200,000 to $249,999	5,029	6.6	1,457	9.3	29.0
$250,000 to $299,999	3,024	4.0	902	5.8	29.8
$300,000 or more	8,594	11.2	3,558	22.8	41.4
Not reported	4,196	5.5	595	3.8	14.2
Median purchase price	$107,500	–	$165,000	–	–
Received as inheritance or gift	**3,388**	**4.4**	**564**	**3.6**	**16.7**
Not reported	**1,163**	**1.5**	**200**	**1.3**	**17.2**

Note: "–" means not applicable.
Source: Bureau of the Census, American Housing Survey for the United States: 2009, Internet site http://www.census.gov/hhes/
www/housing/ahs/ahs09/ahs09.html; calculations by New Strategist

Table 4.56. Homeowners by Value of Home, 2009: Northeast

The median value of homes in the Northeast was 35 percent greater
than the national median in 2009—$230,000 versus $170,000.

(number and percent distribution of total homeowners and homeowners in the Northeast by current self-reported value of home, 2009; numbers in thousands)

	total		Northeast		
	number	percent distribution	number	percent distribution	percent of total
Total homeowners	**76,428**	**100.0%**	**13,378**	**100.0%**	**17.5%**
Under $10,000	1,696	2.2	209	1.6	12.3
$10,000 to $19,999	1,311	1.7	154	1.2	11.8
$20,000 to $29,999	1,073	1.4	134	1.0	12.5
$30,000 to $39,999	1,187	1.6	174	1.3	14.7
$40,000 to $59,999	3,155	4.1	410	3.1	13.0
$60,000 to $79,999	5,261	6.9	633	4.7	12.0
$80,000 to $99,999	6,002	7.9	754	5.6	12.6
$100,000 to $119,999	4,980	6.5	524	3.9	10.5
$120,000 to $149,999	7,629	10.0	836	6.3	11.0
$150,000 to $199,999	11,141	14.6	1,682	12.6	15.1
$200,000 to $299,999	13,494	17.7	2,640	19.7	19.6
$300,000 to $399,999	7,924	10.4	2,025	15.1	25.6
$400,000 to $499,999	4,200	5.5	1,342	10.0	32.0
$500,000 to $749,999	4,577	6.0	1,268	9.5	27.7
$750,000 or more	2,798	3.7	591	4.4	21.1
Median home value	$170,000	–	$230,000	–	–

Note: "–" means nonapplicable.
Source: Bureau of the Census, American Housing Survey for the United States: 2009, Internet site http://www.census.gov/hhes/ www/housing/ahs/ahs09/ahs09.html; calculations by New Strategist

Table 4.57 Homeowners by Value of Home, 2007 and 2009: Northeast

Median home value fell 12 percent in the Northeast between 2007 and 2009.

(number of homeowners in the Northeast by current self-reported value of home, 2007 and 2009, percent change in number of homeowners by value and in median home value, 2007–09; numbers in thousands)

	2009	2007	percent change
Total homeowners in the Northeast	**13,378**	**13,339**	**0.3%**
Under $10,000	209	200	4.7
$10,000 to $19,999	154	91	69.6
$20,000 to $29,999	134	146	−8.0
$30,000 to $39,999	174	184	−5.4
$40,000 to $59,999	410	355	15.6
$60,000 to $79,999	633	509	24.3
$80,000 to $99,999	754	672	12.2
$100,000 to $119,999	524	578	−9.4
$120,000 to $149,999	836	868	−3.6
$150,000 to $199,999	1,682	1,381	21.8
$200,000 to $299,999	2,640	2,698	−2.1
$300,000 to $399,999	2,025	2,080	−2.6
$400,000 to $499,999	1,342	1,339	0.2
$500,000 to $749,999	1,268	1,495	−15.2
$750,000 or more	591	745	−20.7
Median home value	$230,000	$262,526	−12.4

Source: Bureau of the Census, American Housing Survey for the United States: 2009, Internet site http://www.census.gov/hhes/ www/housing/ahs/ahs09/ahs09.html; calculations by New Strategist

Table 4.58 Homeowners by Value of Home, 2009: Midwest

The median value of homes in the Midwest was 21 percent less
than the national median in 2009—$134,000 versus $170,000.

(number and percent distribution of total homeowners and homeowners in the Midwest by current self-reported value of home, 2009; numbers in thousands)

	total		Midwest		
	number	percent distribution	number	percent distribution	percent of total
Total homeowners	**76,428**	**100.0%**	**18,249**	**100.0%**	**23.9%**
Under $10,000	1,696	2.2	323	1.8	19.0
$10,000 to $19,999	1,311	1.7	307	1.7	23.4
$20,000 to $29,999	1,073	1.4	251	1.4	23.4
$30,000 to $39,999	1,187	1.6	261	1.4	22.0
$40,000 to $59,999	3,155	4.1	968	5.3	30.7
$60,000 to $79,999	5,261	6.9	1,841	10.1	35.0
$80,000 to $99,999	6,002	7.9	1,958	10.7	32.6
$100,000 to $119,999	4,980	6.5	1,728	9.5	34.7
$120,000 to $149,999	7,629	10.0	2,487	13.6	32.6
$150,000 to $199,999	11,141	14.6	3,162	17.3	28.4
$200,000 to $299,999	13,494	17.7	2,857	15.7	21.2
$300,000 to $399,999	7,924	10.4	1,087	6.0	13.7
$400,000 to $499,999	4,200	5.5	415	2.3	9.9
$500,000 to $749,999	4,577	6.0	400	2.2	8.7
$750,000 or more	2,798	3.7	204	1.1	7.3
Median home value	$170,000	–	$134,000	–	–

Note: "–" means nonapplicable.
Source: Bureau of the Census, American Housing Survey for the United States: 2009, Internet site http://www.census.gov/hhes/ www/housing/ahs/ahs09/ahs09.html; calculations by New Strategist

Table 4.59 Homeowners by Value of Home, 2007 and 2009: Midwest

Median home value fell 7 percent in the Midwest between 2007 and 2009.

(number of homeowners in the Midwest by current self-reported value of home, 2007 and 2009, percent change in number of homeowners by value and in median home value, 2007–09; numbers in thousands)

	2009	2007	percent change
Total homeowners in the Midwest	**18,249**	**18,194**	**0.3%**
Under $10,000	323	298	8.3
$10,000 to $19,999	307	315	–2.6
$20,000 to $29,999	251	239	5.0
$30,000 to $39,999	261	260	0.5
$40,000 to $59,999	968	785	23.3
$60,000 to $79,999	1,841	1,685	9.3
$80,000 to $99,999	1,958	2,008	–2.5
$100,000 to $119,999	1,728	1,495	15.6
$120,000 to $149,999	2,487	2,550	–2.5
$150,000 to $199,999	3,162	3,099	2.0
$200,000 to $299,999	2,857	3,090	–7.5
$300,000 to $399,999	1,087	1,198	–9.2
$400,000 to $499,999	415	507	–18.2
$500,000 to $749,999	400	452	–11.6
$750,000 or more	204	214	–4.8
Median home value	$134,000	$143,675	–6.7

Source: Bureau of the Census, American Housing Survey for the United States: 2009, Internet site http://www.census.gov/hhes/ www/housing/ahs/ahs09/ahs09.html; calculations by New Strategist

Table 4.60 Homeowners by Value of Home, 2009: South

The median value of homes in the South was 18 percent less than
the national median in 2009—$140,000 versus $170,000.

(number and percent distribution of total homeowners and homeowners in the South by current self-reported value of home, 2009; numbers in thousands)

	total		South		
	number	percent distribution	number	percent distribution	percent of total
Total homeowners	**76,428**	**100.0%**	**29,193**	**100.0%**	**38.2%**
Under $10,000	1,696	2.2	783	2.7	46.2
$10,000 to $19,999	1,311	1.7	660	2.3	50.4
$20,000 to $29,999	1,073	1.4	577	2.0	53.8
$30,000 to $39,999	1,187	1.6	620	2.1	52.3
$40,000 to $59,999	3,155	4.1	1,468	5.0	46.5
$60,000 to $79,999	5,261	6.9	2,341	8.0	44.5
$80,000 to $99,999	6,002	7.9	2,882	9.9	48.0
$100,000 to $119,999	4,980	6.5	2,281	7.8	45.8
$120,000 to $149,999	7,629	10.0	3,573	12.2	46.8
$150,000 to $199,999	11,141	14.6	4,494	15.4	40.3
$200,000 to $299,999	13,494	17.7	4,549	15.6	33.7
$300,000 to $399,999	7,924	10.4	2,390	8.2	30.2
$400,000 to $499,999	4,200	5.5	993	3.4	23.7
$500,000 to $749,999	4,577	6.0	980	3.4	21.4
$750,000 or more	2,798	3.7	602	2.1	21.5
Median home value	$170,000	–	$140,000	–	–

Note: "–" means nonapplicable.
Source: Bureau of the Census, American Housing Survey for the United States: 2009, Internet site http://www.census.gov/hhes/www/housing/ahs/ahs09/ahs09.html; calculations by New Strategist

Table 4.61 Homeowners by Value of Home, 2007 and 2009: South

Median home value fell 10 percent in the South between 2007 and 2009.

(number of homeowners in the South by current self-reported value of home, 2007 and 2009, percent change in number of homeowners by value and in median home value, 2007–09; numbers in thousands)

	2009	2007	percent change
Total homeowners in the South	**29,193**	**28,508**	**2.4%**
Under $10,000	783	826	−5.2
$10,000 to $19,999	660	647	2.0
$20,000 to $29,999	577	546	5.7
$30,000 to $39,999	620	591	4.9
$40,000 to $59,999	1,468	1,673	−12.3
$60,000 to $79,999	2,341	2,160	8.4
$80,000 to $99,999	2,882	2,458	17.2
$100,000 to $119,999	2,281	1,996	14.3
$120,000 to $149,999	3,573	2,856	25.1
$150,000 to $199,999	4,494	4,117	9.2
$200,000 to $299,999	4,549	4,671	−2.6
$300,000 to $399,999	2,390	2,545	−6.1
$400,000 to $499,999	993	1,280	−22.4
$500,000 to $749,999	980	1,359	−27.9
$750,000 or more	602	783	−23.1
Median home value	$140,000	$156,092	−10.3

Source: Bureau of the Census, American Housing Survey for the United States: 2009, Internet site http://www.census.gov/hhes/ www/housing/ahs/ahs09/ahs09.html; calculations by New Strategist

Table 4.62 Homeowners by Value of Home, 2009: West

The median value of homes in the West was 59 percent greater
than the national median in 2009—$270,000 versus $170,000.

*(number and percent distribution of total homeowners and homeowners in the West by current self-reported value
of home, 2009; numbers in thousands)*

	total		West		
	number	percent distribution	number	percent distribution	percent of total
Total homeowners	**76,428**	**100.0%**	**15,607**	**100.0%**	**20.4%**
Under $10,000	1,696	2.2	381	2.4	22.4
$10,000 to $19,999	1,311	1.7	190	1.2	14.5
$20,000 to $29,999	1,073	1.4	110	0.7	10.3
$30,000 to $39,999	1,187	1.6	131	0.8	11.1
$40,000 to $59,999	3,155	4.1	309	2.0	9.8
$60,000 to $79,999	5,261	6.9	447	2.9	8.5
$80,000 to $99,999	6,002	7.9	409	2.6	6.8
$100,000 to $119,999	4,980	6.5	447	2.9	9.0
$120,000 to $149,999	7,629	10.0	732	4.7	9.6
$150,000 to $199,999	11,141	14.6	1,803	11.6	16.2
$200,000 to $299,999	13,494	17.7	3,447	22.1	25.5
$300,000 to $399,999	7,924	10.4	2,421	15.5	30.6
$400,000 to $499,999	4,200	5.5	1,449	9.3	34.5
$500,000 to $749,999	4,577	6.0	1,930	12.4	42.2
$750,000 or more	2,798	3.7	1,402	9.0	50.1
Median home value	$170,000	–	$270,000	–	–

Note: "–" means nonapplicable.
Source: Bureau of the Census, American Housing Survey for the United States: 2009, Internet site http://www.census.gov/hhes/
www/housing/ahs/ahs09/ahs09.html; calculations by New Strategist

Table 4.63 Homeowners by Value of Home, 2007 and 2009: West

Median home value fell 24 percent in the West between 2007 and 2009.

(number of homeowners in the West by current self-reported value of home, 2007 and 2009, percent change in number of homeowners by value and in median home value, 2007–09; numbers in thousands)

	2009	2007	percent change
Total homeowners in the West	**15,607**	**15,607**	**0.0%**
Under $10,000	381	663	–42.6
$10,000 to $19,999	190	122	55.7
$20,000 to $29,999	110	157	–29.9
$30,000 to $39,999	131	162	–18.9
$40,000 to $59,999	309	298	3.7
$60,000 to $79,999	447	368	21.4
$80,000 to $99,999	409	361	13.2
$100,000 to $119,999	447	244	83.1
$120,000 to $149,999	732	462	58.5
$150,000 to $199,999	1,803	1,046	72.4
$200,000 to $299,999	3,447	2,673	29.0
$300,000 to $399,999	2,421	2,237	8.2
$400,000 to $499,999	1,449	1,614	–10.2
$500,000 to $749,999	1,930	2,928	–34.1
$750,000 or more	1,402	2,272	–38.3
Median home value	$270,000	$355,752	–24.1

Source: Bureau of the Census, American Housing Survey for the United States: 2009, Internet site http://www.census.gov/hhes/www/housing/ahs/ahs09/ahs09.html; calculations by New Strategist

Table 4.64 Homeowners by Major Source of Down Payment and Region, 2009

The 52 percent majority of homeowners in the Northeast used
savings or cash on hand as their primary source of down payment.

(number and percent distribution of total homeowners and homeowners by region, by primary source of down payment, 2009; numbers in thousands)

	total	Northeast	Midwest	South	West
Home purchased or built	**71,877**	**12,346**	**17,380**	**27,307**	**14,843**
Sale of previous home	21,946	3,387	5,861	7,760	4,938
Savings or cash on hand	31,437	6,474	7,094	11,680	6,189
Sale of other investment	750	106	150	247	246
Borrowing, other than mortgage on this property	2,409	385	589	959	477
Inheritance or gift	1,358	271	355	390	343
Land where building built used for financing	639	64	142	378	55
Other	3,125	430	786	1,279	630
No down payment	8,346	871	2,049	3,808	1,619
Not reported	1,867	359	354	808	347

PERCENT DISTRIBUTION BY SOURCE OF DOWNPAYMENT

	total	Northeast	Midwest	South	West
Home purchased or built	**100.0%**	**100.0%**	**100.0%**	**100.0%**	**100.0%**
Sale of previous home	30.5	27.4	33.7	28.4	33.3
Savings or cash on hand	43.7	52.4	40.8	42.8	41.7
Sale of other investment	1.0	0.9	0.9	0.9	1.7
Borrowing, other than mortgage on this property	3.4	3.1	3.4	3.5	3.2
Inheritance or gift	1.9	2.2	2.0	1.4	2.3
Land where building built used for financing	0.9	0.5	0.8	1.4	0.4
Other	4.3	3.5	4.5	4.7	4.2
No down payment	11.6	7.1	11.8	13.9	10.9
Not reported	2.6	2.9	2.0	3.0	2.3

PERCENT DISTRIBUTION BY REGION

	total	Northeast	Midwest	South	West
Home purchased or built	**100.0%**	**17.2%**	**24.2%**	**38.0%**	**20.7%**
Sale of previous home	100.0	15.4	26.7	35.4	22.5
Savings or cash on hand	100.0	20.6	22.6	37.2	19.7
Sale of other investment	100.0	14.1	20.1	33.0	32.8
Borrowing, other than mortgage on this property	100.0	16.0	24.4	39.8	19.8
Inheritance or gift	100.0	19.9	26.2	28.7	25.2
Land where building built used for financing	100.0	10.0	22.2	59.1	8.6
Other	100.0	13.8	25.1	40.9	20.2
No down payment	100.0	10.4	24.6	45.6	19.4
Not reported	100.0	19.2	18.9	43.2	18.6

Source: Bureau of the Census, American Housing Survey for the United States: 2009, Internet site http://www.census.gov/hhes/ www/housing/ahs/ahs09/ahs09.html; calculations by New Strategist

Table 4.65 Homeowners by First Home and Mortgage Status, 2009: Northeast

The 51 percent majority of homeowners in the Northeast are in their first home. Sixty-six percent of homeowners in the region have a mortgage or home equity loan, while 31 percent own their home free and clear.

(number and percent distribution of total homeowners and homeowners in the Northeast, by mortgage status, 2009; numbers in thousands)

	total		Northeast		
	number	percent distribution	number	percent distribution	percent of total
FIRST-TIME HOME STATUS					
Total homeowners	**76,428**	**100.0%**	**13,378**	**100.0%**	**17.5%**
First home ever owned	31,676	41.4	6,761	50.5	21.3
Not first home	43,233	56.6	6,243	46.7	14.4
Not reported	1,519	2.0	374	2.8	24.6
MORTGAGE STATUS					
Total homeowners	**76,428**	**100.0**	**13,378**	**100.0**	**17.5**
None, owned free and clear	24,206	31.7	4,122	30.8	17.0
Reverse mortgage	252	0.3	33	0.2	13.2
With regular and/or home-equity mortgages	50,300	65.8	8,839	66.1	17.6
Regular mortgage(s)	46,703	61.1	7,848	58.7	16.8
Home-equity lump-sum mortgage	4,022	5.3	984	7.4	24.5
Home-equity line of credit	9,184	12.0	1,935	14.5	21.1
Not reported	1,670	2.2	384	2.9	23.0

Source: Bureau of the Census, American Housing Survey for the United States: 2009, Internet site http://www.census.gov/hhes/www/housing/ahs/ahs09/ahs09.html; calculations by New Strategist

Table 4.66 Homeowners by First Home and Mortgage Status, 2009: Midwest

Only 40 percent of homeowners in the Midwest are in their first home. Sixty-eight percent of homeowners in the region have a mortgage or home equity loan, while 31 percent own their home free and clear.

(number and percent distribution of total homeowners and homeowners in the Midwest, by mortgage status, 2009; numbers in thousands)

	total		Midwest		
	number	percent distribution	number	percent distribution	percent of total
FIRST-HOME STATUS					
Total homeowners	**76,428**	**100.0%**	**18,249**	**100.0%**	**23.9%**
First home ever owned	31,676	41.4	7,362	40.3	23.2
Not first home	43,233	56.6	10,625	58.2	24.6
Not reported	1,519	2.0	263	1.4	17.3
MORTGAGE STATUS					
Total homeowners	**76,428**	**100.0**	**18,249**	**100.0**	**23.9**
None, owned free and clear	24,206	31.7	5,566	30.5	23.0
Reverse mortgage	252	0.3	33	0.2	13.0
With regular and/or home-equity mortgages	50,300	65.8	12,357	67.7	24.6
Regular mortgage(s)	46,703	61.1	11,461	62.8	24.5
Home-equity lump-sum mortgage	4,022	5.3	1,139	6.2	28.3
Home-equity line of credit	9,184	12.0	2,408	13.2	26.2
Not reported	1,670	2.2	294	1.6	17.6

Source: Bureau of the Census, American Housing Survey for the United States: 2009, Internet site http://www.census.gov/hhes/ www/housing/ahs/ahs09/ahs09.html; calculations by New Strategist

Table 4.67 Homeowners by First Home and Mortgage Status, 2009: South

Only 40 percent of homeowners in the South are in their first home. Sixty-one percent of homeowners in the region have a mortgage or home equity loan, while 36 percent own their home free and clear.

(number and percent distribution of total homeowners and homeowners in the South, by mortgage status, 2009; numbers in thousands)

	total		South		
	number	percent distribution	number	percent distribution	percent of total
FIRST-HOME STATUS					
Total homeowners	**76,428**	**100.0%**	**29,193**	**100.0%**	**38.2%**
First home ever owned	31,676	41.4	11,616	39.8	36.7
Not first home	43,233	56.6	16,995	58.2	39.3
Not reported	1,519	2.0	583	2.0	38.4
MORTGAGE STATUS					
Total homeowners	**76,428**	**100.0**	**29,193**	**100.0**	**38.2**
None, owned free and clear	24,206	31.7	10,502	36.0	43.4
Reverse mortgage	252	0.3	106	0.4	42.1
With regular and/or home-equity mortgages	50,300	65.8	17,900	61.3	35.6
Regular mortgage(s)	46,703	61.1	16,753	57.4	35.9
Home-equity lump-sum mortgage	4,022	5.3	1,084	3.7	27.0
Home-equity line of credit	9,184	12.0	2,681	9.2	29.2
Not reported	1,670	2.2	684	2.3	41.0

Source: Bureau of the Census, American Housing Survey for the United States: 2009, Internet site http://www.census.gov/hhes/ www/housing/ahs/ahs09/ahs09.html; calculations by New Strategist

Table 4.68 Homeowners by First Home and Mortgage Status, 2009: West

Only 38 percent of homeowners in the West are in their first home. Seventy-two percent of homeowners in the region have a mortgage or home equity loan, while 26 percent own their home free and clear.

(number and percent distribution of total homeowners and homeowners in the West, by mortgage status, 2009; numbers in thousands)

	total		West		
	number	percent distribution	number	percent distribution	percent of total
FIRST-HOME STATUS					
Total homeowners	**76,428**	**100.0%**	**15,607**	**100.0%**	**20.4%**
First home ever owned	31,676	41.4	5,938	38.0	18.7
Not first home	43,233	56.6	9,370	60.0	21.7
Not reported	1,519	2.0	300	1.9	19.7
MORTGAGE STATUS					
Total homeowners	**76,428**	**100.0**	**15,607**	**100.0**	**20.4**
None, owned free and clear	24,206	31.7	4,015	25.7	16.6
Reverse mortgage	252	0.3	80	0.5	31.7
With regular and/or home-equity mortgages	50,300	65.8	11,203	71.8	22.3
Regular mortgage(s)	46,703	61.1	10,640	68.2	22.8
Home-equity lump-sum mortgage	4,022	5.3	816	5.2	20.3
Home-equity line of credit	9,184	12.0	2,160	13.8	23.5
Not reported	1,670	2.2	308	2.0	18.4

Source: Bureau of the Census, American Housing Survey for the United States: 2009, Internet site http://www.census.gov/hhes/ www/housing/ahs/ahs09/ahs09.html; calculations by New Strategist

Table 4.69 Homeowners by Year of Origination of Primary Mortgage and Region, 2009

The percentage of homeowners with recently originated mortgages ranges from a low of 38 percent in the Northeast to a high of 48 percent in the West.

(number and percent distribution of total homeowners with mortgages and homeowners with mortgages by region, by year primary mortgage originated, 2009; numbers in thousands)

	total	Northeast	Midwest	South	West
Total homeowners with mortgages	**47,945**	**8,237**	**11,775**	**17,118**	**10,815**
2005 to 2009	21,064	3,147	5,145	7,558	5,213
2000 to 2004	14,175	2,444	3,631	4,868	3,233
1995 to 1999	6,152	1,200	1,457	2,328	1,167
1990 to 1994	2,953	651	676	1,057	569
1985 to 1989	1,808	401	431	629	347
1980 to 1984	767	183	174	307	103
1975 to 1979	564	115	153	201	94
1970 to 1974	434	83	103	165	83
1969 or earlier	28	13	5	6	5
Median year of origination	2004	2003	2004	2004	2004

PERCENT DISTRIBUTION BY YEAR OF ORIGINATION

	total	Northeast	Midwest	South	West
Total homeowners with mortgages	**100.0%**	**100.0%**	**100.0%**	**100.0%**	**100.0%**
2005 to 2009	43.9	38.2	43.7	44.2	48.2
2000 to 2004	29.6	29.7	30.8	28.4	29.9
1995 to 1999	12.8	14.6	12.4	13.6	10.8
1990 to 1994	6.2	7.9	5.7	6.2	5.3
1985 to 1989	3.8	4.9	3.7	3.7	3.2
1980 to 1984	1.6	2.2	1.5	1.8	0.9
1975 to 1979	1.2	1.4	1.3	1.2	0.9
1970 to 1974	0.9	1.0	0.9	1.0	0.8
1969 or earlier	0.1	0.2	0.0	0.0	0.0

PERCENT DISTRIBUTION BY REGION

	total	Northeast	Midwest	South	West
Total homeowners with mortgages	**100.0%**	**17.2%**	**24.6%**	**35.7%**	**22.6%**
2005 to 2009	100.0	14.9	24.4	35.9	24.8
2000 to 2004	100.0	17.2	25.6	34.3	22.8
1995 to 1999	100.0	19.5	23.7	37.8	19.0
1990 to 1994	100.0	22.1	22.9	35.8	19.3
1985 to 1989	100.0	22.2	23.9	34.8	19.2
1980 to 1984	100.0	23.9	22.7	40.0	13.4
1975 to 1979	100.0	20.4	27.2	35.7	16.7
1970 to 1974	100.0	19.2	23.7	37.9	19.2
1969 or earlier	100.0	44.6	17.6	19.5	18.4

Source: Bureau of the Census, American Housing Survey for the United States: 2009, Internet site http://www.census.gov/hhes/www/housing/ahs/ahs09/ahs09.html; calculations by New Strategist

Table 4.70 Mortgage Years Remaining and Principal Outstanding, 2009: Northeast

Homeowners with mortgages in the Northeast have an average of 21 years remaining on their mortgage and still owe a median of $110,806.

(number and percent distribution of homeowners with mortgages and homeowners with mortgages in the Northeast, by remaining years mortgaged and outstanding principal, 2009; numbers in thousands)

	total number	percent distribution	Northeast number	percent distribution	percent of total
Total homeowners	76,428	100.0%	13,378	100.0%	17.5%
Homeowners with mortgages	47,945	62.7	8,237	61.6	17.2
REMAINING YEARS MORTGAGED					
Homeowners with mortgages	47,945	100.0	8,237	100.0	17.2
Less than 8 years	6,160	12.8	1,276	15.5	20.7
8 to 12 years	5,188	10.8	974	11.8	18.8
13 to 17 years	5,077	10.6	998	12.1	19.7
18 to 22 years	6,568	13.7	1,186	14.4	18.1
23 to 27 years	14,948	31.2	2,369	28.8	15.8
28 to 32 years	9,569	20.0	1,369	16.6	14.3
33 years or more	164	0.3	21	0.3	12.8
Variable	271	0.6	44	0.5	16.4
Median years remaining	23	–	21	–	–
TOTAL OUTSTANDING PRINCIPAL					
Homeowners with mortgages	47,945	100.0	8,237	100.0	17.2
Under $10,000	2,797	5.8	525	6.4	18.8
$10,000 to $19,999	1,972	4.1	386	4.7	19.6
$20,000 to $29,999	1,877	3.9	354	4.3	18.9
$30,000 to $39,999	1,978	4.1	343	4.2	17.3
$40,000 to $49,999	2,338	4.9	424	5.1	18.1
$50,000 to $59,999	2,328	4.9	334	4.1	14.3
$60,000 to $69,999	2,504	5.2	350	4.2	14.0
$70,000 to $79,999	2,484	5.2	371	4.5	14.9
$80,000 to $99,999	4,420	9.2	719	8.7	16.3
$100,000 to $119,999	3,751	7.8	604	7.3	16.1
$120,000 to $149,999	5,029	10.5	741	9.0	14.7
$150,000 to $199,999	5,926	12.4	1,090	13.2	18.4
$200,000 to $249,999	3,575	7.5	714	8.7	20.0
$250,000 to $299,999	2,267	4.7	428	5.2	18.9
$300,000 or more	4,700	9.8	855	10.4	18.2
Median outstanding principal	$106,909	–	$110,806	–	–

Note: "–" means not applicable.
Source: Bureau of the Census, American Housing Survey for the United States: 2009, Internet site http://www.census.gov/hhes/www/housing/ahs/nationaldata.html; calculations by New Strategist

Table 4.71 Mortgage Years Remaining and Principal Outstanding, 2009: Midwest

Homeowners with mortgages in the Midwest have an average of 23 years remaining on their mortgage and still owe a median of $88,069.

(number and percent distribution of homeowners with mortgages and homeowners with mortgages in the Midwest, by remaining years mortgaged and outstanding principal, 2009; numbers in thousands)

	total		Midwest		
	number	percent distribution	number	percent distribution	percent of total
Total homeowners	**76,428**	**100.0%**	**18,249**	**100.0%**	**23.9%**
Homeowners with mortgages	47,945	62.7	11,775	64.5	24.6
REMAINING YEARS MORTGAGED					
Homeowners with mortgages	**47,945**	**100.0**	**11,775**	**100.0**	**24.6**
Less than 8 years	6,160	12.8	1,506	12.8	24.4
8 to 12 years	5,188	10.8	1,404	11.9	27.1
13 to 17 years	5,077	10.6	1,291	11.0	25.4
18 to 22 years	6,568	13.7	1,590	13.5	24.2
23 to 27 years	14,948	31.2	3,732	31.7	25.0
28 to 32 years	9,569	20.0	2,137	18.1	22.3
33 years or more	164	0.3	37	0.3	22.4
Variable	271	0.6	78	0.7	28.8
Median years remaining	23	–	23	–	–
TOTAL OUTSTANDING PRINCIPAL					
Homeowners with mortgages	**47,945**	**100.0**	**11,775**	**100.0**	**24.6**
Under $10,000	2,797	5.8	701	6.0	25.1
$10,000 to $19,999	1,972	4.1	522	4.4	26.5
$20,000 to $29,999	1,877	3.9	566	4.8	30.1
$30,000 to $39,999	1,978	4.1	536	4.6	27.1
$40,000 to $49,999	2,338	4.9	734	6.2	31.4
$50,000 to $59,999	2,328	4.9	733	6.2	31.5
$60,000 to $69,999	2,504	5.2	756	6.4	30.2
$70,000 to $79,999	2,484	5.2	785	6.7	31.6
$80,000 to $99,999	4,420	9.2	1,343	11.4	30.4
$100,000 to $119,999	3,751	7.8	1,096	9.3	29.2
$120,000 to $149,999	5,029	10.5	1,332	11.3	26.5
$150,000 to $199,999	5,926	12.4	1,319	11.2	22.3
$200,000 to $249,999	3,575	7.5	664	5.6	18.6
$250,000 to $299,999	2,267	4.7	238	2.0	10.5
$300,000 or more	4,700	9.8	450	3.8	9.6
Median outstanding principal	$106,909	–	$88,069	–	–

Note: "–" means not applicable.
Source: Bureau of the Census, American Housing Survey for the United States: 2009, Internet site http://www.census.gov/hhes/www/housing/ahs/nationaldata.html; calculations by New Strategist

Table 4.72 Mortgage Years Remaining and Principal Outstanding, 2009: South

Homeowners with mortgages in the South have an average of 23 years
remaining on their mortgage and still owe a median of $93,171.

*(number and percent distribution of homeowners with mortgages and homeowners with mortgages in the South,
by remaining years mortgaged and outstanding principal, 2009; numbers in thousands)*

	total		South		
	number	percent distribution	number	percent distribution	percent of total
Total homeowners	**76,428**	**100.0%**	**29,193**	**100.0%**	**38.2%**
Homeowners with mortgages	47,945	62.7	17,118	58.6	35.7
REMAINING YEARS MORTGAGED					
Homeowners with mortgages	**47,945**	**100.0**	**17,118**	**100.0**	**35.7**
Less than 8 years	6,160	12.8	2,378	13.9	38.6
8 to 12 years	5,188	10.8	1,831	10.7	35.3
13 to 17 years	5,077	10.6	1,787	10.4	35.2
18 to 22 years	6,568	13.7	2,427	14.2	36.9
23 to 27 years	14,948	31.2	5,187	30.3	34.7
28 to 32 years	9,569	20.0	3,393	19.8	35.5
33 years or more	164	0.3	30	0.2	18.4
Variable	271	0.6	85	0.5	31.2
Median years remaining	23	–	23	–	–
TOTAL OUTSTANDING PRINCIPAL					
Homeowners with mortgages	**47,945**	**100.0**	**17,118**	**100.0**	**35.7**
Under $10,000	2,797	5.8	1,218	7.1	43.5
$10,000 to $19,999	1,972	4.1	838	4.9	42.5
$20,000 to $29,999	1,877	3.9	732	4.3	39.0
$30,000 to $39,999	1,978	4.1	854	5.0	43.2
$40,000 to $49,999	2,338	4.9	864	5.0	37.0
$50,000 to $59,999	2,328	4.9	967	5.6	41.5
$60,000 to $69,999	2,504	5.2	1,027	6.0	41.0
$70,000 to $79,999	2,484	5.2	979	5.7	39.4
$80,000 to $99,999	4,420	9.2	1,662	9.7	37.6
$100,000 to $119,999	3,751	7.8	1,440	8.4	38.4
$120,000 to $149,999	5,029	10.5	1,879	11.0	37.4
$150,000 to $199,999	5,926	12.4	1,950	11.4	32.9
$200,000 to $249,999	3,575	7.5	965	5.6	27.0
$250,000 to $299,999	2,267	4.7	657	3.8	29.0
$300,000 or more	4,700	9.8	1,085	6.3	23.1
Median outstanding principal	$106,909	–	$93,171	–	–

Note: "–" means not applicable.
*Source: Bureau of the Census, American Housing Survey for the United States: 2009, Internet site http://www.census.gov/hhes/
www/housing/ahs/nationaldata.html; calculations by New Strategist*

Table 4.73 Mortgage Years Remaining and Principal Outstanding, 2009: West

Homeowners with mortgages in the West have an averagae of 24 years remaining on their mortgage and still owe a median of $170,531.

(number and percent distribution of homeowners with mortgages and homeowners with mortgages in the West, by remaining years mortgaged and outstanding principal, 2009; numbers in thousands)

	total		West		
	number	percent distribution	number	percent distribution	percent of total
Total homeowners	**76,428**	**100.0%**	**15,607**	**100.0%**	**20.4%**
Homeowners with mortgages	47,945	62.7	10,815	69.3	22.6
REMAINING YEARS MORTGAGED					
Homeowners with mortgages	**47,945**	**100.0**	**10,815**	**100.0**	**22.6**
Less than 8 years	6,160	12.8	1,001	9.3	16.2
8 to 12 years	5,188	10.8	978	9.0	18.9
13 to 17 years	5,077	10.6	1,001	9.3	19.7
18 to 22 years	6,568	13.7	1,366	12.6	20.8
23 to 27 years	14,948	31.2	3,660	33.8	24.5
28 to 32 years	9,569	20.0	2,670	24.7	27.9
33 years or more	164	0.3	76	0.7	46.4
Variable	271	0.6	64	0.6	23.6
Median years remaining	23	–	24	–	–
TOTAL OUTSTANDING PRINCIPAL					
Homeowners with mortgages	**47,945**	**100.0**	**10,815**	**100.0**	**22.6**
Under $10,000	2,797	5.8	353	3.3	12.6
$10,000 to $19,999	1,972	4.1	226	2.1	11.5
$20,000 to $29,999	1,877	3.9	225	2.1	12.0
$30,000 to $39,999	1,978	4.1	245	2.3	12.4
$40,000 to $49,999	2,338	4.9	316	2.9	13.5
$50,000 to $59,999	2,328	4.9	294	2.7	12.6
$60,000 to $69,999	2,504	5.2	370	3.4	14.8
$70,000 to $79,999	2,484	5.2	349	3.2	14.0
$80,000 to $99,999	4,420	9.2	696	6.4	15.7
$100,000 to $119,999	3,751	7.8	611	5.6	16.3
$120,000 to $149,999	5,029	10.5	1,076	10.0	21.4
$150,000 to $199,999	5,926	12.4	1,567	14.5	26.4
$200,000 to $249,999	3,575	7.5	1,232	11.4	34.5
$250,000 to $299,999	2,267	4.7	944	8.7	41.6
$300,000 or more	4,700	9.8	2,310	21.4	49.1
Median outstanding principal	$106,909	–	$170,531	–	–

Note: "–" means not applicable.
Source: Bureau of the Census, American Housing Survey for the United States: 2009, Internet site http://www.census.gov/hhes/www/housing/ahs/nationaldata.html; calculations by New Strategist

Table 4.74 Mortgages as a Percent of Home Value, 2007 and 2009: Northeast

As home values have declined, mortgage loans as a percent of
home value in the Northeast have increased from 45 to 51 percent.

*(number and percent distribution of homeowners with mortgages in the Northeast by current total loan as a percent
of home value, 2007 and 2009; numbers in thousands)*

	2009		2007	
	number	percent	number	percent
Total homeowners in the Northeast	**13,378**	**100.0%**	**13,339**	**100.0%**
Homeowners with mortgages	8,237	61.6	7,899	59.2
CURRENT TOTAL LOAN AS PERCENT OF VALUE				
Homeowners with mortgages	**8,237**	**100.0**	**7,899**	**100.0**
Less than 20 percent	1,489	18.1	1,660	21.0
20 to 39 percent	1,669	20.3	1,899	24.0
40 to 59 percent	1,635	19.8	1,692	21.4
60 to 79 percent	1,536	18.7	1,421	18.0
80 to 89 percent	732	8.9	540	6.8
90 to 99 percent	556	6.7	375	4.7
100 percent or more	620	7.5	312	3.9
Median percent of value	51.0%	–	44.6%	–

Note: "–" means not applicable.
*Source: Bureau of the Census, American Housing Survey for the United States: 2007 and 2009, Internet site http://www.census
.gov/hhes/www/housing/ahs/nationaldata.html; calculations by New Strategist*

Table 4.75 Mortgages as a Percent of Home Value, 2007 and 2009: Midwest

As home values have declined, mortgage loans as a percent of home value in the Midwest have increased from 61 to 67 percent.

(number and percent distribution of homeowners with mortgages in the Midwest by current total loan as a percent of home value, 2007 and 2009; numbers in thousands)

	2009		2007	
	number	percent	number	percent
Total homeowners in the Midwest	**18,249**	**100.0%**	**18,194**	**100.0%**
Homeowners with mortgages	11,775	64.5	11,352	62.4
CURRENT TOTAL LOAN AS PERCENT OF VALUE				
Homeowners with mortgages	**11,775**	**100.0**	**11,352**	**100.0**
Less than 20 percent	1,316	11.2	1,462	12.9
20 to 39 percent	1,488	12.6	1,737	15.3
40 to 59 percent	2,090	17.8	2,293	20.2
60 to 79 percent	2,684	22.8	2,939	25.9
80 to 89 percent	1,453	12.3	1,342	11.8
90 to 99 percent	1,346	11.4	987	8.7
100 percent or more	1,398	11.9	592	5.2
Median percent of value	67.0%	–	61.2%	–

Note: "–" means not applicable.
Source: Bureau of the Census, American Housing Survey for the United States: 2007 and 2009, Internet site http://www.census.gov/hhes/www/housing/ahs/nationaldata.html; calculations by New Strategist

Table 4.76 Mortgages as a Percent of Home Value, 2007 and 2009: South

As home values have declined, mortgage loans as a percent of
home value in the South have increased from 58 to 65 percent.

*(number and percent distribution of homeowners with mortgages in the South by current total loan as a percent
of home value, 2007 and 2009; numbers in thousands)*

	2009		2007	
	number	percent	number	percent
Total homeowners in the South	**29,193**	**100.0%**	**28,508**	**100.0%**
Homeowners with mortgages	17,118	58.6	16,494	57.9
CURRENT TOTAL LOAN AS PERCENT OF VALUE				
Homeowners with mortgages	**17,118**	**100.0**	**16,494**	**100.0**
Less than 20 percent	2,072	12.1	2,242	13.6
20 to 39 percent	2,557	14.9	3,006	18.2
40 to 59 percent	2,973	17.4	3,366	20.4
60 to 79 percent	3,713	21.7	3,941	23.9
80 to 89 percent	1,956	11.4	1,783	10.8
90 to 99 percent	1,873	10.9	1,270	7.7
100 percent or more	1,974	11.5	886	5.4
Median percent of value	65.0%	–	57.8%	–

Note: "–" means not applicable.
*Source: Bureau of the Census, American Housing Survey for the United States: 2007 and 2009, Internet site http://www.census
.gov/hhes/www/housing/ahs/nationaldata.html; calculations by New Strategist*

Table 4.77 Mortgages as a Percent of Home Value, 2007 and 2009: West

As home values have declined, mortgage loans as a percent of
home value in the West have increased from 49 to 65 percent.

*(number and percent distribution of homeowners with mortgages in the West by current total loan as a percent of
home value, 2007 and 2009; numbers in thousands)*

	2009		2007	
	number	percent	number	percent
Total homeowners in the West	**15,607**	**100.0%**	**15,607**	**100.0%**
Homeowners with mortgages	10,815	69.3	10,716	68.7
CURRENT TOTAL LOAN AS PERCENT OF VALUE				
Homeowners with mortgages	**10,815**	**100.0**	**10,716**	**100.0**
Less than 20 percent	1,297	12.0	1,840	17.2
20 to 39 percent	1,763	16.3	2,459	22.9
40 to 59 percent	1,826	16.9	2,275	21.2
60 to 79 percent	1,991	18.4	2,063	19.3
80 to 89 percent	987	9.1	824	7.7
90 to 99 percent	1,154	10.7	588	5.5
100 percent or more	1,797	16.6	666	6.2
Median percent of value	65.0%	–	49.3%	–

Note: "–" means not applicable.
Source: Bureau of the Census, American Housing Survey for the United States: 2007 and 2009, Internet site http://www.census
.gov/hhes/www/housing/ahs/nationaldata.html; calculations by New Strategist

Table 4.78 Homeowners Who Refinanced Their Primary Mortgage, 2009: Northeast

Twenty-four percent of homeowners with mortgages in the Northeast have refinanced their primary mortgage. Most did so to get a lower interest rate.

(number and percent distribution of homeowners with mortgages and homeowners with mortgages in the Northeast, by refinancing of primary mortgage status, reason for refinancing, and cash received, 2009; numbers in thousands)

	total		Northeast		
	number	percent distribution	number	percent distribution	percent of total
Homeowners with mortgages	**47,945**	**100.0%**	**8,237**	**100.0%**	**17.2%**
Homeowners with a refinanced primary mortgage	12,220	25.5	1,950	23.7	16.0
REASON FOR REFINANCING OF PRIMARY MORTGAGE					
Homeowners with refinanced primary mortgage	**12,220**	**100.0**	**2,896**	**100.0**	**23.7**
To get lower interest rate	9,228	75.5	1,505	52.0	16.3
To reduce the monthly payment	1,552	12.7	215	7.4	13.8
To increase payment period	180	1.5	32	1.1	17.6
To reduce payment period	573	4.7	67	2.3	11.7
To renew or extend a loan that has fallen due	123	1.0	21	0.7	17.0
To receive cash	1,587	13.0	265	9.2	16.7
Other reasons	1,655	13.5	234	8.1	14.2
CASH RECEIVED IN PRIMARY MORTGAGE REFINANCING					
Homeowners receiving cash in mortgage refinancing	**1,587**	**100.0**	**265**	**100.0**	**16.7**
Under $10,000	125	7.9	12	4.7	10.0
$10,000 to $19,999	231	14.5	13	4.8	5.6
$20,000 to $29,999	226	14.3	34	13.0	15.2
$30,000 to $39,999	157	9.9	32	12.1	20.4
$40,000 to $49,999	93	5.9	11	4.2	11.8
$50,000 to $59,999	99	6.3	22	8.2	21.8
$60,000 to $69,999	46	2.9	3	1.0	5.9
$70,000 to $79,999	25	1.6	8	3.0	31.5
$80,000 to $99,999	93	5.9	12	4.7	13.3
$100,000 to $119,999	90	5.7	11	4.0	11.7
$120,000 to $149,999	30	1.9	6	2.2	19.4
$150,000 or more	95	6.0	19	7.2	20.1
Not reported	276	17.4	82	31.0	29.8
Median amount of cash received	$30,000	–	$37,500	–	–

Note: "–" means not applicable.
Source: Bureau of the Census, American Housing Survey for the United States: 2009, Internet site http://www.census.gov/hhes/ www/housing/ahs/ahs09/ahs09.html; calculations by New Strategist

Table 4.79 Homeowners Who Refinanced Their Primary Mortgage, 2009: Midwest

Twenty-eight percent of homeowners with mortgages in the Midwest have refinanced their primary mortgage. Most did so to get a lower interest rate.

(number and percent distribution of homeowners with mortgages and homeowners with mortgages in the Midwest, by refinancing of primary mortgage status, reason for refinancing, and cash received, 2009; numbers in thousands)

	total		Midwest		
	number	percent distribution	number	percent distribution	percent of total
Homeowners with mortgages	**47,945**	**100.0%**	**11,775**	**100.0%**	**24.6%**
Homeowners with a refinanced primary mortgage	12,220	25.5	3,337	28.3	27.3
REASON FOR REFINANCING OF PRIMARY MORTGAGE					
Homeowners with refinanced primary mortgage	**12,220**	**100.0**	**3,337**	**100.0**	**27.3**
To get lower interest rate	9,228	75.5	2,595	77.8	28.1
To reduce the monthly payment	1,552	12.7	413	12.4	26.6
To increase payment period	180	1.5	47	1.4	26.1
To reduce payment period	573	4.7	158	4.7	27.5
To renew or extend a loan that has fallen due	123	1.0	38	1.1	31.1
To receive cash	1,587	13.0	333	10.0	21.0
Other reasons	1,655	13.5	466	14.0	28.2
CASH RECEIVED IN PRIMARY MORTGAGE REFINANCING					
Homeowners receiving cash in mortgage refinancing	**1,587**	**100.0**	**333**	**100.0**	**21.0**
Under $10,000	125	7.9	23	6.8	18.1
$10,000 to $19,999	231	14.5	90	27.0	39.0
$20,000 to $29,999	226	14.3	51	15.4	22.6
$30,000 to $39,999	157	9.9	20	6.1	12.8
$40,000 to $49,999	93	5.9	20	5.9	21.2
$50,000 to $59,999	99	6.3	15	4.4	14.8
$60,000 to $69,999	46	2.9	10	3.0	22.2
$70,000 to $79,999	25	1.6	3	1.0	13.0
$80,000 to $99,999	93	5.9	16	4.7	16.9
$100,000 to $119,999	90	5.7	5	1.6	5.7
$120,000 to $149,999	30	1.9	5	1.5	16.8
$150,000 or more	95	6.0	10	2.9	10.3
Not reported	276	17.4	65	19.6	23.7
Median amount of cash received	$30,000	–	$20,000	–	–

Note: "–" means not applicable.
Source: Bureau of the Census, American Housing Survey for the United States: 2009, Internet site http://www.census.gov/hhes/ www/housing/ahs/ahs09/ahs09.html; calculations by New Strategist

Table 4.80 Homeowners Who Refinanced Their Primary Mortgage, 2009: South

Nineteen percent of homeowners with mortgages in the South have refinanced their primary mortgage. Most did so to get a lower interest rate.

(number and percent distribution of homeowners with mortgages and homeowners with mortgages in the South, by refinancing of primary mortgage status, reason for refinancing, and cash received, 2009; numbers in thousands)

	total		South		
	number	percent distribution	number	percent distribution	percent of total
Homeowners with mortgages	**47,945**	**100.0%**	**17,118**	**100.0%**	**35.7%**
Homeowners with a refinanced primary mortgage	12,220	25.5	3,321	19.4	27.2
REASON FOR REFINANCING OF PRIMARY MORTGAGE					
Homeowners with refinanced primary mortgage	**12,220**	**100.0**	**3,321**	**100.0**	**27.2**
To get lower interest rate	9,228	75.5	2,490	75.0	27.0
To reduce the monthly payment	1,552	12.7	469	14.1	30.2
To increase payment period	180	1.5	27	0.8	15.1
To reduce payment period	573	4.7	188	5.7	32.8
To renew or extend a loan that has fallen due	123	1.0	35	1.0	28.0
To receive cash	1,587	13.0	443	13.3	27.9
Other reasons	1,655	13.5	403	12.1	24.4
CASH RECEIVED IN PRIMARY MORTGAGE REFINANCING					
Homeowners receiving cash in mortgage refinancing	**1,587**	**100.0**	**443**	**100.0**	**27.9**
Under $10,000	125	7.9	61	13.7	48.7
$10,000 to $19,999	231	14.5	75	17.0	32.6
$20,000 to $29,999	226	14.3	52	11.7	22.9
$30,000 to $39,999	157	9.9	46	10.5	29.5
$40,000 to $49,999	93	5.9	23	5.2	24.7
$50,000 to $59,999	99	6.3	22	5.0	22.1
$60,000 to $69,999	46	2.9	8	1.8	17.4
$70,000 to $79,999	25	1.6	6	1.3	23.4
$80,000 to $99,999	93	5.9	25	5.6	26.7
$100,000 to $119,999	90	5.7	18	4.1	20.1
$120,000 to $149,999	30	1.9	10	2.2	31.6
$150,000 or more	95	6.0	34	7.7	36.1
Not reported	276	17.4	63	14.2	22.9
Median amount of cash received	$30,000	–	$30,000	–	–

Note: "–" means not applicable.
Source: Bureau of the Census, American Housing Survey for the United States: 2009, Internet site http://www.census.gov/hhes/ www/housing/ahs/ahs09/ahs09.html; calculations by New Strategist

Table 4.81 Homeowners Who Refinanced Their Primary Mortgage, 2009: West

Thirty-three percent of homeowners with mortgages in the West have refinanced their primary mortgage. Most did so to get a lower interest rate.

(number and percent distribution of homeowners with mortgages and homeowners with mortgages in the West, by refinancing of primary mortgage status, reason for refinancing, and cash received, 2009; numbers in thousands)

	total		West		
	number	percent distribution	number	percent distribution	percent of total
Homeowners with mortgages	**47,945**	**100.0%**	**10,815**	**100.0%**	**22.6%**
Homeowners with a refinanced primary mortgage	12,220	25.5	3,613	33.4	29.6
REASON FOR REFINANCING OF PRIMARY MORTGAGE					
Homeowners with refinanced primary mortgage	**12,220**	**100.0**	**3,613**	**100.0**	**29.6**
To get lower interest rate	9,228	75.5	2,638	73.0	28.6
To reduce the monthly payment	1,552	12.7	456	12.6	29.3
To increase payment period	180	1.5	74	2.1	41.2
To reduce payment period	573	4.7	160	4.4	27.9
To renew or extend a loan that has fallen due	123	1.0	29	0.8	23.9
To receive cash	1,587	13.0	546	15.1	34.4
Other reasons	1,655	13.5	551	15.2	33.3
CASH RECEIVED IN PRIMARY MORTGAGE REFINANCING					
Homeowners receiving cash in mortgage refinancing	**1,587**	**100.0**	**546**	**100.0**	**34.4**
Under $10,000	125	7.9	29	5.3	23.2
$10,000 to $19,999	231	14.5	53	9.7	22.9
$20,000 to $29,999	226	14.3	89	16.3	39.3
$30,000 to $39,999	157	9.9	59	10.7	37.3
$40,000 to $49,999	93	5.9	39	7.2	42.2
$50,000 to $59,999	99	6.3	41	7.5	41.3
$60,000 to $69,999	46	2.9	25	4.5	54.5
$70,000 to $79,999	25	1.6	8	1.5	32.1
$80,000 to $99,999	93	5.9	40	7.4	43.1
$100,000 to $119,999	90	5.7	57	10.4	62.6
$120,000 to $149,999	30	1.9	10	1.8	32.2
$150,000 or more	95	6.0	32	5.8	33.6
Not reported	276	17.4	65	12.0	23.7
Median amount of cash received	$30,000	–	$40,000	–	–

Note: "–" means not applicable.
Source: Bureau of the Census, American Housing Survey for the United States: 2009, Internet site http://www.census.gov/hhes/www/housing/ahs/ahs09/ahs09.html; calculations by New Strategist

Table 4.82 Homeowners by Home Equity Line of Credit Status, 2009: Northeast

Only 23 percent of homeowners with mortgages in the
Northeast have a home equity line of credit, and just
14 percent have an outstanding balance on their loan.

(number and percent distribution of total homeowners and homeowners in the Northeast with a home equity line of credit, outstanding loan amount, and monthly payment, 2009; numbers in thousands

	total		Northeast		
	number	percent distribution	number	percent distribution	percent of total
Homeowners with mortgages	**47,945**	**100.0%**	**8,237**	**100.0%**	**17.2%**
Homeowners with home equity line-of-credit	9,184	19.2	1,935	23.5	21.1
Homeowners with home equity loan outstanding	5,306	11.1	1,179	14.3	22.2
LINE-OF-CREDIT LOANS OUTSTANDING					
Homeowners with outstanding line-of-credit loans	**5,306**	**100.0**	**1,179**	**100.0**	**22.2**
Under $10,000	837	15.8	174	14.8	20.8
$10,000 to $19,999	982	18.5	199	16.9	20.3
$20,000 to $29,999	748	14.1	162	13.8	21.7
$30,000 to $39,999	460	8.7	106	9.0	23.1
$40,000 to $49,999	354	6.7	70	6.0	19.9
$50,000 to $59,999	227	4.3	61	5.1	26.7
$60,000 to $69,999	237	4.5	44	3.7	18.5
$70,000 to $79,999	151	2.9	36	3.1	24.1
$80,000 to $99,999	264	5.0	44	3.7	16.7
$100,000 to $119,999	159	3.0	48	4.1	30.5
$120,000 to $149,999	111	2.1	17	1.5	15.8
$150,000 or more	245	4.6	61	5.2	25.1
Not reported	523	9.9	152	12.9	29.0
Median outstanding line-of-credit loan	$26,000	–	$27,000	–	–
LINE-OF-CREDIT MONTHLY PAYMENT					
Homeowners with outstanding line-of-credit loans	**5,306**	**100.0**	**1,179**	**100.0**	**22.2**
Less than $100	532	10.0	128	10.9	24.1
$100 to $199	1,010	19.0	176	15.0	17.5
$200 to $299	965	18.2	171	14.5	17.8
$300 to $399	594	11.2	134	11.4	22.6
$400 to $499	349	6.6	70	5.9	20.0
$500 to $599	414	7.8	97	8.2	23.3
$600 to $699	183	3.5	37	3.2	20.2
$700 to $799	109	2.1	20	1.7	18.4
$800 to $999	146	2.8	29	2.5	20.0
$1,000 or more	457	8.6	126	10.7	27.6
Not reported	546	10.3	190	16.1	34.8
Median monthly payment	$260	–	$300	–	–

Note: "–" means not applicable.
Source: Bureau of the Census, American Housing Survey for the United States: 2009, Internet site http://www.census.gov/hhes/ www/housing/ahs/ahs09/ahs09.html; calculations by New Strategist

Table 4.83 Homeowners by Home Equity Line of Credit Status, 2009: Midwest

Only 20 percent of homeowners with mortgages in the Midwest
have a home equity line of credit, and just 12 percent
have an outstanding balance on their loan.

(number and percent distribution of total homeowners and homeowners in the Midwest with a home equity line of credit, outstanding loan amount, and monthly payment, 2009; numbers in thousands

	total		Midwest		
	number	percent distribution	number	percent distribution	percent of total
Homeowners with mortgages	**47,945**	**100.0%**	**11,775**	**100.0%**	**24.6%**
Homeowners with home equity line-of-credit	9,184	19.2	2,408	20.5	26.2
Homeowners with home equity loan outstanding	5,306	11.1	1,395	11.8	26.3
LINE-OF-CREDIT LOANS OUTSTANDING					
Homeowners with outstanding line-of-credit loans	**5,306**	**100.0**	**1,395**	**100.0**	**26.3**
Under $10,000	837	15.8	289	20.7	34.6
$10,000 to $19,999	982	18.5	312	22.4	31.8
$20,000 to $29,999	748	14.1	195	14.0	26.1
$30,000 to $39,999	460	8.7	137	9.8	29.8
$40,000 to $49,999	354	6.7	100	7.2	28.3
$50,000 to $59,999	227	4.3	42	3.0	18.5
$60,000 to $69,999	237	4.5	43	3.1	18.3
$70,000 to $79,999	151	2.9	29	2.1	19.1
$80,000 to $99,999	264	5.0	44	3.1	16.5
$100,000 to $119,999	159	3.0	17	1.2	10.5
$120,000 to $149,999	111	2.1	9	0.6	7.9
$150,000 or more	245	4.6	47	3.3	19.0
Not reported	523	9.9	132	9.5	25.2
Median outstanding line-of-credit loan	$26,000	–	$20,000	–	–
LINE-OF-CREDIT MONTHLY PAYMENT					
Homeowners with outstanding line-of-credit loans	**5,306**	**100.0**	**1,395**	**100.0**	**26.3**
Less than $100	532	10.0	156	11.2	29.4
$100 to $199	1,010	19.0	303	21.7	30.0
$200 to $299	965	18.2	274	19.6	28.3
$300 to $399	594	11.2	127	9.1	21.5
$400 to $499	349	6.6	92	6.6	26.2
$500 to $599	414	7.8	97	6.9	23.4
$600 to $699	183	3.5	35	2.5	18.9
$700 to $799	109	2.1	27	2.0	25.0
$800 to $999	146	2.8	41	3.0	28.2
$1,000 or more	457	8.6	127	9.1	27.7
Not reported	546	10.3	117	8.4	21.4
Median monthly payment	$260	–	$240	–	–

Note: "–" means not applicable.
Source: Bureau of the Census, American Housing Survey for the United States: 2009, Internet site http://www.census.gov/hhes/www/housing/ahs/ahs09/ahs09.html; calculations by New Strategist

Table 4.84 Homeowners by Home Equity Line of Credit Status, 2009: South

Only 16 percent of homeowners with mortgages in the South have a home equity line of credit, and just 8 percent have an outstanding balance on their loan.

(number and percent distribution of total homeowners and homeowners in the South with a home equity line of credit, outstanding loan amount, and monthly payment, 2009; numbers in thousands

	total		South		
	number	percent distribution	number	percent distribution	percent of total
Homeowners with mortgages	**47,945**	**100.0%**	**17,118**	**100.0%**	**35.7%**
Homeowners with home equity line-of-credit	9,184	19.2	2,681	15.7	29.2
Homeowners with home equity loan outstanding	5,306	11.1	1,431	8.4	27.0
LINE-OF-CREDIT LOANS OUTSTANDING					
Homeowners with outstanding line-of-credit loans	**5,306**	**100.0**	**1,431**	**100.0**	**27.0**
Under $10,000	837	15.8	265	18.5	31.7
$10,000 to $19,999	982	18.5	287	20.1	29.3
$20,000 to $29,999	748	14.1	222	15.5	29.7
$30,000 to $39,999	460	8.7	99	6.9	21.6
$40,000 to $49,999	354	6.7	88	6.1	24.8
$50,000 to $59,999	227	4.3	62	4.3	27.4
$60,000 to $69,999	237	4.5	63	4.4	26.5
$70,000 to $79,999	151	2.9	30	2.1	19.8
$80,000 to $99,999	264	5.0	74	5.2	28.1
$100,000 to $119,999	159	3.0	40	2.8	25.0
$120,000 to $149,999	111	2.1	39	2.7	35.4
$150,000 or more	245	4.6	35	2.4	14.2
Not reported	523	9.9	124	8.7	23.8
Median outstanding line-of-credit loan	$26,000	–	$23,000	–	–
LINE-OF-CREDIT MONTHLY PAYMENT					
Homeowners with outstanding line-of-credit loans	**5,306**	**100.0**	**1,431**	**100.0**	**27.0**
Less than $100	532	10.0	138	9.6	25.9
$100 to $199	1,010	19.0	297	20.7	29.4
$200 to $299	965	18.2	284	19.9	29.5
$300 to $399	594	11.2	163	11.4	27.4
$400 to $499	349	6.6	103	7.2	29.5
$500 to $599	414	7.8	125	8.7	30.2
$600 to $699	183	3.5	42	3.0	23.1
$700 to $799	109	2.1	27	1.9	24.6
$800 to $999	146	2.8	30	2.1	20.4
$1,000 or more	457	8.6	101	7.1	22.1
Not reported	546	10.3	122	8.5	22.3
Median monthly payment	$260	–	$250	–	–

Note: "–" means not applicable.
Source: Bureau of the Census, American Housing Survey for the United States: 2009, Internet site http://www.census.gov/hhes/ www/housing/ahs/ahs09/ahs09.html; calculations by New Strategist

Table 4.85 Homeowners by Home Equity Line of Credit Status, 2009: West

Only 20 percent of homeowners with mortgages in the West have a home equity line of credit, and just 12 percent have an outstanding balance on their loan.

(number and percent distribution of total homeowners and homeowners in the West with a home equity line of credit, outstanding loan amount, and monthly payment, 2009; numbers in thousands

	total		West		
	number	percent distribution	number	percent distribution	percent of total
Homeowners with mortgages	**47,945**	**100.0%**	**10,815**	**100.0%**	**22.6%**
Homeowners with home equity line-of-credit	9,184	19.2	2,160	20.0	23.5
Homeowners with home equity loan outstanding	5,306	11.1	1,301	12.0	24.5
LINE-OF-CREDIT LOANS OUTSTANDING					
Homeowners with outstanding line-of-credit loans	**5,306**	**100.0**	**1,301**	**100.0**	**24.5**
Under $10,000	837	15.8	109	8.4	13.0
$10,000 to $19,999	982	18.5	183	14.1	18.7
$20,000 to $29,999	748	14.1	168	12.9	22.5
$30,000 to $39,999	460	8.7	117	9.0	25.5
$40,000 to $49,999	354	6.7	96	7.4	27.0
$50,000 to $59,999	227	4.3	62	4.8	27.4
$60,000 to $69,999	237	4.5	87	6.7	36.7
$70,000 to $79,999	151	2.9	56	4.3	37.1
$80,000 to $99,999	264	5.0	102	7.9	38.7
$100,000 to $119,999	159	3.0	54	4.2	34.0
$120,000 to $149,999	111	2.1	45	3.5	41.0
$150,000 or more	245	4.6	102	7.9	41.7
Not reported	523	9.9	115	8.8	21.9
Median outstanding line-of-credit loan	$26,000	–	$40,000	–	–
LINE-OF-CREDIT MONTHLY PAYMENT					
Homeowners with outstanding line-of-credit loans	**5,306**	**100.0**	**1,301**	**100.0**	**24.5**
Less than $100	532	10.0	110	8.4	20.6
$100 to $199	1,010	19.0	234	18.0	23.2
$200 to $299	965	18.2	236	18.1	24.4
$300 to $399	594	11.2	170	13.0	28.6
$400 to $499	349	6.6	85	6.5	24.3
$500 to $599	414	7.8	96	7.4	23.2
$600 to $699	183	3.5	69	5.3	37.7
$700 to $799	109	2.1	35	2.7	32.0
$800 to $999	146	2.8	46	3.5	31.4
$1,000 or more	457	8.6	103	7.9	22.6
Not reported	546	10.3	118	9.0	21.6
Median monthly payment	$260	–	$300	–	–

Note: "–" means not applicable.
Source: Bureau of the Census, American Housing Survey for the United States: 2009, Internet site http://www.census.gov/hhes/ www/housing/ahs/ahs09/ahs09.html; calculations by New Strategist

Table 4.86 Homeowners by Monthly Principal and Interest Payments and Region, 2009

Median monthly principal and interest payments for the nation's
homeowners with mortgages range from a low of $736
in the Midwest to a high of $1,275 in the West.

*(number and percent distribution of homeowners with mortgages by monthly payment for principal and interest,
by region, 2009; numbers in thousands)*

	total	Northeast	Midwest	South	West
Homeowners with mortgages	**47,945**	**8,237**	**11,775**	**17,118**	**10,815**
Less than $100	1,327	279	265	580	203
$100 to $199	1,072	208	290	438	136
$200 to $299	1,757	272	516	792	177
$300 to $399	2,873	451	880	1,240	302
$400 to $499	3,338	502	1,119	1,391	325
$500 to $599	3,816	511	1,239	1,647	420
$600 to $699	3,859	540	1,143	1,580	596
$700 to $799	3,443	493	1,084	1,372	493
$800 to $999	6,162	1,016	1,648	2,372	1,126
$1,000 to $1,249	5,879	1,054	1,443	1,897	1,485
$1,250 to $1,499	4,059	796	810	1,247	1,207
$1,500 to $1,999	4,786	1,019	759	1,325	1,682
$2,000 or more	5,574	1,097	578	1,236	2,663
Median monthly payment	$878	$966	$736	$760	$1,275

PERCENT DISTRIBUTION BY MONTHLY PAYMENT

	total	Northeast	Midwest	South	West
Homeowners with mortgages	**100.0%**	**100.0%**	**100.0%**	**100.0%**	**100.0%**
Less than $100	2.8	3.4	2.3	3.4	1.9
$100 to $199	2.2	2.5	2.5	2.6	1.3
$200 to $299	3.7	3.3	4.4	4.6	1.6
$300 to $399	6.0	5.5	7.5	7.2	2.8
$400 to $499	7.0	6.1	9.5	8.1	3.0
$500 to $599	8.0	6.2	10.5	9.6	3.9
$600 to $699	8.0	6.6	9.7	9.2	5.5
$700 to $799	7.2	6.0	9.2	8.0	4.6
$800 to $999	12.9	12.3	14.0	13.9	10.4
$1,000 to $1,249	12.3	12.8	12.3	11.1	13.7
$1,250 to $1,499	8.5	9.7	6.9	7.3	11.2
$1,500 to $1,999	10.0	12.4	6.4	7.7	15.6
$2,000 or more	11.6	13.3	4.9	7.2	24.6

	total	Northeast	Midwest	South	West
PERCENT DISTRIBUTION BY REGION					
Homeowners with mortgages	**100.0%**	**17.2%**	**24.6%**	**35.7%**	**22.6%**
Less than $100	100.0	21.0	20.0	43.7	15.3
$100 to $199	100.0	19.4	27.1	40.8	12.7
$200 to $299	100.0	15.5	29.4	45.1	10.1
$300 to $399	100.0	15.7	30.6	43.2	10.5
$400 to $499	100.0	15.0	33.5	41.7	9.7
$500 to $599	100.0	13.4	32.5	43.1	11.0
$600 to $699	100.0	14.0	29.6	40.9	15.4
$700 to $799	100.0	14.3	31.5	39.9	14.3
$800 to $999	100.0	16.5	26.7	38.5	18.3
$1,000 to $1,249	100.0	17.9	24.5	32.3	25.3
$1,250 to $1,499	100.0	19.6	19.9	30.7	29.7
$1,500 to $1,999	100.0	21.3	15.9	27.7	35.2
$2,000 or more	100.0	19.7	10.4	22.2	47.8

Source: Bureau of the Census, American Housing Survey for the United States: 2009, Internet site http://www.census.gov/hhes/ www/housing/ahs/ahs09/ahs09.html, calculations by New Strategist

Table 4.87 Homeowners by Monthly Housing Costs and Region, 2009

Median monthly housing costs for the nation's homeowners range
from a low of $827 in the South to a high of $1,389 in the West.

(number and percent distribution of homeowners by monthly housing costs, by region, 2009; numbers in thousands)

	total	Northeast	Midwest	South	West
Total homeowners	**76,428**	**13,378**	**18,249**	**29,193**	**15,607**
Less than $100	475	43	61	182	190
$100 to $199	2,161	149	369	1,186	457
$200 to $299	5,351	366	1,087	3,026	873
$300 to $399	6,022	653	1,549	2,835	984
$400 to $499	5,308	738	1,528	2,190	852
$500 to $599	4,407	898	1,130	1,715	663
$600 to $699	3,735	784	962	1,547	442
$700 to $799	3,597	698	998	1,451	449
$800 to $999	7,139	1,239	2,073	2,824	1,003
$1,000 to $1,249	8,156	1,440	2,388	3,109	1,219
$1,250 to $1,499	6,828	1,139	1,910	2,454	1,326
$1,500 or $1,999	9,445	1,877	2,223	2,949	2,396
$2,000 to $2,499	5,422	1,316	988	1,615	1,502
$2,500 or more	8,383	2,039	982	2,111	3,251
Median monthly cost	$1,000	$1,196	$937	$827	$1,389

PERCENT DISTRIBUTION BY MONTHLY COSTS

	total	Northeast	Midwest	South	West
Total homeowners	**100.0%**	**100.0%**	**100.0%**	**100.0%**	**100.0%**
Less than $100	0.6	0.3	0.3	0.6	1.2
$100 to $199	2.8	1.1	2.0	4.1	2.9
$200 to $299	7.0	2.7	6.0	10.4	5.6
$300 to $399	7.9	4.9	8.5	9.7	6.3
$400 to $499	6.9	5.5	8.4	7.5	5.5
$500 to $599	5.8	6.7	6.2	5.9	4.3
$600 to $699	4.9	5.9	5.3	5.3	2.8
$700 to $799	4.7	5.2	5.5	5.0	2.9
$800 to $999	9.3	9.3	11.4	9.7	6.4
$1,000 to $1,249	10.7	10.8	13.1	10.7	7.8
$1,250 to $1,499	8.9	8.5	10.5	8.4	8.5
$1,500 or $1,999	12.4	14.0	12.2	10.1	15.4
$2,000 to $2,499	7.1	9.8	5.4	5.5	9.6
$2,500 or more	11.0	15.2	5.4	7.2	20.8

	total	Northeast	Midwest	South	West
PERCENT DISTRIBUTION BY REGION					
Total homeowners	**100.0%**	**17.5%**	**23.9%**	**38.2%**	**20.4%**
Less than $100	100.0	9.1	12.8	38.2	39.9
$100 to $199	100.0	6.9	17.1	54.9	21.2
$200 to $299	100.0	6.8	20.3	56.5	16.3
$300 to $399	100.0	10.8	25.7	47.1	16.3
$400 to $499	100.0	13.9	28.8	41.3	16.0
$500 to $599	100.0	20.4	25.6	38.9	15.1
$600 to $699	100.0	21.0	25.8	41.4	11.8
$700 to $799	100.0	19.4	27.7	40.3	12.5
$800 to $999	100.0	17.4	29.0	39.6	14.1
$1,000 to $1,249	100.0	17.7	29.3	38.1	14.9
$1,250 to $1,499	100.0	16.7	28.0	35.9	19.4
$1,500 or $1,999	100.0	19.9	23.5	31.2	25.4
$2,000 to $2,499	100.0	24.3	18.2	29.8	27.7
$2,500 or more	100.0	24.3	11.7	25.2	38.8

Note: Housing costs include utilities, mortgages, real estate taxes, property insurance, and regime fees.
Source: Bureau of the Census, American Housing Survey for the United States: 2009, Internet site http://www.census.gov/hhes/ www/housing/ahs/ahs09/ahs09.html; calculations by New Strategist

Table 4.88 Homeowners by Monthly Utility Costs, 2009: Northeast

Homeowners in the Northeast pay much more for piped
gas than the average homeowner does, a median of
$118 per month versus $80 per month nationally.

(number and percent distribution of total homeowners and homeowners in the Northeast by average monthly costs for utilities, 2009; numbers in thousands)

	total		Northeast		
	number	percent distribution	number	percent distribution	percent of total
MONTHLY COST OF ELECTRICITY					
Households using electricity	**76,378**	**100.0%**	**13,364**	**100.0%**	**17.5%**
Less than $25	442	0.6	65	0.5	14.6
$25 to $49	4,425	5.8	945	7.1	21.4
$50 to $74	11,016	14.4	2,611	19.5	23.7
$75 to $99	12,975	17.0	2,559	19.2	19.7
$100 to $149	21,237	27.8	3,311	24.8	15.6
$150 to $199	12,164	15.9	1,732	13.0	14.2
$200 or more	12,110	15.9	2,018	15.1	16.7
Included in other fee or obtained free	2,010	2.6	123	0.9	6.1
Median monthly cost	$117	–	$105	–	–
MONTHLY COST OF PIPED GAS					
Households using piped gas	**46,700**	**100.0**	**7,819**	**100.0**	**16.7**
Less than $25	1,410	3.0	169	2.2	12.0
$25 to $49	7,933	17.0	475	6.1	6.0
$50 to $74	11,196	24.0	598	7.7	5.3
$75 to $99	8,595	18.4	1,235	15.8	14.4
$100 to $149	9,694	20.8	2,523	32.3	26.0
$150 to $199	3,698	7.9	1,300	16.6	35.2
$200 or more	2,682	5.7	1,094	14.0	40.8
Included in other fee or obtained free	1,494	3.2	426	5.4	28.5
Median monthly cost	$80	–	$118	–	–
MONTHLY COST OF FUEL OIL					
Households using fuel oil	**6,409**	**100.0**	**4,846**	**100.0**	**75.6**
Less than $25	176	2.8	90	1.9	51.1
$25 to $49	325	5.1	179	3.7	55.0
$50 to $74	490	7.6	307	6.3	62.6
$75 to $99	725	11.3	480	9.9	66.2
$100 to $149	1,403	21.9	945	19.5	67.4
$150 to $199	1,052	16.4	886	18.3	84.2
$200 or more	1,701	26.5	1,540	31.8	90.5
Included in other fee or obtained free	536	8.4	419	8.6	78.2
Median monthly cost	$133	–	$167	–	–

	total		Northeast		
	number	percent distribution	number	percent distribution	percent of total
Water paid separately	53,552	–	8,710	–	16.3%
Median monthly cost	$38	–	$38	–	–
Trash paid separately	44,974	–	4,921	–	10.9
Median monthly cost	$21	–	$21	–	–
Property insurance paid	72,313	–	12,930	–	17.9
Median monthly cost	$55	–	$58	–	–

Note: "–" means not applicable.
Source: Bureau of the Census, American Housing Survey for the United States: 2009, Internet site http://www.census.gov/hhes/ www/housing/ahs/ahs09/ahs09.html; calculations by New Strategist

Table 4.89 Homeowners by Monthly Utility Costs, 2009: Midwest

Homeowners in the Midwest pay more for piped gas than the average homeowner does, a median of $92 per month versus $80 per month nationally.

(number and percent distribution of total homeowners and homeowners in the Midwest by average monthly costs for utilities, 2009; numbers in thousands)

	total		Midwest		
	number	percent distribution	number	percent distribution	percent of total
MONTHLY COST OF ELECTRICITY					
Households using electricity	**76,378**	**100.0%**	**18,223**	**100.0%**	**23.9%**
Less than $25	442	0.6	116	0.6	26.2
$25 to $49	4,425	5.8	1,363	7.5	30.8
$50 to $74	11,016	14.4	3,397	18.6	30.8
$75 to $99	12,975	17.0	3,889	21.3	30.0
$100 to $149	21,237	27.8	5,237	28.7	24.7
$150 to $199	12,164	15.9	2,187	12.0	18.0
$200 or more	12,110	15.9	1,530	8.4	12.6
Included in other fee or obtained free	2,010	2.6	504	2.8	25.1
Median monthly cost	$117	–	$100	–	–
MONTHLY COST OF PIPED GAS					
Households using piped gas	**46,700**	**100.0**	**13,959**	**100.0**	**29.9**
Less than $25	1,410	3.0	112	0.8	8.0
$25 to $49	7,933	17.0	1,573	11.3	19.8
$50 to $74	11,196	24.0	2,959	21.2	26.4
$75 to $99	8,595	18.4	2,854	20.4	33.2
$100 to $149	9,694	20.8	3,845	27.5	39.7
$150 to $199	3,698	7.9	1,403	10.1	38.0
$200 or more	2,682	5.7	851	6.1	31.7
Included in other fee or obtained free	1,494	3.2	360	2.6	24.1
Median monthly cost	$80	–	$92	–	–
MONTHLY COST OF FUEL OIL					
Households using fuel oil	**6,409**	**100.0**	**550**	**100.0**	**8.6**
Less than $25	176	2.8	39	7.0	22.0
$25 to $49	325	5.1	63	11.4	19.4
$50 to $74	490	7.6	60	10.9	12.3
$75 to $99	725	11.3	81	14.7	11.1
$100 to $149	1,403	21.9	164	29.8	11.7
$150 to $199	1,052	16.4	50	9.0	4.7
$200 or more	1,701	26.5	64	11.6	3.8
Included in other fee or obtained free	536	8.4	30	5.5	5.6
Median monthly cost	$133	–	$100	–	–

	total		Midwest		
	number	percent distribution	number	percent distribution	percent of total
Water paid separately	53,552	–	12,504	–	23.3%
Median monthly cost	$38	–	$35	–	–
Trash paid separately	44,974	–	11,498	–	25.6
Median monthly cost	$21	–	$20	–	–
Property insurance paid	72,313	–	17,656	–	24.4
Median monthly cost	$55	–	$50	–	–

Note: "–" means not applicable.
Source: Bureau of the Census, American Housing Survey for the United States: 2009, Internet site http://www.census.gov/hhes/ www/housing/ahs/ahs09/ahs09.html; calculations by New Strategist

Table 4.90 Homeowners by Monthly Utility Costs, 2009: South

Homeowners in the South pay more for electricity than the average homeowner does, a median of $145 per month versus $117 per month nationally.

(number and percent distribution of total homeowners and homeowners in the South by average monthly costs for utilities, 2009; numbers in thousands)

	total		South		
	number	percent distribution	number	percent distribution	percent of total
MONTHLY COST OF ELECTRICITY					
Households using electricity	**76,378**	**100.0%**	**29,183**	**100.0%**	**38.2%**
Less than $25	442	0.6	28	0.1	6.3
$25 to $49	4,425	5.8	477	1.6	10.8
$50 to $74	11,016	14.4	1,994	6.8	18.1
$75 to $99	12,975	17.0	3,582	12.3	27.6
$100 to $149	21,237	27.8	9,145	31.3	43.1
$150 to $199	12,164	15.9	6,397	21.9	52.6
$200 or more	12,110	15.9	6,791	23.3	56.1
Included in other fee or obtained free	2,010	2.6	770	2.6	38.3
Median monthly cost	$117	–	$145	–	–
MONTHLY COST OF PIPED GAS					
Households using piped gas	**46,700**	**100.0**	**12,638**	**100.0**	**27.1**
Less than $25	1,410	3.0	547	4.3	38.8
$25 to $49	7,933	17.0	2,494	19.7	31.4
$50 to $74	11,196	24.0	3,156	25.0	28.2
$75 to $99	8,595	18.4	2,656	21.0	30.9
$100 to $149	9,694	20.8	2,192	17.3	22.6
$150 to $199	3,698	7.9	685	5.4	18.5
$200 or more	2,682	5.7	490	3.9	18.3
Included in other fee or obtained free	1,494	3.2	417	3.3	27.9
Median monthly cost	$80	–	$73	–	–
MONTHLY COST OF FUEL OIL					
Households using fuel oil	**6,409**	**100.0**	**845**	**100.0**	**13.2**
Less than $25	176	2.8	44	5.3	25.2
$25 to $49	325	5.1	74	8.7	22.6
$50 to $74	490	7.6	101	12.0	20.7
$75 to $99	725	11.3	139	16.5	19.2
$100 to $149	1,403	21.9	241	28.6	17.2
$150 to $199	1,052	16.4	95	11.2	9.0
$200 or more	1,701	26.5	82	9.7	4.8
Included in other fee or obtained free	536	8.4	68	8.0	12.7
Median monthly cost	$133	–	$167	–	–

	total		South		
	number	percent distribution	number	percent distribution	percent of total
Water paid separately	53,552	–	20,914	–	39.1%
Median monthly cost	$38	–	$35	–	–
Trash paid separately	44,974	–	16,876	–	37.5
Median monthly cost	$21	–	$21	–	–
Property insurance paid	72,313	–	26,972	–	37.3
Median monthly cost	$55	–	$58	–	–

Note: "–" means not applicable.
Source: Bureau of the Census, American Housing Survey for the United States: 2009, Internet site http://www.census.gov/hhes/www/housing/ahs/ahs09/ahs09.html; calculations by New Strategist

Table 4.91 Homeowners by Monthly Utility Costs, 2009: West

Homeowners in the West pay more for water than the average homeowner does, a median of $46 per month versus $38 per month nationally.

(number and percent distribution of total homeowners and homeowners in the West by average monthly costs for utilities, 2009; numbers in thousands)

	total		West		
	number	percent distribution	number	percent distribution	percent of total
MONTHLY COST OF ELECTRICITY					
Households using electricity	**76,378**	**100.0%**	**15,607**	**100.0%**	**20.4%**
Less than $25	442	0.6	234	1.5	52.8
$25 to $49	4,425	5.8	1,640	10.5	37.1
$50 to $74	11,016	14.4	3,014	19.3	27.4
$75 to $99	12,975	17.0	2,944	18.9	22.7
$100 to $149	21,237	27.8	3,543	22.7	16.7
$150 to $199	12,164	15.9	1,849	11.8	15.2
$200 or more	12,110	15.9	1,770	11.3	14.6
Included in other fee or obtained free	2,010	2.6	613	3.9	30.5
Median monthly cost	$117	–	$97	–	–
MONTHLY COST OF PIPED GAS					
Households using piped gas	**46,700**	**100.0**	**12,284**	**100.0**	**26.3**
Less than $25	1,410	3.0	581	4.7	41.3
$25 to $49	7,933	17.0	3,391	27.6	42.7
$50 to $74	11,196	24.0	4,481	36.5	40.0
$75 to $99	8,595	18.4	1,850	15.1	21.5
$100 to $149	9,694	20.8	1,133	9.2	11.7
$150 to $199	3,698	7.9	309	2.5	8.4
$200 or more	2,682	5.7	247	2.0	9.2
Included in other fee or obtained free	1,494	3.2	291	2.4	19.5
Median monthly cost	$80	–	$59	–	–
MONTHLY COST OF FUEL OIL					
Households using fuel oil	**6,409**	**100.0**	**167**	**100.0**	**2.6**
Less than $25	176	2.8	3	1.8	1.7
$25 to $49	325	5.1	10	5.9	3.0
$50 to $74	490	7.6	22	13.0	4.4
$75 to $99	725	11.3	26	15.3	3.5
$100 to $149	1,403	21.9	52	31.3	3.7
$150 to $199	1,052	16.4	22	12.9	2.0
$200 or more	1,701	26.5	15	9.1	0.9
Included in other fee or obtained free	536	8.4	18	10.8	3.4
Median monthly cost	$133	–	$117	–	–

	total		West		
	number	percent distribution	number	percent distribution	percent of total
Water paid separately	53,552	–	11,424	–	21.3%
Median monthly cost	$38	–	$46	–	–
Trash paid separately	44,974	–	11,679	–	26.0
Median monthly cost	$21	–	$25	–	–
Property insurance paid	72,313	–	14,736	–	20.4
Median monthly cost	$55	–	$58	–	–

Note: "–" means not applicable.
Source: Bureau of the Census, American Housing Survey for the United States: 2009, Internet site http://www.census.gov/hhes/www/housing/ahs/ahs09/ahs09.html; calculations by New Strategist

Table 4.92 Homeowners by Real Estate Taxes, 2009: Northeast

Homeowners in the Northeast pay higher property taxes than the average homeowner, a median of $280 per month versus $150 per month nationally.

(number and percent distribution of total homeowners and homeowners in the Northeast by average monthly costs for real estate taxes and taxes per $1,000 assessed value, 2009; numbers in thousands)

	total		Northeast		
	number	percent distribution	number	percent distribution	percent of total
Total homeowners	**76,428**	**100.0%**	**13,378**	**100.0%**	**17.5%**
Monthly cost of real estate taxes					
Less than $25	7,751	10.1	479	3.6	6.2
$25 to $49	6,017	7.9	361	2.7	6.0
$50 to $74	6,565	8.6	483	3.6	7.4
$75 to $99	5,883	7.7	573	4.3	9.7
$100 to $124	6,494	8.5	629	4.7	9.7
$125 to $149	4,880	6.4	593	4.4	12.2
$150 to $199	9,140	12.0	1,442	10.8	15.8
$200 to $299	11,727	15.3	2,581	19.3	22.0
$300 to $399	6,171	8.1	1,783	13.3	28.9
$400 to $499	3,655	4.8	1,264	9.4	34.6
$500 to $599	2,884	3.8	1,103	8.2	38.2
$600 or more	5,260	6.9	2,088	15.6	39.7
Median monthly cost	$150	–	$280	–	–
Annual taxes paid per $1,000 value					
Less than $5	12,710	16.6	796	5.9	6.3
$5 to $9	21,383	28.0	2,129	15.9	10.0
$10 to $14	17,473	22.9	3,417	25.5	19.6
$15 to $19	9,992	13.1	2,798	20.9	28.0
$20 to $24	6,058	7.9	1,777	13.3	29.3
$25 or more	8,812	11.5	2,462	18.4	27.9
Median amount per $1,000 assessed	$10	–	$15	–	–

Note: "–" means not applicable.
Source: Bureau of the Census, American Housing Survey for the United States: 2009, Internet site http://www.census.gov/hhes/ www/housing/ahs/ahs09/ahs09.html; calculations by New Strategist

Table 4.93 Homeowners by Real Estate Taxes, 2009: Midwest

Homeowners in the Midwest pay about the same amount as
the average homeowner in real estate taxes, a median of
$154 per month versus $150 per month nationally.

*(number and percent distribution of total homeowners and homeowners in the Midwest by average monthly costs
for real estate taxes and taxes per $1,000 assessed value, 2009; numbers in thousands)*

	total		Midwest		
	number	percent distribution	number	percent distribution	percent of total
Total homeowners	**76,428**	**100.0%**	**18,249**	**100.0%**	**23.9%**
Monthly cost of real estate taxes					
Less than $25	7,751	10.1	1,056	5.8	13.6
$25 to $49	6,017	7.9	1,232	6.8	20.5
$50 to $74	6,565	8.6	1,508	8.3	23.0
$75 to $99	5,883	7.7	1,478	8.1	25.1
$100 to $124	6,494	8.5	1,828	10.0	28.1
$125 to $149	4,880	6.4	1,518	8.3	31.1
$150 to $199	9,140	12.0	2,677	14.7	29.3
$200 to $299	11,727	15.3	3,216	17.6	27.4
$300 to $399	6,171	8.1	1,581	8.7	25.6
$400 to $499	3,655	4.8	768	4.2	21.0
$500 to $599	2,884	3.8	532	2.9	18.4
$600 or more	5,260	6.9	854	4.7	16.2
Median monthly cost	$150	–	$154	–	–
Annual taxes paid per $1,000 value					
Less than $5	12,710	16.6	1,227	6.7	9.7
$5 to $9	21,383	28.0	3,355	18.4	15.7
$10 to $14	17,473	22.9	5,018	27.5	28.7
$15 to $19	9,992	13.1	3,830	21.0	38.3
$20 to $24	6,058	7.9	2,191	12.0	36.2
$25 or more	8,812	11.5	2,628	14.4	29.8
Median amount per $1,000 assessed	$10	–	$14	–	–

Note: "–" means not applicable.
Source: Bureau of the Census, American Housing Survey for the United States: 2009, Internet site http://www.census.gov/hhes/ www/housing/ahs/ahs09/ahs09.html; calculations by New Strategist

Table 4.94 Homeowners by Real Estate Taxes, 2009: South

Homeowners in the South pay much less in property taxes than the average homeowner, a median of $99 per month versus $150 per month nationally.

(number and percent distribution of total homeowners and homeowners in the South by average monthly costs for real estate taxes and taxes per $1,000 assessed value, 2009; numbers in thousands)

	total		South		
	number	percent distribution	number	percent distribution	percent of total
Total homeowners	**76,428**	**100.0%**	**29,193**	**100.0%**	**38.2%**
Monthly cost of real estate taxes					
Less than $25	7,751	10.1	5,107	17.5	65.9
$25 to $49	6,017	7.9	3,495	12.0	58.1
$50 to $74	6,565	8.6	3,455	11.8	52.6
$75 to $99	5,883	7.7	2,575	8.8	43.8
$100 to $124	6,494	8.5	2,585	8.9	39.8
$125 to $149	4,880	6.4	1,680	5.8	34.4
$150 to $199	9,140	12.0	2,904	9.9	31.8
$200 to $299	11,727	15.3	3,313	11.3	28.2
$300 to $399	6,171	8.1	1,411	4.8	22.9
$400 to $499	3,655	4.8	864	3.0	23.6
$500 to $599	2,884	3.8	598	2.0	20.7
$600 or more	5,260	6.9	1,207	4.1	23.0
Median monthly cost	$150	–	$99	–	–
Annual taxes paid per $1,000 value					
Less than $5	12,710	16.6	7,266	24.9	57.2
$5 to $9	21,383	28.0	9,467	32.4	44.3
$10 to $14	17,473	22.9	5,539	19.0	31.7
$15 to $19	9,992	13.1	2,376	8.1	23.8
$20 to $24	6,058	7.9	1,692	5.8	27.9
$25 or more	8,812	11.5	2,854	9.8	32.4
Median amount per $1,000 assessed	$10	–	$8	–	–

Note: "–" means not applicable.
Source: Bureau of the Census, American Housing Survey for the United States: 2009, Internet site http://www.census.gov/hhes/ www/housing/ahs/ahs09/ahs09.html; calculations by New Strategist

Table 4.95 Homeowners by Real Estate Taxes, 2009: West

Homeowners in the West pay higher property taxes than the average homeowner, a median of $167 per month versus $150 per month nationally.

(number and percent distribution of total homeowners and homeowners in the West by average monthly costs for real estate taxes and taxes per $1,000 assessed value, 2009; numbers in thousands)

	total		West		
	number	percent distribution	number	percent distribution	percent of total
Total homeowners	**76,428**	**100.0%**	**15,607**	**100.0%**	**20.4%**
Monthly cost of real estate taxes					
Less than $25	7,751	10.1	1,110	7.1	14.3
$25 to $49	6,017	7.9	929	6.0	15.4
$50 to $74	6,565	8.6	1,119	7.2	17.0
$75 to $99	5,883	7.7	1,257	8.1	21.4
$100 to $124	6,494	8.5	1,452	9.3	22.4
$125 to $149	4,880	6.4	1,089	7.0	22.3
$150 to $199	9,140	12.0	2,117	13.6	23.2
$200 to $299	11,727	15.3	2,617	16.8	22.3
$300 to $399	6,171	8.1	1,397	8.9	22.6
$400 to $499	3,655	4.8	759	4.9	20.8
$500 to $599	2,884	3.8	652	4.2	22.6
$600 or more	5,260	6.9	1,110	7.1	21.1
Median monthly cost	$150	–	$167	–	–
Annual taxes paid per $1,000 value					
Less than $5	12,710	16.6	3,422	21.9	26.9
$5 to $9	21,383	28.0	6,431	41.2	30.1
$10 to $14	17,473	22.9	3,499	22.4	20.0
$15 to $19	9,992	13.1	988	6.3	9.9
$20 to $24	6,058	7.9	399	2.6	6.6
$25 or more	8,812	11.5	868	5.6	9.9
Median amount per $1,000 assessed	$10	–	$8	–	–

Note: "–" means not applicable.
Source: Bureau of the Census, American Housing Survey for the United States: 2009, Internet site http://www.census.gov/hhes/ www/housing/ahs/ahs09/ahs09.html; calculations by New Strategist

Table 4.96 Homeowners by Opinion of Home and Region, 2009

Regardless of region, about the same proportion of homeowners (30 to 33 percent) rate their home a 10 on a scale of 1 (worst) to 10 (best).

(number and percent distribution of homeowners by opinion of home, by region, 2009; numbers in thousands)

	total	Northeast	Midwest	South	West
Total homeowners	**76,428**	**13,378**	**18,249**	**29,193**	**15,607**
1 (worst)	203	28	43	95	38
2	122	2	25	45	50
3	175	29	41	56	49
4	444	71	110	192	70
5	2,365	381	601	946	436
6	2,655	482	686	967	520
7	8,899	1,584	2,225	3,247	1,843
8	21,042	3,666	5,255	7,690	4,431
9	13,627	2,424	3,184	5,062	2,957
10 (best)	23,967	4,169	5,547	9,606	4,646
Not reported	2,926	542	531	1,286	568
PERCENT DISTRIBUTION BY RATING					
Total homeowners	**100.0%**	**100.0%**	**100.0%**	**100.0%**	**100.0%**
1 (worst)	0.3	0.2	0.2	0.3	0.2
2	0.2	0.0	0.1	0.2	0.3
3	0.2	0.2	0.2	0.2	0.3
4	0.6	0.5	0.6	0.7	0.5
5	3.1	2.9	3.3	3.2	2.8
6	3.5	3.6	3.8	3.3	3.3
7	11.6	11.8	12.2	11.1	11.8
8	27.5	27.4	28.8	26.3	28.4
9	17.8	18.1	17.4	17.3	18.9
10 (best)	31.4	31.2	30.4	32.9	29.8
Not reported	3.8	4.0	2.9	4.4	3.6
PERCENT DISTRIBUTION BY REGION					
Total homeowners	**100.0%**	**17.5%**	**23.9%**	**38.2%**	**20.4%**
1 (worst)	100.0	13.7	21.2	46.6	18.5
2	100.0	1.6	20.6	36.9	40.9
3	100.0	16.4	23.5	31.9	28.2
4	100.0	16.1	24.8	43.3	15.8
5	100.0	16.1	25.4	40.0	18.4
6	100.0	18.1	25.8	36.4	19.6
7	100.0	17.8	25.0	36.5	20.7
8	100.0	17.4	25.0	36.5	21.1
9	100.0	17.8	23.4	37.1	21.7
10 (best)	100.0	17.4	23.1	40.1	19.4
Not reported	100.0	18.5	18.2	43.9	19.4

Source: Bureau of the Census, American Housing Survey for the United States: 2009, Internet site http://www.census.gov/hhes/www/housing/ahs/ahs09/ahs09.html; calculations by New Strategist

Table 4.97 Homeowners by Opinion of Neighborhood and Region, 2009

Homeowners in the West are less likely than those in the other regions to rate their neighborhood a 10.

(number and percent distribution of homeowners by opinion of neighborhood, by region, 2009; numbers in thousands)

	total	Northeast	Midwest	South	West
Total homeowners	**76,428**	**13,378**	**18,249**	**29,193**	**15,607**
1 (worst)	338	41	77	160	61
2	289	40	77	120	52
3	459	62	132	192	73
4	766	84	220	246	216
5	3,356	477	768	1,399	713
6	3,454	590	791	1,322	751
7	9,603	1,643	2,250	3,571	2,138
8	20,808	3,678	4,966	7,778	4,386
9	13,454	2,287	3,308	4,945	2,915
10 (best)	20,891	3,934	5,118	8,120	3,718
No neighborhood	31	4	1	20	6
Not reported	2,979	541	542	1,320	577
PERCENT DISTRIBUTION BY RATING					
Total homeowners	**100.0%**	**100.0%**	**100.0%**	**100.0%**	**100.0%**
1 (worst)	0.4	0.3	0.4	0.5	0.4
2	0.4	0.3	0.4	0.4	0.3
3	0.6	0.5	0.7	0.7	0.5
4	1.0	0.6	1.2	0.8	1.4
5	4.4	3.6	4.2	4.8	4.6
6	4.5	4.4	4.3	4.5	4.8
7	12.6	12.3	12.3	12.2	13.7
8	27.2	27.5	27.2	26.6	28.1
9	17.6	17.1	18.1	16.9	18.7
10 (best)	27.3	29.4	28.0	27.8	23.8
Not reported	0.0	0.0	0.0	0.1	0.0
No neighborhood	3.9	4.0	3.0	4.5	3.7
PERCENT DISTRIBUTION BY REGION					
Total homeowners	**100.0%**	**17.5%**	**23.9%**	**38.2%**	**20.4%**
1 (worst)	100.0	12.0	22.8	47.3	17.9
2	100.0	13.7	26.8	41.5	18.0
3	100.0	13.4	28.7	41.9	15.9
4	100.0	11.0	28.7	32.1	28.2
5	100.0	14.2	22.9	41.7	21.2
6	100.0	17.1	22.9	38.3	21.7
7	100.0	17.1	23.4	37.2	22.3
8	100.0	17.7	23.9	37.4	21.1
9	100.0	17.0	24.6	36.8	21.7
10 (best)	100.0	18.8	24.5	38.9	17.8
Not reported	100.0	12.6	2.4	65.4	19.5
No neighborhood	100.0	18.1	18.2	44.3	19.4

Source: Bureau of the Census, American Housing Survey for the United States: 2009, Internet site http://www.census.gov/hhes/ www/housing/ahs/ahs09/ahs09.html; calculations by New Strategist

Table 4.98 Homeowners with Neighborhood Problems by Region, 2009

Twelve percent of Northeastern homeowners say serious crime has been
a problem in their neighborhood in the past year, well below the
17 percent of homeowners in the West who complain about crime.

(number and percent distribution of homeowners with neighborhood problems, by region, 2009: numbers in thousands)

	total	Northeast	Midwest	South	West
Total homeowners	**76,428**	**13,378**	**18,249**	**29,193**	**15,607**
Bothersome street noise or heavy traffic	15,223	2,926	3,793	5,343	3,161
Serious crime in neighborhood, past 12 months	11,649	1,567	2,679	4,779	2,624
Bothersome odor problem	3,278	563	895	1,071	749
Noise problem	1,733	344	402	541	446
Litter or housing deterioration	1,101	160	268	444	229
Poor city or county services	440	59	106	199	77
Undesirable commercial, institutional, industrial establishments	247	65	56	77	49
People problem	2,706	372	704	1,042	587
Other problems	6,748	1,091	1,403	2,564	1,691
PERCENT DISTRIBUTION BY PROBLEM					
Total homeowners	**100.0%**	**100.0%**	**100.0%**	**100.0%**	**100.0%**
Bothersome street noise or heavy traffic	19.9	21.9	20.8	18.3	20.3
Serious crime in neighborhood, past 12 months	15.2	11.7	14.7	16.4	16.8
Bothersome odor problem	4.3	4.2	4.9	3.7	4.8
Noise problem	2.3	2.6	2.2	1.9	2.9
Litter or housing deterioration	1.4	1.2	1.5	1.5	1.5
Poor city or county services	0.6	0.4	0.6	0.7	0.5
Undesirable commercial, institutional, industrial establishments	0.3	0.5	0.3	0.3	0.3
People problem	3.5	2.8	3.9	3.6	3.8
Other problems	8.8	8.2	7.7	8.8	10.8
PERCENT DISTRIBUTION BY REGION					
Total homeowners	**100.0%**	**17.5%**	**23.9%**	**38.2%**	**20.4%**
Bothersome street noise or heavy traffic	100.0	19.2	24.9	35.1	20.8
Serious crime in neighborhood, past 12 months	100.0	13.5	23.0	41.0	22.5
Bothersome odor problem	100.0	17.2	27.3	32.7	22.9
Noise problem	100.0	19.8	23.2	31.2	25.7
Litter or housing deterioration	100.0	14.5	24.3	40.3	20.8
Poor city or county services	100.0	13.3	24.1	45.2	17.4
Undesirable commercial, institutional, industrial establishments	100.0	26.4	22.7	31.1	19.8
People problem	100.0	13.8	26.0	38.5	21.7
Other problems	100.0	16.2	20.8	38.0	25.1

Source: Bureau of the Census, American Housing Survey for the United States: 2009, Internet site http://www.census.gov/hhes/ www/housing/ahs/ahs09/ahs09.html; calculations by New Strategist

Table 4.99 Homeowners by Community Characteristics, 2009: Northeast

Only 5 percent of homeowners in the Northeast live in a gated community. Forty-five percent have open space, park, woods, farm, or ranch land within 300 feet of their home.

(number and percent distribution of total homeowners and homeowners in the Northeast, by community characteristics, 2009; numbers in thousands)

	total		Northeast		
	number	percent distribution	number	percent distribution	percent of total
Total homeowners	**76,428**	**100.0%**	**13,378**	**100.0%**	**17.5%**
SECURED COMMUNITIES					
Total homeowners	**76,428**	**100.0**	**13,378**	**100.0**	**17.5**
Community access secured with walls or fences	5,337	7.0	606	4.5	11.4
Special entry system present	2,682	3.5	239	1.8	8.9
Special entry system not present	2,648	3.5	367	2.7	13.9
Community access not secured	70,410	92.1	12,680	94.8	18.0
SENIOR CITIZEN COMMUNITIES					
Households with persons aged 55 or older	**36,591**	**100.0**	**6,629**	**100.0**	**18.1**
Community age restricted	1,457	4.0	223	3.4	15.3
No age restriction	35,134	96.0	6,406	96.6	18.2
Community age specific	8,867	24.2	1,393	21.0	15.7
Community not age specific	24,100	65.9	4,588	69.2	19.0
COMMUNITY AMENITIES					
Total homeowners	**76,428**	**100.0**	**13,378**	**100.0**	**17.5**
Community center or clubhouse	14,707	19.2	2,307	17.2	15.7
Golf in community	12,762	16.7	2,307	17.2	18.1
Trails in community	15,300	20.0	2,619	19.6	17.1
Shuttle bus available	5,718	7.5	1,303	9.7	22.8
Daycare center	10,633	13.9	2,318	17.3	21.8
Private or restricted beach, park, or shoreline	15,124	19.8	2,982	22.3	19.7
DESCRIPTION OF AREA WITHIN 300 FEET OF HOME					
Total homeowners	**76,428**	**100.0**	**13,378**	**100.0**	**17.5**
Single-family detached homes	68,909	90.2	12,034	90.0	17.5
Single-family attached homes	10,973	14.4	2,583	19.3	23.5
Multiunit residential buildings	11,514	15.1	2,507	18.7	21.8
One-to-three-story multiunit is tallest	9,014	11.8	1,567	11.7	17.4
Four-to-six-story multiunit is tallest	1,464	1.9	562	4.2	38.4
Seven-or-more-story multiunit is tallest	929	1.2	348	2.6	37.5
Manufactured/mobile homes	10,276	13.4	969	7.2	9.4
Commercial or institutional	16,992	22.2	3,641	27.2	21.4
Industrial or factories	2,520	3.3	585	4.4	23.2
Open space, park, woods, farm, or ranch	33,110	43.3	6,027	45.0	18.2
Four-or-more-lane highway, railroad, or airport	10,380	13.6	1,569	11.7	15.1

	total		Northeast		
	number	percent distribution	number	percent distribution	percent of total
BODIES OF WATER WITHIN 300 FEET OF HOME					
Total homeowners	**76,428**	**100.0%**	**13,378**	**100.0%**	**17.5%**
Water in area	13,824	18.1	2,575	19.2	18.6
With waterfront property	2,653	3.5	423	3.2	16.0
With flood plain	1,929	2.5	360	2.7	18.7
No water in area	62,083	81.2	10,683	79.9	17.2

Note: Numbers may not add to total because "not reported" is not shown.
Source: Bureau of the Census, American Housing Survey for the United States: 2009, Internet site http://www.census.gov/hhes/ www/housing/ahs/ahs09/ahs09.html; calculations by New Strategist

Table 4.100 Homeowners by Community Characteristics, 2009: Midwest

Only 3 percent of homeowners in the Midwest live in a
gated community. Forty-seven percent have open space, park,
woods, farm, or ranch land within 300 feet of their home.

(number and percent distribution of total homeowners and homeowners in the Midwest, by community character-istics, 2009; numbers in thousands)

	total		Midwest		
	number	percent distribution	number	percent distribution	percent of total
Total homeowners	**76,428**	**100.0%**	**18,249**	**100.0%**	**23.9%**
SECURED COMMUNITIES					
Total homeowners	**76,428**	**100.0**	**18,249**	**100.0**	**23.9**
Community access secured with walls or fences	5,337	7.0	480	2.6	9.0
Special entry system present	2,682	3.5	113	0.6	4.2
Special entry system not present	2,648	3.5	364	2.0	13.7
Community access not secured	70,410	92.1	17,644	96.7	25.1
SENIOR CITIZEN COMMUNITIES					
Households with persons aged 55 or older	**36,591**	**100.0**	**8,363**	**100.0**	**22.9**
Community age restricted	1,457	4.0	113	1.4	7.8
No age restriction	35,134	96.0	8,250	98.6	23.5
Community age specific	8,867	24.2	2,164	25.9	24.4
Community not age specific	24,100	65.9	5,700	68.2	23.7
COMMUNITY AMENITIES					
Total homeowners	**76,428**	**100.0**	**18,249**	**100.0**	**23.9**
Community center or clubhouse	14,707	19.2	4,016	22.0	27.3
Golf in community	12,762	16.7	5,041	27.6	39.5
Trails in community	15,300	20.0	4,925	27.0	32.2
Shuttle bus available	5,718	7.5	1,923	10.5	33.6
Daycare center	10,633	13.9	4,242	23.2	39.9
Private or restricted beach, park, or shoreline	15,124	19.8	5,282	28.9	34.9
DESCRIPTION OF AREA WITHIN 300 FEET OF HOME					
Total homeowners	**76,428**	**100.0**	**18,249**	**100.0**	**23.9**
Single-family detached homes	68,909	90.2	16,618	91.1	24.1
Single-family attached homes	10,973	14.4	2,075	11.4	18.9
Multiunit residential buildings	11,514	15.1	2,801	15.3	24.3
One-to-three-story multiunit is tallest	9,014	11.8	2,352	12.9	26.1
Four-to-six-story multiunit is tallest	1,464	1.9	245	1.3	16.8
Seven-or-more-story multiunit is tallest	929	1.2	174	1.0	18.8
Manufactured/mobile homes	10,276	13.4	1,630	8.9	15.9
Commercial or institutional	16,992	22.2	4,158	22.8	24.5
Industrial or factories	2,520	3.3	743	4.1	29.5
Open space, park, woods, farm, or ranch	33,110	43.3	8,566	46.9	25.9
Four-or-more-lane highway, railroad, or airport	10,380	13.6	2,529	13.9	24.4

	total		Midwest		
	number	percent distribution	number	percent distribution	percent of total
BODIES OF WATER WITHIN 300 FEET OF HOME					
Total homeowners	**76,428**	**100.0%**	**18,249**	**100.0%**	**23.9%**
Water in area	13,824	18.1	3,454	18.9	25.0
With waterfront property	2,653	3.5	623	3.4	23.5
With flood plain	1,929	2.5	236	1.3	12.2
No water in area	62,083	81.2	14,699	80.5	23.7

Note: Numbers may not add to total because "not reported" is not shown.
Source: Bureau of the Census, American Housing Survey for the United States: 2009, Internet site http://www.census.gov/hhes/ www/housing/ahs/ahs09/ahs09.html; calculations by New Strategist

Table 4.101 Homeowners by Community Characteristics, 2009: South

Eight percent of homeowners in the South live in a gated community.
Ten percent have a golf course in their community, and
18 percent have a community center or clubhouse.

(number and percent distribution of total homeowners and homeowners in the South, by community characteristics, 2009; numbers in thousands)

	total		South		
	number	percent distribution	number	percent distribution	percent of total
Total homeowners	**76,428**	**100.0%**	**29,193**	**100.0%**	**38.2%**
SECURED COMMUNITIES					
Total homeowners	**76,428**	**100.0**	**29,193**	**100.0**	**38.2**
Community access secured with walls or fences	5,337	7.0	2,281	7.8	42.8
Special entry system present	2,682	3.5	1,281	4.4	47.8
Special entry system not present	2,648	3.5	996	3.4	37.6
Community access not secured	70,410	92.1	26,614	91.2	37.8
SENIOR CITIZEN COMMUNITIES					
Households with persons aged 55 or older	**36,591**	**100.0**	**14,189**	**100.0**	**38.8**
Community age restricted	1,457	4.0	683	4.8	46.9
No age restriction	35,134	96.0	13,506	95.2	38.4
Community age specific	8,867	24.2	3,726	26.3	42.0
Community not age specific	24,100	65.9	8,881	62.6	36.8
COMMUNITY AMENITIES					
Total homeowners	**76,428**	**100.0**	**29,193**	**100.0**	**38.2**
Community center or clubhouse	14,707	19.2	5,260	18.0	35.8
Golf in community	12,762	16.7	3,064	10.5	24.0
Trails in community	15,300	20.0	4,416	15.1	28.9
Shuttle bus available	5,718	7.5	1,196	4.1	20.9
Daycare center	10,633	13.9	2,441	8.4	23.0
Private or restricted beach, park, or shoreline	15,124	19.8	3,693	12.7	24.4
DESCRIPTION OF AREA WITHIN 300 FEET OF HOME					
Total homeowners	**76,428**	**100.0**	**29,193**	**100.0**	**38.2**
Single-family detached homes	68,909	90.2	26,160	89.6	38.0
Single-family attached homes	10,973	14.4	3,662	12.5	33.4
Multiunit residential buildings	11,514	15.1	3,346	11.5	29.1
One-to-three-story multiunit is tallest	9,014	11.8	2,682	9.2	29.8
Four-to-six-story multiunit is tallest	1,464	1.9	385	1.3	26.3
Seven-or-more-story multiunit is tallest	929	1.2	242	0.8	26.0
Manufactured/mobile homes	10,276	13.4	5,713	19.6	55.6
Commercial or institutional	16,992	22.2	5,590	19.1	32.9
Industrial or factories	2,520	3.3	830	2.8	32.9
Open space, park, woods, farm, or ranch	33,110	43.3	12,502	42.8	37.8
Four-or-more-lane highway, railroad, or airport	10,380	13.6	4,218	14.4	40.6

	total		South		
	number	percent distribution	number	percent distribution	percent of total
BODIES OF WATER WITHIN 300 FEET OF HOME					
Total homeowners	**76,428**	**100.0%**	**29,193**	**100.0%**	**38.2%**
Water in area	13,824	18.1	6,126	21.0	44.3
With waterfront property	2,653	3.5	1,322	4.5	49.8
With flood plain	1,929	2.5	1,108	3.8	57.4
No water in area	62,083	81.2	22,898	78.4	36.9

Note: Numbers may not add to total because "not reported" is not shown.
Source: Bureau of the Census, American Housing Survey for the United States: 2009, Internet site http://www.census.gov/hhes/ www/housing/ahs/ahs09/ahs09.html; calculations by New Strategist

Table 4.102 Homeowners by Community Characteristics, 2009: West

Thirteen percent of homeowners in the West live in a gated community.
Twenty-one percent have trails in their community.

(number and percent distribution of total homeowners and homeowners in the West, by community characteristics, 2009; numbers in thousands)

	total		West		
	number	percent distribution	number	percent distribution	percent of total
Total homeowners	**76,428**	**100.0%**	**15,607**	**100.0%**	**20.4%**
SECURED COMMUNITIES					
Total homeowners	**76,428**	**100.0**	**15,607**	**100.0**	**20.4**
Community access secured with walls or fences	5,337	7.0	1,969	12.6	36.9
Special entry system present	2,682	3.5	1,048	6.7	39.1
Special entry system not present	2,648	3.5	921	5.9	34.8
Community access not secured	70,410	92.1	13,472	86.3	19.1
SENIOR CITIZEN COMMUNITIES					
Households with persons aged 55 or older	**36,591**	**100.0**	**7,409**	**100.0**	**20.2**
Community age restricted	1,457	4.0	437	5.9	30.0
No age restriction	35,134	96.0	6,972	94.1	19.8
Community age specific	8,867	24.2	1,584	21.4	17.9
Community not age specific	24,100	65.9	4,931	66.6	20.5
COMMUNITY AMENITIES					
Total homeowners	**76,428**	**100.0**	**15,607**	**100.0**	**20.4**
Community center or clubhouse	14,707	19.2	3,125	20.0	21.2
Golf in community	12,762	16.7	2,350	15.1	18.4
Trails in community	15,300	20.0	3,339	21.4	21.8
Shuttle bus available	5,718	7.5	1,297	8.3	22.7
Daycare center	10,633	13.9	1,632	10.5	15.3
Private or restricted beach, park, or shoreline	15,124	19.8	3,167	20.3	20.9
DESCRIPTION OF AREA WITHIN 300 FEET OF HOME					
Total homeowners	**76,428**	**100.0**	**15,607**	**100.0**	**20.4**
Single-family detached homes	68,909	90.2	14,097	90.3	20.5
Single-family attached homes	10,973	14.4	2,653	17.0	24.2
Multiunit residential buildings	11,514	15.1	2,860	18.3	24.8
One-to-three-story multiunit is tallest	9,014	11.8	2,413	15.5	26.8
Four-to-six-story multiunit is tallest	1,464	1.9	271	1.7	18.5
Seven-or-more-story multiunit is tallest	929	1.2	165	1.1	17.7
Manufactured/mobile homes	10,276	13.4	1,964	12.6	19.1
Commercial or institutional	16,992	22.2	3,603	23.1	21.2
Industrial or factories	2,520	3.3	363	2.3	14.4
Open space, park, woods, farm, or ranch	33,110	43.3	6,015	38.5	18.2
Four-or-more-lane highway, railroad, or airport	10,380	13.6	2,065	13.2	19.9

	total		West		
	number	percent distribution	number	percent distribution	percent of total
BODIES OF WATER WITHIN 300 FEET OF HOME					
Total homeowners	**76,428**	**100.0%**	**15,607**	**100.0%**	**20.4%**
Water in area	13,824	18.1	1,668	10.7	12.1
With waterfront property	2,653	3.5	286	1.8	10.8
With flood plain	1,929	2.5	225	1.4	11.7
No water in area	62,083	81.2	13,803	88.4	22.2

Note: Numbers may not add to total because "not reported" is not shown.
Source: Bureau of the Census, American Housing Survey for the United States: 2009, Internet site http://www.census.gov/hhes/www/housing/ahs/ahs09/ahs09.html; calculations by New Strategist

Table 4.103 Homeowners by Public Services Available, 2009: Northeast

The 56 percent majority of homeowners in the Northeast have public transportation in their area, and 17 percent of those with public transportation use it regularly for their commute to work or school.

(number and percent distribution of total homeowners and homeowners in the Northeast by public services available in neighborhood, 2009; numbers in thousands)

	total		Northeast		
	number	percent distribution	number	percent distribution	percent of total
Total homeowners	**76,428**	**100.0%**	**13,378**	**100.0%**	**17.5%**
LOCAL ELEMENTARY SCHOOL					
Homeowners with children under age 14	**20,490**	**100.0**	**3,485**	**100.0**	**17.0**
Satisfactory public elementary school	16,966	82.8	2,924	83.9	17.2
Unsatisfactory public elementary school	1,422	6.9	218	6.2	15.3
Unsatisfactory public elementary school	**1,422**	**100.0**	**218**	**100.0**	**15.3**
Better than other area elementary schools	154	10.8	19	8.9	12.7
Same as other area elementary schools	490	34.4	88	40.5	18.0
Worse than other area elementary schools	696	49.0	95	43.5	13.6
Homeowners with children under age 14	**20,490**	**100.0**	**3,485**	**100.0**	**17.0**
Public elementary school less than one mile	11,571	56.5	1,969	56.5	17.0
Public elementary school more than one mile	7,785	38.0	1,318	37.8	16.9
PUBLIC TRANSPORTATION IN AREA					
Total homeowners	**76,428**	**100.0**	**13,378**	**100.0**	**17.5**
With public transportation	35,616	46.6	7,543	56.4	21.2
No public transportation	38,848	50.8	5,570	41.6	14.3
With public transportation, travel time to nearest stop	**35,616**	**100.0**	**7,543**	**100.0**	**21.2**
Less than 5 minutes	10,929	30.7	2,392	31.7	21.9
5 to 9 minutes	12,830	36.0	2,619	34.7	20.4
10 to 14 minutes	5,853	16.4	1,303	17.3	22.3
15 to 29 minutes	3,125	8.8	740	9.8	23.7
30 minutes or longer	449	1.3	70	0.9	15.5
With public transportation	**35,616**	**100.0**	**7,543**	**100.0**	**21.2**
Household uses it regularly for commute to school or work	3,817	10.7	1,260	16.7	33.0
Household does not use it regularly for commute to school or work	31,606	88.7	6,204	82.3	19.6

	total		Northeast		
	number	percent distribution	number	percent distribution	percent of total
SHOPPING IN AREA					
Total homeowners	**76,428**	**100.0%**	**13,378**	**100.0%**	**17.5%**
Grocery stores or drugstores within 15 minutes of home	72,548	94.9	12,732	95.2	17.5
Satisfactory	70,400	92.1	12,374	92.5	17.6
Not satisfactory	1,805	2.4	300	2.2	16.6
No grocery stores or drugstores within 15 minutes of home	2,819	3.7	499	3.7	17.7
POLICE PROTECTION					
Total homeowners	**76,428**	**100.0**	**13,378**	**100.0**	**17.5**
Satisfactory police protection	69,633	91.1	12,283	91.8	17.6
Unsatisfactory police protection	4,800	6.3	786	5.9	16.4

Note: Numbers may not add to total because "not reported" is not shown.
Source: Bureau of the Census, American Housing Survey for the United States: 2009, Internet site http://www.census.gov/hhes/ www/housing/ahs/ahs09/ahs09.html; calculations by New Strategist

Table 4.104 Homeowners by Public Services Available, 2009: Midwest

Only 44 percent of homeowners in the Midwest have public transportation in their area. Just 9 percent of those with public transportation use it regularly for their commute to work or school.

(number and percent distribution of total homeowners and homeowners in the Midwest by public services available in neighborhood, 2009; numbers in thousands)

	total		Midwest		
	number	percent distribution	number	percent distribution	percent of total
Total homeowners	**76,428**	**100.0%**	**18,249**	**100.0%**	**23.9%**
LOCAL ELEMENTARY SCHOOL					
Homeowners with children under age 14	**20,490**	**100.0**	**4,995**	**100.0**	**24.4**
Satisfactory public elementary school	16,966	82.8	4,246	85.0	25.0
Unsatisfactory public elementary school	1,422	6.9	265	5.3	18.6
Unsatisfactory public elementary school	**1,422**	**100.0**	**265**	**100.0**	**18.6**
Better than other area elementary schools	154	10.8	25	9.4	16.3
Same as other area elementary schools	490	34.4	102	38.5	20.8
Worse than other area elementary schools	696	49.0	110	41.8	15.9
Homeowners with children under age 14	**20,490**	**100.0**	**4,995**	**100.0**	**24.4**
Public elementary school less than one mile	11,571	56.5	2,820	56.5	24.4
Public elementary school more than one mile	7,785	38.0	1,921	38.4	24.7
PUBLIC TRANSPORTATION IN AREA					
Total homeowners	**76,428**	**100.0**	**18,249**	**100.0**	**23.9**
With public transportation	35,616	46.6	8,055	44.1	22.6
No public transportation	38,848	50.8	9,757	53.5	25.1
With public transportation, travel time to nearest stop	**35,616**	**100.0**	**8,055**	**100.0**	**22.6**
Less than 5 minutes	10,929	30.7	2,947	36.6	27.0
5 to 9 minutes	12,830	36.0	2,744	34.1	21.4
10 to 14 minutes	5,853	16.4	1,079	13.4	18.4
15 to 29 minutes	3,125	8.8	524	6.5	16.8
30 minutes or longer	449	1.3	83	1.0	18.4
With public transportation	**35,616**	**100.0**	**8,055**	**100.0**	**22.6**
Household uses it regularly for commute to school or work	3,817	10.7	726	9.0	19.0
Household does not use it regularly for commute to school or work	31,606	88.7	7,311	90.8	23.1

	total		Midwest		
	number	percent distribution	number	percent distribution	percent of total
SHOPPING IN AREA					
Total homeowners	**76,428**	**100.0%**	**18,249**	**100.0%**	**23.9%**
Grocery stores or drugstores within 15 minutes of home	72,548	94.9	17,526	96.0	24.2
Satisfactory	70,400	92.1	17,153	94.0	24.4
Not satisfactory	1,805	2.4	318	1.7	17.6
No grocery stores or drugstores within 15 minutes of home	2,819	3.7	537	2.9	19.1
POLICE PROTECTION					
Total homeowners	**76,428**	**100.0**	**18,249**	**100.0**	**23.9**
Satisfactory police protection	69,633	91.1	16,927	92.8	24.3
Unsatisfactory police protection	4,800	6.3	943	5.2	19.6

Note: Numbers may not add to total because "not reported" is not shown.
Source: Bureau of the Census, American Housing Survey for the United States: 2009, Internet site http://www.census.gov/hhes/ www/housing/ahs/ahs09/ahs09.html; calculations by New Strategist

Table 4.105 Homeowners by Public Services Available, 2009: South

Only 33 percent of homeowners in the South have public transportation in their area. Just 8 percent of those with public transportation use it regularly for their commute to work or school.

(number and percent distribution of total homeowners and homeowners in the South by public services available in neighborhood, 2009; numbers in thousands)

	total		South		
	number	percent distribution	number	percent distribution	percent of total
Total homeowners	**76,428**	**100.0%**	**29,193**	**100.0%**	**38.2%**
LOCAL ELEMENTARY SCHOOL					
Homeowners with children under age 14	**20,490**	**100.0**	**7,654**	**100.0**	**37.4**
Satisfactory public elementary school	16,966	82.8	6,302	82.3	37.1
Unsatisfactory public elementary school	1,422	6.9	587	7.7	41.3
Unsatisfactory public elementary school	**1,422**	**100.0**	**587**	**100.0**	**41.3**
Better than other area elementary schools	154	10.8	76	12.9	49.2
Same as other area elementary schools	490	34.4	201	34.3	41.1
Worse than other area elementary schools	696	49.0	287	48.9	41.2
Homeowners with children under age 14	**20,490**	**100.0**	**7,654**	**100.0**	**37.4**
Public elementary school less than one mile	11,571	56.5	3,656	47.8	31.6
Public elementary school more than one mile	7,785	38.0	3,592	46.9	46.1
PUBLIC TRANSPORTATION IN AREA					
Total homeowners	**76,428**	**100.0**	**29,193**	**100.0**	**38.2**
With public transportation	35,616	46.6	9,598	32.9	26.9
No public transportation	38,848	50.8	18,754	64.2	48.3
With public transportation, travel time to nearest stop	**35,616**	**100.0**	**9,598**	**100.0**	**26.9**
Less than 5 minutes	10,929	30.7	2,606	27.2	23.8
5 to 9 minutes	12,830	36.0	3,392	35.3	26.4
10 to 14 minutes	5,853	16.4	1,757	18.3	30.0
15 to 29 minutes	3,125	8.8	968	10.1	31.0
30 minutes or longer	449	1.3	203	2.1	45.1
With public transportation	**35,616**	**100.0**	**9,598**	**100.0**	**26.9**
Household uses it regularly for commute to school or work	3,817	10.7	726	7.6	19.0
Household does not use it regularly for commute to school or work	31,606	88.7	8,826	92.0	27.9

	total		South		
	number	percent distribution	number	percent distribution	percent of total
SHOPPING IN AREA					
Total homeowners	**76,428**	**100.0%**	**29,193**	**100.0%**	**38.2%**
Grocery stores or drugstores within 15 minutes of home	72,548	94.9	27,288	93.5	37.6
Satisfactory	70,400	92.1	26,473	90.7	37.6
Not satisfactory	1,805	2.4	643	2.2	35.6
No grocery stores or drugstores within 15 minutes of home	2,819	3.7	1,398	4.8	49.6
POLICE PROTECTION					
Total homeowners	**76,428**	**100.0**	**29,193**	**100.0**	**38.2**
Satisfactory police protection	69,633	91.1	26,267	90.0	37.7
Unsatisfactory police protection	4,800	6.3	2,072	7.1	43.2

Note: Numbers may not add to total because "not reported" is not shown.
Source: Bureau of the Census, American Housing Survey for the United States: 2009, Internet site http://www.census.gov/hhes/ www/housing/ahs/ahs09/ahs09.html; calculations by New Strategist

Table 4.106 Homeowners by Public Services Available, 2009: West

The 67 percent majority of homeowners in the West have public transportation in their area, and 11 percent of those with public transportation use it regularly for their commute to work or school.

(number and percent distribution of total homeowners and homeowners in the West by public services available in neighborhood, 2009; numbers in thousands)

	total		West		
	number	percent distribution	number	percent distribution	percent of total
Total homeowners	**76,428**	**100.0%**	**15,607**	**100.0%**	**20.4%**
LOCAL ELEMENTARY SCHOOL					
Homeowners with children under age 14	**20,490**	**100.0**	**4,355**	**100.0**	**21.3**
Satisfactory public elementary school	16,966	82.8	3,494	80.2	20.6
Unsatisfactory public elementary school	1,422	6.9	353	8.1	24.8
Unsatisfactory public elementary school	**1,422**	**100.0**	**353**	**100.0**	**24.8**
Better than other area elementary schools	154	10.8	34	9.5	21.9
Same as other area elementary schools	490	34.4	99	27.9	20.2
Worse than other area elementary schools	696	49.0	204	57.9	29.3
Homeowners with children under age 14	**20,490**	**100.0**	**4,355**	**100.0**	**21.3**
Public elementary school less than one mile	11,571	56.5	3,125	71.8	27.0
Public elementary school more than one mile	7,785	38.0	955	21.9	12.3
PUBLIC TRANSPORTATION IN AREA					
Total homeowners	**76,428**	**100.0**	**15,607**	**100.0**	**20.4**
With public transportation	35,616	46.6	10,421	66.8	29.3
No public transportation	38,848	50.8	4,767	30.5	12.3
With public transportation, travel time to nearest stop	**35,616**	**100.0**	**10,421**	**100.0**	**29.3**
Less than 5 minutes	10,929	30.7	2,983	28.6	27.3
5 to 9 minutes	12,830	36.0	4,075	39.1	31.8
10 to 14 minutes	5,853	16.4	1,715	16.5	29.3
15 to 29 minutes	3,125	8.8	892	8.6	28.6
30 minutes or longer	449	1.3	94	0.9	20.9
With public transportation	**35,616**	**100.0**	**10,421**	**100.0**	**29.3**
Household uses it regularly for commute to school or work	3,817	10.7	1,104	10.6	28.9
Household does not use it regularly for commute to school or work	31,606	88.7	9,265	88.9	29.3

	total		West		
	number	percent distribution	number	percent distribution	percent of total
SHOPPING IN AREA					
Total homeowners	**76,428**	**100.0%**	**15,607**	**100.0%**	**20.4%**
Grocery stores or drugstores within 15 minutes of home	72,548	94.9	15,002	96.1	20.7
Satisfactory	70,400	92.1	14,401	92.3	20.5
Not satisfactory	1,805	2.4	543	3.5	30.1
No grocery stores or drugstores within 15 minutes of home	2,819	3.7	385	2.5	13.7
POLICE PROTECTION					
Total homeowners	**76,428**	**100.0**	**15,607**	**100.0**	**20.4**
Satisfactory police protection	69,633	91.1	14,156	90.7	20.3
Unsatisfactory police protection	4,800	6.3	999	6.4	20.8

Note: Numbers may not add to total because "not reported" is not shown.
Source: Bureau of the Census, American Housing Survey for the United States: 2009, Internet site http://www.census.gov/hhes/
www/housing/ahs/ahs09/ahs09.html; calculations by New Strategist

Table 4.107 Homeowners Who Moved by Changes in Housing and Costs, 2009: Northeast

Among homeowners in the Northeast who moved in the past year,
66 percent saw their housing costs increase with the move.

(number and percent distribution of total homeowners and homeowners in the Northeast who moved in the past year, by structure type of previous residence, ownership of previous residence, and change in housing costs, 2009; numbers in thousands)

	total		Northeast		
	number	percent distribution	number	percent distribution	percent of total
STRUCTURE TYPE OF PREVIOUS RESIDENCE					
Homeowners who moved within United States	**4,341**	**100.0%**	**582**	**100.0%**	**13.4%**
House	2,595	59.8	339	58.3	13.1
Apartment	1,208	27.8	210	36.1	17.4
Mobile home	238	5.5	7	1.2	2.9
Other	119	2.7	9	1.6	7.6
Not reported	182	4.2	17	2.9	9.2
OWNERSHIP OF PREVIOUS RESIDENCE					
Homeowners who moved from house, apartment, or mobile home within United States	**4,041**	**100.0**	**556**	**100.0**	**13.8**
Owner-occupied	2,032	50.3	284	51.1	14.0
Renter-occupied	2,009	49.7	272	48.9	13.5
CHANGE IN HOUSING COSTS					
Homeowners who moved from house, apartment, or mobile home within United States	**4,041**	**100.0**	**556**	**100.0**	**13.8**
Increased with move	2,455	60.8	364	65.5	14.8
Decreased	801	19.8	87	15.6	10.9
Stayed about the same	663	16.4	86	15.4	12.9
Don't know	60	1.5	10	1.7	16.1
Not reported	62	1.5	9	1.7	14.9

Source: Bureau of the Census, American Housing Survey for the United States: 2009, Internet site http://www.census.gov/hhes/ www/housing/ahs/ahs09/ahs09.html; calculations by New Strategist

Table 4.108 Homeowners Who Moved by Changes in Housing and Costs, 2009: Midwest

Among homeowners in the Midwest who moved in the past year,
62 percent saw their housing costs increase with the move.

(number and percent distribution of total homeowners and homeowners in the Midwest who moved in the past year, by structure type of previous residence, ownership of previous residence, and change in housing costs, 2009; numbers in thousands)

	total		Midwest		
	number	percent distribution	number	percent distribution	percent of total
STRUCTURE TYPE OF PREVIOUS RESIDENCE					
Homeowners who moved within United States	**4,341**	**100.0%**	**966**	**100.0%**	**22.2%**
House	2,595	59.8	615	63.7	23.7
Apartment	1,208	27.8	233	24.2	19.3
Mobile home	238	5.5	63	6.5	26.4
Other	119	2.7	25	2.6	21.0
Not reported	182	4.2	30	3.1	16.4
OWNERSHIP OF PREVIOUS RESIDENCE					
Homeowners who moved from house, apartment, or mobile home within United States	**4,041**	**100.0**	**911**	**100.0**	**22.5**
Owner-occupied	2,032	50.3	475	52.1	23.4
Renter-occupied	2,009	49.7	436	47.9	21.7
CHANGE IN HOUSING COSTS					
Homeowners who moved from house, apartment, or mobile home within United States	**4,041**	**100.0**	**911**	**100.0**	**22.5**
Increased with move	2,455	60.8	564	61.9	23.0
Decreased	801	19.8	173	19.0	21.7
Stayed about the same	663	16.4	153	16.8	23.0
Don't know	60	1.5	9	1.0	14.7
Not reported	62	1.5	12	1.3	19.1

Source: Bureau of the Census, American Housing Survey for the United States: 2009, Internet site http://www.census.gov/hhes/ www/housing/ahs/ahs09/ahs09.html; calculations by New Strategist

Table 4.109 Homeowners Who Moved by Changes in Housing and Costs, 2009: South

Among homeowners in the South who moved in the past year,
59 percent saw their housing costs increase with the move.

(number and percent distribution of total homeowners and homeowners in the South who moved in the past year, by structure type of previous residence, ownership of previous residence, and change in housing costs, 2009; numbers in thousands)

	total		South		
	number	percent distribution	number	percent distribution	percent of total
STRUCTURE TYPE OF PREVIOUS RESIDENCE					
Homeowners who moved within United States	**4,341**	**100.0%**	**1,665**	**100.0%**	**38.4%**
House	2,595	59.8	986	59.2	38.0
Apartment	1,208	27.8	459	27.6	38.0
Mobile home	238	5.5	123	7.4	51.7
Other	119	2.7	27	1.6	22.9
Not reported	182	4.2	70	4.2	38.4
OWNERSHIP OF PREVIOUS RESIDENCE					
Homeowners who moved from house, apartment, or mobile home within United States	**4,041**	**100.0**	**1,568**	**100.0**	**38.8**
Owner-occupied	2,032	50.3	811	51.7	39.9
Renter-occupied	2,009	49.7	757	48.3	37.7
CHANGE IN HOUSING COSTS					
Homeowners who moved from house, apartment, or mobile home within United States	**4,041**	**100.0**	**1,568**	**100.0**	**38.8**
Increased with move	2,455	60.8	918	58.5	37.4
Decreased	801	19.8	354	22.6	44.2
Stayed about the same	663	16.4	246	15.7	37.1
Don't know	60	1.5	19	1.2	32.5
Not reported	62	1.5	30	1.9	48.9

Source: Bureau of the Census, American Housing Survey for the United States: 2009, Internet site http://www.census.gov/hhes/ www/housing/ahs/ahs09/ahs09.html; calculations by New Strategist

Table 4.110 Homeowners Who Moved by Changes in Housing and Costs, 2009: West

Among homeowners in the West who moved in the past year,
60 percent saw their housing costs increase with the move.

(number and percent distribution of total homeowners and homeowners in the West who moved in the past year, by structure type of previous residence, ownership of previous residence, and change in housing costs, 2009; numbers in thousands)

	total		West		
	number	percent distribution	number	percent distribution	percent of total
STRUCTURE TYPE OF PREVIOUS RESIDENCE					
Homeowners who moved within United States	**4,341**	**100.0%**	**1,129**	**100.0%**	**26.0%**
House	2,595	59.8	655	58.0	25.2
Apartment	1,208	27.8	306	27.1	25.3
Mobile home	238	5.5	45	4.0	19.0
Other	119	2.7	58	5.1	48.5
Not reported	182	4.2	65	5.8	36.0
OWNERSHIP OF PREVIOUS RESIDENCE					
Homeowners who moved from house, apartment, or mobile home within United States	**4,041**	**100.0**	**1,006**	**100.0**	**24.9**
Owner-occupied	2,032	50.3	463	46.0	22.8
Renter-occupied	2,009	49.7	544	54.0	27.1
CHANGE IN HOUSING COSTS					
Homeowners who moved from house, apartment, or mobile home within United States	**4,041**	**100.0**	**1,006**	**100.0**	**24.9**
Increased with move	2,455	60.8	609	60.5	24.8
Decreased	801	19.8	186	18.5	23.3
Stayed about the same	663	16.4	179	17.8	27.0
Don't know	60	1.5	22	2.2	36.7
Not reported	62	1.5	11	1.1	17.1

Source: Bureau of the Census, American Housing Survey for the United States: 2009, Internet site http://www.census.gov/hhes/ www/housing/ahs/ahs09/ahs09.html; calculations by New Strategist

Table 4.111 Homeowners Who Moved by Reasons for Choosing Home, 2009: Northeast

Among homeowners in the Northeast who moved in the past year,
the largest share chose their present home for financial reasons.
Sixty-four percent say their current home is better than their previous home.

(number and percent distribution of total homeowning respondents and homeowning respondents in the Northeast who moved in the past year, by reasons for choosing home, 2009; numbers in thousands)

	total		Northeast		
	number	percent distribution	number	percent distribution	percent of total
Total homeowning respondents who moved	**4,623**	**100.0%**	**603**	**100.0%**	**13.0%**
Main reason for choice of present home					
All reported reasons equal	808	17.5	105	17.3	12.9
Financial reasons	1,008	21.8	97	16.0	9.6
Room layout/design	797	17.2	89	14.8	11.2
Kitchen	33	0.7	11	1.8	32.9
Size	377	8.2	53	8.8	14.0
Exterior appearance	125	2.7	15	2.6	12.3
Yard/trees/view	287	6.2	67	11.1	23.3
Quality of construction	186	4.0	33	5.5	17.7
Only one available	76	1.6	15	2.5	19.6
Other	636	13.7	87	14.4	13.6
Not reported	290	6.3	33	5.4	11.2
Present home compared with previous home					
Better	3,017	65.3	385	63.8	12.8
Worse	426	9.2	63	10.4	14.8
About the same	920	19.9	130	21.6	14.2
Not reported	261	5.6	25	4.2	9.7
Home search					
Now in house	3,929	100.0	505	100.0	12.8
Did not look at apartments	3,430	87.3	412	81.7	12.0
Looked at apartments too	305	7.8	70	13.9	23.1
Now in manufactured/mobile home	410	100.0	31	100.0	7.7
Did not look at apartments	304	74.1	23	73.3	7.6
Looked at apartments too	69	16.9	8	26.7	12.1
Now in apartment	285	100.0	67	100.0	23.7
Did not look at houses	181	63.6	48	70.9	26.4
Looked at houses too	92	32.2	16	24.0	17.6

Note: Total number of movers does not equal total movers in other tables because this table shows survey respondents who moved, not necessarily householders. Numbers may not add to total because "not reported" may not be shown.
Source: Bureau of the Census, American Housing Survey for the United States: 2009, Internet site http://www.census.gov/hhes/ www/housing/ahs/ahs09/ahs09.html; calculations by New Strategist

Table 4.112 Homeowners Who Moved by Reasons for Choosing Home, 2009: Midwest

Among homeowners in the Midwest who moved in the past year, the largest
share chose their present home for financial reasons. Sixty-four percent
say their current home is better than their previous home.

*(number and percent distribution of total homeowning respondents and homeowning respondents in the Midwest
who moved in the past year, by reasons for choosing home, 2009; numbers in thousands)*

	total		Midwest		
	number	percent distribution	number	percent distribution	percent of total
Total homeowning respondents who moved	**4,623**	**100.0%**	**1,030**	**100.0%**	**22.3%**
Main reason for choice of present home					
All reported reasons equal	808	17.5	214	20.8	26.5
Financial reasons	1,008	21.8	236	22.9	23.4
Room layout/design	797	17.2	160	15.5	20.1
Kitchen	33	0.7	12	1.2	37.0
Size	377	8.2	106	10.3	28.1
Exterior appearance	125	2.7	21	2.0	16.6
Yard/trees/view	287	6.2	47	4.6	16.5
Quality of construction	186	4.0	39	3.8	21.1
Only one available	76	1.6	11	1.1	14.5
Other	636	13.7	149	14.4	23.4
Not reported	290	6.3	34	3.3	11.8
Present home compared with previous home					
Better	3,017	65.3	660	64.1	21.9
Worse	426	9.2	89	8.6	20.8
About the same	920	19.9	244	23.7	26.5
Not reported	261	5.6	37	3.6	14.1
Home search					
Now in house	3,929	100.0	864	100.0	22.0
Did not look at apartments	3,430	87.3	767	88.8	22.4
Looked at apartments too	305	7.8	70	8.1	22.9
Now in manufactured/mobile home	410	100.0	121	100.0	29.5
Did not look at apartments	304	74.1	79	65.7	26.1
Looked at apartments too	69	16.9	37	31.0	54.2
Now in apartment	285	100.0	45	100.0	15.9
Did not look at houses	181	63.6	39	85.5	21.4
Looked at houses too	92	32.2	5	10.7	5.3

*Note: Total number of movers does not equal total movers in other tables because this table shows survey respondents who
moved, not necessarily householders. Numbers may not add to total because "not reported" may not be shown.*
*Source: Bureau of the Census, American Housing Survey for the United States: 2009, Internet site http://www.census.gov/hhes/
www/housing/ahs/ahs09/ahs09.html; calculations by New Strategist*

Table 4.113 Homeowners Who Moved by Reasons for Choosing Home, 2009: South

Among homeowners in the South who moved in the past year, the
largest share chose their present home for financial reasons.
Sixty-seven percent say their current home is better than their previous home.

(number and percent distribution of total homeowning respondents and homeowning respondents in the South who moved in the past year, by reasons for choosing home, 2009; numbers in thousands)

	total		South		
	number	percent distribution	number	percent distribution	percent of total
Total homeowning respondents who moved	**4,623**	**100.0%**	**1,802**	**100.0%**	**39.0%**
Main reason for choice of present home					
All reported reasons equal	808	17.5	297	16.5	36.7
Financial reasons	1,008	21.8	393	21.8	39.0
Room layout/design	797	17.2	313	17.4	39.3
Kitchen	33	0.7	10	0.6	30.0
Size	377	8.2	123	6.8	32.6
Exterior appearance	125	2.7	65	3.6	52.0
Yard/trees/view	287	6.2	105	5.8	36.6
Quality of construction	186	4.0	86	4.8	46.1
Only one available	76	1.6	24	1.3	31.9
Other	636	13.7	254	14.1	40.0
Not reported	290	6.3	131	7.3	45.1
Present home compared with previous home					
Better	3,017	65.3	1,206	67.0	40.0
Worse	426	9.2	178	9.9	41.8
About the same	920	19.9	310	17.2	33.7
Not reported	261	5.6	107	6.0	41.2
Home search					
Now in house	3,929	100.0	1,538	100.0	39.1
Did not look at apartments	3,430	87.3	1,366	88.8	39.8
Looked at apartments too	305	7.8	90	5.8	29.4
Now in manufactured/mobile home	410	100.0	181	100.0	44.2
Did not look at apartments	304	74.1	149	82.0	49.0
Looked at apartments too	69	16.9	12	6.7	17.5
Now in apartment	285	100.0	83	100.0	29.3
Did not look at houses	181	63.6	46	55.2	25.4
Looked at houses too	92	32.2	31	36.8	33.5

Note: Total number of movers does not equal total movers in other tables because this table shows survey respondents who moved, not necessarily householders. Numbers may not add to total because "not reported" may not be shown.
Source: Bureau of the Census, American Housing Survey for the United States: 2009, Internet site http://www.census.gov/hhes/ www/housing/ahs/ahs09/ahs09.html; calculations by New Strategist

Table 4.114 Homeowners Who Moved by Reasons for Choosing Home, 2009: West

Among homeowners in the West who moved in the past year, the
largest share chose their present home for financial reasons.
Sixty-four percent say their current home is better than their previous home.

(number and percent distribution of total homeowning respondents and homeowning respondents in the West who moved in the past year, by reasons for choosing home, 2009; numbers in thousands)

	total		West		
	number	percent distribution	number	percent distribution	percent of total
Total homeowning respondents who moved	**4,623**	**100.0%**	**1,188**	**100.0%**	**25.7%**
Main reason for choice of present home					
All reported reasons equal	808	17.5	192	16.2	23.8
Financial reasons	1,008	21.8	282	23.7	28.0
Room layout/design	797	17.2	234	19.7	29.4
Kitchen	33	0.7	0	0.0	0.0
Size	377	8.2	96	8.0	25.3
Exterior appearance	125	2.7	24	2.0	19.1
Yard/trees/view	287	6.2	68	5.7	23.6
Quality of construction	186	4.0	28	2.4	15.1
Only one available	76	1.6	26	2.2	34.0
Other	636	13.7	146	12.3	23.0
Not reported	290	6.3	92	7.8	31.9
Present home compared with previous home					
Better	3,017	65.3	765	64.4	25.4
Worse	426	9.2	97	8.1	22.7
About the same	920	19.9	235	19.8	25.5
Not reported	261	5.6	91	7.7	35.0
Home search					
Now in house	3,929	100.0	1,023	100.0	26.0
Did not look at apartments	3,430	87.3	884	86.5	25.8
Looked at apartments too	305	7.8	75	7.4	24.6
Now in manufactured/mobile home	410	100.0	76	100.0	18.6
Did not look at apartments	304	74.1	53	69.1	17.4
Looked at apartments too	69	16.9	11	14.7	16.2
Now in apartment	285	100.0	89	100.0	31.1
Did not look at houses	181	63.6	49	54.9	26.8
Looked at houses too	92	32.2	40	45.1	43.6

Note: Total number of movers does not equal total movers in other tables because this table shows survey respondents who moved, not necessarily householders. Numbers may not add to total because "not reported" may not be shown.
Source: Bureau of the Census, American Housing Survey for the United States: 2009, Internet site http://www.census.gov/hhes/ www/housing/ahs/ahs09/ahs09.html; calculations by New Strategist

Table 4.115 Homeowners Who Moved by Reasons for Choosing Neighborhood, 2009: Northeast

Most Northeastern homeowners who moved in the past year looked at more than one neighborhood before choosing where to live. The biggest factor in choosing their current neigbhorhood was the house itself (18 percent).

(number and percent distribution of total homeowning respondents and homeowning respondents in the Northeast who moved in the past year, by reasons for choosing neighborhood, 2009; numbers in thousands)

	total		Northeast		
	number	percent distribution	number	percent distribution	percent of total
Total homeowning respondents who moved	**4,623**	**100.0%**	**603**	**100.0%**	**13.0%**
Neighborhood search					
Looked at just this neighborhood	1,590	34.4	247	41.0	15.6
Looked at other neighborhoods	2,802	60.6	337	55.9	12.0
Not reported	231	5.0	19	3.2	8.2
Main reason for choice of present neighborhood					
All reported reasons equal	551	11.9	89	14.8	16.2
Convenient to job	611	13.2	98	16.3	16.0
Convenient to friends or relatives	570	12.3	80	13.2	14.0
Convenient to leisure activities	87	1.9	1	0.2	1.5
Convenient to public transportation	29	0.6	6	1.0	19.6
Good schools	289	6.3	51	8.4	17.6
Other public services	36	0.8	1	0.1	1.7
Looks/design of neighborhood	635	13.7	71	11.8	11.2
House was most important consideration	801	17.3	111	18.4	13.9
Other	750	16.2	71	11.8	9.5
Not reported	264	5.7	24	4.0	9.2
Present neighborhood compared with previous neighborhood					
Better	2,253	48.7	286	47.4	12.7
Worse	347	7.5	31	5.1	8.9
About the same	1,555	33.6	236	39.1	15.2
Same neighborhood	179	3.9	16	2.7	9.0
Not reported	290	6.3	35	5.8	12.0

Note: Total number of movers does not equal total movers in other tables because this table shows survey respondents who moved, not necessarily householders.
Source: Bureau of the Census, American Housing Survey for the United States: 2009, Internet site http://www.census.gov/hhes/www/housing/ahs/ahs09/ahs09.html; calculations by New Strategist

Table 4.116 Homeowners Who Moved by Reasons for Choosing Neighborhood, 2009: Midwest

Most Midwestern homeowners who moved in the past year looked at more than one neighborhood before choosing where to live. The biggest factor in choosing their current neigbhorhood was the house itself (21 percent).

(number and percent distribution of total homeowning respondents and homeowning respondents in the Midwest who moved in the past year, by reasons for choosing neighborhood, 2009; numbers in thousands)

	total		Midwest		
	number	percent distribution	number	percent distribution	percent of total
Total homeowning respondents who moved	**4,623**	**100.0%**	**1,030**	**100.0%**	**22.3%**
Neighborhood search					
Looked at just this neighborhood	1,590	34.4	328	31.9	20.6
Looked at other neighborhoods	2,802	60.6	669	65.0	23.9
Not reported	231	5.0	32	3.2	14.1
Main reason for choice of present neighborhood					
All reported reasons equal	551	11.9	117	11.3	21.2
Convenient to job	611	13.2	104	10.1	17.1
Convenient to friends or relatives	570	12.3	141	13.7	24.7
Convenient to leisure activities	87	1.9	28	2.7	32.3
Convenient to public transportation	29	0.6	1	0.1	4.7
Good schools	289	6.3	62	6.0	21.5
Other public services	36	0.8	10	1.0	27.9
Looks/design of neighborhood	635	13.7	171	16.6	26.9
House was most important consideration	801	17.3	221	21.4	27.6
Other	750	16.2	138	13.4	18.4
Not reported	264	5.7	36	3.5	13.6
Present neighborhood compared with previous neighborhood					
Better	2,253	48.7	439	42.6	19.5
Worse	347	7.5	87	8.4	24.9
About the same	1,555	33.6	412	40.0	26.5
Same neighborhood	179	3.9	39	3.8	21.9
Not reported	290	6.3	53	5.1	18.1

Note: Total number of movers does not equal total movers in other tables because this table shows survey respondents who moved, not necessarily householders.
Source: Bureau of the Census, American Housing Survey for the United States: 2009, Internet site http://www.census.gov/hhes/ www/housing/ahs/ahs09/ahs09.html; calculations by New Strategist

Table 4.117 Homeowners Who Moved by Reasons for Choosing Neighborhood, 2009: South

Most Southern homeowners who moved in the past year looked at more than one neighborhood before choosing where to live. The biggest factor in choosing their current neigbhorhood was its convenience to their job (16 percent).

(number and percent distribution of total homeowning respondents and homeowning respondents in the South who moved in the past year, by reasons for choosing neighborhood, 2009; numbers in thousands)

	total		South		
	number	percent distribution	number	percent distribution	percent of total
Total homeowning respondents who moved	**4,623**	**100.0%**	**1,802**	**100.0%**	**39.0%**
Neighborhood search					
Looked at just this neighborhood	1,590	34.4	644	35.7	40.5
Looked at other neighborhoods	2,802	60.6	1,046	58.1	37.3
Not reported	231	5.0	112	6.2	48.5
Main reason for choice of present neighborhood					
All reported reasons equal	551	11.9	202	11.2	36.6
Convenient to job	611	13.2	280	15.5	45.8
Convenient to friends or relatives	570	12.3	221	12.3	38.8
Convenient to leisure activities	87	1.9	28	1.5	31.9
Convenient to public transportation	29	0.6	12	0.7	40.1
Good schools	289	6.3	116	6.4	40.2
Other public services	36	0.8	5	0.3	14.9
Looks/design of neighborhood	635	13.7	216	12.0	34.1
House was most important consideration	801	17.3	247	13.7	30.8
Other	750	16.2	355	19.7	47.3
Not reported	264	5.7	121	6.7	45.8
Present neighborhood compared with previous neighborhood					
Better	2,253	48.7	977	54.2	43.4
Worse	347	7.5	134	7.4	38.5
About the same	1,555	33.6	501	27.8	32.2
Same neighborhood	179	3.9	80	4.4	44.7
Not reported	290	6.3	111	6.1	38.2

Note: Total number of movers does not equal total movers in other tables because this table shows survey respondents who moved, not necessarily householders.
Source: Bureau of the Census, American Housing Survey for the United States: 2009, Internet site http://www.census.gov/hhes/www/housing/ahs/ahs09/ahs09.html; calculations by New Strategist

Table 4.118 Homeowners Who Moved by Reasons for Choosing Neighborhood, 2009: West

Most Western homeowners who moved in the past year looked at more than one neighborhood before choosing where to live. The biggest factor in choosing their current neigbhorhood was the house itself (19 percent).

(number and percent distribution of total homeowning respondents and homeowning respondents in the West who moved in the past year, by reasons for choosing neighborhood, 2009; numbers in thousands)

	total		West		
	number	percent distribution	number	percent distribution	percent of total
Total homeowning respondents who moved	4,623	100.0%	1,188	100.0%	25.7%
Neighborhood search					
Looked at just this neighborhood	1,590	34.4	370	31.2	23.3
Looked at other neighborhoods	2,802	60.6	750	63.1	26.8
Not reported	231	5.0	67	5.7	29.2
Main reason for choice of present neighborhood					
All reported reasons equal	551	11.9	143	12.1	26.0
Convenient to job	611	13.2	129	10.8	21.1
Convenient to friends or relatives	570	12.3	128	10.8	22.5
Convenient to leisure activities	87	1.9	30	2.5	34.3
Convenient to public transportation	29	0.6	10	0.9	35.6
Good schools	289	6.3	60	5.1	20.8
Other public services	36	0.8	20	1.7	55.4
Looks/design of neighborhood	635	13.7	176	14.8	27.8
House was most important consideration	801	17.3	222	18.7	27.7
Other	750	16.2	186	15.6	24.8
Not reported	264	5.7	83	7.0	31.4
Present neighborhood compared with previous neighborhood					
Better	2,253	48.7	551	46.4	24.5
Worse	347	7.5	96	8.1	27.6
About the same	1,555	33.6	406	34.1	26.1
Same neighborhood	179	3.9	44	3.7	24.4
Not reported	290	6.3	92	7.7	31.7

Note: Total number of movers does not equal total movers in other tables because this table shows survey respondents who moved, not necessarily householders.
Source: Bureau of the Census, American Housing Survey for the United States: 2009, Internet site http://www.census.gov/hhes/www/housing/ahs/ahs09/ahs09.html; calculations by New Strategist

Table 4.119 Homeowners Who Moved by Reasons for Moving and Region, 2009

In the South and West, the change from renter to owner was
the single most important reason homeowners moved.

(number and percent distribution of homeowning respondents who moved in the past year by main reason for move, by region, 2009; numbers in thousands)

	total	Northeast	Midwest	South	West
Total homeowning respondents who moved	**4,623**	**603**	**1,030**	**1,802**	**1,188**
All reported reasons equal	203	35	68	63	37
Private displacement	5	0	0	2	3
Government displacement	8	0	0	8	0
Disaster loss (fire, flood, etc.)	24	4	3	16	0
New job or job transfer	370	36	94	177	64
To be closer to work/school/other	217	18	52	94	54
Other financial, employment related	119	2	36	36	45
To establish own household	594	70	147	218	158
Needed larger house or apartment	431	72	107	148	103
Married, widowed, divorced, or separated	284	37	80	99	69
Other family, personal reasons	368	71	72	133	91
Wanted better home	305	41	65	124	76
Change from renter to owner	685	70	120	255	239
Wanted lower maintenance	60	11	10	18	20
Other housing related reasons	168	38	47	55	29
Evicted from residence	14	1	1	6	6
Other	484	69	78	224	113
Not reported	286	29	48	127	81

PERCENT DISTRIBUTION BY REASON FOR MOVE

	total	Northeast	Midwest	South	West
Total homeowning respondents who moved	**100.0%**	**100.0%**	**100.0%**	**100.0%**	**100.0%**
All reported reasons equal	4.4	5.7	6.6	3.5	3.1
Private displacement	0.1	0.0	0.0	0.1	0.3
Government displacement	0.2	0.0	0.0	0.4	0.0
Disaster loss (fire, flood, etc.)	0.5	0.7	0.3	0.9	0.0
New job or job transfer	8.0	5.9	9.1	9.8	5.4
To be closer to work/school/other	4.7	2.9	5.1	5.2	4.5
Other financial, employment related	2.6	0.3	3.5	2.0	3.8
To establish own household	12.8	11.6	14.3	12.1	13.3
Needed larger house or apartment	9.3	12.0	10.4	8.2	8.7
Married, widowed, divorced, or separated	6.1	6.1	7.7	5.5	5.8
Other family, personal reasons	8.0	11.8	7.0	7.4	7.7
Wanted better home	6.6	6.8	6.3	6.9	6.4
Change from renter to owner	14.8	11.6	11.7	14.1	20.1
Wanted lower maintenance	1.3	1.8	1.0	1.0	1.7
Other housing related reasons	3.6	6.3	4.6	3.0	2.4
Evicted from residence	0.3	0.1	0.1	0.3	0.5
Other	10.5	11.5	7.6	12.4	9.5
Not reported	6.2	4.8	4.7	7.1	6.8

	total	Northeast	Midwest	South	West
PERCENT DISTRIBUTION BY REGION					
Total homeowning respondents who moved	**100.0%**	**13.0%**	**22.3%**	**39.0%**	**25.7%**
All reported reasons equal	100.0	17.0	33.5	31.2	18.2
Private displacement	100.0	0.0	0.0	40.7	59.3
Government displacement	100.0	0.0	0.0	100.0	0.0
Disaster loss (fire, flood, etc.)	100.0	16.9	14.0	69.1	0.0
New job or job transfer	100.0	9.6	25.4	47.8	17.2
To be closer to work/school/other	100.0	8.1	24.0	43.1	24.8
Other financial, employment related	100.0	1.5	30.3	30.0	38.2
To establish own household	100.0	11.8	24.8	36.7	26.7
Needed larger house or apartment	100.0	16.8	24.9	34.3	24.0
Married, widowed, divorced, or separated	100.0	12.9	28.1	34.8	24.3
Other family, personal reasons	100.0	19.4	19.7	36.2	24.7
Wanted better home	100.0	13.5	21.2	40.5	24.7
Change from renter to owner	100.0	10.3	17.6	37.2	34.9
Wanted lower maintenance	100.0	18.1	17.3	30.5	34.0
Other housing related reasons	100.0	22.5	28.1	32.4	17.0
Evicted from residence	100.0	5.9	5.5	44.5	44.1
Other	100.0	14.3	16.1	46.3	23.3
Not reported	100.0	10.2	16.8	44.5	28.4

Note: Total number of movers does not equal total movers in other tables because this table shows survey respondents who moved, not necessarily householders.
Source: Bureau of the Census, American Housing Survey for the United States: 2009, Internet site http://www.census.gov/hhes/www/housing/ahs/ahs09/ahs09.html; calculations by New Strategist

5

Renters by Region

There are important differences in renters by region.

Renters are youngest in the South (median age of 37) and oldest in the Northeast (median age of 43). Nationally, 45 percent of renters are Asian, black, Hispanic, or another minority. The proportion ranges from a low of 33 percent in the Midwest to a high of 50 percent in the South. Fully 77 percent of renters in the Northeast live in multiunit buildings compared with only 54 percent of renters in the South.

■ Most renters moved into their home recently. The median year in which renters moved into their current home is 2006 in the Northeast and 2007 in the other regions.

■ Many renters move to be closer to their place of employment. Between 10 and 12 percent of renters who recently moved did so to be closer to work. This is the single biggest reason for moving among renters in the Northeast and West.

■ Monthly housing costs for renters are highest in the West ($956 on average) and lowest in the Midwest ($691).

Minorities account for a large share of renters in every region

(percent of renters who are Asian, black, Hispanic, or another minority, by region, 2009)

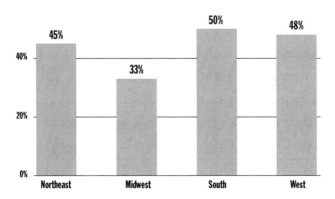

Table 5.1 Renters by Age and Region, 2009

The median age of renters ranges from a low of 37
in the South to a high of 43 in the Northeast.

(number and percent distribution of total renters and renters by region, by age of householder; 2009; numbers in thousands)

	total	Northeast	Midwest	South	West
Total renters	**35,378**	**7,073**	**7,119**	**12,392**	**8,794**
Under age 25	4,799	628	1,143	1,883	1,145
Aged 25 to 29	5,072	827	1,068	1,959	1,219
Aged 30 to 34	4,561	871	796	1,653	1,240
Aged 35 to 44	6,976	1,420	1,202	2,482	1,872
Aged 45 to 54	5,762	1,181	1,139	1,974	1,469
Aged 55 to 64	3,585	875	685	1,175	850
Aged 65 to 74	2,120	569	435	641	475
Aged 75 or older	2,503	701	652	626	524
Median age (years)	39	43	39	37	38

PERCENT DISTRIBUTION BY AGE

	total	Northeast	Midwest	South	West
Total renters	**100.0%**	**100.0%**	**100.0%**	**100.0%**	**100.0%**
Under age 25	13.6	8.9	16.1	15.2	13.0
Aged 25 to 29	14.3	11.7	15.0	15.8	13.9
Aged 30 to 34	12.9	12.3	11.2	13.3	14.1
Aged 35 to 44	19.7	20.1	16.9	20.0	21.3
Aged 45 to 54	16.3	16.7	16.0	15.9	16.7
Aged 55 to 64	10.1	12.4	9.6	9.5	9.7
Aged 65 to 74	6.0	8.0	6.1	5.2	5.4
Aged 75 or older	7.1	9.9	9.2	5.1	6.0

PERCENT DISTRIBUTION BY REGION

	total	Northeast	Midwest	South	West
Total renters	**100.0%**	**20.0%**	**20.1%**	**35.0%**	**24.9%**
Under age 25	100.0	13.1	23.8	39.2	23.9
Aged 25 to 29	100.0	16.3	21.0	38.6	24.0
Aged 30 to 34	100.0	19.1	17.4	36.3	27.2
Aged 35 to 44	100.0	20.4	17.2	35.6	26.8
Aged 45 to 54	100.0	20.5	19.8	34.3	25.5
Aged 55 to 64	100.0	24.4	19.1	32.8	23.7
Aged 65 to 74	100.0	26.8	20.5	30.2	22.4
Aged 75 or older	100.0	28.0	26.1	25.0	20.9

Source: Bureau of the Census, American Housing Survey for the United States: 2009, Internet site http://www.census.gov/hhes/ www/housing/ahs/ahs09/ahs09.html; calculations by New Strategist

Table 5.2 Renters by Household Type and Age of Householder, 2009: Northeast

Forty-one percent of renter households in the Northeast are people who live alone. Only 24 percent are headed by married couples.

(number and percent distribution of total renters and renters in the Northeast, and Northeastern renters as a percent of total, by type of household and age of householder, 2009; numbers in thousands)

| | total | | Northeast | | |
	number	percent distribution	number	percent distribution	percent of total
Total renters	**35,378**	**100.0%**	**7,073**	**100.0%**	**20.0%**
MARRIED-COUPLE HOUSEHOLDS	**8,808**	**24.9**	**1,716**	**24.3**	**19.5**
Under age 25	707	2.0	64	0.9	9.0
Aged 25 to 29	1,313	3.7	198	2.8	15.1
Aged 30 to 34	1,497	4.2	239	3.4	16.0
Aged 35 to 44	2,168	6.1	436	6.2	20.1
Aged 45 to 64	2,329	6.6	546	7.7	23.4
Aged 65 or older	793	2.2	234	3.3	29.5
TWO-OR-MORE-PERSON HOUSEHOLDS					
Female householder, no spouse present	**8,565**	**24.2**	**1,670**	**23.6**	**19.5**
Under age 45	6,119	17.3	1,106	15.6	18.1
Aged 45 to 64	2,030	5.7	452	6.4	22.3
Aged 65 or older	417	1.2	113	1.6	27.0
Male householder, no spouse present	**4,673**	**13.2**	**803**	**11.3**	**17.2**
Under age 45	3,629	10.3	568	8.0	15.6
Aged 45 to 64	895	2.5	196	2.8	21.9
Aged 65 or older	150	0.4	39	0.6	26.0
SINGLE-PERSON HOUSEHOLDS	**13,331**	**37.7**	**2,884**	**40.8**	**21.6**
Female householder	**6,743**	**19.1**	**1,554**	**22.0**	**23.0**
Under age 45	2,434	6.9	484	6.8	19.9
Aged 45 to 64	1,981	5.6	436	6.2	22.0
Aged 65 or older	2,328	6.6	634	9.0	27.3
Male householder	**6,588**	**18.6**	**1,330**	**18.8**	**20.2**
Under age 45	3,540	10.0	653	9.2	18.4
Aged 45 to 64	2,112	6.0	427	6.0	20.2
Aged 65 or older	936	2.6	251	3.5	26.8

Source: Bureau of the Census, American Housing Survey for the United States: 2009, Internet site http://www.census.gov/hhes/www/housing/ahs/ahs09/ahs09.html; calculations by New Strategist

Table 5.3 Renters by Household Type and Age of Householder, 2009: Midwest

Forty-three percent of renter households in the Midwest are people who live alone. Only 20 percent are headed by married couples.

(number and percent distribution of total renters and renters in the Midwest, and Midwestern renters as a percent of total, by type of household and age of householder, 2009; numbers in thousands)

	total		Midwest		
	number	percent distribution	number	percent distribution	percent of total
Total renters	**35,378**	**100.0%**	**7,119**	**100.0%**	**20.1%**
MARRIED-COUPLE HOUSEHOLDS	**8,808**	**24.9**	**1,397**	**19.6**	**15.9**
Under age 25	707	2.0	110	1.5	15.6
Aged 25 to 29	1,313	3.7	225	3.2	17.1
Aged 30 to 34	1,497	4.2	229	3.2	15.3
Aged 35 to 44	2,168	6.1	299	4.2	13.8
Aged 45 to 64	2,329	6.6	383	5.4	16.5
Aged 65 or older	793	2.2	150	2.1	19.0
TWO-OR-MORE-PERSON HOUSEHOLDS					
Female householder, no spouse present	**8,565**	**24.2**	**1,764**	**24.8**	**20.6**
Under age 45	6,119	17.3	1,378	19.4	22.5
Aged 45 to 64	2,030	5.7	315	4.4	15.5
Aged 65 or older	417	1.2	71	1.0	17.1
Male householder, no spouse present	**4,673**	**13.2**	**930**	**13.1**	**19.9**
Under age 45	3,629	10.3	743	10.4	20.5
Aged 45 to 64	895	2.5	156	2.2	17.4
Aged 65 or older	150	0.4	31	0.4	20.7
SINGLE-PERSON HOUSEHOLDS	**13,331**	**37.7**	**3,029**	**42.5**	**22.7**
Female householder	**6,743**	**19.1**	**1,571**	**22.1**	**23.3**
Under age 45	2,434	6.9	468	6.6	19.2
Aged 45 to 64	1,981	5.6	479	6.7	24.2
Aged 65 or older	2,328	6.6	624	8.8	26.8
Male householder	**6,588**	**18.6**	**1,457**	**20.5**	**22.1**
Under age 45	3,540	10.0	756	10.6	21.4
Aged 45 to 64	2,112	6.0	491	6.9	23.2
Aged 65 or older	936	2.6	211	3.0	22.5

Source: Bureau of the Census, American Housing Survey for the United States: 2009, Internet site http://www.census.gov/hhes/ www/housing/ahs/ahs09/ahs09.html; calculations by New Strategist

Table 5.4 Renters by Household Type and Age of Householder, 2009: South

Thirty-six percent of renter households in the South are people
who live alone. Twenty-six percent are female-headed families.

(number and percent distribution of total renters and renters in the South, and Southern renters as a percent of total, by type of household and age of householder, 2009; numbers in thousands)

| | total | | South | | |
	number	percent distribution	number	percent distribution	percent of total
Total renters	**35,378**	**100.0%**	**12,392**	**100.0%**	**35.0%**
MARRIED-COUPLE HOUSEHOLDS	**8,808**	**24.9**	**3,109**	**25.1**	**35.3**
Under age 25	707	2.0	305	2.5	43.2
Aged 25 to 29	1,313	3.7	517	4.2	39.4
Aged 30 to 34	1,497	4.2	564	4.5	37.7
Aged 35 to 44	2,168	6.1	753	6.1	34.7
Aged 45 to 64	2,329	6.6	750	6.1	32.2
Aged 65 or older	793	2.2	220	1.8	27.7
TWO-OR-MORE-PERSON HOUSEHOLDS					
Female householder, no spouse present	**8,565**	**24.2**	**3,178**	**25.6**	**37.1**
Under age 45	6,119	17.3	2,282	18.4	37.3
Aged 45 to 64	2,030	5.7	750	6.1	36.9
Aged 65 or older	417	1.2	146	1.2	35.0
Male householder, no spouse present	**4,673**	**13.2**	**1,642**	**13.3**	**35.1**
Under age 45	3,629	10.3	1,301	10.5	35.8
Aged 45 to 64	895	2.5	298	2.4	33.3
Aged 65 or older	150	0.4	44	0.4	29.3
SINGLE-PERSON HOUSEHOLDS	**13,331**	**37.7**	**4,463**	**36.0**	**33.5**
Female householder	**6,743**	**19.1**	**2,230**	**18.0**	**33.1**
Under age 45	2,434	6.9	959	7.7	39.4
Aged 45 to 64	1,981	5.6	654	5.3	33.0
Aged 65 or older	2,328	6.6	616	5.0	26.5
Male householder	**6,588**	**18.6**	**2,234**	**18.0**	**33.9**
Under age 45	3,540	10.0	1,297	10.5	36.6
Aged 45 to 64	2,112	6.0	696	5.6	33.0
Aged 65 or older	936	2.6	241	1.9	25.7

Source: Bureau of the Census, American Housing Survey for the United States: 2009, Internet site http://www.census.gov/hhes/www/housing/ahs/ahs09/ahs09.html; calculations by New Strategist

Table 5.5 Renters by Household Type and Age of Householder, 2009: West

Thirty-four percent of renter households in the West are people who live alone. Twenty-nine percent are headed by married couples.

(number and percent distribution of total renters and renters in the West, and Western renters as a percent of total, by type of household and age of householder, 2009; numbers in thousands)

	total		West		
	number	percent distribution	number	percent distribution	percent of total
Total renters	35,378	100.0%	8,794	100.0%	24.9%
MARRIED-COUPLE HOUSEHOLDS	8,808	24.9	2,587	29.4	29.4
Under age 25	707	2.0	228	2.6	32.3
Aged 25 to 29	1,313	3.7	373	4.2	28.4
Aged 30 to 34	1,497	4.2	465	5.3	31.1
Aged 35 to 44	2,168	6.1	681	7.7	31.4
Aged 45 to 64	2,329	6.6	650	7.4	27.9
Aged 65 or older	793	2.2	189	2.2	23.9
TWO-OR-MORE-PERSON HOUSEHOLDS					
Female householder, no spouse present	8,565	24.2	1,953	22.2	22.8
Under age 45	6,119	17.3	1,353	15.4	22.1
Aged 45 to 64	2,030	5.7	513	5.8	25.3
Aged 65 or older	417	1.2	87	1.0	20.9
Male householder, no spouse present	4,673	13.2	1,299	14.8	27.8
Under age 45	3,629	10.3	1,018	11.6	28.0
Aged 45 to 64	895	2.5	246	2.8	27.5
Aged 65 or older	150	0.4	36	0.4	24.0
SINGLE-PERSON HOUSEHOLDS	13,331	37.7	2,954	33.6	22.2
Female householder	6,743	19.1	1,388	15.8	20.6
Under age 45	2,434	6.9	523	5.9	21.5
Aged 45 to 64	1,981	5.6	412	4.7	20.8
Aged 65 or older	2,328	6.6	453	5.2	19.5
Male householder	6,588	18.6	1,566	17.8	23.8
Under age 45	3,540	10.0	835	9.5	23.6
Aged 45 to 64	2,112	6.0	498	5.7	23.6
Aged 65 or older	936	2.6	234	2.7	25.0

Source: Bureau of the Census, American Housing Survey for the United States: 2009, Internet site http://www.census.gov/hhes/ www/housing/ahs/ahs09/ahs09.html; calculations by New Strategist

Table 5.6 Renters by Race, Hispanic Origin, and Region, 2009

Non-Hispanic whites account for only 50 to 52 percent of renters in
the South and West and for 67 percent of renters in the Midwest.

*(number and percent distribution of total renters and renters by region, by race and Hispanic origin of householder,
2009; numbers in thousands)*

	total	Northeast	Midwest	South	West
Total renters	**35,378**	**7,073**	**7,119**	**12,392**	**8,794**
American Indian	466	43	131	82	209
Asian	1,487	333	181	269	704
Black	7,446	1,525	1,413	3,706	802
Hispanic	6,300	1,358	468	2,062	2,412
White, non-Hispanic	19,427	3,886	4,797	6,208	4,537

PERCENT DISTRIBUTION BY RACE AND HISPANIC ORIGIN

	total	Northeast	Midwest	South	West
Total renters	**100.0%**	**100.0%**	**100.0%**	**100.0%**	**100.0%**
American Indian	1.3	0.6	1.8	0.7	2.4
Asian	4.2	4.7	2.5	2.2	8.0
Black	21.0	21.6	19.8	29.9	9.1
Hispanic	17.8	19.2	6.6	16.6	27.4
White, non-Hispanic	54.9	54.9	67.4	50.1	51.6

PERCENT DISTRIBUTION BY REGION

	total	Northeast	Midwest	South	West
Total renters	**100.0%**	**20.0%**	**20.1%**	**35.0%**	**24.9%**
American Indian	100.0	9.2	28.2	17.7	45.0
Asian	100.0	22.4	12.2	18.1	47.4
Black	100.0	20.5	19.0	49.8	10.8
Hispanic	100.0	21.5	7.4	32.7	38.3
White, non-Hispanic	100.0	20.0	24.7	32.0	23.4

*Note: American Indians, Asians, blacks, and whites are those who identify themselves as being of the race alone. Numbers do
not add to total because not all races are shown and Hispanics may be of any race.*
*Source: Bureau of the Census, American Housing Survey for the United States: 2009, Internet site http://www.census.gov/hhes/
www/housing/ahs/ahs09/ahs09.html; calculations by New Strategist*

Table 5.7 Renters by Household Income and Region, 2009

Renters in the Midwest have the lowest incomes, a median of $25,200 in 2009.
Renters in the West have the highest incomes, a median of $34,000.

(number and percent distribution of total renters and renters by region, by household income, 2009; numbers in thousands)

	total	Northeast	Midwest	South	West
Total renters	**35,378**	**7,073**	**7,119**	**12,392**	**8,794**
Under $10,000	6,109	1,269	1,492	2,276	1,072
$10,000 to $19,999	6,115	1,112	1,324	2,303	1,376
$20,000 to $29,999	5,981	1,122	1,191	2,278	1,390
$30,000 to $39,999	4,477	839	898	1,616	1,123
$40,000 to $49,999	3,438	679	710	1,111	939
$50,000 to $59,999	2,326	448	449	737	693
$60,000 to $79,999	3,244	684	581	1,022	958
$80,000 to $99,999	1,663	374	260	501	528
$100,000 to $119,999	833	231	120	209	272
$120,000 or more	1,192	315	94	340	442
Median income	$28,400	$30,000	$25,200	$25,670	$34,000

PERCENT DISTRIBUTION BY HOUSEHOLD INCOME

	total	Northeast	Midwest	South	West
Total renters	**100.0%**	**100.0%**	**100.0%**	**100.0%**	**100.0%**
Under $10,000	17.3	17.9	21.0	18.4	12.2
$10,000 to $19,999	17.3	15.7	18.6	18.6	15.6
$20,000 to $29,999	16.9	15.9	16.7	18.4	15.8
$30,000 to $39,999	12.7	11.9	12.6	13.0	12.8
$40,000 to $49,999	9.7	9.6	10.0	9.0	10.7
$50,000 to $59,999	6.6	6.3	6.3	5.9	7.9
$60,000 to $79,999	9.2	9.7	8.2	8.2	10.9
$80,000 to $99,999	4.7	5.3	3.6	4.0	6.0
$100,000 to $119,999	2.4	3.3	1.7	1.7	3.1
$120,000 or more	3.4	4.5	1.3	2.7	5.0

PERCENT DISTRIBUTION BY REGION

	total	Northeast	Midwest	South	West
Total renters	**100.0%**	**20.0%**	**20.1%**	**35.0%**	**24.9%**
Under $10,000	100.0	20.8	24.4	37.3	17.5
$10,000 to $19,999	100.0	18.2	21.7	37.7	22.5
$20,000 to $29,999	100.0	18.8	19.9	38.1	23.2
$30,000 to $39,999	100.0	18.7	20.1	36.1	25.1
$40,000 to $49,999	100.0	19.7	20.6	32.3	27.3
$50,000 to $59,999	100.0	19.2	19.3	31.7	29.8
$60,000 to $79,999	100.0	21.1	17.9	31.5	29.5
$80,000 to $99,999	100.0	22.5	15.6	30.1	31.8
$100,000 to $119,999	100.0	27.8	14.4	25.1	32.7
$120,000 or more	100.0	26.4	7.9	28.5	37.1

Source: Bureau of the Census, American Housing Survey for the United States: 2009, Internet site http://www.census.gov/hhes/ www/housing/ahs/ahs09/ahs09.html; calculations by New Strategist

Table 5.8 Renters by Educational Attainment and Region, 2009

Renters in the Northeast have the highest level of education.
Twenty-five percent are college graduates. In the Midwest and
South, a smaller 19 percent of renters are college graduates.

(number and percent distribution of total renters and renters by region, by educational attainment of householder, 2009; numbers in thousands)

	total	Northeast	Midwest	South	West
Total renters	**35,378**	**7,073**	**7,119**	**12,392**	**8,794**
Not a high school graduate	6,687	1,398	1,094	2,539	1,656
High school graduate only	11,724	2,315	2,576	4,255	2,578
Some college, no degree	6,924	1,069	1,575	2,418	1,862
Associate's degree	2,522	516	524	815	667
Bachelor's degree	5,183	1,209	959	1,634	1,382
Graduate or professional degree	2,338	567	391	732	648
High school graduate or higher	28,691	5,675	6,025	9,854	7,137
Some college or higher	16,967	3,361	3,449	5,598	4,559
Bachelor's degree or higher	7,521	1,776	1,350	2,366	2,030

PERCENT DISTRIBUTION BY EDUCATIONAL ATTAINMENT

Total renters	**100.0%**	**100.0%**	**100.0%**	**100.0%**	**100.0%**
Not a high school graduate	18.9	19.8	15.4	20.5	18.8
High school graduate only	33.1	32.7	36.2	34.3	29.3
Some college, no degree	19.6	15.1	22.1	19.5	21.2
Associate's degree	7.1	7.3	7.4	6.6	7.6
Bachelor's degree	14.7	17.1	13.5	13.2	15.7
Graduate or professional degree	6.6	8.0	5.5	5.9	7.4
High school graduate or higher	81.1	80.2	84.6	79.5	81.2
Some college or higher	48.0	47.5	48.4	45.2	51.8
Bachelor's degree or higher	21.3	25.1	19.0	19.1	23.1

PERCENT DISTRIBUTION BY REGION

Total renters	**100.0%**	**20.0%**	**20.1%**	**35.0%**	**24.9%**
Not a high school graduate	100.0	20.9	16.4	38.0	24.8
High school graduate only	100.0	19.7	22.0	36.3	22.0
Some college, no degree	100.0	15.4	22.7	34.9	26.9
Associate's degree	100.0	20.4	20.8	32.3	26.5
Bachelor's degree	100.0	23.3	18.5	31.5	26.7
Graduate or professional degree	100.0	24.3	16.7	31.3	27.7
High school graduate or higher	100.0	19.8	21.0	34.3	24.9
Some college or higher	100.0	19.8	20.3	33.0	26.9
Bachelor's degree or higher	100.0	23.6	17.9	31.5	27.0

Source: Bureau of the Census, American Housing Survey for the United States: 2009, Internet site http://www.census.gov/hhes/ www/housing/ahs/ahs09/ahs09.html; calculations by New Strategist

Table 5.9 Renters by Household Size and Region, 2009

Although only 25 percent of the nation's renters live in the West, the region is home to 36 percent of renters with the largest households—those that include seven or more people.

(number and percent distribution of total renters and renters by region, by number of persons living in home, 2009; numbers in thousands)

	total	Northeast	Midwest	South	West
Total renters	**35,378**	**7,073**	**7,119**	**12,392**	**8,794**
1 person	13,331	2,884	3,029	4,463	2,954
2 persons	9,453	1,935	1,938	3,259	2,321
3 persons	5,345	1,001	986	2,062	1,296
4 persons	4,016	751	689	1,418	1,157
5 persons	1,910	284	291	725	611
6 persons	780	125	102	292	261
7 or more persons	543	92	84	173	194

PERCENT DISTRIBUTION BY HOUSEHOLD SIZE

	total	Northeast	Midwest	South	West
Total renters	**100.0%**	**100.0%**	**100.0%**	**100.0%**	**100.0%**
1 person	37.7	40.8	42.5	36.0	33.6
2 persons	26.7	27.4	27.2	26.3	26.4
3 persons	15.1	14.2	13.9	16.6	14.7
4 persons	11.4	10.6	9.7	11.4	13.2
5 persons	5.4	4.0	4.1	5.8	6.9
6 persons	2.2	1.8	1.4	2.4	3.0
7 or more persons	1.5	1.3	1.2	1.4	2.2

PERCENT DISTRIBUTION BY REGION

	total	Northeast	Midwest	South	West
Total renters	**100.0%**	**20.0%**	**20.1%**	**35.0%**	**24.9%**
1 person	100.0	21.6	22.7	33.5	22.2
2 persons	100.0	20.5	20.5	34.5	24.5
3 persons	100.0	18.7	18.5	38.6	24.2
4 persons	100.0	18.7	17.2	35.3	28.8
5 persons	100.0	14.9	15.2	37.9	32.0
6 persons	100.0	16.1	13.1	37.5	33.4
7 or more persons	100.0	17.0	15.5	31.8	35.7

Source: Bureau of the Census, American Housing Survey for the United States: 2009, Internet site http://www.census.gov/hhes/ www/housing/ahs/ahs09/ahs09.html; calculations by New Strategist

Table 5.10 Renters by Type of Structure and Region, 2009

The Northeast is home to a disproportionate share of renters
who live in apartment buildings. More than half the renters
of manufactured/mobile homes live in the South.

(number and percent distribution of total renters and renters by region, by type of structure, 2009; numbers in thousands)

	total	Northeast	Midwest	South	West
Total renters	**35,378**	**7,073**	**7,119**	**12,392**	**8,794**
One, detached	9,755	992	1,980	4,140	2,644
One, attached	2,021	516	374	670	461
Multiunit buildings	22,181	5,461	4,564	6,737	5,419
Two to four	6,998	1,964	1,541	1,874	1,619
Five to nine	4,637	830	940	1,632	1,235
10 to 19	4,178	666	860	1,653	999
20 to 49	3,131	781	609	872	870
50 or more	3,237	1,220	614	707	696
Manufactured or mobile home	1,421	104	201	845	270
PERCENT DISTRIBUTION BY UNITS IN STRUCTURE					
Total renters	**100.0%**	**100.0%**	**100.0%**	**100.0%**	**100.0%**
One, detached	27.6	14.0	27.8	33.4	30.1
One, attached	5.7	7.3	5.2	5.4	5.2
Multiunit buildings	62.7	77.2	64.1	54.4	61.6
Two to four	19.8	27.8	21.6	15.1	18.4
Five to nine	13.1	11.7	13.2	13.2	14.0
10 to 19	11.8	9.4	12.1	13.3	11.4
20 to 49	8.9	11.0	8.6	7.0	9.9
50 or more	9.1	17.2	8.6	5.7	7.9
Manufactured or mobile home	4.0	1.5	2.8	6.8	3.1
PERCENT DISTRIBUTION BY REGION					
Total renters	**100.0%**	**20.0%**	**20.1%**	**35.0%**	**24.9%**
One, detached	100.0	10.2	20.3	42.4	27.1
One, attached	100.0	25.5	18.5	33.2	22.8
Multiunit buildings	100.0	24.6	20.6	30.4	24.4
Two to four	100.0	28.1	22.0	26.8	23.1
Five to nine	100.0	17.9	20.3	35.2	26.6
10 to 19	100.0	15.9	20.6	39.6	23.9
20 to 49	100.0	24.9	19.4	27.8	27.8
50 or more	100.0	37.7	19.0	21.8	21.5
Manufactured or mobile home	100.0	7.3	14.2	59.5	19.0

Source: Bureau of the Census, American Housing Survey for the United States: 2009, Internet site http://www.census.gov/hhes/ www/housing/ahs/ahs09/ahs09.html; calculations by New Strategist

Table 5.11 Renters by Year Structure Built and Region, 2009

Renters in the Northeast live in the oldest homes, with half built before 1950.
Renters in the South live in the newest homes, with half built since 1976.

(number and percent distribution of total renters and renters by region, by year structure was built, 2009; numbers in thousands)

	total	Northeast	Midwest	South	West
Total renters	**35,378**	**7,073**	**7,119**	**12,392**	**8,794**
2005 to 2009	1,283	146	160	579	397
2000 to 2004	1,731	165	324	743	500
1995 to 1999	1,603	84	335	753	433
1990 to 1994	1,280	113	271	539	358
1985 to 1989	2,489	248	388	982	872
1980 to 1984	2,179	179	296	1,187	517
1975 to 1979	4,364	570	984	1,688	1,121
1970 to 1974	3,718	597	729	1,499	893
1960 to 1969	4,409	787	824	1,555	1,242
1950 to 1959	3,243	641	696	1,031	876
1940 to 1949	2,322	581	380	740	621
1930 to 1939	1,924	624	433	459	409
1920 to 1929	1,811	749	470	307	285
1919 or earlier	3,021	1,590	830	331	270
Median year	1971	1950	1969	1976	1974

PERCENT DISTRIBUTION BY YEAR BUILT

	total	Northeast	Midwest	South	West
Total renters	**100.0%**	**100.0%**	**100.0%**	**100.0%**	**100.0%**
2005 to 2009	3.6	2.1	2.2	4.7	4.5
2000 to 2004	4.9	2.3	4.5	6.0	5.7
1995 to 1999	4.5	1.2	4.7	6.1	4.9
1990 to 1994	3.6	1.6	3.8	4.3	4.1
1985 to 1989	7.0	3.5	5.5	7.9	9.9
1980 to 1984	6.2	2.5	4.2	9.6	5.9
1975 to 1979	12.3	8.1	13.8	13.6	12.8
1970 to 1974	10.5	8.4	10.2	12.1	10.2
1960 to 1969	12.5	11.1	11.6	12.5	14.1
1950 to 1959	9.2	9.1	9.8	8.3	10.0
1940 to 1949	6.6	8.2	5.3	6.0	7.1
1930 to 1939	5.4	8.8	6.1	3.7	4.7
1920 to 1929	5.1	10.6	6.6	2.5	3.2
1919 or earlier	8.5	22.5	11.7	2.7	3.1

	total	Northeast	Midwest	South	West
PERCENT DISTRIBUTION BY REGION					
Total renters	**100.0%**	**20.0%**	**20.1%**	**35.0%**	**24.9%**
2005 to 2009	100.0	11.4	12.5	45.1	31.0
2000 to 2004	100.0	9.5	18.7	42.9	28.9
1995 to 1999	100.0	5.2	20.9	46.9	27.0
1990 to 1994	100.0	8.8	21.1	42.1	28.0
1985 to 1989	100.0	9.9	15.6	39.4	35.0
1980 to 1984	100.0	8.2	13.6	54.5	23.7
1975 to 1979	100.0	13.1	22.6	38.7	25.7
1970 to 1974	100.0	16.1	19.6	40.3	24.0
1960 to 1969	100.0	17.9	18.7	35.3	28.2
1950 to 1959	100.0	19.8	21.4	31.8	27.0
1940 to 1949	100.0	25.0	16.4	31.9	26.7
1930 to 1939	100.0	32.4	22.5	23.8	21.3
1920 to 1929	100.0	41.4	25.9	16.9	15.7
1919 or earlier	100.0	52.6	27.5	11.0	8.9

Source: Bureau of the Census, American Housing Survey for the United States: 2009, Internet site http://www.census.gov/hhes/ www/housing/ahs/ahs09/ahs09.html; calculations by New Strategist

Table 5.12 Renters by Year Moved into Home and Region, 2009

There is little variation by region in the median year renters moved into their home, 2007 being the median year in the Midwest, South, and West.

(number and percent distribution of total renters and renters by region, by year householder moved into unit, 2009; numbers in thousands)

	total	Northeast	Midwest	South	West
Total renters	**35,378**	**7,073**	**7,119**	**12,392**	**8,794**
2005 to 2009	25,982	4,286	5,359	9,892	6,444
2000 to 2004	4,970	1,216	1,004	1,396	1,354
1995 to 1999	1,914	544	342	511	517
1990 to 1994	1,057	367	186	254	249
1985 to 1989	482	168	84	131	98
1980 to 1984	312	145	56	58	53
1975 to 1979	244	139	30	53	22
1970 to 1974	151	64	19	42	25
1960 to 1969	158	94	15	34	15
1950 to 1959	70	31	11	16	11
1940 to 1949	23	6	7	4	6
1939 or earlier	17	12	5	0	0
Median year moved into home	2007	2006	2007	2007	2007
PERCENT DISTRIBUTION BY YEAR					
Total renters	**100.0%**	**100.0%**	**100.0%**	**100.0%**	**100.0%**
2005 to 2009	73.4	60.6	75.3	79.8	73.3
2000 to 2004	14.0	17.2	14.1	11.3	15.4
1995 to 1999	5.4	7.7	4.8	4.1	5.9
1990 to 1994	3.0	5.2	2.6	2.1	2.8
1985 to 1989	1.4	2.4	1.2	1.1	1.1
1980 to 1984	0.9	2.0	0.8	0.5	0.6
1975 to 1979	0.7	2.0	0.4	0.4	0.3
1970 to 1974	0.4	0.9	0.3	0.3	0.3
1960 to 1969	0.4	1.3	0.2	0.3	0.2
1950 to 1959	0.2	0.4	0.2	0.1	0.1
1940 to 1949	0.1	0.1	0.1	0.0	0.1
1939 or earlier	0.0	0.2	0.1	0.0	0.0

	total	Northeast	Midwest	South	West
PERCENT DISTRIBUTION BY REGION					
Total renters	**100.0%**	**20.0%**	**20.1%**	**35.0%**	**24.9%**
2005 to 2009	100.0	16.5	20.6	38.1	24.8
2000 to 2004	100.0	24.5	20.2	28.1	27.2
1995 to 1999	100.0	28.4	17.8	26.7	27.0
1990 to 1994	100.0	34.8	17.6	24.1	23.5
1985 to 1989	100.0	34.9	17.5	27.2	20.4
1980 to 1984	100.0	46.4	18.1	18.4	17.1
1975 to 1979	100.0	57.2	12.1	21.6	9.2
1970 to 1974	100.0	42.7	12.6	28.0	16.6
1960 to 1969	100.0	59.7	9.2	21.8	9.3
1950 to 1959	100.0	45.1	15.7	23.6	15.5
1940 to 1949	100.0	24.5	31.7	19.4	24.4
1939 or earlier	100.0	71.3	28.7	0.0	0.0

Source: Bureau of the Census, American Housing Survey for the United States: 2009, Internet site http://www.census.gov/hhes/ www/housing/ahs/ahs09/ahs09.html; calculations by New Strategist

Table 5.13 Renters by Square Footage of Unit and Lot Size, 2009: Northeast

The average renter in a single-family detached or mobile home in the Northeast has a median of 1,500 square feet of living space, more than the average renter.

(number and percent distribution of total renters and renters in the Northeast, by square footage of unit and lot size, 2009; numbers in thousands)

	total		Northeast		
	number	percent distribution	number	percent distribution	percent of total
Square footage of home, total*	**11,176**	**100.0%**	**1,096**	**100.0%**	**9.8%**
Less than 500 sq. ft.	220	2.0	28	2.6	12.9
500 to 749 sq. ft.	686	6.1	67	6.1	9.8
750 to 999 sq. ft.	1,495	13.4	122	11.1	8.1
1,000 to 1,499 sq. ft.	3,441	30.8	219	20.0	6.4
1,500 to 1,999 sq. ft.	2,235	20.0	211	19.2	9.4
2,000 to 2,499 sq. ft.	1,134	10.1	104	9.5	9.2
2,500 to 2,999 sq. ft.	429	3.8	49	4.5	11.5
3,000 to 3,999 sq. ft.	301	2.7	49	4.5	16.4
4,000 or more sq. ft.	243	2.2	54	5.0	22.4
Not reported	992	8.9	193	17.6	19.4
Median square footage	1,300	–	1,500	–	–
Lot size, total**	**12,823**	**100.0**	**1,554**	**100.0**	**12.1**
Less than one-eighth acre	2,717	21.2	435	28.0	16.0
One-eighth up to one-quarter acre	4,022	31.4	320	20.6	8.0
One-quarter up to one-half acre	2,084	16.3	207	13.3	9.9
One-half up to one acre	1,162	9.1	171	11.0	14.7
One to five acres	2,120	16.5	301	19.4	14.2
Five to 10 acres	205	1.6	39	2.5	19.1
10 or more acres	513	4.0	82	5.3	15.9
Median lot size (acres)	0.22	–	0.25	–	–

* Single-family detached and mobile homes only.
** Homes in two-or-more-unit buildings are excluded.
Note: "–" means not applicable.
Source: Bureau of the Census, American Housing Survey for the United States: 2009, Internet site http://www.census.gov/hhes/ www/housing/ahs09/ahs09.html; calculations by New Strategist

Table 5.14 Renters by Square Footage of Unit and Lot Size, 2009: Midwest

The average renter in a single-family detached or mobile home
in the Midwest has a median of 1,248 square feet of
living space, about the same as the average renter.

(number and percent distribution of total renters and renters in the Midwest, by square footage of unit and lot size, 2009; numbers in thousands)

	total		Midwest		
	number	percent distribution	number	percent distribution	percent of total
Square footage of home, total*	**11,176**	**100.0%**	**2,181**	**100.0%**	**19.5%**
Less than 500 sq. ft.	220	2.0	18	0.8	8.3
500 to 749 sq. ft.	686	6.1	150	6.9	21.9
750 to 999 sq. ft.	1,495	13.4	354	16.2	23.7
1,000 to 1,499 sq. ft.	3,441	30.8	647	29.7	18.8
1,500 to 1,999 sq. ft.	2,235	20.0	367	16.8	16.4
2,000 to 2,499 sq. ft.	1,134	10.1	228	10.5	20.1
2,500 to 2,999 sq. ft.	429	3.8	65	3.0	15.1
3,000 to 3,999 sq. ft.	301	2.7	83	3.8	27.6
4,000 or more sq. ft.	243	2.2	43	2.0	17.7
Not reported	992	8.9	225	10.3	22.7
Median square footage	1,300	–	1,248	–	–
Lot size, total**	**12,823**	**100.0**	**2,482**	**100.0**	**19.4**
Less than one-eighth acre	2,717	21.2	503	20.3	18.5
One-eighth up to one-quarter acre	4,022	31.4	863	34.8	21.5
One-quarter up to one-half acre	2,084	16.3	390	15.7	18.7
One-half up to one acre	1,162	9.1	146	5.9	12.6
One to five acres	2,120	16.5	388	15.6	18.3
Five to 10 acres	205	1.6	44	1.8	21.4
10 or more acres	513	4.0	149	6.0	29.0
Median lot size (acres)	0.22	–	0.20	–	–

* Single-family detached and mobile homes only.
** Homes in two-or-more-unit buildings are excluded.
Note: "–" means not applicable.
Source: Bureau of the Census, American Housing Survey for the United States: 2009, Internet site http://www.census.gov/hhes/www/housing/ahs/ahs09/ahs09.html; calculations by New Strategist

Table 5.15 Renters by Square Footage of Unit and Lot Size, 2009: South

The average renter in a single-family detached or mobile home in the South has a median of 1,280 square feet of living space, about the same as the average renter.

(number and percent distribution of total renters and renters in the South, by square footage of unit and lot size, 2009; numbers in thousands)

	total		South		
	number	percent distribution	number	percent distribution	percent of total
Square footage of home, total*	11,176	100.0%	4,985	100.0%	44.6%
Less than 500 sq. ft.	220	2.0	101	2.0	45.8
500 to 749 sq. ft.	686	6.1	318	6.4	46.3
750 to 999 sq. ft.	1,495	13.4	695	14.0	46.5
1,000 to 1,499 sq. ft.	3,441	30.8	1,641	32.9	47.7
1,500 to 1,999 sq. ft.	2,235	20.0	979	19.6	43.8
2,000 to 2,499 sq. ft.	1,134	10.1	487	9.8	43.0
2,500 to 2,999 sq. ft.	429	3.8	196	3.9	45.8
3,000 to 3,999 sq. ft.	301	2.7	88	1.8	29.2
4,000 or more sq. ft.	243	2.2	77	1.5	31.7
Not reported	992	8.9	403	8.1	40.6
Median square footage	1,300	–	1,280	–	–
Lot size, total**	12,823	100.0	5,510	100.0	43.0
Less than one-eighth acre	2,717	21.2	859	15.6	31.6
One-eighth up to one-quarter acre	4,022	31.4	1,548	28.1	38.5
One-quarter up to one-half acre	2,084	16.3	1,030	18.7	49.4
One-half up to one acre	1,162	9.1	683	12.4	58.8
One to five acres	2,120	16.5	1,106	20.1	52.2
Five to 10 acres	205	1.6	94	1.7	45.9
10 or more acres	513	4.0	190	3.4	37.0
Median lot size (acres)	0.22	–	0.25	–	–

* Single-family detached and mobile homes only.
** Homes in two-or-more-unit buildings are excluded.
Note: "–" means not applicable.
Source: Bureau of the Census, American Housing Survey for the United States: 2009, Internet site http://www.census.gov/hhes/www/housing/ahs/ahs09/ahs09.html; calculations by New Strategist

Table 5.16 Renters by Square Footage of Unit and Lot Size, 2009: West

The average renter in a single-family detached or mobile home in the West has a median of 1,400 square feet of living space, a bit more than the average renter.

(number and percent distribution of total renters and renters in the West, by square footage of unit and lot size, 2009; numbers in thousands)

	total		West		
	number	percent distribution	number	percent distribution	percent of total
Square footage of home, total*	**11,176**	**100.0%**	**2,914**	**100.0%**	**26.1%**
Less than 500 sq. ft.	220	2.0	73	2.5	33.0
500 to 749 sq. ft.	686	6.1	151	5.2	22.1
750 to 999 sq. ft.	1,495	13.4	324	11.1	21.7
1,000 to 1,499 sq. ft.	3,441	30.8	934	32.1	27.1
1,500 to 1,999 sq. ft.	2,235	20.0	679	23.3	30.4
2,000 to 2,499 sq. ft.	1,134	10.1	314	10.8	27.7
2,500 to 2,999 sq. ft.	429	3.8	118	4.1	27.6
3,000 to 3,999 sq. ft.	301	2.7	81	2.8	26.9
4,000 or more sq. ft.	243	2.2	68	2.3	28.2
Not reported	992	8.9	171	5.9	17.3
Median square footage	1,300	–	1,400	–	–
Lot size, total**	**12,823**	**100.0**	**3,276**	**100.0**	**25.5**
Less than one-eighth acre	2,717	21.2	920	28.1	33.9
One-eighth up to one-quarter acre	4,022	31.4	1,291	39.4	32.1
One-quarter up to one-half acre	2,084	16.3	457	14.0	21.9
One-half up to one acre	1,162	9.1	162	5.0	14.0
One to five acres	2,120	16.5	325	9.9	15.3
Five to 10 acres	205	1.6	28	0.8	13.6
10 or more acres	513	4.0	93	2.8	18.1
Median lot size (acres)	0.22	–	0.13	–	–

* Single-family detached and mobile homes only.
** Homes in two-or-more-unit buildings are excluded.
Note: "–" means not applicable.
Source: Bureau of the Census, American Housing Survey for the United States: 2009, Internet site http://www.census.gov/hhes/www/housing/ahs/ahs09/ahs09.html; calculations by New Strategist

Table 5.17 Renters by Number of Rooms in Home, 2009: Northeast

Eighty-one percent of renters in the Northeast have only one bathroom.
Three out of four have two or fewer bedrooms.

(number and percent distribution of total renters and renters in the Northeast, by number and type of rooms in home, 2009; numbers in thousands)

	total		Northeast		
	number	percent distribution	number	percent distribution	percent of total
Total renters	**35,378**	**100.0%**	**7,073**	**100.0%**	**20.0%**
Number of rooms					
One room	326	0.9	106	1.5	32.4
Two rooms	879	2.5	248	3.5	28.3
Three rooms	7,675	21.7	1,932	27.3	25.2
Four rooms	11,354	32.1	2,130	30.1	18.8
Five rooms	8,212	23.2	1,423	20.1	17.3
Six rooms	4,232	12.0	791	11.2	18.7
Seven rooms	1,735	4.9	265	3.8	15.3
Eight rooms	622	1.8	110	1.6	17.6
Nine rooms	214	0.6	37	0.5	17.4
10 or more rooms	130	0.4	31	0.4	23.8
Number of bedrooms					
None	744	2.1	209	3.0	28.1
One bedroom	9,720	27.5	2,447	34.6	25.2
Two bedrooms	14,200	40.1	2,684	37.9	18.9
Three bedrooms	8,359	23.6	1,327	18.8	15.9
Four or more bedrooms	2,354	6.7	406	5.7	17.2
Number of bathrooms					
None	229	0.6	73	1.0	32.1
One bathroom	22,894	64.7	5,713	80.8	25.0
One-and-one-half bathrooms	3,575	10.1	654	9.3	18.3
Two or more bathrooms	8,680	24.5	632	8.9	7.3
With room used for business	**8,040**	**22.7**	**1,329**	**18.8**	**16.5**
Business only	3,757	10.6	681	9.6	18.1
Business and other use	4,283	12.1	649	9.2	15.1

Source: Bureau of the Census, American Housing Survey for the United States: 2009, Internet site http://www.census.gov/hhes/www/housing/ahs/ahs09/ahs09.html; calculations by New Strategist

Table 5.18 Renters by Number of Rooms in Home, 2009: Midwest

Seventy-two percent of renters in the Midwest have only one bathroom.
Nearly three out of four have two or fewer bedrooms.

(number and percent distribution of total renters and renters in the Midwest, by number and type of rooms in home, 2009; numbers in thousands)

	total		Midwest		
	number	percent distribution	number	percent distribution	percent of total
Total renters	**35,378**	**100.0%**	**7,119**	**100.0%**	**20.1%**
Number of rooms					
One room	326	0.9	53	0.7	16.2
Two rooms	879	2.5	128	1.8	14.5
Three rooms	7,675	21.7	1,670	23.5	21.8
Four rooms	11,354	32.1	2,312	32.5	20.4
Five rooms	8,212	23.2	1,608	22.6	19.6
Six rooms	4,232	12.0	817	11.5	19.3
Seven rooms	1,735	4.9	352	4.9	20.3
Eight rooms	622	1.8	121	1.7	19.5
Nine rooms	214	0.6	38	0.5	17.8
10 or more rooms	130	0.4	19	0.3	14.9
Number of bedrooms					
None	744	2.1	132	1.9	17.8
One bedroom	9,720	27.5	2,026	28.5	20.8
Two bedrooms	14,200	40.1	3,055	42.9	21.5
Three bedrooms	8,359	23.6	1,472	20.7	17.6
Four or more bedrooms	2,354	6.7	434	6.1	18.4
Number of bathrooms					
None	229	0.6	42	0.6	18.3
One bathroom	22,894	64.7	5,093	71.5	22.2
One-and-one-half bathrooms	3,575	10.1	895	12.6	25.0
Two or more bathrooms	8,680	24.5	1,090	15.3	12.6
With room used for business	**8,040**	**22.7**	**1,511**	**21.2**	**18.8**
Business only	3,757	10.6	675	9.5	18.0
Business and other use	4,283	12.1	836	11.7	19.5

Source: Bureau of the Census, American Housing Survey for the United States: 2009, Internet site http://www.census.gov/hhes/ www/housing/ahs/ahs09/ahs09.html; calculations by New Strategist

Table 5.19 Renters by Number of Rooms in Home, 2009: South

Fifty-six percent of renters in the South have only one bathroom.
Sixty-four percent have two or fewer bedrooms.

(number and percent distribution of total renters and renters in the South, by number and type of rooms in home, 2009; numbers in thousands)

	total		South		
	number	percent distribution	number	percent distribution	percent of total
Total renters	**35,378**	**100.0%**	**12,392**	**100.0%**	**35.0%**
Number of rooms					
One room	326	0.9	30	0.2	9.2
Two rooms	879	2.5	186	1.5	21.1
Three rooms	7,675	21.7	2,231	18.0	29.1
Four rooms	11,354	32.1	3,997	32.3	35.2
Five rooms	8,212	23.2	3,303	26.7	40.2
Six rooms	4,232	12.0	1,685	13.6	39.8
Seven rooms	1,735	4.9	613	4.9	35.3
Eight rooms	622	1.8	229	1.8	36.8
Nine rooms	214	0.6	64	0.5	30.1
10 or more rooms	130	0.4	55	0.4	41.8
Number of bedrooms					
None	744	2.1	92	0.7	12.4
One bedroom	9,720	27.5	2,883	23.3	29.7
Two bedrooms	14,200	40.1	4,993	40.3	35.2
Three bedrooms	8,359	23.6	3,561	28.7	42.6
Four or more bedrooms	2,354	6.7	863	7.0	36.7
Number of bathrooms					
None	229	0.6	43	0.3	18.9
One bathroom	22,894	64.7	6,893	55.6	30.1
One-and-one-half bathrooms	3,575	10.1	1,261	10.2	35.3
Two or more bathrooms	8,680	24.5	4,196	33.9	48.3
With room used for business	**8,040**	**22.7**	**2,958**	**23.9**	**36.8**
Business only	3,757	10.6	1,457	11.8	38.8
Business and other use	4,283	12.1	1,501	12.1	35.1

Source: Bureau of the Census, American Housing Survey for the United States: 2009, Internet site http://www.census.gov/hhes/ www/housing/ahs/ahs09/ahs09.html; calculations by New Strategist

Table 5.20 Renters by Number of Rooms in Home, 2009: West

Fifty-nine percent of renters in the West have only one bathroom.
Seventy percent have two or fewer bedrooms.

(number and percent distribution of total renters and renters in the West, by number and type of rooms in home, 2009; numbers in thousands)

	total		West		
	number	percent distribution	number	percent distribution	percent of total
Total renters	**35,378**	**100.0%**	**8,794**	**100.0%**	**24.9%**
Number of rooms					
One room	326	0.9	137	1.6	42.2
Two rooms	879	2.5	317	3.6	36.0
Three rooms	7,675	21.7	1,841	20.9	24.0
Four rooms	11,354	32.1	2,915	33.1	25.7
Five rooms	8,212	23.2	1,878	21.4	22.9
Six rooms	4,232	12.0	939	10.7	22.2
Seven rooms	1,735	4.9	505	5.7	29.1
Eight rooms	622	1.8	162	1.8	26.1
Nine rooms	214	0.6	74	0.8	34.7
10 or more rooms	130	0.4	25	0.3	19.5
Number of bedrooms					
None	744	2.1	311	3.5	41.7
One bedroom	9,720	27.5	2,364	26.9	24.3
Two bedrooms	14,200	40.1	3,468	39.4	24.4
Three bedrooms	8,359	23.6	1,999	22.7	23.9
Four or more bedrooms	2,354	6.7	652	7.4	27.7
Number of bathrooms					
None	229	0.6	70	0.8	30.7
One bathroom	22,894	64.7	5,196	59.1	22.7
One-and-one-half bathrooms	3,575	10.1	765	8.7	21.4
Two or more bathrooms	8,680	24.5	2,762	31.4	31.8
With room used for business	**8,040**	**22.7**	**2,241**	**25.5**	**27.9**
Business only	3,757	10.6	944	10.7	25.1
Business and other use	4,283	12.1	1,297	14.7	30.3

Source: Bureau of the Census, American Housing Survey for the United States: 2009, Internet site http://www.census.gov/hhes/ www/housing/ahs/ahs09/ahs09.html; calculations by New Strategist

Table 5.21 Renters by Presence of Kitchen, Laundry, and Safety Equipment, 2009: Northeast

Only 28 percent of renters in the Northeast have a dishwasher.
Thirty-nine percent have a washing machine.

(number and percent of total renters and renters in the Northeast, by presence of kitchen, laundry, and safety equipment, 2009; numbers in thousands)

	total		Northeast		
	number	percent distribution	number	percent distribution	percent of total
Total renters	**35,378**	**100.0%**	**7,073**	**100.0%**	**20.0%**
With complete kitchen equipment	34,004	96.1	6,992	98.9	20.6
Dishwasher	16,393	46.3	2,016	28.5	12.3
Washing machine	19,545	55.2	2,751	38.9	14.1
Clothes dryer	18,343	51.8	2,291	32.4	12.5
Disposal in kitchen sink	15,933	45.0	1,222	17.3	7.7
Trash compactor	730	2.1	137	1.9	18.8
Working smoke detector	32,565	92.0	6,659	94.1	20.4
Fire extinguisher	11,980	33.9	2,259	31.9	18.9
Sprinkler system inside home	3,081	8.7	643	9.1	20.9
Carbon monoxide detector	9,007	25.5	3,726	52.7	41.4

Note: Complete kitchen equipment includes a sink, refrigerator, and oven or burners.
Source: Bureau of the Census, American Housing Survey for the United States: 2009, Internet site http://www.census.gov/hhes/www/housing/ahs/ahs09/ahs09.html; calculations by New Strategist

Table 5.22 Renters by Presence of Kitchen, Laundry, and Safety Equipment, 2009: Midwest

Only 39 percent of renters in the Midwest have a dishwasher.
The 53 percent majority has a washing machine.

(number and percent of total renters and renters in the Midwest, by presence of kitchen, laundry, and safety equipment, 2009; numbers in thousands)

	total		Midwest		
	number	percent distribution	number	percent distribution	percent of total
Total renters	**35,378**	**100.0%**	**7,119**	**100.0%**	**20.1%**
With complete kitchen equipment	34,004	96.1	6,817	95.8	20.0
Dishwasher	16,393	46.3	2,783	39.1	17.0
Washing machine	19,545	55.2	3,775	53.0	19.3
Clothes dryer	18,343	51.8	3,707	52.1	20.2
Disposal in kitchen sink	15,933	45.0	3,137	44.1	19.7
Trash compactor	730	2.1	110	1.5	15.0
Working smoke detector	32,565	92.0	6,742	94.7	20.7
Fire extinguisher	11,980	33.9	2,323	32.6	19.4
Sprinkler system inside home	3,081	8.7	570	8.0	18.5
Carbon monoxide detector	9,007	25.5	2,268	31.9	25.2

Note: Complete kitchen equipment includes a sink, refrigerator, and oven or burners.
Source: Bureau of the Census, American Housing Survey for the United States: 2009, Internet site http://www.census.gov/hhes/ www/housing/ahs/ahs09/ahs09.html; calculations by New Strategist

Table 5.23 **Renters by Presence of Kitchen, Laundry, and Safety Equipment, 2009: South**

The 55 percent majority of renters in the South has a dishwasher.
Most also have a washer and dryer.

(number and percent of total renters and renters in the South, by presence of kitchen, laundry, and safety equipment, 2009; numbers in thousands)

	total		South		
	number	percent distribution	number	percent distribution	percent of total
Total renters	**35,378**	**100.0%**	**12,392**	**100.0%**	**35.0%**
With complete kitchen equipment	34,004	96.1	12,106	97.7	35.6
Dishwasher	16,393	46.3	6,813	55.0	41.6
Washing machine	19,545	55.2	8,211	66.3	42.0
Clothes dryer	18,343	51.8	7,720	62.3	42.1
Disposal in kitchen sink	15,933	45.0	5,711	46.1	35.8
Trash compactor	730	2.1	304	2.5	41.6
Working smoke detector	32,565	92.0	11,109	89.6	34.1
Fire extinguisher	11,980	33.9	4,684	37.8	39.1
Sprinkler system inside home	3,081	8.7	1,078	8.7	35.0
Carbon monoxide detector	9,007	25.5	1,797	14.5	20.0

Note: Complete kitchen equipment includes a sink, refrigerator, and oven or burners.
Source: Bureau of the Census, American Housing Survey for the United States: 2009, Internet site http://www.census.gov/hhes/www/housing/ahs/ahs09/ahs09.html; calculations by New Strategist

Table 5.24 Renters by Presence of Kitchen, Laundry, and Safety Equipment, 2009: West

The 54 percent majority of renters in the West has a dishwasher.
Most also have a washer and dryer.

(number and percent of total renters and renters in the West, by presence of kitchen, laundry, and safety equipment, 2009; numbers in thousands)

	total		West		
	number	percent distribution	number	percent distribution	percent of total
Total renters	**35,378**	**100.0%**	**8,794**	**100.0%**	**24.9%**
With complete kitchen equipment	34,004	96.1	8,389	95.4	24.7
Dishwasher	16,393	46.3	4,782	54.4	29.2
Washing machine	19,545	55.2	4,808	54.7	24.6
Clothes dryer	18,343	51.8	4,625	52.6	25.2
Disposal in kitchen sink	15,933	45.0	5,863	66.7	36.8
Trash compactor	730	2.1	180	2.0	24.6
Working smoke detector	32,565	92.0	8,055	91.6	24.7
Fire extinguisher	11,980	33.9	2,715	30.9	22.7
Sprinkler system inside home	3,081	8.7	790	9.0	25.6
Carbon monoxide detector	9,007	25.5	1,216	13.8	13.5

Note: Complete kitchen equipment includes a sink, refrigerator, and oven or burners.
Source: Bureau of the Census, American Housing Survey for the United States: 2009, Internet site http://www.census.gov/hhes/ www/housing/ahs/ahs09/ahs09.html; calculations by New Strategist

Table 5.25 Renters by Type of Heating Equipment, 2009: Northeast

Most renters in the Northeast use a steam or hot water system as their main heating equipment. Nine percent also use portable electric heaters.

(number and percent distribution of total renters and renters in the Northeast, by presence and type of heating equipment, 2009; numbers in thousands)

	total		Northeast		
	number	percent distribution	number	percent distribution	percent of total
Total renters	35,378	100.0%	7,073	100.0%	20.0%
Main heating equipment					
Warm-air furnace	19,450	55.0	2,466	34.9	12.7
Steam or hot water system	5,012	14.2	3,547	50.2	70.8
Electric heat pump	3,500	9.9	75	1.1	2.1
Built-in electric units	2,641	7.5	614	8.7	23.2
Floor, wall, or other built-in hot air units without ducts	2,760	7.8	235	3.3	8.5
Room heaters with flue	370	1.0	54	0.8	14.5
Room heaters without flue	414	1.2	11	0.2	2.6
Portable electric heaters	632	1.8	22	0.3	3.4
Stoves	190	0.5	14	0.2	7.1
Fireplaces with inserts	18	0.0	3	0.0	17.0
Fireplaces without inserts	7	0.0	0	0.0	0.0
Other	154	0.4	16	0.2	10.3
Cooking stove	49	0.1	18	0.3	35.9
None	180	0.5	0	0.0	0.0
Renters with additional heating equipment					
Warm-air furnace	26	0.1	3	0.0	10.0
Steam or hot water system	5	0.0	0	0.0	0.0
Electric heat pump	6	0.0	0	0.0	0.0
Built-in electric units	454	1.3	60	0.8	13.2
Floor, wall, or other built-in hot air units without ducts	12	0.0	3	0.0	22.2
Room heaters with flue	106	0.3	15	0.2	13.7
Room heaters without flue	264	0.7	34	0.5	13.0
Portable electric heaters	3,832	10.8	655	9.3	17.1
Stoves	425	1.2	89	1.3	20.9
Fireplaces with inserts	464	1.3	32	0.5	6.9
Fireplaces without inserts	896	2.5	56	0.8	6.3
Other	83	0.2	20	0.3	24.5
Cooking stove	17	0.0	2	0.0	14.3
None	28,863	81.6	6,094	86.2	21.1

Source: Bureau of the Census, American Housing Survey for the United States: 2009, Internet site http://www.census.gov/hhes/ www/housing/ahs/ahs09/ahs09.html; calculations by New Strategist

Table 5.26 Renters by Type of Heating Equipment, 2009: Midwest

More than 70 percent of renters in the Midwest use a warm-air furnace as their main heating equipment. Thirteen percent also use portable electric heaters.

(number and percent distribution of total renters and renters in the Midwest, by presence and type of heating equipment, 2009; numbers in thousands)

	total		Midwest		
	number	percent distribution	number	percent distribution	percent of total
Total renters	**35,378**	**100.0%**	**7,119**	**100.0%**	**20.1%**
Main heating equipment					
Warm-air furnace	19,450	55.0	5,017	70.5	25.8
Steam or hot water system	5,012	14.2	943	13.2	18.8
Electric heat pump	3,500	9.9	160	2.2	4.6
Built-in electric units	2,641	7.5	674	9.5	25.5
Floor, wall, or other built-in hot air units without ducts	2,760	7.8	211	3.0	7.6
Room heaters with flue	370	1.0	34	0.5	9.3
Room heaters without flue	414	1.2	23	0.3	5.5
Portable electric heaters	632	1.8	22	0.3	3.4
Stoves	190	0.5	25	0.4	13.3
Fireplaces with inserts	18	0.0	0	0.0	0.0
Fireplaces without inserts	7	0.0	0	0.0	0.0
Other	154	0.4	8	0.1	5.0
Cooking stove	49	0.1	0	0.0	0.0
None	180	0.5	3	0.0	1.4
Renters with additional heating equipment					
Warm-air furnace	26	0.1	7	0.1	28.7
Steam or hot water system	5	0.0	0	0.0	0.0
Electric heat pump	6	0.0	0	0.0	0.0
Built-in electric units	454	1.3	66	0.9	14.6
Floor, wall, or other built-in hot air units without ducts	12	0.0	3	0.0	21.5
Room heaters with flue	106	0.3	9	0.1	8.5
Room heaters without flue	264	0.7	55	0.8	20.9
Portable electric heaters	3,832	10.8	952	13.4	24.8
Stoves	425	1.2	57	0.8	13.4
Fireplaces with inserts	464	1.3	72	1.0	15.5
Fireplaces without inserts	896	2.5	99	1.4	11.1
Other	83	0.2	22	0.3	26.3
Cooking stove	17	0.0	4	0.1	26.7
None	28,863	81.6	5,800	81.5	20.1

Source: Bureau of the Census, American Housing Survey for the United States: 2009, Internet site http://www.census.gov/hhes/ www/housing/ahs/ahs09/ahs09.html; calculations by New Strategist

Table 5.27 Renters by Type of Heating Equipment, 2009: South

Most renters in the South use a warm-air furnace as their main heating equipment. Nine percent also use portable electric heaters.

(number and percent distribution of total renters and renters in the South, by presence and type of heating equipment, 2009; numbers in thousands)

	total		South		
	number	percent distribution	number	percent distribution	percent of total
Total renters	**35,378**	**100.0%**	**12,392**	**100.0%**	**35.0%**
Main heating equipment					
Warm-air furnace	19,450	55.0	7,406	59.8	38.1
Steam or hot water system	5,012	14.2	204	1.6	4.1
Electric heat pump	3,500	9.9	2,790	22.5	79.7
Built-in electric units	2,641	7.5	325	2.6	12.3
Floor, wall, or other built-in hot air units without ducts	2,760	7.8	476	3.8	17.3
Room heaters with flue	370	1.0	176	1.4	47.5
Room heaters without flue	414	1.2	358	2.9	86.5
Portable electric heaters	632	1.8	405	3.3	64.1
Stoves	190	0.5	76	0.6	39.7
Fireplaces with inserts	18	0.0	6	0.0	34.4
Fireplaces without inserts	7	0.0	0	0.0	0.0
Other	154	0.4	106	0.9	68.9
Cooking stove	49	0.1	24	0.2	48.7
None	180	0.5	39	0.3	21.8
Renters with additional heating equipment					
Warm-air furnace	26	0.1	11	0.1	44.1
Steam or hot water system	5	0.0	3	0.0	65.6
Electric heat pump	6	0.0	6	0.0	100.0
Built-in electric units	454	1.3	148	1.2	32.6
Floor, wall, or other built-in hot air units without ducts	12	0.0	0	0.0	0.0
Room heaters with flue	106	0.3	37	0.3	34.7
Room heaters without flue	264	0.7	134	1.1	50.7
Portable electric heaters	3,832	10.8	1,166	9.4	30.4
Stoves	425	1.2	119	1.0	28.0
Fireplaces with inserts	464	1.3	191	1.5	41.2
Fireplaces without inserts	896	2.5	329	2.7	36.7
Other	83	0.2	20	0.2	23.8
Cooking stove	17	0.0	3	0.0	20.1
None	28,863	81.6	10,281	83.0	35.6

Source: Bureau of the Census, American Housing Survey for the United States: 2009, Internet site http://www.census.gov/hhes/www/housing/ahs/ahs09/ahs09.html; calculations by New Strategist

Table 5.28 Renters by Type of Heating Equipment, 2009: West

Most renters in the West use a warm-air furnace as their main heating equipment. Twelve percent also use portable electric heaters.

(number and percent distribution of total renters and renters in the West, by presence and type of heating equipment, 2009; numbers in thousands)

	total		West		
	number	percent distribution	number	percent distribution	percent of total
Total renters	**35,378**	**100.0%**	**8,794**	**100.0%**	**24.9%**
Main heating equipment					
Warm-air furnace	19,450	55.0	4,560	51.9	23.4
Steam or hot water system	5,012	14.2	318	3.6	6.3
Electric heat pump	3,500	9.9	474	5.4	13.6
Built-in electric units	2,641	7.5	1,029	11.7	39.0
Floor, wall, or other built-in hot air units without ducts	2,760	7.8	1,838	20.9	66.6
Room heaters with flue	370	1.0	107	1.2	28.8
Room heaters without flue	414	1.2	22	0.3	5.4
Portable electric heaters	632	1.8	184	2.1	29.1
Stoves	190	0.5	76	0.9	39.8
Fireplaces with inserts	18	0.0	9	0.1	48.6
Fireplaces without inserts	7	0.0	7	0.1	100.0
Other	154	0.4	24	0.3	15.8
Cooking stove	49	0.1	8	0.1	15.4
None	180	0.5	138	1.6	76.7
Renters with additional heating equipment					
Warm-air furnace	26	0.1	4	0.1	17.3
Steam or hot water system	5	0.0	2	0.0	34.4
Electric heat pump	6	0.0	0	0.0	0.0
Built-in electric units	454	1.3	180	2.0	39.6
Floor, wall, or other built-in hot air units without ducts	12	0.0	7	0.1	56.3
Room heaters with flue	106	0.3	46	0.5	43.2
Room heaters without flue	264	0.7	41	0.5	15.4
Portable electric heaters	3,832	10.8	1,059	12.0	27.6
Stoves	425	1.2	160	1.8	37.7
Fireplaces with inserts	464	1.3	169	1.9	36.4
Fireplaces without inserts	896	2.5	412	4.7	46.0
Other	83	0.2	21	0.2	25.3
Cooking stove	17	0.0	6	0.1	38.9
None	28,863	81.6	6,688	76.0	23.2

Source: Bureau of the Census, American Housing Survey for the United States: 2009, Internet site http://www.census.gov/hhes/ www/housing/ahs/ahs09/ahs09.html; calculations by New Strategist

Table 5.29 Renters with Air Conditioning, 2009: Northeast

Only 17 percent of renters in the Northeast have central air conditioning. Sixty-one percent have room air conditioners.

(number and percent distribution of total renters and renters in the Northeast, by presence of air conditioning equipment, 2009; numbers in thousands)

	total		Northeast		
	number	percent distribution	number	percent distribution	percent of total
Total renters	**35,378**	**100.0%**	**7,073**	**100.0%**	**20.0%**
Households with air conditioning	29,035	82.1	5,549	78.5	19.1
Central	18,161	51.3	1,229	17.4	6.8
Additional central	920	2.6	33	0.5	3.6
One room unit	6,229	17.6	2,075	29.3	33.3
Two room units	3,332	9.4	1,596	22.6	47.9
Three or more room units	1,314	3.7	649	9.2	49.4

Source: Bureau of the Census, American Housing Survey for the United States: 2009, Internet site http://www.census.gov/hhes/ www/housing/ahs/ahs09/ahs09.html; calculations by New Strategist

Table 5.30 Renters with Air Conditioning, 2009: Midwest

Nearly half (49 percent) of renters in the Midwest have central air conditioning. An additional 37 percent have room air conditioners.

(number and percent distribution of total renters and renters in the Midwest, by presence of air conditioning equipment, 2009; numbers in thousands)

	total		Midwest		
	number	percent distribution	number	percent distribution	percent of total
Total renters	**35,378**	**100.0%**	**7,119**	**100.0%**	**20.1%**
Households with air conditioning	29,035	82.1	6,181	86.8	21.3
Central	18,161	51.3	3,519	49.4	19.4
Additional central	920	2.6	84	1.2	9.1
One room unit	6,229	17.6	1,862	26.2	29.9
Two room units	3,332	9.4	647	9.1	19.4
Three or more room units	1,314	3.7	153	2.1	11.6

Source: Bureau of the Census, American Housing Survey for the United States: 2009, Internet site http://www.census.gov/hhes/ www/housing/ahs/ahs09/ahs09.html; calculations by New Strategist

Table 5.31 Renters with Air Conditioning, 2009: South

Eighty percent of renters in the South have central air conditioning.
Only 3 percent have no air conditioning.

(number and percent distribution of total renters and renters in the South, by presence of air conditioning equipment, 2009; numbers in thousands)

	total		South		
	number	percent distribution	number	percent distribution	percent of total
Total renters	**35,378**	**100.0%**	**12,392**	**100.0%**	**35.0%**
Households with air conditioning	29,035	82.1	12,059	97.3	41.5
Central	18,161	51.3	9,923	80.1	54.6
Additional central	920	2.6	658	5.3	71.6
One room unit	6,229	17.6	946	7.6	15.2
Two room units	3,332	9.4	770	6.2	23.1
Three or more room units	1,314	3.7	421	3.4	32.0

Source: Bureau of the Census, American Housing Survey for the United States: 2009, Internet site http://www.census.gov/hhes/www/housing/ahs/ahs09/ahs09.html; calculations by New Strategist

Table 5.32 Renters with Air Conditioning, 2009: West

Only 40 percent of renters in the West have central air conditioning.
Another 20 percent have room units.

(number and percent distribution of total renters and renters in the West, by presence of air conditioning equipment, 2009; numbers in thousands)

	total		West		
	number	percent distribution	number	percent distribution	percent of total
Total renters	**35,378**	**100.0%**	**8,794**	**100.0%**	**24.9%**
Households with air conditioning	29,035	82.1	5,246	59.7	18.1
Central	18,161	51.3	3,490	39.7	19.2
Additional central	920	2.6	145	1.6	15.7
One room unit	6,229	17.6	1,346	15.3	21.6
Two room units	3,332	9.4	319	3.6	9.6
Three or more room units	1,314	3.7	92	1.0	7.0

Source: Bureau of the Census, American Housing Survey for the United States: 2009, Internet site http://www.census.gov/hhes/www/housing/ahs/ahs09/ahs09.html; calculations by New Strategist

Table 5.33 Renters by Primary Source of Water and Sewage Disposal System, 2009: Northeast

Nine percent of renters in the Northeast say their
primary source of water is not safe to drink.

(number and percent distribution of total renters and renters in the Northeast, by primary source of water and type of sewage disposal system, 2009; numbers in thousands)

	total		Northeast		
	number	percent distribution	number	percent distribution	percent of total
Total renters	**35,378**	**100.0%**	**7,073**	**100.0%**	**20.0%**
Source of water					
Public system or private company	33,655	95.1	6,685	94.5	19.9
Well	1,660	4.7	371	5.2	22.4
Safety of primary source of water					
Safe to drink	31,095	87.9	6,342	89.7	20.4
Not safe to drink	3,882	11.0	643	9.1	16.6
Sewage disposal system					
Public sewer	32,732	92.5	6,602	93.3	20.2
Septic tank, cesspool, chemical toilet	2,640	7.5	468	6.6	17.7

Note: Numbers do not sum to total because "other" and "not reported" are not shown.
Source: Bureau of the Census, American Housing Survey for the United States: 2009, Internet site http://www.census.gov/hhes/ www/housing/ahs/ahs09/ahs09.html; calculations by New Strategist

Table 5.34 **Renters by Primary Source of Water and Sewage Disposal System, 2009: Midwest**

Seven percent of renters in the Midwest say their
primary source of water is not safe to drink.

(number and percent distribution of total renters and renters in the Midwest, by primary source of water and type of sewage disposal system, 2009; numbers in thousands)

	total		Midwest		
	number	percent distribution	number	percent distribution	percent of total
Total renters	**35,378**	**100.0%**	**7,119**	**100.0%**	**20.1%**
Source of water					
Public system or private company	33,655	95.1	6,715	94.3	20.0
Well	1,660	4.7	399	5.6	24.0
Safety of primary source of water					
Safe to drink	31,095	87.9	6,582	92.5	21.2
Not safe to drink	3,882	11.0	470	6.6	12.1
Sewage disposal system					
Public sewer	32,732	92.5	6,635	93.2	20.3
Septic tank, cesspool, chemical toilet	2,640	7.5	483	6.8	18.3

Note: Numbers do not sum to total because "other" and "not reported" are not shown.
Source: Bureau of the Census, American Housing Survey for the United States: 2009, Internet site http://www.census.gov/hhes/www/housing/ahs/ahs09/ahs09.html; calculations by New Strategist

Table 5.35 Renters by Primary Source of Water and Sewage Disposal System, 2009: South

Ten percent of renters in the South say their primary
source of water is not safe to drink.

(number and percent distribution of total renters and renters in the South, by primary source of water and type of sewage disposal system, 2009; numbers in thousands)

	total		South		
	number	percent distribution	number	percent distribution	percent of total
Total renters	**35,378**	**100.0%**	**12,392**	**100.0%**	**35.0%**
Source of water					
Public system or private company	33,655	95.1	11,702	94.4	34.8
Well	1,660	4.7	657	5.3	39.5
Safety of primary source of water					
Safe to drink	31,095	87.9	10,959	88.4	35.2
Not safe to drink	3,882	11.0	1,276	10.3	32.9
Sewage disposal system					
Public sewer	32,732	92.5	11,114	89.7	34.0
Septic tank, cesspool, chemical toilet	2,640	7.5	1,276	10.3	48.3

Note: Numbers do not sum to total because "other" and "not reported" are not shown.
Source: Bureau of the Census, American Housing Survey for the United States: 2009, Internet site http://www.census.gov/hhes/ www/housing/ahs/ahs09/ahs09.html; calculations by New Strategist

Table 5.36 Renters by Primary Source of Water and Sewage Disposal System, 2009: West

Seventeen percent of renters in the West say their
primary source of water is not safe to drink.

(number and percent distribution of total renters and renters in the West, by primary source of water and type of sewage disposal system, 2009; numbers in thousands)

	total		West		
	number	percent distribution	number	percent distribution	percent of total
Total renters	**35,378**	**100.0%**	**8,794**	**100.0%**	**24.9%**
Source of water					
Public system or private company	33,655	95.1	8,552	97.3	25.4
Well	1,660	4.7	234	2.7	14.1
Safety of primary source of water					
Safe to drink	31,095	87.9	7,212	82.0	23.2
Not safe to drink	3,882	11.0	1,492	17.0	38.4
Sewage disposal system					
Public sewer	32,732	92.5	8,381	95.3	25.6
Septic tank, cesspool, chemical toilet	2,640	7.5	413	4.7	15.6

Note: Numbers do not sum to total because "other" and "not reported" are not shown.
Source: Bureau of the Census, American Housing Survey for the United States: 2009, Internet site http://www.census.gov/hhes/ www/housing/ahs/ahs09/ahs09.html; calculations by New Strategist

Table 5.37 Renters by Fuels Used by Region, 2009

Sixty percent of renters in the South have all-electric homes compared
with only 12 percent of renters in the Northeast.

(number and percent distribution of total renters and renters by region, by types of fuels used, 2009; numbers in thousands)

	total	Northeast	Midwest	South	West
Total renters	**35,378**	**7,073**	**7,119**	**12,392**	**8,794**
Electricity	35,368	7,067	7,119	12,389	8,794
All-electric homes	12,215	836	1,740	7,385	2,254
Piped gas	21,186	5,230	5,046	4,444	6,466
Bottled gas	1,425	318	336	595	175
Fuel oil	2,800	2,428	144	174	55
Kerosene or other liquid fuel	164	40	3	110	11
Coal or coke	7	5	0	2	0
Wood	278	38	33	96	110
Solar energy	17	0	0	2	15
Other	151	11	65	22	52

PERCENT DISTRIBUTION BY FUELS USED

	total	Northeast	Midwest	South	West
Total renters	**100.0%**	**100.0%**	**100.0%**	**100.0%**	**100.0%**
Electricity	100.0	99.9	100.0	100.0	100.0
All-electric homes	34.5	11.8	24.4	59.6	25.6
Piped gas	59.9	73.9	70.9	35.9	73.5
Bottled gas	4.0	4.5	4.7	4.8	2.0
Fuel oil	7.9	34.3	2.0	1.4	0.6
Kerosene or other liquid fuel	0.5	0.6	0.0	0.9	0.1
Coal or coke	0.0	0.1	0.0	0.0	0.0
Wood	0.8	0.5	0.5	0.8	1.3
Solar energy	0.0	0.0	0.0	0.0	0.2
Other	0.4	0.2	0.9	0.2	0.6

PERCENT DISTRIBUTION BY REGION

	total	Northeast	Midwest	South	West
Total renters	**100.0%**	**20.0%**	**20.1%**	**35.0%**	**24.9%**
Electricity	100.0	20.0	20.1	35.0	24.9
All-electric homes	100.0	6.8	14.2	60.5	18.5
Piped gas	100.0	24.7	23.8	21.0	30.5
Bottled gas	100.0	22.3	23.6	41.8	12.3
Fuel oil	100.0	86.7	5.1	6.2	2.0
Kerosene or other liquid fuel	100.0	24.1	2.1	66.8	7.0
Coal or coke	100.0	69.2	0.0	30.8	0.0
Wood	100.0	13.8	12.0	34.4	39.8
Solar energy	100.0	0.0	0.0	13.5	86.5
Other	100.0	7.5	43.4	14.5	34.6

Note: Numbers do not add to total because many households use more than one fuel.
Source: Bureau of the Census, American Housing Survey for the United States: 2009, Internet site http://www.census.gov/hhes/ www/housing/ahs/ahs09/ahs09.html; calculations by New Strategist

Table 5.38 Renters by Primary Heating Fuel Used, 2009: Northeast

Piped gas is the most common primary heating fuel of renters in the Northeast. A substantial 31 percent use fuel oil.

(number and percent distribution of total renters and renters in the Northeast, by primary heating fuel used, 2009; numbers in thousands)

	total		Northeast		
	number	percent distribution	number	percent distribution	percent of total
Total renters	**35,378**	**100.0%**	**7,073**	**100.0%**	**20.0%**
Renters using heating fuel	35,198	100.0	7,073	100.0	20.1
Electricity	15,632	44.4	1,307	18.5	8.4
Piped gas	15,573	44.2	3,344	47.3	21.5
Bottled gas	929	2.6	138	1.9	14.8
Fuel oil	2,521	7.2	2,197	31.1	87.1
Kerosene or other liquid fuel	154	0.4	36	0.5	23.3
Coal or coke	7	0.0	5	0.1	69.2
Wood	277	0.8	38	0.5	13.6
Solar energy	3	0.0	0	0.0	0.0
Other	101	0.3	8	0.1	8.1

Source: Bureau of the Census, American Housing Survey for the United States: 2009, Internet site http://www.census.gov/hhes/ www/housing/ahs/ahs09/ahs09.html; calculations by New Strategist

Table 5.39 Renters by Primary Heating Fuel Used, 2009: Midwest

Piped gas is the most common primary heating fuel of renters in the Midwest. A substantial 32 percent use electricity.

(number and percent distribution of total renters and renters in the Midwest, by primary heating fuel used, 2009; numbers in thousands)

	total		Midwest		
	number	percent distribution	number	percent distribution	percent of total
Total renters	**35,378**	**100.0%**	**7,119**	**100.0%**	**20.1%**
Renters using heating fuel	35,198	100.0	7,116	100.0	20.2
Electricity	15,632	44.4	2,250	31.6	14.4
Piped gas	15,573	44.2	4,367	61.4	28.0
Bottled gas	929	2.6	282	4.0	30.4
Fuel oil	2,521	7.2	126	1.8	5.0
Kerosene or other liquid fuel	154	0.4	3	0.0	2.2
Coal or coke	7	0.0	0	0.0	0.0
Wood	277	0.8	33	0.5	12.0
Solar energy	3	0.0	0	0.0	0.0
Other	101	0.3	54	0.8	53.2

Source: Bureau of the Census, American Housing Survey for the United States: 2009, Internet site http://www.census.gov/hhes/www/housing/ahs/ahs09/ahs09.html; calculations by New Strategist

Table 5.40 Renters by Primary Heating Fuel Used, 2009: South

Seventy percent of renters in the South use electricity as their main heating fuel.

(number and percent distribution of total renters and renters in the South, by primary heating fuel used, 2009; numbers in thousands)

	total		South		
	number	percent distribution	number	percent distribution	percent of total
Total renters	**35,378**	**100.0%**	**12,392**	**100.0%**	**35.0%**
Renters using heating fuel	35,198	100.0	12,353	100.0	35.1
Electricity	15,632	44.4	8,637	69.9	55.2
Piped gas	15,573	44.2	2,969	24.0	19.1
Bottled gas	929	2.6	390	3.2	42.0
Fuel oil	2,521	7.2	148	1.2	5.9
Kerosene or other liquid fuel	154	0.4	103	0.8	67.0
Coal or coke	7	0.0	2	0.0	30.8
Wood	277	0.8	96	0.8	34.5
Solar energy	3	0.0	0	0.0	0.0
Other	101	0.3	8	0.1	7.6

Source: Bureau of the Census, American Housing Survey for the United States: 2009, Internet site http://www.census.gov/hhes/www/housing/ahs/ahs09/ahs09.html; calculations by New Strategist

Table 5.41 Renters by Primary Heating Fuel Used, 2009: West

Piped gas is the most common primary heating fuel of renters
in the West. A substantial 40 percent use electricity.

*(number and percent distribution of total renters and renters in the West, by primary heating fuel used, 2009;
numbers in thousands)*

	total		West		
	number	percent distribution	number	percent distribution	percent of total
Total renters	**35,378**	**100.0%**	**8,794**	**100.0%**	**24.9%**
Renters using heating fuel	35,198	100.0	8,655	100.0	24.6
Electricity	15,632	44.4	3,438	39.7	22.0
Piped gas	15,573	44.2	4,893	56.5	31.4
Bottled gas	929	2.6	119	1.4	12.8
Fuel oil	2,521	7.2	50	0.6	2.0
Kerosene or other liquid fuel	154	0.4	11	0.1	7.4
Coal or coke	7	0.0	0	0.0	0.0
Wood	277	0.8	110	1.3	39.9
Solar energy	3	0.0	3	0.0	100.0
Other	101	0.3	31	0.4	31.1

*Source: Bureau of the Census, American Housing Survey for the United States: 2009, Internet site http://www.census.gov/hhes/
www/housing/ahs/ahs09/ahs09.html; calculations by New Strategist*

Table 5.42 Renters by Cooking, Water Heating, and Clothes Dryer Fuels Used, 2009: Northeast

Renters in the Northeast are far less likely than the average renter
to use electricity as a fuel for cooking or water heating.

(number and percent distribution of total renters and renters in the Northeast, by cooking, water heating, and clothes dryer fuels used, 2009; numbers in thousands)

	total		Northeast		
	number	percent distribution	number	percent distribution	percent of total
COOKING FUEL					
Renters using cooking fuel	**35,235**	**100.0%**	**7,024**	**100.0%**	**19.9%**
Electricity	21,567	61.2	2,624	37.4	12.2
Piped gas	12,923	36.7	4,162	59.3	32.2
Bottled gas	726	2.1	230	3.3	31.7
Kerosene or other liquid fuel	7	0.0	4	0.1	55.5
Wood	12	0.0	4	0.1	32.9
WATER HEATING FUEL					
Renters with hot piped water	**35,319**	**100.0**	**7,038**	**100.0**	**19.9**
Electricity	16,095	45.6	1,558	22.1	9.7
Piped gas	16,865	47.7	3,732	53.0	22.1
Bottled gas	692	2.0	167	2.4	24.2
Fuel oil	1,604	4.5	1,573	22.3	98.0
Kerosene or other liquid fuel	3	0.0	0	0.0	0.0
Wood	9	0.0	6	0.1	69.9
Solar energy	14	0.0	0	0.0	0.0
Other	39	0.1	2	0.0	5.2
CLOTHES DRYER FUEL					
Renters with clothes dryers	**18,343**	**100.0**	**2,291**	**100.0**	**12.5**
Electricity	15,438	84.2	1,699	74.2	11.0
Piped gas	2,785	15.2	568	24.8	20.4
Other	120	0.7	24	1.0	19.8

Source: Bureau of the Census, American Housing Survey for the United States: 2009, Internet site http://www.census.gov/hhes/ www/housing/ahs/ahs09/ahs09.html; calculations by New Strategist

Table 5.43 Renters by Cooking, Water Heating, and Clothes Dryer Fuels Used, 2009: Midwest

Renters in the Midwest are more likely than the average
renter to use piped gas as a fuel for water heating.

(number and percent distribution of total renters and renters in the Midwest, by cooking, water heating, and clothes dryer fuels used, 2009; numbers in thousands)

	total		Midwest		
	number	percent distribution	number	percent distribution	percent of total
COOKING FUEL					
Renters using cooking fuel	**35,235**	**100.0%**	**7,107**	**100.0%**	**20.2%**
Electricity	21,567	61.2	4,579	64.4	21.2
Piped gas	12,923	36.7	2,384	33.5	18.4
Bottled gas	726	2.1	138	1.9	19.0
Kerosene or other liquid fuel	7	0.0	0	0.0	0.0
Wood	12	0.0	6	0.1	49.4
WATER HEATING FUEL					
Renters with hot piped water	**35,319**	**100.0**	**7,108**	**100.0**	**20.1**
Electricity	16,095	45.6	2,760	38.8	17.1
Piped gas	16,865	47.7	4,151	58.4	24.6
Bottled gas	692	2.0	186	2.6	26.9
Fuel oil	1,604	4.5	0	0.0	0.0
Kerosene or other liquid fuel	3	0.0	0	0.0	0.0
Wood	9	0.0	0	0.0	0.0
Solar energy	14	0.0	0	0.0	0.0
Other	39	0.1	11	0.2	28.4
CLOTHES DRYER FUEL					
Renters with clothes dryers	**18,343**	**100.0**	**3,707**	**100.0**	**20.2**
Electricity	15,438	84.2	2,956	79.7	19.1
Piped gas	2,785	15.2	715	19.3	25.7
Other	120	0.7	36	1.0	30.3

Source: Bureau of the Census, American Housing Survey for the United States: 2009, Internet site http://www.census.gov/hhes/ www/housing/ahs/ahs09/ahs09.html; calculations by New Strategist

Table 5.44 Renters by Cooking, Water Heating, and Clothes Dryer Fuels Used, 2009: South

Renters in the South are far more likely than the average renter to use electricity for their cooking, water heating, and clothes drying fuel.

(number and percent distribution of total renters and renters in the South, by cooking, water heating, and clothes dryer fuels used, 2009; numbers in thousands)

| | total | | South | | |
	number	percent distribution	number	percent distribution	percent of total
COOKING FUEL					
Renters using cooking fuel	**35,235**	**100.0%**	**12,355**	**100.0%**	**35.1%**
Electricity	21,567	61.2	9,566	77.4	44.4
Piped gas	12,923	36.7	2,510	20.3	19.4
Bottled gas	726	2.1	275	2.2	37.9
Kerosene or other liquid fuel	7	0.0	4	0.0	50.2
Wood	12	0.0	0	0.0	0.0
WATER HEATING FUEL					
Renters with hot piped water	**35,319**	**100.0**	**12,379**	**100.0**	**35.0**
Electricity	16,095	45.6	8,892	71.8	55.2
Piped gas	16,865	47.7	3,247	26.2	19.3
Bottled gas	692	2.0	204	1.7	29.6
Fuel oil	1,604	4.5	28	0.2	1.7
Kerosene or other liquid fuel	3	0.0	3	0.0	100.0
Wood	9	0.0	0	0.0	0.0
Solar energy	14	0.0	2	0.0	14.2
Other	39	0.1	4	0.0	10.3
CLOTHES DRYER FUEL					
Renters with clothes dryers	**18,343**	**100.0**	**7,720**	**100.0**	**42.1**
Electricity	15,438	84.2	7,405	95.9	48.0
Piped gas	2,785	15.2	283	3.7	10.2
Other	120	0.7	32	0.4	26.7

Source: Bureau of the Census, American Housing Survey for the United States: 2009, Internet site http://www.census.gov/hhes/ www/housing/ahs/ahs09/ahs09.html; calculations by New Strategist

Table 5.45 Renters by Cooking, Water Heating, and Clothes Dryer Fuels Used, 2009: West

Renters in the West are more likely than the average renter to
use piped gas as a fuel for cooking or water heating.

*(number and percent distribution of total renters and renters in the West, by cooking, water heating, and clothes
dryer fuels used, 2009; numbers in thousands)*

	total		West		
	number	percent distribution	number	percent distribution	percent of total
COOKING FUEL					
Renters using cooking fuel	**35,235**	**100.0%**	**8,750**	**100.0%**	**24.8%**
Electricity	21,567	61.2	4,798	54.8	22.2
Piped gas	12,923	36.7	3,867	44.2	29.9
Bottled gas	726	2.1	83	0.9	11.4
Kerosene or other liquid fuel	7	0.0	0	0.0	0.0
Wood	12	0.0	3	0.0	24.7
WATER HEATING FUEL					
Renters with hot piped water	**35,319**	**100.0**	**8,794**	**100.0**	**24.9**
Electricity	16,095	45.6	2,885	32.8	17.9
Piped gas	16,865	47.7	5,734	65.2	34.0
Bottled gas	692	2.0	134	1.5	19.3
Fuel oil	1,604	4.5	4	0.0	0.2
Kerosene or other liquid fuel	3	0.0	0	0.0	0.0
Wood	9	0.0	3	0.0	34.9
Solar energy	14	0.0	12	0.1	84.9
Other	39	0.1	22	0.3	56.8
CLOTHES DRYER FUEL					
Renters with clothes dryers	**18,343**	**100.0**	**4,625**	**100.0**	**25.2**
Electricity	15,438	84.2	3,378	73.0	21.9
Piped gas	2,785	15.2	1,219	26.4	43.8
Other	120	0.7	28	0.6	23.2

*Source: Bureau of the Census, American Housing Survey for the United States: 2009, Internet site http://www.census.gov/hhes/
www/housing/ahs/ahs09/ahs09.html; calculations by New Strategist*

Table 5.46 Renters by Amenities of Home and Region, 2009

More than one-third of renters in the Northeast do not
have an automobile available to the household.

*(number and percent distribution of total renters and renters by region, by selected amenities of home, 2009;
numbers in thousands)*

	total	Northeast	Midwest	South	West
Total renters	**35,378**	**7,073**	**7,119**	**12,392**	**8,794**
Porch, deck, balcony, or patio	24,984	3,325	5,055	10,024	6,580
Telephone available	34,196	6,685	6,877	12,044	8,590
Usable fireplace	4,540	335	550	1,789	1,866
Separate dining room	9,959	2,103	1,963	3,620	2,274
With two or more living or recreation rooms	2,934	390	618	1,060	866
Garage or carport					
Yes	13,258	1,385	2,748	3,612	5,513
No, but off-street parking is included	17,676	3,188	3,717	8,030	2,742
No cars, trucks, or vans	6,669	2,531	1,267	1,734	1,136
PERCENT DISTRIBUTION BY AMENITY					
Total renters	**100.0%**	**100.0%**	**100.0%**	**100.0%**	**100.0%**
Porch, deck, balcony, or patio	70.6	47.0	71.0	80.9	74.8
Telephone available	96.7	94.5	96.6	97.2	97.7
Usable fireplace	12.8	4.7	7.7	14.4	21.2
Separate dining room	28.2	29.7	27.6	29.2	25.9
With two or more living or recreation rooms	8.3	5.5	8.7	8.6	9.9
Garage or carport					
Yes	37.5	19.6	38.6	29.1	62.7
No, but off-street parking is included	50.0	45.1	52.2	64.8	31.2
No cars, trucks, or vans	18.9	35.8	17.8	14.0	12.9
PERCENT DISTRIBUTION BY REGION					
Total renters	**100.0%**	**20.0%**	**20.1%**	**35.0%**	**24.9%**
Porch, deck, balcony, or patio	100.0	13.3	20.2	40.1	26.3
Telephone available	100.0	19.6	20.1	35.2	25.1
Usable fireplace	100.0	7.4	12.1	39.4	41.1
Separate dining room	100.0	21.1	19.7	36.3	22.8
With two or more living or recreation rooms	100.0	13.3	21.0	36.1	29.5
Garage or carport					
Yes	100.0	10.4	20.7	27.2	41.6
No, but off-street parking is included	100.0	18.0	21.0	45.4	15.5
No cars, trucks, or vans	100.0	38.0	19.0	26.0	17.0

*Source: Bureau of the Census, American Housing Survey for the United States: 2009, Internet site http://www.census.gov/hhes/
www/housing/ahs/ahs09/ahs09.html; calculations by New Strategist*

Table 5.47 Renters by Deficiencies of Home and Region, 2009

Few renters report deficiencies in their home, regardless of region.
The most common deficiency in any region is signs of mice, reported
by 10 percent of renters in the Northeast in the past three months.

(number and percent distribution of total renters and renters by region, by selected deficiencies of home, 2009; numbers in thousands)

	total	Northeast	Midwest	South	West
Total renters	**35,378**	**7,073**	**7,119**	**12,392**	**8,794**
Signs of rats in last three months	258	55	26	114	63
Signs of mice in last three months	2,138	707	415	674	342
Signs of rodents, not sure which kind, in last three months	189	57	31	85	16
Holes in floor	560	134	80	244	103
Open cracks or holes (interior)	2,416	545	524	861	487
Broken plaster or peeling paint (interior)	1,132	269	270	375	219
No electrical wiring	26	8	0	12	6
Exposed wiring	134	40	23	43	28
Rooms without electric outlets	624	99	144	272	109
PERCENT DISTRIBUTION BY DEFICIENCY					
Total renters	**100.0%**	**100.0%**	**100.0%**	**100.0%**	**100.0%**
Signs of rats in last three months	0.7	0.8	0.4	0.9	0.7
Signs of mice in last three months	6.0	10.0	5.8	5.4	3.9
Signs of rodents, not sure which kind, in last three months	0.5	0.8	0.4	0.7	0.2
Holes in floor	1.6	1.9	1.1	2.0	1.2
Open cracks or holes (interior)	6.8	7.7	7.4	6.9	5.5
Broken plaster or peeling paint (interior)	3.2	3.8	3.8	3.0	2.5
No electrical wiring	0.1	0.1	0.0	0.1	0.1
Exposed wiring	0.4	0.6	0.3	0.3	0.3
Rooms without electric outlets	1.8	1.4	2.0	2.2	1.2
PERCENT DISTRIBUTION BY REGION					
Total renters	**100.0%**	**20.0%**	**20.1%**	**35.0%**	**24.9%**
Signs of rats in last three months	100.0	21.4	10.1	44.1	24.3
Signs of mice in last three months	100.0	33.1	19.4	31.5	16.0
Signs of rodents, not sure which kind, in last three months	100.0	29.9	16.4	45.2	8.5
Holes in floor	100.0	24.0	14.2	43.5	18.3
Open cracks or holes (interior)	100.0	22.6	21.7	35.6	20.1
Broken plaster or peeling paint (interior)	100.0	23.7	23.8	33.1	19.4
No electrical wiring	100.0	31.9	0.0	44.3	23.8
Exposed wiring	100.0	29.7	17.5	31.9	20.8
Rooms without electric outlets	100.0	15.8	23.1	43.6	17.5

Source: Bureau of the Census, American Housing Survey for the United States: 2009, Internet site http://www.census.gov/hhes/ www/housing/ahs/ahs09/ahs09.html; calculations by New Strategist

Table 5.48 Renters by Housing Equipment Failures, 2009: Northeast

Thirteen percent of renters in the Northeast said they were
uncomfortably cold for 24 or more hours last winter. The
most common reason was a breakdown in heating equipment.

(number and percent distribution of total renters and renters in the Northeast, and Northeastern renters as a percent of total, by type of equipment failure, 2009; numbers in thousands)

	total		Northeast		
	number	percent distribution	number	percent distribution	percent of total
WATER SUPPLY STOPPAGE					
Renters with piped water	**35,319**	**100.0%**	**7,038**	**100.0%**	**19.9%**
No stoppage in last three months	33,370	94.5	6,694	95.1	20.1
With stoppage in last three months	1,601	4.5	275	3.9	17.2
Not reported	348	1.0	69	1.0	19.9
FLUSH TOILET BREAKDOWNS					
Renters with flush toilets	**35,313**	**100.0**	**7,046**	**100.0**	**20.0**
With at least one working toilet at all times, last three months	33,766	95.6	6,741	95.7	20.0
With no working toilet at least once in last three months	1,210	3.4	237	3.4	19.6
Not reported	337	1.0	68	1.0	20.2
WATER LEAKAGE DURING LAST 12 MONTHS					
Total renters	**35,378**	**100.0**	**7,073**	**100.0**	**20.0**
No leakage from within structure	31,184	88.1	6,204	87.7	19.9
With leakage from within structure*	3,836	10.8	786	11.1	20.5
Fixtures backed up or overflowed	952	2.7	164	2.3	17.2
Pipes leaked	1,664	4.7	395	5.6	23.7
Broken water heater	327	0.9	60	0.8	18.4
Other or unknown	1,088	3.1	193	2.7	17.8
Leakage not reported	357	1.0	83	1.2	23.3
No leakage from outside structure	31,906	90.2	6,369	90.0	20.0
With leakage from outside structure*	3,121	8.8	625	8.8	20.0
Roof	1,579	4.5	306	4.3	19.4
Basement	538	1.5	157	2.2	29.3
Walls, windows, or doors	795	2.2	128	1.8	16.1
Other or not reported	410	1.2	80	1.1	19.4
Leakage not reported	350	1.0	79	1.1	22.5

	total		Northeast		
	number	percent distribution	number	percent distribution	percent of total
HEATING PROBLEMS					
Renters with heating equipment and occupying home last winter	**31,244**	**100.0%**	**6,541**	**100.0%**	**20.9%**
Not uncomfortably cold for 24 or more hours last winter	26,957	86.3	5,452	83.4	20.2
Uncomfortably cold for 24 or more hours last winter*	3,622	11.6	881	13.5	24.3
Equipment breakdown	1,144	3.7	338	5.2	29.6
Utility interruption	496	1.6	123	1.9	24.9
Inadequate heating capacity	675	2.2	153	2.3	22.7
Inadequate insulation	523	1.7	96	1.5	18.4
Cost of heating	421	1.3	85	1.3	20.1
Other	677	2.2	163	2.5	24.1
Not reported	666	2.1	207	3.2	31.1
ELECTRICAL PROBLEMS					
Renters with electrical wiring	**35,351**	**100.0**	**7,065**	**100.0**	**20.0**
No fuses or breakers blown in last three months	31,879	90.2	6,455	91.4	20.2
With fuses or breakers blown in last three months	3,082	8.7	552	7.8	17.9
Not reported	391	1.1	58	0.8	14.8

Figures do not add to total because more than one problem may have occurred.
Source: Bureau of the Census, American Housing Survey for the United States: 2009, Internet site http://www.census.gov/hhes/ www/housing/ahs/ahs09/ahs09.html; calculations by New Strategist

Table 5.49 Renters by Housing Equipment Failures, 2009: Midwest

Fourteen percent of renters in the Midwest said they were uncomfortably cold for 24 or more hours last winter. The most common reason was a breakdown in heating equipment.

(number and percent distribution of total renters and renters in the Midwest, and Midwestern renters as a percent of total, by type of equipment failure, 2009; numbers in thousands)

	total		Midwest		
	number	percent distribution	number	percent distribution	percent of total
WATER SUPPLY STOPPAGE					
Renters with piped water	**35,319**	**100.0%**	**7,108**	**100.0%**	**20.1 %**
No stoppage in last three months	33,370	94.5	6,768	95.2	20.3
With stoppage in last three months	1,601	4.5	306	4.3	19.1
Not reported	348	1.0	34	0.5	9.8
FLUSH TOILET BREAKDOWNS					
Renters with flush toilets	**35,313**	**100.0**	**7,112**	**100.0**	**20.1**
With at least one working toilet at all times, last three months	33,766	95.6	6,823	95.9	20.2
With no working toilet at least once in last three months	1,210	3.4	258	3.6	21.3
Not reported	337	1.0	31	0.4	9.2
WATER LEAKAGE DURING LAST 12 MONTHS					
Total renters	**35,378**	**100.0**	**7,119**	**100.0**	**20.1**
No leakage from within structure	31,184	88.1	6,287	88.3	20.2
With leakage from within structure*	3,836	10.8	792	11.1	20.7
Fixtures backed up or overflowed	952	2.7	223	3.1	23.4
Pipes leaked	1,664	4.7	304	4.3	18.3
Broken water heater	327	0.9	50	0.7	15.4
Other or unknown	1,088	3.1	243	3.4	22.4
Leakage not reported	357	1.0	40	0.6	11.1
No leakage from outside structure	31,906	90.2	6,126	86.1	19.2
With leakage from outside structure*	3,121	8.8	945	13.3	30.3
Roof	1,579	4.5	386	5.4	24.4
Basement	538	1.5	314	4.4	58.3
Walls, windows, or doors	795	2.2	247	3.5	31.1
Other or not reported	410	1.2	80	1.1	19.6
Leakage not reported	350	1.0	48	0.7	13.7

	total		Midwest		
	number	percent distribution	number	percent distribution	percent of total
HEATING PROBLEMS					
Renters with heating equipment and occupying home last winter	**31,244**	**100.0%**	**6,352**	**100.0%**	**20.3%**
Not uncomfortably cold for 24 or more hours last winter	26,957	86.3	5,388	84.8	20.0
Uncomfortably cold for 24 or more hours last winter*	3,622	11.6	873	13.7	24.1
Equipment breakdown	1,144	3.7	292	4.6	25.5
Utility interruption	496	1.6	113	1.8	22.8
Inadequate heating capacity	675	2.2	141	2.2	20.9
Inadequate insulation	523	1.7	142	2.2	27.1
Cost of heating	421	1.3	102	1.6	24.3
Other	677	2.2	172	2.7	25.4
Not reported	666	2.1	91	1.4	13.6
ELECTRICAL PROBLEMS					
Renters with electrical wiring	**35,351**	**100.0**	**7,119**	**100.0**	**20.1**
No fuses or breakers blown in last three months	31,879	90.2	6,349	89.2	19.9
With fuses or breakers blown in last three months	3,082	8.7	719	10.1	23.3
Not reported	391	1.1	51	0.7	13.0

* Figures do not add to total because more than one problem may have occurred.
Source: Bureau of the Census, American Housing Survey for the United States: 2009, Internet site http://www.census.gov/hhes/www/housing/ahs/ahs09/ahs09.html; calculations by New Strategist

Table 5.50 Renters by Housing Equipment Failures, 2009: South

Only 9 percent of renters in the South said they were
uncomfortably cold for 24 or more hours last winter,
below the 12 percent who reported the problem nationally.

(number and percent distribution of total renters and renters in the South, and Southern renters as a percent of total, by type of equipment failure, 2009; numbers in thousands)

	total		South		
	number	percent distribution	number	percent distribution	percent of total
WATER SUPPLY STOPPAGE					
Renters with piped water	**35,319**	**100.0%**	**12,379**	**100.0%**	**35.0 %**
No stoppage in last three months	33,370	94.5	11,722	94.7	35.1
With stoppage in last three months	1,601	4.5	475	3.8	29.7
Not reported	348	1.0	183	1.5	52.5
FLUSH TOILET BREAKDOWNS					
Renters with flush toilets	**35,313**	**100.0**	**12,388**	**100.0**	**35.1**
With at least one working toilet at all times, last three months	33,766	95.6	11,788	95.2	34.9
With no working toilet at least once in last three months	1,210	3.4	427	3.4	35.3
Not reported	337	1.0	173	1.4	51.4
WATER LEAKAGE DURING LAST 12 MONTHS					
Total renters	**35,378**	**100.0**	**12,392**	**100.0**	**35.0**
No leakage from within structure	31,184	88.1	10,864	87.7	34.8
With leakage from within structure*	3,836	10.8	1,354	10.9	35.3
Fixtures backed up or overflowed	952	2.7	335	2.7	35.1
Pipes leaked	1,664	4.7	552	4.5	33.2
Broken water heater	327	0.9	153	1.2	46.7
Other or unknown	1,088	3.1	395	3.2	36.3
Leakage not reported	357	1.0	174	1.4	48.7
No leakage from outside structure	31,906	90.2	11,206	90.4	35.1
With leakage from outside structure*	3,121	8.8	1,019	8.2	32.6
Roof	1,579	4.5	631	5.1	40.0
Basement	538	1.5	38	0.3	7.1
Walls, windows, or doors	795	2.2	258	2.1	32.5
Other or not reported	410	1.2	142	1.1	34.7
Leakage not reported	350	1.0	168	1.4	48.0

	total		South		
	number	percent distribution	number	percent distribution	percent of total
HEATING PROBLEMS					
Renters with heating equipment and occupying home last winter	**31,244**	**100.0%**	**10,802**	**100.0%**	**34.6%**
Not uncomfortably cold for 24 or more hours last winter	26,957	86.3	9,516	88.1	35.3
Uncomfortably cold for 24 or more hours last winter*	3,622	11.6	1,014	9.4	28.0
Equipment breakdown	1,144	3.7	313	2.9	27.3
Utility interruption	496	1.6	200	1.9	40.3
Inadequate heating capacity	675	2.2	176	1.6	26.0
Inadequate insulation	523	1.7	141	1.3	27.0
Cost of heating	421	1.3	92	0.9	21.9
Other	677	2.2	173	1.6	25.6
Not reported	666	2.1	272	2.5	40.9
ELECTRICAL PROBLEMS					
Renters with electrical wiring	**35,351**	**100.0**	**12,381**	**100.0**	**35.0**
No fuses or breakers blown in last three months	31,879	90.2	11,156	90.1	35.0
With fuses or breakers blown in last three months	3,082	8.7	1,019	8.2	33.1
Not reported	391	1.1	206	1.7	52.7

* Figures do not add to total because more than one problem may have occurred.
Source: Bureau of the Census, American Housing Survey for the United States: 2009, Internet site http://www.census.gov/hhes/www/housing/ahs/ahs09/ahs09.html; calculations by New Strategist

Table 5.51 Renters by Housing Equipment Failures, 2009: West

Renters in the West were no more likely than the average renter
to have been uncomfortably cold for 24 or more hours last winter.

(number and percent distribution of total renters and renters in the West, and Western renters as a percent of total, by type of equipment failure, 2009; numbers in thousands)

	total		West		
	number	percent distribution	number	percent distribution	percent of total
WATER SUPPLY STOPPAGE					
Renters with piped water	**35,319**	**100.0%**	**8,794**	**100.0%**	**24.9%**
No stoppage in last three months	33,370	94.5	8,187	93.1	24.5
With stoppage in last three months	1,601	4.5	545	6.2	34.0
Not reported	348	1.0	62	0.7	17.8
FLUSH TOILET BREAKDOWNS					
Renters with flush toilets	**35,313**	**100.0**	**8,768**	**100.0**	**24.8**
With at least one working toilet at all times, last three months	33,766	95.6	8,415	96.0	24.9
With no working toilet at least once in last three months	1,210	3.4	288	3.3	23.8
Not reported	337	1.0	65	0.7	19.3
WATER LEAKAGE DURING LAST 12 MONTHS					
Total renters	**35,378**	**100.0**	**8,794**	**100.0**	**24.9**
No leakage from within structure	31,184	88.1	7,829	89.0	25.1
With leakage from within structure*	3,836	10.8	904	10.3	23.6
Fixtures backed up or overflowed	952	2.7	231	2.6	24.2
Pipes leaked	1,664	4.7	413	4.7	24.8
Broken water heater	327	0.9	64	0.7	19.5
Other or unknown	1,088	3.1	256	2.9	23.6
Leakage not reported	357	1.0	60	0.7	16.9
No leakage from outside structure	31,906	90.2	8,205	93.3	25.7
With leakage from outside structure*	3,121	8.8	533	6.1	17.1
Roof	1,579	4.5	257	2.9	16.3
Basement	538	1.5	29	0.3	5.3
Walls, windows, or doors	795	2.2	162	1.8	20.3
Other or not reported	410	1.2	108	1.2	26.3
Leakage not reported	350	1.0	56	0.6	15.9

	total		West		
	number	percent distribution	number	percent distribution	percent of total
HEATING PROBLEMS					
Renters with heating equipment and occupying home last winter	**31,244**	**100.0%**	**7,550**	**100.0%**	**24.2%**
Not uncomfortably cold for 24 or more hours last winter	26,957	86.3	6,601	87.4	24.5
Uncomfortably cold for 24 or more hours last winter*	3,622	11.6	853	11.3	23.6
Equipment breakdown	1,144	3.7	201	2.7	17.6
Utility interruption	496	1.6	60	0.8	12.1
Inadequate heating capacity	675	2.2	205	2.7	30.4
Inadequate insulation	523	1.7	144	1.9	27.5
Cost of heating	421	1.3	142	1.9	33.8
Other	677	2.2	169	2.2	24.9
Not reported	666	2.1	96	1.3	14.4
ELECTRICAL PROBLEMS					
Renters with electrical wiring	**35,351**	**100.0**	**8,787**	**100.0**	**24.9**
No fuses or breakers blown in last three months	31,879	90.2	7,919	90.1	24.8
With fuses or breakers blown in last three months	3,082	8.7	792	9.0	25.7
Not reported	391	1.1	77	0.9	19.7

Figures do not add to total because more than one problem may have occurred.
Source: Bureau of the Census, American Housing Survey for the United States: 2009, Internet site http://www.census.gov/hhes/ www/housing/ahs/ahs09/ahs09.html; calculations by New Strategist

Table 5.52 Renters by Monthly Housing Costs and Region, 2009

Median monthly housing costs for the nation's renters range
from a low of $691 in the South to a high of $956 in the West.

(number and percent distribution of renters by monthly housing costs, by region, 2009; numbers in thousands)

	total	Northeast	Midwest	South	West
Total renters	**35,378**	**7,073**	**7,119**	**12,392**	**8,794**
Less than $100	248	56	56	83	52
$100 to $199	728	134	211	268	116
$200 to $299	1,381	357	333	408	283
$300 to $399	1,359	352	371	441	194
$400 to $499	2,094	335	616	783	360
$500 to $599	2,985	477	800	1,214	493
$600 to $699	3,808	578	1,044	1,498	688
$700 to $799	3,709	558	895	1,477	779
$800 to $999	6,060	1,170	1,187	2,218	1,486
$1,000 to $1,249	4,777	1,154	668	1,537	1,417
$1,250 to $1,499	2,631	664	272	734	960
$1,500 or $1,999	2,247	567	174	501	1,005
$2,000 to $2,499	718	160	48	147	363
$2,500 or more	596	169	45	137	245
No cash rent	2,037	341	398	945	352
Median monthly cost	$808	$877	$691	$764	$956

PERCENT DISTRIBUTION BY MONTHLY COSTS

Total renters	**100.0%**	**100.0%**	**100.0%**	**100.0%**	**100.0%**
Less than $100	0.7	0.8	0.8	0.7	0.6
$100 to $199	2.1	1.9	3.0	2.2	1.3
$200 to $299	3.9	5.1	4.7	3.3	3.2
$300 to $399	3.8	5.0	5.2	3.6	2.2
$400 to $499	5.9	4.7	8.7	6.3	4.1
$500 to $599	8.4	6.8	11.2	9.8	5.6
$600 to $699	10.8	8.2	14.7	12.1	7.8
$700 to $799	10.5	7.9	12.6	11.9	8.9
$800 to $999	17.1	16.5	16.7	17.9	16.9
$1,000 to $1,249	13.5	16.3	9.4	12.4	16.1
$1,250 to $1,499	7.4	9.4	3.8	5.9	10.9
$1,500 or $1,999	6.4	8.0	2.4	4.0	11.4
$2,000 to $2,499	2.0	2.3	0.7	1.2	4.1
$2,500 or more	1.7	2.4	0.6	1.1	2.8
No cash rent	5.8	4.8	5.6	7.6	4.0

	total	Northeast	Midwest	South	West
PERCENT DISTRIBUTION BY REGION					
Total renters	**100.0%**	**20.0%**	**20.1%**	**35.0%**	**24.9%**
Less than $100	100.0	22.6	22.6	33.7	21.1
$100 to $199	100.0	18.4	28.9	36.8	15.9
$200 to $299	100.0	25.9	24.1	29.6	20.5
$300 to $399	100.0	25.9	27.3	32.5	14.3
$400 to $499	100.0	16.0	29.4	37.4	17.2
$500 to $599	100.0	16.0	26.8	40.7	16.5
$600 to $699	100.0	15.2	27.4	39.3	18.1
$700 to $799	100.0	15.0	24.1	39.8	21.0
$800 to $999	100.0	19.3	19.6	36.6	24.5
$1,000 to $1,249	100.0	24.2	14.0	32.2	29.7
$1,250 to $1,499	100.0	25.3	10.3	27.9	36.5
$1,500 or $1,999	100.0	25.2	7.7	22.3	44.7
$2,000 to $2,499	100.0	22.3	6.7	20.5	50.5
$2,500 or more	100.0	28.3	7.5	23.0	41.1
No cash rent	100.0	16.8	19.6	46.4	17.3

Note: Housing costs include rent, utilities, and property insurance.
Source: Bureau of the Census, American Housing Survey for the United States: 2009, Internet site http://www.census.gov/hhes/www/housing/ahs/ahs09/ahs09.html; calculations by New Strategist

Table 5.53 Renters by Monthly Utility Costs, 2009: Northeast

Renters in the Northeast pay more for piped gas than the average renter,
a median of $71 per month versus $55 per month nationally.

(number and percent distribution of total renters and renters in the Northeast by average monthly costs for utilities, 2009; numbers in thousands)

	total		Northeast		
	number	percent distribution	number	percent distribution	percent of total
MONTHLY COST OF ELECTRICITY					
Renters using electricity	**35,368**	**100.0%**	**7,067**	**100.0%**	**20.0%**
Less than $25	1,259	3.6	129	1.8	10.3
$25 to $49	5,426	15.3	1,389	19.6	25.6
$50 to $74	6,535	18.5	1,529	21.6	23.4
$75 to $99	5,469	15.5	1,040	14.7	19.0
$100 to $149	6,589	18.6	1,026	14.5	15.6
$150 to $199	2,795	7.9	320	4.5	11.5
$200 or more	2,341	6.6	354	5.0	15.1
Incl. in rent, other fee, or obtained free	4,954	14.0	1,279	18.1	25.8
Median monthly cost	$84	–	$71	–	–
MONTHLY COST OF PIPED GAS					
Renters using piped gas	**21,186**	**100.0%**	**5,230**	**100.0%**	**24.7%**
Less than $25	2,447	11.5	466	8.9	19.0
$25 to $49	4,469	21.1	531	10.2	11.9
$50 to $74	3,581	16.9	722	13.8	20.2
$75 to $99	2,054	9.7	513	9.8	25.0
$100 to $149	1,884	8.9	673	12.9	35.7
$150 to $199	643	3.0	225	4.3	34.9
$200 or more	518	2.4	174	3.3	33.6
Incl. in rent, other fee, or obtained free	5,588	26.4	1,927	36.8	34.5
Median monthly cost	$55	–	$71	–	–
MONTHLY COST OF FUEL OIL					
Renters using fuel oil	**2,800**	**100.0%**	**2,428**	**100.0%**	**86.7%**
Less than $25	52	1.9	11	0.5	22.0
$25 to $49	70	2.5	40	1.6	56.9
$50 to $74	91	3.3	68	2.8	74.4
$75 to $99	100	3.6	66	2.7	66.1
$100 to $149	163	5.8	127	5.2	77.7
$150 to $199	108	3.9	79	3.2	72.7
$200 or more	146	5.2	131	5.4	89.8
Incl. in rent, other fee, or obtained free	2,068	73.9	1,905	78.5	92.1
Median monthly cost	$100	–	$125	–	–

	total		Northeast		
	number	percent distribution	number	percent distribution	percent of total
Water paid separately	**9,237**	–	**640**	–	**6.9%**
Median monthly cost	$29	–	$33	–	–
Trash paid separately	**7,551**	–	**436**	–	**5.8**
Median monthly cost	$20	–	$18	–	–
Property insurance paid	**9,397**	–	**1,532**	–	**16.3**
Median monthly cost	$16	–	$17	–	–

Note: "–" means not applicable.
Source: Bureau of the Census, American Housing Survey for the United States: 2009, Internet site http://www.census.gov/hhes/ www/housing/ahs/ahs09/ahs09.html; calculations by New Strategist

Table 5.54 Renters by Monthly Utility Costs, 2009: Midwest

Renters in the Midwest pay more for piped gas than the average renter, a median of $74 per month versus $55 per month nationally.

(number and percent distribution of total renters and renters in the Midwest by average monthly costs for utilities, 2009; numbers in thousands)

	total		Midwest		
	number	percent distribution	number	percent distribution	percent of total
MONTHLY COST OF ELECTRICITY					
Renters using electricity	**35,368**	**100.0%**	**7,119**	**100.0%**	**20.1%**
Less than $25	1,259	3.6	411	5.8	32.6
$25 to $49	5,426	15.3	1,403	19.7	25.9
$50 to $74	6,535	18.5	1,490	20.9	22.8
$75 to $99	5,469	15.5	1,057	14.8	19.3
$100 to $149	6,589	18.6	1,118	15.7	17.0
$150 to $199	2,795	7.9	376	5.3	13.4
$200 or more	2,341	6.6	299	4.2	12.8
Incl. in rent, other fee, or obtained free	4,954	14.0	966	13.6	19.5
Median monthly cost	$84	–	$70	–	–
MONTHLY COST OF PIPED GAS					
Renters using piped gas	**21,186**	**100.0%**	**5,046**	**100.0%**	**23.8%**
Less than $25	2,447	11.5	176	3.5	7.2
$25 to $49	4,469	21.1	725	14.4	16.2
$50 to $74	3,581	16.9	898	17.8	25.1
$75 to $99	2,054	9.7	667	13.2	32.5
$100 to $149	1,884	8.9	701	13.9	37.2
$150 to $199	643	3.0	234	4.6	36.4
$200 or more	518	2.4	191	3.8	36.8
Incl. in rent, other fee, or obtained free	5,588	26.4	1,454	28.8	26.0
Median monthly cost	$55	–	$74	–	–
MONTHLY COST OF FUEL OIL					
Renters using fuel oil	**2,800**	**100.0%**	**144**	**100.0%**	**5.1%**
Less than $25	52	1.9	25	17.5	48.0
$25 to $49	70	2.5	5	3.4	6.9
$50 to $74	91	3.3	3	1.9	3.0
$75 to $99	100	3.6	9	6.1	8.7
$100 to $149	163	5.8	19	12.9	11.4
$150 to $199	108	3.9	8	5.3	7.0
$200 or more	146	5.2	7	4.7	4.6
Incl. in rent, other fee, or obtained free	2,068	73.9	69	48.0	3.3
Median monthly cost	$100	–	$75	–	–

	total		Midwest		
	number	percent distribution	number	percent distribution	percent of total
Water paid separately	**9,237**	–	**1,877**	–	**20.3%**
Median monthly cost	$29	–	$28	–	–
Trash paid separately	**7,551**	–	**1,627**	–	**21.5**
Median monthly cost	$20	–	$17	–	–
Property insurance paid	**9,397**	–	**2,476**	–	**26.3**
Median monthly cost	$16	–	$13	–	–

Note: "–" means not applicable.
Source: Bureau of the Census, American Housing Survey for the United States: 2009, Internet site http://www.census.gov/hhes/ www/housing/ahs/ahs09/ahs09.html; calculations by New Strategist

Table 5.55 Renters by Monthly Utility Costs, 2009: South

Renters in the South pay more for electricity than the average renter,
a median of $111 per month versus $84 per month nationally.

(number and percent distribution of total renters and renters in the South by average monthly costs for utilities, 2009; numbers in thousands)

	total		South		
	number	percent distribution	number	percent distribution	percent of total
MONTHLY COST OF ELECTRICITY					
Renters using electricity	**35,368**	**100.0%**	**12,389**	**100.0%**	**35.0%**
Less than $25	1,259	3.6	49	0.4	3.9
$25 to $49	5,426	15.3	513	4.1	9.5
$50 to $74	6,535	18.5	1,725	13.9	26.4
$75 to $99	5,469	15.5	2,248	18.1	41.1
$100 to $149	6,589	18.6	3,388	27.4	51.4
$150 to $199	2,795	7.9	1,622	13.1	58.0
$200 or more	2,341	6.6	1,359	11.0	58.1
Incl. in rent, other fee, or obtained free	4,954	14.0	1,485	12.0	30.0
Median monthly cost	$84	–	$111	–	–
MONTHLY COST OF PIPED GAS					
Renters using piped gas	**21,186**	**100.0%**	**4,444**	**100.0%**	**21.0%**
Less than $25	2,447	11.5	373	8.4	15.2
$25 to $49	4,469	21.1	1,060	23.9	23.7
$50 to $74	3,581	16.9	867	19.5	24.2
$75 to $99	2,054	9.7	550	12.4	26.8
$100 to $149	1,884	8.9	342	7.7	18.2
$150 to $199	643	3.0	127	2.9	19.7
$200 or more	518	2.4	130	2.9	25.2
Incl. in rent, other fee, or obtained free	5,588	26.4	993	22.3	17.8
Median monthly cost	$55	–	$56	–	–
MONTHLY COST OF FUEL OIL					
Renters using fuel oil	**2,800**	**100.0%**	**174**	**100.0%**	**6.2%**
Less than $25	52	1.9	10	5.7	19.1
$25 to $49	70	2.5	23	13.1	32.5
$50 to $74	91	3.3	17	9.5	18.1
$75 to $99	100	3.6	19	11.0	19.1
$100 to $149	163	5.8	8	4.6	4.9
$150 to $199	108	3.9	22	12.6	20.3
$200 or more	146	5.2	8	4.7	5.6
Incl. in rent, other fee, or obtained free	2,068	73.9	67	38.6	3.2
Median monthly cost	$100	–	$83	–	–

	total		South		
	number	percent distribution	number	percent distribution	percent of total
Water paid separately	**9,237**	–	**4,807**	–	**52.0%**
Median monthly cost	$29	–	$26	–	–
Trash paid separately	**7,551**	–	**3,451**	–	**45.7**
Median monthly cost	$20	–	$20	–	–
Property insurance paid	**9,397**	–	**3,250**	–	**34.6**
Median monthly cost	$16	–	$16	–	–

Note: "–" means not applicable.
Source: Bureau of the Census, American Housing Survey for the United States: 2009, Internet site http://www.census.gov/hhes/www/housing/ahs/ahs09/ahs09.html; calculations by New Strategist

Table 5.56 **Renters by Monthly Utility Costs, 2009: West**

Renters in the West pay less for electricity than the average renter,
a median of $62 per month versus $84 per month nationally.

(number and percent distribution of total renters and renters in the West by average monthly costs for utilities, 2009; numbers in thousands)

	total		West		
	number	percent distribution	number	percent distribution	percent of total
MONTHLY COST OF ELECTRICITY					
Renters using electricity	**35,368**	**100.0%**	**8,794**	**100.0%**	**24.9%**
Less than $25	1,259	3.6	670	7.6	53.2
$25 to $49	5,426	15.3	2,122	24.1	39.1
$50 to $74	6,535	18.5	1,791	20.4	27.4
$75 to $99	5,469	15.5	1,125	12.8	20.6
$100 to $149	6,589	18.6	1,057	12.0	16.0
$150 to $199	2,795	7.9	477	5.4	17.1
$200 or more	2,341	6.6	329	3.7	14.0
Incl. in rent, other fee, or obtained free	4,954	14.0	1,224	13.9	24.7
Median monthly cost	$84	–	$62	–	–
MONTHLY COST OF PIPED GAS					
Renters using piped gas	**21,186**	**100.0%**	**6,466**	**100.0%**	**30.5%**
Less than $25	2,447	11.5	1,432	22.1	58.5
$25 to $49	4,469	21.1	2,153	33.3	48.2
$50 to $74	3,581	16.9	1,094	16.9	30.5
$75 to $99	2,054	9.7	324	5.0	15.8
$100 to $149	1,884	8.9	168	2.6	8.9
$150 to $199	643	3.0	57	0.9	8.9
$200 or more	518	2.4	23	0.3	4.4
Incl. in rent, other fee, or obtained free	5,588	26.4	1,215	18.8	21.7
Median monthly cost	$55	–	$37	–	–
MONTHLY COST OF FUEL OIL					
Renters using fuel oil	**2,800**	**100.0%**	**55**	**100.0%**	**2.0%**
Less than $25	52	1.9	6	10.4	10.9
$25 to $49	70	2.5	3	4.7	3.7
$50 to $74	91	3.3	4	7.5	4.5
$75 to $99	100	3.6	6	11.1	6.1
$100 to $149	163	5.8	10	17.8	6.0
$150 to $199	108	3.9	0	0.0	0.0
$200 or more	146	5.2	0	0.0	0.0
Incl. in rent, other fee, or obtained free	2,068	73.9	27	49.2	1.3
Median monthly cost	$100	–	–	–	–

	total		West		
	number	percent distribution	number	percent distribution	percent of total
Water paid separately	9,237	–	1,913	–	20.7%
Median monthly cost	$29	–	$33	–	–
Trash paid separately	7,551	–	2,037	–	27.0
Median monthly cost	$20	–	$23	–	–
Property insurance paid	9,397	–	2,138	–	22.8
Median monthly cost	$16	–	$17	–	–

Note: "–" means not applicable or sample is too small to make a reliable estimate.
Source: Bureau of the Census, American Housing Survey for the United States: 2009, Internet site http://www.census.gov/hhes/
www/housing/ahs/ahs09/ahs09.html; calculations by New Strategist

Table 5.57 Renters by Opinion of Home and Region, 2009

Regardless of region, about the same proportion of renters (58 to 60 percent) rate their home an 8 or higher on a scale of 1 (worst) to 10 (best).

(number and percent distribution of renters by opinion of home, by region, 2009; numbers in thousands)

	total	Northeast	Midwest	South	West
Total renters	**35,378**	**7,073**	**7,119**	**12,392**	**8,794**
1 (worst)	327	86	51	127	62
2	209	31	54	78	45
3	436	100	69	138	129
4	708	138	151	239	180
5	2,910	482	603	1,124	701
6	2,553	484	551	852	665
7	6,146	1,140	1,236	2,144	1,625
8	9,625	1,933	1,956	3,296	2,439
9	4,217	899	805	1,371	1,143
10 (best)	6,941	1,432	1,443	2,471	1,596
Not reported	1,306	348	200	551	208

PERCENT DISTRIBUTION BY RATING

	total	Northeast	Midwest	South	West
Total renters	**100.0%**	**100.0%**	**100.0%**	**100.0%**	**100.0%**
1 (worst)	0.9	1.2	0.7	1.0	0.7
2	0.6	0.4	0.8	0.6	0.5
3	1.2	1.4	1.0	1.1	1.5
4	2.0	1.9	2.1	1.9	2.1
5	8.2	6.8	8.5	9.1	8.0
6	7.2	6.8	7.7	6.9	7.6
7	17.4	16.1	17.4	17.3	18.5
8	27.2	27.3	27.5	26.6	27.7
9	11.9	12.7	11.3	11.1	13.0
10 (best)	19.6	20.2	20.3	19.9	18.1
Not reported	3.7	4.9	2.8	4.4	2.4

PERCENT DISTRIBUTION BY REGION

	total	Northeast	Midwest	South	West
Total renters	**100.0%**	**20.0%**	**20.1%**	**35.0%**	**24.9%**
1 (worst)	100.0	26.5	15.6	38.9	19.0
2	100.0	15.0	25.8	37.4	21.8
3	100.0	23.0	15.8	31.6	29.7
4	100.0	19.5	21.4	33.7	25.5
5	100.0	16.6	20.7	38.6	24.1
6	100.0	19.0	21.6	33.4	26.1
7	100.0	18.5	20.1	34.9	26.4
8	100.0	20.1	20.3	34.2	25.3
9	100.0	21.3	19.1	32.5	27.1
10 (best)	100.0	20.6	20.8	35.6	23.0
Not reported	100.0	26.6	15.3	42.2	15.9

Source: Bureau of the Census, American Housing Survey for the United States: 2009, Internet site http://www.census.gov/hhes/ www/housing/ahs/ahs09/ahs09.html; calculations by New Strategist

Table 5.58 Renters by Opinion of Neighborhood and Region, 2009

Renters in every region are about equally likely to rate their neighborhood an 8 or higher, with 59 to 61 percent doing so.

(number and percent distribution of renters by opinion, on a scale of 1 (worst) to 10 (best) of neighborhood, by region, 2009; numbers in thousands)

	total	Northeast	Midwest	South	West
Total renters	**35,378**	**7,073**	**7,119**	**12,392**	**8,794**
1 (worst)	499	124	124	163	88
2	348	65	78	148	56
3	543	123	98	179	144
4	867	133	199	289	246
5	2,976	503	555	1,155	763
6	2,465	490	494	798	683
7	5,164	984	1,073	1,773	1,334
8	8,986	1,828	1,785	3,015	2,359
9	4,563	957	912	1,527	1,167
10 (best)	7,575	1,503	1,586	2,752	1,733
No neighborhood	29	9	10	6	5
Not reported	1,362	355	205	586	217
PERCENT DISTRIBUTION BY RATING					
Total renters	**100.0%**	**100.0%**	**100.0%**	**100.0%**	**100.0%**
1 (worst)	1.4	1.7	1.7	1.3	1.0
2	1.0	0.9	1.1	1.2	0.6
3	1.5	1.7	1.4	1.4	1.6
4	2.5	1.9	2.8	2.3	2.8
5	8.4	7.1	7.8	9.3	8.7
6	7.0	6.9	6.9	6.4	7.8
7	14.6	13.9	15.1	14.3	15.2
8	25.4	25.8	25.1	24.3	26.8
9	12.9	13.5	12.8	12.3	13.3
10 (best)	21.4	21.3	22.3	22.2	19.7
No neighborhood	0.1	0.1	0.1	0.1	0.1
Not reported	3.8	5.0	2.9	4.7	2.5
PERCENT DISTRIBUTION BY REGION					
Total renters	**100.0%**	**20.0%**	**20.1%**	**35.0%**	**24.9%**
1 (worst)	100.0	24.8	24.8	32.7	17.7
2	100.0	18.8	22.6	42.6	16.0
3	100.0	22.6	18.0	33.0	26.5
4	100.0	15.3	23.0	33.4	28.3
5	100.0	16.9	18.7	38.8	25.6
6	100.0	19.9	20.0	32.4	27.7
7	100.0	19.1	20.8	34.3	25.8
8	100.0	20.3	19.9	33.5	26.2
9	100.0	21.0	20.0	33.5	25.6
10 (best)	100.0	19.8	20.9	36.3	22.9
Not reported	100.0	30.1	32.5	21.4	15.9
No neighborhood	100.0	26.0	15.0	43.0	15.9

Source: Bureau of the Census, American Housing Survey for the United States: 2009, Internet site http://www.census.gov/hhes/www/housing/ahs/ahs09/ahs09.html; calculations by New Strategist

Table 5.59 Renters with Neighborhood Problems by Region, 2009

Thirty-two percent of Northeastern renters say street noise or heavy traffic is a problem in their neighborhood. A smaller 25 percent of renters in the South say this is a bothersome problem.

(number and percent distribution of renters with neighborhood problems, by region, 2009: numbers in thousands)

	total	Northeast	Midwest	South	West
Total renters	**35,378**	**7,073**	**7,119**	**12,392**	**8,794**
Bothersome street noise or heavy traffic	10,158	2,277	2,213	3,123	2,546
Serious crime in neighborhood in past 12 months	7,650	1,345	1,639	2,702	1,963
Bothersome odor problem	2,156	490	484	661	522
Noise problem	1,217	302	195	424	296
Litter or housing deterioration	590	140	109	215	127
Poor city or county services	254	52	64	93	46
Undesirable commercial, institutional, industrial	168	39	35	56	38
People problem	1,815	307	403	636	468
Other problems	2,791	521	499	1,001	770
PERCENT DISTRIBUTION BY PROBLEM					
Total renters	**100.0%**	**100.0%**	**100.0%**	**100.0%**	**100.0%**
Bothersome street noise or heavy traffic	28.7	32.2	31.1	25.2	28.9
Serious crime in neighborhood in past 12 months	21.6	19.0	23.0	21.8	22.3
Bothersome odor problem	6.1	6.9	6.8	5.3	5.9
Noise problem	3.4	4.3	2.7	3.4	3.4
Litter or housing deterioration	1.7	2.0	1.5	1.7	1.4
Poor city or county services	0.7	0.7	0.9	0.7	0.5
Undesirable commercial, institutional, industrial	0.5	0.6	0.5	0.4	0.4
People problem	5.1	4.3	5.7	5.1	5.3
Other problems	7.9	7.4	7.0	8.1	8.8
PERCENT DISTRIBUTION BY REGION					
Total renters	**100.0%**	**20.0%**	**20.1%**	**35.0%**	**24.9%**
Bothersome street noise or heavy traffic	100.0	22.4	21.8	30.7	25.1
Serious crime in neighborhood in past 12 months	100.0	17.6	21.4	35.3	25.7
Bothersome odor problem	100.0	22.7	22.4	30.7	24.2
Noise problem	100.0	24.8	16.1	34.9	24.3
Litter or housing deterioration	100.0	23.7	18.4	36.3	21.5
Poor city or county services	100.0	20.3	25.1	36.4	18.2
Undesirable commercial, institutional, industrial	100.0	23.3	20.9	33.1	22.7
People problem	100.0	16.9	22.2	35.1	25.8
Other problems	100.0	18.6	17.9	35.9	27.6

Source: Bureau of the Census, American Housing Survey for the United States: 2009, Internet site http://www.census.gov/hhes/ www/housing/ahs/ahs09/ahs09.html; calculations by New Strategist

Table 5.60 Renters by Community Characteristics, 2009: Northeast

Eleven percent of renters in the Northeast live in a gated community. Thirty-six percent have open space, park, woods, farm, or ranch land within 300 feet of their home.

(number and percent distribution of total renters and renters in the Northeast, by community characteristics, 2009; numbers in thousands)

	total		Northeast		
	number	percent distribution	number	percent distribution	percent of total
Total renters	**35,378**	**100.0%**	**7,073**	**100.0%**	**20.0%**
SECURED COMMUNITIES					
Total renters	**35,378**	**100.0**	**7,073**	**100.0**	**20.0**
Community access secured with walls or fences	5,422	15.3	749	10.6	13.8
Special entry system present	3,410	9.6	374	5.3	11.0
Special entry system not present	2,005	5.7	375	5.3	18.7
Community access not secured	29,714	84.0	6,284	88.8	21.1
SENIOR CITIZEN COMMUNITIES					
Renters with persons aged 55 or older	**9,093**	**100.0**	**2,362**	**100.0**	**26.0**
Community age restricted	1,624	17.9	377	16.0	23.2
No age restriction	7,469	82.1	1,984	84.0	26.6
Community age specific	1,435	15.8	351	14.9	24.5
Community not age specific	5,583	61.4	1,497	63.4	26.8
COMMUNITY AMENITIES					
Total renters	**35,378**	**100.0**	**7,073**	**100.0**	**20.0**
Community center or clubhouse	9,703	27.4	1,660	23.5	17.1
Golf in community	3,947	11.2	751	10.6	19.0
Trails in community	6,309	17.8	1,196	16.9	19.0
Shuttle bus available	4,215	11.9	1,005	14.2	23.9
Daycare center	5,249	14.8	1,416	20.0	27.0
Private or restricted beach, park, or shoreline	6,308	17.8	1,445	20.4	22.9
DESCRIPTION OF AREA WITHIN 300 FEET OF HOME					
Total renters	**35,378**	**100.0**	**7,073**	**100.0**	**20.0**
Single-family detached homes	27,007	76.3	5,112	72.3	18.9
Single-family attached homes	10,860	30.7	2,640	37.3	24.3
Multiunit residential buildings	22,121	62.5	4,948	70.0	22.4
One-to-three-story multiunit is tallest	16,130	45.6	2,271	32.1	14.1
Four-to-six-story multiunit is tallest	3,473	9.8	1,435	20.3	41.3
Seven-or-more-story multiunit is tallest	2,243	6.3	1,138	16.1	50.8
Manufactured/mobile homes	3,112	8.8	236	3.3	7.6
Commercial or institutional	18,657	52.7	4,442	62.8	23.8
Industrial or factories	2,856	8.1	865	12.2	30.3
Open space, park, woods, farm, or ranch	12,706	35.9	2,522	35.7	19.9
Four-or-more-lane highway, railroad, or airport	9,232	26.1	1,425	20.1	15.4

	total		Northeast		
	number	percent distribution	number	percent distribution	percent of total
BODIES OF WATER WITHIN 300 FEET OF HOME					
Total renters	**35,378**	**100.0%**	**7,073**	**100.0%**	**20.0%**
Water in area	4,832	13.7	973	13.8	20.1
With waterfront property	678	1.9	131	1.9	19.4
With flood plain	692	2.0	128	1.8	18.4
No water in area	30,390	85.9	6,059	85.7	19.9

Note: Numbers may not add to total because "not reported" is not shown.
Source: Bureau of the Census, American Housing Survey for the United States: 2009, Internet site http://www.census.gov/hhes/ www/housing/ahs/ahs09/ahs09.html; calculations by New Strategist

Table 5.61 Renters by Community Characteristics, 2009: Midwest

Only 6 percent of renters in the Midwest live in a gated community. Forty percent have open space, park, woods, farm, or ranch land within 300 feet of their home.

(number and percent distribution of total renters and renters in the Midwest, by community characteristics, 2009; numbers in thousands)

	total		Midwest		
	number	percent distribution	number	percent distribution	percent of total
Total renters	**35,378**	**100.0%**	**7,119**	**100.0%**	**20.1%**
SECURED COMMUNITIES					
Total renters	**35,378**	**100.0**	**7,119**	**100.0**	**20.1**
Community access secured with walls or fences	5,422	15.3	403	5.7	7.4
Special entry system present	3,410	9.6	207	2.9	6.1
Special entry system not present	2,005	5.7	195	2.7	9.7
Community access not secured	29,714	84.0	6,693	94.0	22.5
SENIOR CITIZEN COMMUNITIES					
Renters with persons aged 55 or older	**9,093**	**100.0**	**1,895**	**100.0**	**20.8**
Community age restricted	1,624	17.9	440	23.2	27.1
No age restriction	7,469	82.1	1,455	76.8	19.5
Community age specific	1,435	15.8	386	20.4	26.9
Community not age specific	5,583	61.4	1,006	53.1	18.0
COMMUNITY AMENITIES					
Total renters	**35,378**	**100.0**	**7,119**	**100.0**	**20.1**
Community center or clubhouse	9,703	27.4	2,245	31.5	23.1
Golf in community	3,947	11.2	1,466	20.6	37.1
Trails in community	6,309	17.8	1,865	26.2	29.6
Shuttle bus available	4,215	11.9	1,075	15.1	25.5
Daycare center	5,249	14.8	1,602	22.5	30.5
Private or restricted beach, park, or shoreline	6,308	17.8	1,916	26.9	30.4
DESCRIPTION OF AREA WITHIN 300 FEET OF HOME					
Total renters	**35,378**	**100.0**	**7,119**	**100.0**	**20.1**
Single-family detached homes	27,007	76.3	5,540	77.8	20.5
Single-family attached homes	10,860	30.7	1,977	27.8	18.2
Multiunit residential buildings	22,121	62.5	4,510	63.3	20.4
One-to-three-story multiunit is tallest	16,130	45.6	3,583	50.3	22.2
Four-to-six-story multiunit is tallest	3,473	9.8	493	6.9	14.2
Seven-or-more-story multiunit is tallest	2,243	6.3	369	5.2	16.5
Manufactured/mobile homes	3,112	8.8	392	5.5	12.6
Commercial or institutional	18,657	52.7	3,608	50.7	19.3
Industrial or factories	2,856	8.1	622	8.7	21.8
Open space, park, woods, farm, or ranch	12,706	35.9	2,864	40.2	22.5
Four-or-more-lane highway, railroad, or airport	9,232	26.1	1,955	27.5	21.2

	total		Midwest		
	number	percent distribution	number	percent distribution	percent of total
BODIES OF WATER WITHIN 300 FEET OF HOME					
Total renters	**35,378**	**100.0%**	**7,119**	**100.0%**	**20.1%**
Water in area	4,832	13.7	1,044	14.7	21.6
With waterfront property	678	1.9	177	2.5	26.2
With flood plain	692	2.0	82	1.2	11.8
No water in area	30,390	85.9	6,051	85.0	19.9

Note: Numbers may not add to total because "not reported" is not shown.
Source: Bureau of the Census, American Housing Survey for the United States: 2009, Internet site http://www.census.gov/hhes/ www/housing/ahs/ahs09/ahs09.html; calculations by New Strategist

Table 5.62 Renters by Community Characteristics, 2009: South

Seventeen percent of renters in the South live in a gated community. Thirty-six percent have open space, park, woods, farm, or ranch land within 300 feet of their home.

(number and percent distribution of total renters and renters in the South, by community characteristics, 2009; numbers in thousands)

	total		South		
	number	percent distribution	number	percent distribution	percent of total
Total renters	**35,378**	**100.0%**	**12,392**	**100.0%**	**35.0%**
SECURED COMMUNITIES					
Total renters	**35,378**	**100.0**	**12,392**	**100.0**	**35.0**
Community access secured with walls or fences	5,422	15.3	2,065	16.7	38.1
Special entry system present	3,410	9.6	1,370	11.1	40.2
Special entry system not present	2,005	5.7	692	5.6	34.5
Community access not secured	29,714	84.0	10,207	82.4	34.4
SENIOR CITIZEN COMMUNITIES					
Renters with persons aged 55 or older	**9,093**	**100.0**	**2,757**	**100.0**	**30.3**
Community age restricted	1,624	17.9	422	15.3	26.0
No age restriction	7,469	82.1	2,334	84.7	31.3
Community age specific	1,435	15.8	480	17.4	33.4
Community not age specific	5,583	61.4	1,710	62.0	30.6
COMMUNITY AMENITIES					
Total renters	**35,378**	**100.0**	**12,392**	**100.0**	**35.0**
Community center or clubhouse	9,703	27.4	3,354	27.1	34.6
Golf in community	3,947	11.2	826	6.7	20.9
Trails in community	6,309	17.8	1,797	14.5	28.5
Shuttle bus available	4,215	11.9	1,080	8.7	25.6
Daycare center	5,249	14.8	1,205	9.7	23.0
Private or restricted beach, park, or shoreline	6,308	17.8	1,399	11.3	22.2
DESCRIPTION OF AREA WITHIN 300 FEET OF HOME					
Total renters	**35,378**	**100.0**	**12,392**	**100.0**	**35.0**
Single-family detached homes	27,007	76.3	9,258	74.7	34.3
Single-family attached homes	10,860	30.7	3,300	26.6	30.4
Multiunit residential buildings	22,121	62.5	6,777	54.7	30.6
One-to-three-story multiunit is tallest	16,130	45.6	5,452	44.0	33.8
Four-to-six-story multiunit is tallest	3,473	9.8	816	6.6	23.5
Seven-or-more-story multiunit is tallest	2,243	6.3	463	3.7	20.7
Manufactured/mobile homes	3,112	8.8	1,633	13.2	52.5
Commercial or institutional	18,657	52.7	5,909	47.7	31.7
Industrial or factories	2,856	8.1	798	6.4	27.9
Open space, park, woods, farm, or ranch	12,706	35.9	4,456	36.0	35.1
Four-or-more-lane highway, railroad, or airport	9,232	26.1	3,628	29.3	39.3

	total		South		
	number	percent distribution	number	percent distribution	percent of total
BODIES OF WATER WITHIN 300 FEET OF HOME					
Total renters	**35,378**	**100.0%**	**12,392**	**100.0%**	**35.0%**
Water in area	4,832	13.7	2,062	16.6	42.7
With waterfront property	678	1.9	273	2.2	40.3
With flood plain	692	2.0	369	3.0	53.3
No water in area	30,390	85.9	10,290	83.0	33.9

Note: Numbers may not add to total because "not reported" is not shown.
Source: Bureau of the Census, American Housing Survey for the United States: 2009, Internet site http://www.census.gov/hhes/www/housing/ahs/ahs09/ahs09.html; calculations by New Strategist

Table 5.63 Renters by Community Characteristics, 2009: West

Twenty-five percent of renters in the West live in a gated community. Thirty-three percent have open space, park, woods, farm, or ranch land within 300 feet of their home.

(number and percent distribution of total renters and renters in the West, by community characteristics, 2009; numbers in thousands)

	total		West		
	number	percent distribution	number	percent distribution	percent of total
Total renters	**35,378**	**100.0%**	**8,794**	**100.0%**	**24.9%**
SECURED COMMUNITIES					
Total renters	**35,378**	**100.0**	**8,794**	**100.0**	**24.9**
Community access secured with walls or fences	5,422	15.3	2,205	25.1	40.7
Special entry system present	3,410	9.6	1,459	16.6	42.8
Special entry system not present	2,005	5.7	743	8.5	37.1
Community access not secured	29,714	84.0	6,530	74.3	22.0
SENIOR CITIZEN COMMUNITIES					
Renters with persons aged 55 or older	**9,093**	**100.0**	**2,080**	**100.0**	**22.9**
Community age restricted	1,624	17.9	384	18.5	23.7
No age restriction	7,469	82.1	1,695	81.5	22.7
Community age specific	1,435	15.8	218	10.5	15.2
Community not age specific	5,583	61.4	1,371	65.9	24.6
COMMUNITY AMENITIES					
Total renters	**35,378**	**100.0**	**8,794**	**100.0**	**24.9**
Community center or clubhouse	9,703	27.4	2,445	27.8	25.2
Golf in community	3,947	11.2	904	10.3	22.9
Trails in community	6,309	17.8	1,451	16.5	23.0
Shuttle bus available	4,215	11.9	1,055	12.0	25.0
Daycare center	5,249	14.8	1,026	11.7	19.5
Private or restricted beach, park, or shoreline	6,308	17.8	1,548	17.6	24.5
DESCRIPTION OF AREA WITHIN 300 FEET OF HOME					
Total renters	**35,378**	**100.0**	**8,794**	**100.0**	**24.9**
Single-family detached homes	27,007	76.3	7,097	80.7	26.3
Single-family attached homes	10,860	30.7	2,942	33.5	27.1
Multiunit residential buildings	22,121	62.5	5,887	66.9	26.6
One-to-three-story multiunit is tallest	16,130	45.6	4,823	54.8	29.9
Four-to-six-story multiunit is tallest	3,473	9.8	728	8.3	21.0
Seven-or-more-story multiunit is tallest	2,243	6.3	272	3.1	12.1
Manufactured/mobile homes	3,112	8.8	851	9.7	27.3
Commercial or institutional	18,657	52.7	4,699	53.4	25.2
Industrial or factories	2,856	8.1	571	6.5	20.0
Open space, park, woods, farm, or ranch	12,706	35.9	2,863	32.6	22.5
Four-or-more-lane highway, railroad, or airport	9,232	26.1	2,224	25.3	24.1

	total		West		
	number	percent distribution	number	percent distribution	percent of total
BODIES OF WATER WITHIN 300 FEET OF HOME					
Total renters	**35,378**	**100.0%**	**8,794**	**100.0%**	**24.9%**
Water in area	4,832	13.7	754	8.6	15.6
With waterfront property	678	1.9	96	1.1	14.2
With flood plain	692	2.0	114	1.3	16.5
No water in area	30,390	85.9	7,990	90.9	26.3

Note: Numbers may not add to total because "not reported" is not shown.
Source: Bureau of the Census, American Housing Survey for the United States: 2009, Internet site http://www.census.gov/hhes/ www/housing/ahs/ahs09/ahs09.html; calculations by New Strategist

Table 5.64 Renters by Public Services Available, 2009: Northeast

The 82 percent majority of renters in the Northeast have public transportation in their area, and 41 percent of those with public transportation use it regularly for their commute to work or school.

(number and percent distribution of total renters and renters in the Northeast by public services available in neighborhood, 2009; numbers in thousands)

	total		Northeast		
	number	percent distribution	number	percent distribution	percent of total
Total renters	**35,378**	**100.0%**	**7,073**	**100.0%**	**20.0%**
LOCAL ELEMENTARY SCHOOL					
Renters with children under age 14	**10,486**	**100.0**	**1,766**	**100.0**	**16.8**
Satisfactory public elementary school	8,331	79.5	1,380	78.2	16.6
Unsatisfactory public elementary school	724	6.9	113	6.4	15.6
Unsatisfactory public elementary school	**724**	**100.0**	**113**	**100.0**	**15.6**
Better than other area elementary schools	63	8.7	11	9.7	17.4
Same as other area elementary schools	224	31.0	36	31.9	16.1
Worse than other area elementary schools	386	53.3	60	53.1	15.6
Renters with children under age 14	**10,486**	**100.0**	**1,766**	**100.0**	**16.8**
Public elementary school less than one mile	7,096	67.7	1,292	73.2	18.2
Public elementary school more than one mile	2,741	26.1	355	20.1	12.9
PUBLIC TRANSPORTATION IN AREA					
Total renters	**35,378**	**100.0**	**7,073**	**100.0**	**20.0**
With public transportation	24,641	69.6	5,832	82.5	23.7
No public transportation	9,684	27.4	1,060	15.0	10.9
With public transportation, travel time to nearest stop	**24,641**	**100.0**	**5,832**	**100.0**	**23.7**
Less than 5 minutes	10,328	41.9	2,403	41.2	23.3
5 to 9 minutes	8,869	36.0	2,072	35.5	23.4
10 to 14 minutes	2,753	11.2	772	13.2	28.1
15 to 29 minutes	1,099	4.5	267	4.6	24.3
30 minutes or longer	169	0.7	37	0.6	21.9
With public transportation	**24,641**	**100.0**	**5,832**	**100.0**	**23.7**
Household uses it regularly for commute to school or work	6,395	26.0	2,378	40.8	37.2
Household does not use it regularly for commute to school or work	18,075	73.4	3,366	57.7	18.6

	total		Northeast		
	number	percent distribution	number	percent distribution	percent of total
SHOPPING IN AREA					
Total renters	**35,378**	**100.0%**	**7,073**	**100.0%**	**20.0%**
Grocery stores or drugstores within 15 minutes of home	34,189	96.6	6,887	97.4	20.1
Satisfactory	33,082	93.5	6,634	93.8	20.1
Not satisfactory	964	2.7	216	3.1	22.5
No grocery stores or drugstores within 15 minutes of home	777	2.2	110	1.6	14.2
POLICE PROTECTION					
Total renters	**35,378**	**100.0**	**7,073**	**100.0**	**20.0**
Satisfactory police protection	31,740	89.7	6,311	89.2	19.9
Unsatisfactory police protection	2,556	7.2	518	7.3	20.3

Note: Numbers may not add to total because "not reported" is not shown.
Source: Bureau of the Census, American Housing Survey for the United States: 2009, Internet site http://www.census.gov/hhes/ www/housing/ahs/ahs09/ahs09.html; calculations by New Strategist

Table 5.65 Renters by Public Services Available, 2009: Midwest

The 66 percent majority of renters in the Midwest have public transportation in their area, and 22 percent of those with public transportation use it regularly for their commute to work or school.

(number and percent distribution of total renters and renters in the Midwest by public services available in neighborhood, 2009; numbers in thousands)

	total		Midwest		
	number	percent distribution	number	percent distribution	percent of total
Total renters	**35,378**	**100.0%**	**7,119**	**100.0%**	**20.1%**
LOCAL ELEMENTARY SCHOOL					
Renters with children under age 14	**10,486**	**100.0**	**1,935**	**100.0**	**18.5**
Satisfactory public elementary school	8,331	79.5	1,516	78.3	18.2
Unsatisfactory public elementary school	724	6.9	157	8.1	21.7
Unsatisfactory public elementary school	**724**	**100.0**	**157**	**100.0**	**21.7**
Better than other area elementary schools	63	8.7	9	5.4	13.6
Same as other area elementary schools	224	31.0	47	30.0	21.0
Worse than other area elementary schools	386	53.3	92	58.5	23.8
Renters with children under age 14	**10,486**	**100.0**	**1,935**	**100.0**	**18.5**
Public elementary school less than one mile	7,096	67.7	1,308	67.6	18.4
Public elementary school more than one mile	2,741	26.1	496	25.6	18.1
PUBLIC TRANSPORTATION IN AREA					
Total renters	**35,378**	**100.0**	**7,119**	**100.0**	**20.1**
With public transportation	24,641	69.6	4,703	66.1	19.1
No public transportation	9,684	27.4	2,182	30.6	22.5
With public transportation, travel time to nearest stop	**24,641**	**100.0**	**4,703**	**100.0**	**19.1**
Less than 5 minutes	10,328	41.9	2,340	49.7	22.7
5 to 9 minutes	8,869	36.0	1,486	31.6	16.8
10 to 14 minutes	2,753	11.2	382	8.1	13.9
15 to 29 minutes	1,099	4.5	123	2.6	11.2
30 minutes or longer	169	0.7	37	0.8	21.6
With public transportation	**24,641**	**100.0**	**4,703**	**100.0**	**19.1**
Household uses it regularly for commute to school or work	6,395	26.0	1,012	21.5	15.8
Household does not use it regularly for commute to school or work	18,075	73.4	3,672	78.1	20.3

	total		Midwest		
	number	percent distribution	number	percent distribution	percent of total
SHOPPING IN AREA					
Total renters	**35,378**	**100.0%**	**7,119**	**100.0%**	**20.1%**
Grocery stores or drugstores within 15 minutes of home	34,189	96.6	6,907	97.0	20.2
Satisfactory	33,082	93.5	6,677	93.8	20.2
Not satisfactory	964	2.7	210	2.9	21.8
No grocery stores or drugstores within 15 minutes of home	777	2.2	162	2.3	20.9
POLICE PROTECTION					
Total renters	**35,378**	**100.0**	**7,119**	**100.0**	**20.1**
Satisfactory police protection	31,740	89.7	6,479	91.0	20.4
Unsatisfactory police protection	2,556	7.2	501	7.0	19.6

Note: Numbers may not add to total because "not reported" is not shown.
Source: Bureau of the Census, American Housing Survey for the United States: 2009, Internet site http://www.census.gov/hhes/ www/housing/ahs/ahs09/ahs09.html; calculations by New Strategist

Table 5.66 Renters by Public Services Available, 2009: South

The 56 percent majority of renters in the South have public transportation in their area, and 18 percent of those with public transportation use it regularly for their commute to work or school.

(number and percent distribution of total renters and renters in the South by public services available in neighborhood, 2009; numbers in thousands)

	total		South		
	number	percent distribution	number	percent distribution	percent of total
Total renters	**35,378**	**100.0%**	**12,392**	**100.0%**	**35.0%**
LOCAL ELEMENTARY SCHOOL					
Renters with children under age 14	**10,486**	**100.0**	**4,079**	**100.0**	**38.9**
Satisfactory public elementary school	8,331	79.5	3,258	79.9	39.1
Unsatisfactory public elementary school	724	6.9	275	6.7	38.0
Unsatisfactory public elementary school	**724**	**100.0**	**275**	**100.0**	**38.0**
Better than other area elementary schools	63	8.7	27	9.9	43.2
Same as other area elementary schools	224	31.0	86	31.4	38.5
Worse than other area elementary schools	386	53.3	141	51.3	36.6
Renters with children under age 14	**10,486**	**100.0**	**4,079**	**100.0**	**38.9**
Public elementary school less than one mile	7,096	67.7	2,402	58.9	33.8
Public elementary school more than one mile	2,741	26.1	1,428	35.0	52.1
PUBLIC TRANSPORTATION IN AREA					
Total renters	**35,378**	**100.0**	**12,392**	**100.0**	**35.0**
With public transportation	24,641	69.6	6,909	55.8	28.0
No public transportation	9,684	27.4	5,040	40.7	52.1
With public transportation, travel time to nearest stop	**24,641**	**100.0**	**6,909**	**100.0**	**28.0**
Less than 5 minutes	10,328	41.9	2,622	37.9	25.4
5 to 9 minutes	8,869	36.0	2,580	37.3	29.1
10 to 14 minutes	2,753	11.2	825	11.9	30.0
15 to 29 minutes	1,099	4.5	348	5.0	31.7
30 minutes or longer	169	0.7	66	1.0	39.2
With public transportation	**24,641**	**100.0**	**6,909**	**100.0**	**28.0**
Household uses it regularly for commute to school or work	6,395	26.0	1,221	17.7	19.1
Household does not use it regularly for commute to school or work	18,075	73.4	5,644	81.7	31.2

	total		South		
	number	percent distribution	number	percent distribution	percent of total
SHOPPING IN AREA					
Total renters	**35,378**	**100.0%**	**12,392**	**100.0%**	**35.0%**
Grocery stores or drugstores within 15 minutes of home	34,189	96.6	11,866	95.8	34.7
Satisfactory	33,082	93.5	11,511	92.9	34.8
Not satisfactory	964	2.7	289	2.3	30.0
No grocery stores or drugstores within 15 minutes of home	777	2.2	330	2.7	42.5
POLICE PROTECTION					
Total renters	**35,378**	**100.0**	**12,392**	**100.0**	**35.0**
Satisfactory police protection	31,740	89.7	11,049	89.2	34.8
Unsatisfactory police protection	2,556	7.2	931	7.5	36.4

Note: Numbers may not add to total because "not reported" is not shown.
Source: Bureau of the Census, American Housing Survey for the United States: 2009, Internet site http://www.census.gov/hhes/ www/housing/ahs/ahs09/ahs09.html; calculations by New Strategist

Table 5.67 Renters by Public Services Available, 2009: West

The 82 percent majority of renters in the West have public transportation in their area, and 25 percent of those with public transportation use it regularly for their commute to work or school.

(number and percent distribution of total renters and renters in the West by public services available in neighborhood, 2009; numbers in thousands)

	total		West		
	number	percent distribution	number	percent distribution	percent of total
Total renters	**35,378**	**100.0%**	**8,794**	**100.0%**	**24.9%**
LOCAL ELEMENTARY SCHOOL					
Renters with children under age 14	**10,486**	**100.0**	**2,706**	**100.0**	**25.8**
Satisfactory public elementary school	8,331	79.5	2,177	80.5	26.1
Unsatisfactory public elementary school	724	6.9	179	6.6	24.7
Unsatisfactory public elementary school	**724**	**100.0**	**179**	**100.0**	**24.7**
Better than other area elementary schools	63	8.7	16	9.0	25.8
Same as other area elementary schools	224	31.0	55	30.7	24.5
Worse than other area elementary schools	386	53.3	93	51.9	24.1
Renters with children under age 14	**10,486**	**100.0**	**2,706**	**100.0**	**25.8**
Public elementary school less than one mile	7,096	67.7	2,094	77.4	29.5
Public elementary school more than one mile	2,741	26.1	463	17.1	16.9
PUBLIC TRANSPORTATION IN AREA					
Total renters	**35,378**	**100.0**	**8,794**	**100.0**	**24.9**
With public transportation	24,641	69.6	7,196	81.8	29.2
No public transportation	9,684	27.4	1,401	15.9	14.5
With public transportation, travel time to nearest stop	**24,641**	**100.0**	**7,196**	**100.0**	**29.2**
Less than 5 minutes	10,328	41.9	2,964	41.2	28.7
5 to 9 minutes	8,869	36.0	2,732	38.0	30.8
10 to 14 minutes	2,753	11.2	774	10.8	28.1
15 to 29 minutes	1,099	4.5	360	5.0	32.8
30 minutes or longer	169	0.7	29	0.4	17.3
With public transportation	**24,641**	**100.0**	**7,196**	**100.0**	**29.2**
Household uses it regularly for commute to school or work	6,395	26.0	1,783	24.8	27.9
Household does not use it regularly for commute to school or work	18,075	73.4	5,394	75.0	29.8

	total		West		
	number	percent distribution	number	percent distribution	percent of total
SHOPPING IN AREA					
Total renters	**35,378**	**100.0%**	**8,794**	**100.0%**	**24.9%**
Grocery stores or drugstores within 15 minutes of home	34,189	96.6	8,530	97.0	24.9
Satisfactory	33,082	93.5	8,259	93.9	25.0
Not satisfactory	964	2.7	249	2.8	25.8
No grocery stores or drugstores within 15 minutes of home	777	2.2	174	2.0	22.4
POLICE PROTECTION					
Total renters	**35,378**	**100.0**	**8,794**	**100.0**	**24.9**
Satisfactory police protection	31,740	89.7	7,900	89.8	24.9
Unsatisfactory police protection	2,556	7.2	606	6.9	23.7

Note: Numbers may not add to total because "not reported" is not shown.
Source: Bureau of the Census, American Housing Survey for the United States: 2009, Internet site http://www.census.gov/hhes/ www/housing/ahs/ahs09/ahs09.html; calculations by New Strategist

Table 5.68 Renters Who Moved by Changes in Housing and Costs, 2009: Northeast

Twenty-three percent of renters in the Northeast who
moved in the past year owned their previous home.
Thirty percent saw their housing costs decline after the move.

*(number and percent distribution of total renters and renters in the Northeast who moved in the past year, by
structure type of previous residence, ownership of previous residence, and change in housing costs, 2009; numbers
in thousands)*

	total		Northeast		
	number	percent distribution	number	percent distribution	percent of total
STRUCTURE TYPE OF PREVIOUS RESIDENCE					
Renters who moved within United States	**12,422**	**100.0%**	**1,608**	**100.0%**	**12.9%**
House	5,936	47.8	652	40.5	11.0
Apartment	5,228	42.1	848	52.7	16.2
Mobile home	545	4.4	23	1.4	4.3
Other	380	3.1	47	2.9	12.3
Not reported	331	2.7	38	2.4	11.6
OWNERSHIP OF PREVIOUS RESIDENCE					
Renters who moved from house, apartment, or mobile home within United States	**11,710**	**100.0**	**1,523**	**100.0**	**13.0**
Owner-occupied	2,991	25.5	344	22.6	11.5
Renter-occupied	8,719	74.5	1,179	77.4	13.5
CHANGE IN HOUSING COSTS					
Renters who moved from house, apartment, or mobile home within United States	**11,710**	**100.0**	**1,523**	**100.0**	**13.0**
Increased with move	5,135	43.8	696	45.7	13.6
Decreased	3,719	31.8	463	30.4	12.4
Stayed about the same	2,444	20.9	274	18.0	11.2
Don't know	250	2.1	59	3.8	23.4
Not reported	161	1.4	32	2.1	19.8

*Source: Bureau of the Census, American Housing Survey for the United States: 2009, Internet site http://www.census.gov/hhes/
www/housing/ahs/ahs09/ahs09.html; calculations by New Strategist*

Table 5.69 Renters Who Moved by Changes in Housing and Costs, 2009: Midwest

Twenty-seven percent of renters in the Midwest who moved
in the past year owned their previous home. Thirty-one percent
saw their housing costs decline after the move.

(number and percent distribution of total renters and renters in the Midwest who moved in the past year, by structure type of previous residence, ownership of previous residence, and change in housing costs, 2009; numbers in thousands)

	total		Midwest		
	number	percent distribution	number	percent distribution	percent of total
STRUCTURE TYPE OF PREVIOUS RESIDENCE					
Renters who moved within United States	**12,422**	**100.0%**	**2,720**	**100.0%**	**21.9%**
House	5,936	47.8	1,341	49.3	22.6
Apartment	5,228	42.1	1,129	41.5	21.6
Mobile home	545	4.4	97	3.6	17.9
Other	380	3.1	99	3.6	26.1
Not reported	331	2.7	53	2.0	16.1
OWNERSHIP OF PREVIOUS RESIDENCE					
Renters who moved from house, apartment, or mobile home within United States	**11,710**	**100.0**	**2,568**	**100.0**	**21.9**
Owner-occupied	2,991	25.5	691	26.9	23.1
Renter-occupied	8,719	74.5	1,877	73.1	21.5
CHANGE IN HOUSING COSTS					
Renters who moved from house, apartment, or mobile home within United States	**11,710**	**100.0**	**2,568**	**100.0**	**21.9**
Increased with move	5,135	43.8	1,161	45.2	22.6
Decreased	3,719	31.8	796	31.0	21.4
Stayed about the same	2,444	20.9	541	21.1	22.1
Don't know	250	2.1	49	1.9	19.5
Not reported	161	1.4	21	0.8	13.2

Source: Bureau of the Census, American Housing Survey for the United States: 2009, Internet site http://www.census.gov/hhes/www/housing/ahs/ahs09/ahs09.html; calculations by New Strategist

Table 5.70 Renters Who Moved by Changes in Housing and Costs, 2009: South

Twenty-six percent of renters in the South who moved
in the past year owned their previous home.
Thirty-one percent saw their housing costs decline after the move.

(number and percent distribution of total renters and renters in the South who moved in the past year, by structure type of previous residence, ownership of previous residence, and change in housing costs, 2009; numbers in thousands)

	total		South		
	number	percent distribution	number	percent distribution	percent of total
STRUCTURE TYPE OF PREVIOUS RESIDENCE					
Renters who moved within United States	**12,422**	**100.0%**	**4,920**	**100.0%**	**39.6%**
House	5,936	47.8	2,406	48.9	40.5
Apartment	5,228	42.1	1,914	38.9	36.6
Mobile home	545	4.4	311	6.3	57.0
Other	380	3.1	123	2.5	32.3
Not reported	331	2.7	167	3.4	50.4
OWNERSHIP OF PREVIOUS RESIDENCE					
Renters who moved from house, apartment, or mobile home within United States	**11,710**	**100.0**	**4,630**	**100.0**	**39.5**
Owner-occupied	2,991	25.5	1,215	26.2	40.6
Renter-occupied	8,719	74.5	3,415	73.8	39.2
CHANGE IN HOUSING COSTS					
Renters who moved from house, apartment, or mobile home within United States	**11,710**	**100.0**	**4,630**	**100.0**	**39.5**
Increased with move	5,135	43.8	1,922	41.5	37.4
Decreased	3,719	31.8	1,453	31.4	39.1
Stayed about the same	2,444	20.9	1,065	23.0	43.6
Don't know	250	2.1	96	2.1	38.3
Not reported	161	1.4	94	2.0	58.3

Source: Bureau of the Census, American Housing Survey for the United States: 2009, Internet site http://www.census.gov/hhes/ www/housing/ahs/ahs09/ahs09.html; calculations by New Strategist

Table 5.71 Renters Who Moved by Changes in Housing and Costs, 2009: West

Twenty-five percent of renters in the West who moved
in the past year owned their previous home. Thirty-four percent
saw their housing costs decline after the move.

(number and percent distribution of total renters and renters in the West who moved in the past year, by structure type of previous residence, ownership of previous residence, and change in housing costs, 2009; numbers in thousands)

	total		West		
	number	percent distribution	number	percent distribution	percent of total
STRUCTURE TYPE OF PREVIOUS RESIDENCE					
Renters who moved within United States	**12,422**	**100.0%**	**3,173**	**100.0%**	**25.5%**
House	5,936	47.8	1,538	48.5	25.9
Apartment	5,228	42.1	1,337	42.1	25.6
Mobile home	545	4.4	114	3.6	20.9
Other	380	3.1	111	3.5	29.3
Not reported	331	2.7	72	2.3	21.8
OWNERSHIP OF PREVIOUS RESIDENCE					
Renters who moved from house, apartment, or mobile home within United States	**11,710**	**100.0**	**2,990**	**100.0**	**25.5**
Owner-occupied	2,991	25.5	740	24.8	24.8
Renter-occupied	8,719	74.5	2,249	75.2	25.8
CHANGE IN HOUSING COSTS					
Renters who moved from house, apartment, or mobile home within United States	**11,710**	**100.0**	**2,990**	**100.0**	**25.5**
Increased with move	5,135	43.8	1,356	45.4	26.4
Decreased	3,719	31.8	1,008	33.7	27.1
Stayed about the same	2,444	20.9	564	18.9	23.1
Don't know	250	2.1	47	1.6	18.9
Not reported	161	1.4	14	0.5	8.7

Source: Bureau of the Census, American Housing Survey for the United States: 2009, Internet site http://www.census.gov/hhes/ www/housing/ahs/ahs09/ahs09.html; calculations by New Strategist

Table 5.72 Renters Who Moved by Reasons for Choosing Home, 2009: Northeast

Among renters in the Northeast who moved in the past year, the largest share chose their present home for financial reasons. Forty-eight percent say their current home is better than their previous one.

(number and percent distribution of total renting respondents and renting respondents in the Northeast who moved in the past year, by reasons for choosing home, 2009; numbers in thousands)

	total		Northeast		
	number	percent distribution	number	percent distribution	percent of total
Total renting respondents who moved	12,840	100.0%	1,690	100.0%	13.2%
Main reason for choice of present home					
All reported reasons equal	1,448	11.3	244	14.5	16.9
Financial reasons	3,846	30.0	479	28.3	12.4
Room layout/design	1,743	13.6	247	14.6	14.1
Kitchen	65	0.5	9	0.5	14.0
Size	1,398	10.9	184	10.9	13.1
Exterior appearance	350	2.7	43	2.5	12.2
Yard/trees/view	412	3.2	30	1.8	7.3
Quality of construction	231	1.8	29	1.7	12.7
Only one available	608	4.7	78	4.6	12.8
Other	2,198	17.1	266	15.7	12.1
Not reported	540	4.2	82	4.9	15.2
Present home compared with previous home					
Better	6,192	48.2	810	47.9	13.1
Worse	2,676	20.8	371	22.0	13.9
About the same	3,498	27.2	442	26.1	12.6
Not reported	474	3.7	67	4.0	14.2
Home search					
Now in house	4,200	100.0	429	100.0	10.2
Did not look at apartments	2,888	68.8	235	54.8	8.1
Looked at apartments too	1,162	27.7	162	37.7	13.9
Now in manufactured/mobile home	551	100.0	19	100.0	3.4
Did not look at apartments	360	65.3	9	49.0	2.5
Looked at apartments too	181	32.8	10	51.0	5.3
Now in apartment	8,090	100.0	1,242	100.0	15.4
Did not look at houses	5,726	70.8	911	73.3	15.9
Looked at houses too	2,056	25.4	287	23.1	13.9

Note: Total number of movers does not equal total movers in other tables because this table shows survey respondents who moved, not necessarily householders. Numbers may not add to total because "not reported" may not be shown.
Source: Bureau of the Census, American Housing Survey for the United States: 2009, Internet site http://www.census.gov/hhes/www/housing/ahs/ahs09/ahs09.html; calculations by New Strategist

Table 5.73 Renters Who Moved by Reasons for Choosing Home, 2009: Midwest

Among renters in the Midwest who moved in the past year, the largest share chose their present home for financial reasons. Forty-nine percent say their current home is better than their previous one.

(number and percent distribution of total renting respondents and renting respondents in the Midwest who moved in the past year, by reasons for choosing home, 2009; numbers in thousands)

	total		Midwest		
	number	percent distribution	number	percent distribution	percent of total
Total renting respondents who moved	12,840	100.0%	2,780	100.0%	21.7%
Main reason for choice of present home					
All reported reasons equal	1,448	11.3	343	12.3	23.7
Financial reasons	3,846	30.0	902	32.5	23.5
Room layout/design	1,743	13.6	367	13.2	21.0
Kitchen	65	0.5	16	0.6	24.8
Size	1,398	10.9	317	11.4	22.7
Exterior appearance	350	2.7	60	2.2	17.2
Yard/trees/view	412	3.2	104	3.7	25.2
Quality of construction	231	1.8	51	1.9	22.3
Only one available	608	4.7	117	4.2	19.2
Other	2,198	17.1	407	14.6	18.5
Not reported	540	4.2	95	3.4	17.6
Present home compared with previous home					
Better	6,192	48.2	1,359	48.9	22.0
Worse	2,676	20.8	597	21.5	22.3
About the same	3,498	27.2	743	26.7	21.3
Not reported	474	3.7	79	2.9	16.7
Home search					
Now in house	4,200	100.0	838	100.0	20.0
Did not look at apartments	2,888	68.8	561	66.9	19.4
Looked at apartments too	1,162	27.7	250	29.9	21.5
Now in manufactured/mobile home	551	100.0	89	100.0	16.1
Did not look at apartments	360	65.3	37	41.4	10.2
Looked at apartments too	181	32.8	52	58.6	28.7
Now in apartment	8,090	100.0	1,853	100.0	22.9
Did not look at houses	5,726	70.8	1,405	75.8	24.5
Looked at houses too	2,056	25.4	400	21.6	19.4

Note: Total number of movers does not equal total movers in other tables because this table shows survey respondents who moved, not necessarily householders. Numbers may not add to total because "not reported" may not be shown.
Source: Bureau of the Census, American Housing Survey for the United States: 2009, Internet site http://www.census.gov/hhes/ www/housing/ahs/ahs09/ahs09.html; calculations by New Strategist

Table 5.74 Renters Who Moved by Reasons for Choosing Home, 2009: South

Among renters in the South who moved in the past year, the largest share chose their present home for financial reasons. Forty-nine percent say their current home is better than their previous one.

(number and percent distribution of total renting respondents and renting respondents in the South who moved in the past year, by reasons for choosing home, 2009; numbers in thousands)

	total		South		
	number	percent distribution	number	percent distribution	percent of total
Total renting respondents who moved	12,840	100.0%	5,056	100.0%	39.4%
Main reason for choice of present home					
All reported reasons equal	1,448	11.3	510	10.1	35.2
Financial reasons	3,846	30.0	1,470	29.1	38.2
Room layout/design	1,743	13.6	682	13.5	39.1
Kitchen	65	0.5	16	0.3	24.7
Size	1,398	10.9	577	11.4	41.3
Exterior appearance	350	2.7	150	3.0	42.9
Yard/trees/view	412	3.2	170	3.4	41.3
Quality of construction	231	1.8	82	1.6	35.5
Only one available	608	4.7	253	5.0	41.5
Other	2,198	17.1	871	17.2	39.6
Not reported	540	4.2	276	5.5	51.1
Present home compared with previous home					
Better	6,192	48.2	2,460	48.7	39.7
Worse	2,676	20.8	961	19.0	35.9
About the same	3,498	27.2	1,398	27.6	40.0
Not reported	474	3.7	237	4.7	50.0
Home search					
Now in house	4,200	100.0	1,845	100.0	43.9
Did not look at apartments	2,888	68.8	1,302	70.6	45.1
Looked at apartments too	1,162	27.7	486	26.3	41.8
Now in manufactured/mobile home	551	100.0	332	100.0	60.3
Did not look at apartments	360	65.3	234	70.5	65.1
Looked at apartments too	181	32.8	88	26.5	48.6
Now in apartment	8,090	100.0	2,879	100.0	35.6
Did not look at houses	5,726	70.8	1,983	68.9	34.6
Looked at houses too	2,056	25.4	754	26.2	36.7

Note: Total number of movers does not equal total movers in other tables because this table shows survey respondents who moved, not necessarily householders. Numbers may not add to total because "not reported" may not be shown.
Source: Bureau of the Census, American Housing Survey for the United States: 2009, Internet site http://www.census.gov/hhes/ www/housing/ahs/ahs09/ahs09.html; calculations by New Strategist

Table 5.75 Renters Who Moved by Reasons for Choosing Home, 2009: West

Among renters in the West who moved in the past year, the largest
share chose their present home for financial reasons. Forty-seven
percent say their current home is better than their previous one.

(number and percent distribution of total renting respondents and renting respondents in the West who moved in the past year, by reasons for choosing home, 2009; numbers in thousands)

	total		West		
	number	percent distribution	number	percent distribution	percent of total
Total renting respondents who moved	**12,840**	**100.0%**	**3,314**	**100.0%**	**25.8%**
Main reason for choice of present home					
All reported reasons equal	1,448	11.3	351	10.6	24.3
Financial reasons	3,846	30.0	995	30.0	25.9
Room layout/design	1,743	13.6	448	13.5	25.7
Kitchen	65	0.5	24	0.7	36.5
Size	1,398	10.9	320	9.7	22.9
Exterior appearance	350	2.7	97	2.9	27.7
Yard/trees/view	412	3.2	108	3.3	26.3
Quality of construction	231	1.8	68	2.1	29.5
Only one available	608	4.7	161	4.9	26.4
Other	2,198	17.1	655	19.8	29.8
Not reported	540	4.2	87	2.6	16.1
Present home compared with previous home					
Better	6,192	48.2	1,563	47.2	25.2
Worse	2,676	20.8	746	22.5	27.9
About the same	3,498	27.2	915	27.6	26.2
Not reported	474	3.7	90	2.7	19.0
Home search					
Now in house	4,200	100.0	1,087	100.0	25.9
Did not look at apartments	2,888	68.8	790	72.6	27.4
Looked at apartments too	1,162	27.7	263	24.2	22.7
Now in manufactured/mobile home	551	100.0	111	100.0	20.2
Did not look at apartments	360	65.3	80	71.7	22.2
Looked at apartments too	181	32.8	32	28.3	17.4
Now in apartment	8,090	100.0	2,116	100.0	26.2
Did not look at houses	5,726	70.8	1,427	67.4	24.9
Looked at houses too	2,056	25.4	616	29.1	29.9

Note: Total number of movers does not equal total movers in other tables because this table shows survey respondents who moved, not necessarily householders. Numbers may not add to total because "not reported" may not be shown.
Source: Bureau of the Census, American Housing Survey for the United States: 2009, Internet site http://www.census.gov/hhes/ www/housing/ahs/ahs09/ahs09.html; calculations by New Strategist

Table 5.76 Renters Who Moved by Reasons for Choosing Neighborhood, 2009: Northeast

The largest share of Northeastern renters who moved in the past year looked at only one neighborhood before choosing where to live. The biggest single factor in choosing their current neighborhood was convenience to their job (21 percent).

(number and percent distribution of total renting respondents and renting respondents in the Northeast who moved in the past year, by reasons for choosing neighborhood, 2009; numbers in thousands)

	total		Northeast		
	number	percent distribution	number	percent distribution	percent of total
Total renting respondents who moved	12,840	100.0%	1,690	100.0%	13.2%
Neighborhood search					
Looked at just this neighborhood	5,900	46.0	832	49.2	14.1
Looked at other neighborhoods	6,533	50.9	795	47.0	12.2
Not reported	407	3.2	64	3.8	15.7
Main reason for choice of present neighborhood					
All reported reasons equal	1,354	10.5	213	12.6	15.7
Convenient to job	2,924	22.8	362	21.4	12.4
Convenient to friends or relatives	1,915	14.9	235	13.9	12.3
Convenient to leisure activities	244	1.9	42	2.5	17.4
Convenient to public transportation	237	1.8	48	2.8	20.2
Good schools	798	6.2	124	7.3	15.5
Other public services	185	1.4	30	1.8	16.0
Looks/design of neighborhood	1,163	9.1	117	6.9	10.1
House most important consideration	964	7.5	100	5.9	10.4
Other	2,563	20.0	339	20.0	13.2
Not reported	493	3.8	82	4.8	16.6
Present neighborhood compared with previous neighborhood					
Better	4,953	38.6	601	35.6	12.1
Worse	1,955	15.2	275	16.3	14.1
About the same	4,916	38.3	650	38.5	13.2
Same neighborhood	520	4.1	88	5.2	17.0
Not reported	496	3.9	76	4.5	15.3

Note: Total number of movers does not equal total movers in other tables because this table shows survey respondents who moved, not necessarily householders.
Source: Bureau of the Census, American Housing Survey for the United States: 2009, Internet site http://www.census.gov/hhes/www/housing/ahs/ahs09/ahs09.html; calculations by New Strategist

Table 5.77 Renters Who Moved by Reasons for Choosing Neighborhood, 2009: Midwest

The 53 percent majority of Midwestern renters who moved in the past year looked at more than one neighborhood before choosing where to live. The biggest single factor in choosing their current neighborhood was convenience to their job (20 percent).

(number and percent distribution of total renting respondents and renting respondents in the Midwest who moved in the past year, by reasons for choosing neighborhood, 2009; numbers in thousands)

	total		Midwest		
	number	percent distribution	number	percent distribution	percent of total
Total renting respondents who moved	12,840	100.0%	2,780	100.0%	21.7%
Neighborhood search					
Looked at just this neighborhood	5,900	46.0	1,242	44.7	21.1
Looked at other neighborhoods	6,533	50.9	1,474	53.0	22.6
Not reported	407	3.2	63	2.3	15.5
Main reason for choice of present neighborhood					
All reported reasons equal	1,354	10.5	289	10.4	21.3
Convenient to job	2,924	22.8	551	19.8	18.8
Convenient to friends or relatives	1,915	14.9	509	18.3	26.6
Convenient to leisure activities	244	1.9	60	2.2	24.8
Convenient to public transportation	237	1.8	50	1.8	21.0
Good schools	798	6.2	153	5.5	19.1
Other public services	185	1.4	47	1.7	25.2
Looks/design of neighborhood	1,163	9.1	255	9.2	21.9
House most important consideration	964	7.5	230	8.3	23.9
Other	2,563	20.0	555	20.0	21.7
Not reported	493	3.8	80	2.9	16.3
Present neighborhood compared with previous neighborhood					
Better	4,953	38.6	1,053	37.9	21.3
Worse	1,955	15.2	431	15.5	22.0
About the same	4,916	38.3	1,112	40.0	22.6
Same neighborhood	520	4.1	94	3.4	18.1
Not reported	496	3.9	89	3.2	18.0

Note: Total number of movers does not equal total movers in other tables because this table shows survey respondents who moved, not necessarily householders.
Source: Bureau of the Census, American Housing Survey for the United States: 2009, Internet site http://www.census.gov/hhes/ www/housing/ahs/ahs09/ahs09.html; calculations by New Strategist

Table 5.78 Renters Who Moved by Reasons for Choosing Neighborhood, 2009: South

The largest share of Southern renters who moved in the past year looked at more than one neighborhood before choosing where to live. The biggest single factor in choosing their current neighborhood was convenience to their job (24 percent).

(number and percent distribution of total renting respondents and renting respondents in the South who moved in the past year, by reasons for choosing neighborhood, 2009; numbers in thousands)

	total		South		
	number	percent distribution	number	percent distribution	percent of total
Total renting respondents who moved	12,840	100.0%	5,056	100.0%	39.4%
Neighborhood search					
Looked at just this neighborhood	5,900	46.0	2,304	45.6	39.1
Looked at other neighborhoods	6,533	50.9	2,546	50.4	39.0
Not reported	407	3.2	206	4.1	50.6
Main reason for choice of present neighborhood					
All reported reasons equal	1,354	10.5	493	9.8	36.4
Convenient to job	2,924	22.8	1,231	24.3	42.1
Convenient to friends or relatives	1,915	14.9	714	14.1	37.3
Convenient to leisure activities	244	1.9	69	1.4	28.3
Convenient to public transportation	237	1.8	67	1.3	28.1
Good schools	798	6.2	295	5.8	37.0
Other public services	185	1.4	74	1.5	40.1
Looks/design of neighborhood	1,163	9.1	501	9.9	43.0
House most important consideration	964	7.5	346	6.8	35.9
Other	2,563	20.0	1,016	20.1	39.6
Not reported	493	3.8	251	5.0	50.9
Present neighborhood compared with previous neighborhood					
Better	4,953	38.6	2,001	39.6	40.4
Worse	1,955	15.2	731	14.5	37.4
About the same	4,916	38.3	1,885	37.3	38.4
Same neighborhood	520	4.1	189	3.7	36.3
Not reported	496	3.9	250	4.9	50.4

Note: Total number of movers does not equal total movers in other tables because this table shows survey respondents who moved, not necessarily householders.
Source: Bureau of the Census, American Housing Survey for the United States: 2009, Internet site http://www.census.gov/hhes/ www/housing/ahs/ahs09/ahs09.html; calculations by New Strategist

Table 5.79 Renters Who Moved by Reasons for Choosing Neighborhood, 2009: West

The 52 percent majority of Western renters who moved in the past year looked at more than one neighborhood before choosing where to live. The biggest single factor in choosing their current neighborhood was convenience to their job (24 percent).

(number and percent distribution of total renting respondents and renting respondents in the West who moved in the past year, by reasons for choosing neighborhood, 2009; numbers in thousands)

	total		West		
	number	percent distribution	number	percent distribution	percent of total
Total renting respondents who moved	12,840	100.0%	3,314	100.0%	25.8%
Neighborhood search					
Looked at just this neighborhood	5,900	46.0	1,522	45.9	25.8
Looked at other neighborhoods	6,533	50.9	1,718	51.8	26.3
Not reported	407	3.2	74	2.2	18.2
Main reason for choice of present neighborhood					
All reported reasons equal	1,354	10.5	359	10.8	26.5
Convenient to job	2,924	22.8	781	23.6	26.7
Convenient to friends or relatives	1,915	14.9	457	13.8	23.9
Convenient to leisure activities	244	1.9	72	2.2	29.6
Convenient to public transportation	237	1.8	73	2.2	30.7
Good schools	798	6.2	226	6.8	28.4
Other public services	185	1.4	34	1.0	18.6
Looks/design of neighborhood	1,163	9.1	290	8.8	25.0
House most important consideration	964	7.5	288	8.7	29.9
Other	2,563	20.0	653	19.7	25.5
Not reported	493	3.8	80	2.4	16.3
Present neighborhood compared with previous neighborhood					
Better	4,953	38.6	1,298	39.2	26.2
Worse	1,955	15.2	519	15.6	26.5
About the same	4,916	38.3	1,268	38.3	25.8
Same neighborhood	520	4.1	149	4.5	28.6
Not reported	496	3.9	81	2.4	16.3

Note: Total number of movers does not equal total movers in other tables because this table shows survey respondents who moved, not necessarily householders.
Source: Bureau of the Census, American Housing Survey for the United States: 2009, Internet site http://www.census.gov/hhes/www/housing/ahs/ahs09/ahs09.html; calculations by New Strategist

Table 5.80 Renters Who Moved by Reasons for Moving and Region, 2009

Employment reasons (new job, closer to work, or other employment) account for a large share of the moves of renters, ranging from a low of 22 percent in the Midwest to a high of 28 percent in the West.

(number and percent distribution of renting respondents who moved in the past year by main reason for move, by region, 2009; numbers in thousands)

	total	Northeast	Midwest	South	West
Total renting respondents who moved	**12,840**	**1,690**	**2,780**	**5,056**	**3,314**
All reported reasons equal	450	85	120	141	104
Private displacement	118	28	9	33	48
Government displacement	45	1	10	12	21
Disaster loss (fire, flood, etc.)	126	11	18	87	10
New job or job transfer	1,220	122	220	542	336
To be closer to work/school/other	1,416	193	290	535	398
Other financial, employment related	527	74	113	156	184
To establish own household	1,282	134	337	503	309
Needed larger house or apartment	1,103	170	222	452	259
Married, widowed, divorced, separated	628	82	144	228	174
Other family, personal reasons	1,004	154	243	396	212
Wanted better home	881	119	230	342	190
Change from owner to renter	120	16	22	52	30
Wanted lower rent or maintenance	867	104	174	366	223
Other housing related reasons	614	80	140	230	163
Evicted from residence	112	10	24	41	37
Other	1,548	208	341	564	436
Not reported	779	100	123	377	179

PERCENT DISTRIBUTION BY REASON FOR MOVE

	total	Northeast	Midwest	South	West
Total renting respondents who moved	**100.0%**	**100.0%**	**100.0%**	**100.0%**	**100.0%**
All reported reasons equal	3.5	5.0	4.3	2.8	3.1
Private displacement	0.9	1.7	0.3	0.7	1.4
Government displacement	0.4	0.1	0.4	0.2	0.6
Disaster loss (fire, flood, etc.)	1.0	0.6	0.6	1.7	0.3
New job or job transfer	9.5	7.2	7.9	10.7	10.1
To be closer to work/school/other	11.0	11.4	10.4	10.6	12.0
Other financial, employment related	4.1	4.4	4.1	3.1	5.6
To establish own household	10.0	7.9	12.1	9.9	9.3
Needed larger house or apartment	8.6	10.0	8.0	8.9	7.8
Married, widowed, divorced, or separated	4.9	4.8	5.2	4.5	5.2
Other family, personal reasons	7.8	9.1	8.7	7.8	6.4
Wanted better home	6.9	7.0	8.3	6.8	5.7
Change from owner to renter	0.9	1.0	0.8	1.0	0.9
Wanted lower rent or maintenance	6.8	6.1	6.3	7.2	6.7
Other housing related reasons	4.8	4.8	5.0	4.5	4.9
Evicted from residence	0.9	0.6	0.9	0.8	1.1
Other	12.1	12.3	12.3	11.1	13.1
Not reported	6.1	5.9	4.4	7.5	5.4

	total	Northeast	Midwest	South	West
PERCENT DISTRIBUTION BY REGION					
Total renting respondents who moved	**100.0%**	**13.2%**	**21.6%**	**39.4%**	**25.8%**
All reported reasons equal	100.0	18.9	26.6	31.3	23.1
Private displacement	100.0	23.8	7.9	27.9	40.4
Government displacement	100.0	3.1	23.0	26.4	47.5
Disaster loss (fire, flood, etc.)	100.0	8.4	14.1	69.5	8.0
New job or job transfer	100.0	10.0	18.1	44.4	27.5
To be closer to work/school/other	100.0	13.6	20.5	37.8	28.1
Other financial, employment related	100.0	14.1	21.5	29.5	34.9
To establish own household	100.0	10.4	26.3	39.2	24.1
Needed larger house or apartment	100.0	15.4	20.1	41.0	23.5
Married, widowed, divorced, separated	100.0	13.0	23.0	36.3	27.7
Other family, personal reasons	100.0	15.3	24.1	39.5	21.1
Wanted better home	100.0	13.5	26.1	38.8	21.6
Change from owner to renter	100.0	13.5	18.5	43.4	24.6
Wanted lower rent or maintenance	100.0	12.0	20.1	42.2	25.8
Other housing related reasons	100.0	13.1	22.8	37.5	26.6
Evicted from residence	100.0	9.1	21.2	36.4	33.3
Other	100.0	13.4	22.0	36.4	28.2
Not reported	100.0	12.8	15.8	48.4	23.0

Note: Total number of movers does not equal total movers in other tables because this table shows survey respondents who moved, not necessarily householders.
Source: Bureau of the Census, American Housing Survey for the United States: 2009, Internet site http://www.census.gov/hhes/ www/housing/ahs/ahs09/ahs09.html; calculations by New Strategist

CHAPTER

6

Owners of New Homes

New home sales have plummeted, prices have declined, and many owners are underwater.

New home sales fell from a peak of 1.3 million in 2005 (see table 39 in chapter 1) to just 375,000 in 2009. As defined by the American Housing Survey, the buyers of new homes are those who own a home built in the past four years (or between 2005 and 2009). In 2009, 3.8 million homeowners lived in a home built in the past four years. They paid a median of $240,000 for their home, and they estimated that their home's current median value was a smaller $220,000 in 2009. Twenty-four percent of the owners of new homes with mortgages are underwater on their loan—owing more than their home is worth.

■ The owners of new homes are substantially younger than the average homeowner, with a median age of 40 versus 52 for all homeowners.

■ The median household income of the owners of new homes was $78,000 in 2009, well above the $60,000 median income of all homeowners. But their housing costs are also much higher, a median of $1,572 per month versus $1,000 per month for the average homeowner.

■ New homes are much larger than average, a median of 2,400 square feet versus 1,800 square feet in the average owned home. Thirty-five percent of new homes are all-electric.

Many owners of new homes are underwater on their mortgage

(percent distribution of owners of new homes with mortgages by current total loan as a percent of home value, 2009)

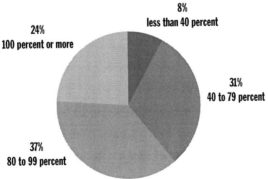

8%
less than 40 percent

24%
100 percent or more

31%
40 to 79 percent

37%
80 to 99 percent

Table 6.1 Owners of New Homes by Age, 2009

The owners of new homes are much younger than the average homeowner, with a median age of 40 versus 52 for all homeowners.

(number and percent distribution of total homeowners and owners of homes built in the past four years, by age of householder, 2009; numbers in thousands)

	total		new homes		
	number	percent distribution	number	percent distribution	percent of total
Total homeowners	**76,428**	**100.0%**	**3,830**	**100.0%**	**5.0%**
Under age 25	1,284	1.7	139	3.6	10.8
Aged 25 to 29	3,541	4.6	480	12.5	13.6
Aged 30 to 34	5,532	7.2	590	15.4	10.7
Aged 35 to 44	14,932	19.5	1,060	27.7	7.1
Aged 45 to 54	17,743	23.2	684	17.9	3.9
Aged 55 to 64	14,924	19.5	554	14.5	3.7
Aged 65 to 74	9,818	12.8	242	6.3	2.5
Aged 75 or older	8,653	11.3	81	2.1	0.9
Median age (years)	52	–	40	–	–

Note: "–" means not applicable.
Source: Bureau of the Census, American Housing Survey for the United States: 2009, Internet site http://www.census.gov/hhes/www/housing/ahs/ahs09/ahs09.html; calculations by New Strategist

Table 6.2 Owners of New Homes by Household Type and Age of Householder, 2009

The owners of new homes are more likely to be married couples
than the average homeowner—69 versus 62 percent.

(number and percent distribution of total homeowners and owners of homes built in the past four years, by household type and age of householder, 2009; numbers in thousands)

	total		new homes		
	number	percent distribution	number	percent distribution	percent of total
Total homeowners	**76,428**	**100.0%**	**3,830**	**100.0%**	**5.0%**
MARRIED-COUPLE HOUSEHOLDS	**47,008**	**61.5**	**2,627**	**68.6**	**5.6**
Under age 25	495	0.6	38	1.0	7.7
Aged 25 to 29	2,007	2.6	305	8.0	15.2
Aged 30 to 34	3,646	4.8	431	11.2	11.8
Aged 35 to 44	10,336	13.5	792	20.7	7.7
Aged 45 to 64	21,352	27.9	867	22.6	4.1
Aged 65 or older	9,174	12.0	195	5.1	2.1
TWO-OR-MORE-PERSON HOUSEHOLDS					
Female householders, no spouse present	**7,931**	**10.4**	**330**	**8.6**	**4.2**
Under age 45	2,948	3.9	205	5.4	7.0
Aged 45 to 64	3,397	4.4	108	2.8	3.2
Aged 65 or older	1,587	2.1	17	0.4	1.1
Male householders, no spouse present	**4,712**	**6.2**	**219**	**5.7**	**4.7**
Under age 45	2,170	2.8	160	4.2	7.4
Aged 45 to 64	1,878	2.5	48	1.2	2.5
Aged 65 or older	663	0.9	11	0.3	1.7
SINGLE-PERSON HOUSEHOLDS	**16,777**	**22.0**	**653**	**17.1**	**3.9**
Female householders	**10,007**	**13.1**	**381**	**9.9**	**3.8**
Under age 45	1,547	2.0	187	4.9	12.1
Aged 45 to 64	3,231	4.2	117	3.1	3.6
Aged 65 or older	5,230	6.8	77	2.0	1.5
Male householders	**6,770**	**8.9**	**272**	**7.1**	**4.0**
Under age 45	2,142	2.8	151	3.9	7.1
Aged 45 to 64	2,810	3.7	99	2.6	3.5
Aged 65 or older	1,818	2.4	22	0.6	1.2

*Source: Bureau of the Census, American Housing Survey for the United States: 2009, Internet site http://www.census.gov/hhes/
www/housing/ahs/ahs09/ahs09.html; calculations by New Strategist*

Table 6.3 Owners of New Homes by Race and Hispanic Origin, 2009

The owners of new homes are more likely to be Asian, Hispanic, or black than is the average homeowner. One in four is a minority.

(number and percent distribution of total homeowners and owners of homes built in the past four years, by race and Hispanic origin, 2009; numbers in thousands)

	total		new homes		
	number	percent distribution	number	percent distribution	percent of total
Total homeowners	**76,428**	**100.0%**	**3,830**	**100.0%**	**5.0%**
American Indian	503	0.7	26	0.7	5.2
Asian	2,516	3.3	217	5.7	8.6
Black	6,547	8.6	364	9.5	5.6
Hispanic	6,439	8.4	339	8.9	5.3
White, non-Hispanic	59,905	78.4	2,856	74.6	4.8

Note: American Indians, Asians, blacks, and whites are those who identify themselves as being of the race alone. Numbers do not add to total because not all races are shown and Hispanics may be of any race.
Source: Bureau of the Census, American Housing Survey for the United States: 2009, Internet site http://www.census.gov/hhes/ www/housing/ahs/ahs09/ahs09.html; calculations by New Strategist

Table 6.4 Owners of New Homes by Household Income, 2009

The owners of new homes have much higher incomes than
the average homeowner, in part because the average
homeowner is much older and more likely to be retired.

(number and percent distribution of total homeowners and owners of homes built in the past four years, by household income, 2009; numbers in thousands)

	total		new homes		
	number	percent distribution	number	percent distribution	percent of total
Total homeowners	**76,428**	**100.0%**	**3,830**	**100.0%**	**5.0%**
Under $10,000	4,423	5.8	127	3.3	2.9
$10,000 to $19,999	5,911	7.7	158	4.1	2.7
$20,000 to $29,999	7,617	10.0	234	6.1	3.1
$30,000 to $39,999	7,082	9.3	249	6.5	3.5
$40,000 to $49,999	6,852	9.0	268	7.0	3.9
$50,000 to $59,999	6,328	8.3	283	7.4	4.5
$60,000 to $79,999	10,535	13.8	636	16.6	6.0
$80,000 to $99,999	8,409	11.0	538	14.0	6.4
$100,000 to $119,999	6,007	7.9	387	10.1	6.4
$120,000 or more	13,264	17.4	950	24.8	7.2
Median income	$60,000	–	$78,000	–	–

Note: "–" means not applicable.
Source: Bureau of the Census, American Housing Survey for the United States: 2009, Internet site http://www.census.gov/hhes/www/housing/ahs/ahs09/ahs09.html; calculations by New Strategist

Table 6.5 Owners of New Homes by Educational Attainment, 2009

The owners of new homes are much better educated than
the average homeowner. Forty-four percent are college
graduates versus 34 percent of all homeowners.

*(number and percent distribution of total homeowners and the owners of homes built in the past four years, by
educational attainment of householder, 2009; numbers in thousands)*

	total		new homes		
	number	percent distribution	number	percent distribution	percent of total
Total homeowners	**76,428**	**100.0%**	**3,830**	**100.0%**	**5.0%**
Not a high school graduate	8,542	11.2	212	5.5	2.5
High school graduate only	22,665	29.7	840	21.9	3.7
Some college, no degree	12,659	16.6	654	17.1	5.2
Associate's degree	6,722	8.8	448	11.7	6.7
Bachelor's degree	15,894	20.8	1,040	27.2	6.5
Graduate or professional degree	9,947	13.0	635	16.6	6.4
High school graduate or higher	67,886	88.8	3,618	94.5	5.3
Some college or higher	45,221	59.2	2,778	72.5	6.1
Bachelor's degree or higher	25,840	33.8	1,676	43.7	6.5

*Source: Bureau of the Census, American Housing Survey for the United States: 2009, Internet site http://www.census.gov/hhes/
www/housing/ahs/ahs09/ahs09.html; calculations by New Strategist*

Table 6.6 Owners of New Homes by Household Size, 2009

Owners of new homes have relatively large households. One-third
of the owners of new homes have four or more people in their
household compared with 26 percent of all homeowners.

(number and percent distribution of total homeowners and owners of homes built in the past four years, by number of persons living in home, 2009; numbers in thousands)

	total		new homes		
	number	percent distribution	number	percent distribution	percent of total
Total homeowners	**76,428**	**100.0%**	**3,830**	**100.0%**	**5.0%**
One person	16,777	22.0	653	17.1	3.9
Two persons	27,633	36.2	1,286	33.6	4.7
Three persons	12,223	16.0	626	16.3	5.1
Four persons	11,791	15.4	760	19.8	6.4
Five persons	5,207	6.8	297	7.8	5.7
Six persons	1,797	2.4	145	3.8	8.1
Seven or more persons	1,000	1.3	63	1.6	6.3

Source: Bureau of the Census, American Housing Survey for the United States: 2009, Internet site http://www.census.gov/hhes/ www/housing/ahs/ahs09/ahs09.html; calculations by New Strategist

Table 6.7 Owners of New Homes by Type of Structure, 2009

Eighty percent of the owners of new homes live in a single-family detached structure. Seven percent live in a mobile home.

(number and percent distribution of total homeowners and owners of homes built in the past four years, by number of units in structure, 2009; numbers in thousands)

	total		new homes		
	number	percent distribution	number	percent distribution	percent of total
Total homeowners	**76,428**	**100.0%**	**3,830**	**100.0%**	**5.0%**
One, detached	63,324	82.9	3,067	80.1	4.8
One, attached	3,952	5.2	324	8.4	8.2
Multiunit buildings	3,734	4.9	167	4.4	4.5
Two to four	1,353	1.8	41	1.1	3.0
Five to nine	632	0.8	38	1.0	6.1
10 to 19	483	0.6	26	0.7	5.4
20 to 49	499	0.7	17	0.4	3.3
50 or more	768	1.0	46	1.2	5.9
Mobile home	5,418	7.1	272	7.1	5.0

Source: Bureau of the Census, American Housing Survey for the United States: 2009, Internet site http://www.census.gov/hhes/www/housing/ahs/ahs09/ahs09.html; calculations by New Strategist

Table 6.8 Owners of New Homes by Square Footage of Unit and Lot Size, 2009

The owners of new homes have much larger houses than the
average homeowner, with a median of 2,400 square feet.

(number and percent distribution of total homeowners and owners of homes built in the past four years, by square footage and lot size, 2009; numbers in thousands)

	total		new homes		
	number	percent distribution	number	percent distribution	percent of total
Square footage of home, total*	**68,742**	**100.0%**	**3,339**	**100.0%**	**4.9%**
Less than 500 sq. ft.	383	0.6	6	0.2	1.5
500 to 749 sq. ft.	1,085	1.6	10	0.3	1.0
750 to 999 sq. ft.	3,519	5.1	67	2.0	1.9
1,000 to 1,499 sq. ft.	14,978	21.8	434	13.0	2.9
1,500 to 1,999 sq. ft.	16,284	23.7	593	17.8	3.6
2,000 to 2,499 sq. ft.	12,057	17.5	618	18.5	5.1
2,500 to 2,999 sq. ft.	6,622	9.6	430	12.9	6.5
3,000 to 3,999 sq. ft.	6,391	9.3	634	19.0	9.9
4,000 or more sq. ft.	3,787	5.5	391	11.7	10.3
Not reported	3,638	5.3	157	4.7	4.3
Median square footage	1,800	–	2,400	–	–
Lot size, total**	**70,643**	**100.0**	**3,472**	**100.0**	**4.9**
Less than one-eighth acre	9,107	12.9	474	13.6	5.2
One-eighth up to one-quarter acre	17,771	25.2	795	22.9	4.5
One-quarter up to one-half acre	13,837	19.6	730	21.0	5.3
One-half up to one acre	8,874	12.6	366	10.5	4.1
One to five acres	14,895	21.1	780	22.5	5.2
Five to 10 acres	2,545	3.6	176	5.1	6.9
10 or more acres	3,614	5.1	152	4.4	4.2
Median lot size (acres)	0.32	–	0.32	–	–

* Single-family detached and mobile homes only.
** Homes in two-or-more-unit buildings are excluded.
Note: "–" means not applicable.
Source: Bureau of the Census, American Housing Survey for the United States: 2009, Internet site http://www.census.gov/hhes/ www/housing/ahs/ahs09/ahs09.html; calculations by New Strategist

Table 6.9 Owners of New Homes by Number of Rooms in Home, 2009

New homes have more rooms than the average owned home.
Forty-three percent have four or more bedrooms, and 94 percent
have two or more bathrooms. Many have a room used for business.

(number and percent distribution of total homeowners and owners of homes built in the past four years, by number and type of rooms, 2009; numbers in thousands)

	total		new homes		
	number	percent distribution	number	percent distribution	percent of total
Total homeowners	**76,428**	**100.0%**	**3,830**	**100.0%**	**5.0%**
Number of rooms					
One room	26	0.0	5	0.1	17.8
Two rooms	68	0.1	3	0.1	3.8
Three rooms	1,036	1.4	41	1.1	4.0
Four rooms	6,475	8.5	147	3.8	2.3
Five rooms	17,232	22.5	825	21.5	4.8
Six rooms	20,364	26.6	821	21.4	4.0
Seven rooms	14,754	19.3	739	19.3	5.0
Eight rooms	9,410	12.3	628	16.4	6.7
Nine rooms	4,130	5.4	323	8.4	7.8
10 or more rooms	2,933	3.8	298	7.8	10.2
Number of bedrooms					
None	45	0.1	5	0.1	10.3
One bedroom	1,714	2.2	43	1.1	2.5
Two bedrooms	13,471	17.6	400	10.4	3.0
Three bedrooms	39,723	52.0	1,746	45.6	4.4
Four or more bedrooms	21,475	28.1	1,636	42.7	7.6
Number of bathrooms					
None	175	0.2	3	0.1	1.5
One bathroom	15,767	20.6	106	2.8	0.7
One-and-one-half bathrooms	12,081	15.8	112	2.9	0.9
Two or more bathrooms	48,405	63.3	3,610	94.3	7.5
With room used for business	**26,108**	**34.2**	**1,676**	**43.8**	**6.4**
Business only	11,479	15.0	751	19.6	6.5
Business and other use	14,629	19.1	925	24.2	6.3

Source: Bureau of the Census, American Housing Survey for the United States: 2009, Internet site http://www.census.gov/hhes/ www/housing/ahs/ahs09/ahs09.html; calculations by New Strategist

Table 6.10 Owners of New Homes by Presence of Kitchen, Laundry, and Safety Equipment, 2009

The owners of new homes are much more likely than the average homeowner to have a dishwasher, 95 versus 75 percent. They are also more likely to have a sprinkler system in their home.

(number and percent of total homeowners and owners of homes built in the past four years, by presence of kitchen, laundry, and safety equipment, 2009; numbers in thousands)

	total		new homes		
	number	percent distribution	number	percent distribution	percent of total
Total homeowners	**76,428**	**100.0%**	**3,830**	**100.0%**	**5.0%**
With complete kitchen equipment	76,050	99.5	3,817	99.7	5.0
Dishwasher	57,191	74.8	3,651	95.3	6.4
Washing machine	73,826	96.6	3,780	98.7	5.1
Clothes dryer	72,562	94.9	3,771	98.4	5.2
Disposal in kitchen sink	40,597	53.1	2,786	72.7	6.9
Trash compactor	3,166	4.1	249	6.5	7.9
Working smoke detector	71,797	93.9	3,730	97.4	5.2
Fire extinguisher	37,922	49.6	1,914	50.0	5.0
Sprinkler system inside home	2,086	2.7	358	9.4	17.2
Carbon monoxide detector	31,691	41.5	1,579	41.2	5.0

Note: Complete kitchen equipment includes a sink, refrigerator, and oven or burners.
Source: Bureau of the Census, American Housing Survey for the United States: 2009, Internet site http://www.census.gov/hhes/ www/housing/ahs/ahs09/ahs09.html; calculations by New Strategist

Table 6.11 Owners of New Homes by Type of Heating Equipment, 2009

The 71 percent majority of new homes are heated by a warm-air furnace, while another 23 percent use an electric heat pump.

(number and percent distribution of total homeowners and owners of homes built in the past four years, by presence and type of heating equipment, 2009; numbers in thousands)

	total		new homes		
	number	percent distribution	number	percent distribution	percent of total
Total homeowners	**76,428**	**100.0%**	**3,830**	**100.0%**	**5.0%**
Main heating equipment					
Warm-air furnace	51,691	67.6	2,701	70.5	5.2
Steam or hot water system	7,494	9.8	80	2.1	1.1
Electric heat pump	9,764	12.8	877	22.9	9.0
Built-in electric units	2,120	2.8	44	1.2	2.1
Floor, wall, or other built-in hot air units without ducts	2,043	2.7	54	1.4	2.6
Room heaters with flue	580	0.8	13	0.3	2.3
Room heaters without flue	694	0.9	8	0.2	1.1
Portable electric heaters	535	0.7	6	0.1	1.1
Stoves	845	1.1	14	0.4	1.6
Fireplaces with inserts	155	0.2	0	0.0	0.0
Fireplaces without inserts	35	0.0	0	0.0	0.0
Other	232	0.3	20	0.5	8.5
Cooking stove	34	0.0	0	0.0	0.0
None	206	0.3	14	0.4	6.8
Homeowners with additional heating equipment					
Warm-air furnace	225	0.3	12	0.3	5.1
Steam or hot water system	51	0.1	3	0.1	5.5
Electric heat pump	91	0.1	9	0.2	9.9
Built-in electric units	1,428	1.9	46	1.2	3.2
Floor, wall, or other built-in hot air units without ducts	63	0.1	14	0.4	21.7
Room heaters with flue	716	0.9	19	0.5	2.7
Room heaters without flue	1,207	1.6	20	0.5	1.7
Portable electric heaters	9,886	12.9	292	7.6	3.0
Stoves	3,740	4.9	85	2.2	2.3
Fireplaces with inserts	4,742	6.2	316	8.2	6.7
Fireplaces without inserts	4,869	6.4	345	9.0	7.1
Other	707	0.9	48	1.2	6.7
Cooking stove	50	0.1	2	0.1	4.4
None	51,171	67.0	2,708	70.7	5.3

Source: Bureau of the Census, American Housing Survey for the United States: 2009, Internet site http://www.census.gov/hhes/www/housing/ahs/ahs09/ahs09.html; calculations by New Strategist

Table 6.12 Owners of New Homes with Air Conditioning, 2009

Ninety percent of the owners of new homes report that
their home has central air conditioning.

(number and percent distribution of total homeowners and owners of homes built in the past four years, by presence and type of air conditioning equipment, 2009; numbers in thousands)

	total		new homes		
	number	percent distribution	number	percent distribution	percent of total
Total homeowners	**76,428**	**100.0%**	**3,830**	**100.0%**	**5.0%**
Homeowners with air conditioning	68,355	89.4	3,574	93.3	5.2
Central	54,647	71.5	3,442	89.9	6.3
Additional central	4,709	6.2	516	13.5	11.0
One room unit	5,303	6.9	49	1.3	0.9
Two room units	4,800	6.3	59	1.5	1.2
Three or more room units	3,604	4.7	24	0.6	0.7

Source: Bureau of the Census, American Housing Survey for the United States: 2009, Internet site http://www.census.gov/hhes/www/housing/ahs/ahs09/ahs09.html; calculations by New Strategist

Table 6.13 Owners of New Homes by Primary Source of Water and Sewage Disposal System, 2009

Owners of new homes are about as likely as the average homeowner to use a well as their source of water. They are slightly less likely to be connected to a public sewer.

(number and percent of total homeowners and owners of homes built in the past four years, by primary source of water and type of sewage disposal system, 2009; numbers in thousands)

	total		new homes		
	number	percent distribution	number	percent distribution	percent of total
Total homeowners	**76,428**	**100.0%**	**3,830**	**100.0%**	**5.0%**
Source of water					
Public system or private company	64,372	84.2	3,238	84.6	5.0
Well	11,769	15.4	580	15.1	4.9
Safety of primary source of water					
Safe to drink	71,152	93.1	3,507	91.6	4.9
Not safe to drink	4,530	5.9	267	7.0	5.9
Sewage disposal system					
Public sewer	56,736	74.2	2,700	70.5	4.8
Septic tank, cesspool, chemical toilet	19,667	25.7	1,130	29.5	5.7

Note: Numbers do not sum to total because "other" and "not reported" are not shown.
Source: Bureau of the Census, American Housing Survey for the United States: 2009, Internet site http://www.census.gov/hhes/ www/housing/ahs/ahs09/ahs09.html; calculations by New Strategist

Table 6.14 Owners of New Homes by Fuels Used, 2009

The owners of new homes are more likely than the average homeowner to have all-electric homes. Thirty-five percent of the owners of new homes have all-electric units compared with 23 percent of all homeowners.

(number and percent of total homeowners and owners of homes built in the past four years, by types of fuels used, 2009; numbers in thousands)

	total		new homes		
	number	percent distribution	number	percent distribution	percent of total
Total homeowners	**76,428**	**100.0%**	**3,830**	**100.0%**	**5.0%**
Electricity	76,378	99.9	3,822	99.8	5.0
All-electric homes	17,951	23.5	1,331	34.8	7.4
Piped gas	46,700	61.1	2,125	55.5	4.6
Bottled gas	8,391	11.0	441	11.5	5.3
Fuel oil	6,409	8.4	55	1.4	0.9
Kerosene or other liquid fuel	451	0.6	18	0.5	4.0
Coal or coke	97	0.1	3	0.1	2.8
Wood	1,510	2.0	28	0.7	1.9
Solar energy	130	0.2	8	0.2	6.0
Other	254	0.3	19	0.5	7.4

Note: Numbers do not add to total because many households use more than one fuel.
Source: Bureau of the Census, American Housing Survey for the United States: 2009, Internet site http://www.census.gov/hhes/www/housing/ahs/ahs09/ahs09.html; calculations by New Strategist

Table 6.15 Owners of New Homes by Primary Heating Fuel Used, 2009

Few homeowners use solar energy as their primary heating fuel,
but among those who do 34 percent are the owners of new homes.

(number and percent of total homeowners and owners of homes built in the past four years, by primary heating fuel used, 2009; numbers in thousands)

	total		new homes		
	number	percent distribution	number	percent distribution	percent of total
TOTAL HOMEOWNERS	**76,428**	**100.0%**	**3,830**	**100.0%**	**5.0%**
Homeowners using heating fuel	76,222	100.0	3,816	100.0	5.0
Electricity	22,219	29.2	1,750	45.9	7.9
Piped gas	41,233	54.1	1,726	45.2	4.2
Bottled gas	4,889	6.4	231	6.1	4.7
Fuel oil	5,693	7.5	47	1.2	0.8
Kerosene or other liquid fuel	444	0.6	18	0.5	4.1
Coal or coke	91	0.1	3	0.1	2.9
Wood	1,503	2.0	28	0.7	1.9
Solar energy	8	0.0	3	0.1	34.2
Other	142	0.2	9	0.2	6.5

Source: Bureau of the Census, American Housing Survey for the United States: 2009, Internet site http://www.census.gov/hhes/www/housing/ahs/ahs09/ahs09.html; calculations by New Strategist

Table 6.16 Owners of New Homes by Cooking, Water Heating, and Clothes Dryer Fuels Used, 2009

The owners of new homes are slightly more likely than the average homeowner to use electricity as their water heating fuel.

(number and percent of total homeowners and owners of homes built in the past four years, by cooking, water heating, and clothes dryer fuels used, 2009; numbers in thousands)

	total		new homes		
	number	percent distribution	number	percent distribution	percent of total
COOKING FUEL					
Homeowners using cooking fuel	**76,388**	**100.0%**	**3,826**	**100.0%**	**5.0%**
Electricity	45,512	59.6	2,227	58.2	4.9
Piped gas	26,553	34.8	1,348	35.2	5.1
Bottled gas	4,274	5.6	247	6.5	5.8
Kerosene or other liquid fuel	7	0.0	0	0.0	0.0
Wood	17	0.0	0	0.0	0.0
Other	25	0.0	4	0.1	17.1
WATER HEATING FUEL					
Homeowners with hot piped water	**76,371**	**100.0**	**3,830**	**100.1**	**5.0**
Electricity	29,341	38.4	1,710	44.7	5.8
Piped gas	40,280	52.7	1,814	47.4	4.5
Bottled gas	3,365	4.4	251	6.6	7.5
Fuel oil	3,087	4.0	32	0.8	1.0
Kerosene or other liquid fuel	18	0.0	4	0.1	0.0
Coal or coke	23	0.0	0	0.0	0.0
Wood	96	0.1	10	0.3	0.0
Solar energy	121	0.2	5	0.1	4.1
Other	40	0.1	4	0.1	0.0
CLOTHES DRYER FUEL					
Homeowners with clothes dryers	**72,562**	**100.0**	**3,771**	**98.5**	**5.2**
Electricity	55,059	75.9	3,031	79.2	5.5
Piped gas	16,326	22.5	680	17.8	4.2
Other	1,178	1.6	60	1.6	5.1

Source: Bureau of the Census, American Housing Survey for the United States: 2009, Internet site http://www.census.gov/hhes/ www/housing/ahs/ahs09/ahs09.html; calculations by New Strategist

Table 6.17 Owners of New Homes by Amenities of Home, 2009

The owners of new homes are more likely than the average homeowner to have a garage or carport—90 versus 80 percent.

(number and percent of total homeowners and owners of homes built in the past four years, by selected amenities of home, 2009; numbers in thousands)

	total		new homes		
	number	percent distribution	number	percent distribution	percent of total
Total homeowners	**76,428**	**100.0%**	**3,830**	**100.0%**	**5.0%**
Porch, deck, balcony, or patio	70,421	92.1	3,506	91.5	5.0
Telephone available	75,129	98.3	3,601	94.0	4.8
Usable fireplace	34,458	45.1	2,085	54.4	6.1
Separate dining room	43,717	57.2	2,208	57.7	5.1
With two or more living or recreation rooms	30,978	40.5	1,736	45.3	5.6
Garage or carport					
Yes	60,979	79.8	3,429	89.5	5.6
No, but off-street parking included	13,287	17.4	352	9.2	2.6
No cars, trucks, or vans	2,069	2.7	22	0.6	1.1

Source: Bureau of the Census, American Housing Survey for the United States: 2009, Internet site http://www.census.gov/hhes/www/housing/ahs/ahs09/ahs09.html; calculations by New Strategist

Table 6.18 Owners of New Homes by Deficiencies of Home, 2009

The owners of new homes are less likely than the average
homeowner to have homes with deficiencies.

*(number and percent distribution of total homeowners and owners of homes built in the past four years, by selected
deficiencies of housing unit, 2009; numbers in thousands)*

	total		new homes		
	number	percent distribution	number	percent distribution	percent of total
Total homeowners	**76,428**	**100.0%**	**3,830**	**100.0%**	**5.0%**
Signs of rats in last three months	354	0.5	7	0.2	1.9
Signs of mice in last three months	3,984	5.2	78	2.0	2.0
Signs of rodents, not sure which kind, in last three months	164	0.2	9	0.2	5.7
Holes in floor	581	0.8	14	0.4	2.4
Open cracks or holes (interior)	3,101	4.1	57	1.5	1.8
Broken plaster, peeling paint (interior)	1,246	1.6	24	0.6	1.9
No electrical wiring	57	0.1	8	0.2	14.6
Exposed wiring	221	0.3	10	0.3	4.4
Rooms without electric outlets	650	0.8	33	0.9	5.1

*Source: Bureau of the Census, American Housing Survey for the United States: 2009, Internet site http://www.census.gov/hhes/
www/housing/ahs/ahs09/ahs09.html; calculations by New Strategist*

Table 6.19 Owners of New Homes by Housing Equipment Failures, 2009

The owners of new homes are less likely than the average homeowner to experience a variety of problems such as water leakage from inside or outside the structure and being uncomfortably cold for a day or more during the past winter.

(number and percent distribution of total homeowners and owners of homes built in the past four years, by type of equipment failure, 2009; numbers in thousands)

	total		new homes		
	number	percent distribution	number	percent distribution	percent of total
WATER SUPPLY STOPPAGE					
Homeowners with piped water	**76,371**	**100.0%**	**3,830**	**100.0%**	**5.0%**
No stoppage in last three months	73,494	96.2	3,687	96.3	5.0
With stoppage in last three months	2,031	2.7	93	2.4	4.6
Not reported	846	1.1	50	1.3	5.9
FLUSH TOILET BREAKDOWNS					
Homeowners with flush toilets	**76,391**	**100.0**	**3,830**	**100.0**	**5.0**
With at least one working toilet at all times, last three months	74,674	97.8	3,771	98.5	5.0
With no working toilet at least once in last three months	884	1.2	12	0.3	1.4
Not reported	833	1.1	47	1.2	5.6
WATER LEAKAGE DURING LAST 12 MONTHS					
Total homeowners	**76,428**	**100.0**	**3,830**	**100.0**	**5.0**
No leakage from within structure	70,356	92.1	3,595	93.9	5.1
With leakage from within structure*	5,170	6.8	185	4.8	3.6
Fixtures backed up or overflowed	1,188	1.6	33	0.9	2.8
Pipes leaked	2,145	2.8	78	2.0	3.7
Broken water heater	714	0.9	29	0.7	4.0
Other or unknown	1,263	1.7	45	1.2	3.6
Leakage not reported	902	1.2	50	1.3	5.6
No leakage from outside structure	67,686	88.6	3,593	93.8	5.3
With leakage from outside structure*	7,842	10.3	187	4.9	2.4
Roof	4,168	5.5	65	1.7	1.5
Basement	2,309	3.0	38	1.0	1.6
Walls, windows, or doors	1,165	1.5	71	1.9	6.1
Other or not reported	691	0.9	18	0.5	2.6
Leakage not reported	900	1.2	50	1.3	5.6

	total		new homes		
	number	percent distribution	number	percent distribution	percent of total
HEATING PROBLEMS					
Homeowners with heating equipment and occupying home last winter	**75,215**	**100.0%**	**3,626**	**100.0%**	**4.8%**
Not uncomfortably cold for 24 or more hours last winter	67,769	90.1	3,390	93.5	5.0
Uncomfortably cold for 24 or more hours last winter*	6,055	8.1	190	5.2	3.1
Equipment breakdown	1,594	2.1	39	1.1	2.4
Utility interruption	2,139	2.8	88	2.4	4.1
Inadequate heating capacity	350	0.5	8	0.2	2.4
Inadequate insulation	394	0.5	7	0.2	1.9
Cost of heating	778	1.0	32	0.9	4.1
Other	1,022	1.4	30	0.8	2.9
Not reported	1,391	1.8	46	1.3	3.3
ELECTRICAL PROBLEMS					
Homeowners with electrical wiring	**76,371**	**100.0**	**3,822**	**100.0**	**5.0**
No fuses or breakers blown in last three months	68,697	90.0	3,431	89.8	5.0
With fuses or breakers blown in last three months	6,685	8.8	339	8.9	5.1
Not reported	989	1.3	52	1.4	5.3

Figures do not add to total because more than one problem may have occurred.
Source: Bureau of the Census, American Housing Survey for the United States: 2009, Internet site http://www.census.gov/hhes/ www/housing/ahs/ahs09/ahs09.html; calculations by New Strategist

Table 6.20 Owners of New Homes by Purchase Price, 2009

The owners of new homes paid more than twice as much as the average homeowner for their home, a median of $240,000. Thirty-three percent paid $300,000 or more.

(number and percent distribution of total homeowners and owners of homes built in the past four years, by purchase price of home, 2009; numbers in thousands)

	total		new homes		
	number	percent distribution	number	percent distribution	percent of total
TOTAL HOMEOWNERS	**76,428**	**100.0%**	**3,830**	**100.0%**	**5.0%**
Home purchased or built	**71,877**	**94.0**	**3,706**	**96.8**	**5.2**
Under $10,000	2,799	3.7	13	0.3	0.5
$10,000 to $19,999	4,229	5.5	8	0.2	0.2
$20,000 to $29,999	3,648	4.8	12	0.3	0.3
$30,000 to $39,999	3,489	4.6	44	1.1	1.2
$40,000 to $49,999	3,002	3.9	17	0.4	0.6
$50,000 to $59,999	3,076	4.0	23	0.6	0.7
$60,000 to $69,999	3,126	4.1	29	0.8	0.9
$70,000 to $79,999	2,968	3.9	37	1.0	1.2
$80,000 to $99,999	5,662	7.4	136	3.6	2.4
$100,000 to $119,999	4,288	5.6	109	2.9	2.5
$120,000 to $149,999	6,691	8.8	262	6.9	3.9
$150,000 to $199,999	8,055	10.5	602	15.7	7.5
$200,000 to $249,999	5,029	6.6	521	13.6	10.4
$250,000 to $299,999	3,024	4.0	335	8.7	11.1
$300,000 or more	8,594	11.2	1,266	33.1	14.7
Not reported	4,196	5.5	293	7.6	7.0
Median purchase price	$107,500	–	$240,000	–	–
Received as inheritance or gift	**3,388**	**4.4**	**16**	**0.4**	**0.5**
Not reported	**1,163**	**1.5**	**108**	**2.8**	**9.2**

Note: "–" means not applicable.
Source: Bureau of the Census, American Housing Survey for the United States: 2009, Internet site http://www.census.gov/hhes/ www/housing/ahs/ahs09/ahs09.html; calculations by New Strategist

Table 6.21 Owners of New Homes by Value of Home, 2007 and 2009

The self-reported value of newly built homes (built in the past four years) fell 17 percent between 2007 and 2009.

(number and percent distribution of the owners of homes built in the past four years by self-reported value of home, 2007 and 2009; percent change, 2007–09; numbers in thousands)

	2009	2007	percent change
Owners of new homes	**3,830**	**4,710**	**–18.7%**
Under $100,000	501	593	–15.5
$100,000 to $119,999	122	109	11.8
$120,000 to $149,999	310	281	10.3
$150,000 to $199,999	644	588	9.5
$200,000 to $299,999	984	1,178	–16.5
$300,000 to $399,999	512	797	–35.7
$400,000 to $499,999	288	400	–28.0
$500,000 to $749,999	290	460	–37.0
$750,000 or more	179	303	–40.9
Median home value	$220,000	$266,480	–17.4

Source: Bureau of the Census, American Housing Survey for the United States: 2009, Internet site http://www.census.gov/hhes/ www/housing/ahs/ahs09/ahs09.html; calculations by New Strategist

Table 6.22 Owners of New Homes by Major Source of Down Payment, 2009

Sixteen percent of the owners of new homes made no
down payment when they bought their home.

*(number and percent distribution of total homeowners and owners of homes built in the past four years, by major
source of down payment, 2009; numbers in thousands)*

	total		new homes		
	number	percent distribution	number	percent distribution	percent of total
Total homes purchased or built	**71,877**	**100.0%**	**3,706**	**100.0%**	**5.2%**
Sale of previous home	21,946	30.5	1,330	35.9	6.1
Savings or cash on hand	31,437	43.7	1,193	32.2	3.8
Sale of other investment	750	1.0	42	1.1	5.5
Borrowing, other than mortgage on this property	2,409	3.4	88	2.4	3.6
Inheritance or gift	1,358	1.9	44	1.2	3.2
Land where building built used for financing	639	0.9	83	2.2	13.0
Other	3,125	4.3	145	3.9	4.6
No down payment	8,346	11.6	602	16.3	7.2
Not reported	1,867	2.6	181	4.9	9.7

*Source: Bureau of the Census, American Housing Survey for the United States: 2009, Internet site http://www.census.gov/hhes/
www/housing/ahs/ahs09/ahs09.html; calculations by New Strategist*

Table 6.23 Owners of New Homes by First Home and Mortgage Status, 2009

Only 28 percent of the owners of new homes are first-time homeowners compared with a larger 41 percent of all homeowners. Nearly one-third of all homeowners own their home free and clear compared with 13 percent of the owners of new homes.

(number and percent distribution of total homeowners and owners of homes built in the past four years, by first-home and mortgage status, 2009; numbers in thousands)

	total		new homes		
	number	percent distribution	number	percent distribution	percent of total
FIRST-HOME STATUS					
Total homeowners	76,428	100.0%	3,830	100.0%	5.0%
First home ever owned	31,676	41.4	1,066	27.8	3.4
Not first home	43,233	56.6	2,648	69.1	6.1
Not reported	1,519	2.0	117	3.0	7.7
MORTGAGE STATUS					
Total homeowners	76,428	100.0	3,830	100.0	5.0
None, owned free and clear	24,206	31.7	499	13.0	2.1
Reverse mortgage	252	0.3	3	0.1	1.0
With regular and/or home-equity mortgages	50,300	65.8	3,251	84.9	6.5
Regular mortgage(s)	46,703	61.1	3,174	82.9	6.8
Home-equity lump-sum mortgage	4,022	5.3	154	4.0	3.8
Home-equity line of credit	9,184	12.0	297	7.8	3.2
Not reported	1,670	2.2	78	2.0	4.7

Source: Bureau of the Census, American Housing Survey for the United States: 2009, Internet site http://www.census.gov/hhes/www/housing/ahs/ahs09/ahs09.html; calculations by New Strategist

Table 6.24 Owners of New Homes by Mortgage Characteristics, 2009

The owners of new homes with mortgages owe a median of $189,805, or 86 percent of the median value of such homes. Twenty-four percent have mortgages that equal or exceed the value of their home.

(number and percent distribution of total homeowners and owners of homes built in the past four years, by mortgage characteristics, 2009; numbers in thousands)

	total		new homes		
	number	percent distribution	number	percent distribution	percent of total
Total homeowners	**76,428**	**100.0%**	**3,830**	**100.0%**	**5.0%**
Homeowners with mortgages	47,945	62.7	3,197	83.5	6.7
REMAINING YEARS MORTGAGED					
Homeowners with mortgages	**47,945**	**100.0**	**3,197**	**100.0**	**6.7**
Less than 8 years	6,160	12.8	53	1.7	0.9
8 to 12 years	5,188	10.8	97	3.0	1.9
13 to 17 years	5,077	10.6	162	5.1	3.2
18 to 22 years	6,568	13.7	63	2.0	1.0
23 to 27 years	14,948	31.2	971	30.4	6.5
28 to 32 years	9,569	20.0	1,808	56.6	18.9
33 years or more	164	0.3	16	0.5	9.9
Variable	271	0.6	26	0.8	9.4
Median years remaining	23	–	28	–	–
TOTAL OUTSTANDING PRINCIPAL					
Homeowners with mortgages	**47,945**	**100.0**	**3,197**	**100.0**	**6.7**
Under $10,000	2,797	5.8	24	0.7	0.8
$10,000 to $19,999	1,972	4.1	95	3.0	4.8
$20,000 to $29,999	1,877	3.9	32	1.0	1.7
$30,000 to $39,999	1,978	4.1	32	1.0	1.6
$40,000 to $49,999	2,338	4.9	37	1.2	1.6
$50,000 to $59,999	2,328	4.9	39	1.2	1.7
$60,000 to $69,999	2,504	5.2	73	2.3	2.9
$70,000 to $79,999	2,484	5.2	124	3.9	5.0
$80,000 to $99,999	4,420	9.2	161	5.0	3.6
$100,000 to $119,999	3,751	7.8	212	6.6	5.7
$120,000 to $149,999	5,029	10.5	314	9.8	6.3
$150,000 to $199,999	5,926	12.4	587	18.4	9.9
$200,000 to $249,999	3,575	7.5	447	14.0	12.5
$250,000 to $299,999	2,267	4.7	273	8.5	12.1
$300,000 or more	4,700	9.8	745	23.3	15.8
Median outstanding principal	$106,909	–	$189,805	–	–

	total		new homes		
	number	percent distribution	number	percent distribution	percent of total
CURRENT TOTAL LOAN AS PERCENT OF VALUE					
Homeowners with mortgages	**47,945**	**100.0%**	**3,197**	**100.0%**	**6.7%**
Less than 20 percent	6,174	12.9	94	2.9	1.5
20 to 39 percent	7,478	15.6	167	5.2	2.2
40 to 59 percent	8,524	17.8	330	10.3	3.9
60 to 79 percent	9,924	20.7	647	20.2	6.5
80 to 89 percent	5,128	10.7	521	16.3	10.2
90 to 99 percent	4,928	10.3	671	21.0	13.6
100 percent or more	5,789	12.1	766	23.9	13.2
Median percent of value	63.0%	–	86.0%	–	–

Note: "–" means not applicable.
Source: Bureau of the Census, American Housing Survey for the United States: 2009, Internet site http://www.census.gov/hhes/ www/housing/ahs/nationaldata.html; calculations by New Strategist

Table 6.25 Owners of New Homes by Monthly Principal and Interest Payments, 2009

The owners of new homes pay more per month than the average homeowner in principal and interest payments, a median of $1,198 versus $878. One in five pay $2,000 or more per month.

(number and percent distribution of total homeowners with mortgages and owners of homes built in the past four years, by monthly payment for principal and interest, 2009; numbers in thousands)

	total		new homes		
	number	percent distribution	number	percent distribution	percent of total
Homeowners with mortgages	**47,945**	**100.0%**	**3,197**	**100.0%**	**6.7%**
Less than $100	1,327	2.8	140	4.4	10.6
$100 to $199	1,072	2.2	49	1.5	4.6
$200 to $299	1,757	3.7	70	2.2	4.0
$300 to $399	2,873	6.0	89	2.8	3.1
$400 to $499	3,338	7.0	65	2.0	2.0
$500 to $599	3,816	8.0	75	2.3	2.0
$600 to $699	3,859	8.0	159	5.0	4.1
$700 to $799	3,443	7.2	185	5.8	5.4
$800 to $999	6,162	12.9	377	11.8	6.1
$1,000 to $1,249	5,879	12.3	478	15.0	8.1
$1,250 to $1,499	4,059	8.5	371	11.6	9.1
$1,500 to $1,999	4,786	10.0	489	15.3	10.2
$2,000 or more	5,574	11.6	649	20.3	11.7
Median monthly payment	$878	–	$1,198	–	–

Note: "–" means not applicable.
Source: Bureau of the Census, American Housing Survey for the United States: 2009, Internet site http://www.census.gov/hhes/www/housing/ahs/ahs09/ahs09.html; calculations by New Strategist

Table 6.26 Owners of New Homes by Monthly Housing Costs, 2009

Housing costs are much higher for the owners of new homes than for the average homeowner—a monthly median of $1,572 versus $1,000.

(number and percent distribution of total homeowners and owners of homes built in the past four years, by monthly housing costs, 2009; numbers in thousands)

	total		new homes		
	number	percent distribution	number	percent distribution	percent of total
Total homeowners	**76,428**	**100.0%**	**3,830**	**100.0%**	**5.0%**
Less than $100	475	0.6	3	0.1	0.5
$100 to $199	2,161	2.8	36	0.9	1.7
$200 to $299	5,351	7.0	166	4.3	3.1
$300 to $399	6,022	7.9	147	3.8	2.4
$400 to $499	5,308	6.9	131	3.4	2.5
$500 to $599	4,407	5.8	127	3.3	2.9
$600 to $699	3,735	4.9	86	2.2	2.3
$700 to $799	3,597	4.7	97	2.5	2.7
$800 to $999	7,139	9.3	196	5.1	2.7
$1,000 to $1,249	8,156	10.7	366	9.6	4.5
$1,250 to $1,499	6,828	8.9	422	11.0	6.2
$1,500 or $1,999	9,445	12.4	719	18.8	7.6
$2,000 to $2,499	5,422	7.1	466	12.2	8.6
$2,500 or more	8,383	11.0	870	22.7	10.4
Median monthly cost	$1,000	–	$1,572	–	–

Note: Housing costs include utilities, mortgages, real estate taxes, property insurance, and regime fees. "–" means not applicable.
Source: Bureau of the Census, American Housing Survey for the United States: 2009, Internet site http://www.census.gov/hhes/www/housing/ahs/ahs09/ahs09.html; calculations by New Strategist

Table 6.27 Owners of New Homes by Monthly Utility and Property Insurance Costs, 2009

The owners of new homes pay more for electricity than
the average homeowner, but less for piped gas.

(number and percent distribution of total homeowners and owners of homes built in the past four years, by average monthly costs for utilities, 2009; numbers in thousands)

	total		new homes		
	number	percent distribution	number	percent distribution	percent of total
MONTHLY COST OF ELECTRICITY					
Households using electricity	**76,378**	**100.0%**	**3,822**	**100.0%**	**5.0%**
Less than $25	442	0.6	12	0.3	2.6
$25 to $49	4,425	5.8	144	3.8	3.2
$50 to $74	11,016	14.4	385	10.1	3.5
$75 to $99	12,975	17.0	540	14.1	4.2
$100 to $149	21,237	27.8	1,251	32.7	5.9
$150 to $199	12,164	15.9	742	19.4	6.1
$200 or more	12,110	15.9	674	17.6	5.6
Included in rent, other fee, or obtained free	2,010	2.6	75	2.0	3.7
Median monthly cost	$117	–	$129	–	–
MONTHLY COST OF PIPED GAS					
Households using piped gas	**46,700**	**100.0**	**2,125**	**100.0**	**4.6**
Less than $25	1,410	3.0	81	3.8	5.8
$25 to $49	7,933	17.0	439	20.7	5.5
$50 to $74	11,196	24.0	511	24.0	4.6
$75 to $99	8,595	18.4	394	18.5	4.6
$100 to $149	9,694	20.8	440	20.7	4.5
$150 to $199	3,698	7.9	102	4.8	2.8
$200 or more	2,682	5.7	99	4.7	3.7
Included in rent, other fee, or obtained free	1,494	3.2	59	2.8	3.9
Median monthly cost	$80	–	$75	–	–
MONTHLY COST OF FUEL OIL					
Households using fuel oil	**6,409**	**100.0**	**55**	**100.0**	**0.9**
Less than $25	176	2.8	0	0.0	0.0
$25 to $49	325	5.1	6	10.4	1.8
$50 to $74	490	7.6	1	1.6	0.2
$75 to $99	725	11.3	5	8.6	0.7
$100 to $149	1,403	21.9	12	21.2	0.8
$150 to $199	1,052	16.4	7	12.7	0.7
$200 or more	1,701	26.5	16	28.7	0.9
Included in rent, other fee, or obtained free	536	8.4	9	16.3	1.7
Median monthly cost	$133	–	–	–	–

	total		new homes		
	number	percent distribution	number	percent distribution	percent of total
Water paid separately	**53,552**	–	**2,566**	–	**4.8%**
Median monthly cost	$38	–	$30	–	–
Trash paid separately	**44,974**	–	**2,068**	–	**4.6**
Median monthly cost	$21	–	$17	–	–
Property insurance paid	**72,313**	–	**3,749**	–	**5.2**
Median monthly cost	$55	–	$56	–	–

Note: "–" means not applicable or sample is too small to make a reliable estimate.
Source: Bureau of the Census, American Housing Survey for the United States: 2009, Internet site http://www.census.gov/hhes/ www/housing/ahs/ahs09/ahs09.html; calculations by New Strategist

Table 6.28 Owners of New Homes by Real Estate Taxes, 2009

The owners of new homes pay more in real estate taxes than the average homeowner, a median of $183 per month versus $150.

(number and percent distribution of total homeowners and owners of homes built in the past four years, by monthly cost of real estate taxes and taxes per $1,000 assessed value, 2009; numbers in thousands)

	total		new homes		
	number	percent distribution	number	percent distribution	percent of total
Total homeowners	**76,428**	**100.0%**	**4,673**	**100.0%**	**6.1%**
Monthly cost of real estate taxes					
Less than $25	7,751	10.1	423	9.0	5.5
$25 to $49	6,017	7.9	214	4.6	3.6
$50 to $74	6,565	8.6	240	5.1	3.7
$75 to $99	5,883	7.7	231	5.0	3.9
$100 to $124	6,494	8.5	272	5.8	4.2
$125 to $149	4,880	6.4	193	4.1	3.9
$150 to $199	9,140	12.0	434	9.3	4.7
$200 to $299	11,727	15.3	605	12.9	5.2
$300 to $399	6,171	8.1	379	8.1	6.1
$400 to $499	3,655	4.8	257	5.5	7.0
$500 to $599	2,884	3.8	181	3.9	6.3
$600 or more	5,260	6.9	401	8.6	7.6
Median monthly cost	$150	–	$183	–	–
Annual taxes paid per $1,000 value					
Less than $5	12,710	16.6	804	17.2	6.3
$5 to $9	21,383	28.0	1,057	22.6	4.9
$10 to $14	17,473	22.9	854	18.3	4.9
$15 to $19	9,992	13.1	407	8.7	4.1
$20 to $24	6,058	7.9	301	6.4	5.0
$25 or more	8,812	11.5	408	8.7	4.6
Median amount per $1,000 assessed	$10	–	$10	–	–

Note: "–" means not applicable.
Source: Bureau of the Census, American Housing Survey for the United States: 2009, Internet site http://www.census.gov/hhes/www/housing/ahs/ahs09/ahs09.html; calculations by New Strategist

Table 6.29 Owners of New Homes by Opinion of Home, 2009

Forty-eight percent of the owners of new homes rate their home a 10 on a scale of 1 (worst) to 10 (best), a much higher share than the 31 percent of all homeowners who give their home a top rating.

(number and percent distribution of total homeowners and owners of homes built in the past four years, by opinion of home, 2009; numbers in thousands)

	total		new homes		
	number	percent distribution	number	percent distribution	percent of total
Total homeowners	**76,428**	**100.0%**	**3,830**	**100.0%**	**5.0%**
1 (worst)	203	0.3	0	0.0	0.0
2	122	0.2	4	0.1	3.1
3	175	0.2	4	0.1	2.2
4	444	0.6	9	0.2	2.0
5	2,365	3.1	57	1.5	2.4
6	2,655	3.5	49	1.3	1.8
7	8,899	11.6	261	6.8	2.9
8	21,042	27.5	794	20.7	3.8
9	13,627	17.8	684	17.9	5.0
10 (best)	23,967	31.4	1,821	47.5	7.6
Not reported	2,926	3.8	149	3.9	5.1

Source: Bureau of the Census, American Housing Survey for the United States: 2009, Internet site http://www.census.gov/hhes/ www/housing/ahs/ahs09/ahs09.html; calculations by New Strategist

Table 6.30 Owners of New Homes by Opinion of Neighborhood, 2009

The owners of new homes have a higher opinion of their
neighborhood than the average homeowner, 37 percent
giving their neighborhood the highest rating.

(number and percent distribution of total homeowners and owners of homes built in the past four years, by opinion of neighborhood, 2009; numbers in thousands)

	total		new homes		
	number	percent distribution	number	percent distribution	percent of total
Total homeowners	**76,428**	**100.0%**	**3,830**	**100.0%**	**5.0%**
1 (worst)	338	0.4	10	0.3	3.1
2	289	0.4	24	0.6	8.4
3	459	0.6	12	0.3	2.5
4	766	1.0	35	0.9	4.6
5	3,356	4.4	144	3.8	4.3
6	3,454	4.5	151	3.9	4.4
7	9,603	12.6	371	9.7	3.9
8	20,808	27.2	891	23.3	4.3
9	13,454	17.6	628	16.4	4.7
10 (best)	20,891	27.3	1,419	37.1	6.8
No neighborhood	31	0.0	0	0.0	0.0
Not reported	2,979	3.9	145	3.8	4.9

Source: Bureau of the Census, American Housing Survey for the United States: 2009, Internet site http://www.census.gov/hhes/ www/housing/ahs/ahs09/ahs09.html; calculations by New Strategist

Table 6.31 Owners of New Homes by Neighborhood Problems, 2009

The owners of new homes are less likely than the average
homeowner to have bothersome street noise in their
neighborhood, but just as likely to have serious crime.

*(number and percent distribution of total homeowners and owners of homes built in the past four years, by selected
neighborhood problems, 2009; numbers in thousands)*

	total		new homes		
	number	percent distribution	number	percent distribution	percent of total
Total homeowners	**76,428**	**100.0%**	**3,830**	**100.0%**	**5.0%**
Bothersome street noise or heavy traffic	15,223	19.9	482	12.6	3.2
Serious crime in neighborhood in past 12 months	11,649	15.2	598	15.6	5.1
Bothersome odor problem	3,278	4.3	125	3.3	3.8
Noise problem	1,733	2.3	58	1.5	3.4
Litter or housing deterioration	1,101	1.4	18	0.5	1.6
Poor city or county services	440	0.6	11	0.3	2.5
Undesirable commercial, institutional, industrial establishments	247	0.3	20	0.5	8.1
People problem	2,706	3.5	129	3.4	4.8
Other problems	6,748	8.8	475	12.4	7.0

*Source: Bureau of the Census, American Housing Survey for the United States: 2009, Internet site http://www.census.gov/hhes/
www/housing/ahs/ahs09/ahs09.html; calculations by New Strategist*

Table 6.32 Owners of New Homes by Community Characteristics, 2009

Twelve percent of the owners of new homes live in gated communities.
Nine percent live in age-restricted communities. More than half have
open space, park, woods, farms, or ranches within 300 feet of their home.

(number and percent distribution of total homeowners and owners of homes built in the past four years, by community characteristics, 2009; numbers in thousands)

	total		new homes		
	number	percent distribution	number	percent distribution	percent of total
Total homeowners	**76,428**	**100.0%**	**3,830**	**100.0%**	**5.0%**
SECURED COMMUNITIES					
Total homeowners	**76,428**	**100.0**	**3,830**	**100.0**	**5.0**
Community access secured with walls or fences	5,337	7.0	459	12.0	8.6
Special entry system present	2,682	3.5	284	7.4	10.6
Special entry system not present	2,648	3.5	175	4.6	6.6
Community access not secured	70,410	92.1	3,336	87.1	4.7
SENIOR CITIZEN COMMUNITIES					
Households with persons aged 55 or older	**36,591**	**100.0**	**1,021**	**100.0**	**2.8**
Community age restricted	1,457	4.0	94	9.2	6.5
No age restriction	35,134	96.0	927	90.8	2.6
Community age specific	8,867	24.2	125	12.3	1.4
Community not age specific	24,100	65.9	735	72.0	3.1
COMMUNITY AMENITIES					
Total homeowners	**76,428**	**100.0**	**3,830**	**100.0**	**5.0**
Community center or clubhouse	14,707	19.2	818	21.4	5.6
Golf in community	12,762	16.7	329	8.6	2.6
Trails in community	15,300	20.0	839	21.9	5.5
Shuttle bus available	5,718	7.5	106	2.8	1.9
Daycare center	10,633	13.9	251	6.6	2.4
Private or restricted beach, park, or shoreline	15,124	19.8	584	15.2	3.9
DESCRIPTION OF AREA WITHIN 300 FEET OF HOME					
Total homeowners	**76,428**	**100.0**	**3,830**	**100.0**	**5.0**
Single-family detached homes	68,909	90.2	3,347	87.4	4.9
Single-family attached homes	10,973	14.4	521	13.6	4.8
Multiunit residential buildings	11,514	15.1	364	9.5	3.2
One-to-three-story multiunit is tallest	9,014	11.8	259	6.8	2.9
Four-to-six-story multiunit is tallest	1,464	1.9	65	1.7	4.4
Seven-or-more-story multiunit is tallest	929	1.2	40	1.1	4.3
Manufactured/mobile homes	10,276	13.4	512	13.4	5.0
Commercial or institutional	16,992	22.2	492	12.8	2.9
Industrial or factories	2,520	3.3	81	2.1	3.2
Open space, park, woods, farm, or ranch	33,110	43.3	2,169	56.6	6.6
Four-or-more-lane highway, railroad, or airport	10,380	13.6	324	8.5	3.1

	total		new homes		
	number	percent distribution	number	percent distribution	percent of total
BODIES OF WATER WITHIN 300 FEET OF HOME					
Total homeowners	**76,428**	**100.0%**	**3,830**	**100.0%**	**5.0%**
Water in area	13,824	18.1	859	22.4	6.2
With waterfront property	2,653	3.5	139	3.6	5.2
With flood plain	1,929	2.5	77	2.0	4.0
No water in area	62,083	81.2	2,920	76.2	4.7

Note: Numbers may not add to total because "not reported" is not shown.
Source: Bureau of the Census, American Housing Survey for the United States: 2009, Internet site http://www.census.gov/hhes/ www/housing/ahs/ahs09/ahs09.html; calculations by New Strategist

Table 6.33 Owners of New Homes by Public Services Available, 2009

The owners of new homes have fewer public services available to them. Only 26 percent have public transportation in their area. Among those with children under age 14, only 44 percent say the public elementary school is within one mile of their home.

(number and percent distribution of total homeowners and owners of homes built in the past four years, by public services available in neighborhood, 2009; numbers in thousands)

	total		new homes		
	number	percent distribution	number	percent distribution	percent of total
Total homeowners	**76,428**	**100.0%**	**3,830**	**100.0%**	**5.0%**
LOCAL ELEMENTARY SCHOOL					
Homeowners with children under age 14	**20,490**	**100.0**	**1,520**	**100.0**	**7.4**
Satisfactory public elementary school	16,966	82.8	1,223	80.5	7.2
Unsatisfactory public elementary school	1,422	6.9	119	7.8	8.4
Unsatisfactory public elementary school	**1,422**	**100.0**	**119**	**100.0**	**8.4**
Better than other area elementary schools	154	10.8	16	13.6	10.6
Same as other area elementary schools	490	34.4	55	46.5	11.3
Worse than other area elementary schools	696	49.0	41	34.1	5.8
Homeowners with children under age 14	**20,490**	**100.0**	**1,520**	**100.0**	**7.4**
Public elementary school less than one mile	11,571	56.5	662	43.6	5.7
Public elementary school more than one mile	7,785	38.0	756	49.7	9.7
PUBLIC TRANSPORTATION IN AREA					
Total homeowners	**76,428**	**100.0**	**3,830**	**100.0**	**5.0**
With public transportation	35,616	46.6	994	26.0	2.8
No public transportation	38,848	50.8	2,686	70.1	6.9
With public transportation, travel time to nearest stop	**35,616**	**100.0**	**994**	**100.0**	**2.8**
Less than 5 minutes	10,929	30.7	278	27.9	2.5
5 to 9 minutes	12,830	36.0	346	34.8	2.7
10 to 14 minutes	5,853	16.4	175	17.6	3.0
15 to 29 minutes	3,125	8.8	76	7.7	2.4
30 minutes or longer	449	1.3	13	1.3	2.9
With public transportation	**35,616**	**100.0**	**994**	**100.0**	**2.8**
Household uses it regularly for commute to school or work	3,817	10.7	100	10.0	2.6
Household does not use it regularly for commute to school or work	31,606	88.7	887	89.2	2.8

	total		new homes		
	number	percent distribution	number	percent distribution	percent of total
SHOPPING IN AREA					
Total homeowners	**76,428**	**100.0%**	**3,830**	**100.0%**	**5.0%**
Grocery stores or drugstores within 15 minutes of home	72,548	94.9	3,537	92.3	4.9
Satisfactory	70,400	92.1	3,386	88.4	4.8
Not satisfactory	1,805	2.4	135	3.5	7.5
No grocery stores or drugstores within 15 minutes of home	2,819	3.7	182	4.7	6.4
POLICE PROTECTION					
Total homeowners	**76,428**	**100.0**	**3,830**	**100.0**	**5.0**
Satisfactory police protection	69,633	91.1	3,399	88.7	4.9
Unsatisfactory police protection	4,800	6.3	294	7.7	6.1

Note: Numbers may not add to total because "not reported" is not shown.
Source: Bureau of the Census, American Housing Survey for the United States: 2009, Internet site http://www.census.gov/hhes/ www/housing/ahs/ahs09/ahs09.html; calculations by New Strategist

Table 6.34 Owners of New Homes Who Moved by Changes in Housing and Costs, 2009

The owners of new homes who recently moved are more likely than
the average homeowner who moved to have owned their previous residence,
and their housing costs are more likely to have increased with their move.

(number and percent distribution of total homeowners who have moved in the past year and those who moved into homes built in the past four years, by structure type of previous residence, tenure of previous residence, and change in housing costs, 2009; numbers in thousands)

	total		new homes		
	number	percent distribution	number	percent distribution	percent of total
STRUCTURE TYPE OF PREVIOUS RESIDENCE					
Homeowners who moved within United States	**4,341**	**100.0%**	**956**	**100.0%**	**22.0%**
House	2,595	59.8	631	66.0	24.3
Apartment	1,208	27.8	213	22.3	17.6
Mobile home	238	5.5	56	5.8	23.5
Other	119	2.7	25	2.6	20.6
Not reported	182	4.2	31	3.2	17.0
OWNERSHIP OF PREVIOUS RESIDENCE					
Homeowners who moved from house, apartment, or mobile home within United States	**4,041**	**100.0**	**900**	**100.0**	**22.3**
Owner-occupied	2,032	50.3	538	59.7	26.5
Renter-occupied	2,009	49.7	362	40.3	18.0
CHANGE IN HOUSING COSTS					
Homeowners who moved from house, apartment, or mobile home within United States	**4,041**	**100.0**	**900**	**100.0**	**22.3**
Increased with move	2,455	60.8	648	72.0	26.4
Decreased	801	19.8	94	10.4	11.7
Stayed about the same	663	16.4	127	14.2	19.2
Don't know	60	1.5	19	2.2	32.6
Not reported	62	1.5	11	1.2	17.8

Source: Bureau of the Census, American Housing Survey for the United States: 2009, Internet site http://www.census.gov/hhes/www/housing/ahs/ahs09/ahs09.html; calculations by New Strategist

Table 6.35 Owners of New Homes Who Moved by Reasons for Choosing Home, 2009

The owners of new homes who recently moved are far more likely than the average homeowner who recently moved to have chosen their home for its room layout/design—29 versus 17 percent. They are also more likely to say their present home is better than their previous home.

(number and percent distribution of total homeowning respondents who have moved in the past year and those who moved into homes built in the past four years, by reasons for choosing home, 2009; numbers in thousands)

	total		new homes		
	number	percent distribution	number	percent distribution	percent of total
Total homeowning respondents who moved	**4,623**	**100.0%**	**965**	**100.0%**	**20.9%**
Main reason for choice of present home					
All reported reasons equal	808	17.5	178	18.4	22.0
Financial reasons	1,008	21.8	143	14.8	14.2
Room layout/design	797	17.2	276	28.6	34.6
Kitchen	33	0.7	0	0.0	0.0
Size	377	8.2	75	7.8	20.0
Exterior appearance	125	2.7	14	1.5	11.4
Yard/trees/view	287	6.2	30	3.1	10.5
Quality of construction	186	4.0	85	8.8	45.7
Only one available	76	1.6	10	1.1	13.4
Other	636	13.7	94	9.8	14.9
Not reported	290	6.3	60	6.2	20.6
Present home compared with previous home					
Better	3,017	65.3	756	78.4	25.1
Worse	426	9.2	40	4.1	9.3
About the same	920	19.9	122	12.6	13.2
Not reported	261	5.6	47	4.9	18.2
Home search					
Now in house	3,929	100.0	893	100.0	22.7
Did not look at apartments	3,430	87.3	796	89.2	23.2
Looked at apartments too	305	7.8	68	7.6	22.3
Now in manufactured/mobile home	410	100.0	29	100.0	7.0
Did not look at apartments	304	74.1	22	77.7	7.3
Looked at apartments too	69	16.9	3	11.7	4.8
Now in apartment	285	100.0	44	100.0	15.4
Did not look at houses	181	63.6	22	49.3	11.9
Looked at houses too	92	32.2	19	42.8	20.4

Note: Total number of movers does not equal total movers in other tables because this table shows survey respondents who moved, not necessarily householders. Numbers may not add to total because "not reported" may not be shown.
Source: Bureau of the Census, American Housing Survey for the United States: 2009, Internet site http://www.census.gov/hhes/www/housing/ahs/ahs09/ahs09.html; calculations by New Strategist

Table 6.36 Owners of New Homes Who Moved by Reasons for Choosing Neighborhood, 2009

The owners of new homes who recently moved are more likely than the average homeowner who recently moved to say their new neighborhood is better. Their reasons for choosing their new neighborhood vary, convenience to job being the single most important factor.

(number and percent distribution of total homeowning respondents who moved in the past year, and those who moved into homes built in the past four years, by reasons for choosing neighborhood, 2009; numbers in thousands)

	total		new homes		
	number	percent distribution	number	percent distribution	percent of total
Total homeowning respondents who moved	**4,623**	**100.0%**	**965**	**100.0%**	**20.9%**
Neighborhood search					
Looked at just this neighborhood	1,590	34.4	314	32.5	19.7
Looked at other neighborhoods	2,802	60.6	619	64.2	22.1
Not reported	231	5.0	32	3.3	13.8
Main reason for choice of present neighborhood					
All reported reasons equal	551	11.9	108	11.2	19.6
Convenient to job	611	13.2	183	19.0	30.0
Convenient to friends or relatives	570	12.3	79	8.2	13.9
Convenient to leisure activities	87	1.9	15	1.6	17.2
Convenient to public transportation	29	0.6	0	0.0	0.0
Good schools	289	6.3	48	5.0	16.6
Other public services	36	0.8	12	1.3	34.2
Looks/design of neighborhood	635	13.7	145	15.0	22.8
House was most important consideration	801	17.3	153	15.9	19.1
Other	750	16.2	179	18.5	23.8
Not reported	264	5.7	43	4.4	16.1
Present neighborhood compared with previous neighborhood					
Better	2,253	48.7	544	56.4	24.1
Worse	347	7.5	42	4.3	12.0
About the same	1,555	33.6	279	28.9	17.9
Same neighborhood	179	3.9	49	5.0	27.3
Not reported	290	6.3	52	5.3	17.8

Note: Total number of movers does not equal total movers in other tables because this table shows survey respondents who moved, not necessarily householders.
Source: Bureau of the Census, American Housing Survey for the United States: 2009, Internet site http://www.census.gov/hhes/ www/housing/ahs/ahs09/ahs09.html; calculations by New Strategist

Table 6.37 Owners of New Homes Who Moved by Main Reason for Moving, 2009

The single most important reason for moving among owners of new homes who recently moved was to establish their own household, mentioned by 14 percent.

(number and percent distribution of total homeowning respondents who moved in the past year and those moving into homes built in the past four years, by main reason for move, 2009; numbers in thousands)

	total		new homes		
	number	percent distribution	number	percent distribution	percent of total
Total homeowning respondents who moved	**4,623**	**100.0%**	**965**	**100.0%**	**20.9%**
All reported reasons equal	203	4.4	36	3.7	17.6
Private displacement	5	0.1	0	0.0	0.0
Government displacement	8	0.2	2	0.3	32.7
Disaster loss (fire, flood, etc.)	24	0.5	9	1.0	39.2
New job or job transfer	370	8.0	101	10.5	27.4
To be closer to work/school/other	217	4.7	41	4.2	18.9
Other financial, employment related	119	2.6	27	2.8	23.0
To establish own household	594	12.8	138	14.3	23.3
Needed larger house or apartment	431	9.3	129	13.4	29.9
Married, widowed, divorced, or separated	284	6.1	41	4.2	14.4
Other family, personal reasons	368	8.0	44	4.5	11.9
Wanted better home	305	6.6	103	10.7	33.7
Change from renter to owner	685	14.8	88	9.1	12.8
Wanted lower maintenance	60	1.3	3	0.3	5.5
Other housing related reasons	168	3.6	39	4.1	23.4
Evicted from residence	14	0.3	0	0.0	0.0
Other	484	10.5	128	13.2	26.4
Not reported	286	6.2	35	3.6	12.3

Note: Total number of movers does not equal total movers in other tables because this table shows survey respondents who moved, not necessarily householders.
Source: Bureau of the Census, American Housing Survey for the United States: 2009, Internet site http://www.census.gov/hhes/ www/housing/ahs/ahs09/ahs09.html; calculations by New Strategist

7

Renters of New Homes

Nearly 1 million renters live in new homes.

With the rental market heating up, it is becoming increasingly important to determine the wants and needs of renters who choose to live in new housing units. In 2009, nearly 1 million renters were in new units. These renters are more likely than the average renter to be non-Hispanic white (61 versus 55 percent), have higher incomes (median household income of $37,000 versus $28,400), and have a college degree (28 versus 21 percent). The wants and needs of renters in new housing units may reveal the best opportunities for real estate developers in the years ahead.

■ Renters of new units are in larger-than-average homes. They have a median of 1,904 square feet versus 1,300 square feet in the average rental unit.

■ Renters of new units have more bathrooms than the average renter. Two-thirds are in units with two or more bathrooms. Among all renters, only 25 percent have two or more bathroom.

■ Renters of new units pay more per month for housing than the average renter (a median of $1,045 versus $808). But they have more amenities than the average renter: 51 percent have a community center or clubhouse in their development; 79 percent have a porch, deck, balcony, or patio; and 85 percent have central air conditioning.

Jobs are the most important reason for moving among renters of new homes who recently moved

(percent distribution by main reason for moving among renters who live in new homes and recently moved, 2009)

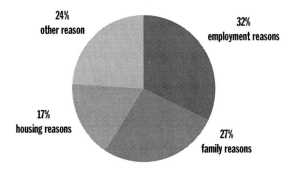

24% other reason

32% employment reasons

17% housing reasons

27% family reasons

Table 7.1 Renters of New Homes by Age, 2009

The renters of new homes are younger than the average renter,
with a median age of 35 versus 39 for all renters.

(number and percent distribution of total renters and renters of homes built in the past four years, by age of householder, 2009; numbers in thousands)

	total		new homes		
	number	percent distribution	number	percent distribution	percent of total
Total renters	**35,378**	**100.0%**	**941**	**100.0%**	**2.7%**
Under age 25	4,799	13.6	171	18.2	3.6
Aged 25 to 29	5,072	14.3	154	16.4	3.0
Aged 30 to 34	4,561	12.9	137	14.5	3.0
Aged 35 to 44	6,976	19.7	187	19.9	2.7
Aged 45 to 54	5,762	16.3	124	13.1	2.1
Aged 55 to 64	3,585	10.1	81	8.6	2.3
Aged 65 to 74	2,120	6.0	53	5.6	2.5
Aged 75 or older	2,503	7.1	35	3.7	1.4
Median age	39	–	35	–	–

Note: "–" means not applicable.
Source: Bureau of the Census, American Housing Survey for the United States: 2009, Internet site http://www.census.gov/hhes/ www/housing/ahs/ahs09/ahs09.html; calculations by New Strategist

Table 7.2 Renters of New Homes by Household Type and Age of Householder, 2009

The renters of new homes are more likely to be married
couples than the average renter—30 versus 25 percent.

(number and percent distribution of total renters and renters of homes built in the past four years, by household type and age of householder, 2009; numbers in thousands)

	total		new homes		
	number	percent distribution	number	percent distribution	percent of total
Total renters	**35,378**	**100.0%**	**941**	**100.0%**	**2.7%**
MARRIED-COUPLE HOUSEHOLDS	**8,808**	**24.9**	**285**	**30.3**	**3.2**
Under age 25	707	2.0	26	2.8	3.7
Aged 25 to 29	1,313	3.7	52	5.6	4.0
Aged 30 to 34	1,497	4.2	43	4.5	2.9
Aged 35 to 44	2,168	6.1	75	8.0	3.5
Aged 45 to 64	2,329	6.6	63	6.7	2.7
Aged 65 or older	793	2.2	25	2.7	3.2
TWO-OR-MORE-PERSON HOUSEHOLDS					
Female householders, no spouse present	**8,565**	**24.2**	**225**	**23.9**	**2.6**
Under age 45	6,119	17.3	178	19.0	2.9
Aged 45 to 64	2,030	5.7	42	4.4	2.1
Aged 65 or older	417	1.2	5	0.5	1.1
Male householders, no spouse present	**4,673**	**13.2**	**108**	**11.5**	**2.3**
Under age 45	3,629	10.3	97	10.4	2.7
Aged 45 to 64	895	2.5	8	0.9	0.9
Aged 65 or older	150	0.4	2	0.3	1.7
SINGLE-PERSON HOUSEHOLDS	**13,331**	**37.7**	**385**	**40.9**	**2.9**
Female householders	**6,743**	**19.1**	**187**	**19.9**	**2.8**
Under age 45	2,434	6.9	62	6.6	2.6
Aged 45 to 64	1,981	5.6	63	6.7	3.2
Aged 65 or older	2,328	6.6	62	6.6	2.7
Male householders	**6,588**	**18.6**	**198**	**21.1**	**3.0**
Under age 45	3,540	10.0	101	10.8	2.9
Aged 45 to 64	2,112	6.0	57	6.0	2.7
Aged 65 or older	936	2.6	40	4.3	4.3

Source: Bureau of the Census, American Housing Survey for the United States: 2009, Internet site http://www.census.gov/hhes/www/housing/ahs/ahs09/ahs09.html; calculations by New Strategist

Table 7.3 Renters of New Homes by Race and Hispanic Origin, 2009

The renters of new homes are more likely to be non-Hispanic
white than the average renter—61 versus 55 percent.

(number and percent distribution of total renters and renters of homes built in the past four years, by race and Hispanic origin, 2009; numbers in thousands)

	total		new homes		
	number	percent distribution	number	percent distribution	percent of total
Total renters	**35,378**	**100.0%**	**941**	**100.0%**	**2.7%**
American Indian	466	1.3	7	0.7	1.5
Asian	1,487	4.2	46	4.9	3.1
Black	7,446	21.0	196	20.8	2.6
Hispanic	6,300	17.8	98	10.4	1.6
White, non-Hispanic	19,427	54.9	576	61.2	3.0

Note: American Indians, Asians, blacks, and whites are those who identify themselves as being of the race alone. Numbers do not add to total because not all races are shown and Hispanics may be of any race.
Source: Bureau of the Census, American Housing Survey for the United States: 2009, Internet site http://www.census.gov/hhes/ www/housing/ahs/ahs09/ahs09.html; calculations by New Strategist

Table 7.4 Renters of New Homes by Household Income, 2009

The renters of new homes have higher household
incomes than the average renter, a median of $37,000.

(number and percent distribution of total renters and renters of homes built in the past four years, by household income, 2009; numbers in thousands)

	total		new homes		
	number	percent distribution	number	percent distribution	percent of total
Total renters	**35,378**	**100.0%**	**941**	**100.0%**	**2.7%**
Under $10,000	6,109	17.3	142	15.1	2.3
$10,000 to $19,999	6,115	17.3	98	10.4	1.6
$20,000 to $29,999	5,981	16.9	127	13.5	2.1
$30,000 to $39,999	4,477	12.7	130	13.8	2.9
$40,000 to $49,999	3,438	9.7	96	10.2	2.8
$50,000 to $59,999	2,326	6.6	55	5.8	2.4
$60,000 to $79,999	3,244	9.2	93	9.9	2.9
$80,000 to $99,999	1,663	4.7	84	8.9	5.1
$100,000 to $119,999	833	2.4	51	5.4	6.1
$120,000 or more	1,192	3.4	66	7.0	5.5
Median income	$28,400	–	$37,000	–	–

Note: "–" means not applicable.
Source: Bureau of the Census, American Housing Survey for the United States: 2009, Internet site http://www.census.gov/hhes/www/housing/ahs/ahs09/ahs09.html; calculations by New Strategist

Table 7.5 Renters of New Homes by Educational Attainment, 2009

The renters of new homes are more educated than the average renter.
Twenty-eight percent are college graduates versus 21 percent of all renters.

(number and percent distribution of total renters and the renters of homes built in the past four years, by educational attainment of householder, 2009; numbers in thousands)

	total		new homes		
	number	percent distribution	number	percent distribution	percent of total
Total renters	**35,378**	**100.0%**	**941**	**100.0%**	**2.7%**
Not a high school graduate	6,687	18.9	101	10.7	1.5
High school graduate only	11,724	33.1	291	30.9	2.5
Some college, no degree	6,924	19.6	214	22.8	3.1
Associate's degree	2,522	7.1	69	7.3	2.7
Bachelor's degree	5,183	14.7	189	20.1	3.6
Graduate or professional degree	2,338	6.6	77	8.2	3.3
High school graduate or higher	28,691	81.1	840	89.3	2.9
Some college or higher	16,967	48.0	549	58.3	3.2
Bachelor's degree or higher	7,521	21.3	266	28.3	3.5

Source: Bureau of the Census, American Housing Survey for the United States: 2009, Internet site http://www.census.gov/hhes/www/housing/ahs/ahs09/ahs09.html; calculations by New Strategist

Table 7.6 Renters of New Homes by Household Size, 2009

Renters of new homes are slightly less likely to live alone than all renters. Thirty-four percent live by themselves compared with 38 percent of all renters.

(number and percent distribution of total renters and renters of homes built in the past four years, by number of persons living in home, 2009; numbers in thousands)

	total		new homes		
	number	percent distribution	number	percent distribution	percent of total
Total renters	**35,378**	**100.0%**	**941**	**100.0%**	**2.7%**
One person	13,331	37.7	323	34.4	2.4
Two persons	9,453	26.7	271	28.8	2.9
Three persons	5,345	15.1	145	15.4	2.7
Four persons	4,016	11.4	121	12.9	3.0
Five persons	1,910	5.4	50	5.4	2.6
Six persons	780	2.2	13	1.4	1.7
Seven or more persons	543	1.5	17	1.8	3.2

Source: Bureau of the Census, American Housing Survey for the United States: 2009, Internet site http://www.census.gov/hhes/ www/housing/ahs/ahs09/ahs09.html; calculations by New Strategist

Table 7.7 Renters of New Homes by Type of Structure, 2009

Sixty-one percent of renters living in new homes are in multiunit buildings. Only 26 percent live in a single-family detached house.

(number and percent distribution of total renters and renters of homes built in the past four years, by number of units in structure, 2009; numbers in thousands)

	total		new homes		
	number	percent distribution	number	percent distribution	percent of total
Total renters	**35,378**	**100.0%**	**941**	**100.0%**	**2.7%**
One, detached	9,755	27.6	244	25.9	2.5
One, attached	2,021	5.7	93	9.9	4.6
Multiunit buildings	22,181	62.7	576	61.2	2.6
Two to four	6,998	19.8	116	12.3	1.7
Five to nine	4,637	13.1	78	8.3	1.7
10 to 19	4,178	11.8	118	12.5	2.8
20 to 49	3,131	8.9	119	12.6	3.8
50 or more	3,237	9.1	145	15.4	4.5
Mobile home	1,421	4.0	28	3.0	2.0

Source: Bureau of the Census, American Housing Survey for the United States: 2009, Internet site http://www.census.gov/hhes/ www/housing/ahs/ahs09/ahs09.html; calculations by New Strategist

Table 7.8 Renters of New Homes by Square Footage of Unit and Lot Size, 2009

The renters of new homes have much larger houses than the
average renter, with a median of 1,904 square feet.

(number and percent distribution of total renters and renters of homes built in the past four years, by square footage and lot size, 2009; numbers in thousands)

	total		new homes		
	number	percent distribution	number	percent distribution	percent of total
Square footage of home, total*	**11,176**	**100.0%**	**272**	**100.0%**	**2.4%**
Less than 500 sq. ft.	220	2.0	0	0.0	0.0
500 to 749 sq. ft.	686	6.1	4	1.5	0.6
750 to 999 sq. ft.	1,495	13.4	0	0.0	0.0
1,000 to 1,499 sq. ft.	3,441	30.8	44	16.3	1.3
1,500 to 1,999 sq. ft.	2,235	20.0	74	27.1	3.3
2,000 to 2,499 sq. ft.	1,134	10.1	79	29.1	7.0
2,500 to 2,999 sq. ft.	429	3.8	25	9.3	5.9
3,000 to 3,999 sq. ft.	301	2.7	9	3.3	3.0
4,000 or more sq. ft.	243	2.2	8	2.9	3.2
Not reported	992	8.9	29	10.7	2.9
Median square footage	1,300	–	1,904	–	–
Lot size, total**	**12,823**	**100.0**	**342**	**100.0**	**2.7**
Less than one-eighth acre	2,717	21.2	78	22.9	2.9
One-eighth up to one-quarter acre	4,022	31.4	112	32.8	2.8
One-quarter up to one-half acre	2,084	16.3	75	21.9	3.6
One-half up to one acre	1,162	9.1	23	6.6	1.9
One to five acres	2,120	16.5	26	7.6	1.2
Five to ten acres	205	1.6	7	2.1	3.5
10 or more acres	513	4.0	21	6.1	4.0
Median lot size (acres)	0.22	–	0.21	–	–

* Single-family detached and mobile homes only.
** Homes in two-or-more-unit buildings are excluded.
Note: "–" means not applicable.
Source: Bureau of the Census, American Housing Survey for the United States: 2009, Internet site http://www.census.gov/hhes/
www/housing/ahs/ahs09/ahs09.html; calculations by New Strategist

Table 7.9 Renters of New Homes by Number of Rooms in Home, 2009

The renters of new homes have more rooms than the average renter. Forty-six percent have three or more bedrooms, and 66 percent have two or more bathrooms. More than one in four have a room used for business.

(number and percent distribution of total renters and renters of homes built in the past four years, by number and type of rooms, 2009; numbers in thousands)

	total		new homes		
	number	percent distribution	number	percent distribution	percent of total
Total renters	**35,378**	**100.0%**	**941**	**100.0%**	**2.7%**
Number of rooms					
One room	326	0.9	2	0.2	0.6
Two rooms	879	2.5	10	1.1	1.2
Three rooms	7,675	21.7	160	17.0	2.1
Four rooms	11,354	32.1	237	25.2	2.1
Five rooms	8,212	23.2	260	27.6	3.2
Six rooms	4,232	12.0	161	17.1	3.8
Seven rooms	1,735	4.9	75	8.0	4.3
Eight rooms	622	1.8	18	1.9	2.9
Nine rooms	214	0.6	10	1.1	4.8
10 or more rooms	130	0.4	8	0.8	5.8
Number of bedrooms					
None	744	2.1	12	1.3	1.7
One bedroom	9,720	27.5	185	19.7	1.9
Two bedrooms	14,200	40.1	314	33.4	2.2
Three bedrooms	8,359	23.6	341	36.3	4.1
Four or more bedrooms	2,354	6.7	88	9.3	3.7
Number of bathrooms					
None	229	0.6	0	0.0	0.0
One bathroom	22,894	64.7	284	30.1	1.2
One-and-one-half bathrooms	3,575	10.1	36	3.9	1.0
Two or more bathrooms	8,680	24.5	621	66.0	7.2
With room used for business	**8,040**	**22.7**	**246**	**26.1**	**3.1**
Business only	3,757	10.6	130	13.8	3.5
Business and other use	4,283	12.1	116	12.3	2.7

Source: Bureau of the Census, American Housing Survey for the United States: 2009, Internet site http://www.census.gov/hhes/ www/housing/ahs/ahs09/ahs09.html; calculations by New Strategist

Table 7.10 Renters of New Homes by Presence of Kitchen, Laundry, and Safety Equipment, 2009

The renters of new homes are much more likely than the average renter to have a dishwasher, 93 versus 46 percent. They are also more likely to have a washer, dryer, and sprinkler system in their home.

(number and percent of total renters and renters of homes built in the past four years, by presence of kitchen, laundry, and safety equipment, 2009; numbers in thousands)

	total		new homes		
	number	percent distribution	number	percent distribution	percent of total
Total renters	**35,378**	**100.0%**	**941**	**100.0%**	**2.7%**
With complete kitchen equipment	34,004	96.1	915	97.2	2.7
Dishwasher	16,393	46.3	874	92.9	5.3
Washing machine	19,545	55.2	819	87.1	4.2
Clothes dryer	18,343	51.8	791	84.0	4.3
Disposal in kitchen sink	15,933	45.0	739	78.5	4.6
Trash compactor	730	2.1	54	5.7	7.4
Working smoke detector	32,565	92.0	926	98.4	2.8
Fire extinguisher	11,980	33.9	385	40.9	3.2
Sprinkler system inside home	3,081	8.7	415	44.1	13.5
Carbon monoxide detector	9,007	25.5	254	27.0	2.8

Note: Complete kitchen equipment includes a sink, refrigerator, and oven or burners.
Source: Bureau of the Census, American Housing Survey for the United States: 2009, Internet site http://www.census.gov/hhes/ www/housing/ahs/ahs09/ahs09.html; calculations by New Strategist

Table 7.11 Renters of New Homes by Type of Heating Equipment, 2009

The 68 percent majority of rented new homes are heated by a warm-air furnace, while another 23 percent use an electric heat pump.

(number and percent distribution of total renters and renters of homes built in the past four years, by presence and type of heating equipment, 2009; numbers in thousands)

	total		new homes		
	number	percent distribution	number	percent distribution	percent of total
Total renters	35,378	100.0%	941	100.0%	2.7%
Main heating equipment					
Warm-air furnace	19,450	55.0	639	67.9	3.3
Steam or hot water system	5,012	14.2	29	3.1	0.6
Electric heat pump	3,500	9.9	218	23.1	6.2
Built-in electric units	2,641	7.5	33	3.5	1.2
Floor, wall, or other built-in hot air units without ducts	2,760	7.8	15	1.6	0.5
Room heaters with flue	370	1.0	3	0.3	0.8
Room heaters without flue	414	1.2	0	0.0	0.0
Portable electric heaters	632	1.8	0	0.0	0.0
Stoves	190	0.5	0	0.0	0.0
Fireplaces with inserts	18	0.0	0	0.0	0.0
Fireplaces without inserts	7	0.0	0	0.0	0.0
Other	154	0.4	2	0.2	1.5
Cooking stove	49	0.1	0	0.0	0.0
None	180	0.5	3	0.3	1.5
Renters with additional heating equipment					
Warm-air furnace	26	0.1	2	0.3	9.7
Steam or hot water system	5	0.0	0	0.0	0.0
Electric heat pump	6	0.0	0	0.0	0.0
Built-in electric units	454	1.3	8	0.9	1.8
Floor, wall, or other built-in hot air units without ducts	12	0.0	0	0.0	0.0
Room heaters with flue	106	0.3	0	0.0	0.0
Room heaters without flue	264	0.7	0	0.0	0.0
Portable electric heaters	3,832	10.8	42	4.5	1.1
Stoves	425	1.2	13	1.4	3.2
Fireplaces with inserts	464	1.3	41	4.3	8.8
Fireplaces without inserts	896	2.5	25	2.6	2.8
Other	83	0.2	4	0.5	5.2
Cooking stove	17	0.0	0	0.0	0.0
None	28,863	81.6	813	86.4	2.8

Source: Bureau of the Census, American Housing Survey for the United States: 2009, Internet site http://www.census.gov/hhes/ www/housing/ahs/ahs09/ahs09.html; calculations by New Strategist

Table 7.12 Renters of New Homes with Air Conditioning, 2009

Eighty-five percent of the renters of new homes report that
their home has central air conditioning, a much greater
share than the 51 percent of all renters with central air.

(number and percent distribution of total renters and renters of homes built in the past four years, by presence and type of air conditioning equipment, 2009; numbers in thousands)

	total		new homes		
	number	percent distribution	number	percent distribution	percent of total
Total renters	**35,378**	**100.0%**	**941**	**100.0%**	**2.7%**
Renters with air conditioning	29,035	82.1	852	90.5	2.9
Central	18,161	51.3	797	84.7	4.4
Additional central	920	2.6	60	6.4	6.6
One room unit	6,229	17.6	22	2.3	0.4
Two room units	3,332	9.4	26	2.7	0.8
Three or more room units	1,314	3.7	6	0.7	0.5

Source: Bureau of the Census, American Housing Survey for the United States: 2009, Internet site http://www.census.gov/hhes/ www/housing/ahs/ahs09/ahs09.html; calculations by New Strategist

Table 7.13 Renters of New Homes by Primary Source of Water and Sewage Disposal System, 2009

Renters of new homes are more likely than the average renter
to use a well as their source of water. They are slightly more
likely to say their water is safe to drink.

(number and percent of total renters and renters of homes built in the past four years, by primary source of water and type of sewage disposal system, 2009; numbers in thousands)

	total		new homes		
	number	percent distribution	number	percent distribution	percent of total
Total renters	35,378	100.0%	941	100.0%	2.7%
Source of water					
Public system or private company	33,655	95.1	879	93.4	2.6
Well	1,660	4.7	62	6.6	3.8
Safety of primary source of water					
Safe to drink	31,095	87.9	855	90.9	2.8
Not safe to drink	3,882	11.0	77	8.2	2.0
Sewage disposal system					
Public sewer	32,732	92.5	858	91.2	2.6
Septic tank, cesspool, chemical toilet	2,640	7.5	83	8.8	3.2

Note: Numbers do not sum to total because "other" and "not reported" are not shown.
Source: Bureau of the Census, American Housing Survey for the United States: 2009, Internet site http://www.census.gov/hhes/ www/housing/ahs/ahs09/ahs09.html; calculations by New Strategist

Table 7.14 Renters of New Homes by Fuels Used, 2009

The renters of new homes are much more likely than the average renter to have all-electric homes. Fifty-six percent of the renters of new homes have all-electric units compared with 35 percent of all renters.

(number and percent of total renters and renters of homes built in the past four years, by types of fuels used, 2009; numbers in thousands)

	total		new homes		
	number	percent distribution	number	percent distribution	percent of total
Total renters	**35,378**	**100.0%**	**941**	**100.0%**	**2.7%**
Electricity	35,368	100.0	941	100.0	2.7
All-electric homes	12,215	34.5	531	56.4	4.3
Piped gas	21,186	59.9	381	40.5	1.8
Bottled gas	1,425	4.0	32	3.4	2.2
Fuel oil	2,800	7.9	19	2.1	0.7
Kerosene or other liquid fuel	164	0.5	3	0.3	1.7
Coal or coke	7	0.0	0	0.0	0.0
Wood	278	0.8	13	1.4	4.8
Solar energy	17	0.0	0	0.0	0.0
Other	151	0.4	0	0.0	0.0

Note: Numbers do not add to total because many households use more than one fuel.
Source: Bureau of the Census, American Housing Survey for the United States: 2009, Internet site http://www.census.gov/hhes/ www/housing/ahs/ahs09/ahs09.html; calculations by New Strategist

Table 7.15 Renters of New Homes by Primary Heating Fuel Used, 2009

The 66 percent majority of the renters of new homes
use electricity as their primary heating fuel.

(number and percent of total renters and renters of homes built in the past four years, by primary heating fuel used, 2009; numbers in thousands)

	total		new homes		
	number	percent distribution	number	percent distribution	percent of total
TOTAL RENTERS	**35,378**	**100.0%**	**941**	**100.0%**	**2.7%**
Renters using heating fuel	**35,198**	**100.0**	**938**	**100.0**	**2.7**
Electricity	15,632	44.4	619	66.0	4.0
Piped gas	15,573	44.2	265	28.3	1.7
Bottled gas	929	2.6	28	3.0	3.0
Fuel oil	2,521	7.2	9	1.0	0.4
Kerosene or other liquid fuel	154	0.4	3	0.3	1.8
Coal or coke	7	0.0	0	0.0	0.0
Wood	277	0.8	13	1.4	4.9
Solar energy	3	0.0	0	0.0	0.0
Other	101	0.3	0	0.0	0.0

Source: Bureau of the Census, American Housing Survey for the United States: 2009, Internet site http://www.census.gov/hhes/www/housing/ahs/ahs09/ahs09.html; calculations by New Strategist

Table 7.16 Renters of New Homes by Cooking, Water Heating, and Clothes Dryer Fuels Used, 2009

The renters of new homes are more likely than the average
renter to use electricity as their cooking and water heating fuel.

(number and percent of total renters and renters of homes built in the past four years, by cooking, water heating, and clothes dryer fuels used, 2009; numbers in thousands)

	total		new homes		
	number	percent distribution	number	percent distribution	percent of total
COOKING FUEL					
Renters using cooking fuel	**35,235**	**100.0%**	**941**	**100.0%**	**2.7%**
Electricity	21,567	61.2	706	75.0	3.3
Piped gas	12,923	36.7	214	22.7	1.7
Bottled gas	726	2.1	21	2.2	2.9
Kerosene or other liquid fuel	7	0.0	0	0.0	0.0
Wood	12	0.0	0	0.0	0.0
WATER HEATING FUEL					
Renters with hot piped water	**35,319**	**100.0**	**941**	**100.0**	**2.7**
Electricity	16,095	45.6	605	64.3	3.8
Piped gas	16,865	47.7	305	32.5	1.8
Bottled gas	692	2.0	19	2.1	2.8
Fuel oil	1,604	4.5	11	1.1	0.7
Kerosene or other liquid fuel	3	0.0	0	0.0	0.0
Coal or coke	0	0.0	0	0.0	0.0
Wood	9	0.0	0	0.0	0.0
Solar energy	14	0.0	0	0.0	0.0
Other	39	0.1	0	0.0	0.0
CLOTHES DRYER FUEL					
Renters with clothes dryers	**18,343**	**100.0**	**791**	**84.0**	**4.3**
Electricity	15,438	84.2	682	72.4	4.4
Piped gas	2,785	15.2	107	11.4	3.8
Other	120	0.7	2	0.2	1.8

Source: Bureau of the Census, American Housing Survey for the United States: 2009, Internet site http://www.census.gov/hhes/ www/housing/ahs/ahs09/ahs09.html; calculations by New Strategist

Table 7.17 Renters of New Homes by Amenities of Home, 2009

The renters of new homes are more likely than the average
home renter to have a garage or carport—53 versus 37 percent.

(number and percent of total renters and renters of homes built in the past four years, by selected amenities of home, 2009; numbers in thousands)

	total		new homes		
	number	percent distribution	number	percent distribution	percent of total
Total renters	**35,378**	**100.0%**	**941**	**100.0%**	**2.7%**
Porch, deck, balcony, or patio	24,984	70.6	740	78.7	3.0
Telephone available	34,196	96.7	861	91.5	2.5
Usable fireplace	4,540	12.8	151	16.0	3.3
Separate dining room	9,959	28.2	273	29.0	2.7
With two or more living or recreation rooms	2,934	8.3	143	15.2	4.9
Garage or carport					
Yes	13,258	37.5	497	52.8	3.7
No, but off-street parking included	17,676	50.0	380	40.4	2.2
No cars, trucks, or vans	6,669	18.9	94	10.0	1.4

Source: Bureau of the Census, American Housing Survey for the United States: 2009, Internet site http://www.census.gov/hhes/ www/housing/ahs/ahs09/ahs09.html; calculations by New Strategist

Table 7.18 **Renters of New Homes by Deficiencies of Home, 2009**

Few renters in new homes report any deficiencies.

(number and percent distribution of total renters and renters of homes built in the past four years, by selected deficiencies of housing unit, 2009; numbers in thousands)

	total		new homes		
	number	percent distribution	number	percent distribution	percent of total
Total renters	**35,378**	**100.0%**	**941**	**100.0%**	**2.7%**
Signs of rats in last three months	258	0.7	0	0.0	0.0
Signs of mice in last three months	2,138	6.0	13	1.3	0.6
Signs of rodents, not sure which kind, in last three months	189	0.5	0	0.0	0.0
Holes in floor	560	1.6	0	0.0	0.0
Open cracks or holes (interior)	2,416	6.8	18	1.9	0.7
Broken plaster, peeling paint (interior)	1,132	3.2	3	0.4	0.3
No electrical wiring	26	0.1	3	0.3	10.3
Exposed wiring	134	0.4	4	0.4	2.7
Rooms without electric outlets	624	1.8	11	1.2	1.8

Source: Bureau of the Census, American Housing Survey for the United States: 2009, Internet site http://www.census.gov/hhes/ www/housing/ahs/ahs09/ahs09.html; calculations by New Strategist

Table 7.19 Renters of New Homes by Housing Equipment Failures, 2009

The renters of new homes are less likely than the average renter to experience a variety of problems such as water leakage from inside or outside the structure and being uncomfortably cold for a day or more during the past winter.

(number and percent distribution of total renters and renters of homes built in the past four years, by type of equipment failure, 2009; numbers in thousands)

	total		new homes		
	number	percent distribution	number	percent distribution	percent of total
WATER SUPPLY STOPPAGE					
Renters with piped water	**35,319**	**100.0%**	**941**	**100.0%**	**2.7%**
No stoppage in last three months	33,370	94.5	908	96.5	2.7
With stoppage in last three months	1,601	4.5	18	1.9	1.1
Not reported	348	1.0	15	1.6	4.3
FLUSH TOILET BREAKDOWNS					
Renters with flush toilets	**35,313**	**100.0**	**941**	**100.0**	**2.7**
With at least one working toilet at all times, last three months	33,766	95.6	923	98.1	2.7
With no working toilet at least once in last three months	1,210	3.4	3	0.4	0.3
Not reported	337	1.0	15	1.6	4.4
WATER LEAKAGE DURING LAST 12 MONTHS					
Total renters	**35,378**	**100.0**	**941**	**100.0**	**2.7**
No leakage from within structure	31,184	88.1	884	94.0	2.8
With leakage from within structure*	3,836	10.8	42	4.4	1.1
Fixtures backed up or overflowed	952	2.7	4	0.4	0.4
Pipes leaked	1,664	4.7	22	2.3	1.3
Broken water heater	327	0.9	2	0.2	0.6
Other or unknown	1,088	3.1	14	1.5	1.3
Leakage not reported	357	1.0	15	1.6	4.1
No leakage from outside structure	31,906	90.2	891	94.7	2.8
With leakage from outside structure*	3,121	8.8	35	3.8	1.1
Roof	1,579	4.5	10	1.1	0.7
Basement	538	1.5	8	0.8	1.4
Walls, windows, or doors	795	2.2	6	0.7	0.8
Other or not reported	410	1.2	11	1.2	2.7
Leakage not reported	350	1.0	15	1.6	4.2

	total		new homes		
	number	percent distribution	number	percent distribution	percent of total
HEATING PROBLEMS					
Renters with heating equipment and occupying home last winter	**31,244**	**100.0%**	**749**	**100.0%**	**2.4%**
Not uncomfortably cold for 24 or more hours last winter	26,957	86.3	689	92.1	2.6
Uncomfortably cold for 24 or more hours last winter*	3,622	11.6	43	5.7	1.2
Equipment breakdown	1,144	3.7	9	1.1	0.8
Utility interruption	496	1.6	18	2.4	3.6
Inadequate heating capacity	675	2.2	5	0.7	0.8
Inadequate insulation	523	1.7	6	0.8	1.1
Cost of heating	421	1.3	0	0.0	0.0
Other	677	2.2	3	0.5	0.5
Not reported	666	2.1	17	2.3	2.6
ELECTRICAL PROBLEMS					
Renters with electrical wiring	**35,351**	**100.0**	**938**	**100.0**	**2.7**
No fuses or breakers blown in last three months	31,879	90.2	867	92.4	2.7
With fuses or breakers blown in last three months	3,082	8.7	61	6.5	2.0
Not reported	391	1.1	11	1.2	2.8

Figures do not add to total because more than one problem may have occurred.

Source: Bureau of the Census, American Housing Survey for the United States: 2009, Internet site http://www.census.gov/hhes/www/housing/ahs/ahs09/ahs09.html; calculations by New Strategist

Table 7.20 Renters of New Homes by Monthly Housing Costs, 2009

Housing costs are higher for the renters of new homes than for the average renter—a monthly median of $1,045 versus $808.

(number and percent distribution of total renters and renters of homes built in the past four years, by monthly housing costs, 2009; numbers in thousands)

| | total | | new homes | | |
	number	percent distribution	number	percent distribution	percent of total
Total renters	**35,378**	**100.0%**	**941**	**100.0%**	**2.7%**
Less than $100	248	0.7	5	0.5	2.0
$100 to $199	728	2.1	24	2.6	3.3
$200 to $299	1,381	3.9	19	2.0	1.4
$300 to $399	1,359	3.8	16	1.7	1.2
$400 to $499	2,094	5.9	35	3.7	1.7
$500 to $599	2,985	8.4	49	5.2	1.6
$600 to $699	3,808	10.8	43	4.6	1.1
$700 to $799	3,709	10.5	89	9.5	2.4
$800 to $999	6,060	17.1	151	16.1	2.5
$1,000 to $1,249	4,777	13.5	174	18.5	3.7
$1,250 to $1,499	2,631	7.4	100	10.6	3.8
$1,500 or $1,999	2,247	6.4	114	12.1	5.1
$2,000 to $2,499	718	2.0	46	4.9	6.4
$2,500 or more	596	1.7	53	5.7	9.0
No cash rent	2,037	5.8	23	2.4	1.1
Median monthly cost	$808	–	$1,045	–	–

Note: Housing costs include rent, utilities, and property insurance. "–" means not applicable.
Source: Bureau of the Census, American Housing Survey for the United States: 2009, Internet site http://www.census.gov/hhes/ www/housing/ahs/ahs09/ahs09.html; calculations by New Strategist

Table 7.21 Renters of New Homes by Monthly Utility and Property Insurance Costs, 2009

The renters of new homes pay more for electricity than the average renter, $98 per month versus $84.

(number and percent distribution of total renters and renters of homes built in the past four years, by average monthly costs for utilities, 2009; numbers in thousands)

	total		new homes		
	number	percent distribution	number	percent distribution	percent of total
MONTHLY COST OF ELECTRICITY					
Renters using electricity	**35,368**	**100.0%**	**941**	**100.0%**	**2.7%**
Less than $25	1,259	3.6	22	2.4	1.8
$25 to $49	5,426	15.3	80	8.5	1.5
$50 to $74	6,535	18.5	144	15.3	2.2
$75 to $99	5,469	15.5	188	20.0	3.4
$100 to $149	6,589	18.6	254	27.0	3.9
$150 to $199	2,795	7.9	102	10.8	3.6
$200 or more	2,341	6.6	56	6.0	2.4
Included in rent, other fee, or obtained free	4,954	14.0	94	10.0	1.9
Median monthly cost	$84	–	$98	–	–
MONTHLY COST OF PIPED GAS					
Renters using piped gas	**21,186**	**100.0**	**381**	**100.0**	**1.8**
Less than $25	2,447	11.5	36	9.5	1.5
$25 to $49	4,469	21.1	103	27.0	2.3
$50 to $74	3,581	16.9	90	23.7	2.5
$75 to $99	2,054	9.7	28	7.5	1.4
$100 to $149	1,884	8.9	43	11.2	2.3
$150 to $199	643	3.0	10	2.6	1.5
$200 or more	518	2.4	7	1.9	1.4
Included in rent, other fee, or obtained free	5,588	26.4	64	16.8	1.1
Median monthly cost	$55	–	$54	–	–
Water paid separately	**9,237**	–	**321**	–	**3.5**
Median monthly cost	$29	–	$25	–	–
Trash paid separately	**7,551**	–	**228**	–	**3.0**
Median monthly cost	$20	–	$20	–	–
Property insurance paid	**9,397**	–	**367**	–	**3.9**
Median monthly cost	$16	–	$17	–	–

Note: "–" means not applicable or sample is too small to make a reliable estimate.
Source: Bureau of the Census, American Housing Survey for the United States: 2009, Internet site http://www.census.gov/hhes/ www/housing/ahs/ahs09/ahs09.html; calculations by New Strategist

Table 7.22 Renters of New Homes by Opinion of Home, 2009

Thirty-five percent of the renters of new homes rate their home a 10 on a scale of 1 (worst) to 10 (best), a much higher share than the 20 percent of all renters who give their home a top rating.

(number and percent distribution of total renters and renters of homes built in the past four years, by opinion of home, 2009; numbers in thousands)

	total		new homes		
	number	percent distribution	number	percent distribution	percent of total
Total renters	**35,378**	**100.0%**	**941**	**100.0%**	**2.7%**
1 (worst)	327	0.9	0	0.0	0.0
2	209	0.6	5	0.5	2.3
3	436	1.2	2	0.2	0.5
4	708	2.0	5	0.6	0.7
5	2,910	8.2	20	2.1	0.7
6	2,553	7.2	27	2.8	1.0
7	6,146	17.4	116	12.3	1.9
8	9,625	27.2	212	22.5	2.2
9	4,217	11.9	196	20.8	4.7
10 (best)	6,941	19.6	328	34.8	4.7
Not reported	1,306	3.7	30	3.2	2.3

Source: Bureau of the Census, American Housing Survey for the United States: 2009, Internet site http://www.census.gov/hhes/www/housing/ahs/ahs09/ahs09.html; calculations by New Strategist

Table 7.23 Renters of New Homes by Opinion of Neighborhood, 2009

The renters of new homes have a higher opinion of their neighborhood than the average renter, 26 percent giving their neighborhood the highest rating.

(number and percent distribution of total renters and renters of homes built in the past four years, by opinion of neighborhood, 2009; numbers in thousands)

	total		new homes		
	number	percent distribution	number	percent distribution	percent of total
Total renters	**35,378**	**100.0%**	**941**	**100.0%**	**2.7%**
1 (worst)	499	1.4	13	1.4	2.7
2	348	1.0	5	0.5	1.5
3	543	1.5	3	0.3	0.6
4	867	2.5	23	2.4	2.7
5	2,976	8.4	32	3.4	1.1
6	2,465	7.0	60	6.3	2.4
7	5,164	14.6	118	12.5	2.3
8	8,986	25.4	265	28.2	2.9
9	4,563	12.9	149	15.8	3.3
10 (best)	7,575	21.4	244	25.9	3.2
No neighborhood	29	0.1	0	0.0	0.0
Not reported	1,362	3.8	30	3.2	2.2

Source: Bureau of the Census, American Housing Survey for the United States: 2009, Internet site http://www.census.gov/hhes/ www/housing/ahs/ahs09/ahs09.html; calculations by New Strategist

Table 7.24 Renters of New Homes by Neighborhood Problems, 2009

The renters of new homes are almost as likely as the average renter to have bothersome street noise in their neighborhood and serious crime.

(number and percent distribution of total renters and renters of homes built in the past four years, by selected neighborhood problems, 2009; numbers in thousands)

	total		new homes		
	number	percent distribution	number	percent distribution	percent of total
Total renters	**35,378**	**100.0%**	**941**	**100.0%**	**2.7%**
Bothersome street noise or heavy traffic	10,158	28.7	234	24.9	2.3
Serious crime in neighborhood in past 12 months	7,650	21.6	179	19.1	2.3
Bothersome odor problem	2,156	6.1	34	3.6	1.6
Noise problem	1,217	3.4	22	2.3	1.8
Litter or housing deterioration	590	1.7	8	0.9	1.4
Poor city or county services	254	0.7	0	0.0	0.0
Undesirable commercial, institutional, industrial establishments	168	0.5	6	0.7	3.8
People problem	1,815	5.1	49	5.2	2.7
Other problems	2,791	7.9	108	11.5	3.9

Source: Bureau of the Census, American Housing Survey for the United States: 2009, Internet site http://www.census.gov/hhes/www/housing/ahs/ahs09/ahs09.html; calculations by New Strategist

Table 7.25 Renters of New Homes by Community Characteristics, 2009

Twenty-nine percent of the renters of new homes live in gated communities. Nearly half have open space, park, woods, farms, or ranches within 300 feet of their home.

(number and percent distribution of total renters and renters of homes built in the past four years, by community characteristics, 2009; numbers in thousands)

	total		new homes		
	number	percent distribution	number	percent distribution	percent of total
Total renters	**35,378**	**100.0%**	**941**	**100.0%**	**2.7%**
SECURED COMMUNITIES					
Total renters	**35,378**	**100.0**	**941**	**100.0**	**2.7**
Community access secured with walls or fences	5,422	15.3	277	29.5	5.1
Special entry system present	3,410	9.6	245	26.0	7.2
Special entry system not present	2,005	5.7	32	3.4	1.6
Community access not secured	29,714	84.0	657	69.8	2.2
SENIOR CITIZEN COMMUNITIES					
Households with persons aged 55 or older	**9,093**	**100.0**	**186**	**100.0**	**2.1**
Community age restricted	1,624	17.9	51	27.4	3.1
No age restriction	7,469	82.1	135	72.6	1.8
Community age specific	1,435	15.8	14	7.3	0.9
Community not age specific	5,583	61.4	119	64.0	2.1
COMMUNITY AMENITIES					
Total renters	**35,378**	**100.0**	**941**	**100.0**	**2.7**
Community center or clubhouse	9,703	27.4	479	50.9	4.9
Golf in community	3,947	11.2	55	5.8	1.4
Trails in community	6,309	17.8	175	18.6	2.8
Shuttle bus available	4,215	11.9	79	8.4	1.9
Daycare center	5,249	14.8	70	7.4	1.3
Private or restricted beach, park, or shoreline	6,308	17.8	149	15.8	2.4
DESCRIPTION OF AREA WITHIN 300 FEET OF HOME					
Total renters	**35,378**	**100.0**	**941**	**100.0**	**2.7**
Single-family detached homes	27,007	76.3	552	58.7	2.0
Single-family attached homes	10,860	30.7	289	30.7	2.7
Multiunit residential buildings	22,121	62.5	566	60.2	2.6
One-to-three-story multiunit is tallest	16,130	45.6	405	43.0	2.5
Four-to-six-story multiunit is tallest	3,473	9.8	73	7.8	2.1
Seven-or-more-story multiunit is tallest	2,243	6.3	88	9.4	3.9
Manufactured/mobile homes	3,112	8.8	78	8.3	2.5
Commercial or institutional	18,657	52.7	348	37.0	1.9
Industrial or factories	2,856	8.1	29	3.1	1.0
Open space, park, woods, farm, or ranch	12,706	35.9	441	46.8	3.5
Four-or-more-lane highway, railroad, or airport	9,232	26.1	242	25.7	2.6

	total		new homes		
	number	percent distribution	number	percent distribution	percent of total
BODIES OF WATER WITHIN 300 FEET OF HOME					
Total renters	**35,378**	**100.0%**	**941**	**100.0%**	**2.7%**
Water in area	4,832	13.7	191	20.3	4.0
With waterfront property	678	1.9	28	2.9	4.1
With flood plain	692	2.0	36	3.8	5.2
No water in area	30,390	85.9	743	79.0	2.4

Note: Numbers may not add to total because "not reported" is not shown.
Source: Bureau of the Census, American Housing Survey for the United States: 2009, Internet site http://www.census.gov/hhes/ www/housing/ahs/ahs09/ahs09.html; calculations by New Strategist

Table 7.26 Renters of New Homes by Public Services Available, 2009

The renters of new homes have fewer public services available to them than the average renter. Only 54 percent have public transportation in their area.

(number and percent distribution of total renters and renters of homes built in the past four years, by public services available in neighborhood, 2009; numbers in thousands)

	total		new homes		
	number	percent distribution	number	percent distribution	percent of total
Total renters	**35,378**	**100.0%**	**941**	**100.0%**	**2.7%**
LOCAL ELEMENTARY SCHOOL					
Renters with children under age 14	**10,486**	**100.0**	**303**	**100.0**	**2.9**
Satisfactory public elementary school	8,331	79.5	248	81.8	3.0
Unsatisfactory public elementary school	724	6.9	26	8.6	3.6
Unsatisfactory public elementary school	**724**	**100.0**	**26**	**100.0**	**3.6**
Better than other area elementary schools	63	8.7	0	0.0	0.0
Same as other area elementary schools	224	31.0	4	15.4	1.8
Worse than other area elementary schools	386	53.3	13	49.1	3.3
Renters with children under age 14	**10,486**	**100.0**	**303**	**100.0**	**2.9**
Public elementary school less than one mile	7,096	67.7	170	56.0	2.4
Public elementary school more than one mile	2,741	26.1	127	41.8	4.6
PUBLIC TRANSPORTATION IN AREA					
Total renters	**35,378**	**100.0**	**941**	**100.0**	**2.7**
With public transportation	24,641	69.6	507	53.9	2.1
No public transportation	9,684	27.4	399	42.4	4.1
With public transportation, travel time to nearest stop	**24,641**	**100.0**	**507**	**100.0**	**2.1**
Less than 5 minutes	10,328	41.9	191	37.7	1.8
5 to 9 minutes	8,869	36.0	149	29.3	1.7
10 to 14 minutes	2,753	11.2	95	18.7	3.4
15 to 29 minutes	1,099	4.5	29	5.7	2.6
30 minutes or longer	169	0.7	5	1.0	3.0
With public transportation	**24,641**	**100.0**	**507**	**100.0**	**2.1**
Household uses it regularly for commute to school or work	6,395	26.0	100	19.8	1.6
Household does not use it regularly for commute to school or work	18,075	73.4	392	77.2	2.2

	total		new homes		
	number	percent distribution	number	percent distribution	percent of total
SHOPPING IN AREA					
Total renters	**35,378**	**100.0%**	**941**	**100.0%**	**2.7%**
Grocery stores or drugstores within 15 minutes of home	34,189	96.6	896	95.3	2.6
Satisfactory	33,082	93.5	880	93.6	2.7
Not satisfactory	964	2.7	16	1.7	1.7
No grocery stores or drugstores within 15 minutes of home	777	2.2	20	2.1	2.6
POLICE PROTECTION					
Total renters	**35,378**	**100.0**	**941**	**100.0**	**2.7**
Satisfactory police protection	31,740	89.7	846	89.9	2.7
Unsatisfactory police protection	2,556	7.2	58	6.2	2.3

Note: Numbers may not add to total because "not reported" is not shown.
Source: Bureau of the Census, American Housing Survey for the United States: 2009, Internet site http://www.census.gov/hhes/www/housing/ahs/ahs09/ahs09.html; calculations by New Strategist

Table 7.27 Renters of New Homes Who Moved by Changes in Housing and Costs, 2009

The renters of new homes who recently moved are more likely than
the average renter who moved to have owned their previous residence.

(number and percent distribution of total renters who have moved in the past year and those who moved into homes built in the past four years, by structure type of previous residence, tenure of previous residence, and change in housing costs, 2009; numbers in thousands)

	total		new homes		
	number	percent distribution	number	percent distribution	percent of total
STRUCTURE TYPE OF PREVIOUS RESIDENCE					
Renters who moved within United States	**12,422**	**100.0%**	**555**	**100.0%**	**4.5%**
House	5,936	47.8	266	47.9	4.5
Apartment	5,228	42.1	229	41.2	4.4
Mobile home	545	4.4	23	4.2	4.2
Other	380	3.1	28	5.0	7.3
Not reported	331	2.7	10	1.8	3.0
OWNERSHIP OF PREVIOUS RESIDENCE					
Renters who moved from house, apartment, or mobile home within United States	**11,710**	**100.0**	**518**	**100.0**	**4.4**
Owner-occupied	2,991	25.5	163	31.5	5.5
Renter-occupied	8,719	74.5	355	68.5	4.1
CHANGE IN HOUSING COSTS					
Renters who moved from house, apartment, or mobile home within United States	**11,710**	**100.0**	**518**	**100.0**	**4.4**
Increased with move	5,135	43.8	265	51.1	5.2
Decreased	3,719	31.8	125	24.2	3.4
Stayed about the same	2,444	20.9	118	22.8	4.8
Don't know	250	2.1	3	0.6	1.3
Not reported	161	1.4	7	1.3	4.0

Source: Bureau of the Census, American Housing Survey for the United States: 2009, Internet site http://www.census.gov/hhes/ www/housing/ahs/ahs09/ahs09.html; calculations by New Strategist

Table 7.28 Renters of New Homes Who Moved by Reasons for Choosing Home, 2009

The renters of new homes who recently moved are far more likely than the average renter who recently moved to have chosen their home for its room layout/design—23 versus 14 percent. They are also more likely to say their present home is better than their previous home.

(number and percent distribution of total renting respondents who have moved in the past year and those who moved into homes built in the past four years, by reasons for choosing home, 2009; numbers in thousands)

	total		new homes		
	number	percent distribution	number	percent distribution	percent of total
Total renting respondents who moved	**12,840**	**100.0%**	**564**	**100.0%**	**4.4%**
MAIN REASON FOR CHOICE OF PRESENT HOME					
All reported reasons equal	1,448	11.3	80	14.1	5.5
Financial reasons	3,846	30.0	105	18.6	2.7
Room layout/design	1,743	13.6	129	22.9	7.4
Kitchen	65	0.5	5	0.8	7.0
Size	1,398	10.9	55	9.7	3.9
Exterior appearance	350	2.7	27	4.9	7.8
Yard/trees/view	412	3.2	13	2.3	3.2
Quality of construction	231	1.8	27	4.9	11.9
Only one available	608	4.7	5	0.9	0.9
Other	2,198	17.1	104	18.4	4.7
Not reported	540	4.2	14	2.5	2.6
PRESENT HOME COMPARED WITH PREVIOUS HOME					
Better	6,192	48.2	365	64.7	5.9
Worse	2,676	20.8	63	11.2	2.4
About the same	3,498	27.2	120	21.3	3.4
Not reported	474	3.7	16	2.9	3.4
HOME SEARCH					
Now in house	**4,200**	**100.0**	**191**	**100.0**	**4.6**
Did not look at apartments	2,888	68.8	138	72.2	4.8
Looked at apartments too	1,162	27.7	50	26.3	4.3
Now in manufactured/mobile home	**551**	**100.0**	**4**	**100.0**	**0.7**
Did not look at apartments	360	65.3	0	0.0	0.0
Looked at apartments too	181	32.8	4	100.0	2.2
Now in apartment	**8,090**	**100.0**	**369**	**100.0**	**4.6**
Did not look at houses	5,726	70.8	233	63.1	4.1
Looked at houses too	2,056	25.4	127	34.3	6.2

Note: Total number of movers does not equal total movers in other tables because this table shows survey respondents who moved, not necessarily householders. Numbers may not add to total because "not reported" may not be shown.
Source: Bureau of the Census, American Housing Survey for the United States: 2009, Internet site http://www.census.gov/hhes/ www/housing/ahs/ahs09/ahs09.html; calculations by New Strategist

Table 7.29 Renters of New Homes Who Moved by Reasons for Choosing Neighborhood, 2009

The renters of new homes who recently moved are more
likely than the average renter who recently moved to have
looked at a number of different neighborhoods. Convenience to job
is the single most important factor in their choice of neighborhood.

(number and percent distribution of total renting respondents who moved in the past year, and those who moved into homes built in the past four years, by reasons for choosing neighborhood, 2009; numbers in thousands)

	total		new homes		
	number	percent distribution	number	percent distribution	percent of total
Total renting respondents who moved	**12,840**	**100.0%**	**564**	**100.0%**	**4.4%**
Neighborhood search					
Looked at just this neighborhood	5,900	46.0	206	36.4	3.5
Looked at other neighborhoods	6,533	50.9	347	61.5	5.3
Not reported	407	3.2	12	2.2	3.0
Main reason for choice of present neighborhood					
All reported reasons equal	1,354	10.5	74	13.2	5.5
Convenient to job	2,924	22.8	159	28.2	5.4
Convenient to friends or relatives	1,915	14.9	52	9.1	2.7
Convenient to leisure activities	244	1.9	14	2.6	5.9
Convenient to public transportation	237	1.8	6	1.1	2.7
Good schools	798	6.2	31	5.6	3.9
Other public services	185	1.4	7	1.3	4.0
Looks/design of neighborhood	1,163	9.1	70	12.5	6.1
House was most important consideration	964	7.5	50	8.8	5.2
Other	2,563	20.0	82	14.5	3.2
Not reported	493	3.8	18	3.1	3.6
Present neighborhood compared to previous neighborhood					
Better	4,953	38.6	246	43.6	5.0
Worse	1,955	15.2	62	10.9	3.2
About the same	4,916	38.3	228	40.4	4.6
Same neighborhood	520	4.1	14	2.5	2.7
Not reported	496	3.9	15	2.7	3.0

Note: Total number of movers does not equal total movers in other tables because this table shows survey respondents who moved, not necessarily householders.
Source: Bureau of the Census, American Housing Survey for the United States: 2009, Internet site http://www.census.gov/hhes/www/housing/ahs/ahs09/ahs09.html; calculations by New Strategist

Table 7.30 Renters of New Homes Who Moved by Main Reason for Moving, 2009

The single most important reason for moving among renters of new homes who recently moved was a new job or job transfer, mentioned by 19 percent.

(number and percent distribution of total renting respondents who moved in the past year and those moving into homes built in the past four years, by main reason for move, 2009; numbers in thousands)

	total		new homes		
	number	percent distribution	number	percent distribution	percent of total
Total renting respondents who moved	**12,840**	**100.0%**	**564**	**100.0%**	**4.4%**
All reported reasons equal	450	3.5	22	3.9	4.9
Private displacement	118	0.9	5	0.9	4.5
Government displacement	45	0.4	5	0.8	10.2
Disaster loss (fire, flood, etc.)	126	1.0	0	0.0	0.0
New job or job transfer	1,220	9.5	106	18.8	8.7
To be closer to work/school/other	1,416	11.0	56	9.9	3.9
Other financial, employment related	527	4.1	19	3.4	3.6
To establish own household	1,282	10.0	35	6.3	2.8
Needed larger house or apartment	1,103	8.6	56	10.0	5.1
Married, widowed, divorced, or separated	628	4.9	18	3.2	2.9
Other family, personal reasons	1,004	7.8	41	7.3	4.1
Wanted better home	881	6.9	37	6.6	4.2
Change from owner to renter	120	0.9	10	1.8	8.5
Wanted lower rent or maintenance	867	6.8	19	3.4	2.2
Other housing related reasons	614	4.8	30	5.3	4.9
Evicted from residence	112	0.9	3	0.6	2.9
Other	1,548	12.1	74	13.1	4.8
Not reported	779	6.1	26	4.7	3.4

Note: Total number of movers does not equal total movers in other tables because this table shows survey respondents who moved, not necessarily householders.
Source: Bureau of the Census, American Housing Survey for the United States: 2009, Internet site http://www.census.gov/hhes/ www/housing/ahs/ahs09/ahs09.html; calculations by New Strategist

Owners of Mobile Homes

The owners of mobile homes have lower incomes than the average homeowner.

Mobile homes are much more affordable than the average owned home. The owners of mobile homes paid a median of $27,000 for their home—about one-fourth of the $107,500 median purchase price of the average owned home. The lower price of mobile homes allows those with lower incomes to afford homeownership. The median household income of mobile home owners was just $32,000 in 2009, well below the $60,000 median income of the average homeowner. Despite their already low cost, mobile homes have dropped in value over the past few years. The median value of mobile homes was $25,000 in 2009, down from $32,899 in 2007—a 24 percent decline.

■ The average owner-occupied mobile home is only 1,200 square feet in size, but the 54 percent majority has three or more bedrooms and 66 percent have two or more bathrooms.

■ Sixty percent of the owners of mobile homes own their home free and clear. Among those with a mortgage, a substantial 34 percent owe more than their mobile home is worth.

■ Sixty-eight percent of mobile home owners rate their home at least an 8 on a scale of 1 (worst) to 10 (best).

Mobile homes have lost value

(median value of owned mobile homes, 2007 and 2009)

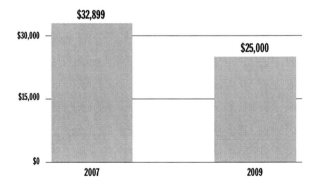

Table 8.1 Owners of Mobile Homes by Age, 2009

Seven percent of all homeowners own a mobile or manufactured home. The owners of mobile homes have a median age of 52, the same as all homeowners.

(number and percent distribution of total homeowners and owners of mobile/manufactured homes by age of householder, 2009; numbers in thousands)

	total		mobile homes		
	number	percent distribution	number	percent distribution	percent of total
Total homeowners	**76,428**	**100.0%**	**5,418**	**100.0%**	**7.1%**
Under age 25	1,284	1.7	179	3.3	14.0
Aged 25 to 29	3,541	4.6	240	4.4	6.8
Aged 30 to 34	5,532	7.2	436	8.1	7.9
Aged 35 to 44	14,932	19.5	937	17.3	6.3
Aged 45 to 54	17,743	23.2	1,169	21.6	6.6
Aged 55 to 64	14,924	19.5	1,079	19.9	7.2
Aged 65 to 74	9,818	12.8	814	15.0	8.3
Aged 75 or older	8,653	11.3	565	10.4	6.5
Median age	52	–	52	–	–

Note: "–" means not applicable.
Source: Bureau of the Census, American Housing Survey for the United States: 2009, Internet site http://www.census.gov/hhes/ www/housing/ahs/ahs09/ahs09.html; calculations by New Strategist

Table 8.2 Owners of Mobile Homes by Household Type and Age of Householder, 2009

The owners of mobile homes are much less likely to be married
couples than the average homeowner—49 versus 62 percent.
They are much more likely to live alone—29 versus 22 percent.

*(number and percent distribution of total homeowners and owners of mobile/manufactured homes, by household
type and age of householder, 2009; numbers in thousands)*

	total		mobile homes		
	number	percent distribution	number	percent distribution	percent of total
Total homeowners	**76,428**	**100.0%**	**5,418**	**100.0%**	**7.1%**
MARRIED-COUPLE HOMEOWNERS	**47,008**	**61.5**	**2,673**	**49.3**	**5.7**
Under age 25	495	0.6	60	1.1	12.2
Aged 25 to 29	2,007	2.6	114	2.1	5.7
Aged 30 to 34	3,646	4.8	272	5.0	7.4
Aged 35 to 44	10,336	13.5	488	9.0	4.7
Aged 45 to 64	21,352	27.9	1,160	21.4	5.4
Aged 65 or older	9,174	12.0	579	10.7	6.3
TWO-OR-MORE-PERSON HOMEOWNERS					
Female householders, no spouse present	**7,931**	**10.4**	**743**	**13.7**	**9.4**
Under age 45	2,948	3.9	282	5.2	9.6
Aged 45 to 64	3,397	4.4	329	6.1	9.7
Aged 65 or older	1,587	2.1	131	2.4	8.3
Male householders, no spouse present	**4,712**	**6.2**	**448**	**8.3**	**9.5**
Under age 45	2,170	2.8	214	3.9	9.8
Aged 45 to 64	1,878	2.5	172	3.2	9.1
Aged 65 or older	663	0.9	62	1.1	9.4
SINGLE-PERSON HOMEOWNERS	**16,777**	**22.0**	**1,555**	**28.7**	**9.3**
Female householders	**10,007**	**13.1**	**893**	**16.5**	**8.9**
Under age 45	1,547	2.0	153	2.8	9.9
Aged 45 to 64	3,231	4.2	296	5.5	9.2
Aged 65 or older	5,230	6.8	444	8.2	8.5
Male householders	**6,770**	**8.9**	**662**	**12.2**	**9.8**
Under age 45	2,142	2.8	209	3.8	9.7
Aged 45 to 64	2,810	3.7	291	5.4	10.3
Aged 65 or older	1,818	2.4	163	3.0	8.9

*Source: Bureau of the Census, American Housing Survey for the United States: 2009, Internet site http://www.census.gov/hhes/
www/housing/ahs/ahs09/ahs09.html; calculations by New Strategist*

Table 8.3 Owners of Mobile Homes by Race and Hispanic Origin, 2009

The owners of mobile homes are more likely to be American Indian
than the average homeowner. More than one in eight
American Indian homeowners live in a mobile home.

*(number and percent distribution of total homeowners and owners of mobile/manufactured homes, by race and
Hispanic origin, 2009; numbers in thousands)*

	total		mobile homes		
	number	percent distribution	number	percent distribution	percent of total
Total homeowners	**76,428**	**100.0%**	**5,418**	**100.0%**	**7.1%**
American Indian	503	0.7	62	1.1	12.3
Asian	2,516	3.3	14	0.3	0.6
Black	6,547	8.6	503	9.3	7.7
Hispanic	6,439	8.4	490	9.0	7.6
White, non-Hispanic	59,905	78.4	4,285	79.1	7.2

*Note: American Indians, Asians, blacks, and whites are those who identify themselves as being of the race alone. Numbers do
not add to total because not all races are shown and Hispanics may be of any race.
Source: Bureau of the Census, American Housing Survey for the United States: 2009, Internet site http://www.census.gov/hhes/
www/housing/ahs/ahs09/ahs09.html; calculations by New Strategist*

Table 8.4 Owners of Mobile Homes by Household Income, 2009

The owners of mobile homes have much lower incomes than
the average homeowner, a median of just $32,000 in 2009.

(number and percent distribution of total homeowners and owners of mobile/manufactured homes by household income, 2009; numbers in thousands)

	total		mobile homes		
	number	percent distribution	number	percent distribution	percent of total
Total homeowners	**76,428**	**100.0%**	**5,418**	**100.0%**	**7.1%**
Under $10,000	4,423	5.8	607	11.2	13.7
$10,000 to $19,999	5,911	7.7	917	16.9	15.5
$20,000 to $29,999	7,617	10.0	926	17.1	12.2
$30,000 to $39,999	7,082	9.3	850	15.7	12.0
$40,000 to $49,999	6,852	9.0	721	13.3	10.5
$50,000 to $59,999	6,328	8.3	416	7.7	6.6
$60,000 to $79,999	10,535	13.8	524	9.7	5.0
$80,000 to $99,999	8,409	11.0	243	4.5	2.9
$100,000 to $119,999	6,007	7.9	87	1.6	1.4
$120,000 or more	13,264	17.4	127	2.3	1.0
Median income	$60,000	–	$32,000	–	–

Note: "–" means not applicable.
Source: Bureau of the Census, American Housing Survey for the United States: 2009, Internet site http://www.census.gov/hhes/www/housing/ahs/ahs09/ahs09.html; calculations by New Strategist

Table 8.5 Owners of Mobile Homes by Educational Attainment, 2009

The owners of mobile homes are much less educated
than the average homeowner. Only 7 percent are
college graduates versus 34 percent of all homeowners.

(number and percent distribution of total homeowners and the owners of mobile/manufactured homes, by educational attainment of householder, 2009; numbers in thousands)

	total		mobile homes		
	number	percent distribution	number	percent distribution	percent of total
Total homeowners	**76,428**	**100.0%**	**5,418**	**100.0%**	**7.1%**
Not a high school graduate	8,542	11.2	1,464	27.0	17.1
High school graduate only	22,665	29.7	2,311	42.7	10.2
Some college, no degree	12,659	16.6	790	14.6	6.2
Associate's degree	6,722	8.8	458	8.5	6.8
Bachelor's degree	15,894	20.8	311	5.7	2.0
Graduate or professional degree	9,947	13.0	85	1.6	0.9
High school graduate or higher	67,886	88.8	3,954	73.0	5.8
Some college or higher	45,221	59.2	1,643	30.3	3.6
Bachelor's degree or higher	25,840	33.8	395	7.3	1.5

Source: Bureau of the Census, American Housing Survey for the United States: 2009, Internet site http://www.census.gov/hhes/www/housing/ahs/ahs09/ahs09.html; calculations by New Strategist

Table 8.6 Owners of Mobile Homes by Household Size, 2009

Owners of mobile homes are more likely to live alone
than the average homeowner, 29 versus 22 percent.

(number and percent distribution of total homeowners and owners of mobile/manufactured homes by number of persons living in home, 2009; numbers in thousands)

	total		mobile homes		
	number	percent distribution	number	percent distribution	percent of total
Total homeowners	**76,428**	**100.0%**	**5,418**	**100.0%**	**7.1%**
One person	16,777	22.0	1,555	28.7	9.3
Two persons	27,633	36.2	1,978	36.5	7.2
Three persons	12,223	16.0	738	13.6	6.0
Four persons	11,791	15.4	585	10.8	5.0
Five persons	5,207	6.8	349	6.4	6.7
Six persons	1,797	2.4	154	2.8	8.5
Seven or more persons	1,000	1.3	59	1.1	5.9

Source: Bureau of the Census, American Housing Survey for the United States: 2009, Internet site http://www.census.gov/hhes/ www/housing/ahs/ahs09/ahs09.html; calculations by New Strategist

Table 8.7 **Owners of Mobile Homes by Year Structure Built, 2009**

The owners of mobile homes live in newer structures
than the average homeowner. Half of the owners of
mobile homes live in a unit built in 1991 or later.

(number and percent distribution of total homeowners and homeowners in mobile/manufactured homes, by year structure was built, 2009; numbers in thousands)

	total		mobile homes		
	number	percent distribution	number	percent distribution	percent of total
Total homeowners	**76,428**	**100.0%**	**5,418**	**100.0%**	**7.1%**
2005 to 2009	4,601	6.0	301	5.6	6.5
2000 to 2004	6,371	8.3	650	12.0	10.2
1995 to 1999	6,221	8.1	1,272	23.5	20.4
1990 to 1994	4,715	6.2	607	11.2	12.9
1985 to 1989	5,159	6.8	511	9.4	9.9
1980 to 1984	4,201	5.5	545	10.1	13.0
1975 to 1979	7,471	9.8	532	9.8	7.1
1970 to 1974	5,696	7.5	595	11.0	10.4
1960 to 1969	8,917	11.7	263	4.9	3.0
1950 to 1959	8,528	11.2	48	0.9	0.6
1940 to 1949	4,423	5.8	48	0.9	1.1
1939 or earlier	10,126	13.2	46	0.9	0.5
Median year	1975	–	1991	–	–

Note: "–" means not applicable.
Source: Bureau of the Census, American Housing Survey for the United States: 2009, Internet site http://www.census.gov/hhes/www/housing/ahs/ahs09/ahs09.html; calculations by New Strategist

Table 8.8 Owners of Mobile Homes by Year Moved into Unit, 2009

The owners of mobile homes have lived in their home for almost the same length of time as the average homeowner. Half moved into their unit in 2000 or later.

(number and percent distribution of total homeowners and owners of mobile/manufactured homes, by year householder moved into unit, 2009; numbers in thousands)

	total		mobile homes		
	number	percent distribution	number	percent distribution	percent of total
Total homeowners	**76,428**	**100.0%**	**5,418**	**100.0%**	**7.1%**
2005 to 2009	20,126	26.3	1,546	28.5	7.7
2000 to 2004	17,520	22.9	1,544	28.5	8.8
1995 to 1999	11,217	14.7	1,206	22.3	10.8
1990 to 1994	7,706	10.1	527	9.7	6.8
1985 to 1989	5,362	7.0	276	5.1	5.1
1980 to 1984	3,124	4.1	140	2.6	4.5
1975 to 1979	3,734	4.9	96	1.8	2.6
1970 to 1974	2,548	3.3	64	1.2	2.5
1960 to 1969	3,142	4.1	17	0.3	0.6
1950 to 1959	1,522	2.0	0	0.0	0.0
1940 to 1949	334	0.4	2	0.0	0.7
1939 or earlier	93	0.1	0	0.0	0.0
Median year moved into home	1999	–	2000	–	–

Note: "–" means not applicable.
Source: Bureau of the Census, American Housing Survey for the United States: 2009, Internet site http://www.census.gov/hhes/www/housing/ahs/ahs09/ahs09.html; calculations by New Strategist

Table 8.9 Owners of Mobile Homes by Square Footage of Unit and Lot Size, 2009

Owned mobile homes are smaller than the average owned home, with a median of 1,200 square feet. Lot size is considerably larger, however, at 1.0 acres per mobile home versus .32 acres on average for all owned homes.

(number and percent distribution of total homeowners and owners of mobile/manufactured homes, by square footage and lot size, 2009; numbers in thousands)

	total		mobile homes		
	number	percent distribution	number	percent distribution	percent of total
Square footage of home, total*	**68,742**	**100.0%**	**5,418**	**100.0%**	**7.9%**
Less than 500 sq. ft.	383	0.6	114	2.1	29.7
500 to 749 sq. ft.	1,085	1.6	452	8.3	41.6
750 to 999 sq. ft.	3,519	5.1	1,052	19.4	29.9
1,000 to 1,499 sq. ft.	14,978	21.8	1,956	36.1	13.1
1,500 to 1,999 sq. ft.	16,284	23.7	916	16.9	5.6
2,000 to 2,499 sq. ft.	12,057	17.5	288	5.3	2.4
2,500 to 2,999 sq. ft.	6,622	9.6	108	2.0	1.6
3,000 to 3,999 sq. ft.	6,391	9.3	51	0.9	0.8
4,000 or more sq. ft.	3,787	5.5	103	1.9	2.7
Not reported	3,638	5.3	379	7.0	10.4
Median square footage	1,800	–	1,200	–	–
Lot size, total*	**70,643**	**100.0**	**5,380**	**100.0**	**7.6**
Less than one-eighth acre	9,107	12.9	1,059	19.7	11.6
One-eighth up to one-quarter acre	17,771	25.2	657	12.2	3.7
One-quarter up to one-half acre	13,837	19.6	375	7.0	2.7
One-half up to one acre	8,874	12.6	534	9.9	6.0
One to five acres	14,895	21.1	1,936	36.0	13.0
Five to ten acres	2,545	3.6	390	7.2	15.3
10 or more acres	3,614	5.1	428	7.9	11.8
Median lot size (acres)	0.32	–	1.00	–	–

* Single-family detached and mobile homes only.
** Homes in two-or-more-unit buildings are excluded.
Note: "–" means not applicable.
Source: Bureau of the Census, American Housing Survey for the United States: 2009, Internet site http://www.census.gov/hhes/www/housing/ahs/ahs09/ahs09.html; calculations by New Strategist

Table 8.10 Owners of Mobile Homes by Number of Rooms in Home, 2009

Most owned mobile homes have three bedrooms and at least two bathrooms.
Twenty-six percent of owned mobile homes have a room used for business.

(number and percent distribution of total homeowners and owners of mobile/manufactured homes, by number and type of rooms, 2009; numbers in thousands)

	total		mobile homes		
	number	percent distribution	number	percent distribution	percent of total
Total homeowners	**76,428**	**100.0%**	**5,418**	**100.0%**	**7.1%**
Number of rooms					
One room	26	0.0	3	0.0	9.8
Two rooms	68	0.1	5	0.1	7.3
Three rooms	1,036	1.4	100	1.8	9.6
Four rooms	6,475	8.5	1,349	24.9	20.8
Five rooms	17,232	22.5	2,028	37.4	11.8
Six rooms	20,364	26.6	1,213	22.4	6.0
Seven rooms	14,754	19.3	531	9.8	3.6
Eight rooms	9,410	12.3	139	2.6	1.5
Nine rooms	4,130	5.4	32	0.6	0.8
10 or more rooms	2,933	3.8	19	0.3	0.6
Number of bedrooms					
None	45	0.1	5	0.1	11.7
One bedroom	1,714	2.2	142	2.6	8.3
Two bedrooms	13,471	17.6	1,854	34.2	13.8
Three bedrooms	39,723	52.0	2,938	54.2	7.4
Four or more bedrooms	21,475	28.1	479	8.8	2.2
Number of bathrooms					
None	175	0.2	13	0.2	7.4
One bathroom	15,767	20.6	1,286	23.7	8.2
One-and-one-half bathrooms	12,081	15.8	535	9.9	4.4
Two or more bathrooms	48,405	63.3	3,584	66.2	7.4
With room used for business	**26,108**	**34.2**	**1,432**	**26.4**	**5.5**
Business only	11,479	15.0	755	13.9	6.6
Business and other use	14,629	19.1	677	12.5	4.6

Source: Bureau of the Census, American Housing Survey for the United States: 2009, Internet site http://www.census.gov/hhes/ www/housing/ahs/ahs09/ahs09.html; calculations by New Strategist

Table 8.11 Owners of Mobile Homes by Presence of Kitchen, Laundry, and Safety Equipment, 2009

The owners of mobile homes are much less likely than the average homeowner to have a dishwasher, 54 versus 75 percent.

(number and percent of total homeowners and owners of mobile/manufactured homes, by presence of kitchen, laundry, and safety equipment, 2009; numbers in thousands)

	total		mobile homes		
	number	percent distribution	number	percent distribution	percent of total
Total homeowners	**76,428**	**100.0%**	**5,418**	**100.0%**	**7.1%**
With complete kitchen equipment	76,050	99.5	5,396	99.6	7.1
Dishwasher	57,191	74.8	2,912	53.7	5.1
Washing machine	73,826	96.6	5,169	95.4	7.0
Clothes dryer	72,562	94.9	5,056	93.3	7.0
Disposal in kitchen sink	40,597	53.1	903	16.7	2.2
Trash compactor	3,166	4.1	39	0.7	1.2
Working smoke detector	71,797	93.9	5,032	92.9	7.0
Fire extinguisher	37,922	49.6	2,469	45.6	6.5
Sprinkler system inside home	2,086	2.7	46	0.9	2.2
Carbon monoxide detector	31,691	41.5	1,264	23.3	4.0

Note: Complete kitchen equipment includes a sink, refrigerator, and oven or burners.
Source: Bureau of the Census, American Housing Survey for the United States: 2009, Internet site http://www.census.gov/hhes/ www/housing/ahs/ahs09/ahs09.html; calculations by New Strategist

Table 8.12 Owners of Mobile Homes by Type of Heating Equipment, 2009

The 74 percent majority of owned mobile homes are heated by a warm-air furnace, while another 15 percent use an electric heat pump.

(number and percent distribution of total homeowners and owners of mobile/manufactured homes, by presence and type of heating equipment, 2009; numbers in thousands)

	total		mobile homes		
	number	percent distribution	number	percent distribution	percent of total
Total homeowners	**76,428**	**100.0%**	**5,418**	**100.0%**	**7.1%**
Main heating equipment					
Warm-air furnace	51,691	67.6	3,986	73.6	7.7
Steam or hot water system	7,494	9.8	20	0.4	0.3
Electric heat pump	9,764	12.8	832	15.3	8.5
Built-in electric units	2,120	2.8	62	1.1	2.9
Floor, wall, or other built-in hot air units without ducts	2,043	2.7	112	2.1	5.5
Room heaters with flue	580	0.8	48	0.9	8.2
Room heaters without flue	694	0.9	94	1.7	13.5
Portable electric heaters	535	0.7	119	2.2	22.3
Stoves	845	1.1	80	1.5	9.5
Fireplaces with inserts	155	0.2	2	0.0	1.0
Fireplaces without inserts	35	0.0	5	0.1	14.7
Other	232	0.3	42	0.8	18.3
Cooking stove	34	0.0	7	0.1	21.5
None	206	0.3	8	0.1	3.7
Households with additional heating equipment					
Warm-air furnace	225	0.3	16	0.3	7.0
Steam or hot water system	51	0.1	0	0.0	0.0
Electric heat pump	91	0.1	13	0.2	14.5
Built-in electric units	1,428	1.9	61	1.1	4.3
Floor, wall, or other built-in hot air units without ducts	63	0.1	0	0.0	0.0
Room heaters with flue	716	0.9	51	0.9	7.1
Room heaters without flue	1,207	1.6	207	3.8	17.1
Portable electric heaters	9,886	12.9	675	12.5	6.8
Stoves	3,740	4.9	238	4.4	6.4
Fireplaces with inserts	4,742	6.2	260	4.8	5.5
Fireplaces without inserts	4,869	6.4	154	2.8	3.2
Other	707	0.9	52	1.0	7.4
Cooking stove	50	0.1	3	0.1	6.8
None	51,171	67.0	3,814	70.4	7.5

Source: Bureau of the Census, American Housing Survey for the United States: 2009, Internet site http://www.census.gov/hhes/ www/housing/ahs/ahs09/ahs09.html; calculations by New Strategist

Table 8.13 Owners of Mobile Homes with Air Conditioning, 2009

Sixty-six percent of the owners of mobile homes have central air conditioning,
below the 72 percent of all homeowners with central air.

(number and percent distribution of total homeowners and owners of mobile homes, by presence of air conditioning equipment, 2009; numbers in thousands)

	total		mobile homes		
	number	percent distribution	number	percent distribution	percent of total
Total homeowners	**76,428**	**100.0%**	**5,418**	**100.0%**	**7.1%**
Households with air conditioning	68,355	89.4	4,929	91.0	7.2
Central	54,647	71.5	3,589	66.2	6.6
Additional central	4,709	6.2	221	4.1	4.7
One room unit	5,303	6.9	591	10.9	11.1
Two room units	4,800	6.3	541	10.0	11.3
Three or more room units	3,604	4.7	208	3.8	5.8

Source: Bureau of the Census, American Housing Survey for the United States: 2009, Internet site http://www.census.gov/hhes/www/housing/ahs/ahs09/ahs09.html; calculations by New Strategist

Table 8.14 Owners of Mobile Homes by Primary Source of Water and Sewage Disposal System, 2009

Owners of mobile homes are much more likely than the
average homeowner to use a well as their source of water and
a septic tank or cesspool as their sewage disposal system.

(number and percent of total homeowners and owners of mobile/manufactured homes, by primary source of water and type of sewage disposal system, 2009; numbers in thousands)

	total		mobile homes		
	number	percent distribution	number	percent distribution	percent of total
Total homeowners	76,428	100.0%	5,418	100.0%	7.1%
Source of water					
Public system or private company	64,372	84.2	3,733	68.9	5.8
Well	11,769	15.4	1,635	30.2	13.9
Safety of primary source of water					
Safe to drink	71,152	93.1	4,865	89.8	6.8
Not safe to drink	4,530	5.9	490	9.0	10.8
Sewage disposal system					
Public sewer	56,736	74.2	2,363	43.6	4.2
Septic tank, cesspool, chemical toilet	19,667	25.7	3,055	56.4	15.5

Note: Numbers do not sum to total because "other" and "not reported" are not shown.
Source: Bureau of the Census, American Housing Survey for the United States: 2009, Internet site http://www.census.gov/hhes/ www/housing/ahs/ahs09/ahs09.html; calculations by New Strategist

Table 8.15 Owners of Mobile Homes by Fuels Used, 2009

The owners of mobile homes are much more likely than the
average homeowner to have all-electric homes, 47 versus 23 percent.

*(number and percent of total homeowners and owners of mobile/manufactured homes, by types of fuels used,
2009; numbers in thousands)*

	total		mobile homes		
	number	percent distribution	number	percent distribution	percent of total
Total homeowners	**76,428**	**100.0%**	**5,418**	**100.0%**	**7.1%**
Electricity	76,378	99.9	5,418	100.0	7.1
All-electric homes	17,951	23.5	2,541	46.9	14.2
Piped gas	46,700	61.1	1,306	24.1	2.8
Bottled gas	8,391	11.0	1,343	24.8	16.0
Fuel oil	6,409	8.4	212	3.9	3.3
Kerosene or other liquid fuel	451	0.6	249	4.6	55.2
Coal or coke	97	0.1	0	0.0	0.0
Wood	1,510	2.0	161	3.0	10.7
Solar energy	130	0.2	0	0.0	0.0
Other	254	0.3	6	0.1	2.5

Note: Numbers do not add to total because many households use more than one fuel.
Source: Bureau of the Census, American Housing Survey for the United States: 2009, Internet site http://www.census.gov/hhes/
www/housing/ahs/ahs09/ahs09.html; calculations by New Strategist

Table 8.16 Owners of Mobile Homes by Heating Fuels Used, 2009

Fifty-three percent of the owners of mobile
homes use electricity as heating fuel.

(number and percent of total homeowners and owners of mobile/manufactured homes, by heating fuels used, 2009; numbers in thousands)

	total		mobile homes		
	number	percent distribution	number	percent distribution	percent of total
TOTAL HOMEOWNERS	**76,428**	**100.0%**	**5,418**	**100.0%**	**7.1%**
Homeowners using heating fuel	**76,222**	**100.0**	**5,410**	**100.0**	**7.1**
Electricity	22,219	29.2	2,847	52.6	12.8
Piped gas	41,233	54.1	1,147	21.2	2.8
Bottled gas	4,889	6.4	881	16.3	18.0
Fuel oil	5,693	7.5	124	2.3	2.2
Kerosene or other liquid fuel	444	0.6	249	4.6	56.0
Coal or coke	91	0.1	0	0.0	0.0
Wood	1,503	2.0	157	2.9	10.4
Solar energy	8	0.0	0	0.0	0.0
Other	142	0.2	6	0.1	4.4

Source: Bureau of the Census, American Housing Survey for the United States: 2009, Internet site http://www.census.gov/hhes/ www/housing/ahs/ahs09/ahs09.html; calculations by New Strategist

Table 8.17 Owners of Mobile Homes by Cooking, Water Heating, and Clothes Dryer Fuels Used, 2009

The owners of mobile homes are more likely than the average homeowner to use electricity as their cooking, water heating, and clothes dryer fuel.

(number and percent of total homeowners and owners of mobile/manufactured homes, by cooking, water heating, and clothes dryer fuels used, 2009; numbers in thousands)

	total		mobile homes		
	number	percent distribution	number	percent distribution	percent of total
COOKING FUEL					
Homeowners using cooking fuel	**76,388**	**100.0%**	**5,413**	**100.0%**	**7.1%**
Electricity	45,512	59.6	3,452	63.8	7.6
Piped gas	26,553	34.8	1,016	18.8	3.8
Bottled gas	4,274	5.6	942	17.4	22.0
Kerosene or other liquid fuel	7	0.0	0	0.0	0.0
Wood	17	0.0	4	0.1	23.7
Other	25	0.0	0	0.0	0.0
WATER HEATING FUEL					
Homeowners with hot piped water	**76,371**	**100.0**	**5,415**	**100.0**	**7.1**
Electricity	29,341	38.4	4,076	75.3	13.9
Piped gas	40,280	52.7	886	16.4	2.2
Bottled gas	3,365	4.4	424	7.8	12.6
Fuel oil	3,087	4.0	10	0.2	0.3
Kerosene or other liquid fuel	18	0.0	7	0.1	39.6
Coal or coke	23	0.0	0	0.0	0.0
Wood	96	0.1	9	0.2	9.4
Solar energy	121	0.2	0	0.0	0.0
Other	40	0.1	2	0.0	5.1
CLOTHES DRYER FUEL					
Homeowners with clothes dryers	**72,562**	**100.0**	**5,056**	**93.4**	**7.0**
Electricity	55,059	75.9	4,615	85.3	8.4
Piped gas	16,326	22.5	316	5.8	1.9
Other	1,178	1.6	124	2.3	10.6

Source: Bureau of the Census, American Housing Survey for the United States: 2009, Internet site http://www.census.gov/hhes/www/housing/ahs/ahs09/ahs09.html; calculations by New Strategist

Table 8.18 Owners of Mobile Homes by Amenities of Home, 2009

Only 44 percent of the owners of mobile homes have a garage
or carport, versus 80 percent of all homeowners.

(number and percent of total homeowners and owners of mobile/manufactured homes, by selected amenities of home, 2009; numbers in thousands)

	total		mobile homes		
	number	percent distribution	number	percent distribution	percent of total
Total homeowners	**76,428**	**100.0%**	**5,418**	**100.0%**	**7.1%**
Porch, deck, balcony, or patio	70,421	92.1	4,744	87.6	6.7
Telephone available	75,129	98.3	5,277	97.4	7.0
Usable fireplace	34,458	45.1	1,072	19.8	3.1
Separate dining room	43,717	57.2	1,820	33.6	4.2
With two or more living or recreation rooms	30,978	40.5	829	15.3	2.7
Garage or carport					
Yes	60,979	79.8	2,357	43.5	3.9
No, but off-street parking included	13,287	17.4	2,843	52.5	21.4
No cars, trucks, or vans	2,069	2.7	177	3.3	8.6

Source: Bureau of the Census, American Housing Survey for the United States: 2009, Internet site http://www.census.gov/hhes/ www/housing/ahs/ahs09/ahs09.html; calculations by New Strategist

Table 8.19 Owners of Mobile Homes by Deficiencies of Home, 2009

Nine percent of the owners of mobile homes have seen
signs of mice in the past three months, a significantly
greater share than the 5 percent of all homeowners with mice.

*(number and percent distribution of total homeowners and owners of mobile/manufactured homes, by selected
deficiencies of housing unit, 2009; numbers in thousands)*

	total		mobile homes		
	number	percent distribution	number	percent distribution	percent of total
Total homeowners	**76,428**	**100.0%**	**5,418**	**100.0%**	**7.1%**
Signs of rats in last three months	354	0.5	45	0.8	12.8
Signs of mice in last three months	3,984	5.2	500	9.2	12.6
Signs of rodents, not sure which kind, in last three months	164	0.2	5	0.1	3.2
Holes in floor	581	0.8	151	2.8	26.1
Open cracks or holes (interior)	3,101	4.1	350	6.5	11.3
Broken plaster, peeling paint (interior)	1,246	1.6	110	2.0	8.8
No electrical wiring	57	0.1	2	0.0	3.5
Exposed wiring	221	0.3	28	0.5	12.6
Rooms without electric outlets	650	0.8	58	1.1	8.9

*Source: Bureau of the Census, American Housing Survey for the United States: 2009, Internet site http://www.census.gov/hhes/
www/housing/ahs/ahs09/ahs09.html; calculations by New Strategist*

Table 8.20 Owners of Mobile Homes by Housing Equipment Failures, 2009

The owners of mobile homes are more likely than the average homeowner to experience problems such as water leakage, being uncomfortably cold, and water stoppages.

(number and percent distribution of total homeowners and owners of mobile/manufactured homes, by type of equipment failure, 2009; numbers in thousands)

	total		mobile homes		
	number	percent distribution	number	percent distribution	percent of total
WATER SUPPLY STOPPAGE					
Homeowners with piped water	**76,371**	**100.0%**	**5,415**	**100.0%**	**7.1%**
No stoppage in last three months	73,494	96.2	4,956	91.5	6.7
With stoppage in last three months	2,031	2.7	414	7.6	20.4
Not reported	846	1.1	45	0.8	5.3
FLUSH TOILET BREAKDOWNS					
Homeowners with flush toilets	**76,391**	**100.0**	**5,418**	**100.0**	**7.1**
With at least one working toilet at all times, last three months	74,674	97.8	5,265	97.2	7.1
With no working toilet at least once in last three months	884	1.2	110	2.0	12.5
Not reported	833	1.1	43	0.8	5.2
WATER LEAKAGE DURING LAST 12 MONTHS					
Total homeowners	**76,428**	**100.0**	**5,418**	**100.0**	**7.1**
No leakage from within structure	70,356	92.1	4,898	90.4	7.0
With leakage from within structure*	5,170	6.8	467	8.6	9.0
Fixtures backed up or overflowed	1,188	1.6	68	1.3	5.7
Pipes leaked	2,145	2.8	228	4.2	10.6
Broken water heater	714	0.9	122	2.3	17.1
Other or unknown	1,263	1.7	65	1.2	5.1
Leakage not reported	902	1.2	53	1.0	5.9
No leakage from outside structure	**67,686**	**88.6**	**4,748**	**87.6**	**7.0**
With leakage from outside structure*	7,842	10.3	617	11.4	7.9
Roof	4,168	5.5	480	8.9	11.5
Basement	2,309	3.0	18	0.3	0.8
Walls, windows, or doors	1,165	1.5	79	1.5	6.7
Other or not reported	691	0.9	60	1.1	8.7
Leakage not reported	900	1.2	53	1.0	5.9

	total		mobile homes		
	number	percent distribution	number	percent distribution	percent of total
HEATING PROBLEMS					
Homeowners with heating equipment and occupying home last winter	**75,215**	**100.0%**	**5,329**	**100.0%**	**7.1%**
Not uncomfortably cold for 24 or more hours last winter	67,769	90.1	4,638	87.0	6.8
Uncomfortably cold for 24 or more hours last winter*	6,055	8.1	586	11.0	9.7
Equipment breakdown	1,594	2.1	168	3.2	10.5
Utility interruption	2,139	2.8	171	3.2	8.0
Inadequate heating capacity	350	0.5	47	0.9	13.3
Inadequate insulation	394	0.5	55	1.0	14.1
Cost of heating	778	1.0	79	1.5	10.2
Other	1,022	1.4	90	1.7	8.8
Not reported	1,391	1.8	105	2.0	7.5
ELECTRICAL PROBLEMS					
Homeowners with electrical wiring	**76,371**	**100.0**	**5,416**	**100.0**	**7.1**
No fuses or breakers blown in last three months	68,691	90.0	4,953	91.4	7.2
With fuses or breakers blown in last three months	6,685	8.8	425	7.8	6.4
Not reported	989	1.3	39	0.7	3.9

* Figures do not add to total because more than one problem may have occurred.
Source: Bureau of the Census, American Housing Survey for the United States: 2009, Internet site http://www.census.gov/hhes/ www/housing/ahs/ahs09/ahs09.html; calculations by New Strategist

Table 8.21 Owners of Mobile Homes by Purchase Price, 2009

The owners of mobile homes paid far less for their home
than the average homeowner, a median of just $27,000.

*(number and percent distribution of total homeowners and owners of mobile/manufactured homes, by purchase
price of home, 2009; numbers in thousands)*

	total		mobile homes		
	number	percent distribution	number	percent distribution	percent of total
TOTAL HOMEOWNERS	**76,428**	**100.0%**	**5,418**	**100.0%**	**7.1%**
Home purchased or built	**71,877**	**94.0**	**5,076**	**93.7**	**7.1**
Under $10,000	2,799	3.7	912	16.8	32.6
$10,000 to $19,999	4,229	5.5	863	15.9	20.4
$20,000 to $29,999	3,648	4.8	750	13.8	20.6
$30,000 to $39,999	3,489	4.6	510	9.4	14.6
$40,000 to $49,999	3,002	3.9	427	7.9	14.2
$50,000 to $59,999	3,076	4.0	279	5.1	9.1
$60,000 to $69,999	3,126	4.1	258	4.8	8.2
$70,000 to $79,999	2,968	3.9	190	3.5	6.4
$80,000 to $99,999	5,662	7.4	236	4.3	4.2
$100,000 to $119,999	4,288	5.6	126	2.3	2.9
$120,000 to $149,999	6,691	8.8	97	1.8	1.4
$150,000 to $199,999	8,055	10.5	19	0.3	0.2
$200,000 to $249,999	5,029	6.6	9	0.2	0.2
$250,000 to $299,999	3,024	4.0	0	0.0	0.0
$300,000 or more	8,594	11.2	3	0.0	0.0
Not reported	4,196	5.5	399	7.4	9.5
Median purchase price	$107,500	–	$27,000	–	–
Received as inheritance or gift	**3,388**	**4.4**	**292**	**5.4**	**8.6**
Not reported	**1,163**	**1.5**	**50**	**0.9**	**4.3**

Note: "–" means not applicable.
*Source: Bureau of the Census, American Housing Survey for the United States: 2009, Internet site http://www.census.gov/hhes/
www/housing/ahs/ahs09/ahs09.html; calculations by New Strategist*

Table 8.22 Mobile Home Owners by Value of Home, 2007 and 2009

The median value of mobile homes fell 24 percent between 2007 and 2009.

(number of mobile/manufactured home owners by current self-reported value of home, 2007 and 2009, percent change in number of homeowners by value, 2007–09; numbers in thousands)

	2009	2007	percent change
Total mobile home owners	**5,418**	**5,419**	**0.0%**
Under $10,000	1,256	1,138	10.4
$10,000 to $19,999	1,001	938	6.7
$20,000 to $29,999	581	514	13.1
$30,000 to $39,999	429	411	4.3
$40,000 to $59,999	611	666	−8.3
$60,000 to $79,999	584	486	20.3
$80,000 to $99,999	290	348	−16.7
$100,000 to $119,999	214	205	4.4
$120,000 to $149,999	251	260	−3.4
$150,000 to $199,999	158	386	−59.1
$200,000 to $299,999	43	67	−35.8
Median home value	$25,000	$32,899	−24.0

Source: Bureau of the Census, American Housing Survey for the United States: 2009, Internet site http://www.census.gov/hhes/ www/housing/ahs/ahs09/ahs09.html; calculations by New Strategist

Table 8.23 Owners of Mobile Homes by Major Source of Down Payment, 2009

The owners of mobile homes are less likely than the average
homeowner to have used money from the sale of a previous home
as their major source of down payment—19 versus 31 percent.

(number and percent distribution of total homeowners and owners of mobile/manufactured homes, by major source of down payment, 2009; numbers in thousands)

	total		mobile homes		
	number	percent distribution	number	percent distribution	percent of total
Total homes purchased or built	**71,877**	**100.0%**	**5,076**	**100.0%**	**7.1%**
Sale of previous home	21,946	30.5	962	19.0	4.4
Savings or cash on hand	31,437	43.7	2,152	42.4	6.8
Sale of other investment	750	1.0	53	1.0	7.1
Borrowing, other than mortgage on this property	2,409	3.4	264	5.2	11.0
Inheritance or gift	1,358	1.9	72	1.4	5.3
Land where building built used for financing	639	0.9	93	1.8	14.6
Other	3,125	4.3	383	7.6	12.3
No down payment	8,346	11.6	893	17.6	10.7
Not reported	1,867	2.6	205	4.0	11.0

Source: Bureau of the Census, American Housing Survey for the United States: 2009, Internet site http://www.census.gov/hhes/ www/housing/ahs/ahs09/ahs09.html; calculations by New Strategist

Table 8.24   Owners of Mobile Homes by First Home and Mortgage Status, 2009

The owners of mobile homes are as likely as the average homeowner to be first-time homeowners. The 60 percent majority own their home free and clear.

(number and percent distribution of total homeowners and owners of mobile/manufactured homes, by first-home and mortgage status, 2009; numbers in thousands)

	total		mobile homes		
	number	percent distribution	number	percent distribution	percent of total
FIRST-HOME STATUS					
Total homeowners	**76,428**	**100.0%**	**5,418**	**100.0%**	**7.1%**
First home ever owned	31,676	41.4	2,196	40.5	6.9
Not first home	43,233	56.6	3,128	57.7	7.2
Not reported	1,519	2.0	94	1.7	6.2
MORTGAGE STATUS					
Total homeowners	**76,428**	**100.0**	**5,418**	**100.0**	**7.1**
None, owned free and clear	24,206	31.7	3,237	59.7	13.4
Reverse mortgage	252	0.3	11	0.2	4.4
With regular and/or home-equity mortgages	50,300	65.8	2,107	38.9	4.2
Regular mortgage(s)	46,703	61.1	2,002	36.9	4.3
Home-equity lump-sum mortgage	4,022	5.3	57	1.1	1.4
Home-equity line of credit	9,184	12.0	106	2.0	1.2
Not reported	1,670	2.2	64	1.2	3.8

Source: Bureau of the Census, American Housing Survey for the United States: 2009, Internet site http://www.census.gov/hhes/ www/housing/ahs/ahs09/ahs09.html; calculations by New Strategist

Table 8.25 Owners of Mobile Homes by Year of Origination of Primary Mortgage, 2009

Owners of the nation's mobile homes were less likely than the average homeowner to have obtained their primary mortgage during the housing bubble.

(number and percent distribution of total homeowners and owners of mobile/manufactured homes, by year primary mortgage originated, 2009; numbers in thousands)

	total		mobile homes		
	number	percent distribution	number	percent distribution	percent of total
Total homeowners with mortgages	**47,945**	**100.0%**	**2,039**	**100.0%**	**4.3%**
2005 to 2009	21,064	43.9	779	38.2	3.7
2000 to 2004	14,175	29.6	545	26.7	3.8
1995 to 1999	6,152	12.8	544	26.7	8.8
1990 to 1994	2,953	6.2	83	4.1	2.8
1985 to 1989	1,808	3.8	41	2.0	2.3
1980 to 1984	767	1.6	27	1.3	3.5
1975 to 1979	564	1.2	15	0.7	2.7
1970 to 1974	434	0.9	6	0.3	1.3
1969 or earlier	28	0.1	0	0.0	0.0
Median year of origination	2004	–	2002	–	–

Note: "–" means not applicable.
Source: Bureau of the Census, American Housing Survey for the United States: 2009, Internet site http://www.census.gov/hhes/ www/housing/ahs/ahs09/ahs09.html; calculations by New Strategist

Table 8.26 Owners of Mobile Homes by Mortgage Characteristics, 2009

Thirty-eight percent of the owners of mobile homes
have mortgages. Among those who do, more than one-third
have mortgages that equal or exceed the value of their home.

(number and percent distribution of total homeowners and owners of mobile/manufactured homes, by mortgage characteristics, 2009; numbers in thousands)

	total		mobile homes		
	number	percent distribution	number	percent distribution	percent of total
Total homeowners	**76,428**	**100.0%**	**5,418**	**100.0%**	**7.1%**
Homeowners with mortgages	47,945	62.7	2,039	37.6	4.3
REMAINING YEARS MORTGAGED					
Homeowners with mortgages	**47,945**	**100.0**	**2,039**	**100.0**	**4.3**
Less than 8 years	6,160	12.8	535	26.3	8.7
8 to 12 years	5,188	10.8	312	15.3	6.0
13 to 17 years	5,077	10.6	277	13.6	5.5
18 to 22 years	6,568	13.7	393	19.3	6.0
23 to 27 years	14,948	31.2	310	15.2	2.1
28 to 32 years	9,569	20.0	200	9.8	2.1
33 years or more	164	0.3	8	0.4	4.9
Variable	271	0.6	3	0.2	1.2
Median years remaining	23	–	16	–	–
TOTAL OUTSTANDING PRINCIPAL					
Homeowners with mortgages	**47,945**	**100.0**	**2,039**	**100.0**	**4.3**
Under $10,000	2,797	5.8	327	16.0	11.7
$10,000 to $19,999	1,972	4.1	246	12.1	12.5
$20,000 to $29,999	1,877	3.9	191	9.3	10.2
$30,000 to $39,999	1,978	4.1	171	8.4	8.7
$40,000 to $49,999	2,338	4.9	73	3.6	3.1
$50,000 to $59,999	2,328	4.9	140	6.9	6.0
$60,000 to $69,999	2,504	5.2	140	6.8	5.6
$70,000 to $79,999	2,484	5.2	165	8.1	6.6
$80,000 to $99,999	4,420	9.2	64	3.1	1.4
$100,000 to $119,999	3,751	7.8	48	2.3	1.3
$120,000 to $149,999	5,029	10.5	42	2.1	0.8
$150,000 to $199,999	5,926	12.4	3	0.2	0.1
$200,000 to $249,999	3,575	7.5	0	0.0	0.0
$250,000 to $299,999	2,267	4.7	8	0.0	0.0
$300,000 or more	4,700	9.8	0	0.0	0.0
Median outstanding principal	$106,909	–	$31,214	–	–

	total		mobile homes		
	number	percent distribution	number	percent distribution	percent of total
CURRENT TOTAL LOAN AS PERCENT OF VALUE					
Homeowners with mortgages	**47,945**	**100.0%**	**2,039**	**100.0%**	**4.3%**
Less than 20 percent	6,174	12.9	240	11.8	3.9
20 to 39 percent	7,478	15.6	219	10.7	2.9
40 to 59 percent	8,524	17.8	229	11.2	2.7
60 to 79 percent	9,924	20.7	295	14.5	3.0
80 to 89 percent	5,128	10.7	195	9.6	3.8
90 to 99 percent	4,928	10.3	170	8.4	3.5
100 percent or more	5,789	12.1	691	33.9	11.9
Median percent of value	63.0%	–	82.0%	–	–

Note: "–" means not applicable.
Source: Bureau of the Census, American Housing Survey for the United States: 2009, Internet site http://www.census.gov/hhes/www/housing/ahs/nationaldata.html; calculations by New Strategist

Table 8.27 Owners of Mobile Homes by Refinancing of Primary Mortgage Status, 2009

Only 13 percent of the owners of mobile homes with a mortgage loan have refinanced their mortgage. Most did so to get a lower interest rate.

(number and percent distribution of total homeowners with mortgages and owners of mobile/manufactured homes with mortgages, by refinancing of primary mortgage status and reason for refinancing, 2009; numbers in thousands)

	total		mobile homes		
	number	percent distribution	number	percent distribution	percent of total
Homeowners with mortgages	**47,945**	**100.0%**	**2,039**	**100.0%**	**4.3%**
Homeowners with refinanced primary mortgage	12,220	25.5	269	13.2	2.2
REASON FOR REFINANCING OF PRIMARY MORTGAGE					
Homeowners with refinanced primary mortgage	**12,220**	**100.0**	**269**	**100.0**	**2.2**
To get lower interest rate	9,228	75.5	172	64.1	1.9
To reduce the monthly payment	1,552	12.7	43	15.9	2.7
To increase payment period	180	1.5	9	3.3	4.9
To reduce payment period	573	4.7	9	3.2	1.5
To renew or extend a loan that has fallen due	123	1.0	2	0.9	2.0
To receive cash	1,587	13.0	32	11.9	2.0
Other reasons	1,655	13.5	58	21.6	3.5

Source: Bureau of the Census, American Housing Survey for the United States: 2009, Internet site http://www.census.gov/hhes/ www/housing/ahs/ahs09/ahs09.html; calculations by New Strategist

Table 8.28 Owners of Mobile Homes by Monthly Principal and Interest Payments, 2009

The owners of mobile homes pay much less per month than the average homeowner in principal and interest payments, a median of $403 versus $878.

(number and percent distribution of total homeowners with mortgages and owners of mobile/manufactured homes, by monthly payment for principal and interest, 2009; numbers in thousands)

	total		mobile homes		
	number	percent distribution	number	percent distribution	percent of total
Homeowners with mortgages	**47,945**	**100.0%**	**2,039**	**100.0%**	**4.3%**
Less than $100	1,327	2.8	132	6.5	9.9
$100 to $199	1,072	2.2	162	7.9	15.1
$200 to $299	1,757	3.7	295	14.5	16.8
$300 to $399	2,873	6.0	375	18.4	13.1
$400 to $499	3,338	7.0	279	13.7	8.4
$500 to $599	3,816	8.0	251	12.3	6.6
$600 to $699	3,859	8.0	165	8.1	4.3
$700 to $799	3,443	7.2	157	7.7	4.6
$800 to $999	6,162	12.9	125	6.1	2.0
$1,000 to $1,249	5,879	12.3	56	2.7	0.9
$1,250 to $1,499	4,059	8.5	23	1.1	0.6
$1,500 to $1,999	4,786	10.0	8	0.4	0.2
$2,000 or more	5,574	11.6	11	0.6	0.2
Median monthly payment	$878	–	$403	–	–

Note: "–" means not applicable.
Source: Bureau of the Census, American Housing Survey for the United States: 2009, Internet site http://www.census.gov/hhes/www/housing/ahs/ahs09/ahs09.html; calculations by New Strategist

Table 8.29 Owners of Mobile Homes by Monthly Housing Costs, 2009

Housing costs are much lower for the owners of mobile homes than for the average homeowner—a monthly median of $332 versus $1,000.

(number and percent distribution of total homeowners and owners of mobile/manufactured homes, by monthly housing costs, 2009; numbers in thousands)

	total		mobile homes		
	number	percent distribution	number	percent distribution	percent of total
Total homeowners	**76,428**	**100.0%**	**5,418**	**100.0%**	**7.1%**
Less than $100	475	0.6	257	4.7	54.1
$100 to $199	2,161	2.8	919	17.0	42.5
$200 to $299	5,351	7.0	1,253	23.1	23.4
$300 to $399	6,022	7.9	675	12.5	11.2
$400 to $499	5,308	6.9	408	7.5	7.7
$500 to $599	4,407	5.8	289	5.3	6.6
$600 to $699	3,735	4.9	283	5.2	7.6
$700 to $799	3,597	4.7	320	5.9	8.9
$800 to $999	7,139	9.3	397	7.3	5.6
$1,000 to $1,249	8,156	10.7	333	6.1	4.1
$1,250 to $1,499	6,828	8.9	156	2.9	2.3
$1,500 or $1,999	9,445	12.4	77	1.4	0.8
$2,000 to $2,499	5,422	7.1	10	0.2	0.2
$2,500 or more	8,383	11.0	41	0.8	0.5
Median monthly cost	$1,000	–	$332	–	–

Note: Housing costs include utilities, mortgages, real estate taxes, property insurance, and regime fees. "–" means not applicable.
Source: Bureau of the Census, American Housing Survey for the United States: 2009, Internet site http://www.census.gov/hhes/www/housing/ahs/ahs09/ahs09.html; calculations by New Strategist

Table 8.30 Owners of Mobile Homes by Monthly Utility and Property Insurance Costs, 2009

The owners of mobile homes pay more for
electricity than the average homeowner.

(number and percent distribution of total homeowners and owners of mobile/manufactured homes, by average monthly costs for utilities, 2009; numbers in thousands)

	total		mobile homes		
	number	percent distribution	number	percent distribution	percent of total
MONTHLY COST OF ELECTRICITY					
Households using electricity	**76,378**	**100.0%**	**5,418**	**100.0%**	**7.1%**
Less than $25	442	0.6	43	0.8	9.7
$25 to $49	4,425	5.8	292	5.4	6.6
$50 to $74	11,016	14.4	728	13.4	6.6
$75 to $99	12,975	17.0	833	15.4	6.4
$100 to $149	21,237	27.8	1,545	28.5	7.3
$150 to $199	12,164	15.9	1,003	18.5	8.2
$200 or more	12,110	15.9	849	15.7	7.0
Included in other fee, or obtained free	2,010	2.6	75	1.4	3.7
Median monthly cost	$117	–	$129	–	–
MONTHLY COST OF PIPED GAS					
Households using piped gas	**46,700**	**100.0**	**1,306**	**100.0**	**2.8**
Less than $25	1,410	3.0	50	3.8	3.5
$25 to $49	7,933	17.0	370	28.3	4.7
$50 to $74	11,196	24.0	339	26.0	3.0
$75 to $99	8,595	18.4	211	16.2	2.5
$100 to $149	9,694	20.8	144	11.0	1.5
$150 to $199	3,698	7.9	47	3.6	1.3
$200 or more	2,682	5.7	23	1.8	0.9
Included in other fee, or obtained free	1,494	3.2	121	9.3	8.1
Median monthly cost	$80	–	$80	–	–
MONTHLY COST OF FUEL OIL					
Households using fuel oil	**6,409**	**100.0**	**212**	**100.0**	**3.3**
Less than $25	176	2.8	15	7.3	8.8
$25 to $49	325	5.1	16	7.4	4.8
$50 to $74	490	7.6	34	16.1	7.0
$75 to $99	725	11.3	40	18.9	5.5
$100 to $149	1,403	21.9	67	31.4	4.7
$150 to $199	1,052	16.4	27	12.8	2.6
$200 or more	1,701	26.5	6	3.0	0.4
Included in other fee, or obtained free	536	8.4	6	2.8	1.1
Median monthly cost	$133	–	$96	–	–

	total		mobile homes		
	number	percent distribution	number	percent distribution	percent of total
Water paid separately	**53,552**	–	**2,566**	–	**4.8%**
Median monthly cost	$38	–	$30	–	–
Trash paid separately	**44,974**	–	**2,066**	–	**4.6**
Median monthly cost	$21	–	$17	–	–
Property insurance paid	**72,313**	–	**4,173**	–	**5.8**
Median monthly cost	$55	–	$38	–	–

Note: "–" means not applicable.
Source: Bureau of the Census, American Housing Survey for the United States: 2009, Internet site http://www.census.gov/hhes/ www/housing/ahs/ahs09/ahs09.html; calculations by New Strategist

Table 8.31 Owners of Mobile Homes by Real Estate Taxes, 2009

The owners of mobile homes pay much less in real estate taxes than
the average homeowner, a median of only $25 per month.

*(number and percent distribution of total homeowners and owners of mobile/manufactured homes, by monthly cost
of real estate taxes and taxes per $1,000 assessed value, 2009; numbers in thousands)*

	total		mobile homes		
	number	percent distribution	number	percent distribution	percent of total
Total homeowners	**76,428**	**100.0%**	**5,418**	**100.0%**	**7.1%**
Monthly cost of real estate taxes					
Less than $25	7,751	10.1	2,688	49.6	34.7
$25 to $49	6,017	7.9	1,071	19.8	17.8
$50 to $74	6,565	8.6	654	12.1	10.0
$75 to $99	5,883	7.7	238	4.4	4.1
$100 to $124	6,494	8.5	225	4.2	3.5
$125 to $149	4,880	6.4	122	2.2	2.5
$150 to $199	9,140	12.0	147	2.7	1.6
$200 to $299	11,727	15.3	136	2.5	1.2
$300 to $399	6,171	8.1	29	0.5	0.5
$400 to $499	3,655	4.8	37	0.7	1.0
$500 to $599	2,884	3.8	20	0.4	0.7
$600 or more	5,260	6.9	51	0.9	1.0
Median monthly cost	$150	–	$25	–	–
Annual taxes paid per $1,000 value					
Less than $5	12,710	16.6	1,606	29.6	12.6
$5 to $9	21,383	28.0	904	16.7	4.2
$10 to $14	17,473	22.9	769	14.2	4.4
$15 to $19	9,992	13.1	458	8.4	4.6
$20 to $24	6,058	7.9	287	5.3	4.7
$25 or more	8,812	11.5	1,394	25.7	15.8
Median amount per $1,000 assessed	$10	–	$10	–	–

Note: "–" means not applicable.
*Source: Bureau of the Census, American Housing Survey for the United States: 2009, Internet site http://www.census.gov/hhes/
www/housing/ahs/ahs09/ahs09.html; calculations by New Strategist*

Table 8.32 Owners of Mobile Homes by Opinion of Home, 2009

The owners of mobile homes are just as likely to rate their home a 10 on a scale of 1 (worst) to 10 (best) as the average homeowner.

(number and percent distribution of total homeowners and owners of mobile/manufactured homes, by opinion of home, 2009; numbers in thousands)

	total		mobile homes		
	number	percent distribution	number	percent distribution	percent of total
Total homeowners	**76,428**	**100.0%**	**5,418**	**100.0%**	**7.1%**
1 (worst)	203	0.3	23	0.4	11.4
2	122	0.2	32	0.6	26.4
3	175	0.2	40	0.7	23.1
4	444	0.6	105	1.9	23.7
5	2,365	3.1	399	7.4	16.9
6	2,655	3.5	279	5.2	10.5
7	8,899	11.6	715	13.2	8.0
8	21,042	27.5	1,311	24.2	6.2
9	13,627	17.8	609	11.2	4.5
10 (best)	23,967	31.4	1,742	32.1	7.3
Not reported	2,926	3.8	162	3.0	5.5

Note: "–" means not applicable.
Source: Bureau of the Census, American Housing Survey for the United States: 2009, Internet site http://www.census.gov/hhes/ www/housing/ahs/ahs09/ahs09.html; calculations by New Strategist

Table 8.33 Owners of Mobile Homes by Opinion of Neighborhood, 2009

The owners of mobile homes are slightly more likely than
the average homeowner to rate their neighborhood
a 10 on a scale of 1 (worst) to 10 (best).

(number and percent distribution of total homeowners and owners of mobile/manufactured homes, by opinion of neighborhood, 2009; numbers in thousands)

	total		mobile homes		
	number	percent distribution	number	percent distribution	percent of total
Total homeowners	**76,428**	**100.0%**	**5,418**	**100.0%**	**7.1%**
1 (worst)	338	0.4	41	0.7	12.0
2	289	0.4	51	0.9	17.6
3	459	0.6	67	1.2	14.5
4	766	1.0	99	1.8	12.9
5	3,356	4.4	368	6.8	11.0
6	3,454	4.5	272	5.0	7.9
7	9,603	12.6	627	11.6	6.5
8	20,808	27.2	1,305	24.1	6.3
9	13,454	17.6	744	13.7	5.5
10 (best)	20,891	27.3	1,678	31.0	8.0
No neighborhood	31	0.0	4	0.1	11.9
Not reported	2,979	3.9	164	3.0	5.5

Source: Bureau of the Census, American Housing Survey for the United States: 2009, Internet site http://www.census.gov/hhes/www/housing/ahs/ahs09/ahs09.html; calculations by New Strategist

Table 8.34 Owners of Mobile Homes by Neighborhood Problems, 2009

The owners of mobile homes are less likely than the average homeowner to have had serious crime in their neighborhood in the past 12 months.

(number and percent distribution of total homeowners and owners of mobile/manufactured homes, by selected neighborhood problems, 2009; numbers in thousands)

	total		mobile homes		
	number	percent distribution	number	percent distribution	percent of total
Total homeowners	**76,428**	**100.0%**	**5,418**	**100.0%**	**7.1%**
Bothersome street noise or heavy traffic	15,223	19.9	1,006	18.6	6.6
Serious crime in neighborhood in past 12 months	11,649	15.2	739	13.6	6.3
Bothersome odor problem	3,278	4.3	311	5.7	9.5
Noise problem	1,733	2.3	114	2.1	6.6
Litter or housing deterioration	1,101	1.4	78	1.4	7.1
Poor city or county services	440	0.6	67	1.2	15.3
Undesirable commercial, institutional, industrial	247	0.3	14	0.3	5.7
People problem	2,706	3.5	303	5.6	11.2
Other problems	6,748	8.8	537	9.9	8.0

Source: Bureau of the Census, American Housing Survey for the United States: 2009, Internet site http://www.census.gov/hhes/www/housing/ahs/ahs09/ahs09.html; calculations by New Strategist

Table 8.35 Owners of Mobile Homes by Community Characteristics, 2009

The owners of mobile homes are more likely than the average homeowner to live in an age-restricted community. Among mobile home owner households that include a person aged 55 or older, 14 percent are in an age-restricted community.

(number and percent distribution of total homeowners and owners of mobile/manufactured homes, by community characteristics, 2009; numbers in thousands)

	total		mobile homes		
	number	percent distribution	number	percent distribution	percent of total
Total homeowners	**76,428**	**100.0%**	**5,418**	**100.0%**	**7.1%**
SECURED COMMUNITIES					
Total homeowners	**76,428**	**100.0**	**5,418**	**100.0**	**7.1**
Community access secured with walls or fences	5,337	7.0	487	9.0	9.1
Special entry system present	2,682	3.5	121	2.2	4.5
Special entry system not present	2,648	3.5	366	6.8	13.8
Community access not secured	70,410	92.1	4,893	90.3	6.9
SENIOR CITIZEN COMMUNITIES					
Households with persons aged 55 or older	**36,591**	**100.0**	**2,669**	**100.0**	**7.3**
Community age restricted	1,457	4.0	366	13.7	25.1
No age restriction	35,134	96.0	2,303	86.3	6.6
Community age specific	8,867	24.2	637	23.9	7.2
Community not age specific	24,100	65.9	1,513	56.7	6.3
COMMUNITY AMENITIES					
Total homeowners	**76,428**	**100.0**	**5,418**	**100.0**	**7.1**
Community center or clubhouse	14,707	19.2	1,178	21.7	8.0
Golf in community	12,762	16.7	447	8.2	3.5
Trails in community	15,300	20.0	451	8.3	2.9
Shuttle bus available	5,718	7.5	216	4.0	3.8
Daycare center	10,633	13.9	339	6.3	3.2
Private or restricted beach, park, or shoreline	15,124	19.8	592	10.9	3.9
DESCRIPTION OF AREA WITHIN 300 FEET OF HOME					
Total homeowners	**76,428**	**100.0**	**5,418**	**100.0**	**7.1**
Single-family detached homes	68,909	90.2	4,020	74.2	5.8
Single-family attached homes	10,973	14.4	242	4.5	2.2
Multiunit residential buildings	11,514	15.1	438	8.1	3.8
One-to-three-story multiunit is tallest	9,014	11.8	398	7.4	4.4
Four-to-six-story multiunit is tallest	1,464	1.9	28	0.5	1.9
Seven-or-more-story multiunit is tallest	929	1.2	6	0.1	0.7
Manufactured/mobile homes	10,276	13.4	4,318	79.7	42.0
Commercial or institutional	16,992	22.2	1,023	18.9	6.0
Industrial or factories	2,520	3.3	269	5.0	10.7
Open space, park, woods, farm, or ranch	33,110	43.3	3,281	60.6	9.9
Four-or-more-lane highway, railroad, or airport	10,380	13.6	882	16.3	8.5

	total		mobile homes		
	number	percent distribution	number	percent distribution	percent of total
BODIES OF WATER WITHIN 300 FEET OF HOME					
Total homeowners	**76,428**	**100.0%**	**5,418**	**100.0%**	**7.1%**
Water in area	13,824	18.1	1,294	23.9	9.4
With waterfront property	2,653	3.5	163	3.0	6.1
With flood plain	1,929	2.5	215	4.0	11.1
No water in area	62,083	81.2	4,094	75.6	6.6

Note: Numbers may not add to total because "not reported" is not shown.
Source: Bureau of the Census, American Housing Survey for the United States: 2009, Internet site http://www.census.gov/hhes/ www/housing/ahs/ahs09/ahs09.html; calculations by New Strategist

Table 8.36 Owners of Mobile Homes by Grouping Status, 2009

Most mobile home owners have no or only a few other mobile homes nearby.
The 73 percent majority are in a mobile home grouping of one to six units.

(number and percent distribution of the owners of mobile homes by group status, 2009; numbers in thousands)

	number	percent
Total mobile home owners	**5,418**	**100.0%**
One to six in area	3,952	72.9
Seven to 20 in area	217	4.0
21 or more in area	1,249	23.1

Source: Bureau of the Census, American Housing Survey for the United States: 2009, Internet site http://www.census.gov/hhes/ www/housing/ahs/ahs09/ahs09.html; calculations by New Strategist

Table 8.37 Owners of Mobile Homes by Public Services Available, 2009

The owners of mobile homes have fewer public services available to them than the average homeowner. Only 22 percent have public transportation in their area.

(number and percent distribution of total homeowners and owners of mobile/manufactured homes, by public services available in neighborhood, 2009; numbers in thousands)

	total		mobile homes		
	number	percent distribution	number	percent distribution	percent of total
Total homeowners	**76,428**	**100.0%**	**5,418**	**100.0%**	**7.1%**
LOCAL ELEMENTARY SCHOOL					
Homeowners with children under age 14	**20,490**	**100.0**	**1,235**	**100.0**	**6.0**
Satisfactory public elementary school	16,966	82.8	1,078	87.3	6.4
Unsatisfactory public elementary school	1,422	6.9	88	7.1	6.2
Unsatisfactory public elementary school	**1,422**	**100.0**	**88**	**100.0**	**6.2**
Better than other area elementary schools	154	10.8	12	13.2	7.5
Same as other area elementary schools	490	34.4	35	39.9	7.1
Worse than other area elementary schools	696	49.0	41	47.0	5.9
Homeowners with children under age 14	**20,490**	**100.0**	**1,235**	**100.0**	**6.0**
Public elementary school less than one mile	11,571	56.5	346	28.0	3.0
Public elementary school more than one mile	7,785	38.0	846	68.5	10.9
PUBLIC TRANSPORTATION IN AREA					
Total homeowners	**76,428**	**100.0**	**5,418**	**100.0**	**7.1**
With public transportation	35,616	46.6	1,183	21.8	3.3
No public transportation	38,848	50.8	4,110	75.9	10.6
With public transportation, travel time to nearest stop	**35,616**	**100.0**	**1,183**	**100.0**	**3.3**
Less than 5 minutes	10,929	30.7	385	32.6	3.5
5 to 9 minutes	12,830	36.0	378	31.9	2.9
10 to 14 minutes	5,853	16.4	144	12.2	2.5
15 to 29 minutes	3,125	8.8	139	11.7	4.4
30 minutes or longer	449	1.3	37	3.1	8.2
With public transportation	**35,616**	**100.0**	**1,183**	**100.0**	**3.3**
Household uses it regularly for commute to school or work	3,817	10.7	117	9.9	3.1
Household does not use it regularly for commute to school or work	31,606	88.7	1,063	89.9	3.4

	total		mobile homes		
	number	percent distribution	number	percent distribution	percent of total
SHOPPING IN AREA					
Total homeowners	**76,428**	**100.0%**	**5,418**	**100.0%**	**7.1%**
Grocery stores or drugstores within 15 minutes of home	72,548	94.9	4,860	89.7	6.7
Satisfactory	70,400	92.1	4,632	85.5	6.6
Not satisfactory	1,805	2.4	207	3.8	11.5
No grocery stores or drugstores within 15 minutes of home	2,819	3.7	451	8.3	16.0
POLICE PROTECTION					
Total homeowners	**76,428**	**100.0**	**5,418**	**100.0**	**7.1**
Satisfactory police protection	69,633	91.1	4,753	87.7	6.8
Unsatisfactory police protection	4,800	6.3	544	10.0	11.3

Note: Numbers may not add to total because "not reported" is not shown.
Source: Bureau of the Census, American Housing Survey for the United States: 2009, Internet site http://www.census.gov/hhes/ www/housing/ahs/ahs09/ahs09.html; calculations by New Strategist

Table 8.38 Owners of Mobile Homes Who Moved by Changes in Housing and Costs, 2009

The owners of mobile homes who recently moved are
more likely than the average homeowner who moved
to have seen their housing costs decrease after their move.

(number and percent distribution of total homeowners who have moved in the past year and those who moved into mobile/manufactured homes, by structure type of previous residence, tenure of previous residence, and change in housing costs, 2009; numbers in thousands)

	total		mobile homes		
	number	percent distribution	number	percent distribution	percent of total
STRUCTURE TYPE OF PREVIOUS RESIDENCE					
Homeowners who moved within United States	**4,341**	**100.0%**	**388**	**100.0%**	**8.9%**
House	2,595	59.8	187	48.3	7.2
Apartment	1,208	27.8	60	15.6	5.0
Mobile home	238	5.5	108	27.9	45.6
Other	119	2.7	11	2.9	9.4
Not reported	182	4.2	21	5.3	11.4
OWNERSHIP OF PREVIOUS RESIDENCE					
Homeowners who moved from house, apartment, or mobile home within United States	**4,041**	**100.0**	**356**	**100.0**	**8.8**
Owner-occupied	2,032	50.3	185	52.1	9.1
Renter-occupied	2,009	49.7	171	47.9	8.5
CHANGE IN HOUSING COSTS					
Homeowners who moved from house, apartment, or mobile home within United States	**4,041**	**100.0**	**356**	**100.0**	**8.8**
Increased with move	2,455	60.8	128	36.0	5.2
Decreased	801	19.8	148	41.6	18.5
Stayed about the same	663	16.4	65	18.4	9.9
Don't know	60	1.5	0	0.0	0.0
Not reported	62	1.5	15	4.2	24.2

Source: Bureau of the Census, American Housing Survey for the United States: 2009, Internet site http://www.census.gov/hhes/www/housing/ahs/ahs09/ahs09.html; calculations by New Strategist

Table 8.39 Owners of Mobile Homes Who Moved by Reasons for Choosing Home, 2009

The owners of mobile homes who recently moved are far more likely than the average homeowner who recently moved to have chosen their home for financial reasons—37 versus 22 percent.

(number and percent distribution of total homeowning respondents who have moved in the past year and those who moved into mobile/manufactured homes, by reasons for choosing home, 2009; numbers in thousands)

	total		mobile homes		
	number	percent distribution	number	percent distribution	percent of total
Total homeowning respondents who moved	**4,623**	**100.0%**	**410**	**100.0%**	**8.9%**
Main reason for choice of present home					
All reported reasons equal	808	17.5	49	12.0	6.1
Financial reasons	1,008	21.8	150	36.6	14.9
Room layout/design	797	17.2	38	9.4	4.8
Kitchen	33	0.7	1	0.3	3.5
Size	377	8.2	24	5.8	6.3
Exterior appearance	125	2.7	6	1.3	4.4
Yard/trees/view	287	6.2	12	2.8	4.0
Quality of construction	186	4.0	15	3.6	8.0
Only one available	76	1.6	18	4.4	24.0
Other	636	13.7	60	14.7	9.5
Not reported	290	6.3	37	9.0	12.8
Present home compared with previous home					
Better	3,017	65.3	211	51.6	7.0
Worse	426	9.2	80	19.5	18.7
About the same	920	19.9	82	20.1	9.0
Not reported	261	5.6	36	8.8	13.9

Note: Total number of movers does not equal total movers in other tables because this table shows survey respondents who moved, not necessarily householders.
Source: Bureau of the Census, American Housing Survey for the United States: 2009, Internet site http://www.census.gov/hhes/www/housing/ahs/ahs09/ahs09.html; calculations by New Strategist

Table 8.40 Owners of Mobile Homes Who Moved by Main Reason for Choosing Neighborhood, 2009

The owners of mobile homes who recently moved are more likely
than the average homeowner who recently moved to say they
chose their present neighborhood to be close to friends or family.

(number and percent distribution of total homeowning respondents who moved in the past year, and those who moved into mobile/manufactured homes, by main reason for choosing neighborhood, 2009; numbers in thousands)

	total		mobile homes		
	number	percent distribution	number	percent distribution	percent of total
Total homeowning respondents who moved	**4,623**	**100.0%**	**410**	**100.0%**	**8.9%**
Neighborhood search					
Looked at just this neighborhood	1,590	34.4	249	60.8	15.7
Looked at other neighborhoods	2,802	60.6	124	30.1	4.4
Not reported	231	5.0	37	9.0	16.0
Main reason for choice of present neighborhood					
All reported reasons equal	551	11.9	38	9.3	6.9
Convenient to job	611	13.2	15	3.7	2.5
Convenient to friends or relatives	570	12.3	102	24.8	17.8
Convenient to leisure activities	87	1.9	6	1.5	6.8
Convenient to public transportation	29	0.6	0	0.0	0.0
Good schools	289	6.3	7	1.8	2.5
Other public services	36	0.8	3	0.7	7.7
Looks/design of neighborhood	635	13.7	41	10.0	6.4
House was most important consideration	801	17.3	59	14.4	7.4
Other	750	16.2	102	24.9	13.6
Not reported	264	5.7	37	9.0	14.0
Present neighborhood compared with previous neighborhood					
Better	2,253	48.7	149	36.3	6.6
Worse	347	7.5	34	8.4	9.9
About the same	1,555	33.6	141	34.4	9.1
Same neighborhood	179	3.9	50	12.1	27.8
Not reported	290	6.3	36	8.8	12.4

Note: Total number of movers does not equal total movers in other tables because this table shows survey respondents who moved, not necessarily householders.
Source: Bureau of the Census, American Housing Survey for the United States: 2009, Internet site http://www.census.gov/hhes/ www/housing/ahs/ahs09/ahs09.html; calculations by New Strategist

Table 8.41 Owners of Mobile Homes Who Moved by Main Reason for Moving, 2009

The single most important reason for moving among owners of mobile homes who recently moved was to establish their own household, mentioned by 16 percent.

(number and percent distribution of total homeowning respondents who moved in the past year and those moving into mobile/manufactured homes, by main reason for move, 2009; numbers in thousands)

	total		mobile homes		
	number	percent distribution	number	percent distribution	percent of total
Total homeowning respondents who moved	**4,623**	**100.0%**	**410**	**100.0%**	**8.9%**
All reported reasons equal	203	4.4	15	3.6	7.2
Private displacement	5	0.1	3	0.8	59.3
Government displacement	8	0.2	3	0.7	35.3
Disaster loss (fire, flood, etc.)	24	0.5	4	0.9	15.3
New job or job transfer	370	8.0	2	0.6	0.7
To be closer to work/school/other	217	4.7	15	3.6	6.9
Other financial, employment related	119	2.6	6	1.4	4.9
To establish own household	594	12.8	65	15.8	10.9
Needed larger house or apartment	431	9.3	17	4.1	3.9
Married, widowed, divorced, or separated	284	6.1	39	9.5	13.7
Other family, personal reasons	368	8.0	55	13.5	15.0
Wanted better home	305	6.6	12	2.9	4.0
Change from renter to owner	685	14.8	41	10.0	6.0
Wanted lower maintenance	60	1.3	13	3.1	21.1
Other housing related reasons	168	3.6	13	3.3	8.0
Evicted from residence	14	0.3	7	1.7	49.2
Other	484	10.5	47	11.5	9.7
Not reported	286	6.2	54	13.1	18.8

Note: Total number of movers does not equal total movers in other tables because this table shows survey respondents who moved, not necessarily householders.
Source: Bureau of the Census, American Housing Survey for the United States: 2009, Internet site http://www.census.gov/hhes/www/housing/ahs/ahs09/ahs09.html; calculations by New Strategist

Renters of Mobile Homes

More than 1 million renters live in mobile homes.

Renters who live in mobile homes are about the same age as the average renter—a median age of 38—but they are much less educated. Only 4 percent have a bachelor's degree compared with 21 percent of all renters. They are also much poorer than the average renter, with a median household income of just $23,000. The 51 percent majority of mobile home renters are people who live alone or female-headed families.

■ Rented mobile homes are much smaller than the average rental unit, with a median of 980 square feet. Nevertheless, most have three or more bedrooms and nearly half have two or more bathrooms.

■ The renters of mobile homes pay on average only $623 per month for housing, much less than the $808 per month paid by the average renter.

■ The 52 percent majority of renters of mobile homes rate their unit at least an 8 on a scale of 1 (worst) to 10 (best). Only 29 percent have a dishwasher, but 86 percent have a washing machine. Eighty-nine percent have air conditioning.

Rented mobile homes are much smaller than the average rented home

(median square footage in the average rental unit and in rented mobile homes, 2009)

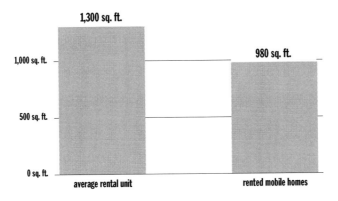

Table 9.1 Renters of Mobile Homes by Age, 2009

Four percent of households that rent live in a mobile or manufactured home. The renters of mobile homes have a median age of 38, about the same as all renters.

(number and percent distribution of total renters and renters of mobile/manufactured homes by age of householder, 2009; numbers in thousands)

	total		mobile homes		
	number	percent distribution	number	percent distribution	percent of total
Total renters	**35,378**	**100.0%**	**1,421**	**100.0%**	**4.0%**
Under age 25	4,799	13.6	216	15.2	4.5
Aged 25 to 29	5,072	14.3	170	12.0	3.4
Aged 30 to 34	4,561	12.9	188	13.2	4.1
Aged 35 to 44	6,976	19.7	323	22.7	4.6
Aged 45 to 54	5,762	16.3	258	18.2	4.5
Aged 55 to 64	3,585	10.1	107	7.5	3.0
Aged 65 to 74	2,120	6.0	95	6.7	4.5
Aged 75 or older	2,503	7.1	63	4.4	2.5
Median age	39	–	38	–	–

Note: "–" means not applicable.
Source: Bureau of the Census, American Housing Survey for the United States: 2009, Internet site http://www.census.gov/hhes/www/housing/ahs/ahs09/ahs09.html; calculations by New Strategist

Table 9.2 Renters of Mobile Homes by Household Type and Age of Householder, 2009

The renters of mobile homes are much more likely to be
married couples than the average renter—34 versus 25 percent.

(number and percent distribution of total renters and renters of mobile/manufactured homes, by household type and age of householder, 2009; numbers in thousands)

	total		mobile homes		
	number	percent distribution	number	percent distribution	percent of total
Total renters	**35,378**	**100.0%**	**1,421**	**100.0%**	**4.0%**
MARRIED-COUPLE HOUSEHOLDS	**8,808**	**24.9**	**484**	**34.1**	**5.5**
Under age 25	707	2.0	58	4.1	8.2
Aged 25 to 29	1,313	3.7	53	3.7	4.0
Aged 30 to 34	1,497	4.2	87	6.1	5.8
Aged 35 to 44	2,168	6.1	130	9.2	6.0
Aged 45 to 64	2,329	6.6	119	8.3	5.1
Aged 65 or older	793	2.2	38	2.6	4.7
TWO-OR-MORE-PERSON HOUSEHOLDS					
Female householders, no spouse present	**8,565**	**24.2**	**341**	**24.0**	**4.0**
Under age 45	6,119	17.3	255	18.0	4.2
Aged 45 to 64	2,030	5.7	73	5.2	3.6
Aged 65 or older	417	1.2	13	0.9	3.0
Male householders, no spouse present	**4,673**	**13.2**	**210**	**14.8**	**4.5**
Under age 45	3,629	10.3	150	10.6	4.1
Aged 45 to 64	895	2.5	54	3.8	6.1
Aged 65 or older	150	0.4	6	0.4	3.7
SINGLE-PERSON HOUSEHOLDS	**13,331**	**37.7**	**385**	**27.1**	**2.9**
Female householders	**6,743**	**19.1**	**187**	**13.2**	**2.8**
Under age 45	2,434	6.9	62	4.4	2.6
Aged 45 to 64	1,981	5.6	63	4.4	3.2
Aged 65 or older	2,328	6.6	62	4.3	2.7
Male householders	**6,588**	**18.6**	**198**	**14.0**	**3.0**
Under age 45	3,540	10.0	101	7.1	2.9
Aged 45 to 64	2,112	6.0	57	4.0	2.7
Aged 65 or older	936	2.6	40	2.8	4.3

Source: Bureau of the Census, American Housing Survey for the United States: 2009, Internet site http://www.census.gov/hhes/ www/housing/ahs/ahs09/ahs09.html; calculations by New Strategist

Table 9.3 Renters of Mobile Homes by Race and Hispanic Origin, 2009

Sixty-nine percent of the renters of mobile homes are
non-Hispanic white, a substantially greater share than the
55 percent of all renters who are non-Hispanic white.

(number and percent distribution of total renters and renters of mobile/manufactured homes, by race and Hispanic origin, 2009; numbers in thousands)

	total		mobile homes		
	number	percent distribution	number	percent distribution	percent of total
Total renters	**35,378**	**100.0%**	**1,421**	**100.0%**	**4.0%**
American Indian	466	1.3	39	2.7	8.4
Asian	1,487	4.2	14	1.0	0.9
Black	7,446	21.0	140	9.9	1.9
Hispanic	6,300	17.8	232	16.3	3.7
White, non-Hispanic	19,427	54.9	987	69.5	5.1

Note: American Indians, Asians, blacks, and whites are those who identify themselves as being of the race alone. Numbers do not add to total because not all races are shown and Hispanics may be of any race.
Source: Bureau of the Census, American Housing Survey for the United States: 2009, Internet site http://www.census.gov/hhes/www/housing/ahs/ahs09.html; calculations by New Strategist

Table 9.4 **Renters of Mobile Homes by Household Income, 2009**

The renters of mobile homes have lower incomes than the
average renter, a median of just $23,000 in 2009.

(number and percent distribution of total renters and renters of mobile/manufactured homes by household income, 2009; numbers in thousands)

	total		mobile homes		
	number	percent distribution	number	percent distribution	percent of total
Total renters	**35,378**	**100.0%**	**1,421**	**100.0%**	**4.0%**
Under $10,000	6,109	17.3	283	19.9	4.6
$10,000 to $19,999	6,115	17.3	321	22.6	5.2
$20,000 to $29,999	5,981	16.9	308	21.7	5.1
$30,000 to $39,999	4,477	12.7	171	12.0	3.8
$40,000 to $49,999	3,438	9.7	96	6.8	2.8
$50,000 to $59,999	2,326	6.6	96	6.8	4.1
$60,000 to $79,999	3,244	9.2	68	4.8	2.1
$80,000 to $99,999	1,663	4.7	26	1.8	1.6
$100,000 to $119,999	833	2.4	21	1.5	2.5
$120,000 or more	1,192	3.4	32	2.3	2.7
Median income	$28,400	–	$23,000	–	–

Note: "–" means not applicable.
Source: Bureau of the Census, American Housing Survey for the United States: 2009, Internet site http://www.census.gov/hhes/ www/housing/ahs/ahs09/ahs09.html; calculations by New Strategist

Table 9.5 Renters of Mobile Homes by Educational Attainment, 2009

The renters of mobile homes are much less educated than the average renter. Nearly one in three did not graduate from high school.

(number and percent distribution of total renters and the renters of mobile/manufactured homes, by educational attainment of householder, 2009; numbers in thousands)

	total		mobile homes		
	number	percent distribution	number	percent distribution	percent of total
Total renters	**35,378**	**100.0%**	**1,421**	**100.0%**	**4.0%**
Not a high school graduate	6,687	18.9	449	31.6	6.7
High school graduate only	11,724	33.1	647	45.5	5.5
Some college, no degree	6,924	19.6	208	14.6	3.0
Associate's degree	2,522	7.1	61	4.3	2.4
Bachelor's degree	5,183	14.7	49	3.5	1.0
Graduate or professional degree	2,338	6.6	7	0.5	0.3
High school graduate or higher	28,691	81.1	973	68.5	3.4
Some college or higher	16,967	48.0	326	22.9	1.9
Bachelor's degree or higher	7,521	21.3	57	4.0	0.8

Source: Bureau of the Census, American Housing Survey for the United States: 2009, Internet site http://www.census.gov/hhes/www/housing/ahs/ahs09/ahs09.html; calculations by New Strategist

Table 9.6 Renters of Mobile Homes by Household Size, 2009

Renters of mobile homes are less likely to live alone
than the average renter, 27 versus 38 percent.

(number and percent distribution of total renters and renters of mobile/manufactured homes by number of persons living in home, 2009; numbers in thousands)

	total		mobile homes		
	number	percent distribution	number	percent distribution	percent of total
Total renters	**35,378**	**100.0%**	**1,421**	**100.0%**	**4.0%**
One person	13,331	37.7	385	27.1	2.9
Two persons	9,453	26.7	365	25.7	3.9
Three persons	5,345	15.1	222	15.6	4.2
Four persons	4,016	11.4	260	18.3	6.5
Five persons	1,910	5.4	105	7.4	5.5
Six persons	780	2.2	50	3.5	6.4
Seven or more persons	543	1.5	33	2.3	6.1

Source: Bureau of the Census, American Housing Survey for the United States: 2009, Internet site http://www.census.gov/hhes/ www/housing/ahs/ahs09/ahs09.html; calculations by New Strategist

Table 9.7 Renters of Mobile Homes by Year Structure Built, 2009

The renters of mobile homes live in newer structures than the average renter.
Half the renters of mobile homes live in a unit built in 1986 or later.

(number and percent distribution of total renters and renters in mobile/manufactured homes, by year structure was built, 2009; numbers in thousands)

	total		mobile homes		
	number	percent distribution	number	percent distribution	percent of total
Total renters	**35,378**	**100.0%**	**1,421**	**100.0%**	**4.0%**
2005 to 2009	1,283	3.6	77	5.4	6.0
2000 to 2004	1,731	4.9	118	8.3	6.8
1995 to 1999	1,603	4.5	187	13.2	11.7
1990 to 1994	1,280	3.6	204	14.4	16.0
1985 to 1989	2,489	7.0	158	11.1	6.4
1980 to 1984	2,179	6.2	153	10.7	7.0
1975 to 1979	4,364	12.3	169	11.9	3.9
1970 to 1974	3,718	10.5	200	14.1	5.4
1960 to 1969	4,409	12.5	138	9.7	3.1
1950 to 1959	3,243	9.2	7	0.5	0.2
1940 to 1949	2,322	6.6	6	0.4	0.2
1930 to 1939	1,924	5.4	3	0.2	0.2
1920 to 1929	1,811	–	–	–	–
1919 or earlier	3,021	–	–	–	–
Median year	1971	–	1986	–	–

Note: "–" means sample is too small to make a reliable estimate.
Source: Bureau of the Census, American Housing Survey for the United States: 2009, Internet site http://www.census.gov/hhes/ www/housing/ahs/ahs09/ahs09.html; calculations by New Strategist

Table 9.8 Renters of Mobile Homes by Year Moved into Unit, 2009

The renters of mobile homes have lived in their home for the same length
of time as the average renter. Half moved into their unit in 2007 or later.

*(number and percent distribution of total renters and renters of mobile/manufactured homes, by year householder
moved into unit, 2009; numbers in thousands)*

	total		mobile homes		
	number	percent distribution	number	percent distribution	percent of total
Total renters	**35,378**	**100.0%**	**1,421**	**100.0%**	**4.0%**
2005 to 2009	25,982	73.4	1,063	74.8	4.1
2000 to 2004	4,970	14.0	231	16.3	4.7
1995 to 1999	1,914	5.4	56	3.9	2.9
1990 to 1994	1,057	3.0	38	2.7	3.6
1985 to 1989	482	1.4	14	1.0	2.9
1980 to 1984	312	0.9	16	1.1	5.0
1975 to 1979	244	0.7	3	0.2	1.1
1970 to 1974	151	0.4	0	0.0	0.0
1960 to 1969	158	0.4	0	0.0	0.0
1950 to 1959	70	0.2	0	0.0	0.0
1940 to 1949	23	0.1	0	0.0	0.0
1939 or earlier	17	0.0	0	0.0	0.0
Median year moved into home	2007	–	2007	–	–

Note: "–" means not applicable.
Source: Bureau of the Census, American Housing Survey for the United States: 2009, Internet site http://www.census.gov/hhes/
www/housing/ahs/ahs09/ahs09.html; calculations by New Strategist

Table 9.9 Renters of Mobile Homes by Square Footage of Unit and Lot Size, 2009

Rented mobile homes are smaller than the average rented home, with a median of 980 square feet. Lot size is larger, however, at .32 acres per mobile home versus .22 acres on average for all rented homes.

(number and percent distribution of total renters and renters of mobile/manufactured homes, by square footage and lot size, 2009; numbers in thousands)

	total renters		mobile home renters		
	number	percent distribution	number	percent distribution	percent of total
Square footage of home, total*	**11,176**	**100.0%**	**1,421**	**100.0%**	**12.7%**
Less than 500 sq. ft.	220	2.0	47	3.3	21.5
500 to 749 sq. ft.	686	6.1	186	13.1	27.1
750 to 999 sq. ft.	1,495	13.4	449	31.6	30.0
1,000 to 1,499 sq. ft.	3,441	30.8	359	25.3	10.4
1,500 to 1,999 sq. ft.	2,235	20.0	166	11.7	7.4
2,000 to 2,499 sq. ft.	1,134	10.1	19	1.3	1.6
2,500 to 2,999 sq. ft.	429	3.8	4	0.3	0.9
3,000 to 3,999 sq. ft.	301	2.7	3	0.2	0.9
4,000 or more sq. ft.	243	2.2	17	1.2	7.0
Not reported	992	8.9	171	12.1	17.3
Median square footage	1,300	–	980	–	–
Lot size, total*	**12,823**	**100.0**	**1,421**	**100.0**	**11.1**
Less than one-eighth acre	2,717	21.2	287	20.2	10.6
One-eighth up to one-quarter acre	4,022	31.4	318	22.4	7.9
One-quarter up to one-half acre	2,084	16.3	154	10.8	7.4
One-half up to one acre	1,162	9.1	156	11.0	13.4
One to five acres	2,120	16.5	399	28.1	18.8
Five to ten acres	205	1.6	43	3.0	20.9
10 or more acres	513	4.0	64	4.5	12.5
Median lot size (acres)	0.22	–	0.32	–	–

* Single-family detached and mobile homes only.
** Homes in two-or-more-unit buildings are excluded.
Note: "–" means not applicable.
Source: Bureau of the Census, American Housing Survey for the United States: 2009, Internet site http://www.census.gov/hhes/www/housing/ahs/ahs09/ahs09.html; calculations by New Strategist

Table 9.10 Renters of Mobile Homes by Number of Rooms in Home, 2009

Most rented mobile homes have three or more bedrooms
and nearly half have two or more bathrooms.

(number and percent distribution of total renters and renters of mobile/manufactured homes, by number and type of rooms, 2009; numbers in thousands)

	total		mobile homes		
	number	percent distribution	number	percent distribution	percent of total
Total renters	**35,378**	**100.0%**	**1,421**	**100.0%**	**4.0%**
Number of rooms					
One room	326	0.9	0	0.0	0.0
Two rooms	879	2.5	2	0.2	0.3
Three rooms	7,675	21.7	55	3.9	0.7
Four rooms	11,354	32.1	539	37.9	4.7
Five rooms	8,212	23.2	550	38.7	6.7
Six rooms	4,232	12.0	170	12.0	4.0
Seven rooms	1,735	4.9	96	6.7	5.5
Eight rooms	622	1.8	4	0.3	0.7
Nine rooms	214	0.6	5	0.3	2.1
10 or more rooms	130	0.4	0	0.0	0.0
Number of bedrooms					
None	744	2.1	2	0.2	0.3
One bedroom	9,720	27.5	60	4.2	0.6
Two bedrooms	14,200	40.1	642	45.2	4.5
Three bedrooms	8,359	23.6	634	44.6	7.6
Four or more bedrooms	2,354	6.7	83	5.9	3.5
Number of bathrooms					
None	229	0.6	3	0.2	1.5
One bathroom	22,894	64.7	612	43.0	2.7
One-and-one-half bathrooms	3,575	10.1	136	9.6	3.8
Two or more bathrooms	8,680	24.5	670	47.1	7.7
With room used for business	**8,040**	**22.7**	**252**	**17.7**	**3.1**
Business only	3,757	10.6	133	9.4	3.5
Business and other use	4,283	12.1	119	8.4	2.8

Source: Bureau of the Census, American Housing Survey for the United States: 2009, Internet site http://www.census.gov/hhes/ www/housing/ahs/ahs09/ahs09.html; calculations by New Strategist

Table 9.11 Renters of Mobile Homes by Presence of Kitchen, Laundry, and Safety Equipment, 2009

The renters of mobile homes are much less likely than the average renter to have a dishwasher, but much more likely to have a washer and dryer.

(number and percent of total renters and renters of mobile/manufactured homes, by presence of kitchen, laundry, and safety equipment, 2009; numbers in thousands)

	total		mobile homes		
	number	percent distribution	number	percent distribution	percent of total
Total renters	**35,378**	**100.0%**	**1,421**	**100.0%**	**4.0%**
With complete kitchen equipment	34,004	96.1	1,415	99.6	4.2
Dishwasher	16,393	46.3	413	29.1	2.5
Washing machine	19,545	55.2	1,225	86.2	6.3
Clothes dryer	18,343	51.8	1,153	81.2	6.3
Disposal in kitchen sink	15,933	45.0	155	10.9	1.0
Trash compactor	730	2.1	15	1.1	2.1
Working smoke detector	32,565	92.0	1,231	86.6	3.8
Fire extinguisher	11,980	33.9	513	36.1	4.3
Sprinkler system inside home	3,081	8.7	23	1.6	0.8
Carbon monoxide detector	9,007	25.5	242	17.0	2.7

Note: Complete kitchen equipment includes a sink, refrigerator, and oven or burners.
Source: Bureau of the Census, American Housing Survey for the United States: 2009, Internet site http://www.census.gov/hhes/ www/housing/ahs/ahs09/ahs09.html; calculations by New Strategist

Table 9.12 Renters of Mobile Homes by Type of Heating Equipment, 2009

The 74 percent majority of rented mobile homes are heated by a warm-air furnace, while another 13 percent use an electric heat pump.

(number and percent distribution of total renters and renters of mobile/manufactured homes, by presence and type of heating equipment, 2009; numbers in thousands)

	total		mobile homes		
	number	percent distribution	number	percent distribution	percent of total
Total renters	**35,378**	**100.0%**	**1,421**	**100.0%**	**4.0%**
Main heating equipment					
Warm-air furnace	19,450	55.0	1,054	74.2	5.4
Steam or hot water system	5,012	14.2	0	0.0	0.0
Electric heat pump	3,500	9.9	178	12.5	5.1
Built-in electric units	2,641	7.5	21	1.5	0.8
Floor, wall, or other built-in hot air units without ducts	2,760	7.8	39	2.8	1.4
Room heaters with flue	370	1.0	11	0.7	2.8
Room heaters without flue	414	1.2	31	2.2	7.5
Portable electric heaters	632	1.8	55	3.9	8.8
Stoves	190	0.5	12	0.8	6.0
Fireplaces with inserts	18	0.0	0	0.0	0.0
Fireplaces without inserts	7	0.0	0	0.0	0.0
Other	154	0.4	12	0.9	8.0
Cooking stove	49	0.1	3	0.2	5.9
None	180	0.5	5	0.3	2.6
Households with additional heating equipment					
Warm-air furnace	26	0.1	0	0.0	0.0
Steam or hot water system	5	0.0	0	0.0	0.0
Electric heat pump	6	0.0	3	0.2	53.9
Built-in electric units	454	1.3	15	1.0	3.2
Floor, wall, or other built-in hot air units without ducts	12	0.0	0	0.0	0.0
Room heaters with flue	106	0.3	6	0.5	6.1
Room heaters without flue	264	0.7	29	2.1	11.1
Portable electric heaters	3,832	10.8	179	12.6	4.7
Stoves	425	1.2	69	4.8	16.2
Fireplaces with inserts	464	1.3	54	3.8	11.7
Fireplaces without inserts	896	2.5	15	1.0	1.6
Other	83	0.2	4	0.3	4.7
Cooking stove	17	0.0	0	0.0	0.0
None	28,863	81.6	1,072	75.4	3.7

Source: Bureau of the Census, American Housing Survey for the United States: 2009, Internet site http://www.census.gov/hhes/ www/housing/ahs/ahs09/ahs09.html; calculations by New Strategist

Table 9.13 Renters of Mobile Homes with Air Conditioning, 2009

Fifty-eight percent of the renters of mobile homes have central air conditioning, a greater share than the 51 percent of all renters with central air.

(number and percent distribution of total renters and renters of mobile/manufactured homes, by presence of air conditioning equipment, 2009; numbers in thousands)

	total		mobile homes		
	number	percent distribution	number	percent distribution	percent of total
Total renters	**35,378**	**100.0%**	**1,421**	**100.0%**	**4.0%**
Households with air conditioning	29,035	82.1	1,264	88.9	4.4
Central	18,161	51.3	817	57.5	4.5
Additional central	920	2.6	48	3.4	5.3
One room unit	6,229	17.6	202	14.2	3.2
Two room units	3,332	9.4	172	12.1	5.2
Three or more room units	1,314	3.7	73	5.2	5.6

Source: Bureau of the Census, American Housing Survey for the United States: 2009, Internet site http://www.census.gov/hhes/ www/housing/ahs/ahs09/ahs09.html; calculations by New Strategist

Table 9.14 Renters of Mobile Homes by Primary Source of Water and Sewage Disposal System, 2009

Renters of mobile homes are much more likely than the
average renter to use a well as their source of water and
a septic tank or cesspool as their sewage disposal system.

(number and percent of total renters and renters of mobile/manufactured homes, by primary source of water and type of sewage disposal system, 2009; numbers in thousands)

	total		mobile homes		
	number	percent distribution	number	percent distribution	percent of total
Total renters	**35,378**	**100.0%**	**1,421**	**100.0%**	**4.0%**
Source of water					
Public system or private company	33,655	95.1	1,106	77.8	3.3
Well	1,660	4.7	306	21.5	18.4
Safety of primary source of water					
Safe to drink	31,095	87.9	1,249	87.9	4.0
Not safe to drink	3,882	11.0	156	11.0	4.0
Sewage disposal system					
Public sewer	32,732	92.5	790	55.6	2.4
Septic tank, cesspool, chemical toilet	2,640	7.5	631	44.4	23.9

Note: Numbers do not sum to total because "other" and "not reported" are not shown.
Source: Bureau of the Census, American Housing Survey for the United States: 2009, Internet site http://www.census.gov/hhes/ www/housing/ahs/ahs09/ahs09.html; calculations by New Strategist

Table 9.15 Renters of Mobile Homes by Fuels Used, 2009

The renters of mobile homes are much more likely than the average renter to have all-electric homes, 45 versus 35 percent.

(number and percent of total renters and renters of mobile/manufactured homes, by types of fuels used, 2009; numbers in thousands)

	total		mobile homes		
	number	percent distribution	number	percent distribution	percent of total
Total renters	**35,378**	**100.0%**	**1,421**	**100.0%**	**4.0%**
Electricity	35,368	100.0	1,421	100.0	4.0
All-electric homes	12,215	34.5	637	44.8	5.2
Piped gas	21,186	59.9	417	29.4	2.0
Bottled gas	1,425	4.0	304	21.4	21.3
Fuel oil	2,800	7.9	37	2.6	1.3
Kerosene or other liquid fuel	164	0.5	50	3.5	30.4
Coal or coke	7	0.0	0	0.0	0.0
Wood	278	0.8	35	2.5	12.7
Solar energy	17	0.0	0	0.0	0.0
Other	151	0.4	3	0.2	2.1

Note: Numbers do not add to total because many households use more than one fuel.
Source: Bureau of the Census, American Housing Survey for the United States: 2009, Internet site http://www.census.gov/hhes/ www/housing/ahs/ahs09/ahs09.html; calculations by New Strategist

Table 9.16 Renters of Mobile Homes by Heating Fuels Used, 2009

Fifty percent of the renters of mobile homes
use electricity as their heating fuel.

(number and percent of total renters and renters of mobile/manufactured homes, by heating fuels used, 2009; numbers in thousands)

	total		mobile homes		
	number	percent distribution	number	percent distribution	percent of total
TOTAL RENTERS	**35,378**	**100.0%**	**1,421**	**100.0%**	**4.0%**
Renters using heating fuel	**35,368**	**100.0**	**1,416**	**100.0**	**4.0**
Electricity	12,215	34.5	712	50.3	5.8
Piped gas	21,186	59.9	362	25.5	1.7
Bottled gas	1,425	4.0	226	16.0	15.9
Fuel oil	2,800	7.9	31	2.2	1.1
Kerosene or other liquid fuel	164	0.5	50	3.5	30.4
Coal or coke	7	0.0	0	0.0	0.0
Wood	278	0.8	35	2.5	12.7
Solar energy	17	0.0	0	0.0	0.0
Other	151	0.4	0	0.0	0.0

Source: Bureau of the Census, American Housing Survey for the United States: 2009, Internet site http://www.census.gov/hhes/ www/housing/ahs/ahs09/ahs09.html; calculations by New Strategist

Table 9.17 Renters of Mobile Homes by Cooking, Water Heating, and Clothes Dryer Fuels Used, 2009

The renters of mobile homes are more likely than the average
renter to use electricity as their water heating fuel.

(number and percent of total renters and renters of mobile/manufactured homes, by cooking, water heating, and clothes dryer fuels used, 2009; numbers in thousands)

	total		mobile homes		
	number	percent distribution	number	percent distribution	percent of total
COOKING FUEL					
Renters using cooking fuel	**35,235**	**100.0%**	**1,417**	**100.0%**	**4.0%**
Electricity	21,567	61.2	853	60.2	4.0
Piped gas	12,923	36.7	348	24.5	2.7
Bottled gas	726	2.1	217	15.3	29.9
Kerosene or other liquid fuel	7	0.0	0	0.0	0.0
Wood	12	0.0	0	0.0	0.0
WATER HEATING FUEL					
Renters with hot piped water	**35,319**	**100.0**	**1,417**	**100.0**	**4.0**
Electricity	16,095	45.6	1,059	74.7	6.6
Piped gas	16,865	47.7	263	18.5	1.6
Bottled gas	692	2.0	95	6.7	13.8
Fuel oil	1,604	4.5	0	0.0	0.0
Kerosene or other liquid fuel	3	0.0	0	0.0	0.0
Wood	9	0.0	0	0.0	0.0
Solar energy	14	0.0	0	0.0	0.0
Other	39	0.1	0	0.0	0.0
CLOTHES DRYER FUEL					
Renters with clothes dryers	**18,343**	**100.0**	**1,153**	**81.4**	**6.3**
Electricity	15,438	84.2	1,074	75.8	7.0
Piped gas	2,785	15.2	51	3.6	1.8
Other	120	0.7	28	2.0	23.4

Source: Bureau of the Census, American Housing Survey for the United States: 2009, Internet site http://www.census.gov/hhes/ www/housing/ahs/ahs09/ahs09.html; calculations by New Strategist

Table 9.18 Renters of Mobile Homes by Amenities of Home, 2009

Only 20 percent of the renters of mobile homes have a garage
or carport, versus 37 percent of all renters.

(number and percent of total renters and renters of mobile/manufactured homes, by selected amenities of home, 2009; numbers in thousands)

	total		mobile homes		
	number	percent distribution	number	percent distribution	percent of total
Total renters	**35,378**	**100.0%**	**1,421**	**100.0%**	**4.0%**
Porch, deck, balcony, or patio	24,984	70.6	1,181	83.1	4.7
Telephone available	34,196	96.7	1,369	96.4	4.0
Usable fireplace	4,540	12.8	123	8.7	2.7
Separate dining room	9,959	28.2	287	20.2	2.9
With two or more living or recreation rooms	2,934	8.3	89	6.2	3.0
Garage or carport					
Yes	13,258	37.5	281	19.8	2.1
No, but off-street parking included	17,676	50.0	1,048	73.8	5.9
No cars, trucks, or vans	6,669	18.9	130	9.1	1.9

Source: Bureau of the Census, American Housing Survey for the United States: 2009, Internet site http://www.census.gov/hhes/ www/housing/ahs/ahs09/ahs09.html; calculations by New Strategist

Table 9.19 **Renters of Mobile Homes by Deficiencies of Home, 2009**

Thirteen percent of the renters of mobile homes have seen
signs of mice in the past three months, a significantly greater
share than the 6 percent of all renters with mice.

(number and percent distribution of total renters and renters of mobile/manufactured homes, by selected deficiencies of housing unit, 2009; numbers in thousands)

	total		mobile homes		
	number	percent distribution	number	percent distribution	percent of total
Total renters	**35,378**	**100.0%**	**1,421**	**100.0%**	**4.0%**
Signs of rats in last three months	258	0.7	18	1.3	6.9
Signs of mice in last three months	2,138	6.0	190	13.4	8.9
Signs of rodents, not sure which kind, in last three months	189	0.5	6	0.4	2.9
Holes in floor	560	1.6	38	2.7	6.8
Open cracks or holes (interior)	2,416	6.8	123	8.6	5.1
Broken plaster, peeling paint (interior)	1,132	3.2	48	3.4	4.2
No electrical wiring	26	0.1	0	0.0	0.0
Exposed wiring	134	0.4	5	0.4	4.1
Rooms without electric outlets	624	1.8	28	2.0	4.4

Source: Bureau of the Census, American Housing Survey for the United States: 2009, Internet site http://www.census.gov/hhes/ www/housing/ahs/ahs09/ahs09.html; calculations by New Strategist

Table 9.20 Renters of Mobile Homes by Housing Equipment Failures, 2009

The renters of mobile homes are more likely than the average
renter to experience problems such as water leakage, being
uncomfortably cold, and water stoppages.

(number and percent distribution of total renters and renters of mobile/manufactured homes, by type of equipment failure, 2009; numbers in thousands)

	total		mobile homes		
	number	percent distribution	number	percent distribution	percent of total
WATER SUPPLY STOPPAGE					
Renters with piped water	**35,319**	**100.0%**	**1,417**	**100.0%**	**4.0%**
No stoppage in last three months	33,370	94.5	1,294	91.3	3.9
With stoppage in last three months	1,601	4.5	103	7.3	6.4
Not reported	348	1.0	20	1.4	5.7
FLUSH TOILET BREAKDOWNS					
Renters with flush toilets	**35,313**	**100.0**	**1,421**	**100.0**	**4.0**
With at least one working toilet at all times, last three months	33,766	95.6	1,366	96.2	4.0
With no working toilet at least once in last three months	1,210	3.4	34	2.4	2.8
Not reported	337	1.0	20	1.4	5.9
WATER LEAKAGE DURING LAST 12 MONTHS					
Total renters	**35,378**	**100.0**	**1,421**	**100.0**	**4.0**
No leakage from within structure	31,184	88.1	1,234	86.9	4.0
With leakage from within structure*	3,836	10.8	168	11.8	4.4
Fixtures backed up or overflowed	952	2.7	28	1.9	2.9
Pipes leaked	1,664	4.7	100	7.0	6.0
Broken water heater	327	0.9	22	1.5	6.6
Other or unknown	1,088	3.1	20	1.4	1.9
Leakage not reported	357	1.0	18	1.3	5.0
No leakage from outside structure	**31,906**	**90.2**	**1,195**	**84.1**	**3.7**
With leakage from outside structure*	3,121	8.8	208	14.6	6.7
Roof	1,579	4.5	140	9.9	8.9
Basement	538	1.5	2	0.2	0.5
Walls, windows, or doors	795	2.2	56	3.9	7.0
Other or not reported	410	1.2	20	1.4	5.0
Leakage not reported	350	1.0	18	1.3	5.1

	total		mobile homes		
	number	percent distribution	number	percent distribution	percent of total
HEATING PROBLEMS					
Renters with heating equipment and occupying home last winter	**31,244**	**100.0%**	**1,261**	**100.0%**	**4.0%**
Not uncomfortably cold for 24 or more hours last winter	26,957	86.3	1,016	80.6	3.8
Uncomfortably cold for 24 or more hours last winter*	3,622	11.6	212	16.9	5.9
Equipment breakdown	1,144	3.7	46	3.7	4.1
Utility interruption	496	1.6	81	6.4	16.3
Inadequate heating capacity	675	2.2	8	0.7	1.3
Inadequate insulation	523	1.7	37	2.9	7.0
Cost of heating	421	1.3	19	1.5	4.6
Other	677	2.2	38	3.0	5.6
Not reported	666	2.1	33	2.6	5.0
ELECTRICAL PROBLEMS					
Renters with electrical wiring	**35,351**	**100.0**	**1,421**	**100.0**	**4.0**
No fuses or breakers blown in last three months	31,879	90.2	1,271	89.4	4.0
With fuses or breakers blown in last three months	3,082	8.7	124	8.7	4.0
Not reported	391	1.1	26	1.8	6.7

* Figures do not add to total because more than one problem may have occurred.
Source: Bureau of the Census, American Housing Survey for the United States: 2009, Internet site http://www.census.gov/hhes/www/housing/ahs/ahs09/ahs09.html; calculations by New Strategist

Table 9.21 Renters of Mobile Homes by Monthly Housing Costs, 2009

Housing costs are lower for the renters of mobile homes than
for the average renter—a monthly median of $623 versus $808.

(number and percent distribution of total renters and renters of mobile/manufactured homes, by monthly housing costs, 2009; numbers in thousands)

	total		mobile homes		
	number	percent distribution	number	percent distribution	percent of total
Total renters	**35,378**	**100.0%**	**1,421**	**100.0%**	**4.0%**
Less than $100	248	0.7	3	0.2	1.2
$100 to $199	728	2.1	8	0.6	1.1
$200 to $299	1,381	3.9	43	3.0	3.1
$300 to $399	1,359	3.8	106	7.5	7.8
$400 to $499	2,094	5.9	144	10.1	6.9
$500 to $599	2,985	8.4	200	14.1	6.7
$600 to $699	3,808	10.8	219	15.4	5.7
$700 to $799	3,709	10.5	195	13.7	5.2
$800 to $999	6,060	17.1	183	12.9	3.0
$1,000 to $1,249	4,777	13.5	40	2.8	0.8
$1,250 to $1,499	2,631	7.4	22	1.6	0.8
$1,500 or $1,999	2,247	6.4	2	0.1	0.1
$2,000 to $2,499	718	2.0	0	0.0	0.0
$2,500 or more	596	1.7	10	0.7	1.7
No cash rent	2,037	5.8	248	17.4	12.2
Median monthly cost	$808	–	$623	–	–

Note: Housing costs include rent, utilities, and property insurance. "–" means not applicable.
Source: Bureau of the Census, American Housing Survey for the United States: 2009, Internet site http://www.census.gov/hhes/
www/housing/ahs/ahs09/ahs09.html; calculations by New Strategist

Table 9.22 Renters of Mobile Homes by Monthly Utility and Property Insurance Costs, 2009

The renters of mobile homes pay more for electricity than the average renter.

(number and percent distribution of total renters and renters of mobile/manufactured homes, by average monthly costs for utilities, 2009; numbers in thousands)

	total		mobile homes		
	number	percent distribution	number	percent distribution	percent of total
MONTHLY COST OF ELECTRICITY					
Renters using electricity	**35,368**	**100.0%**	**1,421**	**100.0%**	**4.0%**
Less than $25	1,259	3.6	9	0.6	0.7
$25 to $49	5,426	15.3	85	6.0	1.6
$50 to $74	6,535	18.5	167	11.8	2.6
$75 to $99	5,469	15.5	229	16.1	4.2
$100 to $149	6,589	18.6	383	27.0	5.8
$150 to $199	2,795	7.9	218	15.4	7.8
$200 or more	2,341	6.6	218	15.3	9.3
Included in other fee or obtained free	4,954	14.0	112	7.9	2.3
Median monthly cost	$84	–	$118	–	–
MONTHLY COST OF PIPED GAS					
Renters using piped gas	**21,186**	**100.0**	**417**	**100.0**	**2.0**
Less than $25	2,447	11.5	54	13.0	2.2
$25 to $49	4,469	21.1	107	25.6	2.4
$50 to $74	3,581	16.9	116	27.7	3.2
$75 to $99	2,054	9.7	41	9.9	2.0
$100 to $149	1,884	8.9	41	9.9	2.2
$150 to $199	643	3.0	4	0.9	0.6
$200 or more	518	2.4	6	1.5	1.2
Included in other fee or obtained free	5,588	26.4	48	11.5	0.9
Median monthly cost	$55	–	$54	–	–
MONTHLY COST OF FUEL OIL					
Renters using fuel oil	**2,800**	**100.0**	**37**	**100.0**	**1.3**
Less than $25	52	1.9	2	6.0	4.3
$25 to $49	70	2.5	4	10.3	5.5
$50 to $74	91	3.3	6	15.8	6.4
$75 to $99	100	3.6	0	0.0	0.0
$100 to $149	163	5.8	5	13.6	3.1
$150 to $199	108	3.9	5	13.8	4.7
$200 or more	146	5.2	4	10.8	2.7
Included in other fee or obtained free	2,068	73.9	11	29.6	0.5
Median monthly cost	$100	–	–	–	–

	total		mobile homes		
	number	percent distribution	number	percent distribution	percent of total
Water paid separately	9,237	–	545	–	5.9%
Median monthly cost	$29	–	$27	–	–
Trash paid separately	7,551	–	414	–	5.5
Median monthly cost	$20	–	$17	–	–
Property insurance paid	9,397	–	157	–	1.7
Median monthly cost	$16	–	$17	–	–

Note: "–" means not applicable or sample is too small to make a reliable estimate.
Source: Bureau of the Census, American Housing Survey for the United States: 2009, Internet site http://www.census.gov/hhes/ www/housing/ahs/ahs09/ahs09.html; calculations by New Strategist

Table 9.23 Renters of Mobile Homes by Opinion of Home, 2009

The renters of mobile homes are just as likely to rate their home a 10
on a scale of 1 (worst) to 10 (best) as the average renter.

(number and percent distribution of total renters and renters of mobile/manufactured homes, by opinion of home, 2009; numbers in thousands)

	total		mobile homes		
	number	percent distribution	number	percent distribution	percent of total
Total renters	**35,378**	**100.0%**	**1,421**	**100.0%**	**4.0%**
1 (worst)	327	0.9	21	1.4	6.3
2	209	0.6	16	1.1	7.8
3	436	1.2	9	0.7	2.1
4	708	2.0	42	3.0	6.0
5	2,910	8.2	196	13.8	6.7
6	2,553	7.2	156	11.0	6.1
7	6,146	17.4	183	12.9	3.0
8	9,625	27.2	330	23.2	3.4
9	4,217	11.9	130	9.1	3.1
10 (best)	6,941	19.6	282	19.8	4.1
Not reported	1,306	3.7	56	3.9	4.3

Source: Bureau of the Census, American Housing Survey for the United States: 2009, Internet site http://www.census.gov/hhes/www/housing/ahs/ahs09/ahs09.html; calculations by New Strategist

Table 9.24 Renters of Mobile Homes by Opinion of Neighborhood, 2009

The renters of mobile homes are more likely than the average renter to
rate their neighborhood a 10 on a scale of 1 (worst) to 10 (best).

(number and percent distribution of total renters and renters of mobile/manufactured homes, by opinion of neighborhood, 2009; numbers in thousands)

	total		mobile homes		
	number	percent distribution	number	percent distribution	percent of total
Total renters	**35,378**	**100.0%**	**1,421**	**100.0%**	**4.0%**
1 (worst)	499	1.4	31	2.2	6.2
2	348	1.0	8	0.6	2.3
3	543	1.5	33	2.3	6.0
4	867	2.5	32	2.3	3.7
5	2,976	8.4	106	7.5	3.6
6	2,465	7.0	108	7.6	4.4
7	5,164	14.6	180	12.7	3.5
8	8,986	25.4	341	24.0	3.8
9	4,563	12.9	130	9.1	2.8
10 (best)	7,575	21.4	395	27.8	5.2
No neighborhood	29	0.1	0	0.0	0.0
Not reported	1,362	3.8	56	3.9	4.1

Source: Bureau of the Census, American Housing Survey for the United States: 2009, Internet site http://www.census.gov/hhes/www/housing/ahs/ahs09/ahs09.html; calculations by New Strategist

Table 9.25 Renters of Mobile Homes by Neighborhood Problems, 2009

The renters of mobile homes are less likely than the average renter to
have had serious crime in their neighborhood in the past 12 months.

(number and percent distribution of total renters and renters of mobile/manufactured homes, by selected neighborhood problems, 2009; numbers in thousands)

	total		mobile homes		
	number	percent distribution	number	percent distribution	percent of total
Total renters	**35,378**	**100.0%**	**1,421**	**100.0%**	**4.0%**
Bothersome street noise or heavy traffic	10,158	28.7	326	22.9	3.2
Serious crime in neighborhood in past 12 months	7,650	21.6	205	14.4	2.7
Bothersome odor problem	2,156	6.1	74	5.2	3.4
Noise problem	1,217	3.4	43	3.0	3.5
Litter or housing deterioration	590	1.7	19	1.3	3.2
Poor city or county services	254	0.7	7	0.5	2.6
Undesirable commercial, institutional, industrial	168	0.5	3	0.2	1.7
People problem	1,815	5.1	90	6.3	5.0
Other problems	2,791	7.9	81	5.7	2.9

*Source: Bureau of the Census, American Housing Survey for the United States: 2009, Internet site http://www.census.gov/hhes/
www/housing/ahs/ahs09/ahs09.html; calculations by New Strategist*

Table 9.26 Renters of Mobile Homes by Community Characteristics, 2009

The renters of mobile homes are less likely than the average renter to live in a gated or age-restricted community. They are more likely to live near open space.

(number and percent distribution of total renters and renters of mobile/manufactured homes, by community characteristics, 2009; numbers in thousands)

	total		mobile homes		
	number	percent distribution	number	percent distribution	percent of total
Total renters	35,378	100.0%	1,421	100.0%	4.0%
SECURED COMMUNITIES					
Total renters	35,378	100.0	1,421	100.0	4.0
Community access secured with walls or fences	5,422	15.3	79	5.6	1.5
Special entry system present	3,410	9.6	13	0.9	0.4
Special entry system not present	2,005	5.7	67	4.7	3.3
Community access not secured	29,714	84.0	1,329	93.5	4.5
SENIOR CITIZEN COMMUNITIES					
Households with persons aged 55 or older	9,093	100.0	320	100.0	3.5
Community age restricted	1,624	17.9	35	10.8	2.1
No age restriction	7,469	82.1	285	89.2	3.8
Community age specific	1,435	15.8	63	19.6	4.4
Community not age specific	5,583	61.4	193	60.4	3.5
COMMUNITY AMENITIES					
Total renters	35,378	100.0	1,421	100.0	4.0
Community center or clubhouse	9,703	27.4	192	13.5	2.0
Golf in community	3,947	11.2	82	5.7	2.1
Trails in community	6,309	17.8	113	8.0	1.8
Shuttle bus available	4,215	11.9	72	5.0	1.7
Daycare center	5,249	14.8	102	7.2	1.9
Private or restricted beach, park, or shoreline	6,308	17.8	168	11.9	2.7
DESCRIPTION OF AREA WITHIN 300 FEET OF HOME					
Total renters	35,378	100.0	1,421	100.0	4.0
Single-family detached homes	27,007	76.3	1,060	74.6	3.9
Single-family attached homes	10,860	30.7	81	5.7	0.7
Multiunit residential buildings	22,121	62.5	140	9.8	0.6
One-to-three-story multiunit is tallest	16,130	45.6	127	8.9	0.8
Four-to-six-story multiunit is tallest	3,473	9.8	6	0.4	0.2
Seven-or-more-story multiunit is tallest	2,243	6.3	4	0.3	0.2
Manufactured/mobile homes	3,112	8.8	1,096	77.1	35.2
Commercial or institutional	18,657	52.7	313	22.0	1.7
Industrial or factories	2,856	8.1	72	5.1	2.5
Open space, park, woods, farm, or ranch	12,706	35.9	851	59.9	6.7
Four-or-more-lane highway, railroad, or airport	9,232	26.1	273	19.2	3.0

	total		mobile homes		
	number	percent distribution	number	percent distribution	percent of total
BODIES OF WATER WITHIN 300 FEET OF HOME					
Total renters	**35,378**	**100.0%**	**1,421**	**100.0%**	**4.0%**
Water in area	4,832	13.7	247	17.4	5.1
With waterfront property	678	1.9	34	2.4	5.0
With flood plain	692	2.0	53	3.7	7.7
No water in area	30,390	85.9	1,169	82.3	3.8

Note: Numbers may not add to total because "not reported" is not shown.
Source: Bureau of the Census, American Housing Survey for the United States: 2009, Internet site http://www.census.gov/hhes/ www/housing/ahs/ahs09/ahs09.html; calculations by New Strategist

Table 9.27 Renters of Mobile Homes by Grouping Status, 2009

Most mobile home renters have no or only a few other mobile homes nearby.
The 68 percent majority are in a mobile home grouping of one to six units.

(number and percent distribution of the renters of mobile homes by group status, 2009; numbers in thousands)

	number	percent
Total mobile home renters	**1,421**	**100.0%**
One to six in area	966	68.0
7 to 20 in area	153	10.8
21 or more in area	301	21.2

Source: Bureau of the Census, American Housing Survey for the United States: 2009, Internet site http://www.census.gov/hhes/ www/housing/ahs/ahs09/ahs09.html; calculations by New Strategist

Table 9.28 Renters of Mobile Homes by Public Services Available, 2009

The renters of mobile homes have fewer public services available to them than the average renter. Only 20 percent have public transportation.

(number and percent distribution of total renters and renters of mobile/manufactured homes, by public services available in neighborhood, 2009; numbers in thousands)

	total		mobile homes		
	number	percent distribution	number	percent distribution	percent of total
Total renters	**35,378**	**100.0%**	**1,421**	**100.0%**	**4.0%**
LOCAL ELEMENTARY SCHOOL					
Renters with children under age 14	**10,486**	**100.0**	**547**	**100.0**	**5.2**
Satisfactory public elementary school	8,331	79.5	460	84.2	5.5
Unsatisfactory public elementary school	724	6.9	31	5.7	4.3
Unsatisfactory public elementary school	**724**	**100.0**	**31**	**100.0**	**4.3**
Better than other area elementary schools	63	8.7	0	0.0	0.0
Same as other area elementary schools	224	31.0	13	40.8	5.7
Worse than other area elementary schools	386	53.3	18	59.2	4.8
Renters with children under age 14	**10,486**	**100.0**	**547**	**100.0**	**5.2**
Public elementary school less than one mile	7,096	67.7	187	34.1	2.6
Public elementary school more than one mile	2,741	26.1	314	57.5	11.5
PUBLIC TRANSPORTATION IN AREA					
Total renters	**35,378**	**100.0**	**1,421**	**100.0**	**4.0**
With public transportation	24,641	69.6	285	20.1	1.2
No public transportation	9,684	27.4	1,081	76.1	11.2
With public transportation, travel time to nearest stop	**24,641**	**100.0**	**285**	**100.0**	**1.2**
Less than 5 minutes	10,328	41.9	93	32.8	0.9
5 to 9 minutes	8,869	36.0	108	37.9	1.2
10 to 14 minutes	2,753	11.2	30	10.6	1.1
15 to 29 minutes	1,099	4.5	22	7.6	2.0
30 minutes or longer	169	0.7	16	5.6	9.4
With public transportation	**24,641**	**100.0**	**285**	**100.0**	**1.2**
Household uses it regularly for commute to school or work	6,395	26.0	39	13.8	0.6
Household does not use it regularly for commute to school or work	18,075	73.4	246	86.2	1.4

	total		mobile homes		
	number	percent distribution	number	percent distribution	percent of total
SHOPPING IN AREA					
Total renters	**35,378**	**100.0%**	**1,421**	**100.0%**	**4.0%**
Grocery stores or drugstores within 15 minutes of home	34,189	96.6	1,282	90.2	3.8
Satisfactory	33,082	93.5	1,244	87.5	3.8
Not satisfactory	964	2.7	31	2.2	3.2
No grocery stores or drugstores within 15 minutes of home	777	2.2	98	6.9	12.6
POLICE PROTECTION					
Total renters	**35,378**	**100.0**	**1,421**	**100.0**	**4.0**
Satisfactory police protection	31,740	89.7	1,240	87.2	3.9
Unsatisfactory police protection	2,556	7.2	134	9.4	5.2

Note: Numbers may not add to total because "not reported" is not shown.
Source: Bureau of the Census, American Housing Survey for the United States: 2009, Internet site http://www.census.gov/hhes/
www/housing/ahs/ahs09/ahs09.html; calculations by New Strategist

Table 9.29 Renters of Mobile Homes Who Moved by Changes in Housing and Costs, 2009

Nearly half (47 percent) the renters of mobile homes who
have recently moved had previously lived in a house.

(number and percent distribution of total renters who have moved in the past year and those who moved into mobile/manufactured homes, by structure type of previous residence, tenure of previous residence, and change in housing costs, 2009; numbers in thousands)

	total		mobile homes		
	number	percent distribution	number	percent distribution	percent of total
STRUCTURE TYPE OF PREVIOUS RESIDENCE					
Renters who moved within United States	**12,422**	**100.0%**	**538**	**100.0%**	**4.3%**
House	5,936	47.8	250	46.5	4.2
Apartment	5,228	42.1	96	17.9	1.8
Mobile home	545	4.4	175	32.5	32.1
Other	380	3.1	5	0.9	1.2
Not reported	331	2.7	11	2.1	3.5
OWNERSHIP OF PREVIOUS RESIDENCE					
Renters who moved from house, apartment, or mobile home within United States	**11,710**	**100.0**	**522**	**100.0**	**4.5**
Owner-occupied	2,991	25.5	136	26.1	4.6
Renter-occupied	8,719	74.5	385	73.9	4.4
CHANGE IN HOUSING COSTS					
Renters who moved from house, apartment, or mobile home within United States	**11,710**	**100.0**	**522**	**100.0**	**4.5**
Increased with move	5,135	43.8	141	27.0	2.7
Decreased	3,719	31.8	187	35.8	5.0
Stayed about the same	2,444	20.9	161	30.9	6.6
Don't know	250	2.1	28	5.4	11.3
Not reported	161	1.4	5	1.0	3.1

Source: Bureau of the Census, American Housing Survey for the United States: 2009, Internet site http://www.census.gov/hhes/ www/housing/ahs/ahs09/ahs09.html; calculations by New Strategist

Table 9.30 Renters of Mobile Homes Who Moved by Reasons for Choosing Home, 2009

The renters of mobile homes who recently moved are far more
likely than the average renter who recently moved to have
chosen their home for financial reasons—44 versus 30 percent.

(number and percent distribution of total renting respondents who have moved in the past year and those who moved into mobile/manufactured homes, by reasons for choosing home, 2009; numbers in thousands)

	total		mobile homes		
	number	percent distribution	number	percent distribution	percent of total
Total renting respondents who moved	**12,840**	**100.0%**	**551**	**100.0%**	**4.3%**
Main reason for choice of present home					
All reported reasons equal	1,448	11.3	55	10.0	3.8
Financial reasons	3,846	30.0	241	43.7	6.3
Room layout/design	1,743	13.6	27	4.9	1.6
Kitchen	65	0.5	0	0.0	0.0
Size	1,398	10.9	35	6.4	2.5
Exterior appearance	350	2.7	13	2.4	3.7
Yard/trees/view	412	3.2	20	3.6	4.7
Quality of construction	231	1.8	0	0.0	0.0
Only one available	608	4.7	42	7.7	6.9
Other	2,198	17.1	92	16.8	4.2
Not reported	540	4.2	25	4.5	4.6
Present home compared with previous home					
Better	6,192	48.2	235	42.6	3.8
Worse	2,676	20.8	129	23.4	4.8
About the same	3,498	27.2	171	31.0	4.9
Not reported	474	3.7	16	3.0	3.5

Note: Total number of movers does not equal total movers in other tables because this table shows survey respondents who moved, not necessarily householders.
Source: Bureau of the Census, American Housing Survey for the United States: 2009, Internet site http://www.census.gov/hhes/www/housing/ahs/ahs09/ahs09.html; calculations by New Strategist

Table 9.31 Renters of Mobile Homes Who Moved by Main Reason for Choosing Neighborhood, 2009

The renters of mobile homes who recently moved are more likely
than the average renter who recently moved to say they chose
their present neighborhood to be close to friends or family.

(number and percent distribution of total renting respondents who moved in the past year, and those who moved into mobile/manufactured homes, by main reason for choosing neighborhood, 2009; numbers in thousands)

	total		mobile homes		
	number	percent distribution	number	percent distribution	percent of total
Total renting respondents who moved	**12,840**	**100.0%**	**551**	**100.0%**	**4.3%**
Neighborhood search					
Looked at just this neighborhood	5,900	46.0	392	71.2	6.6
Looked at other neighborhoods	6,533	50.9	148	26.9	2.3
Not reported	407	3.2	10	1.8	2.5
Main reason for choice of present neighborhood					
All reported reasons equal	1,354	10.5	40	7.2	2.9
Convenient to job	2,924	22.8	101	18.3	3.4
Convenient to friends or relatives	1,915	14.9	168	30.5	8.8
Convenient to leisure activities	244	1.9	12	2.1	4.8
Convenient to public transportation	237	1.8	3	0.5	1.1
Good schools	798	6.2	18	3.3	2.3
Other public services	185	1.4	0	0.0	0.0
Looks/design of neighborhood	1,163	9.1	38	6.8	3.2
House was most important consideration	964	7.5	41	7.4	4.2
Other	2,563	20.0	106	19.3	4.2
Not reported	493	3.8	25	4.4	5.0
Present neighborhood compared with previous neighborhood					
Better	4,953	38.6	260	47.3	5.3
Worse	1,955	15.2	49	8.9	2.5
About the same	4,916	38.3	207	37.5	4.2
Same neighborhood	520	4.1	18	3.2	3.4
Not reported	496	3.9	16	2.9	3.2

Note: Total number of movers does not equal total movers in other tables because this table shows survey respondents who moved, not necessarily householders.
Source: Bureau of the Census, American Housing Survey for the United States: 2009, Internet site http://www.census.gov/hhes/ www/housing/ahs/ahs09/ahs09.html; calculations by New Strategist

Table 9.32 Renters of Mobile Homes Who Moved by Main Reason for Moving, 2009

The single most important reason for moving among renters of mobile homes who recently moved was to establish their own household, mentioned by 15 percent.

(number and percent distribution of total renting respondents who moved in the past year and those moving into mobile/manufactured homes, by main reason for move, 2009; numbers in thousands)

	total		mobile homes		
	number	percent distribution	number	percent distribution	percent of total
Total renting respondents who moved	**12,840**	**100.0%**	**551**	**100.0%**	**4.3%**
All reported reasons equal	450	3.5	24	4.3	5.2
Private displacement	118	0.9	6	1.0	4.8
Government displacement	45	0.4	0	0.0	0.0
Disaster loss (fire, flood, etc.)	126	1.0	9	1.7	7.4
New job or job transfer	1,220	9.5	17	3.0	1.4
To be closer to work/school/other	1,416	11.0	60	10.8	4.2
Other financial, employment related	527	4.1	46	8.3	8.7
To establish own household	1,282	10.0	81	14.7	6.3
Needed larger house or apartment	1,103	8.6	41	7.4	3.7
Married, widowed, divorced, or separated	628	4.9	24	4.4	3.8
Other family, personal reasons	1,004	7.8	47	8.4	4.6
Wanted better home	881	6.9	25	4.5	2.8
Change from owner to renter	120	0.9	3	0.6	2.8
Wanted lower rent or maintenance	867	6.8	36	6.5	4.1
Other housing related reasons	614	4.8	34	6.2	5.6
Evicted from residence	112	0.9	22	3.9	19.4
Other	1,548	12.1	54	9.8	3.5
Not reported	779	6.1	23	4.3	3.0

Note: Total number of movers does not equal total movers in other tables because this table shows survey respondents who moved, not necessarily householders.
Source: Bureau of the Census, American Housing Survey for the United States: 2009, Internet site http://www.census.gov/hhes/www/housing/ahs/ahs09/ahs09.html; calculations by New Strategist

10

Spending of Owners and Renters

Homeowners with mortgages spend much more than those who own their home free and clear.

The average homeowner with a mortgage spent $64,493 in 2009, much greater than the $44,130 spent by homeowners without a mortgage. The reason for the greater spending of those with mortgages is that they are younger (average age 47.8 versus 62.5 for those without mortgages) and less likely to be retired.

Homeowners overall spend 16 percent more than the average household. Homeowners with mortgages spend even more—13 percent more than the average homeowner. They spend more than average on most items, including cell phone service, day care centers, and airline fares. Homeowners without a mortgage spend 23 percent less than the average homeowner, but their spending is above average on maintenance and repair services for owned homes and lawn care service.

In 2009, the average renter household spent $33,404—only 68 percent as much as the average household. Renters spend more than average on only a few items.

■ Homeowners with a mortgage spent an average of $8,030 on mortgage interest in 2009.

■ Homeowners without a mortgage spend more than average on whiskey, lawn and garden supplies, postage, and outdoor furniture.

■ Renters spend more than average on beer, babysitting, coin-operated laundries, mass transit, cigarettes, and child support.

Homeowners spend more than renters

(average annual spending of households by housing tenure and mortgage status, 2009)

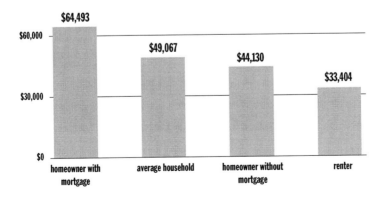

Table 10.1 Household Spending of Homeowners, 2009

Homeowners spend 16 percent more than the average household.
Their spending is above average on nearly every product and service.

(average annual spending of total consumer units and homeowner consumer units on all products and services, 2009; number of consumer units in thousands)

		homeowners	
	total	spending	index to total
Number of households (consumer units)	120,847	80,068	66
Before-tax income	$62,857	$75,858	121
Average age of householder	49.4	53.3	108
Average number of persons in household	2.5	2.6	104
Average number of earners in household	1.3	1.4	108
Average number of vehicles per household	2.0	2.4	120
At least one vehicle owned or leased	88%	96%	109
Average household spending, total	$49,067.20	$57,047.30	116
Food, average spending	6,371.89	7,197.79	113
FOOD AT HOME	3,752.98	4,214.27	112
Cereals and bakery products	506.38	565.90	112
Cereals and cereal products	172.58	185.74	108
Flour	8.67	9.99	115
Prepared flour mixes	14.41	16.73	116
Ready-to-eat and cooked cereals	93.61	101.10	108
Rice	23.99	22.25	93
Pasta, cornmeal, and other cereal products	31.89	35.67	112
Bakery products	333.81	380.16	114
Bread	94.69	105.00	111
White bread	33.84	36.01	106
Bread, other than white	60.85	68.99	113
Cookies and crackers	84.20	96.16	114
Cookies	47.28	53.32	113
Crackers	36.92	42.85	116
Frozen and refrigerated bakery products	27.53	32.04	116
Other bakery products	127.39	146.95	115
Biscuits and rolls	48.83	56.81	116
Cakes and cupcakes	37.40	42.53	114
Bread and cracker products	5.28	6.18	117
Sweetrolls, coffee cakes, doughnuts	21.75	25.16	116
Pies, tarts, turnovers	14.13	16.27	115
Meats, poultry, fish, and eggs	840.92	931.54	111
Beef	226.14	251.70	111
Ground beef	89.03	95.18	107
Roast	34.67	41.16	119
Chuck roast	9.36	11.09	118
Round roast	5.51	6.06	110
Other roast	19.80	24.01	121

		homeowners	
	total	spending	index to total
Steak	$83.00	$94.19	113
Round steak	10.63	10.80	102
Sirloin steak	22.27	25.24	113
Other steak	50.10	58.14	116
Other beef	19.44	21.18	109
Pork	168.37	186.95	111
Bacon	32.26	34.66	107
Pork chops	29.37	31.24	106
Ham	38.10	44.38	116
Ham, not canned	37.06	43.07	116
Canned ham	1.04	1.30	125
Sausage	27.91	30.97	111
Other pork	40.74	45.70	112
Other meats	113.53	130.25	115
Frankfurters	22.60	25.19	111
Lunch meats (cold cuts)	80.36	93.47	116
Bologna, liverwurst, salami	18.98	21.00	111
Other lunch meats	61.38	72.47	118
Lamb, organ meats, and others	10.57	11.59	110
Poultry	154.07	164.84	107
Fresh and frozen chicken	120.63	126.10	105
Fresh and frozen whole chicken	30.60	31.51	103
Fresh and frozen chicken parts	90.03	94.59	105
Other poultry	33.44	38.75	116
Fish and seafood	134.95	151.44	112
Canned fish and seafood	18.35	20.58	112
Fresh fish and shellfish	71.28	80.80	113
Frozen fish and shellfish	45.32	50.06	110
Eggs	43.85	46.35	106
Dairy products	**406.09**	**459.01**	**113**
Fresh milk and cream	143.98	157.75	110
Fresh milk, all types	126.71	137.24	108
Cream	17.28	20.50	119
Other dairy products	262.10	301.27	115
Butter	21.69	25.09	116
Cheese	132.88	152.60	115
Ice cream and related products	62.35	72.18	116
Miscellaneous dairy products	45.18	51.40	114
Fruits and vegetables	**656.45**	**743.55**	**113**
Fresh fruits	219.62	252.42	115
Apples	36.67	42.81	117
Bananas	33.25	36.85	111
Oranges	24.26	26.96	111
Citrus fruits, excluding oranges	19.51	21.54	110
Other fresh fruits	105.92	124.27	117
Fresh vegetables	209.15	237.61	114
Potatoes	37.01	41.78	113
Lettuce	26.58	31.19	117
Tomatoes	36.04	39.64	110
Other fresh vegetables	109.52	125.00	114

	total	homeowners spending	index to total
Processed fruits	$118.05	$130.82	111
Frozen fruits and fruit juices	11.59	13.56	117
Frozen orange juice	2.81	3.04	108
Frozen fruits	6.09	7.53	124
Frozen fruit juices, excluding orange	2.69	3.00	112
Canned fruits	20.44	22.90	112
Dried fruits	8.51	10.10	119
Fresh fruit juice	19.37	21.81	113
Canned and bottled fruit juice	58.13	62.45	107
Processed vegetables	109.64	122.70	112
Frozen vegetables	35.22	40.00	114
Canned and dried vegetables and juices	74.43	82.70	111
Canned beans	15.82	17.39	110
Canned corn	6.49	7.11	110
Canned miscellaneous vegetables	23.40	27.12	116
Dried peas	0.43	0.53	123
Dried beans	3.91	4.08	104
Dried miscellaneous vegetables	9.26	10.08	109
Fresh and canned vegetable juices	14.71	16.00	109
Sugar and other sweets	**140.62**	**163.64**	**116**
Candy and chewing gum	86.20	102.24	119
Sugar	18.91	19.67	104
Artificial sweeteners	5.98	7.40	124
Jams, preserves, other sweets	29.52	34.32	116
Fats and oils	**102.34**	**115.61**	**113**
Margarine	8.11	9.03	111
Fats and oils	35.69	38.51	108
Salad dressings	28.53	32.68	115
Nondairy cream and imitation milk	16.13	18.95	117
Peanut butter	13.88	16.44	118
Miscellaneous foods	**715.06**	**804.54**	**113**
Frozen prepared foods	147.63	159.15	108
Frozen meals	68.96	75.26	109
Other frozen prepared foods	78.67	83.89	107
Canned and packaged soups	47.06	53.55	114
Potato chips, nuts, and other snacks	147.72	172.64	117
Potato chips and other snacks	108.36	124.88	115
Nuts	39.36	47.76	121
Condiments and seasonings	129.79	148.20	114
Salt, spices, and other seasonings	31.28	35.01	112
Olives, pickles, relishes	15.73	17.83	113
Sauces and gravies	55.16	62.35	113
Baking needs and miscellaneous products	27.62	33.00	119
Other canned or packaged prepared foods	242.86	271.01	112
Prepared salads	33.40	38.46	115
Prepared desserts	13.70	15.41	112
Baby food	33.01	28.28	86
Miscellaneous prepared foods	160.29	185.90	116
Nonalcoholic beverages	**336.57**	**368.60**	**110**
Cola	87.70	94.29	108
Other carbonated drinks	49.44	51.48	104
Tea	29.44	33.49	114

		homeowners	
	total	spending	index to total
Coffee	$57.76	$66.48	115
Roasted coffee	38.60	43.78	113
Instant and freeze-dried coffee	19.16	22.71	119
Noncarbonated fruit-flavored drinks	24.58	26.67	109
Other noncarbonated beverages and ice	12.80	14.00	109
Bottled water	56.79	61.52	108
Sports drinks	17.93	20.55	115
Food prepared by consumer unit on trips	**48.55**	**61.87**	**127**
FOOD AWAY FROM HOME	**2,618.91**	**2,983.53**	**114**
Meals at restaurants, carry-outs, other	**2,188.68**	**2,445.08**	**112**
Lunch	733.26	829.83	113
At fast-food restaurants*	354.61	374.94	106
At full-service restaurants	289.80	349.33	121
At vending machines, mobile vendors	8.62	7.41	86
At employer and school cafeterias	80.23	98.16	122
Dinner	1,060.15	1,197.42	113
At fast-food restaurants*	350.72	366.00	104
At full-service restaurants	699.59	823.94	118
At vending machines, mobile vendors	2.82	2.52	89
At employer and school cafeterias	7.02	4.96	71
Snacks and nonalcoholic beverages	167.72	171.48	102
At fast-food restaurants*	110.20	116.74	106
At full-service restaurants	30.85	29.86	97
At vending machines, mobile vendors	21.16	19.90	94
At employer and school cafeterias	5.51	4.98	90
Breakfast and brunch	227.55	246.34	108
At fast-food restaurants*	116.94	122.11	104
At full-service restaurants	96.30	111.73	116
At vending machines, mobile vendors	2.75	2.32	84
At employer and school cafeterias	11.56	10.19	88
Board (including at school)	**45.41**	**62.00**	**137**
Catered affairs	**70.57**	**93.91**	**133**
Food on trips	**222.77**	**279.90**	**126**
School lunches	**64.92**	**80.86**	**125**
Meals as pay	**26.55**	**21.78**	**82**
ALCOHOLIC BEVERAGES	**434.73**	**476.79**	**110**
At home	**246.07**	**281.94**	**115**
Beer and ale	115.25	118.32	103
Whiskey	10.14	12.67	125
Wine	101.18	127.49	126
Other alcoholic beverages	19.50	23.46	120
Away from home	**188.66**	**194.85**	**103**
Beer and ale	69.66	63.86	92
At fast-food restaurants*	12.69	13.29	105
At full-service restaurants	55.66	49.25	88
At vending machines, mobile vendors	1.26	1.32	105
Wine	31.05	35.87	116
At fast-food restaurants*	1.76	1.76	100
At full-service restaurants	29.24	34.10	117
Other alcoholic beverages	46.27	43.90	95
At fast-food restaurants*	5.18	3.74	72
At full-service restaurants	41.02	40.05	98
Alcoholic beverages purchased on trips	41.67	51.22	123

	total	homeowners spending	index to total
HOUSING	**$16,895.11**	**$18,900.95**	**112**
• Shelter	**10,074.80**	**10,732.71**	**107**
Owned dwellings**	**6,542.61**	**9,761.39**	**149**
Mortgage interest and charges	3,593.71	5,346.55	149
Mortgage interest	3,382.93	5,031.81	149
Interest paid, home equity loan	79.27	118.49	149
Interest paid, home equity line of credit	131.52	196.26	149
Property taxes	1,811.04	2,706.76	149
Maintenance, repairs, insurance, other expenses	1,137.86	1,708.08	150
Homeowner's insurance	340.82	510.97	150
Ground rent	51.06	76.30	149
Maintenance and repair services	608.31	914.56	150
Painting and papering	78.28	116.82	149
Plumbing and water heating	57.99	87.25	150
Heat, air conditioning, electrical work	113.09	170.39	151
Roofing and gutters	114.57	172.92	151
Other repair and maintenance services	190.96	287.18	150
Repair, replacement of hard-surface flooring	51.28	76.79	150
Repair of built-in appliances	2.13	3.22	151
Maintenance and repair materials	73.85	111.00	150
Paints, wallpaper, and supplies	12.94	19.44	150
Tools, equipment for painting, wallpapering	1.39	2.09	150
Plumbing supplies and equipment	5.51	8.31	151
Electrical supplies, heating and cooling equipment	6.19	9.34	151
Hard-surface flooring, repair and replacement	6.97	10.52	151
Roofing and gutters	7.73	11.66	151
Plaster, paneling, siding, windows, doors, screens, awnings	13.96	21.05	151
Patio, walk, fence, driveway, masonry, brick, and stucco materials	0.70	1.05	150
Miscellaneous supplies and equipment	18.47	27.56	149
Material for insulation, other maintenance and repair	18.28	27.27	149
Property management and security	57.53	85.79	149
Property management	49.48	73.75	149
Management and upkeep services for security	8.06	12.04	149
Parking	6.29	9.45	150
Rented dwellings	**2,860.24**	**59.81**	**2**
Rent	2,738.81	40.23	1
Rent as pay	79.28	–	–
Maintenance, insurance, and other expenses	42.15	19.58	46
Tenant's insurance	12.40	2.23	18
Maintenance and repair services	19.84	14.82	75
Maintenance and repair materials	9.91	2.53	26
Paints, wallpaper, and supplies	1.35	0.53	39
Electrical supplies, heating and cooling equipment	0.80	0.62	78
Miscellaneous supplies and equipment	5.89	0.53	9
Material for insulation, other maintenance and repair	1.43	0.02	1
Other lodging	**671.95**	**911.51**	**136**
Owned vacation homes	303.02	428.18	141
Mortgage interest and charges	136.53	194.36	142
Property taxes	106.15	147.87	139
Maintenance, insurance, and other expenses	60.34	85.95	142
Housing while attending school	68.47	90.21	132
Lodging on trips	300.46	393.13	131

	total	homeowners	
		spending	index to total
• **Utilities, fuels, and public services**	**$3,644.62**	**$4,275.56**	**117**
Natural gas	**483.21**	**601.80**	**125**
Electricity	**1,376.71**	**1,599.97**	**116**
Fuel oil and other fuels	**141.36**	**192.30**	**136**
Fuel oil	76.71	106.81	139
Coal, wood, and other fuels	10.73	14.12	132
Bottled gas	53.91	71.37	132
Telephone services	**1,161.96**	**1,262.63**	**109**
Residential telephone and pay phones	433.65	516.46	119
Cellular phone service	711.67	732.02	103
Phone cards	9.57	6.51	68
Voice over IP	7.08	7.64	108
Water and other public services	**481.38**	**618.85**	**129**
Water and sewerage maintenance	350.42	442.07	126
Trash and garbage collection	126.56	170.23	135
Septic tank cleaning	4.40	6.56	149
• **Household services**	**1,011.36**	**1,217.16**	**120**
Personal services	**389.44**	**439.07**	**113**
Babysitting and child care in own home	47.07	51.87	110
Babysitting and child care in someone else's home	32.24	26.63	83
Care for elderly, invalids, handicapped, etc.	46.13	56.54	123
Adult day care centers	5.01	7.44	149
Day care centers, nurseries, and preschools	258.99	296.58	115
Other household services	**621.92**	**778.09**	**125**
Housekeeping services	112.08	155.90	139
Gardening, lawn care service	107.33	155.53	145
Water-softening service	3.96	5.08	128
Nonclothing laundry and dry cleaning, sent out	1.03	1.24	120
Nonclothing laundry and dry cleaning, coin-operated	3.59	1.09	30
Termite and pest control services	18.55	26.80	144
Home security system service fee	21.02	30.77	146
Other home services	19.80	26.71	135
Termite and pest control products	2.88	4.10	142
Moving, storage, and freight express	36.78	29.09	79
Appliance repair, including at service center	16.54	23.96	145
Reupholstering and furniture repair	4.33	6.09	141
Repairs and rentals of lawn and garden equipment, hand and power tools, etc.	5.88	7.92	135
Appliance rental	1.36	1.19	88
Repair of computer systems for nonbusiness use	6.75	8.14	121
Computer information services	253.49	285.42	113
Installation of computer	0.38	0.50	132
• **Housekeeping supplies**	**658.76**	**803.97**	**122**
Laundry and cleaning supplies	**155.80**	**174.11**	**112**
Soaps and detergents	85.66	92.43	108
Other laundry cleaning products	70.15	81.67	116
Other household products	**359.87**	**451.86**	**126**
Cleansing and toilet tissue, paper towels, and napkins	110.58	124.21	112
Miscellaneous household products	137.88	168.11	122
Lawn and garden supplies	111.41	159.54	143

	total	homeowners spending	index to total
Postage and stationery	**$143.09**	**$178.00**	**124**
Stationery, stationery supplies, giftwrap	74.63	95.00	127
Postage	64.49	77.56	120
Delivery services	3.97	5.44	137
• Household furnishings and equipment	**1,505.57**	**1,871.55**	**124**
Household textiles	**124.19**	**155.79**	**125**
Bathroom linens	18.41	19.97	108
Bedroom linens	68.26	86.52	127
Kitchen and dining room linens	6.09	7.75	127
Curtains and draperies	17.12	23.36	136
Slipcovers and decorative pillows	3.49	4.21	121
Sewing materials for household items	9.66	12.60	130
Other linens	1.15	1.38	120
Furniture	**342.98**	**404.37**	**118**
Mattresses and springs	56.18	64.04	114
Other bedroom furniture	61.30	69.26	113
Sofas	83.23	96.00	115
Living room chairs	34.50	42.55	123
Living room tables	11.58	13.57	117
Kitchen and dining room furniture	31.91	38.38	120
Infants' furniture	8.00	8.58	107
Outdoor furniture	18.61	25.97	140
Wall units, cabinets, and other furniture	37.67	46.01	122
Floor coverings	**30.31**	**42.20**	**139**
Wall-to-wall carpet	14.36	19.95	139
Floor coverings, nonpermanent	16.52	22.26	135
Major appliances	**193.71**	**256.52**	**132**
Dishwashers (built-in), garbage disposals, range hoods	13.31	19.46	146
Refrigerators, freezers	56.40	76.88	136
Washing machines	32.06	41.09	128
Clothes dryers	23.65	29.57	125
Cooking stoves, ovens	27.28	39.43	145
Microwave ovens	9.79	11.45	117
Portable dishwasher	0.66	0.91	138
Window air conditioners	3.27	3.47	106
Electric floor-cleaning equipment	14.19	15.88	112
Sewing machines	8.19	11.32	138
Miscellaneous household appliances	4.94	7.08	143
Small appliances and miscellaneous housewares	**93.41**	**113.91**	**122**
Housewares	63.95	77.75	122
Plastic dinnerware	2.49	2.35	94
China and other dinnerware	4.89	6.18	126
Flatware	3.66	3.61	99
Glassware	11.25	15.15	135
Silver serving pieces	2.86	3.61	126
Other serving pieces	1.78	2.16	121
Nonelectric cookware	13.38	16.03	120
Tableware, nonelectric kitchenware	23.65	28.66	121
Small appliances	29.46	36.16	123
Small electric kitchen appliances	20.62	23.99	116
Portable heating and cooling equipment	8.84	12.18	138

	total	homeowners	
		spending	index to total
Miscellaneous household equipment	**$720.97**	**$898.77**	**125**
Window coverings	20.62	29.47	143
Infants' equipment	13.91	13.60	98
Laundry and cleaning equipment	16.47	18.88	115
Outdoor equipment	16.91	22.14	131
Lamps and lighting fixtures	28.56	39.91	140
Household decorative items	128.67	167.14	130
Telephones and accessories	47.08	54.83	116
Lawn and garden equipment	56.73	82.60	146
Power tools	35.28	41.11	117
Office furniture for home use	7.47	9.30	124
Hand tools	13.33	17.78	133
Indoor plants and fresh flowers	50.19	64.95	129
Closet and storage items	14.75	17.41	118
Rental of furniture	2.07	1.04	50
Luggage	10.89	12.40	114
Computers and computer hardware for nonbusiness use	156.62	178.54	114
Portable memory	7.70	8.69	113
Computer software and accessories for nonbusiness use	20.52	24.61	120
Personal digital assistants	2.77	2.98	108
Internet services away from home	2.19	2.33	106
Telephone answering devices	0.45	0.58	129
Business equipment for home use	2.82	3.52	125
Other hardware	13.07	17.26	132
Smoke alarms	1.32	1.81	137
Other household appliances	8.81	11.41	130
Miscellaneous household equipment and parts	41.78	54.49	130
APPAREL	**1,725.11**	**1,857.40**	**108**
Men's apparel	**304.32**	**324.40**	**107**
Suits	17.84	18.81	105
Sport coats and tailored jackets	6.83	7.83	115
Coats and jackets	35.07	36.39	104
Underwear	15.83	17.36	110
Hosiery	11.90	12.84	108
Nightwear	1.70	2.11	124
Accessories	28.54	28.05	98
Sweaters and vests	14.42	15.32	106
Active sportswear	16.88	20.24	120
Shirts	84.38	95.05	113
Pants and shorts	67.46	66.50	99
Uniforms	2.73	3.10	114
Costumes	0.72	0.81	113
Boys' (aged 2 to 15) apparel	**78.59**	**87.41**	**111**
Coats and jackets	4.35	4.52	104
Sweaters	1.86	1.91	103
Shirts	24.09	28.79	120
Underwear	6.08	6.92	114
Nightwear	1.08	1.18	109
Hosiery	4.80	4.84	101
Accessories	4.32	5.23	121
Suits, sport coats, and vests	0.93	1.02	110
Pants and shorts	25.79	27.18	105

	total	homeowners	
		spending	index to total
Uniforms	$3.36	$3.61	107
Active sportswear	1.19	1.39	117
Costumes	0.74	0.82	111
Women's apparel	**560.80**	**626.64**	**112**
Coats and jackets	41.98	45.67	109
Dresses	72.15	79.79	111
Sport coats and tailored jackets	4.74	5.80	122
Sweaters and vests	44.10	49.18	112
Shirts, blouses, and tops	111.11	125.93	113
Skirts	9.21	8.83	96
Pants and shorts	91.88	101.26	110
Active sportswear	27.57	30.24	110
Nightwear	21.60	23.19	107
Undergarments	36.16	42.59	118
Hosiery	17.66	19.79	112
Suits	11.31	13.44	119
Accessories	63.37	71.29	112
Uniforms	6.35	7.60	120
Costumes	1.61	2.03	126
Girls' (aged 2 to 15) apparel	**117.65**	**131.62**	**112**
Coats and jackets	7.09	7.27	103
Dresses and suits	13.02	14.48	111
Shirts, blouses, and sweaters	31.15	35.28	113
Skirts, pants, and shorts	26.62	27.89	105
Active sportswear	11.68	14.86	127
Underwear and nightwear	11.30	13.46	119
Hosiery	5.28	5.40	102
Accessories	6.39	7.29	114
Uniforms	3.28	3.37	103
Costumes	1.83	2.33	127
Children's (under age 2) apparel	**91.16**	**88.53**	**97**
Coats, jackets, and snowsuits	2.71	2.58	95
Outerwear including dresses	21.08	21.10	100
Underwear	55.12	52.55	95
Nightwear and loungewear	4.82	5.01	104
Accessories	7.42	7.30	98
Footwear	**323.14**	**329.20**	**102**
Men's	93.22	90.33	97
Boys'	42.89	40.16	94
Women's	150.67	160.83	107
Girls'	36.36	37.87	104
Other apparel products and services	**249.45**	**269.60**	**108**
Material for making clothes	9.68	12.68	131
Sewing patterns and notions	5.59	7.19	129
Watches	25.08	30.00	120
Jewelry	97.87	126.39	129
Shoe repair and other shoe services	1.19	1.44	121
Coin-operated apparel laundry and dry cleaning	41.28	8.47	21
Apparel alteration, repair, and tailoring services	5.73	6.69	117
Clothing rental	2.37	2.80	118
Watch and jewelry repair	3.55	4.52	127
Professional laundry, dry cleaning	55.48	68.50	123
Clothing storage	1.62	0.91	56

	total	homeowners	
		spending	index to total
TRANSPORTATION	**$7,658.25**	**$9,089.32**	**119**
• Vehicle purchases	**2,656.95**	**3,246.92**	**122**
Cars and trucks, new	**1,297.15**	**1,717.86**	**132**
New cars	698.37	905.99	130
New trucks	598.77	811.88	136
Cars and trucks, used	**1,304.35**	**1,459.85**	**112**
Used cars	691.86	767.32	111
Used trucks	612.49	692.53	113
Other vehicles	**55.45**	**69.21**	**125**
New motorcycles	21.79	32.72	150
Used motorcycles	33.66	36.49	108
• Gasoline and motor oil	**1,986.40**	**2,275.58**	**115**
Gasoline	1,831.34	2,084.79	114
Diesel fuel	35.60	48.06	135
Gasoline on trips	108.63	130.62	120
Motor oil	9.73	10.79	111
Motor oil on trips	1.10	1.32	120
• Other vehicle expenses	**2,535.57**	**3,023.11**	**119**
Vehicle finance charges	**281.01**	**326.20**	**116**
Automobile finance charges	119.95	129.60	108
Truck finance charges	136.11	162.01	119
Motorcycle and plane finance charges	4.86	5.72	118
Other vehicle finance charges	20.09	28.86	144
Maintenance and repairs	**732.82**	**862.39**	**118**
Coolant, additives, brake and transmission fluids	3.91	4.01	103
Tires—purchased, replaced, installed	119.17	141.75	119
Parts, equipment, and accessories	43.62	48.83	112
Vehicle audio equipment	2.27	2.18	96
Vehicle products and cleaning services	5.02	5.75	115
Vehicle video equipment	1.99	2.31	116
Miscellaneous auto repair, servicing	55.55	64.34	116
Body work and painting	26.97	34.70	129
Clutch and transmission repair	34.37	39.66	115
Drive shaft and rear-end repair	5.18	5.71	110
Brake work	65.26	76.49	117
Repair to steering or front-end	17.54	21.10	120
Repair to engine cooling system	22.48	25.71	114
Motor tune-up	46.10	54.83	119
Lube, oil change, and oil filters	74.75	88.60	119
Front-end alignment, wheel balance, rotation	12.86	15.56	121
Shock absorber replacement	5.68	5.53	97
Tire repair and other repair work	49.30	60.78	123
Vehicle air conditioning repair	12.47	13.99	112
Exhaust system repair	10.45	11.50	110
Electrical system repair	30.77	34.11	111
Motor repair, replacement	68.89	80.85	117
Auto repair service policy	18.24	24.09	132
Vehicle insurance	**1,075.24**	**1,302.69**	**121**

	total	homeowners	
		spending	index to total
Vehicle rental, leases, licenses, other charges	**$446.50**	**$531.84**	**119**
Leased and rented vehicles	233.03	281.66	121
Rented vehicles	33.06	39.86	121
Auto rental	4.98	4.41	89
Auto rental on trips	23.70	30.24	128
Truck rental	2.27	2.63	116
Truck rental on trips	1.65	2.09	127
Leased vehicles	199.97	241.80	121
Car lease payments	106.66	124.54	117
Truck lease payments	82.37	106.76	130
Vehicle registration, state	95.47	113.94	119
Vehicle registration, local	8.10	9.87	122
Driver's license	7.83	8.23	105
Vehicle inspection	11.36	13.29	117
Parking fees	39.80	44.01	111
Parking fees in home city, excluding residence	32.86	35.15	107
Parking fees on trips	6.94	8.86	128
Tolls	22.33	26.32	118
Tolls on trips	4.49	5.16	115
Towing charges	4.64	4.04	87
Global positioning services	1.92	2.57	134
Automobile service clubs	17.54	22.74	130
• Public transportation	**479.32**	**543.71**	**113**
Airline fares	300.92	364.67	121
Intercity bus fares	9.22	9.75	106
Intracity mass transit fares	65.18	42.47	65
Local transportation on trips	16.97	20.05	118
Taxi fares and limousine service	23.51	21.68	92
Intercity train fares	14.98	17.78	119
Ship fares	48.20	67.15	139
School bus	0.33	0.16	48
HEALTH CARE	**3,126.09**	**3,943.99**	**126**
Health insurance	**1,784.79**	**2,253.26**	**126**
Commercial health insurance	344.11	442.82	129
Traditional fee-for-service health plan (not BCBS)	84.88	110.93	131
Preferred-provider health plan (not BCBS)	259.24	331.89	128
Blue Cross, Blue Shield	527.17	676.92	128
Traditional fee-for-service health plan	86.93	118.05	136
Preferred-provider health plan	214.85	279.24	130
Health maintenance organization	170.01	209.30	123
Commercial Medicare supplement	45.93	59.11	129
Other BCBS health insurance	9.45	11.22	119
Health maintenance plans (HMOs)	285.51	338.05	118
Medicare payments	348.72	434.34	125
Medicare prescription drug premium	62.20	75.15	121
Commercial Medicare supplements and other health insurance	154.13	196.79	128
Commercial Medicare supplement (not BCBS)	102.27	131.86	129
Other health insurance (not BCBS)	51.86	64.93	125
Long-term care insurance	62.94	89.18	142

	total	homeowners	
		spending	index to total
Medical services	$736.32	$932.49	127
Physician's services	184.97	225.50	122
Dental services	268.22	342.82	128
Eye care services	39.86	51.97	130
Service by professionals other than physician	49.47	63.89	129
Lab tests, X-rays	48.19	61.17	127
Hospital room and services	104.86	137.13	131
Care in convalescent or nursing home	16.08	15.36	96
Repair of medical equipment	2.74	3.81	139
Other medical services	21.88	30.80	141
Drugs	486.27	609.41	125
Nonprescription drugs	81.74	96.75	118
Nonprescription vitamins	42.81	56.34	132
Prescription drugs	361.72	456.32	126
Medical supplies	118.71	148.82	125
Eyeglasses and contact lenses	59.81	75.47	126
Hearing aids	16.04	22.46	140
Topicals and dressings	31.84	37.29	117
Medical equipment for general use	2.75	3.35	122
Supportive and convalescent medical equipment	4.83	6.65	138
Rental of medical equipment	1.11	1.38	124
Rental of supportive and convalescent medical equipment	2.34	2.23	95
ENTERTAINMENT	2,692.66	3,255.66	121
Fees and admissions	628.00	785.33	125
Recreation expenses on trips	19.83	24.81	125
Social, recreation, civic club membership	115.41	147.84	128
Fees for participant sports	123.67	161.59	131
Participant sports on trips	21.95	27.58	126
Movie, theater, amusement park, and other admissions	120.38	140.42	117
Movie, other admissions on trips	40.84	50.58	124
Admission to sports events	50.86	61.58	121
Admission to sports events on trips	13.61	16.85	124
Fees for recreational lessons	101.63	129.28	127
Other entertainment services on trips	19.83	24.81	125
Audio and visual equipment and services	974.95	1,092.25	112
Radios	2.24	2.51	112
Television sets	140.39	164.62	117
Tape recorders and players	0.66	0.57	86
Cable and satellite television services	597.38	675.63	113
Miscellaneous sound equipment	1.10	1.55	141
Miscellaneous video equipment	3.64	3.16	87
Satellite radio service	14.01	17.14	122
Sound equipment accessories	10.64	11.12	105
Online gaming services	2.20	2.39	109
VCRs and video disc players	12.46	15.17	122
Video game hardware and software	53.32	51.99	98
Video cassettes, tapes, and discs	30.10	31.01	103
Streamed and downloaded video	1.40	1.57	112
Repair of TV, radio, and sound equipment	3.32	4.16	125
Rental of television sets	0.68	0.14	21
Personal digital audio players	13.01	14.19	109
Sound components and component systems	11.83	14.81	125

		homeowners	
	total	spending	index to total
Satellite dishes	$1.06	$1.31	124
Compact discs, records, and audio tapes	18.46	19.90	108
Streamed and downloaded audio	5.61	6.17	110
Rental of VCR, radio, and sound equipment	0.16	0.17	106
Musical instruments and accessories	23.30	22.66	97
Rental and repair of musical instruments	1.59	1.97	124
Rental of video cassettes, tapes, discs, films	25.49	27.08	106
Rental of computer and video game hardware and software	0.23	0.29	126
Installation of television sets	0.68	0.96	141
Pets, toys, hobbies, and playground equipment	**689.75**	**865.18**	**125**
Pets	542.85	700.27	129
Pet food	168.92	214.71	127
Pet purchase, supplies, and medicines	165.83	201.72	122
Pet services	43.36	56.13	129
Veterinarian services	164.74	227.71	138
Toys, games, hobbies, and tricycles	139.07	154.39	111
Stamp and coin collecting	5.39	7.17	133
Playground equipment	2.45	3.35	137
Other entertainment supplies, equipment, services	**399.95**	**512.91**	**128**
Unmotored recreational vehicles	50.19	72.58	145
Boat without motor and boat trailers	17.14	23.84	139
Trailer and other attachable campers	33.05	48.74	147
Motorized recreational vehicles	109.90	148.20	135
Purchase of motorized camper	31.48	47.51	151
Purchase of other vehicle	40.75	44.52	109
Purchase of boat with motor	37.67	56.16	149
Rental of recreational vehicles	6.53	7.84	120
Docking and landing fees	7.78	11.73	151
Sports, recreation, exercise equipment	129.98	159.55	123
Athletic gear, game tables, exercise equipment	51.67	63.97	124
Bicycles	13.69	14.83	108
Camping equipment	10.73	14.00	130
Hunting and fishing equipment	30.35	36.65	121
Winter sports equipment	3.85	4.58	119
Water sports equipment	3.03	3.80	125
Other sports equipment	5.96	5.98	100
Global positioning system devices	7.98	12.06	151
Rental and repair of miscellaneous sports equipment	2.72	3.68	135
Photographic equipment and supplies	59.08	73.40	124
Film	1.73	1.79	103
Other photographic supplies	1.97	2.78	141
Photo processing	12.87	16.21	126
Repair and rental of photographic equipment	0.59	0.69	117
Photographic equipment	27.57	32.28	117
Photographer fees	14.34	19.64	137
Fireworks	6.39	2.84	44
Souvenirs	2.57	2.75	107
Visual goods	1.41	1.90	135
Pinball, electronic video games	2.61	1.85	71
Live entertainment for catered affairs	8.63	11.40	132
Rental of party supplies for catered affairs	14.09	18.38	130

	total	homeowners spending	index to total
PERSONAL CARE PRODUCTS AND SERVICES	$595.57	$693.14	116
Personal care products	304.22	348.34	115
Hair care products	65.14	74.96	115
Hair accessories	6.38	6.61	104
Wigs and hairpieces	2.95	2.84	96
Oral hygiene products	29.27	33.07	113
Shaving products	16.02	17.86	111
Cosmetics, perfume, and bath products	143.17	166.35	116
Deodorants, feminine hygiene, miscellaneous products	32.61	36.05	111
Electric personal care appliances	8.68	10.60	122
Personal care services	291.35	344.80	118
READING	109.60	135.67	124
Newspaper and magazine subscriptions	43.30	57.68	133
Newspapers and magazines, nonsubscription	14.97	16.46	110
Books	50.31	60.16	120
EDUCATION	1,068.02	1,233.74	116
College tuition	703.66	779.63	111
Elementary and high school tuition	161.87	226.37	140
Vocational and technical school tuition	13.19	17.09	130
Test preparation, tutoring services	8.69	10.93	126
Other school tuition	8.14	9.47	116
Other school expenses including rentals	35.51	41.93	118
Books and supplies for college	66.77	65.01	97
Books and supplies for elementary and high school	18.67	20.24	108
Books and supplies for vocational and technical schools	0.57	0.69	121
Books and supplies for day care and nursery	0.14	0.18	129
Books and suppliesfor other schools	1.50	1.92	128
Miscellaneous school expenses and supplies	49.30	60.27	122
TOBACCO PRODUCTS, SMOKING SUPPLIES	379.69	358.67	94
Cigarettes	347.58	322.63	93
Other tobacco products	30.07	34.26	114
Smoking accessories	1.93	1.74	90
FINANCIAL PRODUCTS AND SERVICES			
Miscellaneous financial	816.36	964.93	118
Miscellaneous fees	5.95	8.40	141
Lottery and gambling losses	74.75	86.87	116
Legal fees	160.64	180.28	112
Funeral expenses	47.61	58.27	122
Safe deposit box rental	3.79	5.17	136
Checking accounts, other bank service charges	23.52	23.68	101
Cemetery lots, vaults, and maintenance fees	14.05	17.63	125
Accounting fees	58.73	74.42	127
Miscellaneous personal services	41.30	44.74	108
Dating services	0.38	0.32	84
Finance charges, except mortgage and vehicles	202.35	235.49	116
Occupational expenses	56.99	69.95	123
Expenses for other properties	107.92	135.81	126
Credit card memberships	1.89	2.21	117
Shopping club membership fees	9.44	12.04	128
Vacation clubs	6.02	8.38	139

	total	homeowners	
		spending	index to total
Cash contributions	**$1,723.08**	**$2,163.61**	**126**
Support for college students	108.91	147.28	135
Alimony expenditures	46.19	60.43	131
Child support expenditures	215.70	193.94	90
Gifts of stocks, bonds, and mutual funds to members of other households	12.54	16.36	130
Cash contributions to charities	208.20	286.43	138
Cash contributions to church, religious organizations	724.60	967.44	134
Cash contributions to educational institutions	30.52	41.69	137
Cash contributions to political organizations	7.11	9.80	138
Cash gifts to members of other households	369.31	440.25	119
Personal insurance and pensions	**5,471.07**	**6,775.63**	**124**
Life and other personal insurance	309.03	417.11	135
Life, endowment, annuity, other personal insurance	292.08	394.52	135
Other nonhealth insurance	16.96	22.59	133
Pensions and Social Security	5,162.04	6,358.52	123
Deductions for government retirement	79.95	105.55	132
Deductions for railroad retirement	7.02	9.61	137
Deductions for private pensions	625.39	852.11	136
Nonpayroll deposit to retirement plans	461.03	625.48	136
Deductions for Social Security	3,988.65	4,765.78	119
Personal taxes	**2,103.78**	**2,823.03**	**134**
Federal income taxes	1,404.46	1,914.88	136
Federal income tax deducted	1,959.52	2,421.66	124
Additional federal income tax paid	451.19	610.92	135
Federal income tax refunds	−1,006.25	−1,117.71	111
State and local income taxes	524.06	657.39	125
State and local income tax deducted	573.97	705.00	123
Additional state and local income tax paid	84.89	111.79	132
State and local income tax refunds	−134.80	−159.40	118
Other taxes	176.56	252.19	143
GIFTS FOR PEOPLE IN OTHER HOUSEHOLDS	**1,067.01**	**1,323.78**	**124**

* The category fast-food restaurants also includes take-out, delivery, concession stands, buffets, and cafeterias other than employer and school.

** Spending on mortgage principal reduction is not included in spending because it is considered an asset.

Note: Numbers may not add to total because not all categories are shown. "−" means zero or sample is too small to make a reliable estimate. Spending on gifts is also included in the preceding product and service categories. The index is calculated by dividing the spending of homeowners by the spending of total households and multiplying by 100.

Source: Bureau of Labor Statistics, unpublished data from the 2009 Consumer Expenditure Survey; calculations by New Strategist

Table 10.2 Household Spending of Homeowners by Mortgage Status, 2009

The 63 percent of homeowners with a mortgage spend 13 percent more on average than the average homeowner, and the 37 percent of homeowners without a mortgage spend 23 percent less. One reason for the lower spending of homeowners without a mortgage is their older age.

(average annual spending of homeowning consumer units (CUs) on all products and services by mortgage status, 2009; number of consumer units in thousands)

		homeowners		index to total homeowners	
	total	with mortgage	without mortgage	with mortgage	without mortgage
Number of homeowner households (CUs)	80,068	50,080	29,988	63	37
Before-tax income	$75,858	$88,237	$55,185	116	73
Average age of householder	53.3	47.8	62.5	90	117
Average number of persons in household	2.6	2.9	2.1	112	81
Average number of earners in household	1.4	1.6	0.9	114	64
Average number of vehicles per household	2.4	2.5	2.2	104	92
At least one vehicle owned or leased	96%	98%	93%	102	97
Average household spending, total	$57,047.30	$64,492.66	$44,129.69	113	77
Food, average spending	7,197.79	7,682.38	6,125.23	107	85
FOOD AT HOME	4,214.27	4,376.86	3,837.36	104	91
Cereals and bakery products	565.90	593.67	500.72	105	88
Cereals and cereal products	185.74	197.72	157.64	106	85
Flour	9.99	10.35	9.15	104	92
Prepared flour mixes	16.73	17.93	13.90	107	83
Ready-to-eat and cooked cereals	101.10	105.75	90.18	105	89
Rice	22.25	25.60	14.39	115	65
Pasta, cornmeal, and other cereal products	35.67	38.08	30.02	107	84
Bakery products	380.16	395.96	343.08	104	90
Bread	105.00	107.06	100.18	102	95
White bread	36.01	36.48	34.91	101	97
Bread, other than white	68.99	70.58	65.27	102	95
Cookies and crackers	96.16	101.18	84.39	105	88
Cookies	53.32	55.28	48.71	104	91
Crackers	42.85	45.90	35.68	107	83
Frozen and refrigerated bakery products	32.04	34.96	25.21	109	79
Other bakery products	146.95	152.76	133.31	104	91
Biscuits and rolls	56.81	57.72	54.66	102	96
Cakes and cupcakes	42.53	46.47	33.30	109	78
Bread and cracker products	6.18	6.61	5.18	107	84
Sweetrolls, coffee cakes, doughnuts	25.16	25.57	24.18	102	96
Pies, tarts, turnovers	16.27	16.40	15.98	101	98
Meats, poultry, fish, and eggs	931.54	965.62	851.55	104	91
Beef	251.70	254.23	245.78	101	98
Ground beef	95.18	98.66	87.01	104	91
Roast	41.16	41.64	40.02	101	97
Chuck roast	11.09	10.52	12.41	95	112
Round roast	6.06	6.17	5.81	102	96
Other roast	24.01	24.95	21.80	104	91

	homeowners			index to total homeowners	
	total	with mortgage	without mortgage	with mortgage	without mortgage
Steak	$94.19	$92.96	$97.08	99	103
Round steak	10.80	10.25	12.10	95	112
Sirloin steak	25.24	27.43	20.13	109	80
Other steak	58.14	55.29	64.85	95	112
Other beef	21.18	20.97	21.67	99	102
Pork	186.95	187.91	184.71	101	99
Bacon	34.66	33.66	37.03	97	107
Pork chops	31.24	32.15	29.12	103	93
Ham	44.38	44.30	44.55	100	100
Ham, not canned	43.07	42.98	43.28	100	100
Canned ham	1.30	1.32	1.26	102	97
Sausage	30.97	31.49	29.74	102	96
Other pork	45.70	46.31	44.27	101	97
Other meats	130.25	133.60	122.38	103	94
Frankfurters	25.19	24.58	26.61	98	106
Lunch meats (cold cuts)	93.47	95.55	88.58	102	95
Bologna, liverwurst, salami	21.00	20.99	21.04	100	100
Other lunch meats	72.47	74.57	67.53	103	93
Lamb, organ meats, and others	11.59	13.46	7.19	116	62
Poultry	164.84	181.00	126.93	110	77
Fresh and frozen chicken	126.10	138.35	97.35	110	77
Fresh and frozen whole chicken	31.51	34.62	24.22	110	77
Fresh and frozen chicken parts	94.59	103.73	73.13	110	77
Other poultry	38.75	42.65	29.58	110	76
Fish and seafood	151.44	161.44	127.97	107	85
Canned fish and seafood	20.58	20.01	21.90	97	106
Fresh fish and shellfish	80.80	87.34	65.47	108	81
Frozen fish and shellfish	50.06	54.09	40.60	108	81
Eggs	46.35	47.45	43.78	102	94
Dairy products	**459.01**	**477.83**	**414.84**	**104**	**90**
Fresh milk and cream	157.75	164.06	142.93	104	91
Fresh milk, all types	137.24	142.70	124.42	104	91
Cream	20.50	21.35	18.51	104	90
Other dairy products	301.27	313.77	271.91	104	90
Butter	25.09	24.68	26.04	98	104
Cheese	152.60	160.64	133.75	105	88
Ice cream and related products	72.18	72.80	70.71	101	98
Miscellaneous dairy products	51.40	55.65	41.41	108	81
Fruits and vegetables	**743.55**	**760.21**	**704.43**	**102**	**95**
Fresh fruits	252.42	253.21	250.59	100	99
Apples	42.81	45.17	37.28	106	87
Bananas	36.85	36.23	38.31	98	104
Oranges	26.96	26.75	27.46	99	102
Citrus fruits, excluding oranges	21.54	21.48	21.67	100	101
Other fresh fruits	124.27	123.58	125.87	99	101
Fresh vegetables	237.61	246.41	216.97	104	91
Potatoes	41.78	43.07	38.75	103	93
Lettuce	31.19	33.24	26.37	107	85
Tomatoes	39.64	40.72	37.10	103	94
Other fresh vegetables	125.00	129.37	114.75	103	92

	homeowners			index to total homeowners	
	total	with mortgage	without mortgage	with mortgage	without mortgage
Processed fruits	$130.82	$134.32	$122.58	103	94
Frozen fruits and fruit juices	13.56	12.86	15.21	95	112
Frozen orange juice	3.04	2.88	3.41	95	112
Frozen fruits	7.53	6.53	9.88	87	131
Frozen fruit juices, excluding orange	3.00	3.45	1.93	115	64
Canned fruits	22.90	22.67	23.43	99	102
Dried fruits	10.10	9.41	11.73	93	116
Fresh fruit juice	21.81	22.73	19.66	104	90
Canned and bottled fruit juice	62.45	66.67	52.55	107	84
Processed vegetables	122.70	126.27	114.30	103	93
Frozen vegetables	40.00	40.79	38.13	102	95
Canned and dried vegetables and juices	82.70	85.48	76.17	103	92
Canned beans	17.39	18.22	15.45	105	89
Canned corn	7.11	7.29	6.67	103	94
Canned miscellaneous vegetables	27.12	28.09	24.83	104	92
Dried peas	0.53	0.65	0.23	123	43
Dried beans	4.08	4.25	3.70	104	91
Dried miscellaneous vegetables	10.08	10.17	9.87	101	98
Fresh and canned vegetable juices	16.00	16.47	14.91	103	93
Sugar and other sweets	**163.64**	**164.25**	**162.22**	**100**	**99**
Candy and chewing gum	102.24	103.28	99.81	101	98
Sugar	19.67	20.11	18.66	102	95
Artificial sweeteners	7.40	6.62	9.25	89	125
Jams, preserves, other sweets	34.32	34.24	34.50	100	101
Fats and oils	**115.61**	**116.71**	**113.03**	**101**	**98**
Margarine	9.03	8.45	10.38	94	115
Fats and oils	38.51	38.66	38.16	100	99
Salad dressings	32.68	33.64	30.44	103	93
Nondairy cream and imitation milk	18.95	18.51	20.00	98	106
Peanut butter	16.44	17.45	14.06	106	86
Miscellaneous foods	**804.54**	**841.73**	**717.25**	**105**	**89**
Frozen prepared foods	159.15	174.40	123.34	110	77
Frozen meals	75.26	80.03	64.06	106	85
Other frozen prepared foods	83.89	94.38	59.28	113	71
Canned and packaged soups	53.55	55.56	48.82	104	91
Potato chips, nuts, and other snacks	172.64	179.09	157.49	104	91
Potato chips and other snacks	124.88	134.03	103.38	107	83
Nuts	47.76	45.06	54.10	94	113
Condiments and seasonings	148.20	155.74	130.49	105	88
Salt, spices, and other seasonings	35.01	36.84	30.74	105	88
Olives, pickles, relishes	17.83	17.42	18.79	98	105
Sauces and gravies	62.35	67.85	49.45	109	79
Baking needs and miscellaneous products	33.00	33.63	31.52	102	96
Other canned or packaged prepared foods	271.01	276.93	257.11	102	95
Prepared salads	38.46	39.94	35.01	104	91
Prepared desserts	15.41	14.76	16.92	96	110
Baby food	28.28	31.70	20.26	112	72
Miscellaneous prepared foods	185.90	188.13	180.64	101	97
Nonalcoholic beverages	**368.60**	**387.97**	**323.12**	**105**	**88**
Cola	94.29	97.61	86.52	104	92
Other carbonated drinks	51.48	53.82	45.99	105	89
Tea	33.49	35.08	29.74	105	89

	homeowners			index to total homeowners	
	total	with mortgage	without mortgage	with mortgage	without mortgage
Coffee	$66.48	$66.21	$67.12	100	101
Roasted coffee	43.78	44.34	42.47	101	97
Instant and freeze-dried coffee	22.71	21.88	24.65	96	109
Noncarbonated fruit-flavored drinks	26.67	27.48	24.76	103	93
Other noncarbonated beverages and ice	14.00	15.71	9.99	112	71
Bottled water	61.52	68.14	45.98	111	75
Sports drinks	20.55	23.84	12.84	116	62
Food prepared by consumer unit on trips	**61.87**	**68.87**	**50.20**	**111**	**81**
FOOD AWAY FROM HOME	**2,983.53**	**3,305.52**	**2,287.87**	**111**	**77**
Meals at restaurants, carry-outs, other	**2,445.08**	**2,678.32**	**1,897.63**	**110**	**78**
Lunch	829.83	915.16	629.56	110	76
At fast-food restaurants*	374.94	421.54	265.57	112	71
At full-service restaurants	349.33	361.06	321.77	103	92
At vending machines, mobile vendors	7.41	8.64	4.52	117	61
At employer and school cafeterias	98.16	123.91	37.70	126	38
Dinner	1,197.42	1,315.15	921.10	110	77
At fast-food restaurants*	366.00	418.85	241.96	114	66
At full-service restaurants	823.94	888.50	672.41	108	82
At vending machines, mobile vendors	2.52	2.85	1.76	113	70
At employer and school cafeterias	4.96	4.96	4.96	100	100
Snacks and nonalcoholic beverages	171.48	192.96	121.07	113	71
At fast-food restaurants*	116.74	131.13	82.97	112	71
At full-service restaurants	29.86	33.61	21.06	113	71
At vending machines, mobile vendors	19.90	22.37	14.09	112	71
At employer and school cafeterias	4.98	5.85	2.95	117	59
Breakfast and brunch	246.34	255.04	225.90	104	92
At fast-food restaurants*	122.11	133.01	96.50	109	79
At full-service restaurants	111.73	107.37	121.95	96	109
At vending machines, mobile vendors	2.32	2.74	1.32	118	57
At employer and school cafeterias	10.19	11.92	6.13	117	60
Board (including at school)	**62.00**	**68.25**	**51.58**	**110**	**83**
Catered affairs	**93.91**	**109.99**	**67.05**	**117**	**71**
Food on trips	**279.90**	**309.56**	**230.36**	**111**	**82**
School lunches	**80.86**	**111.40**	**29.87**	**138**	**37**
Meals as pay	**21.78**	**28.01**	**11.38**	**129**	**52**
ALCOHOLIC BEVERAGES	**476.79**	**524.81**	**370.07**	**110**	**78**
At home	**281.94**	**296.24**	**248.38**	**105**	**88**
Beer and ale	118.32	129.49	92.10	109	78
Whiskey	12.67	9.48	20.17	75	159
Wine	127.49	133.68	112.95	105	89
Other alcoholic beverages	23.46	23.59	23.16	101	99
Away from home	**194.85**	**228.57**	**121.69**	**117**	**62**
Beer and ale	63.86	76.64	33.86	120	53
At fast-food restaurants*	13.29	16.37	6.04	123	45
At full-service restaurants	49.25	58.52	27.48	119	56
At vending machines, mobile vendors	1.32	1.74	0.33	132	25
Wine	35.87	40.29	25.50	112	71
At fast-food restaurants*	1.76	2.40	0.28	136	16
At full-service restaurants	34.10	37.88	25.22	111	74
Other alcoholic beverages	43.90	51.59	25.86	118	59
At fast-food restaurants*	3.74	4.47	2.04	120	55
At full-service restaurants	40.05	47.08	23.54	118	59
Alcoholic beverages purchased on trips	51.22	60.05	36.47	117	71

	homeowners			index to total homeowners	
	total	with mortgage	without mortgage	with mortgage	without mortgage
HOUSING	$18,900.95	$22,846.39	$12,286.91	121	65
• Shelter	10,732.71	14,050.04	5,192.80	131	48
Owned dwellings**	9,761.39	13,059.48	4,253.61	134	44
Mortgage interest and charges	5,346.55	8,455.02	155.42	158	3
Mortgage interest	5,031.81	8,029.87	25.06	160	0
Interest paid, home equity loan	118.49	189.25	0.31	160	0
Interest paid, home equity line of credit	196.26	235.90	130.06	120	66
Property taxes	2,706.76	3,002.37	2,213.10	111	82
Maintenance, repairs, insurance, other expenses	1,708.08	1,602.09	1,885.09	94	110
Homeowner's insurance	510.97	511.84	509.52	100	100
Ground rent	76.30	36.82	142.22	48	186
Maintenance and repair services	914.56	850.87	1,020.94	93	112
Painting and papering	116.82	105.13	136.35	90	117
Plumbing and water heating	87.25	71.38	113.75	82	130
Heat, air conditioning, electrical work	170.39	172.52	166.82	101	98
Roofing and gutters	172.92	144.21	220.87	83	128
Other repair and maintenance services	287.18	253.51	343.41	88	120
Repair, replacement of hard-surface flooring	76.79	100.40	37.36	131	49
Repair of built-in appliances	3.22	3.73	2.36	116	73
Maintenance and repair materials	111.00	112.93	107.78	102	97
Paints, wallpaper, and supplies	19.44	21.72	15.62	112	80
Tools, equipment for painting, wallpapering	2.09	2.33	1.68	111	80
Plumbing supplies and equipment	8.31	8.13	8.62	98	104
Electrical supplies, heating and cooling equipment	9.34	9.47	9.12	101	98
Hard-surface flooring, repair and replacement	10.52	11.22	9.34	107	89
Roofing and gutters	11.66	6.93	19.56	59	168
Plaster, paneling, siding, windows, doors, screens, awnings	21.05	19.94	22.89	95	109
Patio, walk, fence, driveway, masonry, brick, and stucco materials	1.05	1.11	0.95	106	90
Miscellaneous supplies and equipment	27.56	32.09	19.99	116	73
Material for insulation, other maintenance, repair	27.27	32.09	19.21	118	70
Property management and security	85.79	80.42	94.76	94	110
Property management	73.75	70.05	79.92	95	108
Management and upkeep services for security	12.04	10.36	14.85	86	123
Parking	9.45	9.21	9.86	97	104
Rented dwellings	59.81	47.60	80.21	80	134
Rent	40.23	33.07	52.19	82	130
Rent as pay	–	–	–	–	–
Maintenance, insurance, and other expenses	19.58	14.52	28.01	74	143
Tenant's insurance	2.23	1.92	2.74	86	123
Maintenance and repair services	14.82	11.50	20.36	78	137
Maintenance and repair materials	2.53	1.10	4.92	43	194
Paints, wallpaper, and supplies	0.53	0.71	0.23	134	43
Electrical supplies, heating and cooling equipment	0.62	0.16	1.38	26	223
Miscellaneous supplies and equipment	0.53	–	1.40	–	264
Material for insulation, other maintenance, repair	0.02	–	0.04	–	200
Other lodging	911.51	942.97	858.98	103	94
Owned vacation homes	428.18	418.86	443.74	98	104
Mortgage interest and charges	194.36	242.61	113.78	125	59
Property taxes	147.87	120.06	194.32	81	131
Maintenance, insurance, and other expenses	85.95	56.19	135.64	65	158
Housing while attending school	90.21	96.18	80.23	107	89
Lodging on trips	393.13	427.92	335.02	109	85

	homeowners			index to total homeowners	
	total	with mortgage	without mortgage	with mortgage	without mortgage
• **Utilities, fuels, and public services**	**$4,275.56**	**$4,553.72**	**$3,811.03**	**107**	**89**
Natural gas	**601.80**	**642.06**	**534.58**	**107**	**89**
Electricity	**1,599.97**	**1,666.32**	**1,489.15**	**104**	**93**
Fuel oil and other fuels	**192.30**	**184.66**	**205.06**	**96**	**107**
Fuel oil	106.81	101.87	115.06	95	108
Coal, wood, and other fuels	14.12	16.56	10.05	117	71
Bottled gas	71.37	66.23	79.96	93	112
Telephone services	**1,262.63**	**1,391.62**	**1,047.21**	**110**	**83**
Residential telephone and pay phones	516.46	510.39	526.61	99	102
Cellular phone service	732.02	864.80	510.29	118	70
Phone cards	6.51	6.91	5.83	106	90
Voice over IP	7.64	9.52	4.50	125	59
Water and other public services	**618.85**	**669.05**	**535.03**	**108**	**86**
Water and sewerage maintenance	442.07	484.86	370.62	110	84
Trash and garbage collection	170.23	178.15	157.00	105	92
Septic tank cleaning	6.56	6.05	7.41	92	113
• **Household services**	**1,217.16**	**1,423.64**	**873.43**	**117**	**72**
Personal services	**439.07**	**602.22**	**166.61**	**137**	**38**
Babysitting and child care in own home	51.87	71.33	19.37	138	37
Babysitting and child care in someone else's home	26.63	35.04	12.58	132	47
Care for elderly, invalids, handicapped, etc.	56.54	46.24	73.76	82	130
Adult day care centers	7.44	9.15	4.58	123	62
Day care centers, nurseries, and preschools	296.58	440.46	56.31	149	19
Other household services	**778.09**	**821.42**	**706.83**	**106**	**91**
Housekeeping services	155.90	165.56	139.78	106	90
Gardening, lawn care service	155.53	146.70	170.27	94	109
Water-softening service	5.08	5.99	3.56	118	70
Nonclothing laundry and dry cleaning, sent out	1.24	0.99	1.67	80	135
Nonclothing laundry and dry cleaning, coin-operated	1.09	1.24	0.84	114	77
Termite and pest control services	26.80	24.64	30.41	92	113
Home security system service fee	30.77	34.96	23.79	114	77
Other home services	26.71	24.09	31.07	90	116
Termite and pest control products	4.10	3.73	4.72	91	115
Moving, storage, and freight express	29.09	29.98	27.60	103	95
Appliance repair, including at service center	23.96	24.63	22.85	103	95
Reupholstering and furniture repair	6.09	6.05	6.16	99	101
Repairs and rentals of lawn and garden equipment, hand and power tools, etc.	7.92	7.61	8.45	96	107
Appliance rental	1.19	0.93	1.62	78	136
Repair of computer systems for nonbusiness use	8.14	8.73	7.15	107	88
Computer information services	285.42	328.11	214.12	115	75
Installation of computer	0.50	0.63	0.29	126	58
• **Housekeeping supplies**	**803.97**	**804.47**	**802.77**	**100**	**100**
Laundry and cleaning supplies	**174.11**	**176.75**	**167.90**	**102**	**96**
Soaps and detergents	92.43	93.74	89.38	101	97
Other laundry cleaning products	81.67	83.01	78.52	102	96
Other household products	**451.86**	**447.98**	**460.99**	**99**	**102**
Cleansing and toilet tissue, paper towels, and napkins	124.21	124.72	123.00	100	99
Miscellaneous household products	168.11	175.27	151.31	104	90
Lawn and garden supplies	159.54	147.99	186.67	93	117

	homeowners			index to total homeowners	
	total	with mortgage	without mortgage	with mortgage	without mortgage
Postage and stationery	**$178.00**	**$179.75**	**$173.89**	**101**	**98**
Stationery, stationery supplies, giftwrap	95.00	103.22	75.71	109	80
Postage	77.56	71.36	92.10	92	119
Delivery services	5.44	5.17	6.08	95	112
• Household furnishings and equipment	**1,871.55**	**2,014.53**	**1,606.88**	**108**	**86**
Household textiles	**155.79**	**160.21**	**146.99**	**103**	**94**
Bathroom linens	19.97	19.68	20.66	99	103
Bedroom linens	86.52	88.71	81.38	103	94
Kitchen and dining room linens	7.75	7.95	7.28	103	94
Curtains and draperies	23.36	25.10	20.44	107	88
Slipcovers and decorative pillows	4.21	5.05	2.82	120	67
Sewing materials for household items	12.60	12.08	13.47	96	107
Other linens	1.38	1.64	0.95	119	69
Furniture	**404.37**	**441.40**	**347.31**	**109**	**86**
Mattresses and springs	64.04	73.21	48.72	114	76
Other bedroom furniture	69.26	83.47	45.53	121	66
Sofas	96.00	107.62	76.60	112	80
Living room chairs	42.55	36.45	52.74	86	124
Living room tables	13.57	15.07	11.08	111	82
Kitchen and dining room furniture	38.38	45.27	26.88	118	70
Infants' furniture	8.58	10.32	5.68	120	66
Outdoor furniture	25.97	18.90	42.56	73	164
Wall units, cabinets, and other furniture	46.01	51.09	37.53	111	82
Floor coverings	**42.20**	**49.36**	**30.25**	**117**	**72**
Wall-to-wall carpet	19.95	23.93	13.30	120	67
Floor coverings, nonpermanent	22.26	25.43	16.96	114	76
Major appliances	**256.52**	**264.94**	**241.17**	**103**	**94**
Dishwashers (built-in), garbage disposals, range hoods	19.46	19.64	19.15	101	98
Refrigerators, freezers	76.88	71.00	86.71	92	113
Washing machines	41.09	43.88	36.44	107	89
Clothes dryers	29.57	30.69	27.69	104	94
Cooking stoves, ovens	39.43	42.25	34.74	107	88
Microwave ovens	11.45	11.14	11.96	97	104
Portable dishwasher	0.91	1.05	0.67	115	74
Window air conditioners	3.47	3.64	3.17	105	91
Electric floor-cleaning equipment	15.88	18.33	11.77	115	74
Sewing machines	11.32	14.36	6.23	127	55
Miscellaneous household appliances	7.08	8.97	2.65	127	37
Small appliances and miscellaneous housewares	**113.91**	**122.94**	**95.69**	**108**	**84**
Housewares	77.75	83.11	66.09	107	85
Plastic dinnerware	2.35	2.66	1.82	113	77
China and other dinnerware	6.18	5.88	6.86	95	111
Flatware	3.61	4.43	2.24	123	62
Glassware	15.15	15.43	14.50	102	96
Silver serving pieces	3.61	4.03	2.65	112	73
Other serving pieces	2.16	2.39	1.79	111	83
Nonelectric cookware	16.03	16.86	14.09	105	88
Tableware, nonelectric kitchenware	28.66	31.43	22.14	110	77
Small appliances	36.16	39.83	29.60	110	82
Small electric kitchen appliances	23.99	26.99	18.97	113	79
Portable heating and cooling equipment	12.18	12.84	10.63	105	87

	homeowners			index to total homeowners	
	total	with mortgage	without mortgage	with mortgage	without mortgage
Miscellaneous household equipment	**$898.77**	**$975.69**	**$745.46**	**109**	**83**
Window coverings	29.47	33.13	23.35	112	79
Infants' equipment	13.60	14.60	11.26	107	83
Laundry and cleaning equipment	18.88	20.00	16.25	106	86
Outdoor equipment	22.14	16.18	36.11	73	163
Lamps and lighting fixtures	39.91	44.83	28.38	112	71
Household decorative items	167.14	173.76	151.61	104	91
Telephones and accessories	54.83	59.60	43.63	109	80
Lawn and garden equipment	82.60	93.33	57.41	113	70
Power tools	41.11	49.17	22.20	120	54
Office furniture for home use	9.30	12.26	4.34	132	47
Hand tools	17.78	21.59	8.86	121	50
Indoor plants and fresh flowers	64.95	64.43	66.17	99	102
Closet and storage items	17.41	17.73	16.67	102	96
Rental of furniture	1.04	1.12	0.89	108	86
Luggage	12.40	12.20	12.85	98	104
Computers and computer hardware for nonbusiness use	178.54	204.21	135.67	114	76
Portable memory	8.69	10.35	5.92	119	68
Computer software and accessories for nonbusiness use	24.61	28.31	18.42	115	75
Personal digital assistants	2.98	4.36	0.67	146	22
Internet services away from home	2.33	3.03	1.16	130	50
Telephone answering devices	0.58	0.62	0.51	107	88
Business equipment for home use	3.52	3.51	3.54	100	101
Other hardware	17.26	15.95	20.33	92	118
Smoke alarms	1.81	1.96	1.57	108	87
Other household appliances	11.41	11.65	11.00	102	96
Miscellaneous household equipment and parts	54.49	57.80	46.70	106	86
APPAREL	**1,857.40**	**2,084.96**	**1,371.28**	**112**	**74**
Men's apparel	**324.40**	**365.61**	**231.97**	**113**	**72**
Suits	18.81	22.59	12.50	120	66
Sport coats and tailored jackets	7.83	9.31	5.36	119	68
Coats and jackets	36.39	43.49	19.71	120	54
Underwear	17.36	19.10	13.28	110	76
Hosiery	12.84	13.49	11.30	105	88
Nightwear	2.11	2.16	2.01	102	95
Accessories	28.05	32.60	17.36	116	62
Sweaters and vests	15.32	16.83	11.76	110	77
Active sportswear	20.24	18.72	23.81	92	118
Shirts	95.05	108.37	63.78	114	67
Pants and shorts	66.50	74.00	48.88	111	74
Uniforms	3.10	3.76	2.01	121	65
Costumes	0.81	1.18	0.21	146	26
Boys' (aged 2 to 15) apparel	**87.41**	**107.64**	**47.48**	**123**	**54**
Coats and jackets	4.52	5.85	2.29	129	51
Sweaters	1.91	2.49	0.94	130	49
Shirts	28.79	32.81	19.34	114	67
Underwear	6.92	9.05	1.93	131	28
Nightwear	1.18	1.52	0.62	129	53
Hosiery	4.84	5.98	2.16	124	45
Accessories	5.23	7.02	1.02	134	20
Suits, sport coats, and vests	1.02	1.37	0.44	134	43
Pants and shorts	27.18	33.80	16.11	124	59

	homeowners			index to total homeowners	
	total	with mortgage	without mortgage	with mortgage	without mortgage
Uniforms	$3.61	$4.82	$1.58	134	44
Active sportswear	1.39	1.78	0.75	128	54
Costumes	0.82	1.14	0.30	139	37
Women's apparel	**626.64**	**682.25**	**499.18**	**109**	**80**
Coats and jackets	45.67	45.22	46.72	99	102
Dresses	79.79	93.89	46.69	118	59
Sport coats and tailored jackets	5.80	6.33	4.92	109	85
Sweaters and vests	49.18	53.10	39.98	108	81
Shirts, blouses, and tops	125.93	137.36	99.08	109	79
Skirts	8.83	11.44	2.71	130	31
Pants and shorts	101.26	111.15	78.05	110	77
Active sportswear	30.24	33.51	22.58	111	75
Nightwear	23.19	24.81	19.41	107	84
Undergarments	42.59	47.00	32.24	110	76
Hosiery	19.79	18.57	22.68	94	115
Suits	13.44	15.98	9.20	119	68
Accessories	71.29	72.82	67.69	102	95
Uniforms	7.60	8.54	6.04	112	79
Costumes	2.03	2.53	1.20	125	59
Girls' (aged 2 to 15) apparel	**131.62**	**161.34**	**68.90**	**123**	**52**
Coats and jackets	7.27	9.42	2.22	130	31
Dresses and suits	14.48	16.56	9.59	114	66
Shirts, blouses, and sweaters	35.28	41.33	21.10	117	60
Skirts, pants, and shorts	27.89	36.18	14.03	130	50
Active sportswear	14.86	18.17	7.10	122	48
Underwear and nightwear	13.46	15.78	8.01	117	60
Hosiery	5.40	6.98	1.71	129	32
Accessories	7.29	9.14	2.94	125	40
Uniforms	3.37	4.69	1.16	139	34
Costumes	2.33	3.09	1.06	133	45
Children's (under age 2) apparel	**88.53**	**106.45**	**49.86**	**120**	**56**
Coats, jackets, and snowsuits	2.58	3.38	1.25	131	48
Outerwear including dresses	21.10	24.52	15.38	116	73
Underwear	52.55	64.00	25.66	122	49
Nightwear and loungewear	5.01	5.78	3.73	115	74
Accessories	7.30	8.76	3.86	120	53
Footwear	**329.20**	**354.48**	**269.85**	**108**	**82**
Men's	90.33	98.56	71.00	109	79
Boys'	40.16	48.65	20.25	121	50
Women's	160.83	164.76	151.61	102	94
Girls'	37.87	42.51	26.99	112	71
Other apparel products and services	**269.60**	**307.20**	**204.03**	**114**	**76**
Material for making clothes	12.68	13.23	11.40	104	90
Sewing patterns and notions	7.19	7.08	7.47	98	104
Watches	30.00	33.67	21.38	112	71
Jewelry	126.39	139.55	104.43	110	83
Shoe repair and other shoe services	1.44	1.67	1.05	116	73
Coin-operated apparel laundry and dry cleaning	8.47	8.71	8.06	103	95
Apparel alteration, repair, and tailoring services	6.69	7.52	5.31	112	79
Clothing rental	2.80	4.00	0.79	143	28
Watch and jewelry repair	4.52	4.76	4.13	105	91
Professional laundry, dry cleaning	68.50	86.31	38.75	126	57
Clothing storage	0.91	0.71	1.26	78	138

	homeowners			index to total homeowners	
	total	with mortgage	without mortgage	with mortgage	without mortgage
TRANSPORTATION	$9,089.32	$10,004.67	$7,568.14	110	83
• **Vehicle purchases**	3,246.92	3,553.85	2,734.35	109	84
Cars and trucks, new	1,717.86	1,799.99	1,580.71	105	92
New cars	905.99	990.59	764.70	109	84
New trucks	811.88	809.40	816.01	100	101
Cars and trucks, used	1,459.85	1,670.45	1,108.16	114	76
Used cars	767.32	876.01	585.81	114	76
Used trucks	692.53	794.44	522.35	115	75
Other vehicles	69.21	83.41	45.48	121	66
New motorcycles	32.72	40.67	19.44	124	59
Used motorcycles	36.49	42.74	26.04	117	71
• **Gasoline and motor oil**	2,275.58	2,554.89	1,809.13	112	80
Gasoline	2,084.79	2,346.14	1,648.32	113	79
Diesel fuel	48.06	53.12	39.61	111	82
Gasoline on trips	130.62	143.12	109.75	110	84
Motor oil	10.79	11.07	10.34	103	96
Motor oil on trips	1.32	1.45	1.11	110	84
• **Other vehicle expenses**	3,023.11	3,288.17	2,588.74	109	86
Vehicle finance charges	326.20	404.74	195.02	124	60
Automobile finance charges	129.60	158.93	80.64	123	62
Truck finance charges	162.01	202.67	94.10	125	58
Motorcycle and plane finance charges	5.72	7.33	3.03	128	53
Other vehicle finance charges	28.86	35.81	17.25	124	60
Maintenance and repairs	862.39	965.51	687.13	112	80
Coolant, additives, brake and transmission fluids	4.01	4.10	3.86	102	96
Tires—purchased, replaced, installed	141.75	166.97	99.64	118	70
Parts, equipment, and accessories	48.83	50.50	46.05	103	94
Vehicle audio equipment	2.18	2.37	1.86	109	85
Vehicle products and cleaning services	5.75	5.56	6.22	97	108
Vehicle video equipment	2.31	2.43	2.10	105	91
Miscellaneous auto repair, servicing	64.34	69.03	53.34	107	83
Body work and painting	34.70	41.37	23.57	119	68
Clutch and transmission repair	39.66	43.76	32.80	110	83
Drive shaft and rear-end repair	5.71	7.41	2.86	130	50
Brake work	76.49	87.89	57.45	115	75
Repair to steering or front-end	21.10	23.33	17.37	111	82
Repair to engine cooling system	25.71	31.21	16.53	121	64
Motor tune-up	54.83	65.03	37.79	119	69
Lube, oil change, and oil filters	88.60	96.92	74.72	109	84
Front-end alignment, wheel balance, rotation	15.56	16.82	13.47	108	87
Shock absorber replacement	5.53	5.60	5.42	101	98
Tire repair and other repair work	60.78	62.80	57.41	103	94
Vehicle air conditioning repair	13.99	14.76	12.70	106	91
Exhaust system repair	11.50	12.88	9.18	112	80
Electrical system repair	34.11	35.32	32.09	104	94
Motor repair, replacement	80.85	92.80	60.89	115	75
Auto repair service policy	24.09	26.67	19.80	111	82
Vehicle insurance	1,302.69	1,285.97	1,341.94	99	103

| | homeowners | | | index to total homeowners | |
	total	with mortgage	without mortgage	with mortgage	without mortgage
Vehicle rental, leases, licenses, other charges	**$531.84**	**$631.95**	**$364.65**	**119**	**69**
Leased and rented vehicles	281.66	353.01	162.50	125	58
Rented vehicles	39.86	43.44	33.87	109	85
Auto rental	4.41	4.68	3.94	106	89
Auto rental on trips	30.24	34.11	23.76	113	79
Truck rental	2.63	1.68	4.21	64	160
Truck rental on trips	2.09	2.18	1.95	104	93
Leased vehicles	241.80	309.57	128.64	128	53
Car lease payments	124.54	154.13	75.11	124	60
Truck lease payments	106.76	141.70	48.43	133	45
Vehicle registration, state	113.94	122.36	99.88	107	88
Vehicle registration, local	9.87	10.73	8.44	109	86
Driver's license	8.23	9.06	6.85	110	83
Vehicle inspection	13.29	13.98	12.13	105	91
Parking fees	44.01	53.42	28.30	121	64
Parking fees in home city, excluding residence	35.15	42.84	22.30	122	63
Parking fees on trips	8.86	10.58	6.00	119	68
Tolls	26.32	32.90	15.33	125	58
Tolls on trips	5.16	5.81	4.08	113	79
Towing charges	4.04	4.88	2.63	121	65
Global positioning services	2.57	2.60	2.52	101	98
Automobile service clubs	22.74	23.20	21.98	102	97
• Public transportation	**543.71**	**607.76**	**435.91**	**112**	**80**
Airline fares	364.67	413.83	282.59	113	77
Intercity bus fares	9.75	9.14	10.76	94	110
Intracity mass transit fares	42.47	52.46	25.79	124	61
Local transportation on trips	20.05	21.13	18.25	105	91
Taxi fares and limousine service	21.68	22.91	18.79	106	87
Intercity train fares	17.78	18.45	16.66	104	94
Ship fares	67.15	69.59	63.07	104	94
School bus	0.16	0.25	–	156	–
HEALTH CARE	**3,943.99**	**3,626.74**	**4,478.29**	**92**	**114**
Health insurance	**2,253.26**	**2,003.06**	**2,671.11**	**89**	**119**
Commercial health insurance	442.82	488.43	366.65	110	83
Traditional fee-for-service health plan (not BCBS)	110.93	101.22	127.14	91	115
Preferred-provider health plan (not BCBS)	331.89	387.21	239.51	117	72
Blue Cross, Blue Shield	676.92	697.12	643.20	103	95
Traditional fee-for-service health plan	118.05	109.82	131.81	93	112
Preferred-provider health plan	279.24	308.00	231.21	110	83
Health maintenance organization	209.30	230.06	174.63	110	83
Commercial Medicare supplement	59.11	35.39	98.73	60	167
Other BCBS health insurance	11.22	13.86	6.81	124	61
Health maintenance plans (HMOs)	338.05	365.14	292.81	108	87
Medicare payments	434.34	217.09	797.17	50	184
Medicare prescription drug premium	75.15	36.79	139.21	49	185
Commercial Medicare supplements and other health insurance	196.79	144.73	283.74	74	144
Commercial Medicare supplement (not BCBS)	131.86	76.41	224.45	58	170
Other health insurance (not BCBS)	64.93	68.31	59.29	105	91
Long-term care insurance	89.18	53.77	148.33	60	166

	homeowners			index to total homeowners	
	total	with mortgage	without mortgage	with mortgage	without mortgage
Medical services	$932.49	$936.46	$927.51	**100**	**99**
Physician's services	225.50	249.17	185.98	110	82
Dental services	342.82	317.81	384.58	93	112
Eye care services	51.97	57.39	42.91	110	83
Service by professionals other than physician	63.89	67.19	58.38	105	91
Lab tests, X-rays	61.17	65.32	54.23	107	89
Hospital room and services	137.13	146.28	121.85	107	89
Care in convalescent or nursing home	15.36	9.15	25.74	60	168
Repair of medical equipment	3.81	1.38	9.53	36	250
Other medical services	30.80	22.79	44.18	74	143
Drugs	609.41	544.29	722.18	**89**	**119**
Nonprescription drugs	96.75	94.57	101.87	98	105
Nonprescription vitamins	56.34	52.58	65.16	93	116
Prescription drugs	456.32	397.14	555.15	87	122
Medical supplies	148.82	142.93	157.49	**96**	**106**
Eyeglasses and contact lenses	75.47	80.07	67.78	106	90
Hearing aids	22.46	10.26	42.85	46	191
Topicals and dressings	37.29	39.02	33.21	105	89
Medical equipment for general use	3.35	3.45	3.19	103	95
Supportive and convalescent medical equipment	6.65	7.04	5.99	106	90
Rental of medical equipment	1.38	0.64	2.60	46	188
Rental of supportive and convalescent medical equipment	2.23	2.45	1.87	110	84
ENTERTAINMENT	3,255.66	3,578.15	2,654.76	**110**	**82**
Fees and admissions	785.33	932.36	524.80	**119**	**67**
Recreation expenses on trips	24.81	29.09	17.65	117	71
Social, recreation, civic club membership	147.84	164.07	120.72	111	82
Fees for participant sports	161.59	183.72	109.63	114	68
Participant sports on trips	27.58	32.96	18.60	120	67
Movie, theater, amusement park, and other admissions	140.42	165.10	99.20	118	71
Movie, other admissions on trips	50.58	58.75	36.94	116	73
Admission to sports events	61.58	77.68	34.69	126	56
Admission to sports events on trips	16.85	19.57	12.31	116	73
Fees for recreational lessons	129.28	172.32	57.41	133	44
Other entertainment services on trips	24.81	29.09	17.65	117	71
Audio and visual equipment and services	1,092.25	1,186.31	928.96	**109**	**85**
Radios	2.51	2.55	2.44	102	97
Television sets	164.62	180.41	138.26	110	84
Tape recorders and players	0.57	0.35	1.09	61	191
Cable and satellite television services	675.63	709.22	619.53	105	92
Miscellaneous sound equipment	1.55	1.65	1.31	106	85
Miscellaneous video equipment	3.16	3.85	1.55	122	49
Satellite radio service	17.14	18.76	14.42	109	84
Sound equipment accessories	11.12	9.96	13.85	90	125
Online gaming services	2.39	2.99	1.39	125	58
VCRs and video disc players	15.17	18.71	9.27	123	61
Video game hardware and software	51.99	61.73	29.11	119	56
Video cassettes, tapes, and discs	31.01	34.69	24.85	112	80
Streamed and downloaded video	1.57	1.85	1.10	118	70
Repair of TV, radio, and sound equipment	4.16	4.32	3.91	104	94
Rental of television sets	0.14	0.08	0.26	57	186
Personal digital audio players	14.19	17.93	7.94	126	56
Sound components and component systems	14.81	20.79	4.82	140	33

	homeowners			index to total homeowners	
	total	with mortgage	without mortgage	with mortgage	without mortgage
Satellite dishes	$1.31	$1.25	$1.42	95	108
Compact discs, records, and audio tapes	19.90	22.21	16.03	112	81
Streamed and downloaded audio	6.17	7.88	3.32	128	54
Rental of VCR, radio, and sound equipment	0.17	0.24	0.06	141	35
Musical instruments and accessories	22.66	27.10	15.25	120	67
Rental and repair of musical instruments	1.97	1.94	2.02	98	103
Rental of video cassettes, tapes, discs, films	27.08	34.57	14.56	128	54
Rental of computer and video game hardware and software	0.29	0.44	0.04	152	14
Installation of television sets	0.96	0.85	1.14	89	119
Pets, toys, hobbies, and playground equipment	**865.18**	**941.66**	**706.21**	**109**	**82**
Pets	700.27	747.59	610.23	107	87
Pet food	214.71	224.69	191.27	105	89
Pet purchase, supplies, and medicines	201.72	221.25	169.10	110	84
Pet services	56.13	67.67	36.88	121	66
Veterinarian services	227.71	233.98	212.98	103	94
Toys, games, hobbies, and tricycles	154.39	184.29	84.20	119	55
Stamp and coin collecting	7.17	5.06	10.69	71	149
Playground equipment	3.35	4.71	1.08	141	32
Other entertainment supplies, equipment, services	**512.91**	**517.82**	**494.80**	**101**	**96**
Unmotored recreational vehicles	72.58	51.85	107.20	71	148
Boat without motor and boat trailers	23.84	15.49	37.79	65	159
Trailer and other attachable campers	48.74	36.37	69.41	75	142
Motorized recreational vehicles	148.20	135.42	169.54	91	114
Purchase of motorized camper	47.51	33.46	70.98	70	149
Purchase of other vehicle	44.52	45.98	42.08	103	95
Purchase of boat with motor	56.16	55.98	56.47	100	101
Rental of recreational vehicles	7.84	8.87	6.12	113	78
Docking and landing fees	11.73	11.56	12.00	99	102
Sports, recreation, exercise equipment	159.55	175.11	128.22	110	80
Athletic gear, game tables, exercise equipment	63.97	68.05	54.39	106	85
Bicycles	14.83	18.55	8.61	125	58
Camping equipment	14.00	19.22	1.77	137	13
Hunting and fishing equipment	36.65	32.79	45.70	89	125
Winter sports equipment	4.58	5.80	2.56	127	56
Water sports equipment	3.80	4.05	3.37	107	89
Other sports equipment	5.98	7.48	3.47	125	58
Global positioning system devices	12.06	14.54	6.24	121	52
Rental and repair of miscellaneous sports equipment	3.68	4.62	2.10	126	57
Photographic equipment and supplies	73.40	88.26	43.92	120	60
Film	1.79	1.92	1.57	107	88
Other photographic supplies	2.78	3.70	0.65	133	23
Photo processing	16.21	19.59	10.58	121	65
Repair and rental of photographic equipment	0.69	0.82	0.46	119	67
Photographic equipment	32.28	36.62	25.03	113	78
Photographer fees	19.64	25.62	5.63	130	29
Fireworks	2.84	2.68	3.20	94	113
Souvenirs	2.75	1.72	5.18	63	188
Visual goods	1.90	2.28	1.02	120	54
Pinball, electronic video games	1.85	2.49	0.34	135	18
Live entertainment for catered affairs	11.40	16.28	3.26	143	29
Rental of party supplies for catered affairs	18.38	21.31	13.49	116	73

	homeowners			index to total homeowners	
	total	with mortgage	without mortgage	with mortgage	without mortgage
PERSONAL CARE PRODUCTS AND SERVICES	**$693.14**	**$744.03**	**$598.60**	**107**	**86**
Personal care products	**348.34**	**362.37**	**315.33**	**104**	**91**
Hair care products	74.96	85.26	50.78	114	68
Hair accessories	6.61	7.87	3.66	119	55
Wigs and hairpieces	2.84	2.76	2.97	97	105
Oral hygiene products	33.07	33.86	31.20	102	94
Shaving products	17.86	19.05	15.07	107	84
Cosmetics, perfume, and bath products	166.35	166.32	166.40	100	100
Deodorants, feminine hygiene, miscellaneous products	36.05	37.98	31.53	105	87
Electric personal care appliances	10.60	9.27	13.71	87	129
Personal care services	344.80	381.65	283.27	111	82
READING	**135.67**	**134.75**	**137.36**	**99**	**101**
Newspaper and magazine subscriptions	57.68	49.61	71.16	86	123
Newspapers and magazines, nonsubscription	16.46	17.65	14.47	107	88
Books	60.16	66.68	49.25	111	82
EDUCATION	**1,233.74**	**1,502.55**	**777.92**	**122**	**63**
College tuition	779.63	937.24	516.43	120	66
Elementary and high school tuition	226.37	286.30	126.30	126	56
Vocational and technical school tuition	17.09	23.95	5.64	140	33
Test preparation, tutoring services	10.93	14.90	4.31	136	39
Other school tuition	9.47	8.98	10.30	95	109
Other school expenses including rentals	41.93	55.94	18.52	133	44
Books and supplies for college	65.01	75.73	47.11	116	72
Books and supplies for elementary and high school	20.24	26.51	9.78	131	48
Books and supplies for vocational and technical schools	0.69	0.65	0.75	94	109
Books and supplies for day care and nursery	0.18	0.25	0.07	139	39
Books and supplies for other schools	1.92	1.65	2.39	86	124
Miscellaneous school expenses and supplies	60.27	70.46	36.33	117	60
TOBACCO PRODUCTS, SMOKING SUPPLIES	**358.67**	**374.54**	**332.16**	**104**	**93**
Cigarettes	322.63	333.84	303.92	103	94
Other tobacco products	34.26	38.90	26.52	114	77
Smoking accessories	1.74	1.75	1.72	101	99
FINANCIAL PRODUCTS AND SERVICES					
Miscellaneous financial	**964.93**	**1,028.19**	**863.21**	**107**	**89**
Miscellaneous fees	8.40	9.65	5.45	115	65
Lottery and gambling losses	86.87	78.39	106.77	90	123
Legal fees	180.28	156.46	220.05	87	122
Funeral expenses	58.27	56.79	60.74	97	104
Safe deposit box rental	5.17	4.28	6.64	83	128
Checking accounts, other bank service charges	23.68	27.85	16.72	118	71
Cemetery lots, vaults, and maintenance fees	17.63	14.96	22.07	85	125
Accounting fees	74.42	77.99	68.46	105	92
Miscellaneous personal services	44.74	46.16	41.42	103	93
Dating services	0.32	0.36	0.25	113	78
Finance charges, except mortgage and vehicles	235.49	315.88	101.26	134	43
Occupational expenses	69.95	91.62	33.76	131	48
Expenses for other properties	135.81	121.52	159.67	89	118
Credit card memberships	2.21	2.36	1.95	107	88
Shopping club membership fees	12.04	12.43	11.39	103	95
Vacation clubs	8.38	9.91	5.82	118	69

	homeowners			index to total homeowners	
	total	with mortgage	without mortgage	with mortgage	without mortgage
Cash contributions	$2,163.61	$2,078.59	$2,305.59	96	107
Support for college students	147.28	141.53	156.89	96	107
Alimony expenditures	60.43	78.39	30.43	130	50
Child support expenditures	193.94	258.05	86.87	133	45
Gifts of stocks, bonds, and mutual funds to members of other households	16.36	9.00	28.65	55	175
Cash contributions to charities	286.43	247.87	350.81	87	122
Cash contributions to church, religious organizations	967.44	988.82	931.73	102	96
Cash contributions to educational institutions	41.69	27.76	64.97	67	156
Cash contributions to political organizations	9.80	7.66	13.38	78	137
Cash gifts to members of other households	440.25	319.52	641.87	73	146
Personal insurance and pensions	6,775.63	8,281.90	4,260.17	122	63
Life and other personal insurance	417.11	465.82	335.76	112	80
Life, endowment, annuity, other personal insurance	394.52	443.78	312.25	112	79
Other nonhealth insurance	22.59	22.04	23.51	98	104
Pensions and Social Security	6,358.52	7,816.08	3,924.41	123	62
Deductions for government retirement	105.55	134.69	56.89	128	54
Deductions for railroad retirement	9.61	10.45	8.20	109	85
Deductions for private pensions	852.11	1,058.21	507.93	124	60
Nonpayroll deposit to retirement plans	625.48	672.84	546.39	108	87
Deductions for Social Security	4,765.78	5,939.89	2,805.01	125	59
Personal taxes	2,823.03	3,174.38	2,236.26	112	79
Federal income taxes	1,914.88	2,158.47	1,508.09	113	79
Federal income tax deducted	2,421.66	3,014.73	1,431.25	124	59
Additional federal income tax paid	610.92	539.45	730.29	88	120
Federal income tax refunds	−1,117.71	−1,395.71	−653.45	125	58
State and local income taxes	657.39	780.80	451.30	119	69
State and local income tax deducted	705.00	872.57	425.15	124	60
Additional state and local income tax paid	111.79	106.75	120.21	95	108
State and local income tax refunds	−159.40	−198.52	−94.06	125	59
Other taxes	252.19	236.49	278.41	94	110
GIFTS FOR PEOPLE IN OTHER HOUSEHOLDS	1,323.78	1,386.77	1,206.39	105	91

* The category fast-food restaurants also includes take-out, delivery, concession stands, buffets, and cafeterias other than employer and school.
** Spending on mortgage principal reduction is not included in spending because it is considered an asset.
Note: Numbers may not add to total because not all categories are shown. "−" means zero or sample is too small to make a reliable estimate. Spending on gifts is also included in the preceding product and service categories. The index is calculated by dividing the spending of homeowners with and without mortgages by the spending of total homeowners and multiplying by 100.
Source: Bureau of Labor Statistics, unpublished data from the 2009 Consumer Expenditure Survey; calculations by New Strategist

Table 10.3 Household Spending of Renters, 2009

Renters spend only 68 percent as much as the average household. They spend less than average on most products and services. Some exceptions are beer consumed away from home, phone cards, and coin-operated laundries.

(average annual spending of total consumer units and renter consumer units on all products and services, 2009; number of consumer units in thousands)

		renters	
	total	spending	index to total
Number of households (consumer units)	120,847	40,778	34
Before-tax income	$62,857	$37,329	59
Average age of householder	49.4	41.7	84
Average number of persons in household	2.5	2.3	92
Average number of earners in household	1.3	1.1	85
Average number of vehicles per household	2.0	1.2	60
At least one vehicle owned or leased	88%	74%	84
Average household spending, total	$49,067.20	$33,404.45	68
Food, average spending	6,371.89	4,752.77	75
FOOD AT HOME	3,752.98	2,848.87	76
Cereals and bakery products	506.38	389.73	77
Cereals and cereal products	172.58	146.78	85
Flour	8.67	6.08	70
Prepared flour mixes	14.41	9.87	68
Ready-to-eat and cooked cereals	93.61	78.94	84
Rice	23.99	27.41	114
Pasta, cornmeal, and other cereal products	31.89	24.48	77
Bakery products	333.81	242.96	73
Bread	94.69	74.50	79
White bread	33.84	29.59	87
Bread, other than white	60.85	44.91	74
Cookies and crackers	84.20	60.74	72
Cookies	47.28	35.45	75
Crackers	36.92	25.29	68
Frozen and refrigerated bakery products	27.53	18.67	68
Other bakery products	127.39	89.05	70
Biscuits and rolls	48.83	33.19	68
Cakes and cupcakes	37.40	27.35	73
Bread and cracker products	5.28	3.51	66
Sweetrolls, coffee cakes, doughnuts	21.75	15.07	69
Pies, tarts, turnovers	14.13	9.93	70
Meats, poultry, fish, and eggs	840.92	663.30	79
Beef	226.14	176.05	78
Ground beef	89.03	76.97	86
Roast	34.67	21.96	63
Chuck roast	9.36	5.97	64
Round roast	5.51	4.42	80
Other roast	19.80	11.57	58

		renters	
	total	spending	index to total
Steak	$83.00	$61.07	74
Round steak	10.63	10.30	97
Sirloin steak	22.27	16.44	74
Other steak	50.10	34.33	69
Other beef	19.44	16.05	83
Pork	168.37	131.96	78
Bacon	32.26	27.55	85
Pork chops	29.37	25.68	87
Ham	38.10	25.79	68
Ham, not canned	37.06	25.28	68
Canned ham	1.04	0.52	50
Sausage	27.91	21.90	78
Other pork	40.74	31.03	76
Other meats	113.53	80.78	71
Frankfurters	22.60	17.54	78
Lunch meats (cold cuts)	80.36	54.67	68
Bologna, liverwurst, salami	18.98	15.02	79
Other lunch meats	61.38	39.65	65
Lamb, organ meats, and others	10.57	8.57	81
Poultry	154.07	132.94	86
Fresh and frozen chicken	120.63	109.91	91
Fresh and frozen whole chicken	30.60	28.80	94
Fresh and frozen chicken parts	90.03	81.11	90
Other poultry	33.44	23.03	69
Fish and seafood	134.95	102.62	76
Canned fish and seafood	18.35	13.98	76
Fresh fish and shellfish	71.28	52.61	74
Frozen fish and shellfish	45.32	36.03	80
Eggs	43.85	38.95	89
Dairy products	**406.09**	**302.35**	**74**
Fresh milk and cream	143.98	117.00	81
Fresh milk, all types	126.71	106.05	84
Cream	17.28	10.95	63
Other dairy products	262.10	185.35	71
Butter	21.69	15.03	69
Cheese	132.88	94.24	71
Ice cream and related products	62.35	43.10	69
Miscellaneous dairy products	45.18	32.98	73
Fruits and vegetables	**656.45**	**485.76**	**74**
Fresh fruits	219.62	155.32	71
Apples	36.67	24.65	67
Bananas	33.25	26.21	79
Oranges	24.26	18.96	78
Citrus fruits, excluding oranges	19.51	15.53	80
Other fresh fruits	105.92	69.97	66
Fresh vegetables	209.15	153.36	73
Potatoes	37.01	27.67	75
Lettuce	26.58	17.54	66
Tomatoes	36.04	28.99	80
Other fresh vegetables	109.52	79.16	72

	total	renters	
		spending	index to total
Processed fruits	$118.05	$93.02	79
Frozen fruits and fruit juices	11.59	7.74	67
Frozen orange juice	2.81	2.37	84
Frozen fruits	6.09	3.27	54
Frozen fruit juices, excluding orange	2.69	2.09	78
Canned fruits	20.44	15.64	77
Dried fruits	8.51	5.40	63
Fresh fruit juice	19.37	14.58	75
Canned and bottled fruit juice	58.13	49.66	85
Processed vegetables	109.64	84.06	77
Frozen vegetables	35.22	25.84	73
Canned and dried vegetables and juices	74.43	58.22	78
Canned beans	15.82	12.74	81
Canned corn	6.49	5.29	82
Canned miscellaneous vegetables	23.40	16.12	69
Dried peas	0.43	0.24	56
Dried beans	3.91	3.57	91
Dried miscellaneous vegetables	9.26	7.67	83
Fresh and canned vegetable juices	14.71	12.17	83
Sugar and other sweets	**140.62**	**95.50**	**68**
Candy and chewing gum	86.20	54.76	64
Sugar	18.91	17.42	92
Artificial sweeteners	5.98	3.20	54
Jams, preserves, other sweets	29.52	20.12	68
Fats and oils	**102.34**	**76.34**	**75**
Margarine	8.11	6.30	78
Fats and oils	35.69	30.17	85
Salad dressings	28.53	20.38	71
Nondairy cream and imitation milk	16.13	10.61	66
Peanut butter	13.88	8.88	64
Miscellaneous foods	**715.06**	**539.69**	**75**
Frozen prepared foods	147.63	125.06	85
Frozen meals	68.96	56.62	82
Other frozen prepared foods	78.67	68.45	87
Canned and packaged soups	47.06	34.33	73
Potato chips, nuts, and other snacks	147.72	98.88	67
Potato chips and other snacks	108.36	76.00	70
Nuts	39.36	22.88	58
Condiments and seasonings	129.79	93.72	72
Salt, spices, and other seasonings	31.28	23.97	77
Olives, pickles, relishes	15.73	11.61	74
Sauces and gravies	55.16	41.05	74
Baking needs and miscellaneous products	27.62	17.09	62
Other canned or packaged prepared foods	242.86	187.69	77
Prepared salads	33.40	23.49	70
Prepared desserts	13.70	10.37	76
Baby food	33.01	42.28	128
Miscellaneous prepared foods	160.29	110.12	69
Nonalcoholic beverages	**336.57**	**273.79**	**81**
Cola	87.70	74.76	85
Other carbonated drinks	49.44	45.44	92
Tea	29.44	21.51	73

		renters	
	total	spending	index to total
Coffee	$57.76	$40.66	70
Roasted coffee	38.60	28.45	74
Instant and freeze-dried coffee	19.16	12.21	64
Noncarbonated fruit-flavored drinks	24.58	20.49	83
Other noncarbonated beverages and ice	12.80	10.46	82
Bottled water	56.79	47.53	84
Sports drinks	17.93	12.80	71
Food prepared by consumer unit on trips	**48.55**	**22.40**	**46**
FOOD AWAY FROM HOME	**2,618.91**	**1,903.90**	**73**
Meals at restaurants, carry-outs, other	**2,188.68**	**1,686.18**	**77**
Lunch	733.26	544.00	74
At fast-food restaurants*	354.61	314.77	89
At full-service restaurants	289.80	173.14	60
At vending machines, mobile vendors	8.62	10.99	127
At employer and school cafeterias	80.23	45.09	56
Dinner	1,060.15	791.12	75
At fast-food restaurants*	350.72	320.76	91
At full-service restaurants	699.59	455.87	65
At vending machines, mobile vendors	2.82	3.41	121
At employer and school cafeterias	7.02	11.07	158
Snacks and nonalcoholic beverages	167.72	160.35	96
At fast-food restaurants*	110.20	97.39	88
At full-service restaurants	30.85	32.78	106
At vending machines, mobile vendors	21.16	23.64	112
At employer and school cafeterias	5.51	6.54	119
Breakfast and brunch	227.55	190.72	84
At fast-food restaurants*	116.94	106.82	91
At full-service restaurants	96.30	66.05	69
At vending machines, mobile vendors	2.75	3.59	131
At employer and school cafeterias	11.56	14.26	123
Board (including at school)	**45.41**	**12.83**	**28**
Catered affairs	**70.57**	**24.75**	**35**
Food on trips	**222.77**	**110.59**	**50**
School lunches	**64.92**	**33.63**	**52**
Meals as pay	**26.55**	**35.91**	**135**
ALCOHOLIC BEVERAGES	**434.73**	**352.25**	**81**
At home	**246.07**	**175.76**	**71**
Beer and ale	115.25	109.24	95
Whiskey	10.14	5.18	51
Wine	101.18	49.61	49
Other alcoholic beverages	19.50	11.74	60
Away from home	**188.66**	**176.49**	**94**
Beer and ale	69.66	81.05	116
At fast-food restaurants*	12.69	11.52	91
At full-service restaurants	55.66	68.22	123
At vending machines, mobile vendors	1.26	1.14	90
Wine	31.05	21.60	70
At fast-food restaurants*	1.76	1.76	100
At full-service restaurants	29.24	19.73	67
Other alcoholic beverages	46.27	50.92	110
At fast-food restaurants*	5.18	8.00	154
At full-service restaurants	41.02	42.91	105
Alcoholic beverages purchased on trips	41.67	22.92	55

	total	renters spending	index to total
HOUSING	$16,895.11	$12,957.84	77
• **Shelter**	10,074.80	8,782.98	87
Owned dwellings**	6,542.61	222.52	3
Mortgage interest and charges	3,593.71	152.00	4
Mortgage interest	3,382.93	145.34	4
Interest paid, home equity loan	79.27	2.26	3
Interest paid, home equity line of credit	131.52	4.40	3
Property taxes	1,811.04	52.28	3
Maintenance, repairs, insurance, other expenses	1,137.86	18.24	2
Homeowner's insurance	340.82	6.73	2
Ground rent	51.06	1.50	3
Maintenance and repair services	608.31	6.97	1
Painting and papering	78.28	2.62	3
Plumbing and water heating	57.99	0.55	1
Heat, air conditioning, electrical work	113.09	0.58	1
Roofing and gutters	114.57	–	–
Other repair and maintenance services	190.96	2.02	1
Repair, replacement of hard-surface flooring	51.28	1.19	2
Repair of built-in appliances	2.13	–	–
Maintenance and repair materials	73.85	0.91	1
Paints, wallpaper, and supplies	12.94	0.19	1
Tools, equipment for painting, wallpapering	1.39	0.02	1
Plumbing supplies and equipment	5.51	–	–
Electrical supplies, heating and cooling equipment	6.19	–	–
Hard-surface flooring, repair and replacement	6.97	–	–
Roofing and gutters	7.73	–	–
Plaster, paneling, siding, windows, doors, screens, awnings	13.96	0.06	0
Patio, walk, fence, driveway, masonry, brick, and stucco materials	0.70	0.01	1
Miscellaneous supplies and equipment	18.47	0.64	3
Material for insulation, other maintenance and repair	18.28	0.64	4
Property management and security	57.53	2.05	4
Property management	49.48	1.82	4
Management and upkeep services for security	8.06	0.23	3
Parking	6.29	0.08	1
Rented dwellings	2,860.24	8,358.90	292
Rent	2,738.81	8,037.49	293
Rent as pay	79.28	234.94	296
Maintenance, insurance, and other expenses	42.15	86.46	205
Tenant's insurance	12.40	32.37	261
Maintenance and repair services	19.84	29.70	150
Maintenance and repair materials	9.91	24.39	246
Paints, wallpaper, and supplies	1.35	2.96	219
Electrical supplies, heating and cooling equipment	0.80	1.17	146
Miscellaneous supplies and equipment	5.89	16.43	279
Material for insulation, other maintenance, repair	1.43	4.21	294
Other lodging	671.95	201.57	30
Owned vacation homes	303.02	57.27	19
Mortgage interest and charges	136.53	22.99	17
Property taxes	106.15	24.23	23
Maintenance, insurance, and other expenses	60.34	10.05	17
Housing while attending school	68.47	25.78	38
Lodging on trips	300.46	118.52	39

		renters	
	total	spending	index to total
• **Utilities, fuels, and public services**	**$3,644.62**	**$2,405.77**	**66**
Natural gas	**483.21**	**250.34**	**52**
Electricity	**1,376.71**	**938.34**	**68**
Fuel oil and other fuels	**141.36**	**41.32**	**29**
Fuel oil	76.71	17.62	23
Coal, wood, and other fuels	10.73	4.08	38
Bottled gas	53.91	19.62	36
Telephone services	**1,161.96**	**964.30**	**83**
Residential telephone and pay phones	433.65	271.05	63
Cellular phone service	711.67	671.71	94
Phone cards	9.57	15.58	163
Voice over IP	7.08	5.97	84
Water and other public services	**481.38**	**211.46**	**44**
Water and sewerage maintenance	350.42	170.47	49
Trash and garbage collection	126.56	40.81	32
Septic tank cleaning	4.40	0.18	4
• **Household services**	**1,011.36**	**607.28**	**60**
Personal services	389.44	291.99	75
Babysitting and child care in own home	47.07	37.65	80
Babysitting and child care in someone else's home	32.24	43.25	134
Care for elderly, invalids, handicapped, etc.	46.13	25.68	56
Adult day care centers	5.01	0.23	5
Day care centers, nurseries, and preschools	258.99	185.18	72
Other household services	**621.92**	**315.30**	**51**
Housekeeping services	112.08	26.04	23
Gardening, lawn care service	107.33	12.71	12
Water-softening service	3.96	1.76	44
Nonclothing laundry and dry cleaning, sent out	1.03	0.62	60
Nonclothing laundry and dry cleaning, coin-operated	3.59	8.50	237
Termite and pest control services	18.55	2.34	13
Home security system service fee	21.02	1.86	9
Other home services	19.80	6.25	32
Termite and pest control products	2.88	0.47	16
Moving, storage, and freight express	36.78	51.89	141
Appliance repair, including at service center	16.54	1.96	12
Reupholstering and furniture repair	4.33	0.89	21
Repairs and rentals of lawn and garden equipment, hand and power tools, etc.	5.88	1.86	32
Appliance rental	1.36	1.71	126
Repair of computer systems for nonbusiness use	6.75	4.02	60
Computer information services	253.49	190.81	75
Installation of computer	0.38	0.15	39
• **Housekeeping supplies**	**658.76**	**374.17**	**57**
Laundry and cleaning supplies	**155.80**	**119.93**	**77**
Soaps and detergents	85.66	72.37	84
Other laundry cleaning products	70.15	47.56	68
Other household products	**359.87**	**179.56**	**50**
Cleansing and toilet tissue, paper towels, and napkins	110.58	83.87	76
Miscellaneous household products	137.88	78.62	57
Lawn and garden supplies	111.41	17.06	15

	total	renters	
		spending	index to total
Postage and stationery	**$143.09**	**$74.68**	**52**
Stationery, stationery supplies, giftwrap	74.63	34.72	47
Postage	64.49	38.89	60
Delivery services	3.97	1.07	27
• Household furnishings and equipment	**1,505.57**	**787.63**	**52**
Household textiles	**124.19**	**62.21**	**50**
Bathroom linens	18.41	15.35	83
Bedroom linens	68.26	32.46	48
Kitchen and dining room linens	6.09	2.84	47
Curtains and draperies	17.12	4.88	29
Slipcovers and decorative pillows	3.49	2.08	60
Sewing materials for household items	9.66	3.89	40
Other linens	1.15	0.69	60
Furniture	**342.98**	**222.47**	**65**
Mattresses and springs	56.18	40.74	73
Other bedroom furniture	61.30	45.66	74
Sofas	83.23	58.16	70
Living room chairs	34.50	18.70	54
Living room tables	11.58	7.67	66
Kitchen and dining room furniture	31.91	19.20	60
Infants' furniture	8.00	6.85	86
Outdoor furniture	18.61	4.19	23
Wall units, cabinets, and other furniture	37.67	21.30	57
Floor coverings	**30.31**	**6.96**	**23**
Wall-to-wall carpeting	14.36	3.38	24
Floor coverings, nonpermanent	16.52	5.27	32
Major appliances	**193.71**	**70.41**	**36**
Dishwashers (built-in), garbage disposals, range hoods	13.31	1.23	9
Refrigerators, freezers	56.40	16.17	29
Washing machines	32.06	14.32	45
Clothes dryers	23.65	12.02	51
Cooking stoves, ovens	27.28	3.41	13
Microwave ovens	9.79	6.51	66
Portable dishwasher	0.66	0.19	29
Window air conditioners	3.27	2.88	88
Electric floor-cleaning equipment	14.19	10.87	77
Sewing machines	8.19	2.05	25
Miscellaneous household appliances	4.94	0.76	15
Small appliances and miscellaneous housewares	**93.41**	**53.23**	**57**
Housewares	63.95	36.92	58
Plastic dinnerware	2.49	2.78	112
China and other dinnerware	4.89	2.37	48
Flatware	3.66	3.76	103
Glassware	11.25	3.60	32
Silver serving pieces	2.86	1.39	49
Other serving pieces	1.78	1.02	57
Nonelectric cookware	13.38	8.18	61
Tableware, nonelectric kitchenware	23.65	13.82	58
Small appliances	29.46	16.31	55
Small electric kitchen appliances	20.62	14.01	68
Portable heating and cooling equipment	8.84	2.30	26

	total	renters spending	index to total
Miscellaneous household equipment	**$720.97**	**$372.35**	**52**
Window coverings	20.62	3.25	16
Infants' equipment	13.91	14.50	104
Laundry and cleaning equipment	16.47	11.75	71
Outdoor equipment	16.91	6.66	39
Lamps and lighting fixtures	28.56	6.30	22
Household decorative items	128.67	53.28	41
Telephones and accessories	47.08	31.89	68
Lawn and garden equipment	56.73	6.05	11
Power tools	35.28	23.85	68
Office furniture for home use	7.47	3.90	52
Hand tools	13.33	4.59	34
Indoor plants and fresh flowers	50.19	21.28	42
Closet and storage items	14.75	9.52	65
Rental of furniture	2.07	4.10	198
Luggage	10.89	7.93	73
Computers and computer hardware for nonbusiness use	156.62	113.58	73
Portable memory	7.70	5.75	75
Computer software and accessories for nonbusiness use	20.52	12.49	61
Personal digital assistants	2.77	2.37	86
Internet services away from home	2.19	1.91	87
Telephone answering devices	0.45	0.20	44
Business equipment for home use	2.82	1.43	51
Other hardware	13.07	4.86	37
Smoke alarms	1.32	0.36	27
Other household appliances	8.81	3.69	42
Miscellaneous household equipment and parts	41.78	16.88	40
APPAREL	**1,725.11**	**1,465.76**	**85**
Men's apparel	**304.32**	**264.95**	**87**
Suits	17.84	15.94	89
Sport coats and tailored jackets	6.83	4.87	71
Coats and jackets	35.07	32.50	93
Underwear	15.83	12.85	81
Hosiery	11.90	10.06	85
Nightwear	1.70	0.90	53
Accessories	28.54	29.51	103
Sweaters and vests	14.42	12.65	88
Active sportswear	16.88	10.30	61
Shirts	84.38	63.46	75
Pants and shorts	67.46	69.35	103
Uniforms	2.73	2.00	73
Costumes	0.72	0.54	75
Boys' (aged 2 to 15) apparel	**78.59**	**61.31**	**78**
Coats and jackets	4.35	4.03	93
Sweaters	1.86	1.76	95
Shirts	24.09	14.89	62
Underwear	6.08	4.43	73
Nightwear	1.08	0.89	82
Hosiery	4.80	4.71	98
Accessories	4.32	2.54	59
Suits, sport coats, and vests	0.93	0.75	81
Pants and shorts	25.79	23.07	89

	total	renters	
		spending	index to total
Uniforms	$3.36	$2.88	86
Active sportswear	1.19	0.79	66
Costumes	0.74	0.57	77
Women's apparel	**560.80**	**431.72**	**77**
Coats and jackets	41.98	34.74	83
Dresses	72.15	57.19	79
Sport coats and tailored jackets	4.74	2.66	56
Sweaters and vests	44.10	34.13	77
Shirts, blouses, and tops	111.11	82.07	74
Skirts	9.21	9.96	108
Pants and shorts	91.88	73.48	80
Active sportswear	27.57	22.34	81
Nightwear	21.60	18.46	85
Undergarments	36.16	23.57	65
Hosiery	17.66	13.46	76
Suits	11.31	7.14	63
Accessories	63.37	47.85	76
Uniforms	6.35	3.89	61
Costumes	1.61	0.77	48
Girls' (aged 2 to 15) apparel	**117.65**	**90.27**	**77**
Coats and jackets	7.09	6.75	95
Dresses and suits	13.02	10.17	78
Shirts, blouses, and sweaters	31.15	23.04	74
Skirts, pants, and shorts	26.62	24.14	91
Active sportswear	11.68	5.45	47
Underwear and nightwear	11.30	7.09	63
Hosiery	5.28	5.04	95
Accessories	6.39	4.63	72
Uniforms	3.28	3.12	95
Costumes	1.83	0.85	46
Children's (under age 2) apparel	**91.16**	**96.31**	**106**
Coats, jackets, and snowsuits	2.71	2.97	110
Outerwear including dresses	21.08	21.04	100
Underwear	55.12	60.17	109
Nightwear and loungewear	4.82	4.46	93
Accessories	7.42	7.67	103
Footwear	**323.14**	**311.28**	**96**
Men's	93.22	98.89	106
Boys'	42.89	48.24	112
Women's	150.67	130.75	87
Girls'	36.36	33.40	92
Other apparel products and services	**249.45**	**209.92**	**84**
Material for making clothes	9.68	3.81	39
Sewing patterns and notions	5.59	2.46	44
Watches	25.08	15.44	62
Jewelry	97.87	41.86	43
Shoe repair and other shoe services	1.19	0.69	58
Coin-operated apparel laundry and dry cleaning	41.28	105.72	256
Apparel alteration, repair, and tailoring services	5.73	3.84	67
Clothing rental	2.37	1.53	65
Watch and jewelry repair	3.55	1.63	46
Professional laundry, dry cleaning	55.48	29.92	54
Clothing storage	1.62	3.02	186

	total	renters spending	index to total
TRANSPORTATION	$7,658.25	$4,849.18	63
• **Vehicle purchases**	2,656.95	1,498.53	56
Cars and trucks, new	1,297.15	471.07	36
New cars	698.37	290.72	42
New trucks	598.77	180.34	30
Cars and trucks, used	1,304.35	999.03	77
Used cars	691.86	543.69	79
Used trucks	612.49	455.33	74
Other vehicles	55.45	28.44	51
New motorcycles	21.79	0.32	1
Used motorcycles	33.66	28.12	84
• **Gasoline and motor oil**	1,986.40	1,418.61	71
Gasoline	1,831.34	1,333.71	73
Diesel fuel	35.60	11.15	31
Gasoline on trips	108.63	65.44	60
Motor oil	9.73	7.65	79
Motor oil on trips	1.10	0.66	60
• **Other vehicle expenses**	2,535.57	1,579.15	62
Vehicle finance charges	281.01	192.30	68
Automobile finance charges	119.95	101.01	84
Truck finance charges	136.11	85.27	63
Motorcycle and plane finance charges	4.86	3.16	65
Other vehicle finance charges	20.09	2.87	14
Maintenance and repairs	732.82	478.44	65
Coolant, additives, brake and transmission fluids	3.91	3.70	95
Tires—purchased, replaced, installed	119.17	74.82	63
Parts, equipment, and accessories	43.62	33.37	77
Vehicle audio equipment	2.27	2.45	108
Vehicle products and cleaning services	5.02	3.57	71
Vehicle video equipment	1.99	1.36	68
Miscellaneous auto repair, servicing	55.55	38.32	69
Body work and painting	26.97	11.80	44
Clutch and transmission repair	34.37	24.00	70
Drive shaft and rear-end repair	5.18	4.15	80
Brake work	65.26	43.20	66
Repair to steering or front-end	17.54	10.56	60
Repair to engine cooling system	22.48	16.16	72
Motor tune-up	46.10	28.97	63
Lube, oil change, and oil filters	74.75	47.54	64
Front-end alignment, wheel balance, rotation	12.86	7.53	59
Shock absorber replacement	5.68	5.97	105
Tire repair and other repair work	49.30	26.74	54
Vehicle air conditioning repair	12.47	9.48	76
Exhaust system repair	10.45	8.39	80
Electrical system repair	30.77	24.21	79
Motor repair, replacement	68.89	45.41	66
Auto repair service policy	18.24	6.73	37
Vehicle insurance	1,075.24	629.46	59

	total	renters spending	renters index to total
Vehicle rental, leases, licenses, other charges	**$446.50**	**$278.95**	**62**
Leased and rented vehicles	233.03	137.53	59
Rented vehicles	33.06	19.71	60
Auto rental	4.98	6.11	123
Auto rental on trips	23.70	10.86	46
Truck rental	2.27	1.55	68
Truck rental on trips	1.65	0.79	48
Leased vehicles	199.97	117.82	59
Car lease payments	106.66	71.56	67
Truck lease payments	82.37	34.48	42
Vehicle registration, state	95.47	59.21	62
Vehicle registration, local	8.10	4.61	57
Driver's license	7.83	7.05	90
Vehicle inspection	11.36	7.57	67
Parking fees	39.80	31.53	79
Parking fees in home city, excluding residence	32.86	28.37	86
Parking fees on trips	6.94	3.16	46
Tolls	22.33	14.49	65
Tolls on trips	4.49	3.17	71
Towing charges	4.64	5.81	125
Global positioning services	1.92	0.64	33
Automobile service clubs	17.54	7.33	42
• Public transportation	**479.32**	**352.88**	**74**
Airline fares	300.92	175.75	58
Intercity bus fares	9.22	8.17	89
Intracity mass transit fares	65.18	109.77	168
Local transportation on trips	16.97	10.92	64
Taxi fares and limousine service	23.51	27.10	115
Intercity train fares	14.98	9.49	63
Ship fares	48.20	11.01	23
School bus	0.33	0.68	206
HEALTH CARE	**3,126.09**	**1,520.26**	**49**
Health insurance	**1,784.79**	**864.95**	**48**
Commercial health insurance	344.11	150.30	44
Traditional fee-for-service health plan (not BCBS)	84.88	33.72	40
Preferred-provider health plan (not BCBS)	259.24	116.58	45
Blue Cross, Blue Shield	527.17	233.14	44
Traditional fee-for-service health plan	86.93	25.83	30
Preferred-provider health plan	214.85	88.41	41
Health maintenance organization	170.01	92.87	55
Commercial Medicare supplement	45.93	20.05	44
Other BCBS health insurance	9.45	5.98	63
Health maintenance plans (HMOs)	285.51	182.34	64
Medicare payments	348.72	180.58	52
Medicare prescription drug premium	62.20	36.80	59
Commercial Medicare supplements and other health insurance	154.13	70.37	46
Commercial Medicare supplement (not BCBS)	102.27	44.19	43
Other health insurance (not BCBS)	51.86	26.19	51
Long-term care insurance	62.94	11.42	18

	total	renters spending	index to total
Medical services	$736.32	$351.13	48
Physician's services	184.97	105.39	57
Dental services	268.22	121.76	45
Eye care services	39.86	16.09	40
Service by professionals other than physician	49.47	21.16	43
Lab tests, X-rays	48.19	22.72	47
Hospital room and services	104.86	41.49	40
Care in convalescent or nursing home	16.08	17.50	109
Repair of medical equipment	2.74	0.65	24
Other medical services	21.88	4.38	20
Drugs	486.27	244.58	50
Nonprescription drugs	81.74	52.32	64
Nonprescription vitamins	42.81	16.30	38
Prescription drugs	361.72	175.96	49
Medical supplies	118.71	59.60	50
Eyeglasses and contact lenses	59.81	29.07	49
Hearing aids	16.04	3.42	21
Topicals and dressings	31.84	21.16	66
Medical equipment for general use	2.75	1.56	57
Supportive and convalescent medical equipment	4.83	1.26	26
Rental of medical equipment	1.11	0.58	52
Rental of supportive and convalescent medical equipment	2.34	2.54	109
ENTERTAINMENT	2,692.66	1,587.89	59
Fees and admissions	628.00	319.23	51
Recreation expenses on trips	19.83	10.07	51
Social, recreation, civic club membership	115.41	51.73	45
Fees for participant sports	123.67	49.36	40
Participant sports on trips	21.95	10.89	50
Movie, theater, amusement park, and other admissions	120.38	81.03	67
Movie, other admissions on trips	40.84	21.71	53
Admission to sports events	50.86	29.80	59
Admission to sports events on trips	13.61	7.23	53
Fees for recreational lessons	101.63	47.34	47
Other entertainment services on trips	19.83	10.07	51
Audio and visual equipment and services	974.95	744.63	76
Radios	2.24	1.71	76
Television sets	140.39	92.82	66
Tape recorders and players	0.66	0.83	126
Cable and satellite television services	597.38	443.72	74
Miscellaneous sound equipment	1.10	0.21	19
Miscellaneous video equipment	3.64	4.57	126
Satellite radio service	14.01	7.86	56
Sound equipment accessories	10.64	9.68	91
Online gaming services	2.20	1.81	82
VCRs and video disc players	12.46	7.14	57
Video game hardware and software	53.32	55.93	105
Video cassettes, tapes, and discs	30.10	28.31	94
Streamed and downloaded video	1.40	1.07	76
Repair of TV, radio, and sound equipment	3.32	1.66	50
Rental of television sets	0.68	1.74	256
Personal digital audio players	13.01	10.71	82
Sound components and component systems	11.83	5.99	51

	total	renters spending	index to total
Satellite dishes	$1.06	$0.57	54
Compact discs, records, and audio tapes	18.46	15.63	85
Streamed and downloaded audio	5.61	4.50	80
Rental of VCR, radio, and sound equipment	0.16	0.13	81
Musical instruments and accessories	23.30	24.56	105
Rental and repair of musical instruments	1.59	0.84	53
Rental of video cassettes, tapes, discs, films	25.49	22.37	88
Rental of computer and video game hardware and software	0.23	0.12	52
Installation of television sets	0.68	0.14	21
Pets, toys, hobbies, and playground equipment	**689.75**	**345.75**	**50**
Pets	542.85	234.14	43
Pet food	168.92	79.18	47
Pet purchase, supplies, and medicines	165.83	95.36	58
Pet services	43.36	18.28	42
Veterinarian services	164.74	41.32	25
Toys, games, hobbies, and tricycles	139.07	109.05	78
Stamp and coin collecting	5.39	1.88	35
Playground equipment	2.45	0.68	28
Other entertainment supplies, equipment, services	**399.95**	**178.27**	**45**
Unmotored recreational vehicles	50.19	6.23	12
Boat without motor and boat trailers	17.14	3.98	23
Trailer and other attachable campers	33.05	2.25	7
Motorized recreational vehicles	109.90	34.71	32
Purchase of motorized camper	31.48	–	–
Purchase of other vehicle	40.75	33.34	82
Purchase of boat with motor	37.67	1.37	4
Rental of recreational vehicles	6.53	3.96	61
Docking and landing fees	7.78	0.03	0
Sports, recreation, exercise equipment	129.98	72.00	55
Athletic gear, game tables, exercise equipment	51.67	27.57	53
Bicycles	13.69	11.45	84
Camping equipment	10.73	4.31	40
Hunting and fishing equipment	30.35	18.00	59
Winter sports equipment	3.85	2.41	63
Water sports equipment	3.03	1.51	50
Other sports equipment	5.96	5.91	99
Global positioning system devices	7.98	–	–
Rental and repair of miscellaneous sports equipment	2.72	0.84	31
Photographic equipment and supplies	59.08	30.98	52
Film	1.73	1.62	94
Other photographic supplies	1.97	0.39	20
Photo processing	12.87	6.30	49
Repair and rental of photographic equipment	0.59	0.41	69
Photographic equipment	27.57	18.32	66
Photographer fees	14.34	3.94	27
Fireworks	6.39	13.35	209
Souvenirs	2.57	2.22	86
Visual goods	1.41	0.43	30
Pinball, electronic video games	2.61	4.11	157
Live entertainment for catered affairs	8.63	3.18	37
Rental of party supplies for catered affairs	14.09	5.67	40

	total	renters spending	index to total
PERSONAL CARE PRODUCTS AND SERVICES	**$595.57**	**$404.15**	**68**
Personal care products	**304.22**	**217.75**	**72**
Hair care products	65.14	45.91	70
Hair accessories	6.38	5.92	93
Wigs and hairpieces	2.95	3.16	107
Oral hygiene products	29.27	21.84	75
Shaving products	16.02	12.41	77
Cosmetics, perfume, and bath products	143.17	97.74	68
Deodorants, feminine hygiene, miscellaneous products	32.61	25.86	79
Electric personal care appliances	8.68	4.92	57
Personal care services	**291.35**	**186.41**	**64**
READING	**109.60**	**58.40**	**53**
Newspaper and magazine subscriptions	43.30	15.06	35
Newspapers and magazines, nonsubscription	14.97	12.03	80
Books	50.31	31.00	62
EDUCATION	**1,068.02**	**742.67**	**70**
College tuition	703.66	554.50	79
Elementary and high school tuition	161.87	35.22	22
Vocational and technical school tuition	13.19	5.54	42
Test preparation, tutoring services	8.69	4.27	49
Other school tuition	8.14	5.52	68
Other school expenses including rentals	35.51	22.92	65
Books and supplies for college	66.77	70.22	105
Books and supplies for elementary and high school	18.67	15.58	83
Books and supplies for vocational and technical schools	0.57	0.35	61
Books and supplies for day care and nursery	0.14	0.05	36
Books and suppliesfor other schools	1.50	0.68	45
Miscellaneous school expenses and supplies	49.30	27.81	56
TOBACCO PRODUCTS, SMOKING SUPPLIES	**379.69**	**420.95**	**111**
Cigarettes	347.58	396.56	114
Other tobacco products	30.07	21.83	73
Smoking accessories	1.93	2.30	119
FINANCIAL PRODUCTS AND SERVICES			
Miscellaneous financial	**816.36**	**524.70**	**64**
Miscellaneous fees	5.95	1.15	19
Lottery and gambling losses	74.75	51.00	68
Legal fees	160.64	122.07	76
Funeral expenses	47.61	26.69	56
Safe deposit box rental	3.79	1.10	29
Checking accounts, other bank service charges	23.52	23.19	99
Cemetery lots, vaults, and maintenance fees	14.05	7.02	50
Accounting fees	58.73	27.92	48
Miscellaneous personal services	41.30	34.55	84
Dating services	0.38	0.49	129
Finance charges, except mortgage and vehicles	202.35	137.28	68
Occupational expenses	56.99	31.53	55
Expenses for other properties	107.92	53.17	49
Credit card memberships	1.89	1.27	67
Shopping club membership fees	9.44	4.34	46
Vacation clubs	6.02	1.39	23

	total	renters spending	renters index to total
Cash contributions	**$1,723.08**	**$858.09**	**50**
Support for college students	108.91	33.56	31
Alimony expenditures	46.19	18.22	39
Child support expenditures	215.70	258.43	120
Gifts of stocks, bonds, and mutual funds to members of other households	12.54	5.04	40
Cash contributions to charities	208.20	54.60	26
Cash contributions to church, religious organizations	724.60	247.77	34
Cash contributions to educational institutions	30.52	8.58	28
Cash contributions to political organizations	7.11	1.84	26
Cash gifts to members of other households	369.31	230.04	62
Personal insurance and pensions	**5,471.07**	**2,909.55**	**53**
Life and other personal insurance	309.03	96.83	31
Life, endowment, annuity, other personal insurance	292.08	90.93	31
Other nonhealth insurance	16.96	5.90	35
Pensions and Social Security	5,162.04	2,812.72	54
Deductions for government retirement	79.95	29.70	37
Deductions for railroad retirement	7.02	1.93	27
Deductions for private pensions	625.39	180.21	29
Nonpayroll deposit to retirement plans	461.03	138.13	30
Deductions for Social Security	3,988.65	2,462.75	62
Personal taxes	**2,103.78**	**691.53**	**33**
Federal income taxes	1,404.46	402.25	29
Federal income tax deducted	1,959.52	1,052.11	54
Additional federal income tax paid	451.19	137.54	30
Federal income tax refunds	−1,006.25	−787.41	78
State and local income taxes	524.06	262.26	50
State and local income tax deducted	573.97	316.69	55
Additional state and local income tax paid	84.89	32.06	38
State and local income tax refunds	−134.80	−86.49	64
Other taxes	176.56	28.04	16
GIFTS FOR PEOPLE IN OTHER HOUSEHOLDS	**1,067.01**	**563.14**	**53**

* The category fast-food restaurants also includes take-out, delivery, concession stands, buffets, and cafeterias other than employer and school.
** Spending on mortgage principal reduction is not included in spending because it is considered an asset.
Note: Numbers may not add to total because not all categories are shown. "−" means zero or sample is too small to make a reliable estimate. Spending on gifts is also included in the preceding product and service categories. The index is calculated by dividing the spending of renters by the spending of total households and multiplying by 100.
Source: Bureau of Labor Statistics, unpublished data from the 2009 Consumer Expenditure Survey; calculations by New Strategist

Glossary

additional central air *See* Equipment.

air conditioning *See* Equipment.

amenities

• *Garage or carport* is counted only if it is on the same property, though not necessarily attached to the house.

• *Living rooms, recreation rooms, etc.,* includes family rooms, dens, recreation rooms, or libraries.

• *Off-street parking* includes driveway or parking lot privileges that are paid for as part of the rent or owned with the unit.

• *Porch, deck, balcony, or patio* is counted if it is attached to the unit, not just to the building, or free standing. Porches may be enclosed or open. The porch, deck, balcony, or patio is counted only if it is at least 4 feet by 4 feet.

• *Separate dining room* is an area separated from adjoining rooms by archways or walls that extend at least 6 inches from an intersecting wall.

• *Usable fireplace* excludes the following: fireplaces that have been blocked off or whose chimney or flue has been filled; decorative or artificial fireplaces and wood stoves, even if shaped like a fireplace. Freestanding fireplaces are included in this item.

American Housing Survey The AHS collects national and metropolitan-level data on the nation's housing, including apartments, single-family homes, and mobile homes. The nationally representative survey, with a sample of 60,000 homes, is conducted by the Census Bureau for the Department of Housing and Urban Development every other year.

annual taxes paid per $1,000 value Real estate taxes paid per $1,000 value of the house (and lot, except for manufactured/mobile homes).

baby boom Americans born between 1946 and 1964.

bathrooms *See* Complete bathrooms.

bedrooms The number of bedrooms in a housing unit includes those rooms that are used mainly for sleeping or designed to be a bedroom, even if used for other purposes. A room reserved only for sleeping, such as a guest room, even if used infrequently, is considered a bedroom. A room built as a bedroom, although not used for that purpose, such as a room meant to be a bedroom but used as a sewing room, is counted as a bedroom. On the other hand, a room designed and used mainly for other purposes, such as a den with a sleep sofa used mainly for watching television, is not considered a bedroom. A housing unit consisting of only one room, such as a one-room efficiency apartment, is classified by definition as having no bedroom.

bodies of water within 300 feet These questions determine the proximity of the respondent's property to bodies of water such as ponds, lakes, rivers, or ocean. Swimming pools and temporary pools of water are not included in this definition.

cars, trucks, or vans Included are passenger cars and station wagons owned or regularly used by one or more household members and ordinarily kept at home. Company cars are counted (if used regularly for nonbusiness purposes and kept at home), as are taxicabs (if they are owned by a household member and kept at home). Included are pickups and small panel trucks of one-ton capacity or less, and small vans that are owned or regularly used by one or more members of the household and ordinarily kept at home. Company trucks and vans are included if used regularly for nonbusiness purposes and kept at home.

cash received in primary mortgage refinance An owner can receive cash from a mortgage lender by refinancing the primary mortgage. This increases the outstanding balance of the loan.

change in housing costs For the householder and those who moved with the householder, a comparison is made between the share of the housing costs paid in the previous unit and the share paid in the present residence. Housing costs include mortgage and rent payment, real estate taxes, insurance, utilities, land rent, and mobile home park fees.

choice of present home and home search These data are shown for units into which respondent moved during the 12 months prior to the interview. The respondent was asked a four-part question on choice of present home: (1) whether the respondent looked at both houses or manufactured/mobile homes, and apartments; (2) the reasons why the respondent chose the present home; (3) the main reason why the present home was chosen; and (4) how the respondent found the home. The distribution for choice of present home may not add to the total because respondents were not limited to one response.

choice of present neighborhood and neighborhood search These data are shown for units into which the respondent moved during the 12 months prior to the interview. The respondent was asked a three-part question on choice of present neighborhood: (1) whether the respondent also looked for housing in any other neighborhood; (2) the reasons why the respondent chose the present neighborhood; and (3) the main reason why the present neighborhood was chosen. The distribution for choice of present neighborhood may not add to the total because respondents were not limited to one response.

complete bathrooms A housing unit is classified as having a complete bathroom if it has a room or adjoining areas with a flush toilet, bathtub or shower, sink, and hot and cold piped water. A half bathroom has hot and cold piped water and either a flush toilet or a bathtub or shower, but does not have all the facilities of a complete bathroom.

consumer unit (spending tables only) For convenience, the terms consumer unit and household are used interchangeably in the spending tables, although consumer units are somewhat different from the Census Bureau's households. Related household members form a consumer unit, as does any financially independent households member or group of persons.

current total loan as percent of value This percentage is computed by dividing the outstanding principal amount by the value of the housing unit.

description of area within 300 feet The respondent was asked to describe the area within half a block of the unit.

Commercial or institutional refers to nonresidential buildings such as offices, stores, restaurants, hotels, banks, churches, parking garages, hospitals, schools, and prisons.

Four-or-more-lane highway, railroad, or airport includes divided or undivided highways of at least four lanes, railroad or streetcar tracks, public, private, and military airfields.

Industrial or factory refers to nonresidential buildings such as factories, barns, junkyards, water treatment plants, and pumping stations.

Open space refers to areas such as a park, woods, farm, or ranch within half a block of the home/building. It includes other areas such as cemeteries, golf courses, woods, forest preserves, vacant lots, undeveloped land, airport land, ball fields, and school fields.

down payment The total amount of money used for the down payment or outright purchase of the home. Respondents were allowed to answer by giving a total dollar amount or by giving a percent of the purchase price.

equipment This item refers to selected equipment that is not shared with other households. Refrigerators, burners, ovens, and disposals are counted only if they were in working order or the household planned to have them repaired or replaced soon.

• *Additional central* refers to a second central air conditioning system (e.g., a dual zone heat pump system).

• *Air conditioning* is defined as the cooling of air by a refrigeration unit. This definition excludes evaporative coolers, fans, or blowers that are not connected to a refrigeration unit.

• *Burners* were counted only if a respondent did not report having a cooking stove with oven. Burners built into a stove or counter top are counted, as are burners on a wood-burning stove.

• *Central air conditioning* refers to a central system, which air-conditions the entire housing unit or major portions of it. In an apartment building, a central system may cool all apartments in the building, each apartment may have its own central system, or there may be several systems that provide central air conditioning for a group of apartments. A central installation with individual room controls is a central air conditioning system.

• *Clothes dryers* must have motors to be counted. Hand-operated wringers or hand-turned spin dryers are not counted.

• *Complete kitchen facilities* is defined as having all of the following: (1) kitchen sink; (2) burners, cook stove, or microwave oven; and (3) refrigerator.

• *Cooking stove or range* may be mechanical or wood burning.

• *Dishwashers* do not include counter top dishwashers.

• *Disposal in sink* is a motorized device that grinds waste so it can flow through the wastewater pipe.

• *Kitchen sinks* must be in the unit or on an enclosed porch, but it does not matter whether they are in the kitchen. A bathroom sink, however, does not count as a kitchen sink.

• *Microwave ovens* were counted only if the respondent did not report having a cooking stove with oven or burners.

• *Refrigerators* may or may not have freezers. Kerosene refrigerators are counted, but not ice boxes.

• *Room (air conditioning) unit* refers to an individual air conditioner installed in a window or an outside wall and is generally intended to cool one room, although it may be used to cool several rooms.

• *Trash compactors* are counted only if motorized and built-in.

• *Washing machine* Any kind with a motor is counted.

first-time owners If neither the owner nor any co-owner has ever owned or co-owned another home as a usual residence, then the housing unit is reported as the first home ever owned. Previous homes purchased solely as vacation homes or homes purchased for commercial rental purposes are not considered usual residences. However, if a previously owned home was originally purchased as a usual residence and later used as a vacation home or for commercial or rental purposes, the owner is not a first-time owner.

flush toilet and flush toilet breakdowns A privy or chemical toilet is not considered a flush toilet. Flush toilets outside the unit are not counted. The statistics on breakdowns of flush toilets are shown for housing units with at least one flush toilet for the household's use only. The flush toilet may be completely unusable because of a faulty flushing mechanism, broken pipes, stopped up sewer pipe, lack of water supplied to the flush toilet, or some other reason. For households with more than one toilet, the question asked about times when all toilets were unusable.

fuels

• *Bottled gas* is pressurized gas stored in tanks or bottles that are filled or exchanged when empty.

• *Coal or coke* is usually delivered by truck.

• *Electricity* may be supplied by above- or underground electric power lines or generated at the housing unit.

• *Fuel oil* is heating oil normally supplied by truck to a storage tank for use by the heating system.

• *Kerosene or other liquid fuel* includes kerosene, gasoline, alcohol, and other similar combustible liquids.

• *Piped gas* is gas piped through underground pipes from a central system to serve the neighborhood.

• *Solar energy* refers to the use of energy available from sunlight as a heating fuel source.

• *Wood* refers to the use of wood or wood charcoal as a fuel.

• *Other* includes briquettes made of pitch and sawdust, coal dust, waste material like corncobs, purchased steam, or any other fuel not listed.

fuels, other house heating These are the same types of fuels mentioned above but used in addition to and/or supplementing the main house heating fuel.

fuses or breakers blown The data show whether an electric fuse has blown or circuit breaker has tripped in the home in the three months prior to the interview or while the household was living in the unit if less than three months. A blown fuse or tripped breaker switch results in the temporary loss of electricity until the fuse is replaced or the breaker switch reset. Blown fuses inside major pieces of installed equipment (such as some air conditioners) are counted as blown fuses or tripped breaker switches. The item may identify inadequate wiring, but it also happens commonly when people move into houses and are unfamiliar with which items can be turned on at the same time.

heating equipment Data are shown for the main heating equipment and other heating equipment used in addition to the main heating equipment.

• *Built-in electric units* refer to units permanently installed in floors, walls, ceilings, or baseboards.

• *Cooking stove* refers to gas or electric ranges or stoves originally manufactured to cook food.

• *Electric heat pump* refers to a heating and cooling system that utilizes indoor and outdoor coils, a compressor, and a refrigerant to pump in heat during the winter and pump out heat during the summer. Only heat pumps that are centrally

installed with ducts to the rooms are included in this category. Others are included in wall units.

• *Fireplace with inserts* refers to a fan-forced air circulation system installed in the fireplace to force the heat into the room.

• *Fireplace without inserts* refers to glass door fire screens or fire backs inserted in the back of the fireplace to passively reflect heat.

• *Floor, wall, or other built-in hot-air unit without ducts* refers to a system that delivers warm air to the room right above the furnace or to the room(s) on one or both sides of the wall in which the furnace is installed.

• *Portable electric heater* refers to heaters that receive current from an electrical wall outlet.

• *Room heater with flue* refers to nonportable room heaters in the wall or freestanding heaters that burn liquid fuel, and which are connected to a flue, vent, or chimney to remove smoke and fumes.

• *Room heater without flue* refers to any room heater that burns kerosene, gas, or oil and that does not connect to flue, vent, or chimney.

• *Steam or hot water system* refers to a central heating system in which heat from steam or hot water is delivered through radiators or other outlets. It also includes solar-heated hot water that is circulated throughout the home.

• *Stove* refers to any range or stove that burns solid fuel including wood burning, potbelly, and Franklin stoves.

• *Warm-air furnace* refers to a central system that provides warm air through ducts leading to various rooms.

• *Other* includes any heating equipment that does not fit the any of the previous definitions.

heating problems Statistics are shown for housing units occupied by the householder during the winter prior to the interview and refer only to the main heating equipment. The data are classified by whether the housing unit was uncomfortably cold for 24 hours or more, the number of times equipment breakdowns lasted six hours or more, and causes for the breakdowns. The heating equipment is broken down if it is not providing heat at its normal heating capacity through some fault in the equipment.

• *Cost of heating* refers to the occupants turning down their thermostat or turning the equipment off altogether to save money. This category includes utilities/fuels that are unavailable due to unpaid bills.

• *Inadequate heating capacity* refers to heating equipment that is providing heat at its normal capacity, but the housing unit is still too cold for the occupants.

• *Inadequate insulation* refers to air drafts through window frames, electrical outlets, or walls that are cold.

• *Utility interruptions* occur when there is a cutoff in the gas, electricity, or other fuel supplying the heat.

home-equity line of credit This type of revolving home-equity loan allows the property owner to borrow against the equity up to a fixed limit set by the lender without reapplying for a loan.

home-equity lump-sum loan This type of home-equity loan is paid out in a one-time lump-sum amount and must be repaid over a set period.

home-equity mortgage *See* Mortgages currently on property.

household A household consists of all people who occupy a particular housing unit as their usual residence, or who live there at the time of the interview and have no usual residence elsewhere. The usual residence is the place where the person lives and sleeps most of the time. This place is not necessarily the same as a legal residence, voting residence, or domicile. Households include not only occupants related to the householder but also any lodgers, roomers, boarders, partners, wards, foster children, and resident employees who share the living quarters of the householder. It includes people temporarily away for reasons such as visiting, traveling in connection with their jobs, attending school, in general hospitals, and in other temporary relocations. By definition, the count of households is the same as the count of occupied housing units.

household moves Data are shown for households that moved into the present unit during the 12 months prior to the date of the interview.

household, race/ethnicity of Households are categorized according to the race or ethnicity of the householder only.

householder The householder is the first household member listed on the questionnaire who is an owner or renter of the unit and is aged 18 or older. An owner is a person whose name is on the deed, mortgage, or contract to purchase. A renter is a person whose name is on the lease. If there is no lease, a renter is a person responsible for paying the rent. If no one meets the full criteria, the age requirement is relaxed to 14 years or older before the owner/renter requirement. Where the respondent is one of several unrelated people who all could meet the criteria, the interviewer will select one of them to be listed first who then becomes the householder. The householder is not necessarily the one answering the survey questions.

housing units A housing unit is a house, apartment, group of rooms, or single room occupied or intended for occupancy as separate living quarters. The occupants of each housing unit may be a single family, one person living alone, two or more families living together, or any other group of related or unrelated people who share living arrangements.

• *Group quarters* The following types of living quarters are not classified as housing units and are not covered by the American Housing Survey: institutional group quarters such as children in an orphanage, people in a nursing home, and prisoners in a penitentiary; noninstitutional group quarters such as college dormitories, fraternity and sorority houses. Note that institutional and commercial establishments that have single-family houses or individual apartments with direct access, where staff lives separately, such as some residential hotels and units for college professors, are housing units. Military housing for singles is not covered, but housing where civilian family members live is, if it meets the definition of a housing unit.

• *Hotel rooms* or suites of rooms in hotels, motels, and similar places are classified as housing units only when occupied by permanent residents; that is, people who consider the hotel as their usual residence or who have no usual residence elsewhere.

• *Living quarters* is a general term that includes both housing units and group quarters. Living quarters include structures intended for residential use (such as a house, apartment building, boarding house, or mobile home). Living quarters also include the following, but only if they are occupied as usual residences: (a) places such as tents, caves, boats, and railroad cars; and (b) structures intended for nonresidential use (such as rooms in a warehouse where a guard lives). Living quarters exclude quarters being used entirely for nonresidential purposes, such as a store, an office, or quarters used for storing business supplies, machinery, or agricultural products.

• *New housing units* Units being built are classified as housing units (though they may be vacant) if construction has reached a point where all exterior windows and doors are installed and final usable floors are in place.

• *Rooming houses* If any of the occupants in a rooming or boarding house live separately from everyone else in the building and have direct access, their quarters are classified as separate housing units. The remaining quarters are combined. If the combined quarters contain eight or fewer roomers unrelated to the householder or a person in charge, they are counted as one housing unit. Otherwise they are noninstitutional group quarters.

• *Separate living quarters* are those in which the occupants live separately from any other people in the structure and that have direct access from the outside of the structure or through a common hall, lobby, or vestibule that is used or intended for use by the occupants of more than one unit or by the general public. This means that the hall, lobby, or vestibule is not part of any unit, and must be clearly separate from all units in the structure.

income The survey covers total money income received in the 12 months before the interview. It covers people aged 16 or older currently living in the housing unit, even if they lived elsewhere during some of the previous 12 months. The figures represent the amount of income before any deductions such as taxes, Social Security, union dues, bonds, and insurance. The figures exclude capital gains; lump-sum payments from inheritances or insurance; occasional gifts; other sporadic payments; money borrowed; tax refunds; withdrawal of bank deposits; accrued interest on uncashed savings bonds; payments between household members except wages in a family business; income "in kind," such as free living quarters, housing subsidies, food stamps, or food produced and consumed in the home; and money from the sale of property (unless the recipient was in the business of selling such property). Figures also exclude income of people who have died or moved out of the housing unit, even if they lived in it for part of the previous 12 months. For household members related to the householder, the interviewer asks the respondent for the information. For people not related to the householder, the interviewer tries to ask them directly about their income, but if they are not available, the interviewer asks the respondent.

• *Child support or alimony* Child support is money received for the support of children not living with their father or mother as a result of a legal separation. Alimony is money received periodically from a former spouse after a divorce or legal separation.

• *Disability payments, workers' compensation, veterans' disability, other disability* include payments from companies, unions, and the federal, state, or local government, such as payments from the Social Security Disability Insurance program.

• *Dividends* are money received, credited, or reinvested from ownership of stocks or mutual funds.

• *Interest* is money received or credited to checking and savings accounts, money market funds, certificates of deposit, IRAs, KEOGHs, and government bonds.

• *Public assistance income* includes general assistance and temporary assistance for needy families. This does not include Supplemental Security Income or noncash benefits such as food stamps.

• *Rental income* is money (profits or losses) received from renting land, buildings, real estate, or from roomers or boarders.

• *Retirement pensions and survivor benefits* include benefits from a former employer, company, labor union, or federal, state, or local government, and the U.S. military. Also included are periodic receipts from annuities and insurance, and regular income from IRA and KEOGH plans. This does not include Social Security income.

• *Self-employment income* includes net money income (gross receipts minus expenses) from one's own business, professional practice, partnership, farm, or ranch.

• *Social Security income or railroad retirement* includes Social Security pensions and survivor benefits, permanent disability insurance payments made by the Social Security Administration prior to deductions for medical insurance. Medicare reimbursements are not included.

• *Supplemental Security Income* is a nationwide U.S. assistance program administered by the Social Security Administration that guarantees a minimum level of income for needy, aged, blind, or disabled individuals.

• *Wage or salary income* includes total money earnings received for work performed as an employee during the past 12 months. It includes wages, salary, armed forces pay, commissions, tips, piece-rate payments, and cash bonuses earned before deductions were made for taxes, bonds, pensions, and union dues.

• *All other income.* All other income includes unemployment compensation, Veterans Administration payments, royalties, contributions received periodically from people not living in the household, military family allotments, and other kinds of periodic income other than earnings.

line of credit *See* Home-equity line of credit.

line of credit amount used for home additions, improvements, or repairs This is the percentage of the dollar amount of home-equity loans used for home additions, improvements, or repairs.

line of credit monthly payment This is the monthly payment on the line of credit paid to the bank at the present interest rate.

living quarters *See* Housing units.

lot size Includes all connecting land that is owned or rented with the home. Excluded are two-or-more-unit buildings and two-or-more-unit mobile homes.

major source of down payment Refers to the source of the cash used for down payment or outright purchase of the property (house or lot). If more than one source applied, the one providing the largest amount was recorded.

• *Borrowing other than a mortgage on this property* is shown if the present owner borrowed the down payment, even if the property was mortgaged.

• *Land where building built used for financing* means the land on which the structure was built was used as the present owner's equity in the property.

• *Money received as a gift* regardless of the source was categorized as inheritance or gift.

• *Sale of other investment* includes the sale of real property or real estate other than the previous home or the sale of other investments such as stocks, municipal or corporate bonds, mutual funds, or dissolved business ventures.

• *Sale of previous home* was reported only if the previous home was sold during the 12 months preceding the acquisition of the present home.

• *Savings, or cash on hand,* includes money drawn as bank deposits, share accounts, saving bonds, certificates of deposits, money market funds, and IRA or KEOGH accounts.

• *Other* Sources of down payment that do not fit any of the above categories were recorded in the *other* category.

manufactured/mobile homes A manufactured/mobile home is defined as a housing unit that was originally constructed to be towed on its own chassis (also called HUD Code homes). It may be built in one or more sections. Since the sections are attached side by side at the home site, the final home comprises the number of sections referred to as "wide." A unit composed of two sections is a double-wide; three sections is a triple-wide, etc. Single-wide units come from the factory as one section. It also may have permanent rooms attached at its present site or other structural modifications. The term does not include prefabricated buildings, modular homes, travel campers, boats, or self-propelled vehicles like motor homes. Some people use the term trailer or manufactured housing in the same sense as mobile homes.

manufactured/mobile homes in group Manufactured/mobile homes or mobile home sites gathered close together are considered to be in a "group." This may be a mobile home park or it may be a number grouped together on adjacent individually owned lots not in a mobile home park.

means of sewage disposal A *public sewer* is connected to a city, county, sanitary district, neighborhood, or subdivision sewer system, serving six or more units. A *septic tank* or *cesspool* is an underground tank or pit used for disposal of sewage (serving five or fewer units). A *chemical toilet,* which may be inside or outside the unit, uses chemicals to break down or dissolve sewage. Housing units for which sewage is disposed of in some other way are included in the *other* category.

median The median is the amount that divides the population or households into two equal portions: one below and one above the median. Medians can be calculated for income, age, and many other characteristics.

median income The amount that divides the income distribution into two equal groups, half having incomes above the median, half having incomes below the median.

metropolitan area An area qualifies for recognition as a metropolitan area if: (1) it includes a city of at least 50,000 population, or (2) it includes a Census Bureau–defined urbanized area of at least 50,000 with a total metropolitan population of at least 100,000 (75,000 in New England). In addition to the county containing the main city or urbanized area, a metropolitan area may include other counties having strong commuting ties to the central county.

monthly costs for electricity and piped gas Three separate procedures are used to estimate monthly costs of electricity and piped gas. All respondents are asked if they have records available showing their costs for electricity (or piped gas) separate from other utilities. If they respond "yes," they are asked the amount of their electric (or piped gas) bill for the most recent months of January, April, August, and December. These months are the best predictors of annual

costs. On average, more than one-third of respondents provide answers for at least one of the four months. In some cases, respondents are also asked the amount of the most recent bill, the month that it covered, and the average monthly cost. If the respondent answers "no," that he or she does not have separate records for the electricity (or gas), the respondent is asked to provide an estimate of the average monthly costs.

monthly housing costs Monthly housing costs for *owner-occupied* units include the sum of monthly payments for all mortgages or installment loans or contracts, except reverse annuity mortgages and home-equity lines of credit. Costs also include real estate taxes (including taxes on manufactured/mobile homes, and manufactured/mobile home sites if the site is owned), property insurance, homeowner association fees, cooperative or condominium fees, mobile home park fees, land rent, and utilities. Costs do not include maintenance and repairs. Monthly housing costs for *renter-occupied* housing units include the contract rent, utilities, property insurance, and mobile home park fee. Renter housing units occupied without payment of cash rent are shown separately as "No cash rent." For rental units subsidized by a housing authority, the federal government, or state or local governments, the monthly rental costs reflect only the portion paid by the household and not the portion subsidized. The figures do not adjust for lost security deposits or the benefit of free rent offered by some owners. The term *utilities* here includes electricity, gas, fuels (oil, coal, kerosene, or wood), water, sewage disposal, garbage and trash collection, but not telephones or cable television. Utility costs are counted if they are paid by the occupant or by someone else, such as a relative, welfare agency, or friend. They may be paid separately or included in rent, condominium fee, or mobile home park fee.

monthly payment for principal and interest The data present the monthly dollar amount paid on the mortgage for principal and interest only. They do not include that portion of the monthly payment used for property taxes, homeowner's insurance, and/or other charges.

mortgages currently on property The owner or the owner's spouse was asked the number of mortgages or similar loans (including home equity loans) currently in effect on the home. Data are shown for the number of units with the following mortgage categories: owned free and clear, reverse mortgages, regular, and home equity. A mortgage or similar debt refers to all forms of debt for which the property is pledged as security for payment of the debt. It includes such debt instruments as deeds of trust, trust deeds, mortgage bonds, home-equity lines of credit, home-equity lump-sum loans, and vendors' liens. In trust arrangements, usually a third party, known as the trustee, holds the title to the property until the debt is paid. With home-equity lines of credit, home-equity lump sum loans, and vendors' lien arrangements, the buyer keeps the title but the seller (vendor) reserves, in the deed to the buyer, a lien on the property to secure payment of the balance of the purchase price. Also included, as a mortgage or similar debts, are contracts to purchase, land contracts, and lease-purchase agreements where the title to the property remains with the seller until the agreed-upon payments have been made by the buyer.

neighborhood crime This category refers to any serious crimes that occurred in the respondent's neighborhood in the past 12 months such as burglary, robbery, theft, rape, or murder.

neighborhood odors This category refers to smoke, gas, fumes from motor vehicles, industrial, or commercial operations, odors from sewers, septic tanks, aerial spraying, or bad smells the respondent finds bothersome in the neighborhood.

neighborhood services

• *Elementary schools* If there is at least one child aged 13 or younger in the household, the respondent is asked (1) how the public elementary school compares academically with other public elementary schools in the area; and (2) if that public elementary school is within one mile from the home.

• *Police protection* The respondent is asked if police protection was satisfactory.

• *Public transportation* The respondent is asked whether public transportation is available, whether any member of the household uses it for commuting to work or school, and how many minutes it takes to get to the nearest bus stop, train station, or subway stop.

• *Shopping* The respondent is asked whether grocery stores or drug stores are satisfactory and located within 15 minutes of the housing unit.

neighborhood shopping Satisfactory neighborhood shopping could reflect the availability of goods offered, hours of service, prices, or the service available. Respondents are asked only about the quality of grocery stores and drug stores and if the stores are within 15 minutes of their home. A convenience store, such as a 7-Eleven, is not a grocery store. Shopping at other types of neighborhood businesses does not count as neighborhood shopping.

nonfamily household A household maintained by a householder who lives alone or who lives with people to whom he or she is not related.

nonfamily householder A householder who lives alone or with nonrelatives.

non-Hispanic People who do not identify themselves as Hispanic are classified as non-Hispanic. Non-Hispanics may be of any race.

non-Hispanic white People who do not identify themselves as Hispanic and who say their race is white alone.

nonmetropolitan area Counties that are not classified as metropolitan areas.

occupied housing units A housing unit is classified as occupied if there is at least one person who lives in the unit as a usual resident at the time of the interview, or if the occupants are only temporarily absent, for example, on vacation. However, if the unit is occupied entirely by people with a usual residence elsewhere, the unit is classified as vacant. By definition, the count of occupied housing units is the same as the count of households.

opinion of neighborhood The data presented are based on the respondent's overall opinion of the neighborhood. The respondent defines neighborhood.

opinion of structure The data presented are based on the respondent's overall opinion of the house or apartment as a place to live.

percent change The change (either positive or negative) in a measure that is expressed as a proportion of the starting measure. When median income changes from $20,000 to $25,000, for example, this is a 25 percent increase.

percent of primary mortgage refinanced cash used for home additions, improvements, or repairs This question is asked of homeowners who reported "to receive cash" as a reason for the refinance of their mortgage. These homeowners are asked what percentage was used for additions, improvements, or repairs to the home.

percentage point change The change (either positive or negative) in a value which is already expressed as a percentage. When a labor force participation rate changes from 70 percent to 75 percent, for example, this is a 5 percentage point increase.

plumbing facilities The category "With all plumbing facilities" consists of housing units that have hot and cold piped water as well as a flush toilet and a bathtub or shower. For units with less than two full bathrooms, the facilities are only counted if they are for the exclusive use of the occupants of the unit. Plumbing facilities need not be in the same room. Lacking some plumbing facilities or having no plumbing facilities for exclusive use means that the housing unit does not have all three specified plumbing facilities (hot and cold piped water, flush toilet, and bathtub or shower) inside the housing unit, or that the toilet or bathing facilities are also for the use of the occupants of other housing units.

present and previous units The present unit is the one occupied by the householder or respondent at the time of the interview. The previous unit is the one from which the householder or respondent moved. If the householder or respondent moved more than once during the 12 months prior to the date of the interview, the previous unit is the one last moved from.

primary mortgage Detailed information on regular and lump-sum home-equity mortgages was collected on the first three mortgages reported, even if the unit had four or more mortgages. If the owner(s) had both a regular and a lump-sum home-equity mortgage, priority was given to the regular mortgage(s) for collecting detailed information. On the basis of this information, one of the mortgages was considered to be primary. The definition of primary mortgage may not be the same as the legal definitions of a "first mortgage," which would be paid first after a foreclosure. If there was only one mortgage, it was primary. If two or more mortgages existed, the following hierarchy was used: (1) regular mortgage (as opposed to a lump-sum home-equity loan); (2) Federal Housing Administration, Veterans Administration, or Rural Housing Service/Rural Development mortgage; (3) assumed mortgage; (4) mortgage obtained first; and (5) largest initial amount borrowed.

primary source of water A public system or private company refers to any source supplying running water to six or more housing units. The water may be supplied by a city, county, water district, or private water company, or it may be obtained from a well that supplies six or more housing units. An individual well that provides water for five or fewer housing units is further classified by whether it is drilled or dug. Water sources such as springs, cisterns, streams, lakes, or commercial bottled water are included in the "other" category.

principal The amount of money raised by a mortgage or other loan, as distinct from the interest paid for its use. It is the amount of debt excluding interest.

property insurance Insurance on the structure and/or its contents (such as furniture, appliances, or clothing), it usually contains some liability insurance. Renters usually do not have property insurance (renter's property insurance), but, if they do have it, its cost is counted. The total cost is the most-recent yearly cost for which the occupants have actually been billed. Yearly cost is divided by 12 before calculating a monthly median cost.

proportion or share The value of a part expressed as a percentage of the whole. If there are 4 million people aged 25 and 3 million of them are white, then the white proportion is 75 percent.

public transportation Public transportation includes public bus or subway, taxicabs, trains, ferryboats, or any type of transportation service that is available to the public. Also included are bus or van services provided by the management of a housing development for its residents. School buses are not included.

purchase price The price of the house or apartment and lot at the time the property was purchased. Closing costs are excluded from the purchase price, and for mobile homes the value of the land is excluded.

race and Hispanic origin Race and Hispanic origin is self-reported and appears in five categories in this book: American Indian alone, Asian alone, black alone, Hispanic, and non-Hispanic white. Hispanics may be of any race. A household is assigned the race of the householder.

real estate taxes This item includes special assessments, school taxes, county taxes, and any other real estate taxes. Excluded are payments on delinquent taxes due from prior years. Rebates are subtracted from the total. When the real estate taxes are included with the mortgage, a separate amount for the taxes is obtained. To determine average monthly cost, yearly cost is divided by 12.

reasons for leaving previous unit These data are shown for units from which the respondent moved during the 12 months before the interview. The distribution may not add to the total because the respondent was not limited to one reason.

• *Change from owner to renter* or change from renter to owner indicates a change in tenure.

• *Disaster loss* includes damage by a tornado, storm, flood, earthquake, fire, landslide, or other similar occurrences.

• *Evicted from residence* occurs due to nonpayment of rent or objectionable behavior by the renters.

• *Government displacement* means the respondent was forced to leave by the government (local, state, or federal) because it wanted to use the land for other purposes, for example, to build a road or highway, for urban renewal or other public activity, because the building was condemned, or some other reason.

• *Married, widowed, divorced, or separated* is marked if the respondent moved because of marital reasons.

• *Needed larger house or apartment* refers to moves that were necessary because of crowding or for aesthetic reasons.

• *New job or job transfer* indicates that the respondent moved to begin a new job or was transferred from the previous location to the present location.

• *Other, family/personal related* indicates that the respondent moved because of family or personal reasons such as wanting to live closer to relatives.

• *Other, financial/employment related* refers to financial or employment related reasons, such as wanting to look for a new or different job because the person entered or left the U.S. Armed Forces, retired, or had some other financial/ employment reason.

- *Other housing related reasons* include such reasons as respondent wanted larger yard, different zoning, or a better investment.

- *Private displacement* includes situations in which a private company or person wanted to use the housing unit for some other purpose; for example, to develop the land or build commercially, to occupy the unit, to convert the unit to a condominium or cooperative, or to make repairs and renovate the unit.

- *To be closer to work/school/other* means that the respondent moved because commuting was too far and respondent wanted to live closer to work, school, or some other commuting purpose.

- *To establish own household* means that the respondent left a previous residence, such as parent's home, rooming or boarding house, or shared apartment, to establish an own household.

- *Wanted better home* was marked if the respondent moved because the previous residence was too old, run-down, in need of too many repairs, or if there was nothing wrong with the previous home, the respondent simply wanted to move to a better one.

- *Wanted lower rent or less expensive maintenance* indicates that the respondent moved because the rent (or mortgage) payments, taxes, or upkeep were too high at the previous residence.

- *Other* includes examples such as respondent wanted a change in climate, neighborhood crime problem, and racial or ethnic composition of neighborhood.

recent mover comparison to previous neighborhood This item is based on the respondent's comparison between the present neighborhood and the previous neighborhood. The definition of neighborhood is whatever the respondent considers it to be.

regions

- *Northeast* Maine, New Hampshire, Vermont, Massachusetts, Rhode Island, Connecticut, New York, Pennsylvania, and New Jersey.

- *Midwest* Ohio, Indiana, Illinois, Michigan, Wisconsin, Minnesota, Iowa, Missouri, Kansas, Nebraska, North Dakota, and South Dakota.

- *South* Delaware, Maryland, District of Columbia, Virginia, West Virginia, North Carolina, South Carolina, Georgia, Florida, Alabama, Mississippi, Tennessee, Kentucky, Arkansas, Louisiana, Oklahoma, and Texas.

- *West* Montana, Wyoming, Colorado, New Mexico, Arizona, Utah, Idaho, Alaska, Washington, Oregon, Nevada, California, and Hawaii.

remaining years mortgaged The owner or owner's spouse was asked the length of time it would take to pay off the loan at the current payment rate. The response reflects the amortization schedule. For example, in many balloon mortgages the initial monthly payments are calculated to pay off the loan in 30 years, though the mortgage is due in 5 years, and the 60th payment is very large. Such a mortgage would count here as 30 years, not 5 years, minus whatever number of years have passed.

rooms Counted as rooms are whole rooms used for living purposes, such as bedrooms, living rooms, dining rooms, kitchens, recreation rooms, permanently enclosed porches that are suitable for year-round use, lodger's rooms, and other finished rooms. Also included are rooms used for offices by a person living in the unit. A dining room, to be counted, must be separated from adjoining rooms by built-in archways or walls that extend at least 6 inches from an intersecting wall. Half walls or bookcases count if built-in. Movable or collapsible partitions or partitions consisting solely of shelves or cabinets are not considered built-in walls. Bathrooms, laundry rooms, utility rooms, walk-in closets, pantries, and unfinished rooms are not counted as rooms.

rooms used for business A room used for business is set up for use as an office or business for a business owner, contract worker, self-employed person, commercial use (such as daycare or catering), or regular job. The question asked if rooms were exclusively used for business. Follow-up questions asked if there was direct access to the outside without going through any other room and whether the space was used both as business space and for personal use.

rounding Percentages are rounded to the nearest tenth of a percent; therefore, the percentages in a distribution do not always add exactly to 100.0 percent. The totals, however, are always shown as 100.0. Moreover, individual figures are rounded to the nearest thousand without being adjusted to group totals, which are independently rounded; percentages are based on the unrounded numbers.

safety equipment Safety equipment installed inside the home includes: (1) a working smoke detector powered by electricity, batteries, or both (respondent is asked if the batteries in the smoke detector have been replaced in the last six months); (2) fire extinguishers purchased or recharged in the last two years; (3) sprinkler systems; and (4) working carbon monoxide detectors.

safety of primary source of water Water was considered safe (consumable or potable) if the main water source was used or could be used for drinking. The respondent was asked whether or not the main water source was safe for cooking and drinking. This item excludes units where the primary source of household water was commercial bottled water.

secured communities These types of communities are typically residential communities in which public access by nonresidents is restricted, usually by physical boundaries, such as gates, walls, and fences, or through private security. These communities sometimes require a special entry system, such as entry codes, key cards, or security guard approval. A public access restriction refers to the community, not a building or units. These communities exist in a myriad of locations and development types, including high-rise apartment complexes, retirement developments, and resort and country club communities.

selected deficiencies

• *Broken plaster or peeling paint (interior)* is on the inside walls or ceilings, and at least one area of broken plaster or peeling paint must be larger than 8 inches by 11 inches.

• *Exposed wiring* is any wiring that is not enclosed either in the walls or in metal or plastic coverings. Excluded are appliance cords, extension cords, chandelier cords, and telephone, antenna, or cable television wires.

• *Holes in floors* in the interior floors of the unit. The holes may or may not go all the way through to a lower floor or to the exterior of the unit. The holes are only counted if large enough for someone to trip in.

• *Open cracks or holes (interior)* are in the walls or ceilings of the housing unit. Included are cracks or holes that do not go all the way through to the next room or to the exterior of the housing unit. Hairline cracks or cracks that appear in the walls or ceilings, but are not large enough to insert the edge of a dime, are not counted. Very small holes caused by nails or other similar objects are also not counted.

• *Rooms without electric wall outlets* are rooms without at least one working electric wall outlet. A working electric wall outlet is one that is in operating condition; that is, it can be used when needed. An extension cord used in place of a wall outlet is not considered to be an electric wall outlet.

• *Signs of mice or rats* Respondents reported whether they had seen signs of mice or rats inside the house or building during the three months prior to interview or while the household was living in the unit if less than three months. Signs of mice or rats include droppings, holes in the wall, or ripped or torn food containers.

senior citizen communities These communities are age-restricted, meaning that at least one member of the family must be at least 55 years old. Communities that are age specific means that although no age restriction exists, communities attract people in the 55 or older age group.

sewage disposal breakdowns Sewage disposal breakdowns are limited to housing units in which the means of sewage disposal was a public sewer, septic tank, or cesspool. Breakdowns refer to situations in which the system was completely unusable. Examples include septic tank being pumped because it no longer perked, tank collapsed, tank exploded, sewer main broken, sewer treatment plant not operating as a result of electrical failure, or water service interruption. Data on breakdowns are shown if they occurred in the three months prior to the interview or while the household was living in the unit, if less than three months, and if the breakdown lasted six consecutive hours or more.

sewage disposal, means of *See* Means of sewage disposal.

smoke detector *See* Safety equipment.

source of drinking water These statistics are restricted to units where the respondent answered that water from the primary source of water was not safe to drink. Units where the primary source of water is commercial bottled water are excluded.

square footage of unit Housing size is shown for single-family, detached housing units and manufactured/mobile homes. Excluded from the calculation of square footage are unfinished attics, carports, attached garages, porches that are not protected from weather (such as screened porches), and mobile home hitches. Both finished and unfinished basements are included. Median square footage is rounded to the nearest foot. Square footage is based on the respondent's estimate of the size of the unit.

street noise or heavy street traffic refers to noise in outdoor public areas made by children playing outdoors, noise from a factory or business, or any other sounds that the respondent considers street noise. Traffic refers to the amount of vehicular traffic that the respondent considers "heavy."

structure type of previous residence These data are shown for householders who moved within the United States during the previous 12 months. They are based on the respondent's classification.

taxes *See* Annual taxes paid per $1,000 value and Real estate taxes.

tenure A housing unit is owner occupied (including a cooperative or condominium unit) if someone whose name is on the deed, mortgage, or contract to purchase lives in the unit. Units where the elderly buy a unit to live in for the remainder of their lives, after which it reverts to the seller, are considered owner occupied. All other occupied housing units are classified as renter occupied units, including units rented for cash, if occupants or others pay some rent, and/or occupied without payment of cash rent, such as a life tenancy or a unit that comes free with a job. Households that do not pay cash rent may still pay utilities.

tenure of previous unit These data are shown for householders who moved within the United States during the 12 months prior to the interview. The previous unit was owner occupied if the owner or co-owner lived in the unit. All other previous units were renter occupied.

total outstanding line-of-credit loans The total outstanding line-of-credit loan is the current balance on the home-equity line of credit. The current balance is usually reported on the monthly or quarterly statement.

total outstanding principal amount The statistics represent the total amount of principal that would have to be paid if the loans were paid off in full on the date of interview. The formula used to calculate the outstanding principal amount does not take into account the fact that some households make additional principal payments. The resulting data, therefore, may be an overestimate of the total outstanding principal. The data include all regular mortgages and lump-sum home-equity, but exclude line-of-credit home-equity loans.

units in structure In determining the number of housing units in a structure, all units, occupied and vacant, are counted. The statistics are presented for the number of housing units, not the number of residential structures. A structure either has open space on all sides or is separated from other structures by dividing walls that extend from ground to roof. Structures containing only one housing unit are further classified as: detached, if it has open space on all four sides; or attached, if it has unbroken walls extending from ground to roof that divide it from other adjoining structures, as in many row houses or townhouses. If a unit shares a furnace or boiler with adjoining units, then pipes or ducts pierce the walls and all the units thus joined are included in one structure. Manufactured/mobile homes are shown as a separate category.

utilities *See* Monthly costs paid for electricity and piped gas.

value The respondent's estimate of how much the property (house and lot) would sell for if it were for sale. Any non-residential portions of the property, any rental units, and land cost of mobile homes, are excluded from the value.

water *See* Plumbing facilities, Primary source of water, Safety of primary source of water, Source of drinking water and Water supply stoppage.

water leakage during last 12 months Data on water leakage are shown if the leakage occurred in the 12 months prior to the interview or while the household was living in the unit if less than 12 months. Housing units with water leakage are classified by whether the water leaked in from outside the building, and by the most common areas (roof, basement, walls, closed windows, or doors); or inside the building and the reasons of water leakage (fixtures backed up or overflowed or pipes leaked).

water supply stoppage Water supply stoppage means that the housing unit was completely without running water from its regular source. Completely without running water means that the water system servicing the unit supplied no water at all; that is, no equipment or facility using running water (in kitchen and bathroom sinks, shower, bathtub, flush toilet, dishwasher, and other similar items) had water supplied to it, or all were inoperable. The reason could vary from a stoppage because of a flood or storm, to a broken pipe, to a shutdown of the water system, to a failure to pay the bill, or other reasons. Data on water supply stoppage are shown if they occurred in the three months prior to the interview, or while the household was living in the unit if less than three months, and if the breakdown or failure lasted six consecutive hours or more. Housing units with water supply stoppage also are classified according to the number of times the stoppages occurred.

year householder moved into unit The data are based on the information reported for the householder and refer to the year of latest move. Thus, if the householder moved back into a housing unit previously occupied, the year of the latest move is reported. If the householder moved from one apartment to another in the same building, the year the householder moved into the present unit is reported. The intent is to establish the year that present occupancy by the householder began. The year the householder moves is not necessarily the same year other members of the household move, although, in the great majority of cases the entire household moves at the same time.

year primary mortgage originated is the year the mortgage was signed.

year structure built represents the respondent's estimate of when the building was first constructed, not when it was remodeled, added to, or converted. The figures refer to the number of housing units in structures built during the specified periods and in existence at the time of the interview. For manufactured/mobile homes, the manufacturer's model year was assumed to be the year built. For manufactured/mobile homes, the year the householder moved in can be earlier than the year the structure was built because the manufactured/mobile home site, not the manufactured/mobile home itself, is in sample. The householder could have replaced an older manufactured/mobile home with a newer model.

year unit acquired refers to the year in which the present owner acquired or inherited the house or apartment; for example, the year the contract was signed. This date may be different from the date when the occupants moved in. If the land and building were bought at different times, the year the building was acquired is recorded. If there was a land contract only, the year the contract was signed is recorded.

Indw

Index